PENGUIN BOOKS

ITALY AND ITS DISCONTENTS

areful ... ly than Paul
rg's *Ita* ... nt to critical
adn

...endid, par ... analysis of recent Italian history ... Has the
and complexity of a canvas by the Venetian master, Canaletto,
a precisely drawn cityscape is peopled by real characters,
or eccentric, going heedlessly about daily business' *Scotsman*

...lent ... Ginsborg compares the turbulent state of Italy with the
condition of Britain during the same period'
Alexander Chancellor, *Guardian*

'Thorough and perceptive ... Ginsborg's skills at synthesis and his
impressive grasp of the intricacies of Italian politics come into their own.
It is no easy task to pull together the salient points in some twenty
separate governments, most of them coalitions, but Ginsborg does so
with considerable panache' Caroline Moorehead, *Spectator*

'Essential reading for anyone who wishes to understand how and why
Berlusconi came to power' John Foot, *Guardian*

'Italians have a famed ability to make the best of a bad deal. Their
disregard for the rules has been the undoing of the political system, but it
has created a vital and wonderful people. As well as a valuable reference,
Ginsborg has written a substantial guide to the virtues and misdeeds of
Europe's most foxy political class' Ian Thomson, *Evening Standard*

ABOUT THE AUTHOR

Paul Ginsborg was born in London in 1945. He is currently
Contemporary European History at the University of Floren
formerly Reader in European Politics at Cambridge. His last
Penguin was the now famous *A History of Contemporary Italy, 1*

Italy

and Its Discontents

FAMILY, CIVIL SOCIETY, STATE
1980–2001

PAUL GINSBORG

PENGUIN BOOKS

PENGUIN BOOKS

Published by the Penguin Group
Penguin Books Ltd, 80 Strand, London, WC2R 0RL, England
Penguin Putnam Inc., 375 Hudson Street, New York, New York 10014, USA
Penguin Books Australia Ltd, 250 Camberwell Road, Camberwell, Victoria 3124, Australia
Penguin Books Canada Ltd, 10 Alcorn Avenue, Toronto, Ontario, Canada M4V 3B2
Penguin Books India (P) Ltd, 11, Community Centre, Panchsheel Park, New Delhi – 110 017, India
Penguin Books (NZ) Ltd, Cnr Rosedale and Airborne Roads, Albany, Auckland, New Zealand
Penguin Books (South Africa) (Pty) Ltd, 24 Sturdee Avenue, Rosebank 2196, South Africa

Penguin Books Ltd, Registered Offices: 80 Strand, London, WC2R 0RL, England

www.penguin.com

First published by Allen Lane The Penguin Press 2001
Published in Penguin Books 2003

6

Copyright © Paul Ginsborg, 2001
All rights reserved

The moral right of the author has been asserted

Printed in England by Clays Ltd, St Ives plc

ISBN-13: 978–0–140–24794–7
ISBN-10: 0–140–24794–7

For Ben and Lisa

Contents

Preface

OVER THE LAST twenty years Italy has witnessed a socio-economic transformation as dramatic as that of the 'economic miracle' of the 50s and early 60s, but strikingly different from it in both content and consequences. The 'miracle', with its great flows of emigration first from North-East to North-West, and then from South to North, with its dramatic passages from countryside to city, saw the definitive triumph of a new urban Italy over an older agricultural one. At the heart of this new Italy stood the Fordist factory, dominant not in numerical but in symbolic and technological terms. Paolo Volponi, in his novel *Memoriale*, written in 1962, described the impact of the factory upon those who went to work there for the first time:

The noise was great and the workshops took my breath away. The factory was big then, but still only a third of the size of what it is today. Each workshop was large, clean, well-ordered and luminous. Every worker had his own place, and worked there by himself with great purpose and confidence . . . The noise transported me; I heard and felt the whole factory moving as a single engine which pulled me with it and forced my work into its all-embracing rhythm. I couldn't hold myself back, I was as a leaf on a great tree, all of whose branches were shaken by the wind.[1]

The industrial working class that derived both its sustenance and its oppression from these great machines of mass production emerged as a social and political actor of primary importance. Around it there formed a wider social block, more heterogeneous in geographical and occupational terms, but sharing many of the same aspirations and mobilizations. The 34.4 per cent of the national vote gained by Enrico Berlinguer's Communist party in

1976 was the political high tide of these social trends. In 1977, in a famous speech to his party's intellectuals, Berlinguer described the industrial working class as 'the social force which is today the principal motor of history'.[2]

History can be cruel indeed to those who are confident of reading its line of march. In reality, the mid-1970s were precisely the moment when everything began to change and certainly not, *pace* Tomasi di Lampedusa, in order to stay the same.[3] The defeat of a divided working-class movement at FIAT in the autumn of 1980 was the most visible sign of the end of an epoch, the dramatic finale to a whole cycle of struggles,[4] but the subterranean movement of Italian society had in fact begun some years earlier. Italian capitalism was changing its skin, in line with the prevailing trends in the world economy. The breakthroughs in electronic research and their application to the world of communications initiated a new cycle in the global economy. No workplace was left untouched, no entrepreneur unaffected by the new technological paradigm. The resulting revolution in modes of production and the organization of the firm diminished the massed ranks of the industrial working class, offering those who remained an environment that had been radically transformed, both materially and ideologically.[5]

At the same time the tertiary sector increased its dominion over the patterns of employment and the Gross Domestic Product of the advanced economies. The performance of services of every sort became the habitual activity of the great majority of Italy's working population. Services, indeed, are in structural terms one of the principal protagonists of this book.[6]

The effects or even composition of the newly dominant tertiary sector were, and are, difficult to unravel. On the one hand, the service economy brought in its train a significant increase in the number of highly paid and qualified jobs; on the other, it offered a large number of poorly paid and precarious jobs, in work situations which allowed little space for collective solidarities. Fragmentation became the order of the day. So too did unemployment. The prospect of full employment, which had seemed attainable at least in the Centre and North of Italy in the years of the economic miracle, receded far into the distance. From 1973 to 1993 unemployment in Europe grew from 5–6 million to more than 19 million.[7] In 1995 the unemployment rate for those under twenty-five years of age was 33.3 per cent in Italy, the highest in the European Union after Spain.[8] Capitalism's new turn – the revolution in communications and the dominance of services – did not appear to have resolved, in the advanced European economies, the basic problem of employment.

The economy and the labour market were not the only sites of radical transformation in the period covered by this volume. There were to be profound changes in many other areas: in gender relations, where the influence of the women's movement and the great strides in girls' education made themselves felt; in families, which became both 'longer' and 'thinner', in the sense of an increase in longevity and contact between the generations, accompanied by a decrease in the numbers of children and the complexity of family structures; in fertility rates, which declined to the lowest in the world; in modes of consumption, in patterns of emigration and immigration, and after 1992 in politics as well. As a result, the recent history of the Italian Republic acquires a particular fascination because *both* the public and the private worlds were on the move, simultaneously though not in unison, with connections and consequences that the historian struggles to chart and render visible.

Italian democracy brought to these challenges a number of long-term and structural deficits that limited its capacity to respond, and rendered it vulnerable. One of the most important of these was the continuing relative poverty and degradation of many regions of the South, and the continuing existence in some of them of powerful and ferocious criminal organizations. Another, on a quite different plane, was the weakness of its public administration. In an era dominated by services, to have public services that for the most part did not function in anything like an efficient way was truly to cripple a nation from the outset. Another still, at least until 1992, was the inadequacy and cultural poverty of Italy's political system. Not only did the system prevent the turnover of governmental élites, but it was also profoundly structured on the vertical loyalties of patron–client relations. In the 1980s, this deep-rooted clientelism was accompanied by widespread corruption. Both these meant that the input of the political system to the growth of a culture of citizenship was limited indeed.

However, it would be a grave mistake to conclude that these structural deficits, however grave, were bound to condition, in a genetic way, the nature of Italian democracy. Determinism of this sort, whatever its intellectual origins, should be treated with some suspicion. Contrary to the opinion of many Italian intellectuals, there was no *permanent* handicap which had crippled the country's recent history. Rather, that history is perhaps best presented in terms of deep and unresolved *conflicts*, which allow for a variety of cultural and institutional outcomes.

In the 1980s and 1990s, significant forces emerged, both in society and the state, which tended towards the strengthening of democratic trends in Italy, rather than to their restriction. The broadening of the structural and educational bases of a critical middle class, far more numerous and influential than in previous decades, had a beneficial effect. The development of associationism and of a plural and extensive civil society, in the South as well as the North, amongst women as well as men, injected its own dynamics into modern Italian society.

As for the Republican state, its historical formation had seen a highly democratic Constitution (that of 1948) laid upon older and anti-democratic structures, while its modern complexity and bureaucratic weakness had rendered it refractory to centralized command. These were profound weaknesses. They were mitigated, however, by relative autonomies *within* the state of great importance. None was to be more important than that of the judiciary. A minority of prosecuting magistrates was to show extraordinary courage and determination in opposing the old habits and accommodations, the complicity with the Mafia and the corruption of the '*partitocrazia*'. Other voices, too, merged with resonance and determination over the babble of Roman politics; that of the Bank of Italy in particular, which was to have a very significant role in Italy's most recent history.

In spite of the clarity of these voices, they remained fragile and minoritarian within the Italian state. However, they received indirect sustenance from forces which lay outside the Italian body politic. The 'tyranny of Brussels' is an oft-heard slogan in many countries belonging to the European Union, but probably less so in Italy than elsewhere. The European Community had not been an unmixed blessing for Italy, nor Italy an assiduous member state, but as time passed the positive values of the Union – its firm commitment to democracy and economic stability, its encouragement of competition within clearly defined rules, its single market, its insistence on certain standards of equal opportunity and environmental protection, its social programme and regional funds – all these wrought slow but inexorable change upon its largest southern member. Italy constrained by Europe was Italy improved.

In attempting to analyse and narrate this most recent and dynamic period of Italian history, characterized by its great sense of movement and the uncertainty of its outcomes, I have adopted certain organizational and methodological assumptions which I would like briefly to explain. The short final chapter of my previous work (*A History of Contemporary Italy*), that on the 1980s, has been set aside. In its place has grown a new work, originally intended as an update, but which in its writing has acquired ever greater autonomy from its predecessor, as well as, I am afraid to say, ever greater volume. Every author hopes that those who have read a first volume of his or her work will also read the second, and that those who start with the second will then return to the first. Whether this proves to be true in my case or not, I want to assure the prospective reader of the present volume that it has been conceived of as standing in its own right.

In methodological terms, I have again placed a special emphasis on the role of the family. The field of family studies is a very rich and prolific one, but there is a real danger that it remains closed and compartmentalized within the boundaries of separate academic disciplines. In particular, historical studies have very rarely tried to integrate the family into the wider history of a contemporary nation. If there are, by now, many and excellent studies on the history *of* the family, as well as chapters *on* the family in more general texts, there are none that try to look constantly at the *connections* between individuals, families, society and the state, to treat the relationships between different levels of human aggregation as the complex mechanisms around which the history of a nation is constructed.[9] To undertake that task, admittedly a very ambitious one, is the aim of the present volume, so that greater recognition may be granted to the family, to use the words of Susan Moller Okin, as 'a political institution of primary importance'.[10]

In the case of contemporary Italy, the family has always seemed both to informed foreign observers and to many Italians to occupy a special place in the life of the nation. In this respect Italy is not alone. An even minimal knowledge of China or Japan, of Spain or Greece, is sufficient to understand the often unrecognized significance of family in the contemporary history of many other nations as well, especially if that history is not only conceived of in narrowly political terms. Yet each of these nations is different, for each has formed over time its own highly complex and culturally specific way of combining the elements of family, society and state.[11]

In Italy family is very important, both as metaphor and as reality. In terms of metaphor, it is omnipresent, from the 'family' of managers trained by Enrico Cuccia in Mediobanca, to the 'family' of criminals organized by the Mafia. In analysing this metaphor more closely, in terms of emitting and receiving zones, it is striking how often the family is taken as the metaphor for other social or political aggregations, rather than the other way round.[12] In other words, it is not the state or any organization in society which provides examples for the family, but the family which provides metaphors and role models for society and the state. Only the Catholic Church, itself the single most influential propagator of the family as an emitting metaphor, has had the pre-eminence to reverse the metaphor as well, calling the family, in the words of John Paul II, a 'domestic church'.[13]

As for social reality, the importance of family traverses very many moments of this history, from the dominance of family in the ownership of firms, large and small, to the recruitment to the largest political party by the method described by one political scientist as 'enforced family membership',[14] from the pre-eminence of family-run shops in the physiognomy of Italy's service sector, to the use of family contacts as a means of coping with Italian bureaucracy, from 'family days' at FIAT in the 1980s to widespread nepotism within the state apparatuses. I hope all these points will be sufficiently illustrated as the volume unfolds.

If the primary analytical thrust is, therefore, that described above, it is not the only one. I have tried again to stress the need to write history not only from the top downwards, but also from the bottom upwards, to see how ordinary people experienced these years, to look at 'low' as well as 'high' politics, to glance at the condition of the foreign immigrant as well as that of the *'grande borghese'*. Many of the themes treated are the same as those in my previous volume, but there are others that are quite new or were previously mentioned only briefly: Italy's relationship with Europe, its civil society, gender relations, mass culture and consumption patterns are among the most significant. Some readers may find the first chapter on the economy rather heavy and slow going, but I ask them to persevere, as it is an indispensable base for the ensuing argument and narration.

To write the history of so recent a period as the last two decades entails the almost complete abandonment of the traditional tools of the historian's craft — the patient work in the archives, the attention to primary documentation, the challenging of established interpretations. Instead I have been at work on virgin territory, heavily dependent on sociological surveys, on the anthropologist's eye, on newspaper reports, oral history, economists' texts, judicial transcripts, parliamentary inquiries. But I have tried to retain a sense of the historian's duty to offer a general interpretation, to make some order out of complexity instead of simply being submerged by it, to draw a general picture from many and diverse fragments of evidence.

I am aware that what follows is very much a hybrid — part history, part political argument, part participant observation. I am aware, too, of how much as a foreigner I have failed to understand. Hugh Seton-Watson, in the Preface to his study of the nineteenth-century Russian empire, wrote some words on this theme with which I concur profoundly: 'It is difficult to write the history of another country. The foreigner has not grown up in its physical and mental climate, and he cannot understand them, still less feel them, in the same way as its own people do. He can spend long periods in a foreign land, learn its language, work and live among its citizens, to some extent think as they do, and be accepted as a friend. This is not the same thing as being one of the people of the country, but still it is something.'[15]

One final point. As an intellectual endeavour, preparing this book has felt most like being a cartographer. I have sought to draw a first map of these recent years, a drawing which like an ancient parchment contains many mistakes, with coastlines that are the wrong shape, with some parts of countries that are too short and others that are too long, but which still constitutes a guide, to which future historians of Italy may look back with amusement, curiosity and perhaps even affection.

This book is dedicated to my son and daughter, Ben and Lisa, Cambridge children who have grown up in Florence. Watching them become Italians and hearing them defend the attitudes, styles and passions of their country of adoption have exercised a deep influence upon me.

I also want to thank Ayşe, David and Megan, all of whom have helped me greatly, in different ways.

I owe many other debts of gratitude: to the staff of the Sale di Consultazione of the Biblioteca Nazionale di Firenze for their unfailing courtesy and helpfulness; to Vittorio Foa, whose insight and humanity have continued to enrich the lives of all those around him; to Luigi Bobbio and Andrea Ginzburg, for their great patience and instructive help in their respective fields of expertise, namely the public administration and the economy; to those who read and criticized parts or all of the manuscript: Michele Battini, Luisa Finocchi, Marcello Flores, Claudio Pavone, Francesco Ramella, Mario G. Rossi, and Anna Rossi-Doria. None of the above are responsible for eventual errors in the text.

I was extremely fortunate to have Prisca Giusti as my research assistant during the last months of preparation of this volume; her dedication, intelligence and quick-wittedness were invaluable. My warmest thanks also to Stefania Bernini and Marta Bonsanti for their contributions, and to Giambattista Salinari and Marcella Simoni for their last-minute help. For assistance on individual points I am grateful to Claudia Bona, Anna Bosco, Giovanni Focardi, John Foot, Luca Fonnesu, Stephen Gundle and Luisa Levi D'Ancona. At Penguin, Simon Winder's patience and editorial intelligence were of great comfort; so too was the copy-editing expertise of Annie Lee.

Chapter 1

The Italian Economy: Constraints and Achievements

1. Italy's Place in the World Economy

WHEN SUMMIT meetings between the leaders of the capitalist world's most powerful nations began at Rambouillet in France in November 1975, Italy obtained an invitation only at the last moment. The French President of the time, Valéry Giscard d'Estaing, had wished to exclude her, as he did Canada. In the end he failed on both accounts, and from June 1976 the G7 came into being.[1]

At the reunions of this most exclusive of clubs, Italy's prime ministers have always appeared grateful to be there, happy indeed, along with the Canadians and the Japanese, to take a side or back role in the collective photographs. In the centre of the frame in the 1980s and the 1990s stood the President of the United States and the massive Helmut Kohl, the only seemingly permanent member of the club, whose physical stature (unlike that of his Japanese counterparts) closely corresponded to his country's weight in the world economy. The British and French, as always in the second half of the twentieth century, wanted to count for more than they actually did, and often hassled their way to the front of the stage.

How far was Italy's reticence deserved? Did she belong at all to the club? Economists have always been uncertain in their answers to these questions, sometimes emphasizing the country's economic instability, at others praising its vitality, at others still relegating it to the semiperiphery rather than the core of global capitalism.[2]

Bearing in mind these doubts, I intend in this first chapter to present an overall view of the Italian economy, both with regard to its external

1

performance and to its internal workings. I have paid particular attention to the tertiary sector, not just because services have come to dominate the Italian economy, but also because they rarely receive the specific attention which they deserve.

A good place to begin is by examining the volume and quality of Italy's share of world trade. In the period under consideration, characterized by the rapid growth of the south Asian economies, but also by a growing awareness of the limits and dangers of indiscriminate growth, Italy's presence in world markets stood up well to the test of time. Whereas in 1951 her percentage share of world exports had been just 2.2 per cent, by 1994 it had reached 4.5 per cent. In 1987, in comparative terms Italy's share stood at 5.0 per cent, contrasted to 5.7 per cent for Great Britain, 6.2 per cent for France, 9.9 per cent for Japan, 10.5 per cent for the USA and 12 per cent for West Germany.[3]

a. WORLD COMMERCE IN MANUFACTURES

Beyond these overall figures, a distinction must be made between trade in manufactures and that in services. If we concentrate first on manufactures, it can be seen that Italy's performance on a world scale was an admirable one, for in 1997 her share of global exports in this sector was 5.4 per cent, and of imports 3.5 per cent.[4] Her trade was fully integrated with, and oriented towards, the other advanced economies. In 1987, three-quarters of her trade in manufactures was with OECD nations, and over 50 per cent of it was with her partners in the European Community. Italy exported with particular vigour to West Germany, France and Britain, as well as to southern Europe, but more weakly to Holland, Belgium, Denmark and Ireland. A healthy 10 per cent of her trade went to the United States, and Italian goods were actively present in Middle Eastern and northern African markets.[5]

Unlike Great Britain, whose trade deficit in manufactured goods grew dramatically in the 1980s, and France, whose deficit within Europe was only partially balanced by her exports to developing countries, Italy enjoyed a consistent surplus in her trade of manufactured products with the OECD countries.[6] In 1990 Michael Porter of the Harvard Business School published an important comparative survey of national economic competitivity. Much of what he had to say about Italian manufacturing was highly complimentary. Italian firms had shown 'a remarkable ability to innovate in products as well as to incorporate state-of-the-art manufacturing and other technologies in relatively small and medium-sized firms. Sophisticated and advanced home buyers and the development of world-class supplier industries have contributed to the process.'[7]

However, this picture has to be qualified by examining the *quality* of Italy's exports. World commerce in manufactures can be broadly divided into four major components: a group of *science-based* industries, such as computers and office machines, communication equipment and semi-conductors, pharmaceuticals, all characterized by conspicuous investment in research and development; *scale intensive* industries, marked by a high level of technical and organizational complexity, such as car production, industrial chemicals, rubber and plastics; *specialized supplier* industries, small and medium in size, with notable capacity for incremental technological innovation and a highly diversified range of goods (machine-tools, machines for industry and agriculture, precision instruments); and finally *supplier-dominated* or 'traditional' industries (textiles, clothing, footwear, furniture and interior decoration, leather goods, metal products).[8]

Italy's recent prowess as a commercial nation has been confined principally to the third and fourth of these compartments. In the sector of specialized supplier industries concerned with electrical and non-electrical machinery, especially machines for industry, mechanical components and household appliances, Italy did extremely well in these years. Indeed, faced with the strong Japanese challenge in this sector, Italy alone of the advanced economies improved her share of world trade, and continued to do so throughout the early 1990s.[9]

Her performance in the fourth compartment, that of traditional or supplier-dominated industries, especially textiles and clothing, furniture, ceramics, leather goods and footwear, as well as some metal working, was also very strong. Here too there was considerable evidence of Italian firms' ability to fight off challenges from the south Asian and other developing economies, as will be seen when we examine Italy's industrial districts.

Taking into consideration the whole of the Republican period (from 1946 onwards), some of Italy's most traditional industries, like textiles, demonstrated an enviable capacity not only to survive but also to prosper in a fiercely competitive world market. In 1980 Italy, with 7.6 per cent of world exports in textiles, was the world's third largest exporter after Germany and Hong Kong. By 1997 she had increased her share of the world market to 8.3 per cent, but had slipped to fifth position overall, behind the rapidly emerging China and Republic of Korea.[10]

The country's rating in the other two compartments of world trade in manufactures was very much less satisfactory. Many of the major scale intensive industries, such as automobiles and domestic electric appliances, which had been cornerstones of the 'economic miracle', thirty years later had difficulty in standing the pace. The same was even truer of Italy's ailing chemical industry, which was absolutely unworthy of her overall position in the world economy. Italy's share of world exports in chemicals remained constant at 3.9 per cent in the period 1980–95, but her imports in this sector were far more substantial.[11] Another significant weakness lay with her restricted and declining share of the dynamic global market in science-based goods. Here, in the rapidly changing world of information technology, pharmaceuticals, telecommunications, etc., Italy was a net importer of goods in increasing proportions by the 1990s.[12]

b. WORLD COMMERCE IN SERVICES

World commerce in services, as opposed to manufactures, is both an area difficult to define and in rapid expansion, accounting perhaps for more than 30 per cent of world trade by the early 1990s.[13] The World Trade Organisation divides commercial services into three main categories: transport, which covers all transportation services that are performed by residents of one economy for those of another; travel, a hybrid category which includes all services and goods consumed or acquired by travellers, whether for business or holiday purposes; and, finally, the catch-all 'other commercial services', which include communication, construction, insurance, financial, computer, information, personal, cultural, recreational, and other services. This last category was the largest and fastest growing sector, but travel did not lag too far behind.[14]

At first sight the Italian performance in the world of services was as impressive as that in manufactured goods, with 5.5 per cent of world exports in 1995, and fifth position in global terms, behind the USA (16.2 per cent), France (8.2 per cent), Germany (6.8 per cent), and the UK (5.9 per cent). However, the gap between the value of exports and that of imports was much narrower than in Italy's trade in manufactures, and her real strength in services was concentrated in the category of travel, where she was second in the world in 1997, with 6.9 per cent of 'exports'.

In this category tourism was all-important. Italy's tourist industry, as we shall see, was an ailing giant, and its own population's ever-increasing travels were biting into the trade surplus in the sector. None the less the country's assets in this field, if properly used, were formidable.[15]

In the other categories, Italy's performance was less impressive, above all in the variegated, but very modern third sector. Here the country lagged far behind in the specialized services in finance and insurance in which Great Britain excelled, in the distribution services which were France's speciality, and in other professional services based on information technology and telecommunications. Here again, her failure to develop science-based industries cost her dear. The brightest of her services, though of relatively small volume, was engineering and construction. Italian consultancy and project proposals enjoyed an outstanding reputation abroad, especially in the area connected to continuous flow production (petroleum and petrochemicals, iron and steel and electrical industries).[16]

*

Taking trade in manufactures and services together, Italy's performance at the end of the twentieth century provided ample confirmation of her historic reputation as a great trading nation. The economic sectors where she was strongest were unlikely to suffer sudden contraction, and her enterprises provided ample evidence of their ability to cope with very severe global challenges, and not only when the lira was weak and the price of Italian goods low.

None the less, Italy's overall balance of trade showed a deficit for all of the 1980s (with variations in the current account of −2.2 per cent of GDP in 1980 to −1.8 per cent in 1991), and only returned to a surplus after 1993, with the radical devaluation of the lira. Why was this? One reason was to be sought in structural deficiencies, such as Italy's lack of power resources and of raw materials. Another, far from inevitable, was her very poor performance in agriculture, which resulted in her being a net importer of food from the rest of Europe (see below, pp. 20–22). However, the principal causes lay in the worsening of that part of her balance of payments on current account which went under the name of invisible exports and imports.[17]

Whereas in the 1960s 'invisibles' had played a major role in Italy's balance of payments surplus, accounting for some 8 per cent of total flows, by the 1980s the picture had changed dramatically. The surplus from tourism, which had been so conspicuous in the 1960s, was much diminished some thirty years later. The foreign debt of the country had greatly increased in the 1980s, as high interest rates attracted foreign capital but made debt repayment more onerous. Remittances from emigrants, historically of great importance for the Italian economy, had declined dramatically. The state's transfer payments to abroad, especially to the European Union and in aid to third world countries, had increased.[18] When considering Italy's overall balance of trade, these were all factors which had to be weighed against the country's basic manufacturing dynamism.

c. ITALY AND BRITAIN: VYING FOR PRIMACY

If we turn away from broad structural considerations to Italy's performance in the various economic *conjunctures* of this period, we also find much that was reassuring. In the second half of the 1980s, with falling oil prices and the reflation of the American economy, there was a marked revival in the global economy. Growth rates improved all over Europe, but Italy did better than most. Taking the period 1976 to 1990 as a whole, Italy's real GDP grew by almost 50 per cent, six percentage points above the average of the EC; consumption was thirteen points higher in the same period.[19] The recession of the early 1990s affected Italy as a short, very sharp shock concentrated above all in 1993; this was in marked contrast to Great Britain, which lived the same period as a long and seemingly endless agony. Exit from the EMS in September 1992 represented, as we shall see, a grave blow to Italy's standing in Europe; but the relative devaluation of the lira, when combined with the historic agreement with the unions in 1992 on labour costs (see below, Chapter 9), had very favourable consequences for Italian economy. Exporting blossomed into frenetic activity, without the feared-for inflation, and by 1994–5 the major indicators of Italian trade and growth were telling, not for the first time, a story of outstanding expansion. Only at the end of the decade did these indicators show signs of faltering.

It was in the late 1980s that Italy first prided itself on having overtaken Britain, to become the fifth largest economy of the capitalist world. Giovanni Goria, then Treasury Minister, made this claim in January 1987. It was immediately and hotly disputed by Nigel Lawson, the Chancellor of the Exchequer of the time, but the OECD figures for that year confirmed the '*sorpasso*': in 1986 Italy had a GDP of $599.8 bn, compared to the UK's $547.4 bn. For a decade, the two countries remained almost at level pegging, both in terms of per capita income and overall volume of GDP, but Britain has moved ahead again decisively in the last few years.[20]

The argument over the '*sorpasso*', rather silly in itself, was indicative of deeper lying uncertainties in both countries concerning their economic standing in the world. In Britain the debate concentrated for much of the period on the country's seemingly unstoppable economic decline, the liquidation of its manufacturing base in the 1980s, its inability to revive the entrepreneurship of the nineteenth century. In Italy, on the other hand, there was no imperial past or even golden era to lament, but rather a deep lack of confidence about the future of the nation as an effective collective economic agent. Britain looked with envy at the Italian network of small firms and industrial districts; Italy with awe at the power of the City, the sophistication of its financial services, and the world dominance of certain British multinationals.

This last was a particularly sore point. In the 1980s, when leading Italian entrepreneurs tried to move on to the European scene and take control of significant institutions and companies of other national economies, they were by and large rebuffed. There was a lot of evidence that Italy's small industries could fit brilliantly and swiftly into certain market niches, but little that her leading firms and capitalists could achieve dominant positions in global or even European terms. Seventy per cent of the ingenious games which populated the new Eurodisney outside Paris – Peter Pan, Pinocchio, Biancaneve and so on – were made by one Italian firm from Altavilla Vicentina; but when at the beginning of 1988 Carlo De Benedetti attempted to take over the Société Générale de Belgique, la 'Vieille Dame' of the Belgium economy, his bid ended in costly failure.[21]

2. The Triumph of the Service Sector

a. DEFINITIONS AND DEVELOPMENTS

If we turn from an *external* examination of Italy's economy to an *internal* one, to sending a probe into the country's economic entrails, then the great changes of the most recent period soon become apparent, even if only in shadowy form. Crucial to Italy's whole social structure and indeed to her present politics has been the triumph of the service sector. In 1980 the service sector accounted for 48.3 per cent of employment and 51.6 per cent of added value. By 1995 these figures stood at 60.1 per cent and 65 per cent respectively.[22]

The newly dominant services' sector is a phenomenon whose structure and effects economists and sociologists have been slow to unravel, for various reasons: the difficulty in defining and measuring services, the frequent misreading of their significance in modern economies, the lack of an adequate conceptual framework.[23] Behind the bare statistics, therefore, lurk complicated problems of definition and compartmentalization, which have to be aired before we can proceed.

A highly influential distinction between goods and services is that offered by T. P. Hill.[24] For Hill, goods are physical objects which are appropriable, and therefore transferable, between economic units. Services are not 'immaterial' or 'invisible' goods, but enjoy quite distinct properties, and should be accorded a different conceptual status. Various types of services, like the shipment of goods, the cleaning of a house by a servant, or the extraction of a tooth, share certain common characteristics. In all of them *some change*, of a consensual nature, is brought about in the condition of a person or good; furthermore, that change is the result of the activity of some other economic unit. Taken together, for Hill 'these two points provide the key to the concept of a service'.[25]

The *nature* of the change that takes place in the performance of a service may be small or large – additive, coadiuvant, protective, transformative. Its *destination* has usually been defined in relation to two broad market categories: producer or intermediate services on the one hand, and consumer or final services on the other. Examples of the first would include services to firms like accounting, legal and financial aid, as well as advertising, wholesaling, data processing, etc. Examples of the second would be recreation services, entertainment, health care, education, and so on.[26]

Within this second category of consumer or final services there lies a further distinction, crucial to our understanding of the Italian case: that between *services for final demand*, i.e. those that are consumed directly, such as the examples just mentioned, to which we could add, for example, hairdressing, fitness centres, restaurants and bars; and *services for final trade*, which consist principally in retailing, that is the selling of goods for final consumption or use.[27] In Italy services for final trade, as we shall see in a moment, have had a very particular structure and importance.

This division by markets or destination is a necessary first step, but it must be supplemented by at least one other, as obvious as it is crucial: that between private and public services.[28] Both these operate in producer *and* consumer markets. The state, for instance, will provide a large series of services to industry – in the form of credit, infrastructures, legal protection, etc., and at the same time offers a wide range of consumer services, such as in the fields of health, education and welfare. Private services, too, operate in both markets; indeed, one of the major developments and battlegrounds of this period was the spread of private services into those areas of final demand which had for decades been considered, at least in Europe, the preserve of the state.

Once these preliminary distinctions and definitions have been established, it is necessary to highlight those service sectors which came to play a historically dominant role in this period. The first of these was finance, which in many ways assumed a new global centrality. The convergence of information technology and telecommunications was vital to the growth of money markets, as well as the numerous services and roles connected to them. The range of financial services increased dramatically, both to producers and to consumers. At the same time international money markets were transformed by the sheer volume and mobility of capital, by the volatility of the price of money (interest rates), and that of currencies (exchange rates). Cityscapes reflected the changed nature of the power-houses of capitalism: as the Fordist factories fell into disuse and were pulled down, city centres filled up with the plate-glass skyscrapers of the new Moguls.[29]

A second area of services in dynamic expansion was that of entertainment, recreation and information available via telecommunication networks. This was both a public and a private service, aimed primarily at final demand. Its growth was fostered by constant innovation – the invention of the VCR (video cassette recorder), the development of cable and satellite television alongside traditional broadcasting, the spread, from the mid-1980s onwards, of the 'intelligent network'.[30] Rarely had a service changed so rapidly or become the source of such power and influence in so short a space of time. It was also an ever increasingly global service – in its content, its reception and, as we shall see, its ownership.

A third major area, that of social services, did not share the same meteoric trajectory of growth of the other two, for its development was more to be traced to the changing nature of the family life cycle and of gender relations than to technological innovation; in particular, to the increased ageing of the population and the entry of more women into the labour market. Social services enjoyed their major expansion (at least in western Europe and the USA) in the 1960s and 1970s, only to face a period of protracted crisis in the 1980s and 1990s. They could not boast the same luxurious urban temples of the world of finance, but by the end of the 1980s, the local health authority, offering personal transformative services which were hopefully for the better, was often the greatest single employer in many European cities.[31]

b. THE ITALIAN CASE

To draw a convincing map of the tertiary (i.e. service) sector in Italy is no easy task, because it is an under-studied area and there is harsh disagreement even over the relative weight and dynamism of its component parts.[32] None the less, it is quite clear that certain key sectors of Italian services developed in a far weaker and more deformed way than in most other economies of the same stature.

The case of financial services was emblematic in this respect. In the 1970s and early 1980s, it is true, the Italian banking system flourished as never before, benefiting among other things from indigenous high propensity for saving and lack of involvement in Third World debt. However, Italian banks, to use Giuliano Amato's expression, formed 'a petrified forest';[33] they were too many, too antiquated, too tied to various political factions, and none of them was sufficiently large to compete with the major international groups. Labour costs and the number of personnel were much higher than elsewhere. Large multi-functional groups, capable of generating resources and capacity in all areas of financial services, only began to emerge in the late 1990s. Family saving, which was rapidly moving away from traditional investments (by 1995 some 70 per cent of families owned their own homes), offered a major comparative advantage with other nations, but only if Italian banks were to show themselves able to grasp the opportunity.[34]

What was true of banking was even more so of other financial services. The Italian insurance market remained at a primitive level, with 30 per cent of it in the hands of foreign companies in 1989. Milan's stock exchange enjoyed a magical moment between 1982 and 1987, when share prices and volume of trade increased dramatically, but after the crash of 1987 it relapsed into a depressed and somnolent state, from which it rarely emerged and which confirmed its marginal status in global terms.[35]

By contrast, there could be little doubting the vitality and omnivorous nature of Italian information, entertainment and recreational services. The greater part of these services were consumed by means of the mass media, and the television screen in particular. The arrival of colour television in 1977 led to a great boom in television audiences, which showed no signs of abating with the passing of the years. In the period 1988–95, for instance, peak evening viewing increased dramatically, from 15.8 million spectators to 24.8 million.[36]

The total absence of regulation of the mass media for much of the 1980s led to a unique imbalance of ownership and control in the private sector of this key service industry. Silvio Berlusconi, a capable and dynamic Milanese businessman who had made his fortune in the construction industry, succeeded in the space of a few years in establishing a near monopoly of commercial television and the publicity market that accompanied it. Between 1982 and 1984 he added to his own Canale 5 the other two principal commercial channels, Italia 1 and Rete 4. He then bought one of Italy's leading football clubs, AC Milan, in 1986, and thus established a pioneering fusion between Italy's two leading entertainment services, football and television. Rebuffed in France, where his involvement in the commercial channel La Cinq ended disastrously, Berlusconi maintained an important stake in Spanish television, through the channel Telecinco. Other television and media magnates like Rupert Murdoch had far greater global empires, but none had so firm a grip on the market in their own country. By the end of the 1980s, Berlusconi's company Publitalia had concentrated in its hands 42 per cent of all publicity in the mass media, compared to the 15 per cent of the Springer group and Read International in Germany and Britain respectively, and the 22.5 per cent of Hachette in France.[37]

As regards Italy's public services, it has to be stated immediately and unequivocally that they were one of the great historic weaknesses of the Italian state. If the quality of a nation's public services is a critical variable in its competitive capacity, then Italy must be considered a dismal failure. Italy's public administration, both at national and local level, soaked up labour and expenditure, but in general offered a quality of service that was far below European norms. Sabino Cassese, the reforming minister for the Civil Service in the Ciampi government of 1993–4, estimated at that time that each Italian citizen lost an average of fifteen to twenty working days a year in having to cope with the bureaucracy.[38] While productivity in industry had doubled in the period 1970–88, it had remained all but stationary in the public administration. In the same period wages in the two sectors had risen in almost identical fashion.[39]

Almost wherever one stepped in the field of public services, one sank immediately into a bog. Italy's telecommunications were by and large expensive and inefficient; her postal services were the worst in Europe; her national health service had come into being only in the 1970s. It had levels of expenditure equal to those elsewhere in Europe, but was bedevilled by political interference, bureaucracy and major regional disparities. Italy's railways, in spite of conspicuous subsidies and investments, still suffered from grave deficiencies, especially in the South.[40] Her principal libraries, to mention one other area close to the heart of all scholars of the country, were run lackadaisically from Rome, had poor opening hours and prided themselves on a culture of conservation rather than of service to users.[41]

The list is a seemingly endless one, and some of the reasons for so parlous a situation will be examined below, in Chapter 7. Here it is important to single out the state's responsibilities for the defects of tourism, that sleeping giant which played so significant a role in the country's overall service profile. Italy was a country of extraordinary beauty and immense cultural heritage, but the public services offered to its visitors were inadequate, and sometimes grossly so. At Pompei, to take just one dramatic example, the area visitable by tourists had actually declined from 36 per cent of the ancient city to just 12 per cent in the forty years between 1956 and 1997, while the number of visitors had increased constantly to more than 150,000 per year by 1996. After the earthquake of 1980, whole areas had been closed off, and seventeen years later the Ministry of Beni Culturali, under whose authority the site languished, had not managed to reopen any of them.[42]

The performance of private services was a little more encouraging. There were some dynamic producer services, especially in the major northern cities, and Italy's performance in this sector showed a positive balance throughout the 1990s.[43] However, the OECD estimated that many private services to families in Italy charged exorbitant prices. Financial services, car insurance, hotels, restaurants, laundry and dry cleaning all cost above the EC average. So too did private medical services in general, and dentistry in particular.[44] The input of private services to tourism was certainly more enterprising than that of the state, but the sector was heavily dominated by short-term profit motives, and an incapacity to take long-term decisions which would safeguard the environment and avoid congestion.[45]

Behind these failures lay a series of barriers to competition and dynamism in the service sector. Some were public, such as the consistent poor performance of certain public monopolies, whose activities were over-determined by clientelistic appointments and lax financial controls; others were private, such as the restricted entry and corporativism practised by many professions, or the oligopoly exercised by a small group of companies in a certain service sector.[46]

The last, defining feature of the Italian world of services was the extraordinary importance of small family shops, above all in services for final trade. In 1980 the licences granted for retailing (the best way of calculating the number of shops) had been 1,050,000. In 1995 their number had hardly declined at all, to 1,009,000, and foodshops alone accounted for the greater part of this decrease. To this veritable army of shopkeepers had to be added the so-called '*esercizi pubblici*' (principally restaurants, *trattorie*, bars, and cafés), a category constantly on the increase, and contributing another 250,000 establishments in 1994.[47] These two groups, together with hotels, were responsible for some 5 million work units. Far from declining, shopkeepers were estimated to account for 8 per cent of the active population in 1971, 9 per cent in 1983, and 11 per cent in 1993. The fact that white-collar workers in the private sector also constituted only 11 per cent of the active population in 1993 gives some idea of the peculiar weighting of Italian services.[48]

One element of explanation for the dominant presence of retailing in the Italian service sector was a historic one: the governing parties of the Republic had used the sector as an employment sponge, offering economic protection and privileges to small shopkeepers in return for electoral fidelity.[49] As late as 1971, the law no. 426 of that year made the opening of supermarkets and hypermarkets dependent on the issue of three different types of licence, and the approval of two distinct levels of government (communal and regional). The resultant bureaucracy was forbidding, if not actually prohibitive, to the growth of modern retailing. Whereas in France, Britain and Germany the modern sector (supermarkets, hypermarkets, franchising, etc.) accounted for approximately 50 per cent of all retailing in 1990, in Italy it constituted a mere 6 per cent. There were over 1 million small shops and less than 5,000 supermarkets and large stores.[50]

The survival of such a high quota of small shops had both advantages and drawbacks. In certain sectors, networks of independent retailers could be closely linked to industrial districts and offer their products directly to the consumer. In the textile and clothing industry, an Italian model (Benetton) and a British one (Marks & Spencer) vied with one another. The first moved from production, often made up of innumerable local sub-contractors, down into the organization of small-scale retailing through the franchise system. The second, by contrast, moved from large-scale distribution upstream into production, which was mainly outsourced to the low-cost countries of the Far East.[51] The Italian model undoubtedly had the advantage of maintaining a national link between production and distribution, as well as spreading opportunity more widely. A network of small shops was also crucial to the creation and conservation of cityscapes and neighbourhoods, as well as being an indispensable source of employment, a field in which more modern services and large-scale industry offered few guarantees.

On the other hand, so many small shopkeepers, with Italy having the highest density of shops per inhabitant in the whole of Europe, were unlikely to survive and prosper.[52] Inevitably, their prices were marked-up compared to those in supermarkets, and the sort of employment they offered was often of the dead-end variety. Consumers could gain from the sociality and convenience of small shops, but were attracted like flies to the vast spaces and special offers of the super- and hypermarkets.

In looking at the changing balance between services and manufacturing in different national economies, Rowthorn and Wells have suggested a number of possible scenarios.[53] One, which they call 'positive deindustrialization', sees a dynamic service sector absorbing workers displaced from manufacturing. By contrast, 'negative deindustrialization' is a pathological phenomenon 'which can affect economies at any stage of development'. Labour shed from manufacturing finds no convincing substitute in the service sector, and unemployment rises sharply. Italy in the last part of the twentieth century seemed uncertainly balanced between these two paths. Too much of her tertiary sector is taken up with retailing, too little with efficient and advanced services, either public or private, producer or consumer. As such, her service sector offers few guarantees for the future.

3. Industry, Big and Small

Italian manufacturing industry declined as a percentage of GDP and of employment, but it still remained a formidable force in this period. Taken together with the construction industry, it accounted for 32.5 per cent of employment in 1995 (compared to 37.6 per cent in 1980), and 32.1 per cent of added value (42.1 per cent in 1980). Italy's industrial base, then, was broadly a third of its economy, less than in Germany but more than in Great Britain.

a. LARGE FIRMS IN THE PRIVATE SECTOR
Fabrizio Barca has described the Italian world of medium- and large-sized industrial firms as a Janus made up of 'two parts, one "public" and the other "private", almost equal in their dimensions, but opposites in their structure of ownership and often in their economic results'.[54] The major private firms, faced with widespread worker militancy and rising costs, had already begun a radical process of reorganization and decentralization in the early 70s. In the 1980s many of them took the process a stage further, benefiting from the information technology revolution and the passage to the 'Toyota model' of 'lean production'.

The emphasis was no longer, as in the Fordist era, on purpose-built machines to make standard products, but on general-purpose machines using flexible automation to produce a variety of products. Quality control, attention to the needs of customers conceived of as individuals, ability to respond swiftly to changes in the market, became the order of the day. The transformation worked by major firms like FIAT rippled through the economy, affecting many smaller enterprises and sub-contractors.[55]

FIAT itself, Italy's largest private firm and one of its very few global companies, went through alternate phases in this period. At the end of the 1970s it was suffering from a whole series of ills – undercapitalization, a high level of debt, conflictual industrial relations, an antiquated range of car models, over-extension on the world market. The victory in 1980 over the principal left-wing trade union, the CGIL, was a watershed for the company. Aggressive restructuring resulted in marked revival during the second half of the decade.[56] The launching of the Uno in 1983 proved a great success, and brought FIAT for a brief period to level-pegging with Volkswagen on the European automobile markets. The 1990s, though, proved a rather more difficult decade. Shares of the European market slipped constantly, and the protected home market was gradually opened up to foreign competition. The company responded in two principal ways: with a policy of increased diversification, such as in the agro-food sector, and by developing its strategy for global car and commercial vehicle production and sales – the so-called 'Progetto 178' of 1993. By the end of the century this global project was fully operational in six countries: Brazil, Argentina, Venezuela, Poland, Morocco and Turkey. So, too, was a historic agreement with General Motors.[57]

With regard to the domestic market, the unique position of FIAT within Italian capitalism had a distorting effect upon consumption. Its power as a pressure group, when allied to the weakness and inefficiency of public transport services, pushed Italy ineluctably towards a position of automobile saturation. Between 1970 and 1988, Italy more than doubled its volume of passenger transport by car, the fastest rate of increase in Europe. By the late 90s it had more cars per inhabitant than any country except the United States, but only a small and crowded peninsula in which to put them. There was no clearer example of the pernicious effects of the meeting between an over-powerful, quasi-monopolistic private giant and subservient, short-sighted government.[58]

Elsewhere, big industry in the private sector presented rather a mixed picture. White goods (washing-machines, fridges, etc.), traditionally one of Italy's strongest sectors and one of the great motors of the 'economic miracle', could not maintain the impetus of the 1960s. Italy still had 39 per cent of the European market by the beginning of the 1990s, and three of its first five manufacturers (Zanussi, Merloni and Candy), but Zanussi had run into serious financial difficulties and in 1985 had been taken over by the Swedish multinational Electrolux. It was Electrolux, and not an Italian firm, which emerged as the world leader in the sector, with Zanussi forced into an important but subsidiary role.[59]

14

In the chemical sector, one of Italy's major weak spots as we have just seen, Montedison, the largest Italian company in the sector, changed hands five times in twenty years. In the mid-1980s, the Ferruzzi company, which had begun life as a family run agro-industrial company centred in Ravenna, acquired a dominant holding of the shares in Montedison. The guiding force behind this operation, which briefly made of Ferruzzi the second largest private company in Italy, was Raul Gardini, who had married into the Ferruzzi family. His expansionist, charismatic and unscrupulous leadership culminated in the fusion between Montedison and ENI, the state-owned petrochemical company, to create the chemical giant Enimont. This was a short-lived operation which was to be the source of one of the greatest of the 'Tangentopoli' scandals at the beginning of the 1990s, and which would lead to Gardini's suicide (see below, Chapter 8).[60]

In the field of information technology, home computers and office equipment, Carlo De Benedetti, at the head of Italy's largest company in the sector, Olivetti, initially made dynamic progress in the mid-1980s. However, here too the impetus could not be maintained. By the end of the 1990s, Olivetti had been taken over, and in world trade figures Italy did not even figure in the top fifteen exporting countries of office machines and telecom equipment.[61]

One of the most interesting and characteristic features of modern Italian industrial capitalism is the degree to which it is family-based. The results of a detailed study promoted by the Bank of Italy revealed in 1994 that Italian medium- and large-size firms had by far the most concentrated ownership and control structure of all those in the principal industrialized countries.[62]

Such family-oriented control had more disadvantages than advantages. On the credit side, the elision of family and firm made for very strong identification of the one with the other, and great willingness for personal self-sacrifice. It could also result in the invaluable communication of know-how between one generation and another. However, grave problems occurred when the family firm grew beyond a certain size. All too often Italy's entrepreneurs, faced with the choice of relinquishing control or renouncing external financing for new investment, chose the second path. Even then, the future of the firm was far from secure. Family control had a tendency to enter into grave crisis with the third generation, and problems of succession became the cause of anguish and discord.[63]

Everywhere, 'downsizing' was the dominant characteristic of medium- and large-size private firms in this period. The worst years were those between 1980 and 1986. The shedding of labour stopped briefly at the end of that decade, but resumed strongly in the early 1990s. Furthermore, private industry, especially of the most dynamic kind, was abandoning the territorial rooting which had characterized the Fordist era. Italian firms would maintain their headquarters in Italy, but production was increasingly taking place elsewhere, where labour costs were lower. Trans-national networks coordinated by information technology were replacing old territorial loyalties.[64]

b. THE PUBLIC SECTOR

As for public sector industry, the 1980s saw a fleeting revival before a final decline. The great Italian state enterprises had had their moment of glory in the 1950s, before political interference, poor management, low productivity and the costly absorption of private companies reduced them to a parlous state.[65] The decline was halted by the appointments of Romano Prodi to direct IRI in 1982, and Franco Reviglio to ENI in 1983. Both were university professors of economics who had previously held ministerial posts, and both revealed dynamic managerial capacities during their periods of office.

Prodi told the American journalist Alan Friedman: 'When I arrived at IRI I found an oppressive climate of demotivation and schizophrenia; the human resources of the company were being squandered.'[66] Losses stood at 2,672 *miliardi** of lire and debt at 35,000 *miliardi*. Prodi reacted with a vigorous programme of rationalization: Alfa Romeo, amid many polemics and an official inquiry on the part of the European Community, was sold to FIAT rather than to Ford.[67] Another thirty IRI companies were privatized, and the group opened up to internationalization for the first time. By 1988 it was showing a profit of 1,300 billion lire, including 600 billion in its industrial sector. The structural problems of IRI were far from solved, especially in the steel and shipbuilding sectors, but distinct progress had been made.[68]

Much the same story can be told of Reviglio's ENI, which converted losses of 1,500 billion lire in 1982 into profits of 1,316 billion in 1988. Here too privatizations and rationalizations were the order of the day. By 1987 even the disaster-ridden chemical sector had moved into the black.[69]

These limited but still significant successes of the 'two professors' were not to be repeated in the following years, and the arguments in favour of privatization slowly tightened their grip. The dynamic performance of certain public sector companies, like Nuovo Pignone at Florence, which built compressors, turbines, pumps, natural gas stations, etc., and exported them all over the world,[70] was not enough to cast into doubt the prevailing economic wisdom of the time; namely, that public ownership was necessarily bad and private necessarily good. In the early 90s a slow and painful transition towards privatization began.

* *Miliardo* is one thousand million, i.e. one US billion. It is here translated as billion throughout.

At the same time, ferocious de-industrialization descended on major sections of the public sector, especially steel and shipbuilding. Genoa, historically so dependent on the state sector, became for a period something of a ghost city. The statistics on major job losses in state firms tell a drastic story for the 1980s and much of the 1990s.[71]

c. THE NETWORKS OF SMALL INDUSTRY

This grim picture was in some way counterbalanced by the continuing success of Italy's extensive network of small firms and industrial districts. The world of the small firm is a kaleidoscopic and multiform one, and the Italian reality of these years was no exception. At one end of the spectrum it was possible to find firms that were little more than artisan shops, often in a highly dependent relationship with other larger firms, producing components or partly finished goods for them, employing casual labour on low wages. At the other end were autonomous enterprises producing sophisticated goods for particular niches in world markets, with a significant part of their workforces highly specialized and integrated into the life of the firm. In between there existed innumerable local variations – in size, in degree of autonomy, in relationship to markets, in treatment of the workforce.

The brightest elements in this universe of 'molecular capitalism', as Bonomi has called it,[72] were clustered in Italy's industrial districts, a socioeconomic reality of constantly growing proportions, and one which has attracted considerable international attention.[73] The definition of an industrial district is a complicated affair, but has been effectively summarized by Brusco and Paba as 'a community of persons and firms who operate in a limited territorial space, marked by the presence of economies external to the firms, but internal to the district in question. These economies solicit the formation and development of a specialized productive apparatus, in which small firms have a highly relevant role.'[74] The nature of production in such districts was dominated by those supply-side industries which formed so significant a sector of Italy's exports – textiles, as at Prato and Carpi, furniture at Poggibonsi and Arquate, ceramics at Sassuolo (the example chosen by Porter in his *The Competitive Advantage of Nations*[75]), shoes at Vigevano; but a considerable minority produced complicated machinery, such as that for agriculture in Emilia-Romagna, or precision instruments, or eye-glasses and frames as at Belluno, or even artificial kidneys, as at Mirandola. By 1991, on a conservative estimate, there were 238 such districts, with 1,700,000 persons employed in them.[76] Taken together they offered extraordinary testimony to the entrepreneurial vitality of much of the country, to its deep-rooted artisanal skills, and to its flair for design and export.

The sector encountered considerable difficulties in the 1980s. It was unprepared for the fierce competition that the products of the south Asian economies suddenly offered. In 1980 ten knives made at Lumezzane, the Italian centre for the production of cutlery, taps and valve fittings, situated in the Val Brembana above Brescia, cost 10,000 lire; their equivalent from south Korea cost just 2,800 lire.[77] The whole district, which counted some 24,000 inhabitants of whom more than 10,000 were employed in small firms, was under threat. Similar problems faced other districts: they were under-capitalized, their marketing and publicity were still at primitive levels, the great majority of their enterprises had under ten employees. Disaster seemed round the corner.

Instead, the great majority of Italy's small firms adapted with exceptional rapidity and flexibility. The synergies of her industrial districts, their blend of cooperation and competition, the 'industrial atmosphere' which led to the pooling of information and new techniques, all came to the rescue.[78] 'Incremental innovations' were the Italians' strong point, not earth-shaking discoveries, but small improvements and constant modifications in a product, which rendered it more attractive and functional.

Producer services, which had been so primitive in the early industrial districts, developed rapidly. In 1986 at Lumezzane, the Comune, the Banca Popolare di Brescia and Italtel got together to form Lumetel, a sort of supermarket for services of every type – marketing, quality control, training, energy saving, telematics.[79] Some districts, as with the shoe industry at Vigevano, decided to make not only shoes but machines for producing them. Others, naturally enough, specialized in '*cartotecnica*', the wrapping up of what they produced. Others still moved into plastics (some 27 per cent of the districts of 1991). Many districts which had first thrived on the basis of traditional Italian industries now generated new products and processes which were in some way complementary to the original ones.[80]

The combination of all these factors meant that in most, if not all, Italian industrial districts the global competition, and not just that from China, Taiwan and Korea, was held at bay. Italian small firms were closer to the key European markets, they had better records for punctuality, their design and quality remained superior.[81]

The fashion industry was a good case in point. By the early 1990s, the three sectors that made up the industry – textiles, clothing, footwear – between them gave work to 1,500,000 persons and contributed around 14 per cent of GDP. The industry was highly fragmented, with more than 100,000 firms at work. At its apex stood not only the great fashion houses, which became internationally famous in this period, but also the mass production empire of Luciano Benetton, who from artisanal beginnings in the Trevisan countryside soon created a global system of clotheswear shops, based as we have seen on a particular relationship between production and distribution, as well as constant innovation in both style and colour.[82]

The original nucleus of regions which contained industrial districts, heavily concentrated in the North and Centre of the country, gradually widened its base. In the decade between 1981 and 1991, a significant number of districts in the Mezzogiorno (twelve in all, principally in the South-East) made their appearance for the first time.[83] The region in most dynamic expansion was undoubtedly the North-East, with the small towns of the Venetian foothills pullulating with activity.

The dominance of family in these networks of entrepreneurship was even more pronounced than that in the medium and large firms. In the Bank of Italy study of 1994 some 83 per cent of firms with less than fifty employees were found to have a model of control which was either 'absolute' or 'familial'. However, there were signs of variation in the nature of this family control. At Prato, Pescarolo discovered that older forms of control exercised by a network of horizontal kinship (brothers, cousins, etc.) were on the decline. Most common instead were those concentrated on a single, nuclear family, with the entrepreneur's wife sharing in the ownership of the firm with increasing frequency. The male entrepreneur, often the founder of the firm, tended to remain in charge of it beyond retirement age, and often until his death.[84] The intense, symbiotic relationship between small enterprise and nuclear family was a very powerful instrument of economic propulsion. It also harboured significant problems, not only of an economic nature, of succession and of participation external to the family, but of a socio-psychological one, to which we will return in the next two chapters.

The networks of small firms and of industrial districts were one of the economic glories of contemporary Italy, but on no account should a mythical picture be presented of them. The small entrepreneurs prospered not only from their capacity for hard work and inventiveness, but also from the ease with which they evaded taxation, at least until the state began to tighten its fiscal grip in the 1990s. The spread of the 'urbanized countryside', as it came to be called in Italy, brought sudden wealth to individual families, but also considerable environmental damage, as urban sprawl grew out in great, uncontrolled swathes on either side of the main transport arteries. Above all, labour relations were not always based on that harmonious cooperation which had become the official mythology of the industrial districts. In the district of Manzano in Friuli, specializing in wooden products of every sort, there were 800 firms with 8,000 workers. To cut costs, many of the workers figured as pseudo-members of non-existent cooperatives. Many others were on short-term contracts and had no social security rights; others still (an estimated 300–400) were 'invisible' figures of the black economy, such as pensioners working at home, and labourers from nearby Slovenia and Croatia.[85]

4. Agriculture

The so-called 'primary' sector, that of agriculture, had long since become the tertiary one in Italy, with just 7.4 per cent of employment and 2.9 per cent of added value in 1995. Its quantitative decline was accompanied by a number of qualitative transformations. One of the most significant was the gradual revolution in Italy's rural physiognomy, a transformation which threatened, in the words of Franco Farinelli, 'to deprive the rural landscape (*paesaggio*) of almost any significance which was not an archaeological one'.[86] Hill and mountain areas had been widely abandoned in the years of the 'economic miracle', and urban sprawl, as we have just seen, had eaten away at much prime agricultural land of the plains. Between the censuses of 1982 and 1990, the amount of agricultural land had decreased by 981,000 hectares, or 4.1 per cent of the total; since 1960 as much as 3.7 million hectares had been lost.[87]

The problem though was not only, or even principally, a quantitative one. That extraordinary relationship between city and countryside, which had slowly formed Italy's landscape over the centuries, rendering it unique, had been interrupted abruptly. The 'capital', to quote Farinelli again, in the sense of the city which governed its own territory, had been detached from 'Capital', in the sense of modern investment in the food and farming industry. The latter's centres of decision-making were increasingly located far from the ancient provincial cities of the peninsula, and its priorities had little to do with the promotion or conservation of the rural landscape.[88]

One of the most startling developments in the Italian economy was indeed the growth of importance of large groups and multi-national food companies in the agricultural sector. Whereas their penetration had been slow and uncertain in industry, their rise in the primary sector was meteoric. In 1980, of the top 100 Italian food companies, multi-nationals counted for only 4.9 per cent of turnover and 3.6 per cent of employees. Just twelve years later these figures had shot up to 32.2 per cent and 42.2 per cent respectively. Nestlé-Italia had become Italy's largest food firm with over 7,000 employees; BSN, Unilever-Italia and Kraft-Italia also figured prominently, along with the Italians Ferrero, Parmalat and Barilla. Their penetration of certain markets was extraordinary; by 1992 Unilever, for instance, had become Italy's largest producer of olive oil and ice-cream![89]

The multi-nationals had been attracted to Italy by the increasing popularity of Italian food products throughout the world, and by the large number of medium-sized farms which could be bought up at reasonable prices. Their control of all four phases of the agro-food system – production, transformation, distribution and consumption – made them unbeatable competitors. The rapid evolution of computer and bio-technology also gave them the possibility of defying seasons and climate in their quest for all-year-round product perfection.

The invasion of these modern giants hit a rural economy that was for the most part sleepy and backward. There were, of course, sharp regional variations. The South not only had a much higher percentage of persons engaged in agriculture (15.1 per cent in 1990), but was constantly slipping behind in terms of productivity. In 1970 the added value per agricultural worker in the South had been 70.4 per cent of that in the Centre-North; by 1990 it was only 55.6 per cent.[90] Certain parts of Italian agriculture were highly productive, and there were even some 'agricultural districts' to set alongside their industrial counterparts. In Emilia-Romagna, for instance, there were those specializing in Parmesan cheese and pork products, as well as the famous orchards in the zone of Vignola.[91]

However, Italian agriculture as a whole lagged behind that of its European neighbours. Thanks principally to the increased presence of the large groups, both national and multi-national, Italy had pushed up its share of world food exports from 2.4 per cent in 1980 to 3.4 per cent in 1995, but imports were far greater in volume. The result was a significance balance-of-trade deficit, in particular with the European Union. The contrast with France was very striking, for the latter was the world's second largest exporter of food, having increased its world share from 8.0 per cent to 9.1 per cent between 1980 and 1995. Overall, Italy had a constant commercial deficit in the agro-food sector for most of this period.[92]

The structural reasons for this poor performance have most often been located in the fragmentation and restricted average size of Italian farms. Unlike in industry, satisfactory market niches for small farms were few and far between. One hectare of land dedicated to floriculture could be very productive, but a traditional farm even five times that size would not produce a living wage. In the 1990 agricultural census Italy had 3 million farms, with an average size of 7.5 hectares per unit, four times smaller than the average size of a French farm.[93] Yet the principal problem was one of agency, not structure. Italian agriculture, thanks to the persistent lobbying and electoral power of its principal organizations, the Coldiretti and the Confagricoltura, had become a sort of protected reserve, where small farmers (and large) had been subsidized for decades, both by the Italian state and the EEC.[94] The sector, although it provided 7.4 per cent of employment, contributed just 1.2 per cent of total taxation, thanks to widespread concessions and tax evasion.[95] Social surveys of the 1990s stressed the lack of agrarian innovation and entrepreneurship, as well as the closed and diffident culture of even the most productive farming families.[96] Services in the sector were fragmented and primitive, organized on a clientelistic basis, and dominated by a deeply corrupt state organization, the Federconsorzi, which brought its ignominious history to a suitable close in 1991, with a major scandal involving fraud and losses totalling some 3,000 billion lire.[97]

In general, the state's intervention in agriculture was less than satisfactory, marked as it was in the 1980s by a whole series of national plans which bore the name of various Ministers of Agriculture (the Piano Marcora, the Piano Pandolfi, the Piano Mannino), but which had little influence on agricultural output. The Regions and the Ministry of Agriculture vied with each other for control of the sector. The Regions proposed, and obtained by means of a popular referendum, the abolition of the Ministry, but the latter simply emerged from the ashes, phoenix-like, with a new name.[98]

In 1992 the MacSharry reform of agriculture in the European Community offered a new, and some commentators added last, hope for Italian agriculture. The Community's farming was to be divided into two major sections: the first competitive, large-scale, and integrated into the international agro-food industry; the second a 'rural space' in which profit was not everything, and environmental and landscape priorities were to be pre-eminent. In this second, and minoritarian type of agriculture, the 'vocation' of some small-scale farming was to be preserved and agro-tourism encouraged. It remained to be seen whether Italy could benefit from this far-sighted reform. Certainly, the first sector would be ever more dominated by the large groups, but the second could either take the path of a new lackadaisical reserve, or that of a thriving area which helped to renew a remarkable rural inheritance. The great boom in central Italian agro-tourism in the period 1998–2001 was one encouraging pointer in the right direction.[99]

5. The South

Running like an open sore through each compartment of Italy's economy – services, industry and agriculture – lay the unresolved problem of the South. Whichever way the statistician looked, the same depressing line of figures rose to meet his or her gaze. In 1990 the number of unemployed youths aged between fourteen and twenty-nine in the South was a terrible 44.1 per cent, as against 14.6 per cent in the Centre-North;[100] the South's GDP in the same year was only, in proportional terms, 59 per cent of that of the rest of the country, lower than it had been in 1980 or in 1970;[101] the South, contrary to popular legend, did not receive more funding per capita from the state, but it paid far less in taxes than the rest of the country: only 18 per cent of Italy's fiscal revenue, for 36.5 per cent of its population.[102] Infant mortality remained 30 per cent higher than elsewhere; 67 per cent of the railways were not electrified, as opposed to 33 per cent in the Centre-North.[103]

This long run of miserable figures should on no account be allowed to mask two crucial facts about the contemporary South – its regional diversity and its greatly improved standard of living.

There had always been radical differences between the various regions of the South; even the most casual visitor could grasp that Sardinia was not Sicily, and that Naples was different from anywhere else, not just in southern Italy but in southern Europe.[104] In the 1980s and 1990s new lines of demarcation appeared and old ones were reinforced. Thriving areas of small industry dotted the southern Adriatic coastline. The provinces of greatest economic dynamism were above all those in the Abruzzi, as well as certain zones of Molise and Apulia. Traditional Italian products – shoes, clothing and furniture – were much to the fore. Some parts of Campania, too, were emerging rapidly, as were two provinces of relative dynamism in Sardinia (Nuoro and Sassari), and two in eastern Sicily (Ragusa and Catania).[105]

On the other hand, there were vast zones of the South whose economy remained peripheral and depressed. This was especially true of Calabria and of western Sicily, while the huge metropolitan districts of Naples and Palermo had great difficulties in transforming themselves into centres of a modern service economy for the South. The dismal performance of the major southern banks in the first half of the 1990s, with the Banco di Napoli losing 3,155 billion lire in 1995 and major credit institutions in grave difficulty in both Sicily and Puglia, was an eloquent illustration of this point. Although commerce and tourism showed signs of revival in the 1990s, antiquated structures made progress slow and difficult.[106]

The centres which had been selected by government in the 1960s as poles for industrialization – Taranto, Syracuse, Matera and Cagliari – had not stood the test of time thirty years later. Their heavy industry, petrochemicals and steel, had often been unable to withstand global competition. Nor had they been able to generate autochthonous growth. Both the type of development chosen and the way it had been managed, with political and assistance criteria dominating economic ones, had proved recipes for disaster.[107]

The southern economy was patchy and unconvincing, yet standards of living continued to rise. In November 1984, when the journalist Nello Ajello visited Matera, at one time with its cave houses the symbol of southern poverty, he found its central streets crowded with well-dressed youths:

These young people are completely different from those desperately poor landless labourers who at the beginning of the century burned down the archives of the local town halls [which contained details of their debts]; but they are also quite different from the protagonists of that 'peasant civilization' immortalized by Carlo Levi and Rocco Scotellaro in mid-century. Today's spectacle would, all in all, be comforting if one didn't know that most of these youths are without work.[108]

Ajello had put his finger on one of the central economic paradoxes of the South in these years: the contrast between its fragile economic structure and relatively high levels of consumption. In fact, the figures comparing family consumption in the South and the rest of Italy were less dramatic than many others: in 1980 southern consumption had been 70.2 per cent of that elsewhere in Italy; in 1992 it was still at much the same level (69.6 per cent).[109] Bearing in mind the dynamic growth in standards of living in the Centre-North, this was not bad going at all.

How was this paradox to be explained? Part of the answer lay in the pattern of state spending in the South. Much more so than elsewhere, it had come to take the form of cash transfers to families rather than public services. Some of these transfers, whether in the form of hand-outs or jobs in public employment, were knowingly granted under false pretences: invalidity pensions for persons who were perfectly healthy, subsidies for farmers who did no farming, jobs for dustmen who collected no rubbish. The result was that family spending power and the internal market were kept buoyant, while public services – hospitals, schools, the supply of water – remained at often abysmal levels. As Augusto Graziani wrote in 1987, 'The lack of public services is today the real element of poverty in the South.'[110]

Economic development of this sort obviously reflected the nature of politics in the South (see below, Chapters 5 and 6). In the Mezzogiorno politics mattered more in economic terms than elsewhere in Italy, because the historic weakness of the private sector made the public one *the* privileged point of reference. The primacy of politics, though, had anything but benign effects. The southern political class, in search of legitimacy in a society characterized by low levels of trust and association, gave priority to interpersonal, clientelistic relations rather than to relatively disinterested works of public utility. Southern politicians mediated between centre and periphery, distributing state subsidies to individuals and families in return for electoral loyalty. In certain regions, above all in Sicily, Calabria and Campania, amongst their principal interlocutors were powerful criminal interests.[111]

The political economy of southern Italy, therefore, did not encourage autonomous economic entrepreneurs, but rather political and criminal ones. The very considerable volume of business that emanated from the activities of the Mafia, Camorra and 'Ndrangheta, tolerated and even encouraged by local politicians, formed another strong element of explanation for the high levels of consumption in some regions of the South.[112] It was in the 1970s, as we shall see in Chapter 7, that many 'men of honour' became really rich through the drug trade. A vicious circle had been created, which allowed the South a certain economic viability, but on improper bases. Internal constraints, even more than external ones, thus blocked the way forward.[113]

In the 1990s these structural problems were further aggravated. First, the central state began to take its distance from the South, gradually lowering the level of its investment and closing down the historic apparatuses and institutions of its intervention in the South. In 1984 the Cassa per il Mezzogiorno closed its offices. Then in 1992 the long-standing programme of 'extraordinary intervention' in the South was brought to a close. New plans for the support of certain 'depressed areas' did not become operative until 1996. As Gianfranco Viesti wrote at that time, 'the Mezzogiorno counts politically much less than in the past and has repeatedly been penalized in the recent choices of political economy'.[114] The few areas of thriving export-led small industry were not enough to compensate for this disattention.

It also became ever clearer that the international flows of private investment were passing the Mezzogiorno by. FIAT, it is true, chose in 1991 to build a major new car factory at Melfi in Basilicata. The agreement signed in April of that year between the company and the Ministry for the South envisaged a factory which would employ 7,000 workers and produce 450,000 vehicles a year. FIAT promised an overall investment of 6,672 billion lire and was to receive in exchange 'financial facilitations' for no less than 3,100 billion lire.[115]

However, even such favourable terms as these were not easily going to attract other private capital, especially foreign capital, to the Mezzogiorno. There were too many drawbacks, too many 'environmental risks'. In Basilicata, organized crime had never had much of a presence, but the independent Turin consultancy firm R and P (Ricerche e Progetti), which chose the Melfi site for FIAT, listed some other negative features in its final report: the low level and quality of infrastructural services; inadequate educational levels and technical skills of the local workforce; insufficient presence of external economies, both with regard to suppliers and service industries; inadequate local institutional responses.[116] This was a sober but telling indictment of the ills of the Mezzogiorno.

6. The Political Economy of the Republican State

The above discussion of the Mezzogiorno leads naturally to a brief review of the overall policies and achievements of the state in the economic sphere. The evolution of economic policy will be dealt with elsewhere in this book – when discussing the relationship between Italy and Europe, and the performance of individual governments. Here, though, it is necessary to say something of the macro-tendencies of the state's political economy, which to the historian's eye are dominated by one element – the growth of the budget deficit and the overall public debt.

Debt had not been a historic feature of the Italian Republic. In 1960, for instance, Italy had a primary surplus, a very low borrowing requirement and a low debt ratio. The situation had deteriorated slowly in the 1970s, and dramatically in the 1980s. In 1981 the Italian public debt had reached 61.1 per cent of GDP; ten years later it had risen to 103.9 per cent, second only in the EEC to that of Belgium (128 per cent) in percentage terms, but by far the largest in volume.[117]

As Luigi Spaventa has pointed out, major capitalist states have in the past run up larger debts than this.[118] For long periods of its history Britain exhibited levels of debt ratio higher than one, and sometimes nearer two; but this was the result of war or of very severe recession, and the level gradually fell as conditions stabilized. Italy's public debt, by contrast, was a peacetime phenomenon, and showed no signs of diminishing for the whole period from 1975 to 1992. As debt piled up year after year, international confidence in the Italian economy ebbed away.

The heart of the problem lay, obviously, in the structures of income and expenditure. Fiscal revenue gradually climbed to a percentage of income equal to that of Italy's European partners (41.9 per cent in 1990), but tax evasion continued to be very widespread, especially among the self-employed.[119] The tax burden was unevenly distributed: in geographical terms the South, as we have seen, provided only 18 per cent; in class terms, those with modest incomes of between 15 and 30 million lire per year contributed some 62 per cent of total tax in 1989.[120]

As for expenditure, the successful trade union struggles of the 1960s and 1970s led to a notable increase in public spending in various sectors: for the pension system in particular, in the wake of the reform of 1969; but also, after 1978, for the national health service, which was to be admired for its aspirations to provide universal coverage, but to be condemned for its wastefulness and low productivity.[121] At the same time the traditional economic mechanisms by which the political parties maintained their consent remained intact. One of the most authoritative and representative members of the Italian political class, Giuliano Amato, described in 1990 'the habitual praxis according to which all the norms and petty provisions of a financial nature are inserted into the Budget. These are not necessarily measures aimed at making savings; on the contrary, they are above all aimed at increasing spending. The Italian Budget is thus transformed into a process of hectic negotiation, and its contents become a variegated and disjointed mass of allocations.'[122] Italian public expenditure, therefore, was an unfortunate combination of long-term particularism and inefficient universalism. The result was a constant primary budget deficit (net of interest on debt).

By the early 1990s, though, it was the financial component (interest payments on the debt) not the primary component (the difference between income and expenditure in the public sector) that had come to dominate the whole problem. The decision to maintain high interests rates played a crucial role here. Both the Bank of Italy and successive governments kept interest rates high in order to combat inflation and to attract inflows of capital. The downside of such politics, however, was not only increasing foreign debt and discouragement of investment, but above all the leaping costs of interest payments on the public debt. These had become so great that the state, at the beginning of each financial year, was left with very little room for manoeuvre.[123] Eugenio Scalfari, in one of his many doomladen but often salutary editorials in *la Repubblica*, summed up the situation in September 1991: 'The truth is that this state is bankrupt. We all know it. A few people admit it openly, but most hide their heads in the sand.'[124] The truth, as we shall see, turned out to be another. From 1992 onwards the Italian state, aided by a buoyant economy and government by bankers, would climb back from the debt precipice.

The other major feature of the state's political economy was the attempt to tie the lira into a stable relationship with the other currencies of the European Community. After the fluctuations and devaluations of the 1970s, Italy gradually moved closer to the European monetary system. In 1979 the lira entered the EMS, and in January 1990 became part of the narrow band of currencies, with possible fluctuations not exceeding 2.25 per cent.[125]

The results of these policies were rather mixed. Inflation, which had been dangerously high for all of the 1970s and the early part of the 1980s, came down gradually to 6.9 per cent in 1991. A stable rate of exchange kept the cost of imports down and high interest rates discouraged a spiral of debt resulting from easy loans. However, the vigour and competitiveness which were supposed to result from the rigid exchange rate materialized only in part. Worse still, the lira's exalted status in the EMS was in gross contradiction with the continuing disastrous state of Italy's public finances. Sooner or later this contradiction was going to explode. It did so, as we shall see, in spectacular fashion, in September 1992, and left in ruins the monetary policy of the previous twelve years.

7. Conclusion

In 1673 Sir William Temple wrote that 'there seem to be grown too many traders in the world. So they can hardly live one by another.'[126] More than 300 years later, the ferocious competition identified by Temple had increased many-fold and assumed global dimensions. Yet it was only one of many economic elements, both exogenous and endogenous, that weighed upon the nation-state, constrained its political autonomy and determined its social well-being.

Italian capacity to meet these challenges, to survive and prosper in the world economy, was undeniable. In Italy, as in few other countries in the world, the *material* bases for democracy were firmly laid in the second half of the twentieth century. A pluri-secular, urban, commercial and productive tradition found a new lease of life, and the prosperity born of the 'economic miracle' was reinforced in the last twenty years of the century.

In the dominant sector of the economy, the tertiary one, Italy demonstrated a number of major weaknesses, above all in public services and public administration, which together formed the gravest of the internal negative constraints upon her economy. In addition, she showed sparse capacity to make the most of unparalleled resources in particular fields, especially those connected to tourism. Yet these weaknesses were strongly compensated for by the dynamism of much of her industry, especially that of the industrial districts. Italian design, 'incremental innovation', entrepreneurial flair and capacity to export, were all appreciated and envied abroad. The overall result was that between 1976 and 1991 Italy's income had increased (at fixed prices) by little less than 50 per cent, pro-capita income by 45 per cent, family consumption by more than 60 per cent.[127] Prosperity and democracy, as the Americans in Italy had always insisted after the Second World War, went hand-in-hand. Or at least, it was possible to have the first without the second, but extremely difficult to have the second without the first.

On the other hand, economic growth and human development are not at all the same thing, and the first came increasingly to menace the second as the century drew to a close.[128] Italy was very much part of that quarter of the world's population which consumed three-quarters of its resources each year and produced the greater part of its pollution and waste. If the population explosion was one part of the equation threatening the world's environment, the other was the production and consumption habits of the world's richest nations. The joint declaration of the American Academy of Sciences and the British Royal Society warned in 1992: 'If the predictions concerning demographic growth prove to be exact, and if the present forms of economic activity on the planet do not change, then science and technology could well prove incapable of preventing the irreversible degradation of the environment and the extension of poverty to the major part of the world.'[129]

If the criteria for judging Italy's economy shift from trading capacity and annual increase in GDP to its contribution to sustainable growth, then the nation's achievement, both in the public and the private spheres, must be judged much more severely.[130] Reconciling ecological necessities with political consensus is hardly an easy balancing act at the best of times, but what was particularly dispiriting in the Italian case was how low such questions came on the nation's agenda. Enrichment was still everything, and longer-term considerations had hardly begun to penetrate the collective consciousness.

In its most recent works, the UNDP (United Nations Development Programme) has established certain criteria for defining the possibility of human development. The extent to which growth is environmentally sustainable is one such. Another is the degree of 'participation' in such growth.[131] On this latter score, the most recent developments in world capitalism have hardly been reassuring. Karl Marx would have gained a certain, if somewhat meagre, satisfaction from seeing how closely the spiralling tendency towards fusion and concentration amongst the world's major firms at the end of the twentieth century have conformed to his mid-nineteenth-century predictions. The great global companies concentrated an ever-increasing share of the world's resources and decision-making powers in the hands of their boards of directors.[132]

The Italian case only partially fitted this model. Widespread small entrepreneurship allowed some real sense of agency to spread far down into the nation's economic activity. So, too, in a rather different way, did the structure of retailing. Both strongly linked families, often in their entirety, to economic activity. Yet if the concept of participation is interpreted in a different way, with relation to a theme long prevalent in the working-class movement, that of a measure of control over major economic structures, then the Italian experience was much more limited. The debate on this issue had been a constant one in Italy between 1945 and 1976, but seemed to have disappeared altogether some twenty years later.

A final element of human development, from which no rich and successful country like Italy could absent itself, was its relationship with the world's poorer nations. Here, as we shall see, Italy's record was a dismal one.[133] The country's own, very recent, emergence from relative poverty, and the closed, homogeneous culture of its population, did not give it a very good perspective from which to view the poverty of others. Yet Italy was a southern, not a northern European country, and the extensive poverty of much of the Mediterranean world, as well as its cultural diversity, were very close at hand. The eruption of this less privileged world on to the Italian scene would prove one of the major tests of the relationship, or lack of it, between economic growth and human development in contemporary Italy.

Chapter 2

The Social Hierarchies of a Prosperous Nation

*B*Y THE end of the twentieth century Italy's economy was, as we have just seen, one of the largest and most successful in the world and one that had made of Italy a place of hitherto unimagined opulence. Yet there were few signs that Italian society, on becoming richer, had become more just. The new wealth did not possess by itself, as some right-wing theorists fondly imagined, alchemic qualities for society as a whole, a capacity for creating greater social cohesion or social happiness, let alone, as we shall see, an increased faith in the *res publica*.

In the 1990s wealth in Italy, as well as the power and privileges that derived from it, continued to be structurally distributed in a profoundly uneven way. Few commentators denounced this state of affairs. The collapse of Communism, combined with the growing complexity of social structure in western societies, had blunted if not destroyed critiques of capitalism's endemic injustices. Instead there reigned nebulous ideas about the intrinsic value of economic growth, or else a poorly masked social Darwinism. Uncomfortable facts about structural inequality, both very old and very new, in the key areas of gender, class and race, were rarely the subject of public debate in Italy. This was a profound change from the cultural climate of the 1960s and 1970s. Few social trends justified such an abandonment.

1. Social Mobility and Income Distribution

All commentators concur that the social structure of advanced capitalist countries at the end of the twentieth century has become increasingly heterogeneous and complex, marked by a proliferation if not indeed a cacophony of interests and voices. The French anthropologist Henri Mendras has written of the dissolution of 'the class system in the classic sense of the term',[1] and the Italian historian Giulio Sapelli of contemporary Italy's 'social disassociation', and of its resemblance to 'a present-day tower of Babel'.[2]

There is a danger, though, of simplifying past social structure in order to emphasize contemporary change. The idea of entirely homogeneous classes was, of course, always a myth. When in the late 1970s Pietro Marcenaro, a former full-time student activist and trade union organizer, chose to go and work on the shopfloor of a medium-sized Turin factory, he at first considered himself, rightly, to be 'a strange sort of worker'. After a few months, though, he discovered 'lots of strange workers', with life stories which were certainly very different from his, but also very diverse one from the other, and every one of them very distant from the usual stereotypes. He discovered in a strike breaker 'a past as a leader of the struggles of the landless labourers who had emigrated to France'; in a young, revolutionary left-wing worker 'the small saver who was putting aside money to buy a flat'. After having reasoned for years in terms of 'multitudes of persons' – *the* working class, *the* peasants, *the* emigrants, *the* students – Marcenaro was forced to come to terms with the profound diversity and individuality of the 'masses'.[3]

Heterogeneity and quite distinct life projects, then, have always formed the real substratum of social classes. Two things were new about the 1980s and 1990s, both in Italy and Europe as a whole: the first was the profound uncertainty and division created by the rapid advance of information technology and the service economy. An already complex society seemed to be fracturing even further. The second was the contemporaneous weakening of institutions and ideologies which had previously formed identities and fostered social cohesion. Trade unions, mass parties, churches, all faced crises of cohesion and participation. Much more so than in the recent past, individuals were cast adrift in a world characterized by significant opportunities, but also by great risks.[4]

For a time, especially in the second half of the 1980s, it seemed as if almost everyone in Italy, in social terms, was destined to drift upwards. In late 1987 William Scobie, then *Observer* correspondent in Italy, accurately caught the mood of the moment: 'Suddenly this is a land of upward mobility, of vital computerised industry, bustling young business managers and slick middle-aged tycoons who have abjured their sixties' ideals in the sacred cause of profit.'[5]

The middle classes in Italian society expanded rapidly, in both numerical and income terms. *Inter-generational* mobility was a commonplace. Antonio Cobalti and Antonio Schizzerotto, in their recent study of Italian social mobility, have estimated that three-fifths of those at work in 1985 enjoyed a higher work status than that of their parents.[6] In the early decades of the Republic this inter-generational mobility had taken various forms: first, the passage from landless labourer or impoverished peasant to urban worker or artisan or shopkeeper; later on, from urban blue-collar to white-collar employment, or to small business. The Italians had become accustomed to thinking of their country as being a land of opportunity; not, according to one international survey published in 1989, on the level of the 'make good' societies such as the USA and Australia, but certainly more so than many other European countries.[7]

However, in the 1990s there were increasing signs that these upward flows were drying up and that the absolute mobility of previous decades had masked latent rigidities. In Italy *intra-generational* or career mobility, the change of status in a single life course, was much less common than that between generations. Cobalti and Schizzerotto noted that the country had one of the lowest levels of social mobility of this sort, second only to Poland in a seven-nation survey.[8] Barriers of various sorts blocked career progress, whether in the universities, the social services, or the public administration. In career terms, much self-employed work, especially the vast small-shop sector, led nowhere. Furthermore, the inter-generational passage from the working-class to the self-employed, so marked in the 1970s, was less frequent twenty years later. The arteries of Italian mobility were beginning to narrow.[9]

The spectre of work scarcity hung over the 1990s, providing a brutal antidote to previous euphorias. At a global level, some American analysts like Jeremy Rifkin painted an Armageddon scenario in which social structure, far from becoming more fluid and complex, would rapidly become simplified in savage fashion: a small, cosmopolitan élite of 'symbolic analysts' would in the future face a mass of workers who had few chances of finding significant or constant employment in the new high-technology global economy.[10]

Even without embracing so extreme a view, the declining prospects for mobility and job security were evident enough, all over Europe. In Italy the cold breath of downward mobility touched the necks of that same middle class which had been transported upwards, in considerable style, in the late 1980s. Even individuals with high qualifications in modern sectors found themselves at risk. In 1996 the journalist Miriam Mafai interviewed Sandro C., a computer programmer who had set up on his own in the 1980s, earning up to 100 million lire a year. Ten years later he found his income halved: 'at fifty I risk being thrown out of the labour market, unless I manage to re-cycle myself.'[11]

For most of its history the Italian Republic had offered families the possibility of bettering themselves. The violent passages from rural to urban life of the 1950s and 1960s, the monotony of the factory, the long hours of shopkeeping, the extraordinary self-sacrifice of the small entrepreneur, all had made sense so long as they provided the key to *opportunity*, for the next generation if not for one's own. Any interruption to this long-established pattern signified a threat to one of the most delicate mechanisms underpinning Italian democracy.

In visual terms, the income structure of contemporary western societies has often been said to resemble that of a diamond, extended at its mid-point to contain most of the population, but narrowing down symmetrically towards top and bottom. This was the way that most Italians thought that their society was shaped in the 1990s.[12] In reality, the image is a distorted one. A more accurate representation would probably be that of a William pear, but with a stalk more than ten times as long as the pear itself; or else, translated into Italian architectonic terms, something resembling the Mole Antonelliana in Turin. A recent analysis of American households by annual income level, divided into ascending sections of $5,000, confirmed an image of this sort.[13] If total wealth had been taken into consideration (i.e. not only annual declared income but physical assets like houses, land and consumer durables, and financial assets like stocks, bonds and bank accounts), the *stretching* effect of the diagram would have been more extreme still.[14]

The United States is a notoriously unequal society, but visual representations of other western societies convey a similar idea. One of the most striking is that of the Dutch economist Jan Pen, who presented an image of the British population in 1971, based on the idea that each person's height was to be determined by their pre-tax income level (without taking into consideration any other assets).[15] Pen imagined a grand parade lasting an hour, during which the entire population of Great Britain trooped by. First past our eyes were tiny gnomes the size of matchsticks, or cigarettes, those who had no annual income to speak of. Afterwards, for five minutes, came other, lesser dwarfs – some young people, old-age pensioners, divorced women, owners of shops doing poor trade, most of the unemployed. In fact, as Pen wrote, *'we keep on seeing dwarfs'*,[16] for it was only twelve minutes before the end that average income recipients passed by – teachers, executive civil servants, insurance agents, supervisors, a few farmers. In the last six minutes came the country's wealthy. At first these were mere six-footers – headmasters, young university graduates in business or the City. Then in the last minute came people ten yards and more high, like top civil servants or a High Court judge, while in the very last seconds the scene was dominated by colossal figures the size of tower blocks, top businessmen, managers of large firms, holders of many directorships, film stars and a few members of the Royal Family.[17]

No such representation of contemporary Italian society has yet been attempted, but there is little reason to believe that the result would be substantially different. A recent study of eleven nations, based on World Bank data for 1991, revealed that Italy and France were the European nations with the highest index of income inequality, with Great Britain not far behind. Japan took pride of place as the most equitable society, with a group of northern European countries (Sweden, Norway and Holland) in second place.[18]

Short of drastic action, long-term structural economic inequality of this sort can only be modified with great difficulty. In the 1980s a significant number of the Italian middle classes moved up the income and wealth scale, but their new prosperity did not, and could not, alter the basic pattern of income distribution. Paradoxically, favourable economic conjunctures, such as that from 1985 to 1992, tended to stretch still further income differentials, with the rich becoming richer and the poor relatively poorer. A 'composition effect' played a crucial role here: better-off families with more disposable wealth were able to invest in state bonds offering very high returns; poorer families, especially in the South, had no such rapid booster mechanisms.[19] Thus, the top of Italy's William pear became more robust, its stalk longer still, but its basic shape remained much the same.

2. Gender and Work

The American historian Joan Scott has suggested that gender in the modern sense of the word is best defined in terms of two inter-connecting propositions: it is a constitutive element of social relationships based on perceived differences between the sexes, and it is a primary way of signifying relationships of power.[20] To study gender in contemporary European history is not, therefore, synonymous with studying women's history. It means, rather, to study asymmetries between men and women, to chart the course of patriarchy in both private and public life, to estimate how present social trends are affecting historic imbalances of power between the two sexes.[21]

Later sections of this book will discuss perceived differences between men and women within the Italian family, in civil society, as well as in that vast reservoir of male power constituted by Italian public institutions and politics. Here the accent is on changes in the labour market in the 1980s and 1990s, with their profound effects upon Italian social life.

For many Italian women the last fifteen to twenty years have signified a striking transformation in their social identity. The shifts in the Italian economy analysed in Chapter 1 – the growth of the service sector, and especially the growth of public welfare services in the late 70s and early 80s – offered possibilities for women's employment which previously had not existed. Women were able to grasp these opportunities for a number of reasons: they were better educated than ever before; equal opportunities legislation (especially the laws of 1977 and 1991) had opened up areas of the labour market previously excluded to them; and they were having fewer children, though whether this was the cause or the consequence of increased women's employment was a moot point.[22]

Time-honoured patterns of gender differences were interrupted. The image of the man as better educated, as the principal breadwinner, as the family figure with exclusive access to the public world of work, and that of the woman as more poorly educated, as mother and housewife, became blurred. Women were moving *out*, making contact with a wider world, and few aspects of modernity were to produce so great a feeling of liberation as well as so much *angst*.

In 1961 the rate of female activity in Italy (the number of women working or actively seeking work as a percentage of all women able to work) stood at a lowly 22 per cent; by 1991 it had risen to around 30 per cent. At the same date the female labour force in Italy had reached 37.2 per cent of the total labour force.[23]

Behind these modest numerical increases lay major social change. There was, for instance, a spectacular rise in the female presence in some high-status professional jobs. The number of female magistrates, to take just one example, more than doubled between 1985 and 1992, increasing from 852 to 1,791.[24] The extension of social and educational services allowed qualified women mass entry into responsible and caring jobs. Above all, women workers became *visible* in great numbers: there were women ticket inspectors on Italian trains, dustwomen shifting heavy containers of rubbish, women police patrolling the streets. To the casual eye, it seemed as if the habitual gender division of work, so heavily centred in the past on the public-private divide, was being radically reformulated.

The reality was much less revolutionary and more uncertain. Marina Piazza has written perceptively of 'a paradoxical phase, in which women have genuinely acquired a new social force, but within a general context that safeguards the basic structure of gender roles'.[25] Her observation can be supported in a number of different ways. The Italian statistics for women's presence in the labour force did show a significant increase, but they were modest by international standards. The 1991 figures regarding the female employment rate (the number of employed women as a percentage of all those in work) placed Italy, at 37.2 per cent, in a lowly position in the European Community, above only Ireland, Spain and Greece, and far distant from Great Britain (61.1 per cent) and Denmark (70.1 per cent). Furthermore, by 1993 this figure had dropped to 36.0 per cent, and had fallen behind that of Ireland and Greece.[26] Women's work in Italy showed a marked tendency to tail off after childbirth; whereas in Britain and Germany women returned in great numbers to the workforce as their children grew up and left home, this was not the case in Italy. Nor did Italy, unlike Holland or Britain, have any significant section of part-time work for mothers with small children.[27]

A closer look at Italy's higher-ranking service and professional jobs reveals their gendered nature very clearly. In the professions women tended to concentrate in particular sectors or offices which were less prestigious and less well remunerated. Often they chose to do so, either because the work was more congenial to them, or because the hours were less demanding and more flexible. Thus in the magistracy women were to be found in great numbers in the juvenile courts. In some professions, like journalism, women were very under-represented. In others of recent formation, like research scientists in high-technology sectors, male domination was all but absolute.[28]

The explanation for these continuing discrepancies was not hard to find. Women had, for the most part, to sustain a dual presence at work and at home, to care for their families, or at the very least their husbands, as well as to hold down jobs. Theirs was what one group of women researchers has called 'the ambiguity of non-choice',[29] the constant sacrificing of one sphere or the other without achieving full satisfaction in either. Time and space constraints ruled out many of the top jobs in business and the professions; it was simply not possible to care for an ageing mother or young children as well as being on call for the punishing demands of the international money-making circuits. Highly qualified women time and again faced these very difficult choices, and no amount of ingenuity or energy could mask the tension. As Rosemary Crampton has pointed out for Great Britain, there were very many 'service wives', women who 'serviced' their career-oriented, service-sector husbands, but very few 'service husbands'.[30]

The women who tried to bridge these gaps found that they had little time for themselves, and that their lives acquired a hectic, adrenalin-ridden rhythm. In the summer of 1993 V.M. was the editor of one of Italy's leading women's journals, as well as being the mother of a small baby. When interviewed by Giovanni Contini, her account of everyday life was a revealing if extreme glimpse of what it was like to be a woman manager in Italy in the 1990s, as well as a fascinating account of relations between and within the sexes:[31]

v.m.: The baby was born in July, which was a real piece of luck, because that way I managed the first fifteen days of July easily enough, then there was the August break which were my holidays in any case, and by September I was back on the road. So I hardly had to stop at all, I directed the journal the whole time. We use Macintoshes to do the pagination by video, and they installed one in my flat, and that way I was in constant touch with the editorial team . . . I don't want claim to be a heroine, I find the very idea an odious one, let me just say banally that it went like this: when I was in hospital, I think the baby was three days old, I managed to design the cover for the next number . . . [In the morning] I have breakfast with the baby, I read the newspapers; always one at least, I have them delivered so that I get some news straight away. I do three things at once: I eat, I read the newspaper and I play a bit with the baby . . . At 8.15 a.m. the nanny arrives, and I give her instructions for the baby and the house, because she cooks as well . . . The baby gets on very well with this woman, he loves her a lot. She started as my cleaner, and then offered to do the nannying as well. I'm very lucky because at a certain point in the day her daughter, who's twenty years old, takes over from her. They're two different female figures, one forty, one twenty, and that's good for the baby . . . I always work, more or less, from ten in the morning to seven in the evening.

CONTINI: And your husband [another journalist]?

V.M.: He comes back at 10.30 at night.

The great majority of new women's work, however, was neither managerial nor professional. The ever-increasing dominance of the service sector meant a higher demand for women as clerks, typists, secretaries, shopworkers and so on. Obviously there was still a considerable sector of women's work in industry – especially in the clotheswear sector, in ceramics and elsewhere – but the prevailing trend was for women to occupy the lower and middle ranks of services, both consumer and producer, as well as those for final demand. Invariably, they had men for bosses.[32]

Women working in chain stores, in office blocks, in the public administration, had less stress but more routine and drudgery in their lives than the minority of career women above them. Their time to work was time to kill, rigidly stipulated by others, with early starts and fixed holidays. Their free time was probably equal to that of professional women, but it was more *residual* in character, what was left from the week rather than what was selected from it.[33]

The social and educational services presented some sort of haven for women workers in the 1980s – a high level of job satisfaction with reasonable pay and status. Yet the welfare sector and the female presence in it were modest indeed compared to those in northern Europe and especially Scandinavia, and little effort had been made to foster or safeguard women's work.[34] By the late 1980s, in any case, the number of job opportunities in the Italian social services was beginning to contract, exactly at the moment when more and more women (and men for that matter) with the right qualifications were coming on to the market. The lack of proper outlets for these women was to reach dramatic proportions in the 1990s, especially in the South, but even in the North in the 1980s there were strong indications of deep frustration.

One such can be found in a survey of cleaning women in Treviso in

1987.[35] The 200 women interviewees worked for a large cooperative in the area, and clearly divided into two cohorts. Those over thirty-five years old were mainly married housewives with low educational qualifications, working part-time to supplement family income. They were reasonably satisfied with their jobs. Those under thirty-five, by contrast, had high educational qualifications, often difficult family situations (divorced or separated, small children to support, etc.) and were much more dissatisfied with their lot. They saw, with every justification, cleaning jobs as the last post in their struggle for an autonomous and satisfying work identity.

In the first half of the 1980s the feminist movement, then in full flow, had expressed great hopes that women, as they entered the labour market, would act as transformative agents within it. Feminist writing laid the emphasis upon the diversity of women's social activity with respect to men's, based as it was upon the ethics of responsibility and of care. Laura Balbo, one of Italy's foremost feminist sociologists, wrote in 1982 that since women were 'guided by a logic oriented towards needs, they cannot entirely accept submission, but on the contrary tend to resist the logic of the dominant ideology'.[36]

In the ensuing decade neither this emphasis – upon women's essentially different and subversive contribution – nor the more modest one which stressed the need for parity between men and women found much sustenance in the real world. In certain jobs, principally those connected with education and the social services, and in certain regions, of which Emilia-Romagna was the foremost, the increased presence of women did lead to a profound process of cultural transformation, and a new phase in the history of relations between the sexes. In all workplaces which were previously male enclaves, the presence of women changed daily discourse, rendering it not only less sexist but also less monotonous and primitive. Yet it would be foolhardy to exaggerate these processes, for even in the most advanced regions of the country those women who acted as transformative agents were a small minority.

Prevailing attitudes, especially in the upwardly mobile climate of the 1980s were far different. Many women, especially career women, tended to ape male attitudes to work rather than try to change them. Women at work could demonstrate extraordinary solidarity, but they could also be divided by quarrels as bitter and personal as those between men, or between the sexes. Most working women in Italy in these years, with jobs in the lower echelons of the labour market, simply accepted or were forced to accept gendered hierarchies and male values. The increasingly uncertain economic climate of the 1990s forced them further on to the defensive. Stable jobs became fewer, and the tendency to fall back on part-time work in the 'informal' economy much greater.[37]

3. Class

Gender was one fundamental cleavage that cut across Italian society. Class was another. The relationship between the two is complex and much debated. Suffice it to say here that capitalism and patriarchy can with difficulty be fused into a single theoretical framework, but can rather be viewed as interacting, if distinct, systems of power relations and social organization.[38]

Class itself is hardly an uncontroversial term, and the distinction between social class and social status is one of the classic *loci* of sociology. The divisions within society can be variously defined, in terms of income and wealth, of employment relations, of cultural accumulation, of consumption, and so on.[39] Recently, too, the gradual overall diminution of time at work has led to a new awareness of the importance of free time in the formation of identity.[40] Once again, this is not the place to air these debates, but rather to ask how they can inform our analysis of modern Italian society. The key question here has a twofold character: first, whether with increased individualization and fragmentation it was still possible to identify social groupings that, broadly speaking, shared common identities, aspirations and interests; and second, whether such communality of interests enabled them to act, as social and political subjects. Of continued relevance in this respect was Marx's fundamental distinction between a class *in* itself and a class *for* itself.[41] Social groups in contemporary Italy may have shared fundamental work, employment or consumption similarities, but did they still have a collective *voice*, and if so how loud was it?[42]

The answer to this critical question was a variable one. Some sections of society maintained or even enhanced their cohesion, others disintegrated or decomposed, new ones came into being in a deeply disorganized form. Much had changed since the 1970s.

4. The *'grande borghesia'*

The highest echelons of Italian society, those few thousand families which lived at the top of the stalk of the William pear, were, hardly surprisingly, a social force of formidable power and influence. In the late 1960s and early 1970s their position and privileges had come under violent attack, and indeed the very stability of Italian capitalism had been called into question. Symptomatic of the climate of that time was the confession, many years later, of one of the principal stockbrokers of the Milan stock exchange, Aldo Ravelli, a man not given to easy panic: 'Those were the years in which – I'm telling you to give you some idea of the atmosphere at that time – I tested out how long it would take me to escape to Switzerland. I set out from my house in Varese, and got to the frontier on foot.'[43] Ravelli never had to make the walk in earnest. The crisis passed, the ruling groups emerged relatively unscathed, and the following period proved much more benign for them.

The Italian *grande borghesia* shared a basic view of the proper hierarchical ordering of society, but was otherwise divided by many tensions and cleavages – geographical, political, economic and cultural. Wealth and power, the two distinguishing traits of this group, did not always coincide. The economic élites had their epicentre in the great families of northern Italian capitalism, the Agnelli, the Pirelli, the Marzotto, and a few others. What was surprising about the Republican era, during which so much changed in social and economic terms, was the *continuity* of this tight group at the heart of Italian capitalism. Their numbers, it is true, had been thinned during the 1980s: the Borletti, for instance, had sold up to FIAT, Augusta to EFIM, Zanussi, as we have seen, to the Wallemberg. The Catholic wing, long represented by Enrico Pesenti, the 'cement king', had been pushed on to the defensive, especially after the crack of the Banco Ambrosiano.[44] None the less, a small number of very powerful figures, linked often by kinship ties and endogamic marriage strategies, members of the same boards of management, beneficiaries of considerable state aid and concessions, accustomed to oligopolistic positions in their respective markets, together exercised a degree of control and influence that was very much greater than that found in other capitalist countries of equal standing.[45]

No institution or personality symbolized better this relatively discreet but immensely powerful grouping than Enrico Cuccia, head of the famous Milanese Mediobanca, Italy's most important investment bank. Over a period of more than fifty years Cuccia, physically ever more bowed and seemingly frail, a man of formidable severity and intelligence, and of very few public appearances, had built up a complex system which linked and protected the major Italian private firms, banks and insurance companies. His mission, often reiterated, was to protect private Italian capitalism from the maraudings of the politicians and from an over-strong public sector, but his method was certainly not one that shunned contact or aid from Rome. Indeed, Cuccia described himself on one occasion as 'a centaur, half public and half private'.[46] He was a centaur used to command, and he forged the identity and behaviour of successive generations of collaborators at Mediobanca, whom he referred to as his family, right up until his death in June 2000.[47]

In Rome lay another centre of immense power, this time primarily political and cultural. Politicians do not fit easily into the analytical category of '*grande borghesia*', but the 1980s in Italy marked an unusually strong elision of economic and political power. Already in the 1950s the Christian Democrats had created with great care their own centres of economic control within the state.[48] Thirty years later, as we will see below in Chapter 6, politicians became entrepreneurs of themselves, building up considerable personal fortunes in the process. Rome, too, was the capital of the only truly global Italian organization, the Roman Catholic Church. The links between this, the greatest cultural force in the land, and the world of the politicians, between Vatican and Montecitorio, had been intense throughout the history of the Republic.

If Enrico Cuccia was the archetypical figure of the Milanese world of finance and industry, that of Roman politics and Catholicism was best represented by another veteran and besuited figure, equally physically slight and bowed, but much more used to the limelight. Giulio Andreotti had moved between the company of politicians and that of cardinals and popes with greater skill and longevity than any other Christian Democrat politician in Europe.[49] He had entered the world of high politics in 1947 at the age of twenty-eight, when he was nominated by De Gasperi as under-secretary at the Presidency of the Council of Ministers. By the beginning of the 1980s he had been prime minister five times and minister countless others. His political astuteness and ability to survive had become legendary, as had his aphorisms, of which the most famous was undoubtedly 'power consumes he who has it not'.[50] If Cuccia's networks were the narrow ones of leading northern industrialists, bankers and insurance agents, Andreotti's were much more widely based, with an organized clientele extending far down into the social structure of Rome and of Lazio, and to a lesser extent of Palermo and Sicily. Indro Montanelli once wrote that 'De Gasperi and Andreotti used to go to Mass together and everyone believed that they went for the same purpose, but this was not the case. In Church De Gasperi spoke to God, Andreotti to the priest.'[51] Montanelli's spirited remark caught perfectly one part of the fascinating and complex character of the man who, as we shall see, was the single most important figure in the history of these years.

The most powerful elements of the bourgeoisie clearly divided into an older, more established sector and one of much more recent origin. From the 1970s onwards the inner court of Italian capitalism, aristocratic and linked by its origins to the world of material goods, was bombarded by a whole number of newcomers, the *nouveaux riches* who emerged violently and startlingly from various parts of the service economy. Some of these rode and fell on the surging waves of financial capital; others were entrepreneurs, performers and symbolic managers from the world of mass communications; others still used the resources of politics as *the* means of rapid elevation.

Some of the principal figures – Michele Sindona, Roberto Calvi, Raul Gardini, Bettino Craxi – were stars who shone too fiercely in the Italian firmament, and who eventually fell to death or disgrace. Others, like Silvio Berlusconi, were to enjoy a love-hate relationship with the establishment of Italian capitalism. The divisions, however, should not be exaggerated.

Assimilation, imitation, the convergence of interests and of lifestyles were all too strong for that.

For most of the Italian *grande borghesia*, of whatever derivation, discretion was not a quality to be valued highly. If there was a role model for them it was not Cuccia, who was said to live like a bank clerk, but Giovanni Agnelli, whose lifestyle was opulent and international, aristocratic and idiosyncratic.[52] The geographical dispersion of the Italian bourgeoisie meant that there was no single city centre in which the homes of the very rich were concentrated, as for instance in Eaton Square and the adjoining terraces of Belgravia in London.[53] None the less, there were clear patterns of taste and location. For the winter some of the newcomers bought up chalets not far from the Agnellis at St Moritz, or else invited each other to lunches and parties at Cortina d'Ampezzo, and in the summer they had themselves photographed at the helm of their large yachts as they cruised around the Mediterranean.[54] Some could not refrain from exaggerating horribly.

The channels by which the upper ranks of the bourgeoisie made their presence felt were not principally formal or explicit ones. Fragmentation and geographical differentiation were mirrored in the organization of Confindustria, the largest interest group of this sector of Italian society. Unlike its British equivalent, the CBI, Confindustria could boast a daily newspaper, *Il Sole-24 Ore*, of growing influence and quality, but in other respects it lagged behind its European counterparts. It represented far fewer firms – 110,000, compared with 260,000 of the CBI, 1,000,000 of the French CNPF and 1,200,000 of the German BDA, and had not extended its umbrella over the world of commerce, finance and the services in general.[55] It was also organized on a strongly territorial basis, which certainly gave coherence to the stronger sections like the Lombard one, but left others prey to very particularistic interests.[56] These were structural defects, deeply rooted in Italian history, and they made it difficult for Italian entrepreneurs, let alone the *grande borghesia* as a whole, to speak with an effective and convincing national voice. Territorial, sectoral and even familial tendencies to dispersion were further heightened by interaction with a political system which displayed, as we shall see below, many of the same characteristics.

5. The Modern Middle Classes

In the last decades of the twentieth century the urban middle classes came to occupy the central position in Italian society. Numerically dominant as never before in the history of the unified state, they were, however, far from being a united force, and their very diversity encourages us to speak at most of middle classes rather than a single middle class. Over the years they have been portrayed frequently in negative terms, and this tendency shows little sign of abating. The sociologist Carlo Donolo, for instance, has recently passed eloquent and scathing judgement upon this 'modernized and americanized middle class', whose interests and sentiments he summarizes as follows: 'defence of the status quo, in the shape of a society which includes only two-thirds of its members; mass hedonism; primacy of middle-class values, but in the form of a rent-seeking society which finds its macro-expression in the connection between tax evasion, investment in lucrative state bonds, growth of the public debt'.[57]

Such judgements have an undoubted foundation, but to leave them unqualified is to create a major obstacle to our understanding of Italian society and politics. All over Europe, side by side with this rampant and even irresponsible *ceto medio*, there developed another middle class, with rather different perspectives. Some sociologists have chosen to call it 'reflexive', in the sense of its turning an increasingly critical eye upon the very development of modernity, upon its own origins and activities.[58] Instead of being swept away by the intense rhythms, the enrichment and the material consumption of the modern world, this middle class has shown a growing awareness of global dangers, of the damage wrought by unthinking consumption on the quality of everyday life, of the connections between private choices and public consequences.

The cultural origins of these critical sections of the European middle class are many: higher levels of education are one, the long-term effects of 1968 another. Henri Mendras has pointed to an 'innovatory nucleus' at the heart of the contemporary French middle classes, middle-aged and unrepentant of its involvement in the May events, committed to voluntary groups and civil rights movements. This nucleus, according to Mendras, is 'tied to a diverse social cosmogony which both negates and contaminates bourgeois ideology without being subversive of it'.[59]

In the early 1990s each of the major European countries offered a different balance between these two conflicting faces of the middle classes, a balance that depended upon differing structural, cultural and political roots. In Britain, for instance, public sector employment grew with extraordinary rapidity in the 1940s, increasing from 2.2 million to 6.3 million in the period 1938–51. A considerable section of the middle classes, mainly professionals and public employees within the social services, was formed in the post-war years, when British political culture was peculiarly progressive and when the long post-war boom ensured high levels of welfare expenditure.[60] These progressive middle classes of the 40s and 50s built in any case upon a long-established liberal ethic of service to the state, fairmindedness and civic culture. In France, paradoxically, both '68 itself and the Gaullist reaction to it (a considerable increase in social spending in the 1970s) contributed to the formation of a reflexive middle class.

The Italian case was different again. Crucially, we find here a weaker structural base for the development of a critical and reflexive middle class. In the Republican period the formation of the Italian middle classes was much more heavily dependent than in the other major European countries upon two sectors – small family capitalism and a very extensive artisanal and shopkeeping class. Those middle classes which flourished elsewhere with the development of strong welfare spending were much later in coming to Italy. Thus in 1961 Italy employed only 170,000 persons in the public health sector, compared to 545,000 in the German Federal Republic, 550,000 in France, and 627,000 in Britain. Twenty years later, after the belated introduction of the Italian health service (1978), Italy still employed little more than half the number of Britain's public health workers. In social security and social work, Italy lagged still further behind. Only in education during the post-war decades did public employment in Italy keep up with France and Germany, though not with Britain.[61] Furthermore, no sooner were public services in the welfare sector firmly established in Italy in the late 1970s than they were constrained by the economic pressures and prevailing ideology of the last two decades of the century. Nor was any strong ethos of service to the state and service to the public ever established in Italy.[62]

The modern European middle classes, then, at the end of the twentieth century spoke with two rather different voices, with two distinct languages of social identity and responsibility. If this was the case, we need next to ask which of the Italian middle class spoke with which voice. Of course, such an enterprise resembles the labours of Sisyphus, for the subtleties of individual formation, and of family tradition, render the task so intricate as to be impossible. It would be foolish indeed to suggest that certain employment relations or even types of education find, in mechanical fashion, their politico-cultural counterparts. None the less, some broad distinctions can be suggested which may be of relevance for contemporary Italy.

6. The Upper Sections of the Middle Class

Antonio Schizzerotto, in the most recent sociological work on the upper sections of Italian society,[63] has suggested a fourfold division for them: *entrepreneurs* (who own and direct places of employment with at least fifteen dependants); *professionals; the service class* (consisting of the high and middle management of firms and of the public administration); *professional politicians*. Like all such categorizations, this is open to objections and comments, but it serves as a useful point of departure.[64]

Schizzerotto and his fellow researchers present convincing evidence that these four sections of Italian society formed an increasingly homogeneous group at the apex of Italian society in the 1980s, with strong tendencies towards inter-marriage, broad similarities of outlook, and a distinct mode of *exclusion* with respect to those below them. As Schizzerotto has written: 'The difficulty of acceding to the ranks of employers, politicians, managers or professionals is minimal if one is dealing with the descendants of these privileged occupational categories. It grows considerably for those of white-collar workers; increases still more in the case of the self-employed, and reaches its maximum level in the case of the children of dependent manual workers.'[65]

However much they formed a 'community of destiny' in the Weberian sense of the term, these four sections of the upper middle classes (Schizzerotto calls them simply 'upper classes') were not identical, and it is worth trying to bring out the distinctions between them. The professional politicians, a smaller group than the others, whose own very particular mechanisms of self-perpetuation will be dealt with below, followed a pattern of rise and fall all of their own: an intense period of accumulation and wheeler-dealing in the mid- and late 1980s, followed by a violent challenge to their very mode of existence in the years 1992–4.

The entrepreneurs faced no such caesura. Their fortunes varied, as befitted their calling. Significant differences existed among them, both in generational and geographical terms, as well as in the size of their enterprises, but all in all the last two decades of the twentieth century were a halcyon period for them. They faced enormous challenges, but had responded with that peculiarly Italian combination of family mobilization, technological adaptation, design flair and extreme hard work. In the process they created a very high standard of living for themselves. Diego Della Valle, for instance, had become very rich by inventing his own clotheswear products in the second half of the 1970s (the shoes 'Tod's' and the heavy jackets 'Fay'). His grandfather had been a simple cobbler in Sant'Elpidio a Mare (Ascoli Piceno), and his father had built up the family footwear firm in the 1960s, but still as a supplier for others. 'The world,' Della Valle told the journalist Marco Moussanet, 'is full of delicious things, often of great use, which no one knows about, and with which one can make a great deal of money. But you need to be constantly on the move and have a very sharp eye.'[66]

This flair and quick-wittedness was not usually accompanied by a high degree of civic consciousness. Italian entrepreneurs often expressed very strong localistic loyalties, to other members of their industrial districts, as well as comprehension and camaraderie towards the workers in their factories,[67] but they rarely transformed these restricted solidarities into a more general reflection upon their place in society. This was a section of Italian society out to make good, out to make family fortunes, and not too worried about the way they did it.

Silvana E., an entrepreneur in the clotheswear trade of the Venetian hinterland, was culturally very distant from Diego Della Valle, but rather typical of a whole swathe of small factory owners of the most recent generation. When asked in 1992 what her objectives were in life, she replied:

Look, I'm after money – just money, only money. I wanted to have a good life, buy myself beautiful clothes, I wanted people to notice me. I was very ambitious, still am, I wanted to be somebody, I didn't want to be ignored by people. Now I have thirty workers under me and I'm doing well. I make between 300 and 350 million a year (circa £150,000 at 1992 prices), but I declare much, much less to the tax man, the rest is all in *nero*. But don't write that down! Otherwise we'll have the tax inspectors here straight away . . . It's funny, but now I don't even have time to enjoy the money I've earned, but I can tell you fifteen days in a luxury hotel at Jesolo are enough for me. They're enough, enough to make me feel *una gran signora* . . .[68]

In the new villas on the peripheries of the small cities of central and northern Italy, complete with their iron railings, their water-sprayed lawns, and flotillas of various-sized cars, the animal spirits of Italian capitalism found their kingdom. In the past these spirits had to some degree been tempered by the Catholic subculture of the North-East and that of the Communists in central Italy. In the 1980s, with the decline of both these seminal ideological influences in modern Italian society (see below, Chapter 5), the individual entrepreneur was cast loose; free, as Pier Paolo Poggio has written, to create 'a new social landscape in which hard work and opulent patterns of consumption describe the horizons of the world'.[69]

This freedom attained its apogee during the great economic boom of the second half of the 1980s, but even then was accompanied by a growing impatience, especially in the provincial cities of Lombardy and Venetia. Small entrepreneurs, and not only they, began to express a new culture. They were free, but wanted to be more so, in the sense that they resented the inefficiency of the central state, its non-functioning services, the 'thieves of Rome' as the political class was called, as well as the increasing fiscal pressure upon them. There were many ways of avoiding this last without putting oneself completely outside the law, but even so a self-image of hard-working *victims* began to form among this section of society. It went hand-in-hand with a more open intolerance, towards southerners and immigrants, towards those who were different or outsiders. Far from the new wealth producing a pluralist and culturally richer society, the principal actors in the advanced sectors of the economy were giving vent to an increasingly *tribal* voice.[70]

The members of the professions, our third sector of the upper middle classes, were intertwined with the entrepreneurs in myriad ways, and their social milieux often overlapped – the same dinner tables, the Rotary Club and

Lions, the same expensive venues and hotels for mid-winter breaks. Yet the professions *were* a distinct grouping, better educated, often closely linked with the universities, and with a greater presence among them of critical spirits.

The professions, like the business classes, grew significantly in this period. By 1980 the state had recognized twenty-four professions as legal corporations exercising a monopoly in their field, with registers for their members. It would be a mistake, though, to consider only these. Many new professions were still waiting to be recognized (and were to wait throughout our period), while some recognized professions, like that of nursing, were in no way similar to the others, and their members could not remotely be defined as members of the upper middle classes. In all, the recognized professions totalled 1,425,471 members by 1996, compared to only 899,174 in 1986.[71]

In a recent study, Willem Tousijn has noted that in all the major sectors of professional activity conflict was the order of the day: within single professions, between them, and in relation to clients. In health work, for instance, the doctors had established a powerful dominion, while in the 'technical' professions engineers and architects engaged in interminable squabbles.[72] In relation to the outside world, to Italian society as a whole, the professions distinguished themselves for their corporatism and rapacity, qualities far removed from the Durkheimian conception of them as oases untouched by the amoral character of economic life.[73]

Italian dentists, safe in the monopoly of their profession, charged fees that were the most exorbitant in Europe, consultant doctors created an ever more lucrative private sector, with clinics that proved inexhaustible founts of enrichment and frenetic activity. Members of the profession were not in the habit of giving tax receipts for their services. Time and again, ordinary citizens were asked to enter into a pact of complicity in return for a discount, and were only too willing to do so. These practices were so endemic as to constitute a culture in their own right. From the very core of the country's trained élite came a dismal message for the public morality of a great democracy. There were exceptions, of course, but not enough of them.

The service class, or senior management (which is a less confusing term), were different again from the entrepreneurs and the members of the professions.[74] Here there was a fundamental distinction to be made between those employed in the private and the public sector. Many managers in private firms were, for obvious reasons, similar in outlook to the northern *grande borghesia* that had formed them, whereas public managers were closer to the political class that had appointed them. In keeping with all their past history, high-level public managers in the ministries, in local government, in the USL, gave few signs of being a culturally dynamic and socially responsible civil service. Instead, cynicism, corporatism and conservatism seemed both at a national and local level to be their main characteristics.

As for private managers, in a recent European comparative study on management, the authors of the section on Italy felt obliged to begin their piece by stressing the centrality of the model of the family: 'The family provides an example for other *structures*, allowing the development of industrial patterns which either follow the ramifications of the family or mimic them.' The attitudes of Italian managers were found to be dominated by individualism, autocracy, paternalism, a stress upon masculinity and a strong sense of hierarchy.[75]

One of the most important questions regarding the upper middle classes was how far the radical changes in the economy had transformed them, and led to the emergence of new figures with innovative voices. Mario Deaglio has argued forcefully that this was indeed the case at a global level.[76] In the new financial and entertainment sectors, in the world of telematics and information technology, in educational and other services, the possessors of 'human capital', creative as well as technically competent, constituted, according to Deaglio, a 'new bourgeoisie', as revolutionary as that identified by Marx in the middle of the last century.[77] They, and above all the 'electronic' mode of production that had produced them, had swept away millions of decrepit middle managers and white-collar workers, and an even greater number of blue-collar workers in the old Fordist industries. The new bourgeoisie was wedded to efficiency, lower taxes, and the absolute freedom of markets; it hated cumbersome bureaucracy, the rigidity of Keynesian labour markets, the restrictive control of trade unions. It was as international as the old bourgeoisie had been national.

Deaglio's is a thought-provoking analysis, but should be treated with some caution. The 'new bourgeoisie' was in no way as clearly antithetical to its older cousins as might appear, just as the nineteenth-century bourgeoisie was at least as interested in assimilation into the aristocracy as it was in combating it. Nor was it by any means clear that the 'new bourgeoisie' constituted an international force, relatively free of nationalist or even localistic interests.

In the Italian case, the analysis of the country's service sector presented in Chapter 1 must lead to a country-specific scepticism. As we have seen, Italy's service sector was deficient in the most dynamic areas of producer or intermediate services, and strong in the most traditional service, final trade, the retailing necessary for the final consumption of material goods (see above, pp. 9–13). As a result, the new figures of the service economy were of numerically modest proportions.

There were exceptions. In Milan the so-called 'advanced tertiary sector' could already in 1988 count over 30,000 members, with publicity and data processing being the most important occupations, heavily concentrated in the centre of the city. Milan could also boast a populated entertainment sector: theatre and television, editing, dubbing and mixing studios gave work to another 25,000 persons, obviously not all in the higher ranks of these professions.[78] A new series of figures in the credit and financial services, of which Milan boasted a considerable history, were also emerging.

Yet the dominant impression was one of a narrow geographical concentration, especially in Milan and Rome, and of a great deal of talk about the new professions without yet the substance. Far from the traditional upper middle classes being bombarded and overwhelmed by a new élite which was the product of the electronic revolution, bringing with it a revolution in culture, there seemed rather to be an almost painless accommodation of the new with the old. The 'advanced tertiary sector' was neither sufficiently numerous nor sufficiently advanced to give rise to a clear voice of its own. And even if it had been, it is by no means clear that it had something distinctive and different to say.[79]

7. The Lower Middle Classes

Between 1974 and 1989 white-collar workers grew from 20.2 per cent of the working population to 32.4 per cent; in the same period the traditional urban lower-middle classes – artisans, shopkeepers and self-employed, far from declining, actually increased their percentage share of the workforce from 16.4 per cent to 19.3 per cent. Their rural counterparts – small farmers and peasants – dropped from 10.1 per cent to 5 per cent. Taken together, these figures indicate clearly that for the first time the urban lower-middle classes – modern and traditional – constituted the majority of Italy's working population (51.7 per cent).[80]

a. SHOPKEEPERS AND ARTISANS

Within these overall trends there lay a strong Italian anomaly. While the American model of mass employment in a service economy was based on a large number of transient 'Macjobs' (badly paid work in food chains and other services, mainly for immigrants and youth), and the Swedish one on a lesser number of stable and usually female occupations in the social services,[81] the Italian was based on the soaking-up of labour in small family shops and artisan firms. The traditional nature of the Italian service economy, based as we have seen on retailing and tourism, translated into a massive presence of shopkeepers, artisans, tourist operators and the like.[82] These three models – American, Swedish and Italian – reflected three different types of service economy, or at least different emphases within them. They led, as can be imagined, to considerable differences of outlook and culture among service workers.

Sadly for our purposes, more research has been done on Italian family shops at the end of the nineteenth century than at the end of the twentieth.[83] From time to time this extensive social group, ignored in Italy for the most part by the modern social sciences, erupted with force upon the national scene, as in 1984 and 1995–6. In analytical terms, retailing is usually divided into four sectors: the food sector, which in Italian terms translates into the kingdom of small grocers (*alimentari*); clothes and textile shops; furniture and articles for the house; other products and articles. To these must be added the '*esercizi pubblici*': bars, cafés, restaurants and *pizzerie*. In 1982 the Lombard regional council carried out a survey of shops in Italy. It found one shop for every eighty inhabitants in Lombardy, one for every sixty-two in central Italy, and one for every fifty-two in the South. These were by far the highest densities to be found in any of the major European countries.[84]

There were wide variations of wealth in this vast galaxy of food counters and imaginative display of goods, of men and women who worked seemingly endless hours in cramped conditions, coming out from time to time on to the doorsteps of their shops for a breath of fresh air and a chat with their neighbours. In some parts of the South impoverished grocers or ironmongers hovered on the brink of viability, their shops empty except for a few cheap, traditional products. At the other extreme the consumerism of the 1980s had been responsible for some remarkable fortunes, which made of shopkeepers shop-owners, and pushed them into the ranks of the upper-middle classes in terms of income, if not of culture. A jaundiced view would single out those terrible twins, the butcher and the chemist, as the symbols of the new Italy: the consumption of meat remained constantly high while that of medicines zoomed upwards between 1986 and 1991.[85]

The shopkeeping class had become accustomed over time to being allowed, for reasons of political convenience, to avoid much of the taxation that they should have paid. Each year the Ministry of Finances produced figures showing that shop-owners and artisans very often declared incomes that were the same or smaller than those of their employees. Thus in 1993 the owners of shops selling electrical household appliances declared an average income of only 16.2 million lire, against the 20.2 million of their shop assistants; jewellers declared just 22.5 million against the 19.8 million of their employees; car repair firms 21.2 million against 18.6 million of their mechanics, but owners of *autosaloni* 15.4 million lire against the 27.2 million of car salesmen.[86] Such figures allowed small shop-owners to survive and to prosper, but created a central block in Italian society, composed of self-employed professionals, small entrepreneurs and shopkeepers who defrauded the state on a massive and habitual basis. To add insult to injury, they then often put the very income that they had denied the Treasury into state bonds offering high interest to finance the public debt. This was a cynical operation, impossible to quantify, but deeply rooted in the folklore of the 1980s.[87]

In that decade, as deindustrialization tightened its grip, regional and local governments were over-liberal in granting shop licences, treating the retail sector as a sort of social shock-absorber. The liquidation payments of many workers were promptly used to open small shops. However, the market could only take so much, and the long-term trend towards supermarkets, hypermarkets and discount stores, although much slower as we have seen than in northern Europe, was inescapable.[88] By the mid-1990s the High Noon of many small retailers had arrived. Legislation against tax evasion had become increasingly insistent (see below, Chapter 8, p. 272), and at the same time families were reining in their expenditure. In 1993 consumption dropped by 2.5 per cent. Small family shops wilted under this many-pronged attack upon their profits. The panic of the shopkeepers was not, or at least not yet, that which had gripped them in 1920 and 1922, for the country as a whole was too prosperous and the political context very different, but by the late 1990s their voice had become increasingly shrill.

b. WHITE-COLLAR WORKERS

The other, still larger, section of the lower middle classes was that of white-collar workers and their families. If the specificity of the modern Italian middle classes consisted in the presence of a dynamic small business class and an extended shopkeeping and artisanal sector, the numerical preponderance of *dependent* work should at no cost be ignored. Indeed, statistics comparing 1960 and 1992 reveal that dependent work had significantly increased in this time span, from 49.1 per cent to 71.8 per cent of those in employment. Much of this difference was to be accounted for by the disappearance of impoverished peasant proprietors and their female 'helpers' ('*coadiuvanti*'). However, these statistics serve to remind us how much the structure of a service economy, as well as an industrial one, was reliant on dependent work, on enduring structures of command and obedience, and of the rigidities of time connected with them. Of dependent workers in Italy in 1992, 4.8 per cent were in agriculture, 36.2 per cent in industry and 58.7 per cent in the tertiary sector.[89]

As service work tightened its grip on the economy, the occupational profiles of the city centres as well as their skylines changed rapidly. Office blocks, banks and centres of consumer spending established a near total domination. In the space of a few years, nearly all the great factories at Sesto San Giovanni, on the outskirts of Milan, were pulled down and redevelopment for offices, supermarkets and the like began. At sleepy Poggibonsi in the heart of the Sienese countryside, suddenly out of nowhere a multi-storey and plate glass '*Centro direzionale*' sprang up from 1980 onwards, to cater for the many service requirements – finance, training, hotel accommodation, etc. – of the dynamic small firms of the area.

The cooler economic climate of the 1990s, combined with the intrinsic long-term job-shrinking qualities of information technology, began to take their toll of white-collar work of this sort. As Miriam Mafai has written:

Once upon a time, not long ago, to say 'bank clerk' meant security: work that was not too tiring, fifteen monthly payments per year, an average salary much superior to an equivalent grade in the civil service, generously subsidized social clubs, a special integrative pension in addition to the state one, employers who provided study scholarships, tennis competitions, a week's skiing holiday.[90]

By 1996, however, the previously unknown word 'excess' began to be whispered among the bank clerks. As one of them confided to Mafai in the spring of that year:

Somebody like me, who for years has been behind the counter, feels humiliated when he's made to understand that his work is practically superfluous. A transaction at the counter costs the banks just over a dollar, but only 35 cents if it's done by telephone and 27 cents by Bancomat (credit card). Faced with figures like these, how can you help but be afraid?[91]

Italy lagged some years behind Britain in its rationalization of this sector, but could not do so indefinitely. In the public sector, white-collar work expanded in two principal directions – geographically, towards local and especially regional government, as new powers and responsibilities were devolved; and descriptively, as new services in health, social work, education and transport were made available. Hospitals, schools and airports became some of the largest single employers in the social geography of the new Italy.

These developments were very much in line with those in other European countries, and it would be quite mistaken to talk of a particularly bloated public sector in Italy compared with elsewhere. By 1991, the number of public-sector employees per 100 inhabitants was 6.5 in Italy, compared to 6.8 in West Germany, 8.8 in France and 9.2 in Great Britain.[92]

The universe of white-collar work in the public sector was vast and heterogeneous, as were its places of employment. The latter varied from the great rhetorical ministerial palaces of late-nineteenth-century Rome to ancient town halls and social insurance institutions of Fascist foundation, from the plate glass and concrete constructions of regional government to dilapidated schools and hospitals. The greatest concentration of personnel was to be found in school education (29.1 per cent of all public sector employment in 1992), followed by local government (21.8 per cent) and the health service

(20.7 per cent). Women were 51.8 per cent of total employees, but this parity was due in great part to their overwhelming presence in the schools; 71.7 per cent of schoolteachers were women.[93]

Overall, that is if it is in any way possible to generalize about so great and variegated a mass, the Italian civil service was an ageing (the average age of employees being forty-four), dispirited and lackadaisical force, in striking contrast to many sections of its French, British and German counterparts. Most Italian civil servants declared themselves satisfied with their jobs, which certainly constituted secure shelters from the bombs dropping outside on to other sectors of employment. The hours of work, too, usually from 8 a.m. until 2 p.m., were not onerous. However, Italian public employees were deeply dissatisfied with their rates of pay, and also with the lack of recognition of individual ability and dedication. Promotion followed time-honoured paths of seniority and was usually limited in extent.[94]

Low productivity and low status produced low morale and a deeply ingrained scepticism and pessimism. The overriding tendency was to feather individual or sectorial nests – the category, division, section or even grade, and to do so by union organization that was for the most part corporate and short-sighted.

None the less, it was among this much-maligned section of Italian society that it was most possible to find the 'reflexive' voices of the modern middle classes. Among the 900,000 dissatisfied, demoralized and poorly paid Italian schoolteachers there were tens of thousands who struggled on in difficult, if not impossible conditions of work, who paid out of their own pockets to go on further training courses, who worked to keep up with the scientific literature in their discipline, and who tried to communicate their enthusiasm to their students, whether large or small.[95] Unlike in Britain, the private sector of schooling did not hive off many of the best teachers, and in Italy it was possible to find a fierce commitment to state education.

The intermediate generation of teachers, those born between 1941 and 1955, was the most affected by what Alessandro Cavalli has called 'the modernization *manqué*', the destruction of all their hopes of a cultural transformation of the schools in the 1970s.[96] Even so, many of them, and especially their younger colleagues, retained a sense of urgency in encouraging school students to reflect critically on the modern world.

In the world of local government, too, cultural, educational and social services had expanded greatly in the period under consideration. Adult education, libraries, children's recreation centres, various types of social and educational services for young people, theatre laboratories, exhibitions, cinema festivals, all these extended by the 1990s, as Carbonaro and Sbordoni have written, into 'the remotest piazzas of the peninsula'.[97] They brought into being new figures, 'social and cultural operators', very often women.

They were precious indeed to contemporary Italy, but they were deemed the most 'expendable' in terms of public sector cuts.

8. The Working Classes

Of all the sections of Italian society, it was the blue-collar working class whose composition, culture and voice changed most drastically in the last twenty years. Once a strong and relatively united force, unusually class-conscious and capable of great acts of solidarity and mobilization, like those of the 'Hot Autumn' of 1969, the Italian working class abruptly fragmented and lost impetus. By the mid-1990s it could with difficulty be described as a class *in* itself, let alone *for* itself. Behind this transformation lay not so much a dramatic numerical decline as a fundamental change in its composition. In 1993 25 per cent of the workforce were still industrial workers, compared to 31 per cent in 1971, but the great factories had ceased to be centres of working-class aggregation and political power.[98]

The working classes, both industrial and in services, were divided into three major components in this period: the most advanced sectors, working for the major companies, but totally transformed in terms of outlook and job description; the composite world of the small factories, whose members and dynamism helped to keep industrial employment reasonably buoyant; and growing numbers of service workers, often on short-term contracts, working in relative isolation, almost always without trade union organization.

a. 'OPERAI' OR 'OPERATORI'?

The process of numerical decline in industrial work has already been briefly described in Chapter 1 (see above, p. 15). Traditional sectors like the metal and mechanical industry, chemical production and textiles were those most affected. In the six years from 1980 to 1986 FIAT cut its workforce by nearly half. Those who remained had to learn very rapidly a different organization of work and work culture, based on radically changed modes of production. As Arnaldo Bagnasco has written,

In the major factories, at all levels, specialization and room for autonomy tended to increase, the quality and content of work improved, investment in training grew, workers created individual careers in line with their professionalism. They diversified and regrouped in small, independent work squads. They were expected to participate and show loyalty to the firm.[99]

In place of the old labour relations of the Fordist factory, based on hierarchy, formality and authority, as well as a profound capital–labour divide, there emerged a conception of the workplace that was hegemonic and monistic. Production was to be an 'organic' act, harmonious and necessarily unifying.[100] Workers were asked to be knowledgeable, flexible, subjectively involved in what they were doing. Informality oiled the wheels of industrial relations, as did collective involvement in the fate of the firm. All these attitudes were well summarized in 1990, in the testimony of S.V., a systems manager in the mechanics workshops at FIAT Mirafiori:

I think that I'll always have something to learn from these machines . . . we all know that to keep up with its competitors, FIAT has to innovate non-stop, and so our expertise has to increase at the same rhythm . . . The dominant criterion is your willingness to take on responsibility and to be extremely flexible. Flexible in the sense that the work of a systems manager like me means being multi-functional . . . It's also important to understand the problems of others. If I imagine myself to be not a wage worker but a client and a supplier at the same time, then I must, like any good manager of a firm, understand the problems of others.[101]

As so often in the history of Italy's industrial relations, FIAT was in the forefront of the new tendencies. These took various forms. One was the adoption of quality circles, consisting of workers who stayed behind in the factory, of their own accord and without pay, to discuss ways of improving the quality of the firm's product. By 1987 more than 5,000 workers were involved. Another were 'family days', parties organized by the firm at the workplace so that FIAT workers could bring their families into the factory. Another still was the network of swimming-pools made available to FIAT employees and their families, and used by 400,000 people per year. Shareholding in the company increased rapidly, with 86,000 employees investing 1.5 million lire per head by the end of the 1980s.[102]

Fewer workers, better trained, highly motivated, fully integrated into the firm; this was the model, of obvious Japanese origin, for the Italian labour aristocracy at the end of the century. It brought both great opportunities and great dangers. Skilled workers had more chance of their talents being recognized, of promotion and pay increases, of professional mobility. They also enjoyed more independence and responsibility, and much less routine and monotony.[103] On the other hand their hours of work were long and the competitive stress considerable. There was also a real danger of a new servility, of the triumph of neo-paternalism or even neo-feudalism, of the return of the organic community from which they could not escape and against which they had lost the will to rebel.

What voice would issue forth from these new high-technology Italian work communities was the subject of considerable debate. Optimists, like the veteran trade-union leader Bruno Trentin, saw new opportunities opening up for the advanced nuclei of the working class: job enlargement had enriched their work, they had more responsibility and autonomy, they had more potential power. For the first time there existed the structural basis on which could be built a real 'co-determination' at the workplace.[104] Pessimists like the sociologist Marco Revelli put the accent instead on the extent to which ruling-class ideas had totally permeated the minds of workers, rendering them loyal, malleable and profoundly subordinate. Such attitudes, argued Revelli, were good for profits but bad for democracy.[105]

b. WORKERS IN SMALL FIRMS

If we turn to workers in small firms, we see some of the same processes at work, but in a less sophisticated and more personalized way. Informality was the name of the game, with workers encouraged to feel, and genuinely feeling, part of a common endeavour. In the 'industrialized countryside' of much of central and northern Italy, *padroni* and *operai* shared common values and symbols, pastimes and eating-places. Their voice was a celebration of localism, sometimes exasperatedly so.

However, behind this localistic camaraderie there lurked tensions of many sorts. Very many of the workers in Italy's small firms were linked by kinship ties to those who owned them. Far too much attention has been dedicated to the benign and productive nature of these relationships, and far too little to their hierarchies, oppressions and tensions, especially with regard to marginal kin and women.

Michael Blim's research into shoe-producing firms in the Marches in the 1980s gives a glimpse of the differentials in kin relationships. One family firm produced inner soles and supports, employing six full-time and two part-time workers. Seven of the eight were kin. They consisted of the brother and sister of the firm's head, Antonio Rovere, his son-in-law, his wife's son-in-law, his niece's husband, and last, but far from least, his two daughters. Blim commented on this firm:

There are kin – it seems – and there are kin. Favored are the lineal rather than the collateral kin – that is, one's children rather than one's siblings. The hope often expressed by the Gentile–Rovere household principals is that ownership of the business will pass to Feliciana and Fulvio [elder daughter and her husband]. In contrast, Antonio's brother and sister along with the other kin are considered employees of the firm. They are not consulted in the firm's operation, nor are they expected to share eventually in its ownership.[106]

Such evidence was very much in line with that described by Pescarolo at Prato: 'vertical' kin was gaining ground at the expense of 'horizontal'.[107]

Given the whole history of Italy's small firms, it was inevitable that many of them would be directed by dominant male figures, unable to conceive of relations that were other than authoritarian and patriarchal. As a result the symbiosis of family and firm, of private and public, could be asphyxiating, with the hierarchies of the one transposed mechanically to the other. No amount of financial compensation was likely to allay these oppressions.

In the 1960s and 1970s industrial workers in Italy had found in the major trade unions (CGIL–CISL–UIL) a collective voice of considerable strength, one dominated by ideas of solidarity and equality which found concrete expression in demands for parity between regions, the narrowing of wage differentials, the raising of workers' educational levels through the *150 ore* scheme.[108]

A decade later, this type of militant trade unionism was in grave crisis. The principal unions were still capable from time to time of mass mobilizations, of filling the piazzas of the major cities with their members; the factory councils, although much diminished as a vehicle of grass-roots representation, were still crucial reference points at times of heightened social tension; the local trade unions in areas of small industry could still hope to establish the broad framework for working conditions, even if their membership in individual factories was scarce.[109] However, what had disappeared almost entirely was the presence of the trade-union movement as a major social and political protagonist.

Italian trade unions were not alone in suffering such a decline. Elsewhere in Europe, and in the United States as well, the 1980s were a period of defensiveness and of defeat. Part of the reason for this was structural, with the radically changed nature of the capitalist economy and the composition of its workforce. Part was political, with the frontal attacks waged upon trade unionism by the Anglo-American neo-conservatives.[110] But part, too, of the responsibility lay with the trade-union movement itself. In the Italian case, there was great reluctance to come to terms with changing realities, to accept for instance that diversity and differentials could not simply be ignored or demonized. The trade-union bureaucracies were top-heavy and poorly oiled machines, the membership was declining and ageing at the same time. By 1990 the CGIL, the largest of the three major unions, had 2 million pensioners out of a total of 5 million members.[111]

As their influence lessened, the trade unions began to quarrel among themselves. In 1984 CISL and UIL agreed to a three-point cut in the wage-index mechanism, the so-called *scala mobile*, designed to protect real wages against inflationary spirals. The cut was fiercely opposed by the Communist-dominated union, the CGIL. There followed a fiercely fought referendum at a national level, called for and lost by the Italian Communist party (see below, Chapter 5, p. 152).

From this time onwards 'competitive unity' replaced any real unity of action between the major unions. More problematic still, radical and militant sectional trade unions, the so-called COBAS, began to stake their claim to represent new as well as old sectors of the workforce. The new organizations were especially strong in the public sector, among groups such as train drivers, schoolteachers and nurses. The COBAS advocated the defence of class interests, but this often led in practice to a clear conflict between the interests of consumers and those of workers in the public services, especially the railways. Faced with a seemingly interminable series of wildcat strikes, public sympathy slipped still further away from the trade unions.[112]

All this induced, at least in some sectors of the working class, growing feelings of frustration and impotence. The average working-class wage in the early 1990s almost equalled that of the *declared* income of jewellers and was supposedly superior to that of hotel owners. Taxation at source meant that dependent workers were bearing the brunt of the fiscal pressures exercised by the state, that other much better-off sectors of the social structure were escaping almost scot-free, but that workers had lost the collective power to do anything about these manifest injustices.

c. SERVICE SECTOR WORKERS AND THE 'BLACK ECONOMY'

An ever more dramatic division was opening up between those who were in steady work and those who had to be content with temporary employment or work in the black economy. One estimate of the early 1990s placed the number of visible 'irregular' workers at 3.5 million, to whom were to be added another 2 million submerged in the black economy.[113] These were dramatic figures. Marx imagined that the lumpenproletariat, as he called it, would slowly be sucked into the great factories, and this was one of the sociological bases for his belief in eventual social revolution. Instead, modern capitalism continued to produce an enormous casual sector, both in industry and services. In Italy many of these were to be found in the sweat-shops of the informal industrial economy, from the metalworking *'boîte'* (small workshops) of Piedmont all the way down to the small textile firms of Apulia, some of which operated in conditions of complete illegality and employed young girls for up to fourteen hours a day.

The problem of *lavoro nero* was certainly most acute in the South, but it was not confined there. A tragic incident of March 1987 in the rich (and left-wing) city of Ravenna revealed the national realities of the informal sector. Thirteen casual labourers lost their lives when they were overcome by fumes while cleaning a ship's hold. The small firm which employed them, McNavi, was a subcontractor which paid 5,900 lire (under £3.00 at 1987 exchange rates) an hour to work in conditions where no safety regulations were applied, and no trade-union organization was permitted. The men who died were aged between seventeen and sixty; most of them were local and the youngest was at his first day of work. One of them, Mohamed Mosad, was an Egyptian whose address was given as a beach-hut at Marina di Ravenna.[114]

An increasing number of these casual workers were in the service sector. In the major city centres, clustering around the great banks, office blocks and stations of the Metro were the shops, sandwich bars and *tavole calde* which served the vast army of daily commuters. The workforce here was mainly young and female, with low educational qualifications, confined to small spaces for long hours.

The micro-firms of the major northern cities were marked by a fragility of relations between employer and employed; informal and irregular agreements over terms of pay and overtime often led to quarrels, sackings and even court cases.[115] Trade unions were unable to make any impact upon this world, nor upon that of shop-workers in traditional retail outlets. From the extreme opposite end of the peninsula, from Acri in the province of Cosenza, Calabria, came a cry of desperation from a teenage girl looking for work:

I'm eighteen years old . . . and at the moment I'm pretty confused. I can't decide if I should just conform or else rebel against the reality of my life. But against whom? . . . perhaps against the way the shop-owners behave here. They make huge profits and at the same time, to avoid paying tax, they make the girls who work regularly for them sign for wages which aren't even half of what they really earn. And let's not even talk about those who work for them without a regular contract! Their day's work is usually between eleven and twelve hours long. Do you think it's just that we should continue to submit to such misuse of their power? And that they should exploit the plight of their fellow citizens in this way?[116]

At the end of this chain came the so-called 'entry jobs' – cleaning of every sort, looking after old people (on the increase), baby-sitting (in decline). These were, once more, female enclaves and poorly paid. Yet the long lists which appeared in all the local papers of people offering to do work of this sort bore testimony to how far demand for work outstripped its supply.

9. Poverty, Unemployment and Urban Peripheries

At the bottom of the social scale came a significant percentage of the Italian population who had benefited marginally, if at all, from the country's new affluence. Poverty is a controversial term, heavily dependent for its meaning upon distinctions of definition and measurement. The international standard-of-poverty line is drawn at the point where a family of two persons has an income inferior or at most equal to that of the average pro-capita income of the nation in question. Such a definition is clearly one that regards *relative*, not *absolute* poverty. It is also exclusively economic in content and allows no space for what Nicola Negri and Chiara Saraceno have called 'the progressive and multi-dimensional character of poverty',[117] the way in which different elements — health, nutrition, work, education, social contact, housing — all interlock. As for the measurement of poverty, different methods (by income or consumption, by person or by family) can lead to radically different results.[118]

With regard to the Italian case, a national Commission on poverty (and later on immigration as well) was first set up in 1984 by the then President of the Republic, Sandro Pertini. Its reports, based on the international standards described above (but calculated by consumption not income), pointed to a persistent hard core of poverty, equivalent to 13 per cent of the resident population in 1983, rising to 15.4 per cent in 1988, and declining again to 11.5 per cent in 1994. The percentage figure of 1994 was equivalent to 6,458,000 persons, out of a total resident population of 56,371,000.[119]

Who were these 6.5 million Italians who lived in relative poverty? The first and most obvious answer was a considerable section of the population of the Mezzogiorno. According to the 1994 statistics, the poor accounted for 4.5 per cent of the northern population, 6.7 per cent of those living in the Centre, but 22.6 per cent of those in the South. Looked at in another way and at another date, the South in 1988 had 37 per cent of the Italian population and the Centre-North 63 per cent, but these proportions were exactly reversed with regard to the number of poor people: 67 per cent of them were to be found in the South, and only 33 per cent in the North.[120]

A disproportionate number of these poor were to be found in large southern families, where often only one low income had to cover a multitude of needs. Children in these families suffered a great deal of relative deprivation. Old people, too, as everywhere in Europe, were much at risk. The older the cohort of the Italian population, the greater the percentage of it living in poverty. Thus in 1988, 20.8 per cent of those between the ages of sixty-six and seventy-five were classified as poor, but the corresponding figure for those over seventy-five was 28.4 per cent.[121] These were not comforting statistics for a country with an ever more imbalanced age structure.

The old and the very young, especially in the South, were thus two obvious categories at risk. A third were those affected by Italy's particular model of unemployment. This model, as Enrico Pugliese has explained, was characterized by strong youth, female and southern elements, and also by very long-term unemployment for certain groups of the population. The other side of this coin was an almost total absence of unemployed males in the North.[122] The level of Italy's unemployment was not much higher than the European average (11 per cent as against 9 per cent in 1991), but in the same year those under twenty-five years of age constituted 49.3 per cent of all Italian unemployed, compared to the European average of 32.4 per cent.[123]

The lack of work for southern youth was one of the Republic's gravest problems, which showed little sign of disappearing as the decades passed. As in many other fields, the dramatic changes and high hopes of the 1960s seemed, when viewed from the end of the century, to have been a parenthesis in the history of the Republic. Much of southern youth was trapped, as it had been in the 1940s and 1950s, by a labour market which gave it the possibility only of casual, part-time, precarious ways of earning money.[124]

There were, of course, great material differences compared to forty or fifty years earlier. The widespread, absolute poverty of that period had disappeared; young people in the South in the 1990s were protected by their families, offered a minimal education, and guaranteed adequate levels of clothing and food, if not always of health and housing. Their real problem, though, consisted of a different but equally fundamental aspect of poverty: the absence of hope. There seemed few acceptable or legal ways of breaking out of their enforced idleness, which produced more apathy than anger.

The prospects for young southern women were particularly grim. Time and again even those women who had continued their studies found no proper jobs at the end of them. The teacher training colleges and professional and technical institutes of the South offered few real hopes for female emancipation and careers.[125] Instead there loomed an almost inevitable life-cycle, made up of housework, bringing up children, caring for elderly relatives. There could be much that was fulfilling in such a life course, as women themselves would testify; but there was also much that could lead to isolation and depression. This last, an especially female illness, was most prevalent in Italy among housewives with low levels of education.[126]

All over Italy, not just in the South, there existed the grave problem of the urban peripheries.[127] By the 1990s the nature of poverty in the peripheries was not so much economic as spatial and social. The periphery had become a category of sociological analysis in its own right, but not the object of proper governmental attention, either local or national. The same mistakes that had characterized urban peripheral planning in earlier decades of the Republic were repeated with depressing frequency.[128] In opulent Florence, a public housing development of the 1980s, the Piagge, was home to some 8,000 people, but without a single shop, playground, chemist or post office. A prefabricated hut, which served as a social centre, was opened in 1996, a decade after the estate had been completed. At the same time major structural faults became apparent in one of the housing blocks.[129]

The syndrome of emargination that derived from abandoned peripheries is well known throughout Europe, from the housing estates of Edinburgh with their high incidence of drug consumption, to the outer ring of the Parisian suburbs, where youth unemployment figures rivalled those in southern Italy. In Italy, the voice of these peripheries was a polyphonous one, if it was *one* at all. Young people in the urban peripheries were often unemployed, bored and alienated. They might dream of glorious futures as football stars, but their chances of success in this or any other field were thin indeed. Recruitment to illegal bands was one possible line of 'exit', especially in certain regions of the South; drug dependence was another.[130]

The Italian peripheries, unlike those in France, Britain and Germany, were white, indigenous and at least nominally Catholic. Giorgio Ruffolo, following Arnold Toynbee, has referred to their populations as an *internal* proletariat, which was rapidly coming into contact with an *external* one. Certainly, those living on the peripheries were not a proletariat in Marx's sense; they were rather economically marginal, deeply divided and inward-looking.[131] Yet Ruffolo was right in one way. One of the clearest voices coming from the periphery was a racist one; the outsider, if he was to arrive, was not wanted or welcome.

10. Immigration and Racism

At the beginning of the 1980s modern Italy reached another watershed; it ceased to be a net exporter of labour, and began to welcome, though that is hardly the correct verb, a significant number of non-European and east European immigrants, known as *'extracomunitari'*, a peculiarly Italian label which in technical terms described immigrants from countries not belonging to the European Community, but which also had strong overtones of exclusion, of describing those who lay outside of the national community.[132]

Their numbers, given the high level of illegal immigration in a Mediterranean country with long coastlines, were always indeterminate. One reliable research of 1991, based on the number of visitors' permits issued by the Ministry of Interior, produced the figure of 409,898 registered *'extracomunitari'*, and estimated the number of illegal immigrants as roughly of the same entity, making for a total of 7–800,000, or between 1.3 per cent and 1.4 per cent of the population.[133] Since then the number has certainly doubled, with a fresh wave of mainly illegal eastern European immigrants. Even so it is far inferior to the percentage presence of immigrants in France or Germany.[134]

The immigrants' provenance was extremely varied, with 176 different nationalities being listed in the census figures of 1991. One major group, probably the largest, was North African Arab (especially Moroccan and Tunisian), though such a denomination masks not only important regional differences, but also distinctions of language, religion and culture. Another was black African, especially Somalian and Senegalese. Another still was Asian, with the Philippines dominant.[135]

After the collapse of Soviet Communism and the outbreak of war in Yugoslavia, Italian attention and apprehension was concentrated on the Adriatic coastline. The attempted exodus from Albania in August 1991 was particularly dramatic, culminating in the terrible scenes in Bari between 8 and 15 August of that year, when thousands of Albanians, among whom there were many women and children, forcibly disembarked from the ancient and rotting ship *Viora* and were herded by the Italian authorities into the old football stadium of the city. Most of the Albanians were immediately repatriated, but not before conditions in the stadium had deteriorated dramatically and violence had broken out. On 12 August Enzo Biagi commented bitterly from the columns of the *Corriere della Sera*:

The dream of the Albanians has dissolved, but so too has that of the Italians. The fifth industrial power in the world has not been capable, in three days, of distributing ten thousand cups of coffee . . . Those plastic sacks of water thrown from above to the dehydrated immigrants, those sandwiches scattered by the soldiers into the scrambling mob — it was like being at the zoo.[136]

The plight of the Albanians and their treatment at Bari acquired international notoriety and were to form the background to Giovanni Amelio's memorable film *Lamerica*.[137]

The immigrants who managed to remain lived in conditions of great poverty and many gained stable work only with difficulty. In the 1980s there were Egyptian foundry workers in Emilia, Tunisians in the Sicilian fishing industry at Mazara del Vallo, Eritreans and Ethiopians working as dishwashers, porters and building workers in Milan. Filipino and Somali women made up the great majority of cleaning ladies, nurses and carers for the elderly, all jobs that were coming on to the market with increasing frequency.[138] Types of work varied between South and North. In the South casual work linked to agriculture, such as tomato-picking and other harvest work, was often the norm. Pay was based on piecework, with the average wage less than half that agreed with the agricultural unions.[139] In the Centre and North of the country there was more chance of a job in industry, especially in the small factories of the Third Italy at the time of the great export boom of 1993–5, and in the Veneto in particular in the last years of the century.

However, many immigrants found no real work of any sort and were reduced to squalid survival in refugee and immigrant camps, in the abandoned *cascine* of the Po plain, in caravan parks and building sites. Segregation from the indigenous Italian population was thus almost total. Significant numbers of these immigrants were drawn into the networks of crime, drug-peddling, prostitution and eventually prison. In the mid-90s the straight tree-lined road that leads from the rich city of Mestre to the even richer one of Treviso was populated at night by long rows of immigrant prostitutes, mainly Nigerian and Albanian, and some very young. This was service work with a vengeance, with many girls deprived of their passports and liberty by the male gangs that controlled them.

As in the 'economic miracle' of 1958–63, when newly arrived immigrants from the South had slept the night in the empty railway carriages of Milan station, the main railway stations became central sites in the drama of immigrant survival in a hostile world.[140] The comparison between the two periods was once again at the expense of the more recent. In the 1990s, at the central station of Milan, the situation deteriorated rapidly as successive waves of the homeless from different countries fought for control of the sleeping space offered by the '*parchi*', the sidings which housed trains being washed and repaired. At first this vast area, which the railway police could not patrol effectively, was the domain of the Moroccans and Italian drug addicts. Then the new arrivals from the East, in particular the Albanians and Romanians, took over the best sidings, forcing out the other groups, which included Serbs, Poles and Croats. In March 1993 knife-fights broke out between the Albanians and the Romanians. The image of these brutal night-time confrontations, taking place in the shadowland of the empty carriages, occasionally illuminated by the bonfires which warmed the rival groups, was one of the most disturbing in contemporary Italy.[141]

Before this recent wave of immigration, the Italian population had been extraordinarily homogeneous – in colour of skin, religion, even increasingly in language. It was, in racial terms, deeply conservative, and was quite unprepared for, and hostile to, the idea of a multi-ethnic Italy. In all Europe in the 1980s racial tension heightened, as the pressure to enter the countries of the European Community intensified. The reasons for immigration were much more of the 'push' rather than the 'pull' variety. Dramatic population growth in southern Mediterranean countries, economic or political disaster, derisory pro-capita incomes, pushed the youth of northern Africa, of the Horn, of eastern Europe, towards opulent western Europe.[142] Often it was the most courageous and the most qualified who sought their fortune in emigration, but what they faced was an uphill struggle against a brutal economic reality: unlike in the 1960s in northern Europe or northern Italy, there was simply not enough regular work to go around.[143]

Given this context, it was not surprising that in Italy hostile reactions to immigrants were widespread. They were true outsiders, viewed with suspicion and horror. When 8,000 schoolchildren from all over Italy were asked by the anthropologist Paola Tabet in 1994–5 to write on the theme 'If my parents were black', their replies not only read for the most part like a lexicon of racism, but unwittingly expressed all the horror of what it was like to be black in Italy in the 1990s. One child, from the fourth year of elementary school in the Sardinian capital of Cagliari, wrote as follows:

One night I had a dream. Suddenly I found myself in a different place that I didn't know. My parents, my sister and me had a different, darker skin. We'd become part of the peoples of the Third World. All my friends wouldn't talk or play with me, and at school it was the same, and so I was even more alone. One day my father went to work and they sacked him. Our family became poor, and we had to suffer hunger and rely on charity. One day I was driven out of the school. So my family decided to go to another place to seek our fortune. We were living in a horrible tent. One night some youths wanted to attack us but we called the police. But instead of believing our story they arrested us. Then I woke up.[144]

The most shocking part of this history was the violence which many *'extracomunitari'* suffered, which far outweighed anything that the Italians themselves had experienced in Germany or Switzerland some thirty years earlier. Immigrants' caravans were set alight in Florence, raids were organized on immigrant camps all round the country, countless beatings took place of foreign workers picked upon at random. Only the most serious cases reached the press, while a whole history of discrimination went by unchecked and unrecorded.

Of all the incidents in this unhappy story – a terrible and continuing discredit to Italy – the death of Jerry Essan Mazlo was perhaps of the greatest significance. In 1989, Mazlo, a political refugee from South Africa, was staying in a camp with other immigrant youth at Villa Literno (Caserta), and earning a living in the tomato fields of the zone. On 24 August of that year he was killed during a night raid on the camp by a gang of local youths. In the wake of his killing, Italy seemed for a time to stir from its torpor and indifference, and confront the new problems it faced; but after the incidents at Bari in August 1991 it relapsed into what Laura Balbo and Luigi Manconi have rightly called a state of 'ordinary racism'.[145]

In June 1997 a research coordinated by Michele Sorice of the university of Rome was presented to the Italian parliament. Statistics collected from twenty newspapers revealed that immigrants suffered more than one aggression a day: 374 in 1996, of which sixty-eight were fatal. The Minister of the Interior, Giorgio Napolitano, who was present at the meeting, corrected this last figure upwards, to 111 fatalities. Of course, not all these were racist attacks; an unspecified number were the result of disputes between bands in the underworld of drugs and prostitution. But it was highly significant that the greatest number of victims of aggressions of every kind were immigrant women.[146]

11. Conclusion

From this long, descending journey through Italian society, a journey that has concentrated principally on work or the lack of it, it has perhaps become apparent that much has changed in the period from 1980 to the present. The long tradition in Italian history which had linked poverty with a dignity of perspective, work with collective organization, had been drastically undermined. Most people were materially richer than ever before, but they seemed poorer in terms of collective identities. In the public sector, there was much evidence of a fragmented and corporatist trade-unionism, incapable of addressing wider problems of reform and consumer service. In the private sector, on the other hand, many workers had lost out in terms of job security and even rights at the workplace. In very many areas of the new service economy, dependent workers (whom, it should be remembered, were still 79 per cent of those in work) increasingly had few mechanisms, other than individual ones, by which they could make themselves heard. Power and opportunity were as unevenly divided as ever. Those who had no work – a category that seemed ineradicable – or those in relative poverty were not likely to make themselves heard with any vehemence. Unemployment, as is well known, is not a stimulant but a depressant. And for those who lay at the lowest level of Italian society, the immigrants, often the only real full-time job on offer was that of survival and self-protection.

The middle classes, the central and decisive block in Italian society, spoke with two rather different voices. One, heavily concentrated among small entrepreneurs and shopkeepers, was localistic, consumerist, strongly oriented both to self-interest and an overriding work ethic. The other, prevalent among those in education and the social services, in reflexive fringes of the professions and the salariat (all areas where a new female presence had made itself most felt), spoke a different language, not puritan but critical, not rejecting of modern individualist consumption but seeking to place it in a social context. The one interpreted modernity in terms of the profit motive and of making good for oneself and one's family. It was exquisitely Thatcherist without Mrs Thatcher. The other, which had no prophet, sought the collective mediation of processes that were leading to grave pollution, both environmental and social. The first, given the way in which state and economy had developed in Italy, was structurally much stronger than the second, and was destined to triumph, in political terms, at the beginning of the new century.

Social stratification in Italy has a very strong geographical identity. In my *History of Contemporary Italy* I suggested a four-part division of the peninsula: the North-West, which constituted the old Industrial Triangle of Milan, Turin and Genoa; the South, consisting of the southern mainland and the islands; the Centre and North-East, which the sociologist Arnaldo Bagnasco has called the 'Third Italy'; and finally the capital, Rome, and the region (Lazio) that surrounded it. Each of these had undergone considerable change. The industrial triangle of the North was no more, with Genoa, and Turin to a lesser extent, undergoing very difficult transitions, as their traditional industrial working class disappeared. Milan and its hinterland, on the other hand, built on what was already a strong tertiary sector, and confirmed Lombardy's absolute primacy in regional economic terms.

The Third Italy also witnessed some significant shifts. The Veneto moved into a period of startling economic dynamism, with its small entrepreneurs among the most successful in all Europe. The central regions, Emilia-Romagna, Tuscany, Umbria, the Marches, continued to do well, but they risked stagnation in some areas during the transition from industry to services. Lombardy and Venetia (or at least certain key provinces therein) therefore seemed to have much in common in socio-economic terms, as they had once had in the first half of the nineteenth century. The political sociology of this refound similitude was to become apparent in the 1990s.

As for Rome, it had never succeeded in becoming the driving force of the country.[147] During the 1980s its image as a centre of consumption and of bureaucracy had become more marked, both in reality and, more importantly, in the collective imagination. Its identity as the *'capitale corrotta'* of the Republic was one it had difficulty in shedding; its dual nature, as capital of the Italian nation but also of world Catholicism, granted it a special but ambiguous status. Rome was splendid but chaotic, full of tourists, pilgrims and lackadaisical civil servants. It was the city of ministries, but not of government, of urban sprawl, but not of urban planning.[148]

In the South, some parts of the Mezzogiorno and the islands, as we have seen in Chapter 1, had made significant economic progress, so much so that by 1996 the comet of small industry had left its trail down the Adriatic coast. However, time and again the outline of social hierarchy has revealed the South as the territorial container of Italy's most socially deprived categories: here there was most unemployment, here children in large families were most at risk, here women had the most difficulty in finding decent jobs, whatever their qualifications. The deep social inequalities of contemporary Italy thus continued to have a uniquely geographical aspect, for none of the other major European countries, not even the recently reunited Germany, suffered from so severe a territorial disequilibrium.

Chapter 3

Families and Consumption

1. Inside the Family

*A*QUITE EXTRAORDINARY unanimity reigns among those who come to Italy from Britain – journalists, historians, sociologists, novelists – regarding the peculiar importance of the family in Italian society and of its centrality in the life of the nation. Peter Nichols, the veteran correspondent of *The Times* in Rome, described the family in 1973 as 'the accredited masterpiece of Italian society over the centuries, the bulwark, the natural unit, the provider of all that the state denies, the semi-sacred group, the avenger and the rewarder'.[1] In *The Economist*'s survey of Italy in May 1990, the family was enthroned as the universal explicandum, as 'the enduring unit of Italian society. It explains the lack of public spirit in Italy, and even of the concept of public good ... It explains the Mafia, the biggest family of them all. It also explains the pattern of business. From the Agnelli down, Italians like to keep control of their affairs within the family.'[2]

More soberly, the distinguished family sociologist Janet Finch, commenting in 1989 on the results of a comparative social survey of seven countries, concluded that 'of all the countries under study, Italy emerges with a particularly distinctive pattern of personal relationships and social networks ... To Italians, relationships with both relatives and friends form a much more integral part of daily life than elsewhere. They are more likely to share a home with their relatives and also to have relatives living nearby. They are more likely to visit or telephone relatives daily and also to be in daily contact with "a best friend". Relationships between parents and children seem particularly important.'[3]

Of course, Italy is not the only country where family matters so much. The international survey just cited did not include any other southern European country, nor an Islamic one. On the southern shores of the Mediterranean the Arab family, with its tradition of endogamic marriage, offers an even stronger example of family cohesion and centrality. Indeed, the perception of Italy on the part of some immigrants to it from that part of the world is of a country where family matters *too little*, with insufficient respect shown towards mothers![4] Comparative truth does depend a great deal upon one's point of departure.

Whatever one's starting point, however, it would be difficult to contest the transformations that beset Italian families in the years under consideration in this book. The most recent history of the Republic acquires a special fascination because both the public and the private worlds underwent major change. Employment and reproduction patterns, gender relations, household forms, types of consumption, attitudes to civil society, and after 1992 politics as well, were all subject to significant shifts. Twilight had set upon Fordist Italy, and at the same time touched the traditional Italian family, child-oriented, patriarchal and Catholic; but this model of family had been one of such longevity as to leave deep impressions upon Italian modernity.

a. FALTERING REPRODUCTION

In all of Europe during the twentieth century there had been a gradual decline in the number of children being born. This trend was interrupted for the twenty years after the Second World War, during the so-called baby boom, but after 1965 resumed again its downward path.[5] The case of Italy was particularly dramatic because its absolute fertility rate (the average number of children per woman) had for a long time been above or around the European average, but then in just twenty years dropped to being the lowest, not only in Europe but in the world. In 1970, the average number of children per woman in Italy was 2.42, around the norm for the European community; by 1980 it was 1.64; by 1990 1.30, and by 1993 1.21.

Behind these national statistics there lay a distinct difference between the Centre-North of the country on the one hand, and the South on the other. From at least 1920 onwards, fertility levels in the Centre-North had been much lower than in the South. In the former the dominant reproductive model in recent decades was that of families with a single child, often conceived by a mother over thirty years of age. In the latter, although there are a relatively high number of women without children, the dominant model remained that of families with at least two children, born one soon after the other. Liguria and Emilia-Romagna are today the regions with the lowest fertility rates in the country.[6]

Italy, though, was only the severest case of a general southern European phenomenon, for Spain, Greece and Portugal all registered sharp drops in fertility rates in the same period. Just when the southern shore of the Mediterranean was undergoing a population explosion, the northern was ceasing to be able to reproduce its population.[7]

The long-term consequences of this imbalance were very considerable, both for the overall history of the Mediterranean, and for each of the countries involved. In Italy's case, the reasoned estimates of the demographer Gian Carlo Blangiardo delineate nothing short of a revolution in population structure over the next forty years.[8] Unless fertility rates suddenly improve (a highly unlikely scenario), or there is a major influx of a fertile immigrant population, the population structure of Italy will come to resemble an inverted pyramid, with an ever smaller cohort of youth at the bottom, and a mass of old people at the top. Whereas in the middle of the 1950s there were twenty-seven Italians under the age of twenty for every ten over sixty, by 2038 (at present fertility levels) the ratio will have been reversed: there will be twenty-five people over sixty years of age for every ten under twenty. By that time Italians over the age of sixty will constitute 40 per cent of the population.[9] The danger, then, is not that denounced by Mussolini in 1929 – of too few Italians to fulfil their country's imperial destiny. In actual fact, a less crowded peninsula could only be welcome. It is, rather, of a serious imbalance in the age structure of the Italian population.

As for families, or more precisely households, their numbers will at first increase, as more old people live by themselves, but will then begin to decline rapidly. Numbers *within* each household, in any case, will continue to contract constantly, as in the whole history of the Republic: 3.3 at the time of the census of 1971, 3.0 in 1981, 2.8 in 1991.[10]

The wider consequences of these demographic trends are difficult to predict. They would appear to be beneficial at only one level, that of employment, as smaller cohorts of young people enter a contracting labour market. For the rest, families (or rather female carers within them) and social services (already inadequate) will be hard put to cope with so great a number of old people. If the trends noted in Chapter 2, of increased economic poverty accompanying increased old age, were to continue, then Italy faces a very disturbing scenario: of a major, not a minor, part of its population being not only old and debilitated, but also poor. At another level, that of politics, it is as well to remember that old societies tend to be conservative ones: there would not only be the risk of gerontocracy, but the certainty of the older generations crushing the younger ones in electoral terms, while being dependent on them economically.[11]

These are scenarios common to the whole of Europe, and much debated throughout it. The reasons for the especially drastic reduction in child-rearing in Italy are very complex and not easily susceptible to a hierarchy of ordering.

Italians of all ages and classes express a clear preference for families with two children, but actually produce those with only one.[12] How can the 'missing child', *'il bambino negato'*, be explained?

An answer to this central question in Italian social history can be constructed on a number of bases. On the level of long-term causality, there can be little doubting the importance of the compressed and convulsive nature of Italian modernization. The 60s and 70s were in these terms key decades, marked by the sudden interruption of long-established cultural and reproductive patterns. The massive internal migration of the early 60s, which returned at a lesser intensity in 1966–74, the liberalization of sexual habits, the diffusion of contraceptive devices, the divorce and abortion laws (and referenda), all created a decisive break in the transmission of codes of conduct between generations.[13]

Growing out of this caesura came a fundamental shift in gender relations. The relative emancipation of women, their higher levels of education and their increased presence in the labour market, signified that very many of them, especially in the Centre-North of the country, took their distance from previous norms governing maternity. Paradoxically, though, it was precisely the *incomplete* nature of their emancipation that was causally most active in this context. Italian women may still have wanted two children, but the pressures of their lives made such symmetry difficult to obtain. Men still did too little to help at home;[14] the principal tasks of caring fell upon the mother of each family; working women found themselves drained by their 'double presence', in their homes and in their jobs.[15] As the new liberty of individual choice and the use of some measure of contraception spread from the élites and permeated Italian families, women's vision of themselves changed. This subjective transformation, when combined with the time constraints and exhaustion of many women's lives, told against the choice for a second or even a third child.

Supplementing this central element – *partial* emancipation leading to self-imposed constraint – were other factors. As opportunities in the labour market narrowed, educational careers lengthened and premarital sexual experiences became the norm. Italians got married ever later. In 1981 62.3 per cent of men aged twenty-eight and 66.2 per cent of women aged twenty-five were married; just ten years later the corresponding figures had dropped to just 36.7 per cent of men and 53.1 per cent of women.[16] At the same time the dominant practice continued to be that of having children only *within* marriage, a choice that revealed the deep residual legacy of Catholic teaching.

These two elements – later marriage and a cultural insistence on having 'legitimate' children – led in only one direction; to that of women having their first child ever later, leaving themselves with less time and energy to repeat the experience. In Italy in 1972 the average age of women at the birth of their first child had been 24.9 years; by 1990 it was 29.0.[17]

The choice not to have children was not only the woman's. Very much less research has been done on putative fathers than on mothers, but their hesitations and fears must form part of any explanation. Work came first, and fathering children – once an important demonstration of virility – was often now subordinate to career patterns and to the search for individual self-fulfilment. Delay, therefore, was the name of the game. At the same time, many men were *afraid* of becoming fathers, using various stratagems to justify their choice. As Gustavo Pietropolli Charmet has written, on the basis of long professional experience in Milan: 'The most common [stratagem] was to repeat, until it became a self-evident truth, that it was irresponsible to bring children into the world in such a terrible moment of its history. In reality the only real danger that the man felt was with regard to himself.'[18]

It would be a mistake, though, to upbraid either men or women, as some commentators have done, for their unbridled egoism. A major contribution to fertility decline came not from a lack of responsibility, but an excess of it. Here was a second paradox: it was the very strength of the Italian family that contributed to its numerical diminution. In contemporary Italy the generation of reproductive age, both men and women, were faced with family responsibilities which urged caution upon them. There were more old people to look after, but also young ones who stayed ever longer at home. If individual strategies had been stronger and family ones weaker, it would have been possible to dispatch old people into homes and eighteen-year-olds out into the world to fend for themselves. This was not the Italian way. Instead the central generation shouldered its responsibilities, but did so with what Dalla Zuanna has rightly called 'an exasperated neo-Malthusian prudence'.[19]

Time was in Italy when having a large number of children could be regarded as making good economic sense. This antiquated view still lingered on, and indeed had some validity in the popular quarters of the great cities of the South.[20] But for most of Italy in the 1980s and 1990s the opposite was true: having offspring signified, in economic terms, not solace but sacrifice. The anthropologist Paola Filippucci, in her study of Bassano in the late 1980s, noted clearly these trends:

'I have to go out to work,' said Bertilla (b. 1945, part-time cleaner, wife of a factory worker), 'because Antonio (her twelve-year-old son) for school, for instance, wants the same bag that his classmates have, and only that costs 60,000 lire.' 'Now it's not like it used to be, that, when you had a baby, you thought it wouldn't matter if he'd have to do without something – now you can't send them out if they don't have everything (Gina).'[21]

Children-become-adults stayed firmly in the parental home, sometimes laboriously acquiring educational qualifications, sometimes already at work, perhaps in the family firm (as in many parts of the Centre and North), sometimes simply under-employed (as in many parts of the South).[22] There they would remain until marriage finally prised them away, or the labour market at last granted them economic autonomy. In these circumstances, children were a considerable drain upon family resources, cuckoo fledglings demanding constant support from exhausted sparrow parents. A single child was already a major investment, and no child at all was a selfish but understandable choice.[23]

A last level of explanation lies with the state. The Republic of the Christian Democrats, in spite of repeated assertions of the importance of family life, had done very little to encourage child-rearing. Service provision for small children, tax relief and allowances for numerous families had not been historic features of public policy in Italy.[24] If maternity leave was adequate, the standards in most maternity hospitals and infant schools were not.[25]

However, to blame the state only takes us so far. The twentieth-century European experience of nations which had tried to increase fertility rates had not, by and large, been either enlightening or successful, as they had concentrated for the most part on an archaic vision of motherhood and family relations, with women rewarded for being baby-producing machines.[26] The most interesting and appealing counter-model was the Swedish one in the years after 1980. Faced with a sharp decline in absolute fertility rates between 1960 and 1980 (from 2.2 children per woman to 1.6), the Swedish state intensified its efforts to support working women who wished to have more than one child, to guarantee them economic autonomy, to allow their partners time off during maternity and early childhood, to try to establish, in other words, a revolutionary link between gender equality and fertility. By 1993, with a marked increase in the number of women over thirty having children, the Swedish fertility rate had risen to 2.0.[27]

The Swedish model was instructive, but it would be a grave mistake to imagine that it could be mechanically transposed, or would slowly filter down to southern Europe.[28] Family culture, socio-economic conditions, public policy were all very different in Sweden and Italy, and were likely to remain that way for some time to come. Furthermore, Italy in the 1980s and 1990s presented some strong evidence against state intervention being decisive. Emilia-Romagna boasted some of the best local services for children and mothers in the whole of Europe; yet the average number of children per woman in the region, exactly 1.00 in 1990, was well below the national average.[29] A caring state was essential but not necessarily enough.

Italy's case, therefore, offered its own peculiar mixture of transformation and continuity. On the one hand there were strong forces pushing towards a European model of modernity, among which were the cultural revolution of the 1960s and 1970s, leading to greater individual choice, the spread of contraception and legalized abortion, the partial emancipation of women and their entry into the labour market. On the other, tradition weighed heavily in both the public and the private spheres: the felt obligation to have children within marriage, the power of the family as an inter-generational collective, the state's disinterest, after the unfortunate Fascist experience, in reproduction politics. It was this complex but powerful intertwining of the old and the new in family strategies that gave Italy its unexpected and unwanted global primacy.

b. COHESION AND CONTINUITY

While reproduction patterns heralded many changes, other indicators tended to confirm the external observer's impression of the great stability and cohesion of Italian family life. The elements of family break-up which so exercised American and British commentators were also present in Italy, especially in the great cities, and were on the increase, but they did not dominate public attention in the same way.

Family statistics in Italy still told a broad story of continuity. In 1994 in Italy there were sixteen separations and eight divorces for every 100 marriages, compared to thirty-five divorces in France and forty-four in Britain.[30] The number of lone parent families in Italy in 1993–4 was 7.2 per cent of all families with small children, in contrast to nearly 20 per cent in Britain.[31] The number of births outside marriage as a percentage of total births was just 7.3 per cent in Italy in 1993, compared to Spain's 10.5 per cent, Germany's 15.4 per cent, Britain's 32 per cent and France's 34.9 per cent.[32]

However, the firmest evidence, though less easily quantifiable, of the links that bound Italian families together came from their inter-generational solidarity, to which passing reference has already been made. Grandparents, parents and children often lived close together and in daily contact one with the other. Italian families were becoming 'long' and 'thin': long in the sense of adult children staying longer at home; thin because of declining fertility rates. They were also characterized by frequent contacts between collaterals, especially cousins. All this caused Italian families to express particular qualities of spatial and emotional proximity.[33]

There had been a moment in the Republic's history when these patterns had risked interruption. The great internal migrations of the late 1950s and early 1960s had weakened the geographical links between the generations. So too had Fordism and the new youth culture, with the possibilities they offered young people of economic independence and alternative lifestyles.

Leone Diena, in his study of young Milanese workers, published in 1960, asserted boldly on the basis of his interviews that 'Almost never does the family seem to constitute an important factor in the life of the workers.'[34]

This brave new world failed to materialize. There was no mechanical connection between industrialism and new, looser family patterns, and in any case the Fordist era in Italy had a very compressed time-span. No sooner was Italy in it than it was out of it. Instead, the service and consumption economy of the last twenty years was characterized, as we have seen, by the very strong overlay between family and economic activity, and by the strong reassertion of traditional proximities between individual family members. The Italian version of the post-modern world thus acquired a profoundly familial flavour.

The relationship between the older generation and the youngest one seemed particularly intense. Even in urban contexts, Italian grandparents remained closely involved in the care of grandchildren, and once threatened by fragility and immobility they in turn received considerable assistance and company, especially from the female members of the younger generations. Such patterns of behaviour enabled researchers to identify a reality, not of isolated conjugal households, but of 'modified extended families'.[35] In one survey of adult women between the ages of twenty-five and fifty-five, carried out in Emilia-Romagna in 1984, it emerged that approximately half of their 'closest relatives' lived either in the same household or block of flats, while another 40 per cent were to be found either in the same quarter or municipality. This was spatial proximity with a vengeance.[36]

If we turn to the youngest generation, there is overwhelming evidence of the Italian nuclear family unit being both numerically restricted and chronologically protracted. In 1982–3, 90 per cent of male youth between twenty and twenty-four years of age still lived at home, in comparison to 43 per cent in West Germany, 52 per cent in France, and 58 per cent in Britain. The corresponding figures for young women were 65 per cent for Italy, 31 per cent for West Germany, 27 per cent for France and 23 per cent for Britain.[37] Ten years later, Alessandro Cavallo and Antonio De Lillo found that by the age of twenty-nine nearly half of Italian sons and more than a quarter of daughters were still living at home.[38] Daughters were more carefully controlled by parents, and perhaps because of it they asserted their independence more precociously. But these statistics can also be read to suggest a particular mother–son dynamic and dependency, to which we shall return in a moment.

One obvious material explanation for the phenomenon of the 'long' family was the lack of suitable low-price rented accommodation for young people.[39] Another, with particular relevance in the South, were very high rates of youth unemployment. Many children stayed at home because they had no economic alternative. However, material explanations alone are not enough. Much emphasis has been put instead on the 'contractual' nature of the modern Italian family.[40] In keeping with trends in other European countries, so it is argued, individual family members had developed a greater tendency towards freedom and autonomy. Yet in Italy this process of individualization had not, by and large, led to family ruptures, estrangements, or distances between parents and children. On the contrary: a process of negotiation, of mutual tolerance, of informal *contract* allowed children and parents to continue to live under the same roof.[41]

In an influential article of 1989, the Catholic sociologist Giuseppe De Rita, head of Italy's principal social research institute, CENSIS, offered a persuasive interpretation along these lines of Italian family patterns.[42] The 1970s and 1980s, he suggested, had constituted a watershed in Italian family history, but one very different from that which had loomed at the time of the 'economic miracle'. In unprecedented fashion, the 'long' family had become a centre of income, investment, consumption and entrepreneurship.[43] For De Rita, the Italian family was a 'firm', to which each generation made its contribution. The male head of the family, although no longer patriarchal, continued to exercise his hegemony, in order to ensure the smooth functioning of this '*azienda-famiglia*'. He was the guarantor, in other words, of 'a richer system of autonomy for the various members of the family, who do not express their freedom as divergence but rather as integration'.[44] Thus at the very moment when the family in the West was considered in grave crisis, the Italian family, in this vision, seemed to have reached its apotheosis.

c. INTERIORS

For any student of contemporary Italy, the picture painted by De Rita in 1988 was an instantly recognizable one. Yet it has to be handled with care, because beneath the external surface of unity, wealth and harmony there lurked many uncertainties and tensions. Two of the most implacable were how these families were going to cope in the not-so-distant future with the major social trends of the age – the diminution of work and the rapid increase in the number of old people.

At the end of the century these were still unanswerable questions, but there were others which already provided important antidotes to an over-idyllic picture. Intense and prosperous family relationships of the sort described above could certainly be founts of great devotion and unity, but also of suffocation and oppression. Close-knit, traditional family life was much praised by Catholic commentators. The danger, though, was of mistaking 'the domestic church'[45] for what was in reality a rumbling volcano.

Some of these internal tensions can be sounded out by examining changing kinship roles. Fathers, by and large, were not the democratic princes of De Rita's scenario. Patriarchy had certainly lost some of its teeth; the authoritarian and absenteeist fathers of the immediate post-war period, with their often violent dominion over the weaker members of the family, had become a small minority.[46] Yet a new model of paternity had great difficulty in emerging.

There was evidence from a region like Emilia-Romagna that young fathers were more involved with their small children than ever before, both in terms of play and affection.[47] Often, though, the impression (and it can be little more than that, given the present state of research) was of men who, if they did not choose the time-honoured path of 'exit', i.e. of spending little time at home, had difficulty in negotiating the dynamics of modern family life. The ground rules had been rewritten, but no one was sure of the new text.[48] Men felt threatened and defensive, often yearning after a lost liberty before the birth of children.[49]

Nearly always, they found great difficulty in being *fathers*, behaving more like elder brothers to their children, or friends and confidants, or even servants. If for rural Calabria in the 1980s Minicuci still recorded severe, distant and authoritarian fathers, for Milan Pietropolli Charmet noted: 'In the last few years there hardly exists any possibility of an adolescent finding in his family a father still willing to let himself be killed in symbolic terms . . . Rather, one finds a father waiting patiently for an audience outside the door of his son's room.'[50] Fathers had become more affectionate, but uncertain, protective and indulgent. As such, they were less able to communicate key values such as autonomy and the assumption of responsibility, essential for the adolescent's process of individuation and separation from his or her family.[51]

Fathers struggled to be fathers, but mothers had few choices about being mothers. They remained at the centre of Italian families, the providers of a constant flow of totalizing care, directed primarily towards their child or children, but also towards their husband, their parents and often their husband's parents as well. The American anthropologist Donald Pitkin, who followed the story of one very ordinary family in lower Lazio for four generations (down to the 1980s), was struck by the degree to which it remained 'matri-centred': 'Giulia in her time and now Maria have constituted the significant other for their children, the object of assured constancy whose love has been unqualified . . . Oral dependency is but one aspect of a much larger configuration . . . The amount of time spent in the daily rituals related to the preparation and consumption of food, as well as the cleaning up afterwards is impressive, and the priestess of this cult of food is the mother.'[52]

Another anthropologist, Victoria Goddard, in her recent study of Neapolitan outworkers, makes much the same sorts of points: 'The division of labour and space, the importance of women's networks, the centrality of children in the family and of food in defining membership within the household, contributed to making women and especially mothers central to household organisation and family life.'[53]

Of course, it is rare indeed, except in male lone-parent situations, to find families that are *not* matri-centred or matri-focal. Such a description, by itself, hardly takes us very far in a quest for the specificity of Italian motherhood. Those who have been brave enough to reflect upon the archetypes that lie at the heart of maternal behaviour in Italy have usually made reference to two figures in particular: the Virgin Mary and the Mediterranean '*Grande Madre*'.

Over a period of many centuries, the Virgin Mary has served historically as a role model in a number of different ways: as the supreme example of purity, as the symbol of motherhood defined as pain and sacrifice borne with wisdom, humility and forgiveness, as a key mediating figure in Catholicism rather than Protestantism, interceding between God the Father and God the Son.[54] (She is also, though it is rather wicked to point it out, a very modern Italian figure, being the mother of a single, male child.)

The Mediterranean Mother-God is a much less obvious point of reference, but it was the distinguished German Jungian psychoanalyst Ernst Bernhard who in 1960, after many years of practice in Rome, made a number of telling observations on the importance of the complex of the '*Grande Madre*' for mother–son relations in contemporary Italy:

The Mediterranean '*Grande Madre*' is in Italy a primitive mother. For the most part she spoils her sons with the maximum of instinctiveness, and as a result her sons are exigent. But the more she spoils them, the more she makes them dependent upon her; and the more natural come to appear her own demands upon her sons, the more they come to feel tied to her. At this point the good mother, protective and nourishing, is transformed into her own negation.[55]

From the literature on these archetypes, there begins to emerge a picture of Italian motherhood couched in terms of sacrifice, purity and possessiveness, with a further key element being the intensity of the mother–son relationship. Anne Parsons, in a seminal article first published in 1964,[56] suggested that the dynamics of the (admittedly few) southern Italian families that she had studied as anthropologist and psychiatrist were built upon the two contrasting axes of mother–son and father–daughter relations. Sons tended to create a feminine rather than a masculine 'super ego', couched in Madonna-like terms, as well as a lasting oral dependence and 'a continual expectation of maternal solace and giving, rather than a gradual or sudden emancipation from it'.[57] The resulting centripetal tendencies made for an 'unbroken continuity of the primary family'.[58] In other words, left to themselves, mothers and sons would never look elsewhere in emotional terms, and indeed often did not.

Father–daughter relations, on the other hand, caused the release of a 'spring mechanism', which broke asunder the original family unit. For Parsons this mechanism derived from the dramatic and explosive quality of father–daughter relations at the time of courtship. As the incest taboo between them was less strong and deep-lying than that between mother and son, the ensuing accumulation of tension forced a revolution, with the exit of the daughter from the family of origin: 'the daughter has to seek an object outside of the family, the father has to rid himself of a woman whom he perceives as very desirable but cannot possess'.[59]

It is all too easy to translate archetypes into stereotypes, and dangerous to use either as the basis for generalizing about contemporary Italian families. Given the limited amount of research on contemporary Italian mothers, it is only possible to stress the *suggestive* nature of the insights briefly outlined above. However, some of the most recent official statistics tended to confirm strongly the picture of mother–son dependencies. According to an ISTAT research of 1993–4, one third of married Italian men still saw their mothers every day, while another 27.5 per cent saw them more than once a week. These patterns were marginally more intense in the South than in the North. Seven out of ten unmarried Italian men over the age of thirty-five lived with their parents, as did one in four of those who had divorced.[60] The journalist Laura Laurenzi, commenting on these statistics, noted: 'therein lies the confirmation that Italian men – whether single, regularly married, co-habiting, separated or divorced – demonstrate an evident reluctance, whether from choice or necessity, to distance themselves from the maternal embrace and from that formidable supplier of services constituted by a matriarchal home in which everything functions.'[61]

For the rest, it is not possible to state with any certainty how far traditional maternal models of behaviour were being abandoned in modern urban contexts. Mothers had adapted, perhaps with more success than fathers, to modern family relations. Less silent and repressive about sexual matters than in the past, they had become the confidantes, even the accomplices, of their adult sons. But the old anxieties remained, and perhaps were even reinforced by new ones, by feelings of inadequacy inculcated by television advertising, which represented perfect mothers and wives, operating simultaneously in a multiplicity of roles.[62] Once upon a time it had been the Catholic Church which had, inadvisedly, presented the Holy Family as an ideal model.[63] Thirty years later, it was television publicity that had taken its place. In both cases, though, mothers were expected to be little short of saints.

The reality of working mothers' lives was a very demanding one, and they received, at least in material terms, very little help from their spouses. One survey of 1988–9 revealed that in the average Italian couple with child (or children) the woman spent five and a half hours every day on normal household tasks, the man forty-eight minutes. Nor did these proportions vary a great deal if the woman also worked *outside* the home, as well as within it.[64] The researchers' conclusions were unequivocal: 'The man dedicates a marginal part of his time to serving and caring for the family, the woman a central one.'[65]

Such findings were, of course, in line with trends in other European countries. If Italian mothers were special, it was perhaps because of the amount of inter-generational care they shouldered, the intensity of their attachment to their sons, the reverence they received as well as the dependency they created.[66]

As for children, the fewer they were, the greater the investment in them. The single Italian child could expect his or her parents and grandparents to gratify desires, whims and the requirements of the peer group from an early age.[67] In the 1990s the copious arsenal of expensive toys in an average Italian home was striking material testimony to this process. Such hyper-attention and hyper-affection had consequences that were at least as negative as they were positive, for they produced, as the psychologist Eugenia Scabini has written, 'a sort of inter-generational glue',[68] which did little to help the autonomous development of the child. They also produced what Padiglione and Pontalti have perceptively called a constant 'preoccupied glance', not only from parent to child, but from child to parent. The net result, according to them, was 'to block the generations in a sort of reciprocal protection [*accudimento*] which was substantially infantilizing'.[69]

A rare statistical glimpse into these processes comes from a 'Eurobarometer' survey of 1993 on Europeans and their families. Asked what values should be encouraged in children, there was a convergence around the qualities of 'Responsibility', 'Tolerance/Respect for others' and, perhaps surprisingly, 'Good manners'. However, the category of 'Self-reliance' revealed sharp national differences. Whereas 59 per cent of Danish and 62.4 per cent of German parents chose it as one of the three key qualities they valued most, only 17.7 per cent of Italian, 16.6 per cent of British, and 14.9 per cent of Spanish parents did so.[70]

Developmental patterns of this sort must cast doubt on over-generous interpretations of the 'long' family or indeed 'the family as a firm'. The Italian model of parent–child relations, premised on emancipation *within* the family, rather than emancipation *from* the family, was more myth than reality. The longevity of these protracted household relationships could lead families in extreme cases to 'implode', to destroy themselves from inside;[71] more often they produced a certain exhaustion, a forced cohabitation made up of silences and incomprehensions. One survey of 1995, conducted among Italian youth between the ages of eighteen and thirty still living at home, found few rows but much dissatisfaction.[72]

Above all, the shape of Italian family life encouraged *dependency*. The sociologist Laura Balbo made this point, to great effect: 'Interdependent roles, specialized roles, the family as the privileged or rather unique site for the maximization of resources, all these signal the existence of very heavy pressure on individuals to define themselves and to live in terms of their ascribed family roles . . . a family of this sort produces individuals but conditions and controls them.'[73]

d. DIFFERENCES AND DEPRIVATION

Up to this point the analysis of Italian families and their members has sought out their common characteristics, with the consequent risk, or rather inevitability, of distortion and simplification. As has often been pointed out, there is no such entity as *the* Italian family. Each family has its own history and destiny, its own secrets, aspirations and delusions, its own conflicts and passions. Each is built on mobile sands, for time is constantly changing its shape and the status of the individuals who compose it. In the same urban spaces, in the same blocks of flats, families live one on top of the other, superficially all the same and each profoundly different. In 1993, from the popular quarter of San Lorenzo in Naples, Stefano De Matteis gave us a glimpse of three such families, who lived in the same building:

C. is an artisan with wife and two children. His rented shop, which serves as workspace and showroom, is on the ground floor, their bedroom is on the first. One of their children sleeps with them, the other with the grandparents who have the shop next door and live in the building opposite. Lunch and supper are at the grandparents'. When there's the market, there are no set meals; everything happens in the shop, with the grandmother cooking and serving out the plates . . . Above them there's a tailor. He's got this to say: 'Once I applied to join the Carabinieri because I liked the idea of riding one of their motorbikes. Then I had second thoughts: who's making me do such a thing! Here I can do exactly what I want.' Still further up there's the greengrocer: wife in the shop and husband between the market and his allotment. Sometimes there's their son to give them a hand. I asked him to give me some strawberries, he told his mother to give them to me, otherwise he'd have got his hands dirty. Father and mother in a little three-wheeled van, son in a FIAT Uno.[74]

It is impossible to do justice to such diversity at the level of synthesis required by a book such as this. None the less, it is worth trying to connect the analysis of family with the principal distinctions of class and region which have emerged in the previous chapters. It is particularly important to draw attention to that large minority of poorer families which least fitted the dominant image of familial prosperity in these years.

In the Centre and North of the country, for most families the balance between opportunities and risks was heavily weighted in favour of the first; for much of the South the opposite was true. While not forgetting the heterogeneity of the South, it is still true that the majority of deprived families lived there. The great urban centres continued to be the homes of an unacceptably high number of poor families. In Palermo in 1984 an estimated 250,000–300,000 people out of a total population of some 700,000 lived below the official poverty line, and there was little reason to suppose that the situation had changed a great deal ten or fifteen years later.[75] Average family size in the popular areas of the great southern cities was declining, but remained higher than elsewhere. Families sought to maximize the number of persons available for what was an unstable and fragile labour market, made up of 'black work', temporary service jobs of the most humble kind, labouring on building sites, illegal employment of minors, foot-soldiering for the criminal organizations.[76] In the absence for most of this period of prescient or even honest local government (see below, Chapter 6, pp. 183ff.), the southern cities confirmed their character of teeming urban jungles, asphyxiated by traffic, and dominated by the collusion between politicians and the local criminal class. In such a hostile environment the family provided an uncertain but vital refuge for the poorest sections of the population.

In all of Italy, and not just in the South, the families most at risk – in terms of health, environmental hazards, violence, break-ups – were to be found on the peripheries of the great cities. These were no longer the families depicted by Pasolini in his earlier writings and films, of shanty towns and slums. They were rather those of Gianni Amelio's film *Il ladro dei bambini*: decomposing, even depraved families living on large, ill-planned and ill-serviced estates, or else in modern urban wastelands.

On the northern periphery of Naples at Scampia, a huge housing estate called 'Le Vele', with seven tower blocks of ingenious but impractical design, was the home to 1,200 families. By 1995, less than twenty years after they had been built, 'Le Vele' were deemed uninhabitable. Here were to be found some of the highest percentages of unemployment and school truancy in all of metropolitan Naples.[77] Here too were alarming levels of illness and of suicide, especially among housewives. Some of those who lived there blamed the buildings above all; others the families themselves. Few doubted the vicious circle that linked the two.[78]

2. Consumption

One of the keys to understanding contemporary Italian families, their potentialities as well as their weaknesses, lies in the world of consumption. The development of consumer behaviour in Italy is an area of inquiry as fascinating as it is little studied. Traditional history and political economy, regardless of their political viewpoint, have concentrated predominantly on production and the public sphere, ignoring for the most part the other half of modern capitalism, consumption, and the principal locus of it, the home and the family.

a. THE DEVELOPMENT OF ITALIAN CONSUMPTION

In the history of the Italian Republic it is possible to discern two reasonably distinct moments of transition in consumption history. The first occurred at the time of the 'economic miracle', which saw the passage from a society where basic needs were not satisfied, to one in which they were for the great majority, if not for all, of the Italian population. The consumption of this period was characterized principally by its relative homogeneity, closely linked to the Fordist nature of production, by its utilitarianism, and by its attention to the newly discovered joys of home living. Typical items such as fridges and washing-machines, as well as new furniture, were purchased for the material enrichment of the home, and for the reduction of women's chores within it.[79] The increased consumption of meat was the dietary symbol of the transition, the celebration of the 'miracle' at family mealtimes.[80]

Yet even in this phase there was a considerable amount of consumption by the average Italian family which did not easily fit a purely utilitarian typology, nor any simple distinction between needs and wants.[81] Cars and scooters can be taken as one example. They certainly facilitated movement and communication, but they also gave individuals and families a previously undreamed-of possibility of the personal selection of travel itineraries, both within the city and beyond it. The FIAT 500 was a dream machine, not just a convenient means of transport.

Television was another, and probably the most important example. In the early years of the 'miracle' many commentators denounced the dangers for poorer families of acquiring 'unnecessary' elements of consumption like televisions, when so much else that was necessary went unpurchased.[82] But this betrayed a very limited view of the connection between commodities and capabilities, that is the degree to which ownership of a television was not just an act of foolish emulation, but an act of enablement. As Amartya Sen has written, with disarming simplicity: 'Given a social context in which certain commodities are generally available for most people, taking part in the life of the community could be very difficult for those who do not possess these commodities.'[83] A television was a passport to modern Italy, rather as Adam Smith had noted that in Britain in the eighteenth century a pair of leather shoes enabled you to 'appear in public without shame'.[84]

Italian consumption, then, even in the 'economic miracle', combined utility, standardization and home-building with wider needs and dreams. From the end of the 1970s onwards, after the grave economic crisis of mid-decade,[85] a further crucial transformation took place. This new phase derived its propulsive force from some of those fundamental economic changes which have been outlined in Chapter 1: the information technology revolution, the shift from standardized goods to more personalized ones, the growth of entertainment as a major service industry, the long favourable economic conjuncture of the late 80s and early 90s. The combination of these factors unleashed a wave of consumption that was much richer, in every sense of the word, and more complex than the preceding one.

At the heart of the new phase lay the marked accentuation of certain characteristics that had been present earlier, and their extension to much wider sections of the population. Of crucial importance was what Colin Campbell has called 'modern autonomous imaginative hedonism'. Central to this concept is the place of day-dreaming and longing in modern consumption: 'The visible practice of consumption is thus no more than a small part of a complex pattern of hedonistic behaviour, the majority of which occurs in the imagination of the consumer.'[86] Individuals enjoy as never before the possibility of 'being their own despot',[87] exercising control over an ever-widening choice of stimulae.

Through the proliferation of television channels and the Internet, through video cassettes and video games, through 'Walkmen' and CD players, to mention only the most obvious instruments, the world of play, of emotions and romance, of dreaming and imagination, became commodified on a mass scale. In terms of single commodities, it was the videocassette recorder that swept fastest into Italian homes. By 1992 45.4 per cent of Italian families had a VCR at home; six years earlier the percentage had been just 3.5.[88]

The new hedonism also refined and developed travel. Airports became modern palaces, with consumption immediately preceding departure, first in rather elementary duty-free shops, and then in ever more sophisticated shopping arcades. Massed cohorts of Italians took to the air, in ever-wider waves of journeying and discovery.[89]

Their children, too, were increasingly well catered for in a modern world that offered the combination of travel and fun. For richer families a trip to Disneyland in Florida was an important appointment; the *ceti medi* could aspire to the Parisian version of the same; Gardaland, on the shores of Lake Garda, was a good fall-back for those with more limited resources. Middle-class families throughout the peninsula increasingly organized their time between two houses: the one the site of everyday life, of the stress of routine, business, work and school; the other, in the mountains or by the sea, that of leisure and escapism.

A second element strongly present in this new phase of consumption was a cognitive one. With the revolution in information technology, the availability and consumption of knowledge in a home environment increased drastically. Personal computers were much less present in Italian homes than were videos or hi-fis. By 1996 7.2 per cent of the Italian population owned a personal computer – a great increase compared to a decade earlier, but in Germany, Britain and France the percentage was almost double, and in the United States had reached 29.7 per cent.[90] As training and education qualifications became essential requirements in the service economy, cognitive consumption became ever more important. For children, hedonist and cognitive consumption could be ideally linked through the use of computers first for video games and then for educational purposes. Some children, of course, never made the transition.

Another central but less innovatory element in the new phase was the aesthetic one. A passionate attention to aesthetics – to appearance, style, fashion – was, of course, deeply rooted in the wider culture of the country as well as in the history of Italian consumption. The spectacular success of the Italian fashion industry in these years, when linked with Italian families' increased disposable income, produced a mass market for Italian *haute couture*. By 1992 a startling 37 per cent of Italians claimed to wear garments that had designer labels.[91] Obsession with look and smell found new and expensive commodities to devour, with after-shave lotions and anti-wrinkle creams enjoying rocketing sales. Nearly one in three Italians (not all female) were habitually using face creams at this time.[92]

Aesthetics went hand-in-hand with health. Young Italians went to gyms, but all Italians consumed a veritable mountain of pills and medicines. In common with other southern European countries, spending per capita on pharmaceuticals was unusually high.[93] At the same time there was a dramatic increase in the number of days spent in hospital, not because Italians were getting iller but because the Italian health system, for reasons that will become clear, had no external imperatives to limit the duration of hospital stays. Pre-op tests and post-op recovery were very lengthy affairs, and hospital visiting a full-time family occupation. This was an odd sort of consumption but a very characteristic one.[94]

Hedonism, cognition, aesthetics and health: these were the four principal, interconnected realms of modern Italian consumption. They were far from the only ones, for just as 60s consumption could not be limited to a typology of utility and convenience, so that of the 90s was not confined to pleasure, knowledge and the body. The key family acquisition in these years remained that of a home, with the statistics showing an inexorable rise in home ownership.[95] The anthropologist Filippucci noted for Bassano:

The better-off live in *ville* set in landscaped gardens, protected by burglar-proof gates and ferocious dogs. A more modest ideal is a flat in a *villetta*, expensively outfitted . . . Arturo, a man in his 40s, son of factory workers, who has a good job as an electrician, and his wife, a schoolteacher, were given by his mother her old four-roomed 'workers' cottage'. In 1988, Arturo was rebuilding it as a two-floor, three-bedroomed house, with a separate flatlet for his mother, a sauna, a laundry room, expensive fittings, and a complicated burglar alarm system.[96]

b. COMMERCIAL TELEVISION AND CONSUMER STYLES

The great boom in consumption, with its innovatory features and mass participation, was vigorously stimulated in 1974 by the arrival of colour, and then commercial, television. The latter, as its name suggests, derived both its *raison d'être* and economic viability from the advertising of commodities. As Nora Rizza has written, the aim of commercial television was *not* 'to know how to produce programmes, which is or should be the rule in public television, but to know how to produce, by means of the programmes on offer, television audiences; that is, the consumers required by the market of investors in publicity'.[97] This was true of all commercial televisions, but the particularly wildcat nature of the Italian case (whose history will be recounted below) made for an especially vigorous commercial assault upon viewers. Forgacs has calculated that in 1984 the RAI showed 46,080 advertisements for a total of 311 hours of advertising, whereas commercial channels showed 494,000 advertisements for a total of 3,468 hours; in all, around 1,500 television advertisements per day were being shown in Italy, more than in all the other European countries put together.[98] The onslaught was not only temporal but aural: volume automatically increased at advertisement time, not only for adults' programmes but for children's as well. Far from being Packard's famous 'hidden persuaders',[99] Italian commercial television advertisements in the 1980s were a noisy, endlessly repetitive, frontal attack upon fledgling consumers as well as hardened veterans of the world of goods.[100]

All this happened at a time when television exercised an extraordinary dominion over leisure time. The Eurisko survey of 1986 compared the frequency of certain key elements of cultural consumption. Of the interviewees 86.3 per cent watched television on a daily basis, compared to only 46.4 per cent who listened to the radio and 41.4 per cent who read a newspaper. Only 17 per cent went to the cinema once or more a month, and 6.1 per cent to a museum. Television was the only daily 'cultural' activity of the average Italian family.[101]

Commercial television, with its endless repetitions and vast cultural deserts, was one of the least attractive elements of the new phase of consumerism. None the less it was central, for it played incessantly upon the key quality of modern consumption – its *insatiability*. This derived not from inherent greed, but from consumption's essentially cyclical quality: from desire to acquisition and use, to disillusionment, discarding and renewed desire. Such a cycle founded its trajectory not just on the 'suggestions' of commercial television, nor simply on Veblenesque qualities of emulation, but on a more deep-rooted and restless searching for identity and meaning through acquisition.[102]

Not all Italians, of course, could acquire in equal measure. Biorcio and Maneri have suggested four different consumption styles for the second half of the 1980s, which if they did not correspond mechanically to different strata of the population, none the less offer some suggestive indications.[103] Opulent styles, which account for approximately 30 per cent of consumers in 1990, varied between '*ricchezza ed immagine*' (with the accent on high spending, fashion, the building of self-identity through the acquisition of exclusive goods), and '*qualità ed equilibrio*' (elegance, sobriety and a greater control over consumption). More women were to be found in the first category, more men in the second. Explorative styles (28 per cent in 1990) were very much those of youth in the 1980s: the celebration of ostentation, of frequent changes of goods (watches, clothes, cars, etc.), of culinary experimentation, of exotic travel; or else, on a lower income level, of a certain curiosity and nonchalance combined. Traditional styles (20.5 per cent) were, as their name suggests, the rockbed of what remained of '*l'Italietta*': well-turned-out and conventional consumers, who had modest incomes and paid much attention to saving, to special offers, to the sales; housewives and pensioners figured strongly in this group. Finally came marginal styles (21 per cent), characterized by consumer poverty, a disattention to fashion, a heavy emphasis on practical buys, on making ends meet; not surprisingly, workers and pensioners were over-represented in this group.

c. THE CRITIQUE OF CONSUMPTION

The dramatic transformation of Italian consumption described briefly above has been the object of strongly negative comment from many quarters. Indeed, in Catholic circles reproductive decline and consumer indulgence have been intimately linked, with the paucities of the former being attributed to the egoistical excesses of the latter. So widespread a condemnation should come as no surprise, for it derives from different parts of a very long-standing and international critique of modern consumption.[104]

Recent critics, if they do not go as far as Pasolini once did, to argue that modern consumption is profoundly anti-democratic,[105] certainly suggest that there is little that links the modern enrichment of material culture to the consolidation of citizenship. Such a contention is well summarized by J. C. Agnew's brutal question: 'How does brand loyalty mediate civic loyalty?'[106] They also suggest that in opulent capitalist economies like the Italian one, individuals are quite unable to deal with, digest, or control the great flux of goods that flutters before their eyes. Daniel Miller, for instance, has argued recently that the spread of objective culture has outstripped the capacity of the subject to absorb it, and has made a passionate plea for the construction of a modern process of 'sublation', by which objects are reabsorbed by their creators, rather than remaining external and alien to them.[107] Yet there seems little in contemporary consumer capitalism to sustain such perspectives. Instead, the admen's cynical view, that a great part of modern consumption is little more than a Pavlovian reaction to their own artful creations, seems to be a sharp if sad account of modern realities.

In Italy, the most resounding and intelligent public voice which criticized consumer tendencies was that of the Communist leader Enrico Berlinguer. As early as 1977, when introducing the theme of 'austerity' into his vision of 'historic compromise' between Catholic and Communist forces, Berlinguer urged the abandonment of 'the illusion that it is possible to perpetuate a type of development founded on that artificial expansion of individual consumption which is the source of waste, of parasitism, of the dissipation of resources, of financial disaster'.[108] In 1983, at the sixteenth congress of the PCI, in a speech that was in many ways his moral and political testament, he returned in apocalyptic terms to these same themes.[109]

At the heart of Berlinguer's denunciation lay the superfluity and damage inherent in modern consumption. Too much was consumed too fast, too much was thrown away;[110] too much in general meant irreparable damage to the environment and to the ecology of everyday life. Furthermore, for Berlinguer the recent advance of material culture was based on profoundly mistaken values: the supreme importance accorded to money, appearance, individual satisfaction, without regard to the wider needs of the community.

The risks associated with irresponsible consumption, so eloquently denounced by Berlinguer in the late 1970s and early 1980s, were there for all to see a decade later: cities overcome by traffic, with overhead electronic boards flashing daily warnings of pollution levels; coastlines and mountain landscapes ruined by unregulated construction of second homes; small élites ostentatiously displaying their riches while millions of Italians, as we have seen, continued to live in relative poverty.

Much of consumption was indeed futile, damaging or simply idiotic, like endless 'zapping' between television channels (which produces, after a time, a profound sense of depression), taking hard drugs (which produces much better, but then much worse effects), or using a portable telephone to say *'Ciao mamma'* or 'I have just got on the train' (which produces no effect at all). Superfluity was *often* the order of the day. One wife of a Tuscan small entrepreneur confided in the mid-80s that she had built four showers into her two bathrooms, one for each member of her family – husband, wife and two sons. That way, she said, there was no queue in the morning, even if the bathrooms had come to resemble the changing rooms of a sports pavilion.[111]

Much, too, was based on obsessive emulation and the desire for show, not only among the upper strata of the population. In the heart of the Calabrian countryside in the late 1970s the anthropologist Fortunata Piselli interviewed a woman who insisted that her husband returned to work in Africa so that she could buy a 'new Salvarani kitchen unit': 'To tell the truth my husband really didn't want to go. "But what shall we do with so much money?" he asked. But this time I'm really going to buy it. It's the television that's shoved the idea into my head! Here at Altopiano nobody's seen a Salvarini.'[112]

d. POSSIBLE REPLIES

Both in Italy and elsewhere, the deep intellectual gloom induced by such patterns of modern consumption has been allayed occasionally by gleams of hope. Some commentators, for instance, have pointed to the shifting and cyclical nature of consumer behaviour. Albert Hirschman has argued that 'each time economic progress has enlarged the availability of consumer goods for some strata of society, strong feelings of disappointment in, or of hostility toward, the new material wealth have come to the fore. Along with appreciation, infatuation and even addiction, affluence seems to produce its own backlash'.[113] Colin Campbell, with a rather different emphasis, has stressed the cyclical pattern of generation – degeneration – regeneration.[114]

These are perspectives certainly preferable to the more habitual ones of unbounded pessimism; but they are perhaps not enough. Italian consumption, like that in other opulent societies, was not *all* waste, excess and emulation; to describe it in those terms is to ignore not only its *attraction* but also its *validity*. Great parts of 'autonomous imaginative hedonism' were in no way damaging, but on the contrary enriching of life. Some indeed could be called ecstatic, like the first experience of using a portable CD player and receiving directly into one's ears an individual concert, be it Mahler or Metallica. This aural experience was the very antithesis of loud television advertising. At the heart of modern consumption, it can be argued, lay the enhancement of life through a greatly increased wealth of experience and personal choice, both in the realm of goods and that of services.

Consumption, therefore, was not just to be criticized or even criminalized; it was also to be celebrated. Nor can any easy typology of good and evil consumption be invented. With few exceptions (like hard drugs), everything depended on degree and context, whether social or personal. As

Colin Campbell concluded, where largely materialistic and utilitarian beliefs prevailed, then dreams would be used primarily to overcome boredom and alienation, rather than 'to raise the vision of an imaginatively apprehended ideal world with which to counter this one'.[115] But if there was a different context, or rather the possibility of *connection* between dreams and action, then very significant synergies could be produced.

This profoundly ambivalent nature of modern consumption and its dependency on context and personal choice can perhaps be best illustrated by taking on one of the acknowledged 'monsters' of modern consumption, the television, and putting it in its family environment in contemporary Italy.[116] The dialogue that follows was recorded in 1993, during the course of a participant observation survey on families and the television.[117] A family from Rimini, of low educational qualifications but described as 'hyper-technological', was recorded as it discussed the origins of the *five* televisions in their home:

YOUNGER DAUGHTER: 'No, wait a second, the story's a long one. My parents had bought me a television, all for me. He kicked up a fuss because he didn't have one: "Elisa, let me have it; Elisa give me the T.V." . . .'

RESEARCHER: 'And why had they bought the television for you?'

YOUNGER DAUGHTER: 'As a present.'

ELDER SON: 'They'd got it as a free gift with the washing machine.'

YOUNGER DAUGHTER: 'Rubbish!'

ELDER SON: 'It came free with some sort of machine for the house.'

FATHER: 'Hang on, it was with the what's it called . . .'

MOTHER: 'When we had the bathroom re-done.'

FATHER: 'Yes, the bathroom, the bathroom. They robbed us of fourteen million lire for the bathroom and gave us a television that costs 100,000 lire . . . Ha, ha, ha!'

YOUNGER DAUGHTER: 'But it works jolly well!'

FATHER: 'It's a Kendo . . .'

MOTHER: 'They didn't rob us of anything. Remember, we got a bath with hydromassage in it.'

YOUNGER DAUGHTER (addressing her brother): 'But you broke my television . . .'

ELDER BROTHER: 'Eh?'

YOUNGER DAUGHTER: 'Yes, it was you who broke the controls, which I'd looked after perfectly. Along he comes, and whoops, there go the controls straight away.'

FATHER: 'Anyway, we got it by collecting Omo stamps . . .'

At first reading (and even on successive ones) this dialogue encapsulates some of the more criticizable patterns of modern Italian consumption: high spending in the bathroom (an item that is by now familiar);[118] in return for that high spending, special offers of other consumer durables, not necessarily wanted; acriticality towards excessive accumulation; disillusionment in the value of the purchase ('they robbed us of fourteen million'); frustration with the breaking of the object; in sum, an accumulation of negatives to lay alongside habitual family tensions like acute sibling rivalry.

However, this was not the whole story. The researchers reported that in this family there reigned 'an atmosphere made up of a chaotic vitality and playfulness, as well as strong emotional attachment'. The family did have five televisions but this had not led to its breaking-up into its component parts, with each member of the household watching their own programmes. Most viewing took place collectively, in the kitchen (the most uncomfortable place in the house), and was accompanied by a stream of caustic and ironic comments.[119] This was a family, then, which offered ample evidence of commodity fetishism, but whose attitudes could not simply be dismissed as passive and servile. Television, especially commercial television, had made its powerful and repetitive suggestions, but these had been filtered through a *family culture* which treated them in its own way.

What was true of the most insidious and omnipresent 'service', the television, was also so of other aspects of modern consumption. It is difficult to agree with Christopher Lasch when he wrote in 1967: 'In reality, the modern intrudes at every point and obliterates its [the family's] privacy . . . The sanctity of the home is a sham in a world dominated by giant corporations and by the apparatus of mass promotion.'[120] The reality of consumption was not so unidirectional and doom-laden. Critical inquiry into the social properties of modern artefacts and services must certainly acknowledge the power and concentration of the forces that are promoting them, but it cannot stop there. It must, in addition, take into account the varying significance given to goods and services by consumers, and the complexity and autonomy of their culture and reactions.[121] In the Italian case, such inquiry would lead to a more balanced attitude towards modern consumption and its impact, one which would necessarily go beyond Berlinguer's sacrosanct, passionate, but limited denunciations.

3. Conclusions

In the 1980s and 1990s changes inside Italian households were complex and far-reaching. The material culture available to families was far richer than ever before, even if they did not make good use of all the possibilities inherent in it, erring instead towards futility, repetition and ostentation. Yet not all consumption was couched or was to be interpreted in these terms. In the world of services there was much evidence among middle-class families of investment in education, such as the huge increase of money and time spent on attending private English language schools.[122] Travel and cultural activities enjoyed unparalleled booms. Aesthetics remained the historic consumer passion of the Italians, body-servicing was a new obsession, but cognitive considerations were taken more seriously than ever, especially for and by the younger generation.

Within the Italian family, the autonomy and liberty of individual members undoubtedly increased in this period. Every family is made up of individuals, some more powerful than others, some more constrained by its confines. In Italy, the formerly weaker members — women and children — made their voices heard as never before (in the case of children rather too loudly). The emancipation of working women was especially marked. If their marriages had broken down, many wives felt free for the first time to go their own way.[123] Gay men and women came out in a brave and unashamed way — something that would have been unthinkable just fifteen years earlier in a society that on these issues was deeply ingrained with hypocrisy and cant.[124]

There was also much stress on the fact that family life was based increasingly on types of informal contracts between members, and that these bases led to a more natural and relaxed intra-familial democracy.[125] There was evidence, too, that the younger generation viewed their families less as a hermetically sealed capsule than had their parents and grandparents, and were as a result more open to extra-familial values and experiences.[126] Here elements of cognitive consumption and the decline of patriarchy had clearly worked together.

On the other hand, there was still a great deal of circumstantial evidence, difficult to quantify but easy to observe, that the balance between 'family time' and 'individual time' in modern Italy was still weighted in favour of the former.[127] Dependency, control, conformity, were strongly present in household structures. The 'long family' could act as a form of chloroform: it offered the security services of the mother, washing, ironing and feeding, and at the same time the instruments of modern hedonist consumption. The net result was more escapism than escape. Traditions, too, still lingered on strongly, leading to families that were sometimes deeply oppressive in their normative requirements and their protracted inter-generational links.

These traditions were closely linked to the reproductive crisis which affected Italy at the end of the millennium. Both the Italian paradoxes mentioned earlier as major contributory features to denatality drew their strength from deeply ingrained family habits and policies. The very emancipation of women, their new 'double presence' in the public and the private spheres, militated against them fulfilling their dreams of maternity, given that they continued to receive sufficient support neither from their partners nor from the state. In addition, the very strength of families, and especially of inter-generational links, discouraged the central generation from shouldering further responsibilities, and led them along the path of neo-Malthusian prudence.

One final and crucial question has been deliberately omitted so far: the degree to which these changes in reproduction, consumption, family roles – in a word, family life – had influenced the relationship between families and the world outside them. Arnaldo Bagnasco, with his customary intelligence, has suggested a possible link between a greater democracy in the family and that in society: 'the values of obedience and of hierarchy are making way for those of discussion and agreement, in families and therefore in society too'.[128] But was this positive connection, between changes within the family and those outside it, so clear a one? It is to a discussion of this theme, in the context of Italy's civil society and mass culture, that we must now turn.

Chapter 4

Civil Society and Mass Culture

IVIL SOCIETY is both a very new and a very old term. In its
classic sense civil society was political society, in contrast to natural
society, which was not.[1] Men, public affairs, government and the law
belonged firmly to the first sphere; women, family and the household to the
second. Later on, the significance of the term and the normative values
associated with it underwent considerable variation. Hegel's civil society, for
instance, lay between the family and the state, and was viewed in predominantly negative terms;[2] while Marx's, which included the family, was the
structure of social organization deriving from a particular mode of production.[3]

In recent times, especially before and during the great transformations
in eastern Europe in 1989, civil society has been seen as a heroic sphere of
associationism and opposition, which dared to raise its voice against the
decaying dictatorship of Communist state apparatuses. In the context of
Poland's Solidarity and Havel's Prague, there was no longer an elision
between political society and civil society. The one was now the realm of
corrupt and bankrupt states; the other of free association and liberty.[4]

In contemporary western European democracies, civil society is a much
used, as well as abused, term. It is possible to discern two distinct and
common usages: the first is a broad, spatial and relatively value-free one,
intended to cover all those activities, institutions and relations that do not
belong primarily to the private sphere or to that of the state. Churches,
political parties, firms, associations and interest groups of all kinds fill this
vast intermediate area. The second usage is much more narrow and normative.
It too covers an intermediate area between family and state, but intends to

distinguish between 'civil' and 'uncivil' society, between those networks and associations which stimulate democracy and pluralism, and those which do not. Civil society, in this definition, is not a catch-all area broadly equivalent to the English term 'society', but rather an area of interaction which fosters the diffusion of power rather than its concentration, builds horizontal solidarities rather than vertical loyalties, encourages debate and autonomy of judgement rather than conformity and obedience. In Michael Walzer's words, 'The citizens of a democratic state are not, in this view, self-sufficient creatures. They must be members elsewhere, in a smaller, more accessible, less demanding, less dangerous place than the modern state. For only in such places can they acquire political competence, learn to win and lose, learn to compromise, make friends and allies, explore oppositionist ideas.'[5]

In this book the term 'civil society' is used very much in this second sense, though hopefully with some awareness of its possible pitfalls. Among these are the temptations to present civil society in over-idealized terms, to see it as a substitute for state power rather than complementary to it in the making of modern democracy, and also to include the family within it as its first association. Civil society, on the contrary, can be identified neither with the state nor with the family but constitutes a sphere of human association intimately connected to, and influencing both. Finally, civil society cannot be properly understood without emphasizing the transient character of many of its manifestations, and the possible conflict between them.

In Italy, society (as opposed to civil society in the narrower sense just outlined above) has long been seen as the site of vibrant activity and, at the same time, the conveyor of essentially negative civic values. Far from being submissive to the state along Germanic lines, Italian society has appeared as an enticing combination of autonomy and delinquency; its culture vital and individualist, but deeply deficient in trust and solidarity. Gabriele Calvi, commenting on one of the recent surveys of Italian values, that of Eurisko in 1986, has confirmed these stereotypes:

Amongst all the heritages that weigh negatively on present-day Italian society, we must put in first place the culture of diffidence, which forms, almost genetically, the mentality of each one of us. The survey confirms that the great majority of Italians have little faith in themselves, less still in others, little in public institutions, almost none in the trade unions and political parties . . . We are a people of saints, heroes, improvisers and artful fixers; above all we are cunning. Our cunningness [*furbizia*] consists in believing that others will take advantage of us if we do not first take advantage of them. The *humus* on which this popular culture grows is extensive.[6]

The most recent period in Italian history has often been seen as one which has brutally reinforced these values. After the era of collective action in the late 1960s and the 1970s, there was a return to the normality of an 'uncivil society'. According to Marco Revelli, only the most eloquent and radical of a whole shoal of commentators, the visible subjects of this society

> have remained almost exclusively the following: the principal public banks and companies, artificially sustained by the state; the so-called 'strong powers' [traditional big industry and Mediobanca], camouflaged behind the rhetoric of the Firm and the mythology of the Entrepreneur as the new Prince of modernity; the Mafia, whose 'dirty' money, circulating internationally, has given us standards of living and consumption well above what we merit; the unending army of tax evaders.[7]

The 1980s, in other words, combined the atavistic diffidence of Italian society with the triumph of some of its most delinquent elements, which were also, not incidentally, its most powerful.

There is much to comfort such an interpretation, but much else that contests it. It is my argument here that Italian social trends developed in two opposing directions, neither of which was clearly dominant. On the one hand, the period was marked by a return to the unquestioned acceptance of hierarchy, by the increased power of monopolies and oligopolies, by the new and deleterious influence exercised by commercial television, by a mass passivity in strong contrast to earlier social patterns of mobilization. On the other, there were distinct signs of the growth, for the first time in Italian history, of an autonomous and active civil society (in the narrow sense outlined above). The post-materialist values identified by Inglehart in 1977,[8] the great strides taken in education, particularly female education, the growth of a new associationism, linked with social commitment and strong in both South and North, all these were inescapable signs of a generational shift, which was also a form of cultural revolution.

The critical and 'reflexive' middle classes referred to in Chapter 2 were certainly at the heart of this construction of civil society, but membership was not just limited to them. Indeed, just how widely civil society could spread was probably one of the crucial demands in contemporary Italian history.

Italian society, then, was the site of considerable, if pacific, cultural conflict at the end of the century. Which of the two trends outlined above would triumph remained a very open question, for neither was archaic. One took its principal force from the slow processes of mass education, the other from the further concentrations of power and ideological control in late twentieth-century capitalism. Both of them tended to be the preserve of different sections of society, sometimes dangerously so.

This chapter is dedicated to a further exploration of these themes and tendencies, their provenance and principal characteristics. The complex picture that emerges of Italy's mass culture, conceived of in the widest sense,[9] is hardly that of a paradigm of civic virtues, but certainly much more than the clienteles of the semi-periphery.[10]

1. The Legacy of the Past

a. FAMILISM

In the formation of Italian mass culture various long-term characteristics have played a critical role. One of these, highly negative in content, has been familism. A discussion of its importance allows us to return to the problem raised at the end of the last chapter, namely the possible connection, or lack of it, between changes in family life and the growth of a more democratic, and thus civil, society. Familism is a highly controversial term, frequently over-used in Italy, and even more often left ill-defined. Its very vagueness and catch-all quality have led some distinguished scholars of contemporary Italy, in particular Gabriella Gribaudi and Marzio Barbagli, to propose its discarding.[11] Others, including the author of this volume, have argued for its continued relevance as an explanatory tool, provided it is carefully defined and historically rooted.[12]

The term 'amoral familism' was coined by Edward Banfield in 1958, to describe the attitudes of the peasants he had studied at Chiaromonte in Basilicata. The extreme backwardness of this village was caused, according to him, by 'the inability of the villagers to act together for their common good, or indeed, for any good transcending the immediate, material interest of the nuclear family'.[13] This was 'amoral familism', and Banfield claimed that such crippling and exclusive concentration on the family did not apply just to the village he had studied, but to many other parts of the rural South.

Banfield's theses were heavily criticized,[14] but the term familism lived on. It did so because in all probability it struck a resonant chord, not simply as a description of attitudes in the backward and primitive South, but also for Italy as a whole. Familism, it emerged, was not just rural and archaic, destined to disappear with American-style modernization, as Banfield envisaged. It was also urban and modern.[15]

In attempting to refine and adapt the term better to the realities of contemporary Italy, I have suggested that it should be viewed as a particular form of the *relationship* between family, society (and, if it exists, civil society) and the state; a form in which the values and interests of the family are counterposed to the other principal moments of human associationism.[16] In this definition, the respective weight of all three elements in the relationship, and not just the family, have to be taken into consideration. In Italy's case, the very strength of family units, outlined in the previous chapter, when linked to the relative weakness of civil society, especially in the South, and to a profound distrust in the state, allowed familism to persist in its modern form. The result has often been, in the words of Norberto Bobbio, that in Italy 'a quantity of energy, commitment and courage is squandered on the family, but little is left for society or for the state'.[17]

The causal responsibilities for this state of affairs have been variously located. Banfield himself went round in circles. Familism caused backwardness, but was itself caused by elements of backwardness, namely high mortality rates and land hunger, which combined with the supposed vices of the nuclear, as opposed to extended, family.[18] Other explanations have tended to be either of an ascending or descending quality. Some scholars, especially those trained in social psychology or psychoanalysis, have identified, predictably, processes within the family, especially mother–son relations or the 'long' family, as deforming Italian families' relations to the outside world, and indeed Italian society in general. These are ascending explanations, originating in the family and moving upwards.[19] Others, especially sociologists, have tended to reverse the process and make familism derive from external forces, which descended upon families and conditioned them. Here it was not family dynamics but the failures of the state, the particularities of Catholic ideology, the clientelism of Italian society, which were principally responsible.[20]

Both these lines of explanation have considerable persuasive force. Looked at from a historian's viewpoint, however, it would seem a mistake to prioritize one or the other. Rather it seems necessary to import a diachronic element into the discussion, to see how family–civil society–state relations changed over time, and the different weight of each in any given period. In this way it may be possible to avoid the widespread idea of a genetic or 'anthropological' nature of Italian familism, deeply inbred into its people. 'What is the character of a people?' asked Benedetto Croce. 'Its history, all its history, nothing but its history.'[21]

As I tried to show in my earlier work on the Republic, in Italy's most recent history there was no simple linear development or affirmation of familism. Rather there were places and moments when family interests and those of civil society strongly intertwined – in the northern cities during the Resistance of 1944–5, in the southern peasant movement of the late 1940s and early 1950s, in many of the social movements from 1968 onwards. By contrast, there were places and periods when family strategies acquired an overridingly private dimension – on the new housing estates in the early years of the 'miracle',[22] in the turn away from the public sphere of the late seventies, in much of the urban South for most of the time.

The key questions, then, concern all three elements of our chain of connections: what forms of family favoured a fruitful relationship between individuals and civil society? What type of society, and even more so civil society, could exercise a benign influence on families? What actions of the state could foster both less familist families, and the burgeoning of a modern civil society?

The answers to such daunting questions lie beyond the scope of this book. Here only a few observations relating to the weakness in Italy of the relationship between family and civil society are in order, while the Italian state's attitudes towards the family will be touched upon in Chapter 7.

Civil society is composed primarily of individuals, not of families. A successful relationship between family and civil society would be one in which family members were encouraged, both by their family background and by the wider society of which they were part, to participate in the activities of civil society as individuals and equals, to become citizens and not just voters. The form of the family (its openness or closedness, its gendered hierarchies or lack of them) and the possibilities of politics are thus intimately linked. J. S. Mill saw this very clearly when he wrote of the condition of women in 1870: 'The family is a school of despotism, in which the virtues of despotism, but also its vices, are largely nourished. Citizenship, in free countries, is partly a school of society in equality; but citizenship fills only a small place in modern life, and does not come near the daily habits or inmost sentiments. The family, justly constituted, would be the real school of the virtues of freedom.'[23]

It may be that recent changes in family forms in Italy, as Bagnasco suggests, are slowly pushing family–civil society relations in this direction; as gender relations change, and individuals become more free *within* the family, it is possible that citizenship will grow *outside* the family. Yet the legacy of the past, while not a uniform one, weighs heavily upon these prospects. Families in Italy have become accustomed to developing defensive, cynical and even predatory attitudes towards much of the outside world, towards the institutions of the state, towards those wider loyalties that transcend kinship or narrow local networks of friendship. The Republic, for all its formal democracy, has done little to combat these tendencies, and the form assumed by the modern socio-economic structures of the country has probably increased rather than decreased these negative trends.

The anthropologist Stefano De Matteis has written perceptively of the vitality of traditional relationships in the *'vicoli'* (back streets, alleys) of Naples, of the links between artisan and shopkeeping families and the world that surrounded them, even up to the present day. Here families are drawn out of their shells: 'It is as if the central family, that of the *bottega* [workshop or shop], is subject to a series of centripetal forces which, while they do not threaten the family's unity, extend it, push it out of its habitual shape, confer upon it a variable rhythm.'[24] To romanticize such relationships would be a grave mistake, but so too would be the failure to recognize that such 'variable rhythms' were not the natural product of the economic and social modernization of modern Italy, and were to be found with difficulty in the many thousands of modern blocks of flats which housed the numerical majority of contemporary Italians.

b. CLIENTELISM

Familism was one negative legacy of the past which rendered the creation of a civil society more difficult; clientelism was another. Clientelism in its original Roman form was a formal pact established between patron and client, in which the client swore loyalty to his master, but received in return a series of legal guarantees as to the conduct of the patron on his behalf. In this vertical diadic relationship, power was unequally distributed between the two persons involved, but was not exclusively the prerogative of one or the other.[25]

The traditional clientelism of rural Italy, though the object of infinite variations and gradations, saw the evolution of another model. The discretionary power of the patron, in this case the landlord, was very much increased, and the contractual power of the client, the peasant or landless labourer, correspondingly diminished. Nowhere was this more apparent than on the great *latifondi* of southern Italy, where the rights of peasants, beholden and dependent on landlords and their agents, were reduced to a minimum.[26]

Schematically speaking, in the history of the Republic a third model can be identified, deriving from the great increase in the resources of the modern state. It was distinguished by two features in particular: first, the benefits to be distributed were no longer primarily those of the private patron, but those of the state; secondly, the pattern of their distribution was not, as in ancient Rome, broadly in accordance with official norms, but in defiance of them.[27]

Modern Italian clientelism has been very usefully defined by the anthropologist Amalia Signorelli as 'a system of interpersonal relations in which private ties of a kinship, ritual kinship, or friendship type are used inside public structures, with the intent of making public resources serve private ends'.[28] In the history of the Italian Republic the public patron, a politician or civil servant, acted as a sort of gatekeeper, distributing selected public resources (jobs, pensions, licences, etc.) to clients, friends and relations in return for fidelity, both personal and electoral.[29] Once again the client had few rights or powers, for agreements were perforce personal and informal, often covert and without legal binding. All took place in a context of servilism, not citizenship. The dominant social values fostered were those of submissiveness and of gratitude.[30]

The longevity of these clientelistic relationships in Italy, and their constantly evolving forms and content, have strong similarities with those in other southern European societies, such as the *cacique* system in nineteenth-century Spain.[31] Their survival and force depended to a great extent upon the failure of the political élites in all these countries in the late nineteenth and early twentieth centuries to make a clear break with established practices. Naturally, all states function not only on the basis of law and regulation, but on interpersonal contact and informal relations. In southern Europe, however, these latter relations heavily outweighed the former, and always threatened to engulf them.

The effect upon Italian public institutions of this pervasive and long-lasting clientele culture will be analysed below, in Chapter 7, which is dedicated to an analysis of the state. In *societal* terms the culture of clientelism led, to quote Signorelli again, to a 'mass socialization in the practices of illegality'.[32] Such illegality could take minor forms, such as using a patron's influence in order to circumvent the more tedious of the bureaucracy's requirements; or it could serve a much more sinister purpose, as the bedrock upon which criminal organizations developed, though not necessarily everywhere or in the same way.[33] Not by chance did Leopoldo Franchetti, in his classic study of the early Mafia in Sicily, make that organization derive directly from patron–client relations of an especially perverse form.[34]

Another consequence was the necessary limiting of the space for horizontal solidarities in Italian society. Vertical diadic relations became *the* norms of society, a natural and honourable way of proceeding, a service performed by the fortunate and the powerful for those who were neither. No one summed up better these attitudes than Giulio Andreotti, when he objected in 1957 to the idea that there was anything wrong in writing a 'raccomandazione':

We would not like anyone to jump to the conclusion that deputies, senators, and also those who hold no public post, react in a way that is less than noble when their help and aid is incessantly solicited. Each one of us is approached, on our Sunday walk-abouts or on other days of the week, by those who ask for help in finding work, for the speeding-up of a pension claim, for advice on applications for public sector job competitions, and so on. One takes the appropriate notes, one writes or telephones, one tries to do something. It is a wearing routine and not devoid of misunderstandings and of bitterness, but it is obligatory. Let tribute be paid . . . to those who serve their neighbours by offering a modest human contact, which sometimes manages to give hope to those who no longer believe in the solidarity of others.[35]

The only problem being that such long-suffering acts of Christian *caritas* were rarely disinterested and frequently illegal. By the 1970s Andreotti and his lieutenants had built up a legendary network of clients, first in Lazio and then in western Sicily. They were not alone in so doing.

Given these long-term practices, it was not surprising to find that in the 1980s and 1990s international social surveys reflected a particular Italian culture of clientelism. When asked about factors influencing 'getting ahead in life', the Italians, more than other nations consulted, consistently put 'knowing the right people' very high on their list of priorities. To have 'political contacts' was also regarded as of unusual importance.[36]

The possible linkages between familism and clientelism remain to be explored. Are these two terms Siamese twins, locked inextricably together in the history of the Republic, are they identical twins, are they twins at all? The question of their connection has never been treated in any great analytical depth, but it is possible to suggest intrinsic, if not mechanical, links between the two. Modern clientelism, by its encouragement of single families to seek individualist solutions to their problems, based on diadic hierarchies, inevitably invited primary social groups to exist in competition and diffidence, one with another. Familist traditions in their turn, based on profound scepticism about external solidarities, formed the intimate cultural basis on which clientelist strategies were grounded. It would be wrong to derive one from the other, and perhaps more useful to suggest that they overlapped in a number of spheres. The clientelist use of godparenthood or ritual kinship would be one such example.[37]

It would also be useful to try to ascribe familism and clientelism predominant spheres of influence and activity. In an interesting study of Sicily in the 1960s,[38] G. Grieco suggested that in the sphere of politics clientelism was pervasive, while familism was occasional, whereas in that of economic activity excessive reliance on the family group far superseded the activities of clienteles. In the murky waters of 'Tangentopoli' ('kick-back city'), as we shall see, the clan or clientelistic group was the dominant form, but exclusive loyalty to the family, both as motive and practice, was certainly not absent.

c. WHITE AND RED

In the early decades of the Republic two great ideological forces in Italian society, the Catholic Church and the Communist party, were very often responsible for organized social and cultural activities which went beyond single families. Both these mass organizations reached out beyond the educated minorities to involve a consistent sector of the popular classes. In the 1940s and 1950s much of social life in northern Italy revolved around the parish; in the central regions much the same could be said for the role of the left-oriented *Case del popolo* ('Houses of the people'). This was not so much a civil society as a society organized (if and where it was organized) according to belief.

The two subcultures,[39] white and red, have often been presented, especially in the recent literature on the 'Third Italy', as having fundamental traits of resemblance, both in appearance and content. There is much to support this view. Both subcultures stressed their difference from, and superiority to, the world that surrounded them, while at the same time practising unceasing proselytism. Both were against the modern world of consumerism, which was denounced roundly, either for its egoism or its commodity fetishism. Both placed great emphasis upon solidarity, or solidarism as the Catholics called it. One boasted the culture of the confessional; the other of public self-criticism. Both offered powerful charismatic and Utopian visions, the one extraterrestrial, the other in the Motherland of world revolution.

However, there is a real danger, especially after the demise of the principal political expressions of these two cultures, the DC and the PCI, of exaggerating their similitude. Catholic culture enjoyed a rootedness and strength to which the Communists could only aspire. As Pius XII claimed in 1946: 'For more than fifteen centuries the Italian people has remained faithful to this order of belief, which appeared to them entirely normal and unquestioned.'[40] If Communism exercised a certain hegemony over high culture in the Republican decades, it was Catholicism that could boast of prestigious universities in Milan and Rome, and which had created over time, as Giorgio Galli wrote in 1968, 'an extended network of associations which has regimented the greater part of the lower and middle-ranking intelligentsia of the professions'.[41]

Communism, on the other hand, was much more closely linked with the dominant intellectual and material trends of the twentieth century. For all its hostility to capitalism, it felt itself to be on the side of history, the natural heir to the tradition of the French Revolution, and the cultural expression of the industrial masses. By contrast, Catholicism was history's critic, extraneous to and critical of the modern world, about which it expressed a fundamental 'eschatological reserve'.[42]

Most importantly, the two subcultures presented quite different attitudes towards authority. Both were hierarchical organizations, but they were diametrically opposed in their basic teaching and their structural siting in Italian society. The Church, as a result of its predominant cultural longevity and by means of the Christian Democrat hold upon the state, was the very essence of institutional authority, both political and moral. The culture it preached *vis-à-vis* authority was fundamentally that of submission and docility, accompanied by the unparalleled virtues of mediation, which all too easily slipped into clientelism. Families were invited to seek mediated and individual, not 'mass', solutions in their relations to the outside world and to authority. The whole tradition of the propitious invocation of the Madonna and of the saints was founded upon these premises.[43]

For the Communists on the other hand, contesting authority, often against the councils of their more prudent leaders, organizing the 'masses', leading strikes, seeking collective solutions to collective problems, was the very heart of the matter. They were the form and sense that the Communists gave to the word 'solidarity'.

The divergences between the two subcultures were thus at least as important as their similarities. They were also to be the profound substrata upon which different parts of the country constructed differing political responses to the crisis of the 1990s.

With the passage of time, the Catholic and Communist hold on the organization of society changed and weakened.[44] Moments of renewal and of high idealistic tension still occurred for both of them: for the Catholics with the extraordinary impulses provided by the papacy and encyclicals of Pope John XXIII (1958–63), as well as by the second Vatican council, which met for the first time in October 1962. It was from this era that a new grass-roots Catholicism developed, less doctrinaire and integralist, more the Catholic component of an imminent civil society. As for the Communists, the wave of student and worker militancy of 1968–9, for all its criticisms of the party's revisionism and orthodoxy, was in time to fill its sections with a new generation of militants.

Yet the very nature of modern society, with its accentuated individualism, its autonomous youth culture, its growing secularization and economic well-being, step by step dismantled the subcultures.[45] Residual ideological influences were to be of great importance in the history of the 1980s and 1990s, but the time of regimented mass culture had gone for ever.

In many ways this was a very good thing. It allowed, eventually, for a new pluralism freed of hierarchy, for the flowering for the first time in Italy of a non-party, non-church civil society. But this civil society, as we shall see, was overwhelmingly the preserve of the educated classes. The cultural, political and religious influences which had permeated deep into society during the early decades of the Republic, and which had given it its peculiar quality, had evaporated. In their place, many millions of working- and lower-middle-class families were left materially richer but more destitute in terms of association, even at the minimal level of involvement in their children's schools.[46] Instead, the main cultural influence in their lives had become the television.

d. GENDER AND CIVIL SOCIETY

Traditionally, in Italian as in other European societies, associationism was male. If we glance inside a working-class bar in a popular quarter of Genoa in 1962, with its habitués gathered around the television to comment upon

Tribuna politica, the party political programme of the time, we find that all those making comments, and perhaps all those present, were men.[47]

In the intensely Catholic province of Vicenza, some years earlier, when a questionnaire of the ACLI (Italian Catholic Workers' Association) was distributed to young people at their places of socialization, there were just fifteen female replies out of a total of nearly 900. In the section of the questionnaire dedicated to 'the family', there were questions about relations with fathers and brothers, but none at all about the female side of the family.[48]

Historically, deep-rooted patriarchal culture allowed no space in the public sphere for women's sociality. Rather, women's networks were those centred around children, housework and kinship. Even in 1980s Bassano, Paola Filippucci came to the conclusion that 'outside socializing is thus enacted by women as a brief chance aside in the course of doing domestic errands'.[49] The neighbourhood, too, was traditionally a female domain; one that could certainly produce sociality and even solidarities, but also the poisons of gossip, competition and spying.[50] However, neighbourhood and street sociality were declining forces in modern Italy. As Siebert and Minicuci noted in Calabria, the new modes of urban construction isolated women rather than pulling them together.[51]

In comparative European terms, Italian women, even though they made great strides in the last two decades of the century, remained among those who had least chance to escape from family constrictions into the official world of work. They were blocked, as we have seen, both by the restricted structures of the Italian labour market and by the limited public care for very young children. There were important sub-national qualifications to be made to this picture, with Emilia-Romagna foremost in attempting to offer an alternative model. Overall, though, Italy occupied a distinctly retrograde place in the diverse worlds of European patriarchy.[52]

These considerations on the exclusion and isolation of women found some substance in the 1986 Eurisko survey on Italy, in which the gendered nature of friendship emerged very strongly.[53] Those who declared that they had few friends were primarily women, especially housewives, and those with low income. Those who had extended friendship networks, by contrast, were men, those with a university education, young people, and rather surprisingly, the unemployed. Men spent much more of their free time in activities outside the home, a factor which according to the survey 'confirms a greater male "liberty" and a greater female "imprisonment" in the domestic sphere'.[54] Clearly, these were long-term historical trends which not only were slow to die, but deeply inhibited the creation of a less gendered civil society.

e. GEOGRAPHY

Finally, a word about geography. In a pioneering study on the performance of regional governments in Italy since their foundation in 1971, the American political scientist Robert Putnam pointed to considerable divergences which seemed to derive principally from their geographical location.[55] Whereas regions in the Centre and the North of the country performed highly creditably in Putnam's assessment, those in the South did much less well. The sites of regional government themselves gave off a different feel: 'Even finding officials of the Puglia regional government in the capital city of Bari proved a challenge for us, as it is for their constituents ... In the dingy anteroom loll several indolent functionaries, though they are likely to be present only an hour or two each day and to be unresponsive even then. The persistent visitor might discover that in the offices beyond stand only ghostly rows of empty desks.'[56] Whereas to visit the corresponding seat of regional government in Emilia-Romagna, in the city of Bologna, was 'like entering a modern high-tech firm. A brisk, courteous receptionist directs visitors to the appropriate office, where, likely as not, the relevant official will call up a computerized database on regional problems and policies.'[57]

The explanation that Putnam offered for so great a divergence lay outside the regional centres of government, or indeed the history of the Republic. It resided instead in the capacity of one part of the country, but not the other, to create over a long historical timespan what he called a 'civic community', 'that is, patterns of civic involvement and social solidarity'.[58] Civic community was not the same as civil society. In Putnam's definition, it lacked the latter's pluralism, democracy and gender parity, but was rather the substrata, the social capital, upon which a civil society could be formed.

For Putnam the key period that established the divergence between North and South was the medieval one. The flowering of the free communes and city republics of the Centre-North was contrasted to the top-down centralism of Frederick II's reign in the South. Here was the original divide. Successive generations were to build upon it, but could not change its basic shape. In the period after Italian Unification, for instance, the Centre-North boasted a rich network of mutual aid associations, of Catholic social initiatives, etc.; the South, by contrast, remained a land almost desolate of association, prey to clientelism and criminality.[59]

Putnam's thesis has been heavily criticized, principally on two grounds. The first was for its obvious tendency to determinism, the second for its undifferentiated approach to the South. Many scholars of the Mezzogiorno were at pains to point out the diversity of regional traditions in the South, as well as their *variation* over time. The South, they argued, was not one, nor was its fate fixed in 1250.

These were just criticisms, sometimes expressed unjustly, but they should not allow us to forget the thrust of Putnam's inquiry – the attempt to explain how Italy's differing regional history resulted in a variable capacity for the creation of a civic community, and eventually of a civil society. For the 1980s and 1990s, though, the hard questions did not concern so much the geo-history and supposed homogeneity of the South as that of the Centre-North.

In the early years of the debate upon the existence of a 'Third Italy',[60] comprising *both* the central regions of the country and those of the North-East, great emphasis was placed upon the possible elements of convergence between these regions: a sharecropping background, extended families, the development of dynamic small industry in the context of an 'urbanized countryside', hegemonic subcultures, efficient local government. Their similarities, it was argued, outweighed their differences and justified an original redrawing of Italy's socio-economic geography. The North-West (Lombardy, Piedmont and Liguria), on the other hand, the traditional geographical location of big industry, was considered a case apart.

Twenty years later it is possible to suggest a quite different reading. The 'white' zones of northern Italy, the historic areas of mass Catholic voting and belief (eastern Lombardy, central and northern Veneto, much of Venezia Giulia), seem to have reaffirmed significant *differences* from the rest of the Third Italy, as well as from the North-West. In these areas, which do not correspond to a simple regional division,[61] there was a startling growth, not so much of a civil society, as of a localist culture based on free market values and hard work, patriarchy and vertical hierarchies, conformity and racialist exclusion. These traits, although certainly present elsewhere in the North and Centre, were not nearly so prevalent. In particular, Emilia-Romagna, Tuscany, Umbria and the Marches were heirs to a different tradition. Though far from perfect societies (or regional governments), they were more heavily committed to the values of a modern civil society.

The rise of the Northern League will be dealt with in detail in the next chapter of this book. For the purposes of the present discussion it is enough to note that the correspondence between the traditional areas of Catholic subculture and the strongholds of the League lends itself to at least two possible interpretations. The first is that the newly dominant culture of these zones was a distinct break with the past, a rejection of, and revolt against, Catholic values. The second is a subtler and more disconcerting reading. It is that there were strong elements in Catholic teaching and practice which laid the very ground for the triumph of the new culture. The Church could condemn the materialism, individualism and xenophobia of the new majority opinion, but its more attentive members reflected on the fact that these were children who had been brought up in their own parishes.[62]

2. Aspects of Contemporary Mass Culture

After having examined some of the most significant legacies of the past, I would like to turn now to consider certain aspects of contemporary mass culture. For reasons of space and competence, I have chosen to concentrate on television and football, though I am aware that in doing so I have omitted other equally important areas, such as that of popular music.

a. TELEVISION AND THE MASS MEDIA

The single greatest constituent element of mass culture in Italy's most recent history has been the television. With the growth of commercial and colour television, the amount of time that Italians spent in front of their television sets increased rapidly: from an average of 2 hours 53 minutes per day in 1988 to 3 hours 35 minutes in 1995.[63] As we have seen, this was the only 'cultural' activity that the great majority of Italians indulged in on a daily basis.[64]

The general reaction to television's dominance has been apocalyptic. Karl Popper's last diatribe against television circulated very widely in Italy in the 1990s. His criticisms were reinforced by those of Norberto Bobbio and repeated by many other intellectuals.[65] Television was diseducative, sly and violent. It penetrated homes and minds, turned ordinary children into potential criminals, produced conformism and passivity. It was not a *medium* but a *subject*, the most powerful cultural actor of the contemporary scene. It was also, according to Popper, 'a colossal political power, potentially the most powerful of all, as if it was God himself who was speaking'.[66] Television had to be stopped, at least in its present form.

So dramatic a view must be treated with some scepticism. In some circumstances, as De Mauro has argued, television has had an invaluable educative function, as in Italy in the 1960s, informing parts of the population which otherwise had no contact with elements of a national or international culture.[67] Joseph Meyrowitz's insistence on the levelling effects of the electronic media is also worthy of serious attention. Following in the steps of McLuhan, he argues that television as a *medium* is at least as important as its content, for it leads to a new 'situational geography' of social life. Hierarchical senses of place and position are broken down, leading to the creation of new and more universal spaces of communication: 'through television rich and poor, young and old, scholars and illiterates . . . often share the same or very similar information at the same moment.'[68] There is no need to embrace some of Meyrowitz's more extreme claims[69] in order to recognize that television, in its redefinition of information in relation to place, is at least potentially a medium more connected with the growth of democracy than might at first appear.

The apocalyptic view also takes very little account of another problematic area: the highly complex interactions between television and its viewers. As we have seen in the previous chapter, television is *mediated* by an individual's or a family's culture and not simply accepted uncritically. Time and again the most perceptive observers have emphasized television's *dualities*: television influences society, but it also reflects it.[70] It 'clamps the family together', as Peter Laslett has written, 'as nothing else has done since the one open fire in the kitchen', but it also 'sets every viewer adrift in an open, boundaryless, standardless world of infinite symbolic gratification'.[71] It wastes time, especially of the young and old, but can help to form the one and comfort the other. It presents stereotypes, but these can incite unexpectedly to action (the American soap of intrepid policewomen can have an extraordinary effect in a traditional patriarchal world). Gunther and Svennevig put it at its simplest: 'television can work both ways.'[72]

Which way television works, though, depends upon the wider context in which it functions. Here there are two key variables: who controls the medium and how culturally rich and varied is the society in which it operates. If control is too narrow and mass culture lacking in autonomy and criticality, then the links between television and *civil* society will indeed be tenuous. Without espousing the apocalyptic view, and bearing in mind the degree of sophistication of much of Italian society, it is still difficult to escape the conclusion that at the end of the twentieth century television was working the wrong way, and quite badly so.

Such an assertion can be supported, in sober fashion, on a number of counts. First, the question of control. The market in television ownership is a very particular one, in no way comparable, for example, to that in which small Italian industry thrives. To prosper in television, especially in the era of rapidly developing global technologies, means to have access to extraordinary resources. Only a few moguls, from Rupert Murdoch downwards, can hope to survive, and even European public televisions find themselves in difficulty in such a context.[73]

The unparalleled concentration of ownership in the last decade has had grave consequences. The global television oligarchy is distinguished, quite naturally, by its insatiable desire for personal profit and aggrandisement, by the corresponding priority given to levels of audience participation, and by a cultural framework that is deeply limited and conformist. All these factors, though with important national variations, have produced commercial television of a particularly repetitive and unedifying quality.

By and large, European public television has not responded to this challenge with an alternative model of its own. Instead it has been pushed into competing with commercial television on the latter's own ground, with deleterious consequences in terms of programming and quality.

To this central structural point must be added others, relating to the consumption and nature of the media. One of these is a question of class. Private television is owned by the hyper-rich, those at the very top of the 'Mole Antonelliana' of Italian social stratification, but consumed most by those at its very bottom. The Eurisko survey of 1986 for Italy showed that those families with the lowest level of education and of income were those most television-dependent. Gender and age also played a central role. The two categories of most habitual viewers, not only in Italy, were housewives, and those between the ages of 65 and 74.[74]

To this mass audience of habitual viewers, modern television offered a certain type of culture, heavily oriented towards light entertainment, films, sport and soap operas; and a certain form for its consumption, based on short timespans of concentration, on frequent breaks and incongruous juxtapositions.[75] The sensory impression thus created was one of rapidity and interruption, but also of repetitive reassurance and constant presence.

Television of this sort took hold of its viewers and rooted them to the home. One middle-aged Italian interviewee, a woman of fifty-eight who lived on the north-west periphery of Milan, explained in 1991 that in her quarter 'television nails people down . . . it makes you lazy; the fear of being on the streets at night is more of an excuse than anything else. At nine in the evening you come home and you don't have any desire to go out again, because there's the television that helps you pass those two or three hours before it's time to go to sleep.'[76]

Television offered frequent viewers alternative spaces to the outside world – symbolic sites as Meyrowitz would have it, or 'non-spaces' according to Augé,[77] which ably substituted the more difficult terrain of the external built environment and its interpersonal relations. It was easier, in other words, to watch *Neighbours* than be neighbours. Poverty, in its widest sense, and modern television were thus intimately linked.[78]

The Italian case exemplified many of these trends, some of them in extreme form. Control was one such. Silvio Berlusconi, as we have seen in Chapter 1, was allowed, and indeed encouraged, to build up a dominant control of commercial television. In 1995 Marialina Marcucci, the owner of Videomusic, an interesting channel much followed by Italian youth, recounted interestingly how she had been squeezed out, principally through the activities of Publitalia, Fininvest's advertising company. By hogging the whole market in television publicity, Publitalia had made it impossible for smaller independent companies such as hers to survive:

I remember once, it was at the end of the eighties, that we had signed an agreement with [the ice-cream company] Algida for their summer campaign of advertisements. It was a contract worth 70 million lire in all: peanuts compared with the sort of sums that were being spent for advertising on Silvio Berlusconi's channels. Even so, the Publitalia sellers of advertising space tried to undercut us. They offered Algida very favourable terms if the company agreed to spend all its advertising budget on the Fininvest channels . . . All in all, you could say that the only company that has never let itself be intimidated by Publitalia has been Coca-Cola . . . Usually, though, the firms give way. And from their point of view it's only just that they do so, for they have their budgets to balance.[79]

Videomusic was eventually bought up and its identity transformed by Vittorio Cecchi Gori, a film producer who had many more resources than Marcucci, and who had also purchased Telemontecarlo. In the 1990s only Cecchi Gori offered any competition, but no real diversity, in the face of Berlusconi's empire.

The narrowness of control in television was mirrored by that in the media in general. In the mid-80s, for example, FIAT controlled *La Stampa*, *Il Corriere della Sera*, *La Gazzetta dello Sport*, and all the magazines of the Rizzoli publishing house. The oil billionaire Attilio Monti owned an extensive press empire in the provinces, including daily papers in Tuscany, Emilia-Romagna and Friuli-Venezia Giulia. Cecchi Gori dominated film production and owned a large string of cinemas. All this added up to an oligopoly unmatched in the other European democracies.

However, it is worth noting a marked difference *between* media. Whereas in the press minority newspapers like *il manifesto* managed to survive and assured themselves of a national distribution, the same was simply impossible in television.[80] There were lots of smaller channels in Italy, but nearly all of them were dominated by carpet-sellers and other television hawkers. Local television offered a few under-financed programmes, often on frequencies that allowed only poor reception.

Faced with the rapid growth of commercial and colour television in the 1980s, the RAI did little to distinguish itself from its rampant rival. As Mauro Wolf has written, 'public television chose a strategy of fighting its commercial counterpart primarily on the terrain of audience levels'.[81] By so doing, quality (not in great supply in any case) was sacrificed to Auditel ratings.

It was also the case that ever since 1976–7 the three channels of the RAI had been divided up amongst the major political parties – the first and most prosperous channel to the DC, the second to the PSI, the third to the PCI. This meant that instead of there being at least one channel dedicated to a long-term strategy of high-quality television, which could hope with growing education levels to attract larger audiences, each public channel offered 'general' television, was politically aligned, and was in competition one with another. RAI 3 was very much the poor cousin and for many years suffered from poor reception in many parts of the peninsula. In 1987 Angelo Guglielmi was appointed its director and gave it a new, critical quality.

Various programmes offered a type of *television verité* that up to then had been completely unknown in Italy. Its satirical capacity increased, especially with the delicious *Blob*, which offered each day 'a selection of the worst horrors (gaffes, vulgarity, technical faults, heated exchange, exhibitions of ignorance) broadcast on all channels in the previous 24 hours'.[82] However, its news programmes were as heavily biased as those of the other two channels. For those interested in relatively balanced and informative news comment, the sermons of Sandro Curzi on RAI 3 in these years were as dispiriting as those of Bruno Vespa on RAI 1. At a critical moment in its development, Italian public television was thus split into factions and culturally subaltern to the dynamic model presented by Silvio Berlusconi.

Taking public and private together, Italian television presented a sorry picture. A massive number of imports from the USA dominated the programmers' weekly fare. RAI made some efforts to encourage and subsidize the Italian film industry, but in general the quality of home products was poor. Chat shows, preferably with a histrionic row or two, were the substitute for in-depth political or social analysis. Documentaries were few and far between, variety shows were more frequent than in the other major western European countries.

All this demonstrated that Italian television was deeply *lazy*. It was also self-referential, a pathology which Umbert Eco described as 'neo-television'.[83] At a time when Italy was changing with great rapidity, the controllers of television showed little desire or capacity to analyse what was happening. Instead, radical transitions were coaxed into traditional and reassuring cultural schemes, with old hands like Ettore Bernabei and new ones like Silvio Berlusconi being past masters at the exercise.[84]

It needs an afternoon in bed with 'flu', wrote Michele Serra,

> to realize what television is capable of doing to people without defences, above all the old and the ill . . . Crimes and miracles, blood and the Madonna, tales about cancer victims who instead of going to the specialist are cured at the Sanctuary. Never a word, or a hint of critical distance on the part of the commentators or the hostess of the programme. On *Italia in diretta* they don't say 'this woman claims to have benefited from a divine intervention' but rather 'this woman has benefited from a divine intervention'. Here lies the difference between journalism and deceit, between culture and ignorance.[85]

b. DEEP PLAY

Clifford Geertz has suggested that games can be considered the hidden metaphors or dramatizations of societies, one of the keys that help to reveal the specificity of cultures. In the case of contemporary Italy the game in question is football.[86] From the time of the two World Cup victories under Fascism in 1934 and 1938, football has always been an abiding passion of the Italians, but in the last twenty years this passion has reached new levels of intensity, to become, in the words of one authoritative anthropologist, a secular religion, 'an elementary symbolic universe, fixed and pliant at the same time, within which it is possible for very different people to define themselves, and themselves in relations to others'.[87]

To see football straightforwardly as a metaphor of Italian society would be to risk some pretty mechanical transpositions. None the less, to look at it in this light throws up a series of suggestive insights and linkages. At one level, football is an ideal game for a family-centred nation, because it links almost effortlessly childhood and adulthood, both within the same person (who remembers his own kickabouts or youth games while watching the professional game), and within the family, especially in relations between fathers and sons.[88]

At the same time, it can be seen as one of the many representations of a strongly male-dominated culture. On the field, and off it, aggression and violence are controlled with some difficulty. The nature of football requires, as Finn writes, that 'hard men who lead by example are made captains'.[89] Football is a man's world, often a 'real' man's world. Women are not totally absent from it, but they nearly always appear, at least in Italy, in subordinate roles: at the ground as the girlfriend or sister *of* someone, or else simply dressing up in the team's colours in order to be noticed;[90] at home, during the televised games, in support roles, as one mother explained to a group of researchers in 1995: 'I do the crossword while they watch . . . I share their enthusiasm if their side wins, but it's not that it interests me all that much.'[91]

At another level still, reactions to the game's rules and refereeing can be seen as a mirror of wider reactions to authority in contemporary Italian society. The sort of game that football is – men fighting for possession of a ball, but only allowed to use a certain number of physical attributes and skills in order to do so – makes for difficult arbitration. What constitutes a foul, what justifies a penalty, whether or not a player is offside, is often difficult to discern. In other words, the rules exist, but they are not easy to interpret. In these circumstances, the referee's authority is perforce uncertain, but it is made much more so in Italy by the almost universal climate of suspicion, if not derision, that accompanies his decisions. The referee is the butt on to which the spectators can project all their fury and disdain, as well as their oft-repeated conviction that he has been corrupted.[92] It is not difficult to discern here a series of emotions – suspicion, contempt, cynicism, even hatred – that characterize the relationship between Italians and their state. 'Deep play', as Geertz tells us, is truly a sort of sentimental education. It is also worth noting that in his example, cockfighting in Bali, the rules were equally difficult to interpret, the game being concluded in a few seconds in a great flurry of feathers and blood, but the authority of the umpire was absolute: 'I have never seen an umpire's judgement questioned on any subject, even by the more despondent losers, nor have I ever heard, even in private, a charge of unfairness directed against one, or, for that matter, complaints about umpires in general.'[93]

Sport in Italy, even football, has had an uncertain trajectory in the Republican period. For many years football and cycling were mass passions but not mass practices. An ISTAT census of 1959 found only 1,300,000 Italians who were '*sportivi*' of any sort. Of these the majority were under fifteen years of age, and 90 per cent were male; a third were so-called 'hunters', and a fifth footballers.[94] The state's input into school sports was very limited. There were no school sporting clubs and little space for physical exercise. In 1963 CONI, the state agency responsible for sport, made known that at least 4,000 elementary and 7,000 middle schools had no gyms.[95]

However, in the same decades, many of Italy's sportsmen were consistently successful at the highest international levels. Her football clubs, especially the Milanese ones, enjoyed a reign of glory in European competitions in the early 60s. Her collection of gold medals at the Olympic games between 1948 and 1980 was twice as large as that of Britain (sixty-five to thirty-three), and far superior to that of France (thirty-seven). Certain 'proletarian' sports (cycling and boxing) combined with more 'aristocratic' ones (fencing and equestrianism) to produce these results.[96] With sporting funds heavily centralized, CONI was able to invest in certain privileged areas, and its strategy had an almost east European flavour to it; the most significant difference being that in Italy, consistent with Catholic ideology, investment in women's sport was very limited.

This peculiar Italian sporting model, which combined a high level of male international achievement with a very low level of mass sporting activity, and the almost total absence of women, gradually changed in the most recent period. Thanks to a slow and sometimes painful decentralization of funding and responsibility, local government was able to spend heavily on sport for the first time. Between 1979 and 1989, sports centres of every sort grew in number from 45,494 to 118,712.[97] Nearly every local government authority undertook to equip itself with a modern sports centre. The possibility of practising sport became a valuable element of social citizenship, and women took part for the first time in significant numbers.

Interest grew rapidly in new and different sports. Skiing and tennis, at one time élite pastimes, became mass ones. The watching and playing of basketball and of volleyball attracted growing numbers. Cross-country skiing, cheap and ecological, appealed to Italian Greens of various hues, and in time produced Italian *women* champions at an international level. For those, by contrast, who preferred their sport rough and masculine, the Italian rugby federation expanded significantly, boasted a respectable national team in the 1990s, and celebrated its entry into the five nations (now six) championship with a famous victory against Scotland at Rome in January 2000.[98]

All this activity and interest gained sustenance from that attention to body and health which, as we have seen above, was one of the driving forces in consumer spending in the 1980s. It was certainly part of that culture of narcissism which Christopher Lasch had analysed memorably with reference to the United States,[99] but it also increased young people's sociability outside narrow school and family circles, their fitness and contact with nature.

As for the dominant sport, football, in 1982 Italy won her first World Cup since the Fascist period. This was a key event both for the game and also for the country's expression of its national identity. Attendances at 'Serie A' (Premiership) matches rose until 1985–6, declined towards the end of the decade, but reached new heights in the 1990s.[100] Massive amounts of money were invested in teams, and also in stadiums at the time of the 1990 World Cup in Italy (in which the home team finished a disappointing third). By the mid-1990s 'Serie A' in Italy, with its large number of highly paid foreign stars, was widely acknowledged as the most entertaining and expensive football championship in the world. Regular and highly successful live broadcasting of it to Britain on Sunday afternoons bore tribute to the place that Italian football had captured on an international scale. The price that was paid, and not only in monetary terms, for such pre-eminence was, as we shall see in a moment, a high one.

At the local level, new clubs and championships sprang up everywhere, though much more so in the Centre-North than in the South, where the footballing culture was much weaker. In the 1990s a city like Florence could boast a thirty-page, self-supporting weekly newspaper, *Calciopiù* (founded in 1981), almost entirely dedicated to the reporting of local and regional non-professional games. Details were given of some 110 different leagues and divisions. 'Deep play' here meant not a high-risk game, but one profoundly woven into the texture of society.

This extensive public sphere of football could not, in all honesty, be said to have contributed much to civil society. The joy and excitement of going to a match, of being on the terraces, was undeniable. In 1991 one young female fan of the Milanese club Inter recounted in this way her feelings on a Sunday afternoon: 'The best thing is the waiting before the game begins. I like it when they sing every imaginable sort of song and your singing along with them becomes important. It's the fact of feeling one part of a whole; a whole load of people who don't know each other but are united by a common "ideal". Something like what happens at the big rock concerts.'[101]

It was also true that the supporters' clubs, the 'Ultras' as they came to be called in Italy, often played an important social role, and certainly did not conform simply to a 'hooligan' stereotype. The leader of one of Naples's largest supporters' clubs, *'Il Commando Ultrà – Curva B'*, stoutly defended his club's role in Neapolitan society: 'We've been at work for fifteen to twenty years trying to create a group where young Neapolitans can meet. In any case being at the ground can be an important moment for kids who live on the margins of society, in the *bassifondi*, in the popular quarters of the city; in many cases it can be a lifeline for them.'[102] This particular supporters' club had made a 'code of non-violence' one of its basic rules.

However, being at the *stadio* was not only about enjoying a football match, or expressing deep-felt group or municipal loyalties. It was also the place where pent-up emotions and frustrations and prejudices were released, where it was possible to shout the crudest of abuse at the opposition fans, where racist slogans were chanted, unchecked, on the terraces of many northern grounds in the 1990s. At Verona it was possible to go to the ground and see a large doll of a black man being dangled from a rope; or else in Florence, as late as 1997, to witness a group of youngsters unfold a foul banner against the Jews. Sunday afternoon at the stadium was sometimes a political, as much as a sentimental, education of a pretty disturbing sort.

By British standards, violence in and around Italian football games was limited, though there were a constant number of serious, and sometimes fatal, incidents. In the Italian case, the crucial nexus between alcohol and football was missing. It was Italian fans who suffered the terrible attack of drunken Liverpool supporters at the Heysel Stadium in Brussels on the night of 29 May 1985, just before the European Championship Cup final between Juventus and Liverpool. With no way to escape, the Italians were crushed against each other and trampled underfoot; thirty-seven of them died.[103]

The atmosphere on the terraces, though not in the other, more expensive parts of Italian football grounds, was one of highly organized and ritualized support. Fan clubs were serious affairs, patronized and subsidized by the club's management, and responsible for an elaborate and theatrical *mise en scène* at the beginning of the game. The supporters were active, not passive participants, both spectacle and spectators at the same time. The major clubs boasted extraordinary networks of supporters throughout the peninsula, which in some way compensated for the South's paucity of major clubs. In the early 1990s the 'Associazione Italiana Milan Club', the supporters' association of A.C. Milan, counted some 200,000 members, with 1,350 sections in all Italy, of which sixty were in Milan but also fifty in Sicily.[104] Juventus was an even more *national* club, with more banners from the rest of Italy than from Turin being displayed at the ground on a Sunday afternoon.

The majority of the Juventus fans who were killed at the Heysel Stadium in 1985 came from Lombardy and the Veneto.[105]

The *form* of the game of football could with difficulty sustain all the expectations invested in it. Soccer is a highly discontinuous sport, with around half of each ninety-minute game lost through interruptions. Although some games could reach extraordinary dramatic peaks — the Italians as a nation have never forgotten the late victory over West Germany in the semi-final of the World Cup of 1970 in Mexico — many others were mundane and even boring affairs, quite lacking in rhythm or fluency. At a football match, 'burn' was a more constant companion than 'peak'. The pattern of emotions experienced in fact bore many similarities to that of modern consumption — expectation, acquisition and use, delusion and discarding. After the intense build-up before the game, the feeling of being let down at the end of it was visible all too often on the faces of those coming away from the ground. Winning or losing obviously made a big difference, but the quality of the experience itself was in general not a reliable one.

This profound gap between what the game could realistically deliver, and the amount of emotional energy and economic resources invested in it, was rendered much the greater by developments in the 1980s and 1990s. Soccer became very big business in Italy, as it was to become in Britain ten years later, as the game was transformed into *the* major entertainment industry, with innumerable product spin-offs. Commercial television and publicity tightened their grip, as sponsored teams, players, boots and so on became a standard form of advertising. The links between club ownership, extraordinarily bloated payments to players and managers, and global markets were everywhere visible. One newspaper cutting, taken almost at random from the sporting pages of one of Italy's major dailies, summed up perfectly this interlinking:

The 20 year old Brazilian phenomenon [Ronaldo] is heading for a break with Barcelona, who have not yet kept their promise of improving his contract; an agreement of last autumn should have given him an increase from three to eight billion lire per year. Over the last few days the prospect has emerged that Nike, who sponsor the world's most famous player, might acquire the rights to his playing activity as well, and pay Barcelona the fine (some 32 million dollars) for his breaking the contract with the club (valid until the year 2006). Nike, at that point, could rent out Ronaldo's magic feet — he has scored 22 goals in the Spanish League this year — to one of the teams in its 'stable'. Parma is about to enter that stable . . . When we assess the possibility [of Ronaldo going to Parma] we have to remember that behind Parma stands the Tanzi dairy products' empire. It's not difficult to imagine the potential that an investment of this sort would have for the global strategies of the Tanzi group. Parmalat is very strong on the Brazilian market, where it also controls Palmeiras, but at the moment it lacks a figure who could have a strong impact on a global level.[106]

Television played a very special role in these commercial strategies. No other programmes in Italy, not even the San Remo song festival, could guarantee such mass audiences, nor could deliver so many millions into the hands of the advertisers. At the time of the 1994 World Cup in the United States, the following were the products that bought commercial space on television at this peak time: Ariel, Beltè, Borotalco, Cereal, Coca Cola 2 litri, Colgate Baking Soda, Diadora, Game Boy Gig, Gatorade, Gillette After Shave Gel, Kinder Delice, Kronenbourg, Lacca Panten, Lancers, Lipton Ice Tea, Lycia Persona, Merit Cup, Moulinex (various products), Neutro Roberts, Nike, Nutella, Pepsi Max, Pilotissimi Agip, Rai, Reebok, Sigma 3 × 2, Skipper, Swatch, Ulysse Fiat, Valtur.[107]

The majority of these products were from major multinational companies, and nearly all of their advertisements portrayed an idealized world of sport, one of frenetic enjoyment, constant movement, and boundless *joie de vivre*. The reality of most of the World Cup, let alone that of everyday life, had some difficulty in living up to these illusions. The World Cup final, between Brazil and Italy, was a dismal affair, even for Italians and Brazilians, though not quite as terrible as that in Rome in 1990 between Argentina and West Germany.

Such let-downs seemed to do little to stem the tide of football's invasion of television time. Whatever its limitations, football seemed to be a cast-iron revenue producer for Italian television magnates. Post-game analyses took up peak viewing time on many channels on Sunday and Monday night, reaching grotesque levels of repetition. With the help of slow-motion playbacks (the '*Moviola*'), it was possible to analyse tediously whether or not a player had been offside or a penalty justly awarded. The '*Moviola*' became a key instrument in mass culture, the ultimate but in the last analysis deeply useless authority.

Football was fun to watch on television, with its sweep of the whole ground, its close-ups of players, its ability to repeat the goals. The iron laws of advertising, though, increasingly interfered with it. Mini-advertisements were slipped in at the time of throw-ins, fouls and goal-kicks, as programmers became aware that football's 'dead' times could be filled up with selling goods. Even in the midst of the game, sponsors' names would trail across the screen, or else be blipped on, accompanied by a short, sharp sound to remind the viewer of his consumer duties. All this amounted to a trap for millions of Italian boys, a lure that was difficult to resist, a pastime that was apparently innocuous but was in reality a drug.

The 'deep play' of football touched every Italian family, though in different ways. It was the pretext for family get-togethers, or, as we have seen, an important moment of inter-generational male contact. It could clear the streets of an Italian city as nothing else could, and establish an amazing conformity of consumption, as each family gathered in front of the screen to view an important local or national match. Football could, through the voices of its champions, convey a deep attachment to traditional family values, one which almost belied the nature of recent developments. In 1993, Roberto Baggio, probably Italy's most famous player of the period, recounted, in highly revealing language, his priorities and way of life: '[After the game] I prefer to go home, to Caldogno, where I've built a small house, a cradle by the side of my parents and those of my wife . . . I was brought up in a big family, there were eight children, we gave emotional warmth one to the other, and I've never wanted to leave. I have a wife, Andreina, and a daughter Valentina, and where they are is my resting-place . . . As for my *miliardi* of lire, my father looks after them, with a friend of ours who works in a bank.'[108]

Yet the way in which football was developing, the way in which it mirrored the wider world, could also be deeply damaging to families. Not only could it glue boys to the television; it also turned them into commodities. The market in young and very young players was a disturbing phenomenon which brought little joy to families, and could fill them with cruel illusions. At the age of twelve a gifted boy player could be worth many millions of lire, and be bought for the youth team of a major club. Schooling and family life were disrupted in the hope that the son would eventually win a place in the senior side, and thus make the family fortune. The chances of this happening were about as high as winning a lottery prize, but the mirage was a very powerful one, and penetrated down to the lowest levels of the sport. Fathers were tense and critical of their son's performance, of the coaching he was receiving, of the club's capacity to realize their son's talent. Mothers, fewer in numbers but distinctly present, were often quietly maternal, but some screamed abuse at the referee and were even known to have assaulted him. Watching one's son play all over Tuscany of a Sunday morning was a glorious experience, but it could also make for an unpleasant and unexpected cocktail of familism, football and commodity fetishism.[109]

3. The Growth of Italian Civil Society

In opposition to many of the negative legacies of the past outlined earlier in this chapter, and to the more deleterious aspects of mass culture, Italian civil society developed with distinct vigour in the period under consideration. It would be too élitist to say that this was *in spite* of mass culture, and too populist to claim that it was *because* of it. Rather civil society grew primarily because of the wealth of cultural instruments available to many Italians, and the greater spaces, both material and of the imagination, in which to use them. The diffusion of education was the key factor here, but so too were some of the opportunities afforded by the electronic media. For instance, by 1994 almost 30 per cent of the material available on video cassettes was of a documentary or scientific nature.[110]

David Forgacs has written recently of 1980 being a watershed in the history of cultural consumption in Italy; not only thanks to the new media, but also to the expansion of the traditional ones.[111] Newspaper readership increased throughout the 1980s, and new bookshops continued to open. Twenty years earlier it had been customary, when travelling on Italian trains, to see young people reading comics, chatting or simply staring out of the window. By the 1990s the change was remarkable, as more and more of the younger generation, especially women, used their train journeys to study and read. In the early 1970s Pier Paolo Pasolini had predicted the inevitable 'homologization' of Italian society, its reduction to an undifferentiated and conformist mass.[112] Certainly, as we have seen, there were tendencies of this sort at work, but there were also very strong countercurrents. What was happening, slowly but surely, as Tullio De Mauro noted as early as 1979, was that 'a growing number of people possess the means with which to move in the world of cultural differences'.[113] Enablement of this sort was the essential underpinning of a pluralist civil society.

The multiple associations of civil society in the 1990s were populated by young people. As in France, but less so in Spain, there were also representatives of an older generation, those who had traversed the dramatic experiences of the late 60s and early 70s, and had emerged the other end neither in total despair nor with total cynicism. These fifty-year-olds were often to be found in leading roles in civil society, but they were not its driving force. That role belonged to the younger, and youngest generations, the children of those vast and variable *ceti medi* described in Chapters 2 and 3. Interestingly, not only the children of the 'reflexive', professional middle classes were involved. The narrow corridors of cultural continuity, often passing through the same restricted group of families generation by generation, were giving way to larger, more inclusive spaces. Many small entrepreneurs and some shopkeepers encouraged their children to gain the education that they had not had. Often this meant that the younger generation turned their backs on that total dedication to the work rituals of the family economy which had so characterized their parents.[114] As Gabriella Turnaturi has written, 'It was from the attention to self, to one's own desires that probably there grew the conscience of being part of a network, or at least of being together with others'.[115] Individualism was not an automatic synonym for disinterest in the fate of society as a whole.

*

The new linkages of civil society were neither those of the traditional Catholic and Communist subcultures, nor those of the militant groups of the 1970s. Gone for the most part were the over-dominant ideologies, the old certainties and fanaticisms, as well as the international context which had given rise to them. In their place was a universe of small groups, often concentrating on single issues, pragmatic rather than ideological, inclusive rather than exclusive, non-violent.[116] Very often their activities involved the need to control the activities of the state, to push it into greater efficiency (or even minimum efficiency), to demand some devolution of the power it wielded.

At the same time there evolved with considerable rapidity that 'third sector' of the economy which has already been mentioned in Chapter 1: a flourishing world of cooperatives, non-profit organizations and volunteer groups which frequently offered alternative services to those tied more narrowly to the market.[117]

On no account should this variegated world of Italian civil society be over-idealized. It remained the expression of a small minority, albeit one that was on the increase, of Italian society at large. Its web of associations was fragile and easily broken. Cooperation could be difficult to obtain, inter-group rivalries were frequent, the aims of different associations could, and often did, conflict. The very informality of the groups often hid a secret power agenda, within which single charismatic leaders dominated. Sometimes, too, older cliques were reluctant to let newcomers in. The formal expressions of horizontal solidarity and democratic decision-making could hide an older culture of clientelism.

None the less, the associationism of the 80s and 90s in Italy was an important contribution to the growth of Italian democracy. Participation in clubs and circles would come and go, as indeed did the associations themselves, but such experiences left important sediments in personal experience, a civil education which was an invaluable resource, and one which could be reactivated at different moments during the long life cycles of individuals and their families.

a. A WOMAN'S WORLD?

In historical terms the most innovative element of this new civil society was the place of women in it. The feminist movement had begun its long war against a patriarchal society in the 1970s, and in its early years had been characterized, not only by mass campaigns such as that over abortion, but also, as Luisa Passerini has written recently, by 'the discovery of other women, of their speech and their bodies, in the almost stifling immediacy of the collective'.[118]

In the 1980s, this intensity and insistence on group identity lessened somewhat, and the Italian feminist movement passed from a pioneering and

121

crusading phase into one which sought to create its own culture and embed itself in civil society.[119] Bookshops, centres, journals, cooperatives were founded in quick succession. So too were professional associations – of women lawyers, managers, historians, and so on. At a more modest level, groups of women got together to discuss and study 'in their workplaces and their homes, in an entirely informal way, and one which can never be properly documented'.[120]

As Anna Rossi-Doria has noted, all this activity did not lead, as in many other European countries, to 'a mere subculture', 'a separate universe for women'.[121] The themes of equality and difference intertwined, as did the activities of the movement within traditional institutions, particularly the trade unions and the left-wing groups and parties. Indeed, from 1986 onwards, there was a distinct move towards the political sphere. To quote Rossi-Doria again: 'It was as if civil society, in which we had been so active, was no longer enough for us, and we wanted to enter into political society, but this time with our own banners held high.'[122] Here, though, in contrast to civil society, the space available was to be much more limited.

It was also true that the praxis of the feminist movement was confined to certain sections of Italian society, beyond which it penetrated with great difficulty. Class proved a formidable barrier to the spreading of the revolution in gender relations. In the educated middle ranks of Italian society, the changing place and consciousness of women was *the* distinctive feature of the age, but it was not so for the working classes. If women from the working classes managed to combat any of the multiple features of patriarchy, it was either because their work brought them into contact with new ideas and solidarities, or because dramatic events *within* their families forced them into the public sphere.

In the 1980s familism was sometimes turned on its head as associations were founded which had as their *raison d'être* family tragedies. One such was the 'Comitato delle mamme contro la droga' (the Committee of Mothers against Drugs), active in a popular quarter of Naples in the second half of the 1980s. The committee, which enjoyed little credit with the local authorities and experts, was formed of middle-aged, working-class mothers whose children, most often sons, were killing themselves on hard drugs. It aimed both to help the addicts, in particular to convince them to join a rehabilitation community, and to provide solidarity for their mothers. One of the latter told Gabriella Turnaturi:

Everyone was against it when I began going to the meetings of the Committee; I'd never been out and about, I was always at home looking after my five kids. Before this experience I wasn't independent, but I am now; if I had to go somewhere I had to ask permission from my husband or my elder sons. Now I've become a proper person, I'm out here in the world too . . . Thanks to the Committee I've learned to tell my son: 'Go your own way.' Before I used to go down on my knees before him, but now I've thrown him out with all his rubbish. But he knows what this means, he knows where to find me if he wants help.[123]

Associations such as the 'Comitato delle mamme', which brought family traumas into a wider, shared arena, survived amid multiple difficulties and contradictions. They were brave and innovatory, but in relation to the needs of millions of working-class women they were all too few and far between.

b. THE SOUTH

In topographical terms, much of the Mezzogiorno in the 1980s resembled a building site. With increasing affluence and the return of many migrants from abroad, a wave of wildcat building swept through the South. Houses were constructed, or half-constructed, anywhere and everywhere. In 1990 the Sicilian writer Peppe Balistreri described the impression produced:

These houses . . . have been left in their rudimentary state, without plaster on their walls, often without fixtures or fittings, so that they appear to have been gutted, almost as if they were the spectral images of what remains after a bombardment. Yellow tufa, the poorest building material that can be used, is everywhere dominant, and from afar it seems as if a huge sandstorm has taken pleasure in creating senseless forms.[124]

The damage done to the built environment was irreparable. Narrow family interests had triumphed, without any connection to wider, collective projects and responsibilities. Yet this deeply depressing *surface* impression of the South does not accurately tell all of its history. Conflicts over long-established value systems, clashes between generations, the startling growth of a new associationism, all these *also* characterized the South in this period.

The conflicts of this transitional period were well illustrated by the research carried out in the early 1980s by a team headed by the anthropologist Amalia Signorelli in a group of villages forming a '*Comunità montana*' (mountain community) in the province of Salerno.[125] This marginal and backward area of the South, with a population of some 25,000 people, was not, historically speaking, a likely location for civic virtue. Indeed, the local economy was highly dependent on women working in the black economy, and specifically for the shoe industry: 'The work is organized on a clientelistic basis: the raw materials are brought in by a boss who gives the orders, fixes the wage levels for piecework, and by increasing, decreasing or cutting off the amount of his orders, rewards fidelity and punishes insubordination.'[126]

Yet this '*Comunità montana*', even as early as 1981, was also marked out by a striking number of educated youth, young women and men of equal numbers enrolled at the universities of Salerno and Naples.[127] Enrolled is perhaps too strong a word, for many of them were simply 'parked' at the university in the absence of any real prospects of employment.

Their attitudes were revelatory. Far from adhering to time-honoured codes, they expressed a profound cultural ambivalence, a terrible tension between 'particularism and universalism, self-interest and equity, clientelism and legality'.[128] At one level, they believed profoundly in equality before the law, in meritocratic and universalistic values, which their studies by and large had emphasized. At another, they knew that preferential treatment, the contacts of *clientela* and *parentela*, were the only way forward. This necessity, as Signorelli noted, served only to increase their anger, as well as their desolation and their sense of impotence.[129]

One anthropological study, however revealing and unexpected, cannot pass muster for the many and divergent realities of southern Italy. Yet there was strong evidence by the end of the 1990s, in all parts of the South, that attitudes were changing. A new associationism was spreading its wings, and with even greater rapidity than in the North. Robert Putnam had argued that the South was condemned by its history to live without 'civic community'. By the 1990s a significant minority of southern youth were out to prove him wrong.

The new associations had a number of distinguishing features: two-thirds of them had been founded since 1980, they had a very strong following among students and the salaried middle class, they were to be found in the minor as well as the major urban centres. Their activities were predominantly in the fields of cultural consumption and civic commitment. The first were more frequent than the second – cultural circles and clubs which promoted debates and discussions on music, cinema, theatre and literature, as well as organizing their consumption and practice. Civic-issue groups were less numerous, but were marked by a high level of intensity and involvement, with environmental issues to the fore.[130]

Particular attention must be paid to those groups which had as their *raison d'être* the dangerous but necessary fight against organized crime in general, and the Mafia in particular. Much more than other associations, their growth was linked specifically to key moments in Italian politics, and to the terrible high points of the Mafia offensive against the state – the killings of general Alberto dalla Chiesa in 1984 and of the judges Falcone and Borsellino in 1992. As such they will be analysed in greater detail in Chapters 6 and 8. Suffice it to say here that there had always been a movement against organized crime both in Palermo and Naples, linked above all with the Communist party ever since the 1940s, and the New Left groups in the 1970s. What emerged, though, in the most recent period was qualitatively different, a spontaneous associationism which was not narrowly party-based, had a strong religious component, and was populated by young and educated militants of both sexes.[131]

Putting all the different types of associations together, Diamanti, Ramella and Trigilia estimated in 1995 that they were over 6,000 in number, with 700,000 members and around 3 million occasional users. Of course, not all of them could be said to have a 'civic' content. Many of those which did were very fragile, with less than fifty members and growing debts. Few of them succeeded in involving the lower classes of southern society.[132]

None the less, as Trigilia concluded, this was a phenomenon of unexpected dimensions and vitality. The absence of any such extended network in the past gave the new southern associationism a peculiar pioneering quality, in contrast to the older and staider organizations of the Centre-North. Its young activists felt that they were, in a modest way, making history.

What sort of history this would be depended in no small part on the links that could be established between the new civil society and the state, both local and national. In other words, civil society had more chance of being 'civil' if it was not the opponent of the state, but its mentor and collaborator. In that 'golden chain' which ideally linked individuals, not only to their families, but also to civil society and to the state, the policies and reactions of the state itself were obviously of crucial importance. There were many dangers. The state, by its inefficiency, indifference or outright hostility, could easily let civil society die. Or else it could swamp it with money and incorporate it in factional and clientelistic fashion.

On the other hand, through an enlightened education system, through the provision and equitable distribution of meeting-halls and social spaces, through the supply of equipment and the offer of information, above all through an openness, transparency and availability, the state could greatly aid the growth of an independent citizenry.

In 1987–8 the geographers King and Killingbeck returned to the village of Aliano in Basilicata, where Carlo Levi had been confined by the Fascist regime in the 1930s, and about which he had written his famous book, *Christ Stopped at Eboli*. They found dramatic change since Levi's time, and not all of it was positive. The number of villagers had declined, but this had not prevented sprawling new settlements, free of any concept of town planning, being constructed in the fractions of San Brancato and Sant'Arcangelo. High rates of youth unemployment accompanied the abandonment of land once cultivated by their land-hungry parents.[133]

Yet standards of living had improved dramatically since Levi's time, and the village was full of shops. Furthermore, part of the primitive agriculture of the zone had been transformed, for the whole of the valley of the river Agri was under irrigation from a large reservoir upstream. Economic associationism had, at long last, reached Aliano. Peach producing, marketing, transport and tourism cooperatives had been founded in the last few years. The local state, in the form of the 'Comunità montana del medio Agri-Sauro', had a tiny but active staff of sixteen technicians and agronomists. Here were the first signs, fragile but distinct, of a different relationship between forgotten communities, civil society and the state.

c. FRIENDSHIP, YOUTH CULTURE, POST-MATERIALISM

In the late 1980s in the northern Veneto, Paola Filippucci found the youth of the city she had chosen to study, Bassano del Grappa, deeply divided in the use of leisure time and the type of networks it created. These divisions revealed different attitudes towards consumption, culture, the nature of friendship and the closeness of kinship ties. On the one hand, she found large *'compagnie'*, of up to forty components, usually having a fixed meeting-place, such as a bar in the centre of the city. The boundaries of the *'compagnia'* were sometimes marked by dress, with its members wearing garments bought in certain shops. The trend-setters were the children of the city's wealthier families, who led the way in expensive pastimes, such as driving in fast cars to far-away discos. 'In 1988, when I met them, most of the members of the *"compagnia"* had a full-time job. Only one or two attended University . . . When I went out with them, only a couple of people spoke to me directly. The conversation consisted mainly of in-jokes, and innuendos about past shared experiences and present relations among the members.'[134] Filippucci, with delightful technical aplomb, described the *'compagnia'* as 'a mixed gender courting group'.[135]

On the other hand, she found smaller groups of friends who tried 'to explore alternative models of consumption and self-realization'.[136] Here the accent was on cultural enrichment, on travel, books, cinema and theatre. Friendship was seen as the cultivation of 'tastes and interests' rather than being based predominantly on geographical loyalty. Many of this second cross-section of Bassano youth were more highly educated than their parents: 'Francesca, a chartered accountant, was the daughter of a municipal clerk; Fiorenza and Ilario, trained nurses, were children of factory workers. Silvano, Simona, Luca, Aldo, university students, were also children of factory workers.'[137] Quite a few of them had moved out of home, and expressed critical attitudes towards their families of origin and the suffocating closeness of kinship ties in Bassano. Friendship, writes Filippucci, was acting upon the family 'both in symbolic and in practical terms'.[138]

The divisions described above should not be considered as rigid polarities. Obviously, there were many young people who expressed a whole range of intermediate attitudes, whose loyalties were composite,[139] and whose culture was fluid and full of conflicting ideas. Yet the broad archetypes outlined by Filippucci could be found, with innumerable local variations, all over the country.[140]

In the Centre and North of the country there was a lot of hard work, expensive clothes, holidays and cars, seasonal rituals like the week's holidays in the mountains ('*la settimana bianca*') and suntanning at summer weekends on the shores of the Adriatic or Tyrrhenian seas; above all, an abiding obsession with making money. As one Venetian priest put it: 'there are people who now recognize only one God – Money. A God who conditions everything: relationships with work, with family, with children, with other people, with politics.'[141]

At the same time, a significant minority of youth networks were marked as never before by spontaneous support for associations which pursued primarily cultural interests, but also civic commitment. The specific foci of attention varied over time: in the early 80s, at the time of the European-wide anti-nuclear campaign, over 600 committees sprang up in neighbourhoods, schools and factories all over the country. Later it was the ecological movement which gained a growing presence in civil society, as issues such as traffic pollution and global warming gradually imposed themselves, though not without considerable difficulties, as youth were reluctant to abandon their motorbikes and families their cars. Individual mobility, in other words, still remained far more important than collective responsibility for the fate of congested and polluted city centres.[142]

A much more unqualified pattern accompanied the development of cultural associations, which enjoyed an enormous boom at national level. ARCI, traditionally left-wing, experienced the fastest increase in its history, more than doubling its membership between 1988 and 1995, from 507,889 to 1,087,531. In some southern regions, like Campania and Abruzzo, the increase was little short of spectacular.[143]

Quite often this new associationism was superimposed upon the old, as if the traditional subculture had found a new lease of life, once liberated from previous orthodoxy and ritual.[144] One of the more acute observers of contemporary Italian *mores*, the English novelist Tim Parks, found just such a superimposition in the village of Montecchio, in the province of Verona, where he lived in the late 1980s. Here the 'Centro Primo Maggio', originally a Communist party social club, had transformed itself into a relaxedly alternative social centre, open to anyone who wanted to pass a long Saturday afternoon, a place where it was possible to eat, play tennis, talk politics, organize a meeting, or drink continuously in habitual English fashion. 'It was', wrote Parks, 'the sort of place ... that Orwell must have dreamed of', and there he found a refuge from 'down-town middle-class Verona', from 'that obsession with fashion and elegance, fur and leather, the scrubbed faces of the men, the heavy make-up of the women, the crinkly dyed blond of respectable girls fanning out on to sheepskin shoulders, the hubbub of posh Veneto la-di-da'.[145]

One of the most vivid elements of the new civil society was the growth of voluntary work. By 1994 nearly 5 million volunteers dedicated part of their spare time to a very wide range of helping activities: work with old people, visiting in hospitals, anti-drug propaganda, campaigning for the national blood bank, work with immigrants and illiterates, helping those who suffered from every kind of illness and affliction. The presence of highly educated youth in this vast movement was widely commented upon.[146]

Youth commitment to civil society in Italy can be seen as part of that long-term international transition which the American social scientist Ronald Inglehart has analysed with care over the course of nearly two decades.[147] Inglehart's argument is a compelling one: each new generational cohort in advanced industrial countries demonstrates a greater commitment to post-materialist values than the preceding one. In Inglehart's surveys, 'post-materialism' was defined as a clear preference for a specific cluster of values: 'seeing that people have more say in how things get decided at work and in the community'; 'progress towards a less impersonal society'; 'protecting freedom of speech'; 'progress towards a society where ideas are more important than money'; 'giving people more say in important government decisions'; 'trying to make our cities and countryside more beautiful'. Material-ism, on the other hand, derived from the following choices: 'maintaining a high rate of economic growth'; 'fighting rising prices'; 'maintaining a stable economy'; 'making sure that this country has strong defence forces'; 'main-taining order in the nation'; 'the fight against crime'.[148]

These were highly suggestive groupings, though naturally they shared the limitations of all purely opinion-based survey analysis. From Inglehart's surveys it emerged that all across Europe, as well in the United States, the generation born between 1946 and 1955, that which was young in the tumultuous 60s and 70s, showed a much greater commitment to post-materialist values than did preceding cohorts. However, this cohort was not a one-off phenomenon. Those that came after, born in the years 1956–65 and 1966–73, were in turn more committed to post-materialism than their predecessors. Nor did the generation of '68 (or any of the others) become more materialist with age, for it expressed broadly the same values in 1988 as it had done in 1970. These values, argued Inglehart, could be dented by specific insecurities and economic crises, but the general trend was inexorably towards post-materialism.[149]

The Italian case, in Inglehart's analysis, demonstrates a number of particularities. Italy, unlike Britain, was not a stagnant society where values changed relatively little between generations. In 1987, 'postmaterialists' were to be found in Italy in much greater numbers among the younger generations than the older ones. This was no great surprise. Yet, unlike in Holland, West Germany or Denmark, in Italy they were not a clear *majority* in any generation. Italy, in fact, lagged far down the list of 'postmaterial' European countries, not only because of the weight of its older generations who had been children in a period of great material scarcity, but also because of the uncertainties of its younger ones. Here was clear evidence of that cultural and normative conflict which has permeated the analysis presented in this chapter.[150]

By 1994, the most recent year of Inglehart's analysis, among the twenty-one nations in the survey Italy was shown to be the country which was most rapidly catching up with regard to post-materialist values. None the less, it was clear that that which he called 'cultural shift' was going to be a slow and much contested transition in Italian society.[151]

d. THE AMBIGUITIES OF THE CATHOLIC CHURCH

In these mobile sands of cultural change, the Catholic Church in the 1980s and 1990s communicated messages which, to the outside eye, seemed deeply contradictory.

Many instances and activities of contemporary Catholicism linked with, and contributed significantly to, the new civil society. At a doctrinal level, the modern Church not only expressed unequivocal support for democracy, but many of its documents urged believers to be responsible, critical and active citizens. This was very much the sense, for instance, of the 'pastoral note' entitled 'Legality and justice', written in October 1991 by one of the commissions of the Italian conference of bishops.[152] Heavily critical of the role of Italy's political parties, it urged the faithful to recognize that civil society, too, had responsibility for formulating projects and denouncing the malfunctions and inertia of the parties and the state. Civil society, argued the commission, had to ensure 'by means of the democratic instruments available to citizens that resources are not just available for those who hold power, but for everyone'.[153]

The long and influential pontificate of Karol Wojtyla, Pope John Paul II, has often been interpreted simply as the reassertion of dogma after a long period of uncertainty and innovation; as the reaffirmation of the centrality of the Church's hierarchy and its institutions; as the re-elaboration, for the rest of the world, of the traditions of the Polish Church, heavily marked as it was by rural millenarianism and the fight for survival against a hostile state.

That these elements existed in John Paul II's pontificate is undeniable, but they were far from the whole picture. Precisely because he came from a national experience where civil society, and principally *Solidarność*, had played a crucial role in ending state oppression, Wojtyla seemed particularly aware of the necessity of linking families, civil society, and the growth of a democratic state. His teaching on the family went beyond that tradition which had found its most succinct summary in a brutal phrase of Pius XII's, of September 1951: 'the family is not there to serve society; it is society which is there to serve the family.'[154] Under the direction of John Paul II the familism of the Church was much less audible than previously.[155]

In *Familiaris Consortio* (1981), John Paul II's most important statement on the subject, he urged Catholic families to step out, to realize their mission in modern society: 'from the family, in fact, citizens are born, and in the family they find that first school of social virtues which animate the life and development of society itself. Precisely because of its nature and vocation, the family, far from closing in upon itself, opens out to other families and to society, thus taking on social duties.'[156]

Another instance, deeply memorable, of John Paul's departure from a long-standing ecclesiastical tradition with regard to Italian society was that of his visit to Sicily in May 1993. In the past the Church, by and large, had paid little more than lip service to the struggle against the Mafia. If there had been honourable exceptions, there had also been long periods of silence on the part of the ecclesiastical authorities.[157] In the first part of his pontificate John Paul II had not paid particular attention to the problem, and indeed had been heavily criticized for not mentioning the Mafia when he visited Palermo in 1982. Ten years later, in 1992 and above all 1993, he made amends. After the deaths of the magistrates Falcone and Borsellino, he spoke out with great vehemence, and in so doing transformed dramatically the history of the attitude of the Church to the Mafia. On 9 May 1993, in the stadium of Agrigento, at the end of a Mass for Sicilian youth, the ageing and enfeebled Pope found the strength to launch an unforgettable message against the Mafia. Banging down his great staff, he exhorted the Sicilians to begin a new era of 'concord, without deaths, without assassinations, without fears, without menaces, without victims. The Sicilian people is one that loves life ... It cannot always live under the pressure of a counter-culture, the culture of death. Here it is the culture of life that is needed! In the name of Christ, crucified and risen again, in the name of this Christ who is Life, who shows us the way forward, who is Truth and Life.'[158]

John Paul's Church, for all its doctrinal certainties and evangelism, also had an ecumenical face. Building on the tolerance and openness expressed by the second Vatican Council, Wojtyla's reign was marked by the acceptance of the coexistence of religions, the impossibility and perhaps even undesirability of total religious conquest. In 1986 this realization found its highest symbolic expression at Assisi, when the religious leaders of the world accepted the Pope's invitation to come to the city of S. Francesco to pray for peace. This was, as Andrea Riccardi has written, 'so disturbing an innovation as to be considered by Mons. Lefebvre as the ultimate expression of "betrayal"'.[159] Further gestures of ecumenicalism, of high symbolic significance, were also to take place during the Jubilee of the year 2000. The Pope visited the Wailing Wall in Jerusalem and there deposited a message begging forgiveness of God for the ambiguous role played by the Catholic Church during the Holocaust. This was not the same thing as begging forgiveness of the Jews, but it was better than nothing. Integralism was slowly being pushed to one side in Catholic attitudes to society, and this was good news for all those who believed in pluralism in Italy and elsewhere.

Above all, the Catholic Church distinguished itself for the variety and depth of its commitment to charitable works in Italian society. This was mainly a northern phenomenon: 56 per cent of the social and charitable work of the Church was located in the North of the country, compared to 16.3 per cent in the Centre, 13.6 per cent on the southern mainland, and 13.9 per cent in Sicily and Sardinia.[160] A small army of volunteers was involved in some 4,500 centres.[161]

The slogan of these years, and one which had many resonances in Catholic history and praxis, was 'begin again from those who are last'. Cardinal Carlo Maria Martini, archbishop of the enormous diocese of Milan (with an adult population of over 5 million), probably the most authoritative and enlightened voice of the Italian Church in these years, explained that 'the last are to be chosen because they are those who Christ loved most; they are those who have most need of the hope that derives from the message of love'.[162]

In his diocese Catholic volunteers helped, and often they were the only ones to do so, many of the most desperate members of Italy's opulent society – the tramps and the homeless (estimated at 2,000 in Milan in 1990), the elderly and abandoned, the victims of AIDS, drug addicts, political refugees, and immigrants in general.[163] Towards these last the Church distinguished itself as no other institution in Italian society, offering not only material aid but also moral protection. It demanded repeatedly and with authority that the immigrants be treated as 'Christians', whether they were Christians or not.[164]

Against these manifestations of Catholic ideology and action must be weighed others, which are much more perplexing in relation to the growth of a modern civil society. The need for moral clarity, even intransigence, in an age of uncertainty, and the quest for consistency in relation to the pluri-secular teachings of the Church, frequently led the Vatican hierarchy away from the frontiers of twentieth-century democracy and back towards nineteenth-century obscurantism. The Church, as always, had to distance itself from modernity, but by so doing it excluded itself from many of the crucial battles in Italian society at the end of the century. What was at stake was not, as the Church would have desired, the dissolving of modernity, but its direction. Individualism, consumerism, materialism, rationalism, even respect for difference, these were some of the key concepts to which the Catholic Church had declared its anathema; but they were also the bases upon which civil society had for the first time put down firm roots.

Nowhere was this great distance between Catholicism and the modern world more apparent than on the question of gender. Karol Wojtyla stressed the equal dignity of men and women, both in the home and in the outside world. He talked of the necessity of 'equal pay for equal work, protection for working mothers, fair promotion for women in their careers, equal rights for both spouses within the family, the recognition of all that is linked to citizens' rights and duties in a democratic regime'.[165]

However, he insisted with even greater vigour that the prime and natural role of a woman was at home and as a mother. Furthermore, at a time when the Church of England was transforming, with enormous difficulty, some of its most fundamental structures and attitudes, the Catholic Church remained obdurate on many of the fundamental gender issues: no women priests, no marriage for male priests, no abortion, no divorce, no artificial contraception; above all, a whole structure of organization, hierarchy and belief which was the very essence of patriarchy.

In the realm of what constituted a family, the Vatican dug in its heels. In one breath John Paul II urged families to participate in society, to work for its improvement; in the next, he was careful to distinguish between 'false marriages' and real (i.e. Christian) ones, between 'regular' families and 'irregular' ones.[166] There was no space in his 'civilization of love' for those who pursued ways of loving and partnership which diverged from the orthodox vision of the family as a 'domestic church';[167] no possibility of inclusion for those who chose not to marry, let alone for homosexuals and lesbians. Such foreclosures meant that the gap between the ideas of the Church and those of civil society remained very large.

The Catholic Church flourished under liberal democracy, but its own internal organization was not conceived on democratic lines.[168] John Paul II turned his back firmly on any interpretation of the pronouncements of the second Vatican council as an invitation to liberalize or democratize the Church. Catholicism's institutional identity had always combined a highly accentuated centralism with a great plurality of expressions and organizations, as well as different models of the relationship between the faithful and society. In the 1980s some of these assumed forms which were in close congruence with the most interesting developments in Italian society: the Sicilian Jesuits under the leadership of padre Bartolomeo Sorge, the rank-and-file Catholics of Don Ciotti, were just two examples. But as always there were others which went in a quite different direction: the integralists of 'Communione e Liberazione', whose undoubted piety[169] was combined with free marketeering and deep immersion in the traditional world of Christian Democrat politics; or the less showy, but internationally powerful figures of the Opus Dei.[170]

However many faces the Church presented to the outside world, it could not mask its ageing profile. Secularization and the growing market in religions – the Protestant sects were particularly active in the North – combined to produce what seemed to be an inexorable decline, in spite of the great popularity and evangelizing energy of Karol Wojtyla. The great rites of passage in human life remained distinctly Catholic affairs. A sense of widespread religiosity, of living in a Catholic country, remained *the* prevailing cultural norm. But the number of active Christians, and indeed of young clergy, was very much reduced. By 1990 the key indicator of regular attendance at Mass on Sundays had reached an all-time low: 19.1 per cent of the adult population in Milan, 15.2 per cent in both Rome and Naples, 7.9 per cent for Florence, just 4 per cent for Bologna.[171] By 1996 Cardinal Ruini summed up very well the preoccupation of the Church even with regard to its capital city: 'The fact that Rome is the diocese of the Pope and has a long Christian history behind it does not render it immune from the world-wide phenomena which have transformed both customs and culture. We are in the presence of philosophical trends and life styles which are deeply alien to a Christian mentality.'[172]

Mass phenomena like the veneration of Padre Pio, which assumed the proportions of a very widespread cult by the year 2000, were signals which went in another direction. They were signs of a distinct need for charismatic figures to worship, for new and modern saints preaching a highly traditionalist message. They were not, though, sufficient to turn the tide, or to offer a fresh start in the modern society of the end of the century.[173]

In 1986, in one of the very few sociological or anthropological studies of parish life, Lorenzo Dani painted a sympathetic but depressing picture of the parish of San Giuseppe fuori Mura, in Padua.[174] The parish was situated in a typically modern urban environment, most of which had been constructed after the Second World War, with a high density of population, shops and services. The parish had 8,900 inhabitants in 1984, but few of them were actively involved in parish life. There were some 290 activists, but 60 per cent of these were involved only in catechism teaching. From the church magazine and parish authorities came a 'continuous and pressing justification of the church and its hierarchy'.[175] This 'ecclesiology', as it was called, was far more dominant than the 'Christology', the return to a reflection on Christ and his message, which had been one of the main thrusts of the second Vatican council. The parish had ample physical and structural resources, but not enough people to fill them. The population was reported as diffident, if not hostile.[176] The most successful, lively and democratic group, regarded with more than a little suspicion by the rest of the parish, was the football team of the 'Unione Sportiva Virtus'.[177]

Finally, there was clear if controversial evidence that while some of the highest organs of the Church urged respect for legality and the duties of democratic citizenship, the body of the clergy was very much more tepid. In 1993 the journalist Pino Nicotri, posing as a repentant Catholic politician or businessman heavily involved in the corruption scandals of the time, went to confess and to ask advice in some of the principal churches of the peninsula. He took his tape recorder with him.[178] His leading question to his confessors was whether or not he should collaborate with the inquiring magistrates. In spite of the fact that Cardinal Martini had recently invited all those involved in 'Tangentopoli' to do precisely this, the priests in confessional took, almost uniformly, quite another view. Their replies were couched in terms which emphasized private repentance over public justice, private and family duties over public ones. There was an overwhelming insistence that no man was obliged to denounce himself. In Milan cathedral one confessor advised: 'If I were you I wouldn't turn myself in.'[179] Another, in the church of Saint Ambrose, Milan: 'No one is obliged to betray themselves . . . It seems to me that there is no real need.'[180] In Naples cathedral: 'I tell you again, you've already shown repentance . . . there is the justice of men, but there is a superior justice! . . . And then think of the consequences, of what it would mean for your family.'[181]

Only one clergyman, in Milan cathedral, was adamant that there could be no absolution without immediate cooperation with the magistrates: 'At stake here is not just the subjective problem of being a certain person, involved in a certain reality, the question of one's own liberty. Here there is also an external obligation, a reference to Christ. It hasn't been understood that there can be no good Christians if there are not honest citizens.'[182]

4. Conclusion

Civil society, in the particular sense in which it has been used here, is a delicate plant. In many ways Italian socio-economic trends of the last twenty years threatened it as much as they aided it.[183] Enumerating these trends does not make for comforting reading. The restrictions of the labour market marginalized a significant section of the country's youth and left dissatisfied many others, especially women. Deep-seated structural inequalities of class showed no signs of disappearing. The dangerous reassertion of the arbitrary power of private employers in the workplace coincided with a weakening or even disappearance of trade-union representation, and resulted in a proliferation of temporary and short-term contracts and a decline in employees' rights. Flexibility at work was one thing, but insecurity and powerlessness was another.

To these trends of the most recent period must be added those negative legacies of the past – clientelism, familism, a part, if not all of Catholic culture – which formed a strongly sedimented layer of values in Italian families.

Developments in the realm of mass culture seemed, at first glance, equally negative. The oligopolistic ownership of the mass media, when combined with the peculiar quality, or rather lack of it, of both public and commercial television, offered an alarmingly vacuous vision of the modern world. Norberto Bobbio, in his reflections on civil society, pointed with great efficacy to the deleterious effects of this sort of cultural modernity.[184] While Rousseau had proposed that those who refused to obey the 'general will' should be constrained to be 'free', the culture of modern mass society worked in a more subtle way, by a continuous manipulation of ideas and information. The individual was convinced, of his or her own free will, to be a slave: 'There [in Rousseau] force is the means to realize liberty; here liberty is a means to realize subjection. The first reality is represented by the figure of the individual who is "free" in spite of himself, the second by that of the contented slave. On the one hand we find the eulogy of force in the name of liberty, on the other the eulogy of liberty in the name of servitude.'[185]

So draconian a view of the relationship between civil society and mass culture must be treated with respect but also with some scepticism. In particular, it underestimates drastically the degree to which other forces were at work in Italian modernity, forces which ran counter to any idea of a facile manipulation of the individual. More Italians than ever before had access to a richly varied series of cultural instruments. The effects of the electronic media were complex and far from unilinear. Education, halting and insufficient, distant light years from providing a real equality of opportunity,[186] none the less provided an ever greater minority with the means to make their own, informed decisions, whatever they were. It also provided an invaluable context for youth socialization, for the first experiences of collective action.[187]

Fifty years of democracy, imperfect but still democratic, had rubbed off in many unexpected ways. They had created, as time passed, a strong cultural tension and a plurality of values; phenomena which had surfaced, as we have seen, even in the far-flung hills of the province of Salerno in the early 1980s.

In their 1963 study on political culture in five different nations, the American political scientists Almond and Verba had described Italian culture as fragmented, passive, alienated, parochial, traditionalist and based on the norms of the patriarchal family.[188] Much had changed for the better since then. How much could still change did not depend just on economic and social trends, but also, crucially, upon the nature and actions of the state. It was the democratic state that could guarantee civil society and give it the space to breathe, or else could limit it and stunt its own citizens. It is to the Italian state, to all its travails and insufficiencies, that we must now turn.

Chapter 5

A Blocked Political System, 1980–92

*T*HE RELATIONSHIP between society and politics in the 1980s bears a striking resemblance to that of the 1960s. Both decades were marked by dynamic changes in the country's economy, in the habits of its people, in the everyday life of its families. At a political level both found a new formula which gave greater responsibility to the Socialist party: in 1962, with the beginning of the centre-left experiment; in 1983, with the first Socialist prime minister of the Republic, Bettino Craxi. Both these political responses proved quite inadequate to the tasks in hand. Neither succeeded in governing the country's many and rapid transitions, and neither communicated to the Italians a clear sense of priorities and necessities. The experience of the 1980s, however, was more dismal than that of twenty years earlier. Not only was there stalemate, but there was also a creeping degradation which further discredited the Republic's institutions and which, to add insult to injury, was justified in the name of modernity and political realism.

There is a danger, though, of presenting too simplistic an interpretative scheme of these years. The recent history of the Republic cannot be read as some sort of morality play, in which a thriving and virtuous economy and society continually encounter a deaf and corrupt state. Society's development, as we have seen, was itself profoundly ambivalent; family life, consumption, mass culture, all contained elements which could be said to have contributed to the demanding goal of living in freedom together, and others which did not. Italian society, in other words, was not all civil society, and even civil society had its faults.

Similarly, given the great complexity of the modern state, and its many and conflicting power centres, not all of its actions flowed in one direction alone. Even if it is difficult to dispute that Italy's political system and its state apparatus were two of the Republic's greatest weaknesses, we must be careful not to treat the public sphere as a monolith. The state, like society, was deeply complicated, and different parts of it had different historical trajectories. The prevailing trends, after more than thirty years of Christian Democrat dominance, were not difficult to identify. Yet they were not the only ones, for other forces, of different intent and tradition, had flourished *within* the state as well as *outside* it. Here too democracy had been at work, sowing seeds in what appeared a barren terrain, but one which in time bore unexpected fruit.

In many parts of western Europe in the 1980s and 1990s, there were clear signs of a decline in the democratic process. Fewer people voted,[1] cynicism about the political process and politicians' motives was even more widespread than usual, idealism as well as ideology seemed to have deserted the political sphere. Democracy, as John Dunn wrote in 1992, badly needed to renew itself, but had no clear ideas of how to do so: 'Analysts of modern economies often stress how urgently these need to reinvent economic agency all the time, and to do so in the face of the strong organizational tendencies to construct monopoly, extract unearned rents, and protect comforting routines. But we have a far less clear and vivid sense of the permanent need to reinvent political and social agency throughout the world in which we now live.'[2]

In the Italian case there was strong evidence of renewed agency both in the economic sphere, with the creation of a highly successful network of small businesses which had attracted global attention, and in the social one, with the flourishing of an autonomous civil society. These two spheres of agency were, as we have seen, far from in harmony, but they were both undeniable signs of the vitality and inventiveness of Italian society. They needed, urgently, to be set in relation one with the other. This was the task of politics, but it was precisely here that Italy's deficit was most marked.

Reinventing democratic political agency could take many forms. One of them was to be discerned in the wake of the students' and workers' movements in Italy in the late 1960s and early 1970s. There had been concerted attempts to introduce elements, if not of direct democracy, at least of citizens' participation into many of Italy's institutions. Councils and committees, with varying degrees of power, had been set up in factories, schools, neighbourhoods, and so on. At the same time the new regional assemblies had slowly taken over from Rome some of the responsibilities of central government.

By and large, with the withering away of collective action, these institutional innovations floundered. The councils and committees were too marginal, and never endowed with sufficient powers or responsibilities. Regional government, with few exceptions, tended to reproduce at a lower level the same pattern of politics which had marked the central government and its administration.[3]

The 1980s, then, were in many ways a period of political restoration. After the disturbances of the previous years, everything seemed to return to normal. Normality, however, was a very relative term in Italian politics. In the complicated set of interconnections between individuals, families, society and the state, the Italian state was peculiar in being so alien from its citizens. Its behaviour was both lackadaisical and punitive, an unappealing combination hardly designed to produce loyalty, let alone any Hegelian sense of individual self-realization in the highest authority of the land. That Italy had democratic institutions was undeniable, but little functioned in them as it ought to have done.

The second part of this book is dedicated to an analysis of these institutions in the most recent period, with regard to various sectors and developments: the political system and its principal actors, the practice of corruption, the complicity with the Mafia, the nature of the public administration and the policy-making process, the image and actions of Italy in Europe and the wider world. Although this history is perforce a gloomy one, it is illuminated from time to time with sharp rays of sunlight.

1. Structural Problems of the Political System

When the political system that defined Italy's democracy was drawn up after the Second World War, its basic imprint was, for obvious reasons, anti-authoritarian and pluralist. Its intent, as David Hine has written, was 'to disperse power rather than concentrate it'.[4] Under the precepts of the Constitution no single part of the state, no institutional force, had a clear and autonomous mandate to govern. Each instead – parliament, government, the president of the Republic, the courts, the public administration, and so on – could constrain, in different ways and to different degrees, the powers of the other. Relations between different elements of the state were thus more horizontal than vertical, lacking in a clear hierarchy of command. Intended as a delicate system of checks and balances, the system rapidly revealed itself as the perpetrator of weak and ineffectual government.

This unintended consequence was further aggravated by the electoral system chosen in these same years. The very pure Italian system of proportional representation could be relied upon to ensure a plurality of voices in parliament, but not to provide governments with clear majorities or clear mandates. Coalition government, centred around one major party with a host of smaller allies, became customary.

However, it would be a mistake to attribute too much responsibility solely to proportional representation. In reality, *whom* people voted for was at least as important as *which system* was used. This very obvious point is nearly always forgotten in the seemingly interminable Italian debate on electoral reform. Only in 1948 did the Christian Democrats obtain a clear majority of seats in the Chamber of Deputies; and only in 1976 did the Left come anywhere near having a majority to oust them. For forty years it was the *stability* of Italian voting patterns, when filtered through the electoral and institutional systems of the post-war settlement, that excluded any chance of alternation in power, and produced the particular pattern of Italian politics.

The unsatisfactory nature of that pattern, from the point of view of effective government, was very evident. In July 1988, Giuliano Amato, the then Socialist minister of the Treasury, explained in an unusually frank way why he, as head of the most powerful ministry in Italy, could do so little:

I have the sensation of moving in an archipelago . . . Single ministries are much less responsive to the collegial will of the government and much more to that of the 'triangle' which each forms with the corresponding parliamentary commission and the interest groups of the sector . . . All in all, the system is centrifugal, everything has to be negotiated, everyone negotiates with everyone else, every procedural step is a negotiation, and at each negotiation either one stops or one loses a part of what one is proposing.[5]

The endless bargaining of coalition government, the lack of authority of key institutions, the absence of alternation, all these created a very ample political space for the ruling parties. They filled it gleefully and short-sightedly, with their appetites directed in two directions. The first of these was internal to the state itself. If its institutions were lacking in *esprit de corps* and traditions of autonomy, then they could be controlled or even 'occupied' by the political parties, or factions thereof.[6] The second line of attack was towards society. By politicizing appointments in nearly every state institution in contact with the public – banks, hospitals, opera houses, etc., often even down to their lowest levels of employment – the parties of the ruling coalitions established long-lasting networks of clientelistic loyalty. This two-pronged attack – the one directed inwards to the state, to its Roman entrails, the other moving from it outwards to society – constituted the essence of that 'partitocracy' which had become endemic by the 1980s.[7] Partitocracy offered excellent prospects for spoils-hunting, but none at all for that reinvention of political agency which Dunn invoked.

As for the opposition, it both opposed and cooperated with the dominant system of politics. One of the strongest and most surprising myths in contemporary Italian politics is that the opposition, principally in the shape of the Italian Communist party (PCI), was in fact no opposition at all, as it was drawn permanently into a series of consociational pacts with the ruling parties.[8] Not only is this a misunderstanding, or to put it benignly a reinterpretation, of a rather abstruse term in political science. It is also a drastic distortion of the historical record.

The myth, as always, had some bases in reality. One of these was the period of collaboration between the PCI and the ruling parties in the years after the 1976 elections. This was not an equal pact, as in Lijphart's original usage of the term consociational, because the PCI was not in the government, and thus controlled no ministries. However, it was certainly drawn into the time-honoured practice of '*lottizzazione*' – the distribution of jobs and zones of influence on the basis of party membership and strength.[9] The fall-out from this period lingered on in the 1980s, and was to be rudely exposed, as we shall see, at the time of the great 'Tangentopoli' judicial inquiry.

Another of the myth's foundations, though a rather weaker one, was the Italian way of dealing with micro-sectional legislation. As parliamentary procedures were cumbersome, slow and unpredictable, it had become common practice to delegate to parliamentary committees the power to legislate on certain categories of business, without having to refer back to the full assembly. At committee stage, therefore, government and opposition often sought agreement, with the result that large, though diminishing, numbers of so-called '*leggini*' were passed in each of the Republic's legislatures.[10]

However, the nature of this cooperation needs to be carefully specified rather than being erected haphazardly into a theory of covert collaboration. The '*leggini*' were small-scale stuff, which undoubtedly served local and sectional interests, but which in other political systems, as Hine has written, would have been 'subsumed in more uniform framework legislation, or would be dealt with by administrative discretion'.[11] Communist voters undoubtedly benefited, but in smaller measure than those of the ruling parties. This was backstairs parliamentary horse-trading, often carried out by individual deputies. It was a far cry from an implicit agreement between the two major parties to maintain the status quo both within the Italian political system and outside it. Rather, the Italian Communists had had a distinguished, if criticizable, record of opposition, which was to become more arid and barren, as we shall see, in the course of the 1980s.

A last and fundamental weakness of the Italian political system needs to be identified. It was not specific to Italy, and constituted one of the most intractable problems in modern democratic politics. In both France and Italy women voted for the first time in national elections in 1946. For the most part, they voted for men. In France, for example, just 8 per cent of the Senate and 7 per cent of the Assembly was female in 1946. So weak was the thrust towards gender equality that in following years the number of women in British, French and Italian parliaments diminished rather than increased.[12] Originally, the secret vote had signified for women an important private moment in the public sphere, a political right that no one else could control;[13] but this conquest had not led to the gradual transformation of the patriarchal nature of the political system, let alone of the state in its entirety.[14] On the contrary. Women voted, but in a system whose origins and structure had been conceived without them in mind.[15] A very grave discrepancy had thus opened up between changes in society in the realm of gender, and the response of politics.

2. In the Shadows of the State

The 1980s were a period of political continuity. After the brief experiment of the years of national solidarity, government politics reverted again to that alliance between the Christian Democrats and Socialists which had dominated Italian politics since the early 1960s. The alliance was anything but pacific. It was, rather, devoid of mutual trust, parity or programmatic accord, and riven by suspicion and by an eternal jockeying for position. These characteristics made any strategic planning very difficult, and led to an extraordinary amount of time and energy being wasted on internal feuding. The two leading politicians of the decade, the Christian Democrat Ciriaco De Mita and the Socialist Bettino Craxi, found it very difficult to agree on anything, and there was little love lost between them. The period 1986–7 was a particularly dismal one in terms of polemics and even histrionics.

From June 1981 the so-called *'pentapartito'* came into being, a governmental alliance between Liberals, Social Democrats, Republicans, Socialists and Christian Democrats which was to last for almost ten years, until April 1991. 'Last' in a manner of speaking, for there were nine different governments in this period. The *amour propre* of each of the parties needed to be satisfied in terms of ministerial responsibilities and positions of power within the state apparatus. The size of the boards of directors and the number of vice-presidents of banks and government agencies reached their peak in this decade.[16] If one of the coalition partners felt dissatisfied, either over policy or position, it could request a *chiarimento* (clarification). And if the skies failed to clear, then there was the *crisi del governo*. These were habitual events, almost seasonal in their repetitiveness, and they lent Italian politics its rhythms and melodrama.

The complex pattern of intra-party bargaining and of *veti incrociati* (overlapping vetoes), so dispiriting for most of the time, could also produce unexpected surprises, which warn against any monochrome interpretation of these years. One such surprise was the election of Sandro Pertini as President of the Republic in July 1978. After the fall from grace of the Christian Democrat Giovanni Leone, Bettino Craxi had insisted that the next President be a Socialist. Pertini was certainly not his first choice, being far too independent-minded and even hostile to the new Socialist leadership. However, Pertini's candidature gained widespread consent in the ranks of both the PCI and the DC, with the result that he was elected with a massive majority of 832 votes out of a possible 995.[17]

This tiny and frail old man, who had been a leading member of the Resistance, reinvigorated rapidly the office of President. His outspoken advocacy of democratic values, his constant re-evocation of his anti-Fascist youth, his invitation every year to thousands of schoolchildren to come and meet him in the Quirinale palace, left an indelible impression on Italian public opinion. Pertini had his faults, among which was an excess of rhetoric, but in the seven years of his term of office he became the most popular President that the Republic had ever had. As a result, Italian democracy was much strengthened.

In constitutional terms, Pertini's presidency raised a number of issues. There had always been discussion as to whether the President of the Republic should play a purely supervisory role, that of a notary registering the acts of the other elements of the state, or whether he (for there had never been a she) should intervene more directly in government. Pertini opted more strongly than his predecessors for the second role. He exercised an autonomy from the parties in his choice of possible prime ministers, he ventilated the idea of forming 'governments of the President', made up more of experts than politicians, he spoke out frequently and undiplomatically on a whole range of issues, exercising what came to be called, rather comically, the *'diritto di esternazione'*, or right to express one's opinions forcefully. All this seemed acceptable enough coming from Pertini, given what he stood for in the history of the Republic. However, it was all too easy to confuse the person with the role. In other circumstances, and in other hands, an interventionist presidency, and one bent on *'esternazioni'* could and would be much more of a mixed blessing.[18]

It was Pertini who took the initiative in 1981 to invite the Republican Giovanni Spadolini to become President of the Council of Ministers. This was the first time since the government of Ferruccio Parri in 1945 that a member of a party other than Christian Democracy had led the country. Spadolini's two brief governments, lasting from June 1981 to November 1982, were not much more than an interim period, but the mould had been broken.

The year 1981 was also highly significant for two other events, of very different origin. A new referendum campaign promoted by the Vatican against the abortion law of 1978 was supported only by the Christian Democrats and the neo-Fascists of the MSI. Karol Wojtyla was here at his least enlightened, leading a doctrinaire campaign which, if successful, would have rendered abortion in Italy once again illegal and dangerous. The referendum initiative was crushingly defeated, with 67.5 per cent of those voting in favour of keeping the 1978 law in its place.

The other event touched one of the deepest constants in post-war Italy, and one that it is most difficult to write about with any degree of historical certainty. Behind the surface of Italian democracy lay a secret history, made up of hidden associations, contacts and even conspiracies, some farcical and others more serious. These secret lobbies gained their motive force from the twin desires to exercise power and make money, and their ideology (if they had one) from an ill-defined anti-Communism. Nearly always they had links with the secret services both Italian and American, and often they were in contact with criminal organizations. Those who lived in the shadows of the Republic used the Communist threat as a justification for relegating democratic rules and procedures to a position of secondary importance. This manifest contradiction – the supposed defence of democracy by its distortion, suspension or even destruction – was the hallmark of their actions.

It is all too easy to exaggerate the significance of this secret history, and seek within it a cohesion and explanatory force which it clearly did not possess. It is, by contrast, extremely difficult, if not impossible, to acquire reliable evidence and assemble it into a convincing picture. In these circumstances the historian can only proceed with great caution and considerable scepticism.

In March 1981 the Milanese magistrates, Gherardo Colombo and Giuliano Turone, while conducting inquiries into the activities of the disgraced banker Michele Sindona,[19] discovered in the office of a certain Licio Gelli at Castiglion Fibocchi in the province of Arezzo the list of 962 persons belonging to a Masonic lodge called Propaganda 2 (the P2), a lodge whose existence had already aroused suspicion and comment, but whose particulars had been kept secret.[20] While the documents which were not only lists but much else besides, were being removed, the colonel of the Guardia di Finanza in charge of the operation, Vincenzo Bianchi, was telephoned by General Orazio Giannini, the chief-in-command of the force. Bianchi later testified to the parliamentary commission of inquiry as to the contents of the conversation. Giannini told him: 'You better know that you've found some lists. I'm in those lists – be careful, because so too are all the highest echelons (I understood "of the state") . . . Watch out, the Force could be overwhelmed by this.'[21]

Giannini's informed opinion of the nature of Gelli's lists was broadly accurate. The membership of the P2 included the names of all the heads of the secret services, 195 officers of the various armed corps of the Republic, among whom were twelve generals of the Carabinieri, five of the Guardia di

Finanza, twenty-two of the army, four of the air force, and eight admirals. There were leading magistrates, a few prefects and heads of police (*questori*), bankers and businessmen, civil servants, journalists and broadcasters. The political world was represented by forty-four members of parliament, forty-one of whom belonged to the *pentapartito* and three to the neo-Fascist MSI. There were the names of three ministers, and one secretary of a leading political party, the Social Democrat Pietro Longo. The membership numbers began at 1,600, which suggested that the complete list had not been found.[22]

On examining the lists, and the other voluminous material which had been confiscated, the two Milanese magistrates realized that they had stumbled across something which was much bigger than they could possibly handle by themselves. One of the documents which they meticulously filed, photocopied and deposited was a note which it is worth reproducing in full:

Ubs-Lugano, current account no. 633369, 'Protezione'. [Account] number corresponding to the name of the Hon. Claudio Martelli on behalf of Bettino Craxi, into which has been paid by Dr Roberto Calvi on 28 October 1980 the sum of 3,500,000 dollars, subsequent to the drawing up by Dr Fiorini of the agreement with ENI. On the signing of the agreement by Dr C.R. [Calvi, Roberto] and D.D.L. [Di Donna, Leonardo], on 20 November 1980, there will be a further payment of 3,500,000 dollars.[23]

Exactly what the banker Roberto Calvi, who was to be found dead, hanging from under Blackfriars Bridge, London, on 18 July 1982, was doing depositing 7 million dollars in a secret Swiss bank to the credit of the secretary of the Socialist party was something which would only emerge, and then not in full, more than ten years later.[24] Nor was it clear why the details of this operation should have finished in the safe of Licio Gelli at Castiglion Fibocchi in the province of Arezzo.

The two magistrates immediately sought an interview with Sandro Pertini, the President of the Republic, but they did not manage to gain an audience with him. Instead, through the good offices of a friend, Umberto Loi, they went to see the then President of the Council of Ministers, the Christian Democrat Arnaldo Forlani. After waiting for hours, they were received by Forlani's *chef de cabinet*, the prefect Mario Semprini who, so it later emerged, was himself a member of the P2. Ushered into the office of the President, Colombo and Turone found a hesitant and sceptical Forlani. They pointed out to him that among the requests for admission to the secret lodge was the autographed letter of the Minister for Justice, the Christian Democrat Adolfo Sarti. Forlani went in search of a document of his own, signed by Sarti, so that he could compare the two. To his apparent surprise, the signatures corresponded. The two magistrates were then sent back to Milan, having received the promise that the matter would be taken seriously.[25]

Slowly, the pieces of the jigsaw began to be assembled, although many were missing from the start, and were to remain that way. After the Second World War, Italian Masonry, which had been outlawed by the Fascist regime, was reborn under American influence. Its Risorgimento traditions of free-thinking gave way to a fervent anti-Communism. The heated social climate of the late 1960s caused the Masons great concern, and in 1971 the Gran Maestro Lino Salvini of the 'Grande Oriente d'Italia', one of Italy's largest Masonic groupings, entrusted Licio Gelli with the task of reorganizing the ancient 'Propaganda' lodge, which then became Propaganda 2.

Its head, Licio Gelli, seemed a relatively insignificant and provincial personality, a man who had dedicated his life to anti-Communist and then to Masonic activities, and who had extensive contacts in Latin America. A few months before the lists of the P2 were discovered, Maurizio Costanzo, a well-known personality of the Italian mass media and himself a member of the P2, had interviewed Gelli at some length for *Corriere della Sera*.[26] Gelli told Costanzo that the Lodge wished 'to work solely for the good of humanity, with the aim, which may appear utopian, of improving it'. Gelli was in favour of rewriting the republican Constitution along the lines of a Gaullist presidential system, and of taking Italy out of the European Community. Asked for his views on democracy, he replied that Aldo Moro had once told him: 'You mustn't be in a hurry, for democracy is like a saucepan of beans: for them to taste good, they must cook very, very, very slowly.' To which Gelli had replied (according to Gelli): 'Be careful, right honourable minister, that the beans do not remain without water, because in that way they would burn.' Costanzo ended the interview by asking Gelli what he had always wanted to be when he was a child, to which he replied, 'A puppet master.'

Behind the relatively innocuous, if vaguely menacing, image which Gelli projected in the interview lay a much more insidious project. The material confiscated from his office not only revealed a secret affiliation of significant parts of the nation's élite, but also unmasked Gelli's role as an information collector. Benefiting from classified information made available to him by his secret service contacts, Gelli had accumulated a series of files which could be, and perhaps were, used as a powerful weapon of control and blackmail. The details of Calvi's secret payment of funds to the Socialist party would seem to belong in this category.

Further details emerged from documents of the P2 which were found by customs officers at Fiumicino airport in July 1982. The documents had been poorly hidden in the false bottom of a suitcase belonging to Gelli's daughter, Maria Grazia, and included two typescripts, probably of the period 1975–6, entitled 'Memorandum sulla situazione italiana' and 'Piano di rinascita democratica'. The principal enemies of Italy, according to these documents, were the PCI and the trade-union movement. To combat them, and to avoid any perilous cooperation with them along the lines which had been proposed by Aldo Moro, the P2 advocated, in appropriately obtuse language, a programme of extensive corruption: 'Political parties, newspapers and trade unions can be the objects of possible solicitations which could take the form of economico-financial manoeuvres. The availability of sums not exceeding 30 to 40 billion lire would seem sufficient to allow carefully chosen men, acting in good faith, to conquer key positions necessary for overall control.'[27]

Elements of such operations are clearly recognizable in some of the history of the 1970s. In 1977 the P2 took control of the *Corriere della Sera*, Italy's leading newspaper. The capital of Rizzoli Editore Spa, which owned the newspaper at that time, was increased from 5 to 25.5 billion lire, with funds coming from, among other sources, the Vatican bank IOR, directed by the bishop Paul Marcinkus. It was in this context of P2 control of the *Corriere della Sera* that Costanzo had interviewed Gelli in 1980.

The exact nature of the P2's other activities can only be hinted at. Members of the Masonic lodge, so it turned out afterwards, figured prominently in some of the most disquieting events of these years. For instance, both Gelli and the secret service chief, Pietro Musumeci, were later condemned for attempting to mislead the police inquiry into the terrible terrorist bombing of Bologna station on 2 August 1980, as a result of which eighty-five people died.[28] It is also the case that the links between the lodge and two of the most disreputable and powerful figures of the 1970s, the bankers Sindona and Calvi, were clearly established.[29] On the other hand, little is known of the international contacts and ramifications of the P2.[30]

The history of the lodge after its unmasking in 1981 is briefly told. In the face of unprecedented public outrage, Forlani appointed a parliamentary commission of inquiry. Headed by a highly unusual figure, an independent-minded Christian Democrat woman, Tina Anselmi, the commission reported its findings in 115 volumes, published in 1984. The majority of the commission concluded that the P2 had devoted itself to '. . . the pollution of the public life of a nation. It aimed to alter, often in decisive fashion, the correct functioning of the institutions of the country, according to a project which . . . intended to undermine our democracy.'[31]

A minority report of the same commission went further still. According to this viewpoint the P2 was not a deviant outgrowth from a basically healthy political and institutional system (for this was the majority opinion), but an intrinsic part of the system itself.[32] Such an interpretation raised a fundamental problem about the body politic in Italy: had the bypassing of democratic norms and procedures become so frequent and habitual as to be the principal (and not occasional) mode of functioning of the Republic? The 1980s, as we shall see, did not give a reassuring answer to this question.

As if to confirm the doubts of the minority of the commission, the legal, as opposed to parliamentary, judgement on the P2 was strikingly different. The judicial inquiry into the activities of the lodge was quickly taken out of the hands of the unaccommodating magistrates of Milan, and transferred to the Procura of Rome, where it languished for many years and with few results. In 1994, thirteen years after the original investigation, the second Assize Court of Rome ruled that the P2 was a 'normal' Masonic lodge, secret only for those who were 'deaf and illiterate'. The final judgement of the Corte di Cassazione, Italy's highest court, was more balanced, but still maintained that the P2 was not a conspiracy but a 'business committee'. Only General Maletti of the secret services was given an unsuspended prison sentence, but he in the meanwhile had fled to South Africa.[33]

3. Ciriaco De Mita and the Christian Democrats

Back at the surface of Italian politics, Christian Democracy, Italy's long-standing ruling party, was unable in these years to break free from the political habits and culture that had characterized it since the early years of the Republic. In the mid-1970s Benigno Zaccagnini's secretaryship had offered the promise of renewal, but ten years later all the major problems of the party were still there: the lack of generational turnover, rampant factionalism and clientelism, the unchecked over-representation of the South (62.3 per cent of total membership in 1982).[34] Sicily and Campania had the highest membership per capita of all the Italian regions, and were thus the key to the control of the party. The number of women members had decreased in the North, but increased in the South, a sure sign of that 'forced-family recruiting'[35] which took place in a context of mass clientelism.

The involvement of many Christian Democrats in the P2, and the fact that the secret organization had flourished undisturbed for some years, deeply discredited Italy's principal political party. It was these events that opened the way for Pertini to choose Spadolini as premier. They also led to some soul-searching within the DC. At the XVth Congress of the party, held at Rome in May 1982, Ciriaco De Mita, the leader of the 'Base' faction, became the new secretary.

De Mita, the son of a tailor from the village of Nusco in the province of Avellino, had some ambitious ideas for the transformation of his party. He was aware of the dangers of leaving the DC unreformed at a time of rapid social change. At the XVth Congress he had spoken of the 'brute force' of new interests emerging in society, and of the failure of the traditional 'cultural and ideological mediation' of the mass parties, and of the DC in particular.[36] The old politics, he argued, had to adapt or perish. He spoke out in favour of the end of factions within the party, against false or bloated membership lists, and any residues of an integralist or confessional party.[37] In the wake of the triumphs of Thatcher and Reagan, he emphasized the need for the party to respond to free enterprise, reduce the public sector and render it more efficient. The political system had to be modified so that the two major parties, the DC and the PCI, could alternate in power. De Mita's was an attempt, the last as it turned out, to push the great white whale (a widely used metaphor for the DC) into fresh waters.

De Mita had the merit of thinking strategically in a party that had become accustomed simply to the exercise of power. His proposals, though, lacked credibility, even though at the time they convinced more than one authoritative commentator. His was a typically juridical and humanist Catholic culture, lacking the sociological and economic sensibility necessary for a society in such rapid transition. He made frequent references to the need to introduce 'rationality' into politics, but this was hardly enough to combat his tendency to verbosity and abstraction.

Furthermore, he was a typical product of the southern clienteles, from which he showed no signs of detaching himself. His power base in Irpinia was organized as the classic fiefdom of a southern notable. In the wake of an earthquake which badly damaged Irpinia (as well as parts of Naples and Campania) in 1980, the Banca Popolare dell'Irpinia, of which De Mita and his family were principal shareholders, was widely accused of benefiting improperly from the funds assigned for the reconstruction of the region.[38] De Mita was too much part of southern political culture to reform it effectively, and too little part of the socio-economic reality of the Centre-North to be able to formulate its needs in effective terms.

The new secretary of the DC was soon put to the test. In 1983 Bettino Craxi, seeking to profit from the DC's crisis, withdrew his support from the government and forced national elections a year ahead of schedule. De Mita responded with a vigorous election campaign based on the need to modernize the DC and the Italian political system. He was rewarded with the worst defeat in the history of the party. The DC fell from 38.3 per cent of the vote to 32.9 per cent, the PSI increased from 9.8 per cent to 11.4 per cent, the PCI lost only 0.5 per cent, polling 29.9 per cent. The smaller parties of the *pentapartito* all did well, especially the Republicans who benefited from Spadolini's presidency to increase their votes from 3.0 per cent to 5.1 per cent.

In the South, De Mita's proposals had been judged as little short of subversive by many sections of his own party. He recounted later that more than once during the election campaign he was asked if he really was a Christian Democrat.[39] Worse still, the sectors of northern society to whom he hoped to appeal, the new *ceti medi* and the small entrepreneurs, remained indifferent to his message. They distrusted this reformer from the deep South, his lack of traditional anti-Communism, his rather abstract appeals for political modernity. In the Veneto, the DC's vote dropped from 50.0 per cent to 42.5 per cent, and there was a small protest vote of some 4.2 per cent in favour of an unknown local movement, the Liga Veneta.[40] With the benefit of hindsight, it is possible to see this as the first stirrings of the electoral revolution which was to hit the government parties in 1992.

De Mita survived the 1983 electoral defeat, but the experience greatly undermined his reforming zeal. From this point onwards he concentrated principally on consolidating his hold on the secretaryship, reverting to a classic pattern introduced by Fanfani when he was secretary of the party in the 1950s. There were some laudable attempts at local reform of the party, especially in Sicily, but the Christian Democrats needed a great deal more than this if they were to respond to the challenges of the 1980s.

4. The Craxi Years, 1983–7

a. THE POLITICAL CULTURE OF THE SOCIALISTS

De Mita's failure was Bettino Craxi's success. After the 1983 elections the way was open for Craxi to become the first Socialist prime minister in the history of the Republic. Against all expectations, Craxi's period in office proved to be of considerable longevity, at least by the unexalted standards of the Italian Republic: his two successive governments were to last from August 1983 until April 1987.

This extended tenure enabled Craxi to stamp his considerable personality upon the politics of the decade. Massive and intimidating, a born polemicist and tactician, Craxi reaffirmed in a modern form certain perennial values of Italian politics, according to which the strongest and the most cunning must perforce prevail. The Craxi years, in fact, saw a radical divorce between politics on the one hand, and morality and the law on the other. The group of Socialists who clustered around their charismatic leader, for the most part intelligent and able men, seemed at times to have learned by heart Machiavelli's famous lines from the fifteenth chapter of *The Prince*: 'How we live is so far removed from how we ought to live, that he who abandons what is done for what ought to be done, will rather learn to bring about his own ruin than his preservation.'[41]

Craxi's politics, however, were a great deal more than Machiavellianism writ large.[42] More than any other Italian politician of the decade, he had an innate understanding of how much was changing in Italian society and offered a spectacular, if ethically unconvincing, reply. Craxi came from Milan, a city whose name, as he declared rhetorically, 'is written in stone on every event that has to do with progress, with modernisation, with democracy'.[43] Milan was a privileged viewpoint from which to construct the politics of modern Italy. In contrast to De Mita's often empty verbal arabesques, the products of 'an intellectual from Magna Grecia' as Giovanni Agnelli had once called him, the Socialist leader offered a 'realist's' view of the individualism and consumerism which so characterized the decade. Modern trends of entrepreneurship, of consumption and individual liberty were to be celebrated as such, without being submitted to any reflexive filters, let alone to the austere and archaic critique of the Communist Berlinguer. 'Innovation' was the keyword, and power was to be exercised for its own, and one's own, sake.

To be a Socialist politician in Italy in these years meant to have a portable telephone and a BMW, to mix with high-flying lawyers and businessmen, to lunch at Matarel or Savini in Milan's Galleria, to have a good line of conversation on information technology and to take exotic holidays. As the historian Giuseppe Tamburrano, himself a leading Socialist in these years, wrote after Craxi had fallen from grace: 'A whole army of careerists, social climbers and yuppies entered the PSI, and used it as an instrument of political and economic promotion.'[44] These trends were not unique to Italy, but were to be found, to varying degrees, in all the southern European Socialist parties of these years.

Under Craxi's leadership, politics were to be personalized and simplified, they were to have a strong showbiz element, their principal medium was to be the television. If their new form was thus very specific, their content was left, for the most part, deliberately vague. Craxi was a fervent anti-Communist, and his long-term ambition was to weaken mortally the PCI and to replace it with a broader Socialist movement with himself at its head. To this aim he even, rather bizarrely, resurrected Proudhon as an antidote to Marx.[45] For the rest, he took care not to espouse a purely Thatcherite attitude to political economy, continuing instead to pay lipservice to the old Socialist ideals of social justice and participation. His youthful lieutenant, Claudio Martelli, was also useful for his advocacy of some elements of the 'new' politics, such as ecological and anti-nuclear issues. All this, though, was so much froth on the top of the *real* politics, which were primarily oriented to increasing the power of the PSI within Italy's political system. The methods used to achieve this objective will be described in detail in Chapter 7.

The transformation in 1984 of the old central committee of the Socialist party into a national assembly was highly significant at a symbolic level. Whereas the old committee, made up of deputies, trade-unionists and full-time officials, had been, for all its factionalism, a forum of discussion and decision-making, the new assembly designed by Craxi was a largely ornamental gathering, with representatives from the professions and the world of business, as well as intellectuals, television celebrities and stars. At the height of his powers, Craxi was re-elected secretary of the party by acclamation; gone were the days of motions and voting.

b. 'GOVERNABILITY'

During his years in office, Craxi claimed to have brought a greater 'governability' to Italy. His powerful personality was certainly in contrast to many lesser and greyer figures of the recent past, but it is difficult to find much empirical evidence of effective government. Given the litigious and tension-ridden nature of the DC–PSI alliance, and the fractious nature of Italy's parliament, government measures were always at risk on the floor of the Chamber of Deputies, and indeed were frequently rejected. Inside the Council of Ministers, life was not much easier. In 1992 Bruno Visentini, the distinguished member of the Republican party who had been Craxi's Minister of Finances, briefly re-evoked his experience of Craxi's Cabinets. For Visentini, Craxi had been 'an eminent President of the Council [of Ministers]', and it had been 'a privilege to have held government responsibility under his Presidency'. Here then was a witness who could hardly be accused of anti-Craxi bias. None the less he had a sorry, if familiar, story to tell. When it came to taking action on *the* crucial issue of the time, the reduction of the public debt and the annual deficit, 'every appeal, even when supported by authoritative voices, including that of the President of the Council, fell on deaf ears. There were those who believed, with a sort of weary disdain, that they were not responsible to the President, nor to the collegial solidarity of the government, nor to parliament, but only to their own party, or faction within it.'[46] This was the very antithesis of 'governability'.

Apologists for the Craxi years, who are now few and far between, but who proliferated in Italian intellectual circles throughout the 1980s, could point to a limited number of achievements. One was his victory, which has already been mentioned, in the referendum on the *scala mobile*, the national scheme of threshold payments. After only a few months in power, Craxi's government cut significantly the extent of these payments. There were widespread workers' protests, with the result that the Communist party organized a referendum to repeal the government decree. Craxi held firm and won the day by 54.3 per cent of the votes against 45.7 per cent. Such a result certainly served to reduce labour costs and to inspire confidence in business circles. Yet this was an isolated act of political economy, and unilateral at that.

These were boom years for the European economies, and all the political leaders of the time, from Thatcher to Kohl to Mitterrand to Felipe Gonzales and Craxi, had the good fortune to exercise power at a time of economic expansion. Some made better use of this opportunity than others. In the Italian case no clear strategy emerged. The economic historian Luciano Cafagna, another erstwhile supporter of Craxi, noted that the Socialist leader had a very ' "Lombard" view of the Italian economy, in the sense that he did not get beyond the level of the "real economy" – production, firms, what economic operators themselves perceived –; for the rest he was distracted and impatient, the exact characteristics of one who has no passion for these problems'.[47]

In the Craxi years from 1983 to 1987, inflation fell significantly from 10.8 per cent to 4.7 per cent, but the annual government spending deficit remained very high, declining only from 14.3 per cent to 11.6 per cent of GDP.[48] Within this context of high spending, investment in key areas such as research and technology remained among the lowest in Europe. At the same time the public debt spiralled gaily out of control, from 72 per cent of GDP to 93 per cent,[49] while every encouragement was given to private savers to cash in on the consequent high interest rates on state bonds. Craxi could boast in 1992: 'I have no self-criticisms . . . I regret the passing of those years and I hope that the country does as well';[50] but the truth was that a historic occasion to put in order Italy's public economy had been lost.

Other achievements were claimed for, and by, Craxi in diverse fields. One was the rewriting of the Concordat between the Italian state and the Vatican.[51] Another was a more powerful presence in foreign affairs, epitomized by the incident at Sigonella in 1985. In October of that year, four Palestine terrorists hijacked the liner *Achille Lauro* and killed a Jewish American passenger. After protracted negotiations, the Italian and Egyptian governments agreed to guarantee them and their leader, Abu Abbas (who had already been sentenced to life imprisonment by an Italian court for a previous act of terrorism), safe passage to Belgrade in return for the lives of the other passengers and of the crew. The United States government violently disagreed with this compromise. American fighter jets forced the aeroplane which was bearing the terrorists to their safe haven to make an emergency landing at the NATO base of Sigonella, in Sicily. There American troops belonging to the garrison demanded that the terrorists be handed over to them, while Italian marines took up positions around the aeroplane to prevent any such action. In this difficult and tense situation Craxi insisted rightly that a question of national sovereignty was at stake, with the result that the United States government backed down.[52]

However, the acid test for any Italian government in the 1980s was not so much in the realm of foreign affairs or of relations with the Vatican, as in the field of domestic reform – economic, social and institutional. Here the Craxi years were distinguished primarily by their silence, and the reformism of the 1980s appears no more consistent, and in many ways less significant, than that of the 1970s.[53] The absence of any strategic economic policy was accompanied by a failure to tackle the structural problems of the Italian state. No attempt was made to reform the public administration, and pro-capita income in the public administration was allowed to rise some 30 per cent in the years 1985–7. Similarly, the health service remained unhappily in the hands of the technically incompetent and frequently corrupt local health authorities, the Unità Sanitarie Locali. As for the reform of the political system, a bicameral commission set up in late 1983 under the presidency of the Liberal Aldo Bozzi had failed to reach any agreement some two years later.[54]

In these years there were only two serious and hard-fought attempts at reform. In 1984 the Republican Minister of Finance, Bruno Visentini, introduced measures to ensure that some control over the taxable income of shopkeepers was finally exercised. The uproar was immense and the *'pentapartito'* hovered on the brink of crisis. Giuseppe Orlando, the veteran leader of the major shop-owners' federation, the Confcommercio, threatened an electoral revolution.[55] In the event, the elections of 1987 saw no such protest and Visentini's reforms carried the day, though in modified form.

The other measure worthy of note was again the work of a Republican, Giuseppe Galasso, who was under-secretary at the strange-sounding Ministry of Cultural Assets (*Beni Culturali*). Galasso introduced a law compelling each region to draw up a regional landscape plan (*Piano paesistico regionale*). The aim was to defend Italy's coastlines and other aspects of her environment from further ruination. This was certainly a case of shutting the stable door after the horse had bolted, but it was still much better than nothing. All Italian regional governments were supposed to have drawn up their landscape plans by the end of 1986, but by that date only three had done so, and no single plan had become operational. In July 1986, with the law no. 349 of that year, the Italian ministry for environmental protection finally came into being.[56]

For the rest, it is difficult indeed to discern a more incisive way of governing during Craxi's premiership. Certainly, the Socialists' limited strength in parliament made it almost impossible for them to initiate a revolution in government, and there can be little doubt that Craxi himself would have relished more effective power. Quite what use he would have made of such power must remain an open question. At the end of the day, he seemed as much committed to perpetuating a spectacular version of patron–client relations as to fighting for efficient and equitable administration. One of the key areas where this became very clear was that of television broadcasting, where it is possible to trace a consistent and blatant policy of partisan *laissez-faire*.

c. THE CRAXI GOVERNMENTS AND COMMERCIAL TELEVISION

In July 1976 the Constitutional Court had laid down guidelines for television transmission. National broadcasting was reserved for public television, but the Court opened the way for private, local transmissions, on the grounds that there were sufficient frequencies available 'to permit the freedom of private initiative without danger of private monopolies or oligopolies'.[57] The Court declared that ether was a collective resource, and asked parliament to legislate with urgency regarding a proper disciplining of the whole area of the mass media.

Parliament was neither able nor willing to do anything of the sort. Years passed, during which an unchecked free-for-all reigned in the world of commercial television. It was in this period that Silvio Berlusconi built up his television empire. He was the most dynamic of the television entrepreneurs, the one who was prepared to sail closest to the wind in legal terms, the one who seemed to have access to the greatest quantities of capital.[58] Naturally enough, he was opposed to any regulation. He told Alberto Statera in 1983: 'For my part, I am convinced that there is no need for any legislation, because the market, here as elsewhere, contains all the antibodies necessary to regulate itself.'[59]

Berlusconi was an intimate friend of Bettino Craxi. They were both Milanese and they took holidays together at Portofino and at Saint Moritz. In 1984 Craxi was godfather to the child born to Berlusconi and Veronica Lario, and six years later Craxi and his wife were the witnesses at their marriage.[60] So close a friendship was deeply to influence government policy towards television broadcasting.

On 16 October 1984, two months after Berlusconi had bought up Rete 4 for 135 billion lire, thus establishing a near monopoly of commercial broadcasting, three magistrates from Turin, Rome and Pescara respectively gave orders for his television stations to be partially blacked out. Their argument was very simple. The ruling of the Constitutional Court in 1976 made provision for *local* but not *national* commercial broadcasting, and Berlusconi's three national channels were flagrantly in breach of these provisions. Rome and Lazio, Turin and Piedmont, the Abruzzi and a part of the Marches suddenly found themselves without Canale 5, Italia 1 and Rete 4. It was a disconcerting experience. That day their programmes included the favourite children's cartoon the *Smurfs, Dallas, Dynasty* and *High Noon* (all scheduled for Canale 5), *The Man from Singapore* (Italia 1), *New York, New York* (Rete 4). It was not a good moment to have a blank screen.[61]

Predictably enough, the popular outcry was considerable. Berlusconi's channels, which continued to transmit in the rest of the country, fanned the

155

flames, demanding respect for a new citizen's right, 'freedom to use the television's automatic controls (*libertà di telecommando*)'. In the face of this mediatic crisis, the first in the history of the Republic, Bettino Craxi reacted with a speed and determination which revealed the depth of his loyalty to his friend as well as a very limited sense of impartiality. The Council of Ministers was summoned to meet on a Saturday, 20 October 1984, and immediately issued a decree law (*decreto legge*), valid for six months, ordering the resumption of national commercial transmissions. At the same time the new Socialist spokesman for telecommunications, Paolo Pillitteri, Craxi's brother-in-law and later to be mayor of Milan, announced: 'The magistrates' initiative is all the more inappropriate at a moment when parliament is in the process of examining and refining a new law on private television transmissions.'[62]

On 28 November 1984, the Craxi–Berlusconi axis received a setback when the Chamber of Deputies declared the decree law of 20 October unconstitutional. The Prime Minister, though, was not to be defeated. He obtained the Christian Democrats' permission to present new temporary legislation on 6 December 1984, and on its expiry the ruling parties deemed that no further legislation was necessary. Commercial television simply lapsed back into its Hobbesian state of nature. Another *five years* passed before any properly deliberated law on television broadcasting was to see the light of day, all the time necessary for Berlusconi to consolidate his quasi-monopoly.[63]

By 1987 Bettino Craxi was well known as a formidable politician on an international level. His was the only statue of a contemporary Italian in Madame Tussaud's famous waxworks museum in London. Yet all was not well. For all Craxi's self-dubbed '*decisionismo*', his record in office was a thin one. Christian Democrat weakness after the defeat of 1983, rather than his own strength, had probably allowed him to survive as long as he had. Furthermore, the Socialists had dreamed of converting the Republic into a presidential system, hopefully with Craxi himself at its head, and of joining their European Socialist colleagues as a major political force.[64] Neither of these ambitions had been realized.

By 1987 it was time for fresh elections. The PSI did gain votes, increasing its share from 11.4 per cent to 14.3 per cent, but it was too little to show for four years in power. The DC, under a more sober De Mita, recovered to 34.3 per cent, and the PCI remained obstinately strong with 26.6 per cent, nearly double the Socialist vote. The Greens were present for the first time in the Italian parliament, with 2.5 per cent of the votes. The Republican slipped back to 3.7 per cent, and an unknown organization, the Lombard League, managed to elect one Senator, a certain Umberto Bossi, and one deputy, his close friend Giuseppe Leoni.

The 'long wave' of Socialist advance was thus proving terribly slow to break on to Italian shores. Craxi relinquished the premiership to the young protégé of De Mita, Giovanni Goria. It seemed at the time as if Craxi's absence from Palazzo Chigi was only temporary. With hindsight, it is possible to see that 1987 was the apogee of his power.

5. The Atrophy of Italian Communism

a. ENRICO BERLINGUER

The last element in Italy's blocked political system was the Communist party. The 1980s proved a very difficult decade for the party, as it did for the European Left as a whole. The rapid changes that were taking place in society were undermining the Left's traditional electorate and bringing into question many of its old ideological certainties.

Enrico Berlinguer was too experienced and intelligent a leader not to realize the novelty of the challenges that were being posed. At an international level, he responded with determination. In the wake of the *coup d'état* in Poland in 1981 and the crushing of the independent trade union Solidarity, Berlinguer declared on Italian television on 15 December that the 'capacity of the eastern European societies, or at least some of them, to act as a driving force for renewal, has now exhausted itself'.[65] This was a carefully phrased sentence, but for an increasingly ageing party such as the PCI, firmly wedded to the idea that some sort of socialism had been achieved in the East, it came as a great shock.[66] On 24 January 1982 the leading Soviet newspaper, *Pravda*, accused the PCI of having taken a position 'against the interests of peace and socialism'.[67] Berlinguer stood firm, and at the XVIth congress of the Italian party, held in 1983, the great majority of delegates approved his critical line.

Many critics and some supporters of the PCI have pointed out that '*lo strappo*', the break, with the Soviet Union came too late in the history of the party. If the Italian Communists, they argue, had found the courage to make their break at the time of the Soviet invasion of Czechoslovakia in 1969, they would have been in a much stronger position to lead the country in the following decades. Berlinguer himself was still claiming publicly in 1975 that workers' conditions were getting better in the East while they deteriorated in the West,[68] even if in private he had little regard for eastern bloc Communism. He confided in Massimo D'Alema while they were in Moscow in 1984 that there were three general laws which characterized the eastern bloc countries: 'The first is this: the leaders always tell lies, even when they are unnecessary; the second is that their agriculture is hopelessly inefficient; the third is that the wrapping paper always sticks to their sweets.'[69]

There is no doubt that the Italian Communists were to pay dearly for the gap that existed between such private scepticism and their residual public loyalty. On the other hand, they had always been more critical of the Soviet Union than any of the other western European Communist parties, and in 1981 Berlinguer once again went further, faster than anyone else.

He was less successful in domestic politics. After the failure of the 'historic compromise', Berlinguer elaborated an alternative strategy, which envisaged the PCI and PSI uniting forces to bring down the Christian Democrat regime. The example of France, where the Left had combined under Mitterrand to conquer power for the first time in the 5th Republic, seemed to be an encouraging one, though naturally Berlinguer took for granted that the respective weight of Socialists and Communists in France would be reversed in Italy. However, there was not the slightest chance of this 'democratic alternative', as it was called, coming into being. Time had long passed when the Socialists might have accepted such an electoral pact, and Craxi was very firmly determined to go his own, anti-Communist way.[70] The 'historic compromise', for all its weaknesses, had been a highly suggestive and deeply thought-out programme for the future of Italy. The 'democratic alternative' was little more than a fallback position.

The Berlinguer of the early 1980s was in very many ways as attractive a political leader as it was possible to find in Europe of that time. The defeat of the 'historic compromise' had rendered him more human, though no less obstinate, more aware of his own limits and those of his party. He was acutely aware of the widespread corruption present in Italian public life, and of the need to reform the political system. He also recognized the revolutionary importance of the new and active presence of women in Italian society, and believed passionately in the need to end the oppression of women by men.[71]

He was not able, though, to adapt his party's politics to the transformations of contemporary Italian society. If De Mita lacked any real social understanding of modernity, and Craxi celebrated some of its worst elements in acritical fashion, Berlinguer substantially viewed modernity as decadence. This gave his voice, as we have seen in Chapter 4, a sharply critical edge, but it also prevented him addressing the question of individual consumption in other than negative terms. Indeed, both consumption and the individual were relatively foreign terrains for the Communist movement as a whole. It had been production, not consumption, industry not services, which had always caught the Communist imagination. Equally, it was not so much the individual as the 'masses' that mattered. In Berlinguer's political vision, whole new cohorts – women, youth, unemployed, old people – were moving on to the historical stage, but it was difficult for him to discern the process which caused the ranks to ripple and sway, and then dissolve into their component parts. As a consequence, civil society, the meeting-place of free individuals, was always unlikely to attain the attention it merited. What mattered was the party, its organization and discipline, its fairs and rituals, its mass assemblies and carefully staged congresses.

The greatest failing of all, which was certainly not Berlinguer's alone, was the ever more apparent nebulosity of the so-called 'third way' to socialism, which was meant to be neither that of the Communist East nor that of western social democracy. Berlinguer believed passionately that the Italian Communists were different, but this difference was not translated into a convincing programme of socialist transformation. In the 1950s and 1960s, great emphasis had been put on the realization of structural reforms, inherently anti-capitalist by nature, as gradual stepping-stones in the construction of socialism.[72] This theory, never entirely satisfactory in itself, was quietly put to one side in the 1970s and 1980s, and nothing much else replaced it.

Berlinguer's contribution to Italian politics was cut tragically short. While delivering a speech at Padua during the European election campaign of 1984 he suffered a cerebral haemorrhage, and he died four days later, on 11 June 1984. More than a million people came to his funeral in Rome, a moving tribute to the last great western Communist. In overall terms, his politics cannot be judged a success, but he left an indelible image of rectitude, intelligence and commitment to democracy.

Berlinguer's sudden death deprived the Communists of the one man of sufficient national and international stature to guide them through the doldrums of the 80s. He was succeeded as party secretary by Alessandro Natta, a cultured and senior figure in the party. Natta was a likeable and sensible leader, but not at all what the Communists needed at that time. Under his interim secretaryship, from 1984 until 1988, the PCI failed to respond with sufficient alacrity or intellectual rigour. In whole areas of modern life – the family, consumption, the new service sector – the party had nothing much to say.[73] After losing electoral ground for nearly a decade, its militants were getting increasingly desperate.

b. THE COLLAPSE OF COMMUNISM AND THE BIRTH OF THE PDS

In 1988 Natta, who had fallen ill, was forced to step down in favour of Achille Occhetto, the vice-secretary of the party. With Occhetto's arrival, a new generation took control of the party. Born in 1936, Occhetto had been the secretary of the FGCI, the youth movement of the party. 'A slight, stocky man with a generous greying moustache',[74] Occhetto, like Berlinguer, had spent his life as a party functionary, but he lacked both Berlinguer's charisma and intellectual clarity, with the result that he was never fully able to dominate his own party or the course of events.

In his first eighteen months as secretary Occhetto, to his considerable credit, pushed firmly for change. At the XVIIIth Congress, held in Rome in March 1989, the women's movement enjoyed an unprecedented importance, reflected both in the debate on gender issues and in the establishment of quotas assuring female representation, varying from one-third to one-fifth, in the various party organisms. This was not much, but was far ahead of the other Italian and most European parties of the time. There was, in addition, a new emphasis on citizenship and rights which reflected the profound influence of liberal thinking upon the European socialism of the 1980s.[75]

All this has to be put in the context of the dramatic events then taking place in the Communist regimes of central and eastern Europe. The reforming policies of Mikhail Gorbachov had unleashed a desire for change and a room for dissent which could not be contained, either in the USSR or in the other eastern bloc countries. The gathering storm in the East acted as a formidable catalyst in the West. The Italian Communists supported Gorbachov to the full, hoping that out of the turmoil there would emerge a profoundly reformed international Communist movement.[76] By the last months of 1989, however, it was becoming ever clearer that international Communism was doomed, and during the night of 9–10 November the Berlin Wall, the single most powerful symbol of Communist oppression, was breached.

The reaction of Achille Occhetto was a precipitate one. On 12 November 1989, in a speech to a group of ex-partisans at the Bolognina section of the party, he announced that the Italian Communist party would change its name, though he did not say what the new name would be, nor when the change would take place. He recalled later: 'I was convinced that the more radical the break, the more it would be possible to save and recuperate the best elements of Italian Communism. I had decided that that was the right choice, I was very determined, and as a result I lived that moment with joy, and I have always remembered it in the same spirit.'[77]

The reaction within the Italian Communist party was somewhat less joyous.[78] Occhetto had acted in a style typical of the former secretaries of his party, for both Togliatti and Berlinguer had always combined authority with autonomy, often elaborating strategy in consultation with a very restricted group of advisers. Occhetto, though, was neither Togliatti nor Berlinguer; nor could the declaration of the end of the party after seventy years of history in any way be compared to a change in strategy, however portentous. Occhetto's decision was, in broad terms, the right one: the end of global Communism necessitated either the dissolution of his party or a radical new beginning. However, the new secretary's action lacked a number of essential ingredients: the necessary authority to carry the old party with him without a deeply damaging internal war; a coherent political project with which the new party could be identified; and even the name by which it was to be called.

Initially, there was considerable support for Ochetto's initiative: from many left-wingers who were not Communists, but who had been appalled by Craxi's 'Socialism'; and from the reformist heartlands of Italian Communism, especially Emilia-Romagna. But for many militants whose whole lives had been dedicated to the party, as well as for many left-wing intellectuals, his proposal seemed an outrage. Natalia Ginzburg, the famous author, declared that the end of the party felt like having an arm amputated. During the fierce discussions in the crowded sections of the party, many members admitted to being completely disorientated. One Milanese militant, immortalized in Nanni Moretti's documentary of these months, *La Cosa*, 'The Thing' (for this was what the new organization, in the absence of any other name, had been unaffectionately dubbed), promised fidelity but not self-annihilation: 'You can count on me, but don't ask me to renounce my history.'

It was in a state of prostration and division that the Italian Communists reached the XXth and last Congress of their party, held at Rimini at the end of January 1991. Sixty-eight per cent of the delegates gave their support to Occhetto and to the new party, which had finally acquired the name of Partito Democratico della Sinistra (PDS). Twenty-seven per cent of the delegates, the supporters of the filo-Soviet Armando Cossutta and of the veteran left-wing leader of the party, Pietro Ingrao, voted no, and founded a new political formation called Rifondazione Comunista (RC). The remaining 5 per cent backed the motion of Antonio Bassolino, which had sought *in extremis* and in vain to heal the divisions. For Occhetto it was to be an inauspicious start. The meeting called at the end of the Congress to elect him secretary of the new party was inquorate, and he was only confirmed as secretary some days later, at a special assembly held in Rome of the new national council of the PDS.[79]

The PCI was the first of the major political forces in Italy to be swept away by the extraordinary crisis which affected Italian politics at the end of the century. Its death marked the end of an era in Italian history. Born as a party intent on making socialist revolution, it gradually became, by one of those exquisite ironies of history, the champion of that very 'bourgeois' democracy it had vowed to destroy. In its internal workings, although strikingly participative, the PCI, like most other parties in modern democracies, was not particularly democratic. Even after the end of the Stalinist period, discipline and loyalty were always to be more important components of 'democratic centralism' than dissent and debate. Yet in relation to external democracy, to that of the new Republic created after the war, the PCI proved its credentials time and again. It combined a lack of adventurism in its own politics – at the end of the Resistance, after the attempted assassination of Togliatti, at the time of the historic compromise – with a determined and salutary opposition every time incipient subversion surfaced among its political opponents: with Tambroni, Segni and De Lorenzo, during the strategy of tension and the machinations of the CIA and the extreme right, against the terrorism of the Red Brigades. Paradoxical as it may appear, Italian democracy was almost certainly safer with the Italian Communists than without them.

The Italian party closed its history without ever having stained its hands with the sort of crimes against humanity which many of its fellow parties had perpetrated on a mass scale during the course of the twentieth century. Yet it was all too reticent about denouncing or even acknowledging the existence of such crimes. The party's loyalty to the Soviet model and the international Communist movement, protracted far into the 1970s at least in public if not in private, deprived it of any chance of making the word communist mean something different in the West. For all Togliatti's talk of polycentrism, for all the originality and distinction of Gramsci's prison reflections, for all the numerical and cultural primacy of the PCI among the Communist parties of the West, the Italian party never broke through to a sufficient political and intellectual autonomy from the eastern model of Communism.

Within Italian society, the PCI played an extraordinary role in the post-war period. Through the organization of Togliatti's mass party and the dedication of its militants, significant minorities of Italian working people were brought, for the first time, into active contact with left-wing politics. The PCI's was a version of that politics based very firmly on social equality and social justice, but much less so on individual liberty. The mass party was an extraordinary experience in political education and activism, in persuading working people that they could do something, collectively, to change their lives.

In the last analysis, though, the PCI has to be considered in terms of its own objectives. To its dying day in January 1991 the party did not only set itself the tasks, however significant, of defending Italian democracy, of integrating the workers' movement into the life of the nation, of encouraging collective solidarities. It nurtured an overriding ambition to transform Italian society in a socialist direction. First with Togliatti's explicitly anti-capitalist strategy of structural reform, and later, rather more mutedly, with Berlinguer's historic compromise, the Communists set their sights on transformative politics. In these terms, their failure was unequivocal. While the very existence of the Communist party influenced profoundly the culture of many millions of Italian families and affected significantly the history of the Republic, it did not succeed in moving Italy, either in socio-economic terms or in political ones, any closer to socialism, however defined.

6. The 'CAF': Craxi, Andreotti and Forlani, 1987–92

a. THE DEFEAT OF DE MITA

In the same period that the Italian Communist party was going through its death throes, the Christian Democrats and Socialists, flanked by their lesser allies in the *'pentapartito'*, consolidated their stranglehold upon Italian politics. After the 1987 elections, Giovanni Goria's government lasted only a few months before being replaced, in April 1988, by one headed by Ciriaco De Mita. After holding the post of secretary of the DC for six years, longer than anyone else in the history of the party, De Mita now became President of the Council of Ministers as well. To all appearances he was the most powerful politician in Italy.

In reality, his position was more precarious than secure. The Christian Democrats had a tendency to conspire against over-powerful figures in their own party, as Fanfani had learned to his cost in 1959. De Mita, in spite of his repeated calls to abandon factionalism in the party, had carefully strengthened his own 'left-wing' current, and steered its men into key positions in the state apparatus. At the end of 1987, in reaction to what was seen as De Mita's increasingly autocratic exercise of power, a new and powerful Christian Democrat faction, Azione Popolare, came into being. Baptized immediately as *'il grande centro'*, the new grouping drew in some of the most powerful figures in the party – from Antonio Gava and Enzo Scotti to Arnaldo Forlani, Emilio Colombo and Flaminio Piccoli. The 'Dorotei' had been reborn. De Mita was aware of the danger they posed to him, and in the formation of his government tried to appease them as far as he could. Antonio Gava, the historic boss of Neapolitan Christian Democratic politics, and one with a most dubious past,[80] became nothing less than Minister of the Interior.

Even so, the bait was not enough. De Mita had other opponents, outside the ranks of the *'neodorotei'*: for different reasons, both Giulio Andreotti and Bettino Craxi were happy to conspire in his downfall.[81] The showdown came at the XVIIIth Congress of the Christian Democrats, held in February 1989.[82] Of the 1,249 delegates (a most baroque affair), 37 per cent backed *'il grande centro'*, 35 per cent the 'Left' of De Mita, 17.8 per cent Andreotti, 7 per cent 'Forze Nuove' of Carlo Donat Cattin, and 3.2 per cent Amintore Fanfani. The congress duly elected the veteran and rather colourless Arnaldo Forlani as the new secretary. In his acceptance speech he emphasized the Christian origins that inspired the party's actions: 'We have received, and we must always remember it, a Mandate and a Mission. We have been invested with a responsibility which is in part different [from that of the other parties], which has more profound roots, and in the face of which we must react with a singular and renewed capacity for devotion and sacrifice.'[83]

The XVIIIth Congress, with its vintage combination of ruthless in-fighting and Catholic rhetoric, was only the first act in De Mita's defenestration. The second came some months later, once again at a Congress, but this time the Socialist one at Milan, of May 1989. Craxi and Forlani met somewhat incongruously in a camper which was Craxi's temporary head-quarters at the Congress. The upshot of the meeting was that De Mita was immediately replaced as prime minister by Giulio Andreotti, who duly formed his sixth government on 23 July 1989. In this way the 'CAF' came into being. Its name derived from the first letters of the names of the three men who had created it: Craxi, Andreotti and Forlani – Italy's most aggressive politician, its most subtle one, and the one who epitomized best the time-honoured qualities of mediation and immobility. The alliance was to last three years, until the fateful general elections of April 1992.

There could be little doubt that with the demise of De Mita, Italy had swung further to the right. Andreotti's faction, intimately linked with the more moderate elements in the Vatican and with *Comunione e Liberazione*, rapidly occupied many of the important positions in the public sector. One of the key changes was the replacement of Romano Prodi by Franco Nobili at the head of IRI. At the same time Franco Reviglio's place at ENI was taken by his fellow Socialist, Gabriele Cagliari. Andreotti's was a peculiarly Roman dominance, with the banks, the municipal government and even the two football teams of the capital (Roma and Lazio) firmly in the hands of his friends. One of their elected meeting places, in fact, was the director's box at the Olympic stadium on a Sunday afternoon, a ritual site where they could receive favoured clients and be admired by the general public.[84]

A certain aura of solidity and permanence soon surrounded the 'CAF', in contrast to the previous period of bitter personal rivalry between Craxi and De Mita. The traditional ways of running the Republic seemed to have taken on a new lease of life, with the political class clustered around the unflappable figure of Giulio Andreotti. He returned to the Presidency of the Council of Ministers with the same style – serene and cynical, understated and sarcastic – that had been his hallmark during the previous forty years. His was a constant and seemingly reassuring presence on television in these years, above all in variety and chat shows.[85] But there was always a mysterious and sinister side to him, a sort of glacial reserve. At Palermo in 1983, Eugenio Scalfari, the editor of *la Repubblica*, asked De Mita, 'Do you trust Andreotti?', to which De Mita replied, after a long silence: 'Who is Andreotti, according to you? Do you know anything about him? Do you really know who he is? I don't.'[86] And Federico Fellini, who was his friend, described him as 'the guardian of an undefined area, a person who has to introduce you into another dimension which you don't fully understand'.[87]

b. REFORMS AND REFORMISM

In the light of what happened after 1992, it is tempting to offer an interpretation of this last summer of Italy's ruling politicians couched principally in terms of arrogant and corrupt indifference, a fiddling by latter-day Neros while Rome burned;[88] or, at the very least, of a steady decline throughout the 1980s and early 1990s in the ruling parties' capacity to govern.[89] Seen in these terms, the fall of the political class was inevitable and consequent primarily upon its incompetence and misdeeds.

The reality was rather more complex, and interesting. The tenth legislature of the Italian parliament (1987–92), and in particular the two Andreotti governments (for he succeeded himself, forming a seventh government in April 1991[90]), were actually a period of considerable reforming zeal. The list of measures passed in this period was, at least on the surface, an impressive one. In the field of European political economy, the most important were the La Pergola[91] law of 9 March 1989, which reorganized Italy's policy making *vis-à-vis* the European Community, the entry of Italy into the narrow band of the European monetary system (January 1990), the abolition in the following six months of all restrictions on the free flow of capital; in the field of internal political economy, the Amato law (30 July 1990), which allowed public sector banks to change their legal status from trusts, foundations and associations into joint stock corporations, the anti-trust law (10 October 1990) and that on insider trading, as well as the law of 1991 which granted the Bank of Italy full autonomy from the Treasury to fix interest rates; in the institutional sphere, the reform of the Presidency of the Council of Ministers (23 August 1988), and that of local government (8 June 1990); in public administration, the law of 7 August 1990, making individual civil servants responsible to the general public for their actions and establishing fixed time limits for single procedures; in the mass media, the Mammì law of August 1990, which at last regulated the free-for-all in this field of the previous fourteen years; in social policy, the Martelli law on immigration of 29 February 1990, the first comprehensive legislation of its kind in Italy, and the equal opportunities law of 21 March 1991; in educational policy, various provisions for increasing the autonomy of the university system; finally, with regard to the environment, the law on land protection (18 May 1989), and that aimed at extending Italy's limited national parks (6 December 1991). All in all, there was no comparison between this record of legislation and that of the Craxi years.

Straight away, and in fairness to previous governments, it must be noted that some of these measures had distant origins, and their slow journey to becoming law only reached fruition in this period. Most, though, were individual initiatives which reflected the peculiar composition of the governments of these years. While many Ministers epitomized continuity and immobility, there were others of considerable intellectual stature and technical expertise, often in key posts. It was as if the party leaders had realized that mere loyalty and a dividing of the spoils were in no way sufficient. Symptomatic of these positions was the ascribing of the key post of the ministry of the Treasury to two very able, if contrasting figures: from 1987 to 1989 to the Socialist Giuliano Amato, who had previously been Craxi's under-secretary at the Presidency of the council of ministers; and thereafter to Guido Carli, who had been the long-serving Governor of the Bank of Italy in the 1960s and 1970s.[92] Carli himself was fully aware of the ambiguous position in which he found himself. He recorded in his *Memoirs*: 'They were three years of hand-to-hand fighting, in which I was often defeated but sometimes managed to extract some sort of result.'[93]

To make sense of, and distinguish between, the reforms of these years, it is perhaps worth returning to the analytical distinctions introduced in my *History of Contemporary Italy*, with reference to the aspirations of the centre-left governments of the 1960s.[94] At that time three distinct lines had emerged. The first was that of *corrective* reform, which sought to strengthen Italian capitalism by remedying the deformations and imbalances endemic in its development. The second was *structural* reform, which did not seek to correct capitalism, but to supersede it. Structural reforms were seen as cumulative, a sort of 'revolutionary reformism', as Riccardo Lombardi called them,[95] a series of measures which would lead to socialism. The third line, the *minimalist* one, was as its name implied. Reforms served, in this vision, only to ensure the status quo, to maintain and reinforce existing equilibriums, above all in the political sphere.

By the 1980s, these categories were in need of adjustment, both for the Italian situation and elsewhere. In particular, a chasm had come to divide two different views regarding the nature of the 'correction' necessary for contemporary capitalism. On the one hand there survived a view of corrective reform, common both to social democracy and to social Catholicism, which stressed the need for strong state intervention and planning. From the 1940s onwards, this tradition had done little to renew itself, and nothing to analyse the macroscopic defects that had emerged in every European public sector. On the other, a new wave of right-wing liberal thinking had broken with force on to the international scene. For its exponents, capitalism was suffering not from a lack of control, but from an excess of it. Modern economies would only realize their true potential if markets were freed to do their jobs, and the state withdrew from its over-protective social and economic role. Far from being minimalist, this latter position implied a drastic revision of post-war relations between economy, society and state.

If these various distinctions are applied to the activities of the tenth legislature of the Italian Republic, important differences emerge. Here it is not my intention to deal with all the laws listed above (many of which will be discussed separately in the chapters that follow), but rather to establish broad distinctions which may permit an overall judgement. Minimalist legislation was certainly present. The Mammì law of 1990 on telecommunications, for instance, was a classic of its kind. Indeed, its proposer, the Republican Oscar Mammì, the Minister for Post and Telecommunications, was at pains to establish his minimalist credentials, constantly making the distinction between 'desirable laws' and 'possible laws'. In the case in question, the only 'possible' law was that which confirmed Berlusconi's dominance of commercial television. The new legislation could with difficulty be described as 'liberal' reformism, because instead of fighting restricted markets and oligopoly, it simply sanctioned them. Furthermore, it contained no strategic thinking about the relationship between television as a public service and television as a commercial enterprise.[96]

The approval of the Mammì law was the occasion for a major parliamentary battle at the end of July 1990. Berlusconi had lobbied parliament in massive fashion,[97] and the left replied with a campaign ably orchestrated by a young leader of the PDS, Walter Veltroni, who was enamoured of the cinema. Neatly combining cultural and political objectives, Veltroni aimed to prevent films shown on television being constantly interrupted for commercial breaks. He assembled an impressive supporting cast which included Federico Fellini, Alberto Moravia and Marcello Mastroianni, and inside parliament he was backed by the left of the DC, who were no friends of the pro-Socialist Silvio Berlusconi. In the Senate the amendment limiting advertisements during films was duly improved.[98]

Faced with this challenge from the Senate, the Socialists pushed Andreotti to call for a vote of confidence in the House of Deputies. Five ministers of the left faction of the Christian Democrats resigned in protest from the government. Such a desertion *en masse* could have been expected in normal circumstances to have led to a government crisis. Instead, Andreotti responded imperturbably, replacing the five ministers in less than twenty-four hours and ensuring the definitive approval of the Mammì law by the beginning of August 1990.

The course of the debate on the regulation of television had been instructive, for it had revealed the 'CAF''s determination and cohesion, which cut across traditional party demarcations. It also revealed the connection between strong vested interests in the new service sector of the economy and a highly reductionist view of reform. However, by no means all the legislation of these years was of this sort. Much of it, instead, belonged firmly to the category of corrective reform, but of a particular kind, with a notable gap separating intent and execution, the letter of the law and its implementation. Here was a recurrent category in the history of the Republic: that of a corrective reform which on paper appeared far-sighted and innovative, but which was left unimplemented in part or in whole, either through flaws in its conception, or through lack of funding, or because of the inadequacy and unwillingness of the state machinery itself.[99]

Compared to the law on television, much of the legislation of the years 1987–92 was indeed less particularist and more ambitious in intent, but was deeply vitiated in its implementation. The Martelli law on immigration of 1990, for instance, contained liberal features aiming at the successful integration of immigrant communities, but these were put into operation only in minimal part. Instead, the repressive aspects of the law were those which received most attention.[100] The environmental reforms put forward by a highly respected Minister and one who had great experience in the problems of planning, the Socialist Giorgio Ruffolo, were to a considerable extent nullified by the absence of scope, funds and personnel accorded to the new ministry.[101] The Amato reform of the banking system had the intent of opening up the public banks to real competition. In the event, vested political interest in the sector profited from the state's 'golden share' of 51 per cent in order to minimize change.[102] The law of August 1990 on the reform of the public administration took corrective reform into the belly of the beast, but resulted principally, as we shall see in Chapter 7, in evasive action on the part of the bureaucrats themselves.

What then remained of the reforming impetus of these years? It is tempting to reply nothing, and thus confirm the broad picture of governmental incompetence, though whether this latter was growing or not remains a moot point. But in certain key areas, all in the realm of political economy, the reformers were successful, and it is vital to understand that *their very success* was an important contributory element to the causation of the crisis which was to explode in 1992. Under Carli, amid many hesitations, the Bank of Italy was granted complete autonomy to decide interest rates.[103] In spite of the fact that the annual deficit in public spending had not diminished, the primary balance (i.e. net of interest repayments) did, and in 1992 actually showed a surplus.[104] In January 1990 Andreotti chose, again on Carli's advice, to place Italy in the narrow band of the EMS. During the six months of the Italian presidency of the European Community (July to December 1990), the country's representatives played a significant role in accelerating the process of monetary union, and then, in 1991, in the drawing up and the voting of the Maastricht treaty. All these were not structural reforms in the old socialist sense, an aspiration which had exited from the language of Italian politics, but structural in another sense, that of tying the fate of Italy very strongly to the economic destiny of Europe.

The European initiatives of the Andreotti governments will be analysed in detail below. What is important here is to reiterate the complexity of the strictly political origins of the crisis, and their derivation from *both* the failures of the ruling groups and from their successes. Time and again, in major political crises, not to speak of revolutions, it is the attempt to reform that causes events to precipitate. In Italy in the early 1990s, the reforming impetus could hardly be called of Gorbachovian proportions, but the choices made in political economy, implying as they did greater rigour and the reduction of public spending, actually tightened the noose around the ruling parties' neck. Nor was this a mere Pavlovian reaction to external constraint. Other options were available: the lira could have been left out of the narrow band of European currencies; it would have been possible to have taken a British and reductionist view of Maastricht; the Bank of Italy could have been, and nearly was, rendered less autonomous. The choices made undermined the consensus for party government, but kept the dialogue with Europe open. They should be recognized for what they were.

7. Warning Signs

Guido Carli had his way, more or less, on Europe, but not on other matters closer to home. His own list of failures, drawn up at the end of his *Memoirs*, was a stark one: no reform of the pension system, no health reform, no privatizations; with the result that while he was at the Treasury 'the public deficit, in spite of [our] continuous corrective action, showed no signs of diminishing'.[105] Nor could the government leaders count any longer on the growth rates of the 1980s to help them along their way. The recession of the early 1990s, as we have noted in Chapter 1, certainly did not hit Italy as hard as it did Britain, but it took money out of people's pockets at a time when fiscal pressure was on the increase. The 'squeeze' was on, not yet in draconian fashion, but sufficiently to begin its habitual corrosive action in terms of electoral consent.

On the surface, the 'CAF' looked strong enough. The tenth legislature (1987–92) was one of the few that ran its full term. In that time, the major opposition party was in complete disarray, the level of intra-party feuding was kept relatively under control, the key posts in the public sector were ascribed to loyal place-men. Yet there were disquieting elements of scandal and dissent which served to raise the temperature of Italian politics in the early 1990s.

a. THE 'PICKAXE' PRESIDENT

One of the most spectacular of these was the activities and pronouncements of no less a figure than the President of the Republic. Among De Mita's few successes had been the construction of a broad consensus around the name of the Christian Democrat politician Francesco Cossiga to succeed Sandro Pertini in 1985. Cossiga was an amiable Sardinian who had been Minister of the Interior at the time of Moro's assassination, and who had resigned, deeply shocked, after his death. He had a reputation for discretion and good sense, as well as a passion for English constitutional history and Cardinal Newman. In the first years of his presidency he maintained a low profile which seemed to imply that he had chosen a notarial vision of the presidency, in contrast to Pertini's more extrovert and interventionist style.

In 1990 Cossiga changed tack in a most remarkable way. He suddenly decided that he would 'empty his shoes of some pebbles', as he colourfully put it, and launched into an extraordinary series of polemics. He attacked the party system for its failure to introduce reform, the magistrates for interfering in the political sphere, the PDS for its 'Stalinism', the press for taking too many liberties (he was particularly incensed at being called a 'March hare' by Tana De Zulueta in the pages of *The Economist*). He addressed the nation with increasing frequency on radio and television, calling for the creation of a Second Republic, with a strong President at its head. The notary had become the *'picconatore'*, the 'pickaxe man'.

At the same time Cossiga launched a series of violent verbal attacks on individuals. No President of the Republic had ever done this before, and Cossiga's language was so vulgar and offensive as to bring the office of the Presidency into disrepute.[106] His justification was that there was an inter-party conspiracy to unseat him, and that he had to reply in kind. He broke openly with both Andreotti and De Mita, was disowned by his own party and resigned from it. The PSI, on the other hand, continued to support him.

Doubts about the sanity of the President were aired very publicly at this time. He was certainly under considerable strain, but a British journalist, Amanda Mitchison, who went to interview him in February 1992, found rather 'a wily operator who hops with suspicious ease from Cossiga One to Cossiga Two'.[107] The President, in fact, had a clear strategy. Sensing a growing insufferance towards the ruling parties, the political system and the state, he wanted to try to lead the protest by portraying himself as an honest, blunt man, different from the rest of the political class. He was neither the first, nor the last, to play this game in Italian politics. It was a classic populist strategy, and earned him considerable support in 1991 and 1992.

Cossiga also left little doubt about the political colouring of his version of a 'Second Republic'. He was fulsome in his praise of the armed forces and the Carabinieri, from whom he received public messages of support, he urged the democratic rehabilitation of the neo-Fascists of the MSI, he defended as 'patriots' those members of the P2 whom he knew, and he belittled the significance of the secret lodge's activity.[108] In 1992, Cossiga's term as President came to an end, and with it his possibility of playing a leading role in the coming crisis. The latter years of his presidency had been deeply disconcerting, and certainly damaging to reasoned democratic discourse. Not since Antonio Segni (Cossiga's first patron in politics) had dabbled with De Lorenzo's counter-insurgency plans in 1964 had there been so unreliable a President.[109]

b. GLADIO

Running parallel to Cossiga's extemporizations, and intimately linked with them, was a fresh scandal which plunged Italy back into fervid debate about its secret history. Once again it was the work of a young investigating magistrate, this time the Venetian Felice Casson, which led to previously hidden facts coming partially into the light. Casson had been investigating one of the unsolved cases of the 'strategy of tension' – the death of three *carabinieri* at Peteano in May 1972 – when he came across evidence of hidden caches of arms and explosives belonging to the secret services. He requested and surprisingly received permission from the President of the Council of Ministers (Andreotti) to work in the archives of the secret services in Forte Boccea in Rome. There he found clear evidence of a hidden armed network called Gladio. He informed Andreotti, who on 3 August 1990 told parliament for the first time of the existence of Gladio.[110]

Some, though by no means all, of the history of the organization was pieced together in the following months. A crucial document relative to it was an agreement signed in 1956 between SIFAR (the Italian military secret service) and the CIA which spoke of a 'Stay-Behind' organization, a clandestine network of groups which would be activated in the case of foreign invasion. Its tasks would include sabotage, guerrilla warfare, propaganda, information collecting, etc. Its training ground was the military base at Capo Marragiu near Alghero in Sardinia, and its arms and explosives were buried in 139 different hiding places spread throughout the peninsula. In all its activities Gladio was to be heavily dependent upon the training and direction provided by the CIA. The names of some 622 recruits emerged from the inquiries, though it was not clear whether this was the full strength of the force.

The discovery of the secret organization created a furore in a country which had lost all faith in its secret services and which had so many unexplained acts of violence in its recent history. The Italian revelations also sparked off investigations into similar organizations in other European countries, especially Belgium and Switzerland. Only the British government, in keeping with its long-standing tradition of secrecy, maintained a steely silence.[111]

Interpretations of the real significance of Gladio varied markedly. Giulio Andreotti minimized its importance and doubted its illegality. It had been a NATO structure, he claimed, which 'had at its disposition a small network of partisans who could keep communications open and help certain people who had to reach safe zones, in the ill-fated case of a war which resulted in the invasion of Italy. That was all there was to it.'[112] Francesco Cossiga shared Andreotti's opinion, though he gravely doubted the latter's motives for responding so solicitously to Casson's requests for help.[113] For Cossiga Gladio had been an organization of patriots of which he had always known the existence and which he had been proud to help. In December 1991 he denounced himself to the magistrates as being as guilty as anyone for the presumed crimes of the organization, and dared them to proceed against him.

No action was taken, either against Cossiga or those responsible for Gladio,[114] but it is difficult to accept the reassuring official version of the organization's history. To begin with, there was no proof that Gladio's activities or existence were formally covered by Italy's membership of NATO, and every indication that the CIA–SIFAR agreement of 1956 was an illegal act between two national secret services.[115] Furthermore, the Italian secret services had chosen selectively whom to inform, however vaguely, of the existence of Gladio. Only certain Presidents of the Council of Ministers knew about it; Fanfani, for instance, had been kept in the dark throughout the 50s and 60s. After the supposed reform of the secret services of 1977 a parliamentary commission of control for the secret services had been instituted. It too had not been informed.

Worse still, there was abundant evidence that Gladio had been not only a Cold War organization set up to respond to a possible foreign invasion, but above all an instrument for surveillance and possible action against internal enemies (of the left). No senior political authority had been informed that this was its principal purpose. Among the documents found in the archives of the 7th Division of the secret services was a disquieting account of a meeting of December 1972 between the chief of station of the CIA in Rome, Howard 'Rocky' Stone, and his counterparts in Gladio. Stone warned that 'there could occur an extraordinary insurrectionary situation in the South, as a result of which certain pockets of territory could in effect be controlled by forces contrary to the government'. For this reason, suggested Stone, Gladio would have to operate in 'exactly the same way' that the CIA had operated in Vietnam.[116]

The secret organization lived on throughout the 1980s, a decade in which internal insurrection or foreign invasion could hardly have been said to have been on the agenda. Instead Gladio continued as a surveillance and information-gathering organization, to be dissolved by Andreotti only at the end of 1990. As with the P2, so with Gladio, senior officials of the Italian state had used anti-Communism as a pretext for illegal and anti-democratic activities. In the case of Gladio, they had used the resources of the state itself for that purpose.

c. THE REFERENDUM OF 9 JUNE 1991

One of the most significant weaknesses of the political system in the 1980s had been its failure to introduce significant electoral or institutional reform. The Bozzi bicameral commission (1983–5), as we have seen, had come to nothing. The only steps forward had been the reorganization of the Presidency of the Council of Ministers, the reduction in secret (and thus wildcat) voting in the two houses of parliament, and the reform of local government; but none of these was sufficient to combat the structural deficiencies outlined at the beginning of this chapter.

In response to the stalemate produced by the parties, a young Christian Democrat deputy, Mario Segni, son of the former President of the Republic, launched a courageous initiative in February 1990. He aimed to correct the system from below, by means of a popular referendum. Referenda in Italy were only of the abrogative variety; that is, they could not propose legislation, but could only exercise the negative power of repealing an existing law. Segni proposed to undermine Italy's very pure system of proportional representation by means of a three-pronged attack: the reduction of the importance of the proportional system in elections for the Senate; its abolition in local elections; and the end of multiple-choice preference votes in elections for the Chamber of Deputies.[117]

In January 1991, the Constitutional Court ruled that only the referendum on preference voting could go ahead. This was a grave blow, for many considered it to be the most marginal of the three issues. None the less, the referendum remained an important test. Being able to choose up to four candidates of the same political party had been a historic vehicle of political clientelism, a means of tying local clients to patrons, and of building factional strength in specific areas. It was much more of a southern than a northern phenomenon, and had been most used by Christian Democrat voters.[118]

Segni was a dissident within his own party, an obstinate moderate who wished to break the stranglehold of party politics in the name of effective government.[119] In support of the referendum he assembled a highly variegated alliance, which included Catholic intellectuals like Pietro Scoppola, the employers' organization Confindustria, the Radical party, and the hesitant and divided 'Cosa' (PCI–PDS). A significant contribution came from Catholic

173

rank-and-file and voluntary organizations such as the ACLI (Associazione Cattolica Lavoratori Italiani), as well as other sections of Catholic civil society, with the Veneto in the forefront. Their presence in an oppositional referendum of this sort was a clear sign of shifting allegiances.[120]

Against them were aligned the rump of the ruling parties as well as the public (and private) mass media. The Socialist Enrico Manca, Director-General of the RAI, justified his failure to accord the referendum any coverage on television by saying that the promoting committee was not an 'institutional subject', thus confirming the unsavoury view that the task of public television was to cover only the utterances of officialdom.[121] The Socialist party as a whole was very hostile to the referendum, as was most of the DC and the President of the Republic. Vittorio Sbardella, Andreotti's lieutenant in Rome, covered the walls of the capital with posters advising abstention, and in Naples Antonio Gava made it known to the party faithful that he was not amused.[122] The date of the referendum was fixed for 9 June, a Sunday in early summer; Bettino Craxi advised the Italians to go to the sea for the day. In the face of such formidable opposition, the task of reaching the necessary quorum of voters (over 50 per cent of those having the right to vote) seemed an arduous one. Achille Occhetto recounted later: 'That evening I went out to dinner on the banks of the Tiber, on the edge of the city of Rome . . . I saw the queues of cars, jammed up as they were coming back from the sea, and I said to myself: we'll never make it, they'll never get home in time to vote.'[123]

Instead, the referendum result proved a great surprise, as well as a significant warning to the 'CAF': 62.5 per cent of the electors had voted, and of these an overwhelming 95.6 per cent had said 'yes' to the abolition of multi-preference voting. A different Italy had made its voice heard, one that was much less servile than either government or opposition had imagined.

d. THE RISE OF THE NORTHERN LEAGUE

The last element of disturbance to the ruling parties was one which initially seemed little more than a passing political joke, but which in the long run proved the most corrosive of all. In the 1987 national elections, as we have seen, the Lombard League had gained representation in the Italian parliament for the first time, with its leader Umberto Bossi elected as a senator for Varese. His rough and ready ways, popular and backwoods origins, badly tailored clothes and undone tie, all fitted in very poorly with the immaculate senior party citizens and the red plush of the Senate's home, Palazzo Madama. To the outside world he appeared at first as another of those fleeting aberrations of Italian politics, similar in duration, though not in form, to the porno star Ilona Staller, whom the Radicals had successfully elected to the Chamber of Deputies in 1983.

Umberto Bossi was not to be dismissed so lightly. His movement was one of many neo-localist organizations which flourished in the Europe of the 1980s, protests against the distance of centralized politics and the narrow careerism of many of its politicians.[124] Initially, the League put down strong roots in a provincial male culture, that of the popular classes of the 'urbanized countryside' of the northern Lombard provinces. This was a culture of the bar and the local football stadium, strongly sexist in its language, with an emphasis on the values of relatively closed communities, of hard work and conspicuous consumption. It celebrated its Lombard particularity through the use of local dialect, and the choice of a symbol destined to make its mark, a twelfth-century warrior, Alberto da Giussano, with raised sword, rallying the Lombard communes against the Emperor Frederick Barbarossa.

After 1987, Bossi expanded cleverly on this rather restricted base. He reduced the narrowly ethnic qualities of his movement, for they were of uncertain appeal or definition: the dialect was no longer widespread, and it was difficult indeed to speak in the name of a Lombard nation which had never existed.[125] Instead, he talked of a community of interests among the 'nation of producers' of all northern Italy, and in November 1989 he formed the Northern League, together with Franco Rocchetta's Liga Veneta and other smaller organizations. The electoral base of his party rapidly expanded: small industrialists as well as their workers, shopkeepers, some of the white-collar urban middle classes, women as well as men. The *leghisti* were distinguished as much by cultural traits as by economic ones – they were not highly educated but highly practical, the unsophisticated but determined inhabitants of that new Italy that lay outside the major cities – a world of corrugated-iron worksheds, of urban sprawl and of *villette*. Suddenly, some of those key social strata which weighed so particularly in post-Fordist Italy, both in industry and in services, had found, at least in many provinces of the North and North-East of the country, a new voice with which they could associate.

What exactly did that voice have to say? It spoke both to the material interests and the *amour propre* of these social groups. It promised revolt and resistance against the Roman politicians and parties, their inefficient bureaucracy and increasingly vexatious taxes. It promised 'freedom' in the sense of autonomy, of liberation from centralized oppression and corruption.[126] The future lay with the Europe of the regions, not that of the nations. Government should be on a local basis, staffed by local people, with taxes locally collected and spent. The values of the North, entrepreneurship, efficiency, the capacity to work hard and to save, were contrasted with those of a lazy and parasitic South, which most certainly included Rome. Sometimes autonomy meant secession, at others federalism. In either case, the Risorgimento had been a bad mistake. A unified Italy, controlled from Rome by a centralized state, had been an undesirable and unrealizable objective. The two parts of the peninsula were irreconcilable; Garibaldi should never have left for Marsala in 1860.[127]

The voice of the League also spoke cleverly to the prejudices and fears of these social strata.[128] The 'other' was not welcome, and the local community, a traditional *Gemeinschaft* transplanted into the modern world, did not make a virtue out of diversity or plurality. The *'terroni'*, the southerners who had 'invaded' the North in such massive numbers during the 'economic miracle', would do well to go back to where they came from.[129] Even less welcome were the *extracomunitari* (and how perfectly that word fitted the League's view of them!), who began to arrive in the North in small but significant numbers in the mid-1980s. Some of them could be used as casual labour, but they would never be considered part of the community.

The overt quality of the League's racism varied on tactical grounds from moment to moment, but it was never far beneath the surface. At the first national congress of the League, held in December 1989, Bossi was shockingly explicit on the subject: assimilation 'could not apply to black immigrants, for whom integration is not foreseeable even at the distance of many centuries. With them the classic mechanisms of social integration, which are marriage and children, do not function, with the result that it would be impossible to build an ethnic link without generating grave racial tensions within society.'[130]

Fears were both xenophobic and material. The provinces of the northern hills and mountains, which were always to be the League's strongholds, had grown rich on hard work, family labour, and tax evasion in the 1970s and 1980s. If we return to Lumezzane, in the hills above Brescia, which had so brilliantly specialized in the making of cutlery (see above, Chapter 1, p. 18), we find it highly prosperous in the early 1990s, but also suffering its first kidnapping (of a rich industrialist's daughter) in November 1991.[131] There were fears that the state, by sending accused Mafiosi awaiting trial into forced exile in northern localities, would introduce southern criminal networks into the North. There was fear, too, that the almost miraculous transformation in family fortunes in the previous twenty years could evaporate as swiftly as it had occurred. The downturn in the economy at the beginning of the 90s preoccupied the 'nation of producers', but not as much as did the prospect of the central state tightening its fiscal net.

Two elements characterized those northern provinces (in Lombardy: Brescia, Bergamo, Varese, Como, Sondrio, Cremona and Pavia; in the Veneto, Verona and Vicenza) whose populations began to vote in significant numbers for the Northern League in the period 1987–92. One was that they were strong areas of traditionally Catholic culture, 'white' zones rather than 'red', which had always turned out *en masse* for the Christian Democrats. The other was that they were provinces of small and medium industry in tumultuous expansion, among the most dynamic in the whole of Italy.[132] Certainly, the one weighed heavily upon the other. Economic and social modernization had brutally diminished church attendance and decimated the Catholic subculture.

However, as has been suggested above, it was not so much the *abandonment* of Catholic values as their *continuation* in another, more secular, form which helps to explain the coincidence between the 'white' zones and the strongholds of the League. Those who supported Bossi took with them from their broadly Catholic education the localism and exclusiveness of northern, small-town Catholic Italy, its sense of hierarchy and mediation, its belief in the networks of a closed community.[133]

As for the local Christian Democrats, they had governed some of these northern provincial cities, such as Brescia, Bergamo and Verona, with a great deal of competence in previous decades. The 1980s, though, saw a decline in the quality of the party's personnel and a marked increase in corruption. This latter phenomenon will be analysed in detail in the next chapter. Suffice it to say here that at Verona the number of DC members increased miraculously, and spuriously, from 27,300 in 1984 to 43,500 in 1992, but the party sections remained ever more empty.[134] The DC also paid the price for its long history of aid for the South and of southern leadership. The Venetian and Lombard DC had always delivered great numbers of votes to the party, but the last northern President of the Council of Ministers had been Mariano Rumor in 1974.

In an era when vast financial resources and constant media presence were considered the *sine qua non* of politics, it is worth pointing out that the Northern League gradually built its support in the most traditional and primitive ways: fly-posting, door-to-door canvassing, local meetings, the spraying of slogans such as 'Via da Roma' on the bridges over the northern motorways. The leaders of the major parties, with Craxi to the forefront, were dismissive of the League's efforts, but it was precisely this David and Goliath syndrome that held considerable appeal at a local level.

Bossi was the undisputed, charismatic and authoritarian leader of the movement, a politician who was consistently underrated in the early years of the League, but who was able to keep the bulk of the Northern League together in the face of innumerable desertions and breakaways. There was no room for democracy in the organization, and never had been. In the statute of the Lombard League, underwritten in 1986 by five founding members (Umberto Bossi, his partner Manuela Marone, his brother-in-law Pierangelo Brivio, and his close friends Giuseppe Leoni and Marino Moroni), all power was concentrated in the hands of the 'ordinary' members, a group of 119 men and eight women, all chosen personally by Bossi.[135] In an interesting, repeated ritual the local councillors and national deputies of the organization were required to swear a solemn oath of loyalty at a gathering of the League's faithful at Pontida, the locality where on 7 April 1167 the Lombard communes had sworn to resist the Emperor Frederick Barbarossa.

Once Bossi had widened the appeal of his organization, and founded the Northern League, his electoral success was very rapid. At the regional and local elections of 1990 he made a major breakthrough, with 18.9 per cent of the votes in the Lombard regional elections, 6.1 per cent in Liguria, 5.9 per cent in Veneto, and 5.1 per cent in Piedmont. Some 750 local councillors had been elected, and the League could boast its first majority in local government – at Cene, 3,700 inhabitants and fifteen minutes from Bergamo. A local policeman told the journalist Giovanna Pajetta: ' "You see, by now we're all involved in this adventure. It's like when the DC had just been founded, straight after the war, and you still didn't have the courage to come out openly in its support" . . . But when I asked him from where this desire for change at all costs had come, the policeman Vismara took offence: "Listen here, we've all got television and radio, you know. We've seen all that squalid and corrupt behaviour, all that waste . . ." [136]

The rise of the League, the referendum of 9 June 1991, the 'pickaxing' of Cossiga, the continuing saga of Italy's scandalous secret history – all these were signals of fractures in Italy's political system at the beginning of the 1990s. However, the system had been in worse trouble before. The crisis of the early 1970s, with its massive social disruption, the 'strategy of tension', the near bankruptcy of the state, had been infinitely graver, but the political class had survived it. To understand better why it was that 1992 proved so fateful and devouring, it is necessary to leave the surface of Italian politics, and to look more deeply at certain key questions and structures in the public sphere. This will be the purpose of the next two chapters, before I return in the third and final part of the book (Chapters 8 and 9) to assemble the complicated causes of the hurricane of 1992–3, and to chart its extraordinary course and outcome.

Chapter 6

Corruption and the Mafia

1. Political Corruption

*I*N THE 1980s the Italian political system was not only blocked but deeply degenerate. From time to time corruption scandals involving politicians hit the headlines. Significantly, some of the most notorious cases came from the North of the country, as if to underline that what was happening was not a question of latitude or longitude, but of national culture. In March 1983 the local council of Turin was brought into disrepute by revelations of the corrupt practices of the deputy mayor and of a group of city councillors. In June of the same year the former President of the Ligurian regional government, the Socialist Alberto Teardo, was arrested and later convicted, together with his closest collaborators, on charges of corruption principally concerning building contracts.[1] On each occasion the national political leadership of the governing parties tried to minimize the extent of corruption, or worse still accused the magistrates involved of political bias. Bettino Craxi, for instance, denounced the Ligurian magistrates in the Teardo case for abusing their position 'for vulgar electoral and political purposes'. He went on: 'I am indignant, because I cannot discern any quest for justice in initiatives of this type, for they are animated instead by a spirit of personal and political vendetta.'[2]

In reality, such cases were only the tip of the iceberg, the most visible evidence of an entire *system* of corruption, whose workings were to be revealed in full only in 1992, when the great 'Tangentopoli' ('Bribesville') scandal exploded at Milan.

Political corruption has been usefully defined by Donatella della Porta and Yves Mény as 'a clandestine exchange between two "markets": on the one hand, the political and/or administrative market, on the other the social and economic'.[3] Exchange of this sort is clandestine because it is illicit. The object of the exchange is usually money in return for privileged treatment or information. All over Europe the actors have been, for the most part, businessmen and professionals from the private sphere, and civil servants and politicians from the public ones. Roles, though, often become blurred, as civil servants moved into politics (as was the long-standing case of France), or ex-politicians became members of the boards of large private firms (as was the case increasingly in Britain in the 1980s and 1990s).

The extent of political corruption in modern democracies depends fundamentally upon the socio-political culture that has developed over time in any given country. The creation of public ethics is a long and complicated process, and certainly not an irreversible one. It will depend upon administrative structures, that is the degree of transparency of modern bureaucracies, the limits upon their discretionary power, the degree to which they are subject to substantive and not merely formal controls; upon political practice, the extent to which the interests and actions of democratic representatives are clearly codified and controllable; upon legal culture, on the tension between custom and the law, for what is corruption in one country may be regarded as standard practice in another; finally and most importantly, upon processes of education both within and outside families, so that the very air that one breathes as a citizen can come to contain the oxygen of certain values and modes of behaviour rather than others. This last factor helps to determine the level of the 'moral costs' of corruption, the extent to which exposure brings not only legal sanctions but social disgrace.[4]

Political corruption can flourish both where there is too much state intervention, with parasitical and overblown public sectors, and where there is too little, as in the rapid and recent processes of deregulation and privatization. All over Europe, the 1980s and early 1990s saw a significant increase in political corruption. Or at least it became more visible.

In the Italian case, in spite of many claims to the contrary, the widespread system of political corruption was not new or merely a child of the 1980s. Its origins, on the contrary, were deeply rooted in the political practice of the country. Because judges are not historians, the mass of evidence that has been accumulated by them refers only to the most recent period, but the collusion between politicians, businessmen and civil servants has a much longer history in the Republic, most of which is completely uncharted. Indeed one of the most disquieting questions about the condition of contemporary Italy, as that of Japan or Russia, concerns its long-term moral standing; the degree that is, to which corruption has become *endemic* in the public life of the country. The chronology of this process is not clear. Certainly, any simplistic distinction between an earlier era of relative honesty and the degenerate 1980s should be treated with some scepticism. However, it is the case that the 1980s witnessed a new and organized rapacity on the part of politicians, a spoils system which extended throughout the peninsula.

a. LOCAL GOVERNMENT AND 'BUSINESS POLITICIANS'

A good way to understand the mechanisms by which this system operated is to concentrate upon local government contracting. Regional, provincial and city politicians – presidents and vice-presidents, mayors and their deputies, *assessori* and councillors – increasingly became what Alessandro Pizzorno has called 'business politicians', interested primarily in the use of office to accumulate capital, and in the use of capital to further their careers.[5] The many levels and offices of local government signified that by the 1990s some 100,000 persons were involved at a political level, while employees numbered nearly 700,000.[6] The majority of these were honest, but a significant minority were willing and anxious to exploit the economic potential of their offices. In Verona, for instance, the old guard of Christian Democrat politicians recounted how they had been displaced and disoriented by an upwardly mobile and unscrupulous new generation. Agostino Montagnoli, one of the veteran leaders of the local party, told the historian Federico Bozzini:

Maybe I'm ingenuous, but I would never have believed that there was such deep-rooted and diffuse corruption. I could certainly imagine that buying packs of membership inscriptions, financing conferences, offering dinners, publishing journals on glossy paper, all cost vast amounts of money. But – and I insist because it is the honest truth – I could never have supposed that they were such blatant thieves. When I learned that the parties and factions were taking regular percentage cuts of public contracts, I was utterly appalled.[7]

The principal *modus operandi* of the business politicians was indeed the collecting of kickbacks from local businessmen. Politicians had many ways of extracting illegal payments from firms. They could exclude them, in one way or another, from the list of businesses able to tender for public contracts. They could deprive them of privileged information on the 'confidential' estimates to which bids had to approximate. They could simply delay payments at their discretion.[8] No business wanted to be excluded from the 'magic circle' of local government work. The price to be paid varied: in Milan it oscillated from the 5 per cent on certain work contracts for the municipal transport company (ATM), to the 13.5 per cent for construction work on the subway. In Rome, it cost 10 per cent of the contract to have the privilege of cleaning the offices of the Lazio Region; in Savona, the same cut applied to various public works contracts.[9]

If local politicians could demonstrate that 'exceptional circumstances' required the suspension of normal administrative controls, then they could operate with even greater impunity. In 1989 the Corte dei Conti, the Republic's court of accounts with responsibility for controlling public expenditure, described with alarm the growth of this phenomenon:

It is therefore not by chance that in recent years in place of regular sectorial spending . . . there have arisen a multiplicity of 'emergencies'. Sometimes these have indeed derived from unforeseeable events (such as earthquakes and other natural calamities), but more often from circumstances in which the event can hardly be said to have happened suddenly and unpredictably. 'Emergencies' of this second type have been the infrastructural work for the World Cup 'Italia '90', the public works connected with the celebrations of 1992 concerning Christopher Columbus, housing shortages, the absence of car parks in the major metropolitan areas.[10]

The money collected from kickbacks flowed in a number of different directions. Sometimes it was channelled directly to party headquarters, sometimes to the leaders of the powerful factions within the parties, sometimes it went directly into private pockets.[11] Often the corrupt local politician would use the kickback to reinforce his own power base, which consisted of the packet of votes, the positions of responsibility and the other resources that he had accumulated. Mario Chiesa, a local Socialist politician in Milan whose confessions launched the 'Tangentopoli' scandal of 1992, described how he had built up what he called, rather lugubriously, his own 'Falange': he controlled 7,000 votes, sporting and recreational facilities, the direction of an old people's home (the Pio Albergo Trivulzio). This last was very useful both for the work contracts that could be offered to local firms and the old people who could be wheeled out to vote for a certain party, or part thereof. In 1989–90 Chiesa switched factional allegiance within the local Socialist party and put his organization at the disposal of Bettino Craxi's son, Bobo, who was duly elected as a municipal councillor.[12]

The system of kickbacks was so common in the 1980s that it came to be considered almost as normal procedure. It was called the 'cost of politics', just as publicity and marketing also had their price. The politicians seemed invulnerable, with the result that it was all too easy and convenient to forget that at stake was the concept of honest and impartial administration, and the belief in fair and reasonable competition for local government contracts. In the absence of both of these, Italian local democracy was a dead horse.

b. THE INPUT FROM SOCIETY

In describing the system of kickbacks, it would be quite wrong to assume that the flow of corruption was in one direction alone. Many businessmen later tried to portray themselves as simple victims of the politicians, but the reality was much more complicated and reciprocal. Mario Chiesa talked of politicians and economic lobbies being in 'symbiosis'; Gherardo Colombo, the Milanese magistrate, recounted that 'in many circumstances, in reality, it is political power which seems dependent upon financial power, and not vice versa'; Donatella della Porta, the foremost Italian scholar of these phenomena, has referred to a whole number of businesses which thrived from privileged contacts with local and national politicians.[13]

Business morals were certainly not identical to public ethics. In order to bring them a little closer together, Guido Carli, when he was at the head of Confindustria in 1978, had proposed a 'Statute for Business'. It aimed at introducing 'transparency in the accounts of firms, in their shareholding structure, in every form of help they receive from the State'.[14] His proposals were unanimously rejected by his colleagues at Confindustria in June of that year, with the result that the economic élites traversed the 1980s without any self-imposed constraints. Networks of corruption flourished in their usual meeting-places, overlaying and intertwining with traditional associations and friendships. The bridge and the golf club, the Rotary and the Lions, the offices of wealthy accountants and lawyers, all were privileged locations for the striking of illicit deals. In the major cities of the South, local criminal organizations were often a habitual and almost natural part of these networks.[15]

Payment of the kickback took pre- and post-modern forms. Sometimes money changed hands by means of complicated circuits involving foreign banks, more often briefcases stashed full of used banknotes were simply handed over at agreed meeting-places. The more senior the politician or the businessman, the more likely he was to pretend that such goings-on were beneath him, and leave the dirty work to a trusted subordinate, usually a private secretary or '*portaborse*' (the potentate's 'bag-carrier').[16]

The widespread practice of clientelism, which has been outlined above in Chapter 4, was the context within which political corruption flourished. The two phenomena are not identical.[17] Clientelism was much less covert, it was much more accepted practice, it more rarely involved the direct exchange of cash. There were differences of arena (open or hidden), differences of degree (asking favours was not the same as paying kickbacks), differences of hierarchy (by its very nature clientelism was a vertical diadic relationship, while corruption could take place between equals). On the other hand, clientelism and corruption are not easily separated.[18] The one was the breeding ground for the other, and neither formed part of the official morality.[19] Clientelism was a great grey area, accepted by many, condemned by some, even accepted and condemned by the same person in different situations. Corruption was much less easily accepted, however 'natural' some politicians tried to make it appear.

The different places that clientelism and corruption occupied on the same continuum can be illustrated by looking at hospitals, for these were classic sites of services, salaries and hierarchies of power. In 1963 the president of the Vittorio Emanuele hospital at Catania, Alfio Di Grazia, a DC senator desperate for re-election, had moved potential voters into hospital beds so that they could vote for him at the right moment in the right constituency. Such action was outrageous and illegal, but it was not covert and it clearly belonged, though bizarrely, to the general framework of patron–client relations.[20]

However, what took place in the late 1980s at the Fatebenefratelli hospital of Milan was clearly corruption. Here it was not a case of moving patients out and voters in, but of fixing appointment committees for the coveted post of consultant. Favoured candidates were prepared to pay up to 100 million lire (about £40,000 at that time) in bribes, and selection of the committee was correspondingly adjusted by the so-called 'frozen ball' technique. The trick functioned in the following way. Selection procedures stipulated that in order to avoid favouritism the external member of the committee would be chosen by a lottery system. The names of possible external members were each enclosed in a small ball, and one ball was then to be chosen at random. However, at the Fatebenefratelli hospital (and presumably not only there and not only in the 1980s), the ball containing the 'preferred' name was placed in a freezer in the hours preceding the draw, so that at the crucial moment the hand of the corrupt official would be suitably cooled by the appropriate ball.[21]

Some of the judges' later reconstruction of these goings-on emphasized the strong clan mentality which linked certain professionals, businessmen, administrators and politicians. One such reconstruction talked of 'the presence of a whole series of links deriving from political militancy, friendships, masonic brotherhood and self-interested collaboration, which have constituted the substratum on which the criminal activity of the accused has been constructed'.[22] Marauding élite groups, each with their clientele, roamed through society and the state, sometimes in collaboration and sometimes in competition with each other.

The role of family in all this is as yet little studied, and until social anthropologists and historians take the place of journalists and judges any conclusions must be tentative. It can, however, be suggested that nepotism, the practice of favouring relatives in the conferring of public offices and contracts, stood in relation to familism much as corruption did to clientelism. Within the framework of a set of uneasy relationships between family, civil society and the state, characterized by strong and cohesive family units, a historically weak civil society, and scant respect for a negligent state, it was to be expected that individual families, both powerful and powerless, would view the public sphere as a plundering ground.

Formal laws forbidding nepotism seemed to be all too easily circumvented. In 1992 at Raccuia in the province of Messina there existed an extraordinary coincidence between the fact that the then under-secretary at the Ministry of Post and Telecommunications, the Christian Democrat Giuseppe Astone, had been born in the town, and the high number of persons from the same zone who had been given jobs in his Ministry under a special law favouring the public employment of the handicapped. The list of the supposed *'invalidi'* was little more than a kinship gathering of Astone's friends and clients: one son of the mayor of Raccuia, two sons of the mayor of San Pietro Patti, one son of the vice-mayor of Furnari, one daughter of a local DC deputy, another daughter of a DC *assessore* at Messina, the wife of another *assessore* of the same city, the son of the political secretary of the mayor of Messina, the sister of the vice-mayor of Terranova, a cousin of Astone himself, and so on.[23] The local medical commissions which had to judge the level of handicap of these persons had shown themselves to be remarkably accommodating.

Once again, geography was not necessarily determinant, for what could be found in Sicily was also present in Milan. In the late 1980s the president of the city's airport company put aside 500 million lire to celebrate the anniversary of the first flight from Malpensa airport. He entrusted this sum to a publicity agent by the name of Gabriele Pillitteri. Gabriele happened to be the brother of the mayor of the city, Paolo Pillitteri, who happened also to be Bettino Craxi's brother-in-law.[24] The Craxi family seemed particularly prone to using public resources for their own purposes, although it may be that this impression is only the result of the intense scrutiny to which this particular family has been subjected. In any case, when Bettino Craxi, the then President of the Council of Ministers, visited China in November 1986, the Italian delegation consisted of fifty-two persons, of whom eleven were part of Craxi's personal retinue. They included Anna, his wife, who was the only member of kin permitted by official protocol, his son Bobo, with his fiancée, his daughter Stefania, three different secretaries, his private photographer and a personal assistant. Giulio Andreotti, who was also there as Minister of Foreign Affairs, commented icily, and memorably, 'I am here in China with Craxi and his dear ones.'[25]

Some tentative hypotheses can be advanced with regard to a hierarchy of kinship in relation to the corruption of these years. Corruption was gendered, for it was directed and organized by male heads of families. Father–daughter relations seemed to be of special significance as a motor for accumulation. Italian fathers believe in celebrating in style the marriage of their daughters, and 'business politicians' took a particular joy in giving away their daughters with extraordinary pomp and circumstance. Fraternal solidarities, especially of elder towards younger brothers, were recurrent. As for wives, some of them took a back seat, and protested their innocence and ignorance once all was revealed. Others organized their own, mainly female networks, in close coordination with those of their husbands.[26] Very rarely indeed a wife denounced her husband. Mrs Chiesa did, because they were separated and he was not paying her sufficient alimony. So did Adriana Rosci, who on the night of 12 July 1991 in melodramatic fashion threw two stacks of banknotes out of the window of the family home in Rome. She then telephoned the *carabinieri* and told them: 'On the pavement you'll find thirteen million lire. At home I've got another ninety million. It's laundered money. My husband brings it home every evening, he's one of the administrators of the USL [the local health authority] in the twelfth district.' Her husband, Gianfranco, fifty-three years old, was an ex-functionary of the neo-fascist MSI who had transferred his allegiances to the dominant DC faction of Vittorio Sbardella, Giulio Andreotti's lieutenant in Rome.[27]

c. THE POLITICAL PARTIES

In many democracies in the 1970s and 1980s, the new modes of communication and techniques of electioneering contributed greatly to raising the cost of politics. Laws were passed stipulating the amount of public money political parties could spend, the modalities by which private donors could make contributions to the party of their choice. By and large, this new legislation proved entirely inadequate to stem the tide of corruption.[28]

In Italy the law of 1974 had been welcomed by all the parties as providing a sound footing for their financing. However, in the following years it was flouted systematically, and no party behaved more flagrantly than the Socialists of Bettino Craxi. His was a highly centralized system of corruption. In the authoritative words of Luciano Cafagna, himself a leading Socialist intellectual in the 1980s: 'By offering from the centre both the partitioning of financial resources and the political legitimacy to procure such resources at a local level, he [Craxi] was able in a very short space of time to have the whole party eating out of his hand.'[29] Craxi's rule was that of an absolute monarchy; his subordinates both admired him and were cowed by him at the same time. When Mario Chiesa was finally received for a short interview in the inner sanctuary of Piazza Duomo 19, Milan, 'Craxi did not even glance up from his table . . . he had his head in his hands and his glasses on his forehead. I confess that I felt like a child on his first day at school.'[30] The Socialists were not only corrupt, they theorized their own corruption. For them modernity was such, and those who failed to understand this were old-style 'moralists' or more simply, to use the brutal expression of the then mayor of Milan, Paolo Pillitteri, 'cretins who still don't understand how the world goes around'.[31] However, such overriding arrogance was an element of their undoing, and Craxi's own peculiar dedication to corrupt practice was, in the long run, to eat away at his considerable political talent.[32]

The Christian Democrats were no less active in this field, but in keeping with the history of their party there was no undisputed leader, no single figure at the centre of the web of corruption, except for the luckless Severino Citaristi, the Treasurer of the party, who was an administrator rather than a politician.[33] Most Christian Democrats also tended to be rather more discreet about what they were up to, as if their religious background in some way inhibited them and caused them the occasional pang of conscience. The minor government parties certainly did not refrain from tucking in. If the Social Democrats had few restraining moral influences in the history of their party, the Republicans had the ghost of Ugo La Malfa to haunt them, but that did not stop them from being an integral part of the system, especially in the South. Whatever their former traditions, for all the governing parties covert and illicit politics became an important activity, running parallel to overt and explicit politics. This metamorphosis signalled a new, or at least intensified role for the parties – that of guarantors of illegal pacts.

The most controversial question of all was the involvement of the Communists. Berlinguer had asserted repeatedly the high moral profile of the PCI, which for him was an essential feature that distinguished it from other political parties. The reality was somewhat less exalted. The consociational practice of the years of historic compromise had left its mark upon the party. In Milan, for instance, some senior local Communists had been sucked into the kickback system, and the rest of the party did not have the courage to denounce them. In 1982 the Communist Luigi Carnevale became the vice-president of the Milanese underground railway company. At first, so he told the magistrates later, the average kickback for works on the new Third Line was a 'modest' 3 per cent, most of which was divided up between the PSI and the DC. The PCI was compensated with a certain number of contracts awarded automatically to the 'red' cooperatives. However, from 1985 onwards it was decided that the party should receive 'money instead of favours'.[34]

The history of corruption within the PCI remains to be written, and it will be no easy task. In its absence, two opposed interpretations have clashed violently. One of them is that the PCI was substantially no different from the other parties, and was only less corrupt because it had had less opportunity. The other, while not denying the facts of the Milanese case, maintains that they formed no part of a general pattern. Communist local government, it is argued, was exceptional in its honesty and transparency, qualities that clearly distinguished it from the Italian norm.

Any firm conclusions to this debate are obviously premature, but it seems likely that the truth lies somewhere between these two extremes. Communist local government, as I tried to show in my *A History of Contemporary Italy*, was often of a distinctly higher quality than elsewhere. The great majority of the party's militants and administrators were transparently honest, and the pattern of self-enrichment, so typical of the Socialists of the 1980s, was quite alien to them. On the other hand, corruption was unlikely to have been confined to Milan. Favouritism for the cooperatives, 'red' clientelism, tax evasion, the receipt of funds from Moscow (at least until Berlinguer's '*strappo*'), were all part of the daily reality of the party. Failure to expose and eliminate them was another symptom of how *tired* the politics of the left had become.

d. THE CENTRAL STATE

Local government corruption was one of the most important aspects of business politics, but it was far from the only one. The role played by the central apparatuses of the state was in many ways more important. However, information on the latter's role is very much more scant than that on local government, at least in part because of the lack of effective internal controls and the long-standing reluctance of the Roman magistrates to conduct any serious investigation into the malpractices of the Ministries and of the state agencies with their headquarters in the capital.

The historian writing at the end of the 1990s can therefore point only to a small number of spectacular cases of central government corruption, but he or she can in no way be sure of their exemplary nature. One such case concerned the Bonifica company, a subsidiary of the huge state-owned Italstat, which operated in the construction industry. It is worth recounting the case in detail because of the graphic and convincing account offered of it by one of its protagonists, Agatino Licandro, the former Christian Democrat mayor of Reggio Calabria.[35]

After his successful election in February 1990, Licandro was quickly drawn into a web of local-central government collusion. The Bonifica company, which had its headquarters in Rome and specialized in 'services and projects', had reached an agreement with the Municipality of Reggio Calabria to plan and direct the building of a new administrative centre at Reggio. The cost of the operation was estimated conservatively at 118 billion lire. Bonifica's role was described by Licandro as follows: 'It speeds up the administrative procedures necessary to gain government finance, draws up the overall plans, organizes the tendering of the contracts, nominates the works' directors.'[36] In other words, it formed part of the service economy, but operated in the quasi-monopolistic conditions which were created by the state. Licandro summarized its role with considerable efficacy: 'people don't know what a "services' company" is and they have some difficulty in grasping the fact that the state organizes one section of the state in order for it to steal from another.'[37]

At the end of 1990 Licandro and Giuseppe Nicolò, one of the Christian Democrat bosses of Calabrian politics, travelled to Rome to reach agreement with Giorgio De Camillis, the managing director of the Bonifica company. At the offices of the company, a large modern palace in the suburb of EUR, they were ushered into the studio of De Camillis on the top floor. The studio was, according to Licandro, 'spacious and full of light'. The managing director of Bonifica was 'sad and ponderous', though 'a real gentleman'. He and Nicolò disagreed over the size of the kickback to be handed over that day, but Nicolò agreed reluctantly to accept only 300 million lire (*circa* £120,000 at that time): 'A young man entered holding under his arm a rigid cardboard container, one of those which has a tin lining around the edges ... The container was placed on the table alongside De Camillis, who with a natural nonchalance pushed it across to Nicolò.'[38]

The two men got up to leave. At the last moment Nicolò remembered something else: '"The diaries. Engineer De Camillis, I beg you, at least the diaries. We're at the end of the year. You know what an effect they have. Everybody asks us for them. It's in your interests as well." "*Onorevole*, don't worry, I've already made the necessary arrangements." Nicolò explained to me: "They cost the earth. We give a few away as presents and we cut a splendid figure. It's lucky I remembered."'[39]

Once they had left the office of De Camillis, Licandro and Nicolò sought refuge in a small side room. There, with the door locked behind him, Nicolò checked the money: '"A hundred million are for the members of the municipal council. Half of what remains goes to the Socialists ... With all the expenses I've had, going up and down from Reggio to Roma, at the end of the day I'll lose money on this operation ... You know the rules: you must look after all the *assessori*. Ours and the Socialists'. And don't forget the Republicans, who are part of the ruling majority. That's the agreement."' What impressed Licandro was that 'the bands which held together the banknotes were commonplace, as were the envelopes in which they were placed, as was the cardboard container. Nobody could ever have found incriminating evidence of the transaction. This was an organization which exuded efficiency, solidity, shrewdness, professionalism. "This lot – I thought – don't do anything else."'[40]

Apart from its moral implications, the system of corruption had grave consequences for the capacity of the central state to plan and execute major public works. In the 1980s, a great deal of money was put aside for this purpose; the Budget for 1987 alone set aside some 190,000 billion lire for the three years 1987–9. These vast sums were not spent well. The accent was more on image than function, more on the construction of vast business, administrative and commercial centres than on less visible or prestigious public works like guarding against landslides and floods.[41] Investment in the arts and in the conservation and restoration of monuments, which were so important not just for the nation's cultural heritage but also for the long-term health of its greatest service industry, tourism, continued to be insufficient.[42]

Public policy became weighted towards those areas where kickbacks could be easily collected and competition from 'outsiders' avoided.[43]

The absence of independent controls upon the functioning of government was crucial in this respect. In Britain and the USA a series of control authorities had been established as far back as the 30s, and had been constantly updated. Their efficacy varied, but they were better than the Italian tradition of turning a blind eye. Freed from the prospect of independent control, the power of the informal networks of complicity increased, to the detriment of any clearly defined idea of planning.

2. The Judiciary

The appalling process described above may have become predominant in the 1980s, but it was not all-conquering. Within the great complex of institutions that made up the Italian state there were counter-tendencies at work, which ensured that pluralism and conflict remained essential features of Italian democracy. For while the governing parties were behaving in a certain way, a significant minority of magistrates was more determined than ever before to stop them in their tracks. In the absence of any other controls, the law was the last recourse, and its deterrent power had in some ways increased as the Republic's history unfolded. Henceforth, the conflict between magistrates and government moved rapidly into the centre of the stage of Italian politics, and the ancient principle of the separation of powers acquired new meaning and urgency.

To understand why this was so, it is worth recapping for a moment. In the early years of the Republic the judiciary had been mainly a conservative corps, beholden to the governing élites and sharing their values and sentiments. However, the Constitution of 1948 had made provision for the institution of a Higher Council of the Judiciary (Consiglio Superiore della Magistratura), on which the elected representatives of the judiciary were to form a clear majority. The Council was finally instituted in 1959, and once it began to function properly in the 1960s the formal freedom of the judiciary from control by the executive became more of a reality.[44] Here was one of those 'virtues' of the Italian Republic, bequeathed from the post-war settlement, and responsible for introducing a certain dynamism and tension into the workings of the state, in contrast to the many elements of continuity with the Fascist period.[45] Slowly, too, the hierarchical control of the most senior judges and prosecuting magistrates weakened, to allow a limited freedom of action for the more junior ranks.

The importance of these developments was heightened by the strong and independent role that public prosecutors play in Italy's civil law system.

Rather than being the mere counterpart of the defence lawyers, as in the British common law system, prosecutors are responsible for undertaking investigations and directing police inquiries, as well as being obliged to pursue the possibility of prosecution for all reported offences. They also form part of the same professional corporation as the judges. Each *Procura* of the major cities enjoys substantial independence, and each prosecutor a significant freedom of action, though under the general supervision of the Procurator-General.[46]

There was a constant risk of abuse of such considerable powers, as there was in the self-government of the Higher Council of the Judiciary. Taken together, however, they signified a greater degree of judicial independence in Italy than in other western democracies. In France in this period the Ministry of Justice exercised a suffocating control over public prosecutors, as witnessed by the constant transfer of their 'over-zealous' elements and the burying of delicate investigations involving politicians.[47] In Britain control was more subtle. The very nature of recruitment resulted in the creation, as David Nelken has written, of 'a small group of middle-aged and middle-minded members of the Establishment'.[48] In Germany public prosecutors were considered state functionaries, organized in hierarchical fashion and dependent upon the political executive.[49]

Judicial autonomy in Italy (in the sense of the independence of action of both public prosecutors and judges) would never have had the effect that it did without the cultural revolution of the years from 1968 onwards. As higher educational opportunities broadened and traditional values were brought into question, the nature of recruitment to the judiciary — by competitive examination immediately after university — brought into its ranks a more socially diverse and open-minded generation.[50] Italian juridical culture finally began to turn its back on the formalism of the past. Some junior magistrates, the so-called *'pretori d'assalto'*, waged war in favour of social justice and against the unchecked position of powerful vested interests in Italian society. Others, as we shall see in a moment, began to take extraordinarily courageous stands against organized crime.

However, these were also the years in which the judiciary began to be organized in political currents, each fighting for proportional representation in the Higher Council of the Judiciary. This was rather more of a mixed blessing. The politicization of the judiciary certainly broke with the conservative homogeneity of the past, and introduced a new pluralism into the corps, but it also meant that judges and prosecutors could be more easily linked to specific political parties (or factions within them), and become instruments in the battle for power within the state. The main organizations were 'Magistratura Democratica', representing left-wing judges, 'Unità per la Costituzione', representing the centre, and 'Magistratura Indipendente' for the right.[51] Of course, the judiciary had always played a political role in the Republic — its

191

very acquiescence to the dominant political and economic powers in the 1940s and 1950s was itself an exquisitely political position. None the less, there was a real danger that heightened political awareness would increase the temptation to use judicial power for narrowly political purposes. Paradoxically, the judiciary's political dependence, expelled from the public arena by the dictates of the Constitution, could come in again through the back door.

Events in the spring of 1979 revealed how great this danger could be. Certain magistrates from the Procura of Rome, Antonio Alibrandi and Achille Gallucci, launched an unprecedented attack upon the leadership of the Bank of Italy, and in particular upon its Governor, Paolo Baffi, and Vice-Director, Mario Sarcinelli, both of whom enjoyed very high reputations as outstandingly honest civil servants. They were accused of pursuing private and personal interests in connection with financial aid obtained from the central bank by the chemical group of Nino Rovelli. Sarcinelli was briefly imprisoned, a humiliation spared to Baffi only on account of his age. The Roman magistrates who launched this attack were known to have right-wing sympathies: Gallucci had close links with the Roman friends of Giulio Andreotti, at that time President of the Council of Ministers, Alibrandi was a well-known sympathizer of the neo-Fascist MSI.[52] When Baffi went to see Andreotti, the latter expressed his esteem both for him and for Sarcinelli, but there lurked the suspicion that Baffi had been too rigid in his treatment of certain of Andreotti's friends, especially the Caltagirone brothers, Roman building constructors, at that time in great financial difficulty and in need of the Banca d'Italia's aid.[53] As Baffi commented bitterly in a letter of 3 March 1983: 'Unfortunately, just as the political class (and the potentates tied to it by the exchange of favours) had to take notice of me, so I had to take stock of the power of that political, judicial and speculative complex that obtained my downfall.'[54] In June 1981 both Baffi and Sarcinelli were cleared of all the accusations against them, but by that time Baffi had already stepped down.

A second, ambivalent development of this same period was the increased use of so-called *'pentiti'* (literally 'repentants') in obtaining convictions. In order to counter the terrorist emergency of the 1970s, new incentives had been introduced to persuade those who had participated in terrorist or other criminal organizations to collaborate with the law. Their confessions were obviously of enormous value, both in unmasking terrorist organization and, as we shall see, in permitting public prosecutors to build up an accurate picture of the structure of criminal organizations. The long-standing tradition of *omertà*, of knowing silence, began to crumble. However, there was always going to be the risk of relying too heavily on the uncorroborated evidence of the collaborators, or on a series of *'pentiti'* who simply corroborated each other. The conflict between the utility of such evidence and the dangers inherent in it, between means and ends in the legal system, was to form the basis for a passionate debate in Italian public life, a debate which was to continue for the next twenty years.[55]

The dangers of relying too heavily on the evidence of *'pentiti'* was brought out very clearly in the tragic case of Enzo Tortora.[56] Tortora, a well-known television personality, was arrested in 1983 and charged with drug-trafficking and association with the 'Nuova Camorra Organizzata' of Raffaele Cutolo. The accusations against him were based on the evidence of a number of *'pentiti'*, principally Giovanni Pandico. Tortora spent some seven months in prison before being brought to trial in 1985, found guilty and sentenced to ten years' imprisonment. The Appeal Court judges, however, threw out the case, showing very conclusively the grave inconsistencies of the *'pentiti'* evidence, and the superficiality of the prosecution case. The Court of Cassation, the highest court in Italy, confirmed the judgment of the Appeal Court. By that time it was too late to save Tortora. His reputation had been utterly besmirched and he developed cancer, from which he died in 1988.[57]

Another case which highlighted the controversial use of *'pentitismo'* was that regarding the assassination of the police commissioner Luigi Calabresi in Milan on 17 May 1972. Sixteen years after the event, Leonardo Marino, who had been a militant in the revolutionary group Lotta Continua, accused himself and Ovidio Bompressi of the killing. He claimed that he had driven their car, while Bompressi had done the actual killing. Marino also accused two ex-leaders of Lotta Continua, Adriano Sofri and Giorgio Pietrostefani, of being his instigators.

The case became a judicial nightmare, lasting more than ten years and involving contrasting sentences at different levels of Italy's complicated legal system. Despite the fact that Marino's 'repentance' had taken place at such a great distance from the event, and that no material proof or other corroborative evidence existed to sustain his claims, Bompressi, Pietrostefani and Sofri were found guilty on 22 January 1997, and began twenty-two-year sentences in the prison of Pisa. Marino, in exchange for his testimony, went free. Later, Bompressi was released on medical grounds and Pietrostefani, briefly freed pending yet another appeal, sought refuge outside of Italy. Sofri, alone, remained in prison.[58]

Another, essential part of the judicial landscape of the 1980s was the unequal battle being waged between the governing parties and those few magistrates who tried to expose their corrupt practices. A well-documented case is that of Michele Del Gaudio, the prosecutor principally responsible for bringing to trial Alberto Teardo, the corrupt Socialist politician who had been President of the Liguria region. Del Gaudio was one of the many young magistrates who had entered the system in the early 1980s, full of idealism and the desire to serve the state.[59]

In his fight against institutional corruption at Savona, Del Gaudio, a Neapolitan, found himself terribly isolated. He received valuable help from a few of his colleagues, especially Francantonio Granero, and an especially precious collaboration from a colonel of the Carabinieri, Nicolò Bozzo. Del Gaudio described their relationship in a letter to his wife in June 1983:

It's four o'clock in the morning. We've just finished signing the arrest warrants. I'm tired, but I'll be able to rest only for two hours on a divan in the Carabinieri barracks. I wanted to tell you about Bozzo, who's a colonel in the Carabinieri. 'Colonel,' I said to him while we were waiting for the Public Prosecutor, 'you're not by any chance one of those Carabinieri who is the butt of everyone's jokes?' 'Sir, we're the subject of fun and we intend to stay that way, but we also mean to remain the pillars of Italian democracy.' And he wasn't joking, he kept his word, in spite of the difficulties we encountered.[60]

Alberto Teardo and his corrupt clan were brought to justice, but not without cost. Del Gaudio and Granero were transferred elsewhere and saw their careers in the judiciary severely compromised. The *carabiniere* Bozzo, too, was transferred, first to Rome and then to Messina.

These punitive measures formed part of a wider offensive launched by the Socialist party against the judiciary.[61] Most magistrates were more than willing not to inquire too vigorously into the system of corruption. Some were actually profiting from it, as was to become clear in the 1990s. But there was an obstinate minority who would not toe the line, and they had to be stopped before they caused too much trouble. The Socialists, for whom control of the post of Minister of Justice was becoming ever more crucial, organized a number of deterrent measures. One such was the referendum of 1987. In the wake of the Tortora case, the PSI launched a campaign in favour of introducing the civil liability of prosecutors, that is of their being liable to pay damages to those whom they had wrongly accused. The referendum, held in November 1987, produced a resounding victory for the Socialists – a clear case of a just cause being pursued for dubious motives.[62] One of Craxi's most valuable allies in the fight against an indocile magistracy was Francesco Cossiga, the President of the Republic. After 1990 he entered on a collision course with the Higher Council of the Judiciary, of which he was nominally the President.

By the beginning of the 1990s, therefore, the reforming magistrates were very much on the defensive. One of them, Gian Carlo Caselli, later to become Procurator-General at Palermo, remembered the late 80s as 'years of arrogance, at the very edge of constitutional propriety; years from which we emerged as if from a tunnel, thanks also, perhaps, to the shameless idiocy with which certain centres of power were convinced that they could continue to act with impunity'.[63]

3. The Mafia and the State

The ebb and flow of the struggle for legality, both within and outside the state, was not confined to the muddy fields of corruption. There was a more historic terrain, that of western Sicily, on which the battle was to be waged with extraordinary ferocity in the 1980s. The stakes were very high, for in this period the Mafia attacked more directly than ever before those servants of the state who were brave or foolhardy enough to try to see the rule of law enforced. Once again, a small minority of magistrates, *carabinieri* and policemen were in the front line.

a. THE NATURE OF THE MAFIA

At the origins of the Mafia lay the failure of the central Italian state both to impose its authority and establish consent in western Sicily. The Mafia filled the space, offering protection where the state could not. Honest government functionaries were left completely isolated, as Franchetti noted as early as 1876, without anyone who would collaborate in the enforcement of the law.[64] It was a measure of how little had changed 100 years later that the most famous of all anti-Mafia prosecuting judges, Giovanni Falcone, admitted frankly to the French journalist Marcelle Padovani: 'I am simply a servant of the State *in terra infidelium*.'[65]

It would be a mistake, however, to maintain that the Mafia was in any way an alternative state. This oft-argued thesis, espoused even by eminent figures of the anti-Mafia struggle like Falcone himself, does not withstand analysis.[66] As Diego Gambetta has argued, the Mafia had no juridical ordering. It was not centralized, but was made up of a number of competing groups. It had no constant normative code.[67] The Mafia did not even resemble a pre-modern state, for it had no absolute monarch and no dependence on a landowning class. Rather, it had grown side by side with the development of capitalism in Sicily and had acquired its identity, both urban and rural, in contradistinction to the modern state, and not in imitation of it. It was deeply embedded in society, an illegal organization which prospered, as we shall see, thanks to the collusion of more than one element of the state itself.

Its habitual mode of action was a discreet one, not the flamboyant presence of an outsider or bandit group, but the social invisibility of respected members of society, the men of honour.[68] Silence more than words was its preferred medium. As Falcone, himself from Palermo, explained: 'The Sicilians' tendency to discretion, not to speak of muteness, is proverbial. In the ambit of Cosa Nostra it reaches levels of paroxysm.'[69] One expression of this was the *omertà*, the knowing silence, of the inhabitants of the great city in which the Mafia thrived. Another was the reduction of the language of the organization to the necessary minimum of phrases and gestures. Tommaso

Buscetta, the most famous of the Mafia bosses who was later to collaborate with the forces of justice, recounted how 'In my ambience no one asks direct questions, but your interlocutor, when he considers it necessary, makes you understand with a phrase, with a nod of the head, with a smile . . . even simply by his silence.'[70]

In economic terms, the Mafia corresponded fundamentally to a *service* organization. If we return to T. P. Hill's definition of services outlined in Chapter 1, it can be seen that the activities of *mafiosi* did not principally involve the production of commodities, but the provision of services.[71] Only that theirs were not always services carried out 'with the agreement of the person concerned or economic unit owning the good', nor were their services necessarily beneficial in intent, other than to themselves.[72] In fact Mafia economic activity took a variety of forms. A central element, as Gambetta has shown convincingly, was the offer of protection in a situation characterized by the uncertainty of market regulation and the inefficacy of the law – a real service offered directly to consumers. However, the distinction between protection and extortion was not a great one, and often the Mafia offered protection against itself. In other words, it created a 'racket' in which it consciously injected elements of uncertainty into market conditions, and then extorted payments for protection from these same conditions. As the Schneiders have written, 'the fine line between protection and a protection racket is an expression of mafia's inherently mixed political economy'.[73] Sometimes, too, the Mafia was heavily involved in services for final demand, that is in the trading of commodities that they did not themselves produce (or only very rarely), principally drugs and arms. On occasions it offered a 'final' service in the most lugubrious sense of the word.

In sorting out the Mafia's different services or disservices, it is essential to keep in mind the wide geographical spread of its operations. At a local level it specialized in offering protection and privilege in certain markets it controlled, as well as extortion rackets. At a national level it offered a political service, packets of votes in return for being able to continue its own operations undisturbed. At an international level it could boast of long-established and reliable networks for illegal trafficking of goods and the laundering of 'dirty' money.

The Mafia maintained its control through the certainty of its sanctions, which were as ruthless and inevitable as those of the state were neither. It was not, though, a smooth-running organization, but rather an uneasy coalition of *cosche* or 'families', shifting and competitive one with another, and all too ready to resort to killing in their fight for supremacy. Death lurked as a constant presence in all Mafia activity. As Buscetta revealed, some overall control was maintained by a 'Cupola' of senior *mafiosi*, the Commissione Provinciale di Palermo, who established, as best they could, lines of demarcation and rules of conduct.

b. MAFIA 'FAMILIES' AND REAL FAMILIES

In the many possible combinations of relationships between individuals, families, society and the state, that proffered by the Mafia was a very particular and extreme one. For the Mafia there was to be no equilibrium between the three principal elements of human aggregation, but rather the exalting of a single organization within society. That organization was the very antithesis of modern civil society, being neither pluralist, nor democratic, nor based on gender equality, but one which had its own value system of honour, shame and revenge. To one side of it lay individuals and families, both of which, according to Mafia codes of conduct, were to be strictly, indeed savagely, subordinated to its needs. To the other lay the state, which was regarded with a mixture of hostility and contempt.

If this was the rudimentary but effective way in which the Mafia theorized these relationships, the reality was far more problematic. In the first place, opposition to the state was accompanied by collusion with many of its constituent elements, a point to which we shall shortly return. In the second, the relationships between the individuals who formed a Mafia 'Family' and those who formed a consanguineous group were anything but straightforward. Some scholars have insisted that the one simply dominated and used the other. Piero Bevilacqua has written, 'In the competition between the interests of the organization and those of kinship, it is the first that prevail . . . The family was, and is to this day, one of the most useful and flexible *instruments* for creating and keeping together a specific and ruthless criminal organization.'[74] Diego Gambetta has suggested instead that there was not only an analogical but a substantial similarity between Mafia Families and real ones. They shared a common view of the world which derived from them both being systems of protection.[75] I find neither of these accounts satisfactory, for they underplay the multiple layers of tension inherent in the relationship between kinship loyalty and Mafia membership.

At one level, it is true, blood loyalties were considered the best guarantees of fidelity. In the Inzerillo clan Giovanni Falcone noted the 'incredible interlacing of kinship ties . . . with each new generation, the links become more binding as a consequence of marriages between cousins . . . which render the group more cohesive and homogeneous'.[76] Mafia loyalties passed from one generation to another. Leonardo Messina, a young *'pentito'* from San Cataldo in the 1980s, boasted: 'Mine is a family which belongs by tradition to Cosa Nostra, and I belong to the seventh generation . . . I did not become a man of honour because I was a thief or because I was capable of killing, but because family traditions meant I was destined to become part of the group.'[77]

However, at another level, the Mafia could not afford to trust entirely the loyalties of close kin ties, for they offered a code of conduct which *could* enter into terrible conflict with the needs of the organization. The boss Pippo Calderone, in his attempt to establish some sort of order in Cosa Nostra in the 1970s, had proposed that there should not be more than two brothers in the same Family, and that two brothers or two blood relatives should not head a Family for fear that they would put the interests and the affections of kin before the needs of the organization.[78] Buscetta could claim that 'Cosa Nostra comes before blood, family or relations', but the reality did not always conform with this principle. In his own case it had been the killing of two of his sons by a rival band, killings which he considered unjust by the Mafia's own code of conduct, which had convinced him of the need to turn state witness.[79]

Again, as in the case of 'Tangentopoli', it is necessary to separate different kin relations, to try to analyse those which were more susceptible to Mafia dictates and those which were less. The Mafia Family, up until very recently, was an exclusively male organization, both patriarchal and fraternal. Each clan had its leader, who not only commanded within the organization, but also used godparenthood (*comparatico*) to widen his sphere of influence, both within his clan and in the wider society outside.[80] But the Mafia was also an organization based strongly on fraternal solidarities between the 'footsoldiers' of the organization. Consanguineal ties traversed both these lines of loyalty — the horizontal/fraternal and the vertical/patriarchal — but appear to have disturbed them in different measure. Sometimes the organization would require one brother to betray or abandon another, and he would respond, even using kinship as a snare to entrap his luckless relative.[81] Sometimes he would insist, in the name of kinship, that he alone should do the killing.[82] On the other hand, there seems to be much less evidence of patricide, and still less of fathers killing sons. Indeed, if a father was killed by a Mafia Family, it was a general rule not to let a son enter the organization, for fear of the conflict thus created.[83]

The greatest potential conflict lay with members of the other sex, and especially with mothers. Women were traditionally excluded from the Mafia because they were considered untrustworthy, because they gossiped, because they could not be expected necessarily to subordinate kin ties to the needs of the organization. Wives could often be the agents of those 'manifest complicities' which Renate Siebert has analysed in detail,[84] but mothers would always put loyalty to their sons before any other consideration. As the '*pentito*' Antonino Calderone told Pino Arlacchi:

Women are uncontrollable if you touch their sons, because no greater love exists in the world. The link between mother and son is stronger than any other, more than that between wife and husband, between daughter and father, between sister and brother. The pain caused by losing a son is unbearable for a mother. If they kill her husband she may in the end accept it (even if there's no guarantee), but if they kill her son . . .[85]

Mafiosi were also traditionalists with regard to gender relations. They declared themselves good Catholic patriarchs, and married off their daughters in church with great show. Daughters were to be virgins before marriage, divorce and adultery were frowned upon, mothers were 'saints'. Pimping was forbidden. The womenfolk of *mafiosi* were symbols, and their propriety and effective protection boosted the reputation of a man of honour.[86] However, such archaic codes contrasted increasingly with the processes of education and emancipation at work in Sicilian society. Even in traditional inland Mafia strongholds, modernizing forces were widening women's horizons, and causing conflicts within the homes of Mafia males.[87]

Layers of tension thus existed at many different levels: between the loyalty inspired by kinship and the shifting, but imperious demands of the Mafia Family; between an exclusively male organization, where the shadow of death was never far distant, and women trying to build up a home and a family; between the cultural conservatism of the Mafia and the transformations in Italian society. All these made for a profoundly uneasy relationship between the two types of families, the real and the *mafioso*. Such uneasiness reinforced the underlying ambiguity and instability of Mafia values.

c. DRUGS AND INTERNECINE WARFARE

In the 1970s the Mafia flourished as never before. The principal reason for this was the great boom of the international drug trade. The former Mafia boss Antonino Calderone remembered that 'we all became millionaires. Suddenly, within a couple of years. Thanks to drugs . . .'[88] The heroin trail, which originated in the opium fields of the East, passed through the refineries of Marseilles and found its markets above all in the United States, came to be controlled in no small part by Cosa Nostra. This was because the organization could offer trans-oceanic lines of communications and guarantees which were necessary in very high-risk operations of this sort. At two key terminals for the trade stood two cousins, Carlo Gambino and Salvatore Inzerillo, representing respectively the most powerful clan in New York and one of the oldest 'families' in Palermo.[89]

The drug trade immensely enriched the Mafia, but it also destabilized it. More so than in the past, *mafiosi* became entrepreneurs in their own right. Some refined opium directly in laboratories at Palermo, others bought and sold at the various stages of transit. In all this frenetic activity, hierarchies and territorial divisions of competence were considerably undermined.

Between 1981 and 1983 clan rivalry combined with the great profits from drugs to give rise to the worst internecine war between Mafia Families in the whole of the Republican period. Although from the outside it was very difficult to distinguish what was happening, on the one side there stood the supporters of the *Corleonesi*, whose origins derived from the inland town of Corleone, and who were headed by Salvatore Riina and Bernardo Provenzano; while on the other were the previously dominant families of Palermo, headed by Stefano Bontate, Salvatore Inzerillo and Gaetano Badalamenti.[90] Between 500 and 1,000 people lost their lives in what became an unstoppable slaughter. In Palermo, General Carlo Alberto dalla Chiesa told Giorgio Bocca in August 1982: 'They are killing people in open daylight, moving their corpses, mutilating them, depositing them in the streets between the police headquarters and the offices of the regional government, burning them at three in the afternoon in one of the main streets of Palermo.'[91] It was a transversal war of intricate personal rivalries which cut across traditional loyalties and even kinship ties. In the end the *Corleonesi* emerged as the winners, a victory pregnant with consequences for both the Mafia and the Italian state.

The 1970s and early 1980s also witnessed the general expansion of organized crime in Italy. Historically the Mafia had been confined to certain geographical areas of Sicily, above all the western part of the island. In the 1970s its influence spread rapidly, and the east coast of Sicily, especially Catania, which had previously been almost untouched, became heavily involved. In the same period Cosa Nostra established a strong presence in Naples, with the founding of the 'Nuova Famiglia' to combat the influence of the Nuova Camorra Organizzata of Raffaele Cutolo, the organization of which Enzo Tortora had wrongly been accused of being a member. The Camorra, the principal criminal organization of Naples and its hinterland, had a history longer than that of the Mafia. It differed from the latter in being a looser, mass organization, consisting of more than 100 bands which appeared and disappeared, changing shape and form continuously. Camorra bands were much more ostentatious than their Mafia counterparts, more likely to be organized horizontally by a group of brothers, more willing to involve adolescents and even whole families in activities such as the peddling of drugs.[92] In the war between the Nuova Camorra Organizzata and the Nuova Famiglia, it was the latter which emerged victorious, but the battle had been as ferocious as that in Palermo, with 284 deaths in the Campania region in 1982 alone.[93]

In Calabria, too, the principal criminal organization of the region, the 'Ndrangheta, expanded greatly its activities in this period. It resembled the Camorra in having a mass membership (an estimated 5,600 persons by 1993) and in being loosely and primitively organized. Narrow territorial control was all important, with the organization being dominated by blood ties, especially between brothers. The clans of the city of Reggio Calabria were the most important and ruthless. The city had about 1 per cent of the Italian population, but 11 per cent of all homicides in the period 1985–91.[94] The 'Ndrangheta specialized in kidnappings and in the arms traffic, and developed ever closer ties with Cosa Nostra.

These were the three principal criminal organizations in Italy, distinguished from petty crime by their territorial control, their political links and their degree of internationalization. They were not the only ones. At the end of 1981, in the prison of Bari, the Sacra Corona Unita came into being, an organization which was to dominate crime in Puglia in the 1980s.[95] Here, contacts with the 'Ndrangheta had helped the new grouping to extend its control over a major part of the region. Indeed, in the 1980s it was possible for the first time to talk of an interlinked even if constantly conflictual southern Italian criminal class, with increasing activities and contacts in the centre and north of the country as well.

This was also the period when contacts between these powerful criminal groupings and certain Masonic lodges became more frequent. From the lists of P2 members, and those of the Gran Loggia d'Italia di Piazza del Gesù, confiscated by the police in 1986, it emerged that many Mafia members had become Masons for the first time in the years from 1976 to 1980. Calabria was the region with the highest ratio of Masons per head of population. These lodges, as the parliamentary anti-Mafia commission wrote in 1993, with commendable understatement, 'are characterized by an over-extended interpretation of the concept of Masonic solidarity'.[96]

The weight of organized crime in the Italian economy was almost impossible to estimate, given the covert nature of so much of its activity. In 1986 it was estimated by CENSIS that some 12.5 per cent of Italian GDP was the fruit of all types of criminal activity, of which nearly half was from the commerce of drugs. Seven years later Luciano Violante, the president of the parliamentary anti-Mafia commission, put the turnover attributable to the major criminal organizations at only 4.4 per cent of GDP, but this still made them the second largest 'firm' in Italy after IRI.[97] It was figures such as these which had made Aldo Ravelli, one of the leading figures of the Milanese stock exchange, refer to the Mafia as one of the three great sections of the Italian bourgeoisie, at least in terms of its financial resources.[98] Clearly, as time passed, the Italian Republic was losing the battle against organized crime.

d. MAFIA AND POLITICIANS

The dramatic explosion of criminal activities outlined above would have been impossible without the active collusion of significant sections of the Italian political class. The continuum examined earlier in this chapter between clientelism and corruption in Italian political culture can be extended to include collusion with organized crime.

When thinking about these connections it is perhaps worth using the metaphor (beloved of Gramsci) of the train and its carriages. Italian politicians and civil servants, when boarding the train of Italian public life, were always able to choose their carriage. In the first could be found many honest functionaries and politicians who attempted to live their public life by the rulebook, without exceptions and favouritisms. The second carriage, always very crowded, was occupied by a veritable clientelist army: administrators who were busy accelerating bureaucratic procedures for friends and relations, politicians writing *'raccomandazioni'* and assembling their files of clients in preparation for voting day. In the third sat the practitioners of corruption, usually very well-dressed gentlemen, sipping aperitifs, waiting for their secretaries to bring them suspiciously full briefcases. In the last carriage, the lighting was dim and the conversation minimal. This was the place of shadowy deals, struck between politicians, some of national importance, and representatives of organized crime, of very different social provenance.

There was no inevitability in such a progression. At each point of passage and of distinction — between disinterested political behaviour and clientelism, between clientelism and corruption, between corruption and the various Mafias — a politician or civil servant could choose not to proceed. How easy it was to do so depended not only upon individual integrity but also upon regional environment and long-standing political practice. Where public ethics had never been created with any force, it was all too natural for clientelistic practice to finish in a Mafia embrace.

In the Sicily of the Republic, the links between Mafia and members of the ruling parties were formed at an early date. Just occasionally in the early years of the Republic the politicians were so indiscreet and confident of impunity as to leave written evidence of the link. Thus in April 1951 the Liberal member of parliament for western Sicily, Giovanni Palazzolo, wrote the following letter to the *mafioso* Frank Coppola, on paper headed 'The Chamber of Deputies':

Dearest Don Ciccio,

The last time we saw each other at the Hotel de Palme you told me rightly that for Partinico we needed a young and quick-witted deputy for the regional parliament, a person who was a friend and who was within the reach of our friends. Totò Motisi is a friend who corresponds to all these requirements and I've decided to help him with all my force. If you give me a hand at Partinico we will get him elected as a deputy.

> With affectionate greetings,
> Yours,
> (Giovanni Palazzolo)[99]

In general, contacts were much more discreet. The Mafia pursued a strategy of '*avvicinamento*', of cautious approach to individual politicians. It could offer the electoral loyalty of those areas and neighbourhoods where its territorial hold was greatest. In return the politician could use his power to favour and protect the Mafia's interests. Historically, as Paolo Pezzino has written, 'between local society and politics it was the *mafioso* who did the mediating; between *mafioso* and institutions this was the job of the politician'.[100]

At Palermo these connections became more structured than ever before at the time of the great construction boom at the end of the 1950s. Mayor of the city was the thirty-year-old Salvo Lima; the *assessore* for public works was Vito Ciancimino. Both formed part, at a national level, of Amintore Fanfani's faction of the Christian Democrats, which was to dominate Sicilian politics until the mid-1970s.[101] It was at this time, as Luciano Violante has written, that Cosa Nostra became 'a modern politico-criminal organization'.[102] Chains of connection were created systematically between the Mafia, building speculators, entrepreneurs, professionals, and both local and national politicians.

Of crucial importance, as with the growth of 'Tangentopoli', was sub-contracting at both national and local level. More than any other political élite in the history of Italy, the politicians of the Republic had at their disposal a great richness of resources. They acted, as we have seen, as gatekeepers of these resources, channelling them in directions often of their own choosing, with the intent to reinforce primarily their own power and clienteles. Criminal organizations sought to insert themselves into these patterns of resource distribution. According to the Camorra member Pasquale Galasso, sub-contracting was more lucrative even than the drug trade.[103] Major public works programmes were particularly significant. The rise of the 'Ndrangheta can be traced to the completion of the Autostrada del Sole, from Salerno to Reggio in the mid-60s; for the Camorra a crucial moment of expansion came with the 'reconstruction' of Naples after the earthquake of November 1980.

Control of municipal government was all-important, for only it could guarantee the Mafia the territorial freedom it needed, the possibility of obtaining building licences where and when it wanted, the chance to ignore any regulations protecting the local environment. As the years passed, the link between Mafia activities and ecological damage became ever clearer — rivers polluted, waste dumped indiscriminately, the environment damaged permanently in return for unbridled profits.[104] Local and national politicians who colluded in, or pretended to ignore, this free-for-all, were accessories to three sorts of crime simultaneously: the organization of unfair competitions for local sub-contracts, the knowing assignment of such contracts to illegal organizations and, gravest of all, irreparable long-term damage to local communities.

In all this, the national state was both present and absent at the same time. It made available a great quantity of resources, but showed little capacity or inclination to control their distribution or limit illegal infiltrations. In spite of the many denunciations of left-wing parties, it was only in 1963 that the first anti-Mafia parliamentary commission was finally set up.[105] At the same time those few servants of the same state who tried to check the growing tide of illegality found that officially the state was on their side, but that they were left without means and without defence. Cruel and coded equivocation of this sort, which left little space between martyrdom and collusion, was to be the hallmark of the state's response for many decades.

In 1968 Salvo Lima, the ex-mayor of Palermo, became a Christian Democrat national deputy for the first time, receiving more than 80,000 preference votes in Palermo. However, he had quarrelled bitterly and indeed usurped his former patron Giovanni Gioia, one of Fanfani's closest collaborators, and thus needed to look for a new patron at the apex of the Democrazia Cristiana. Fatefully, his needs coincided with those of Giulio Andreotti, who was seeking to expand his faction, which was too narrowly based in Rome and Lazio. Franco Evangelisti, one of Andreotti's closest collaborators, has recounted this crucial passage of Lima into Andreotti's camp:

After having founded at Rome our 'Primavera' faction within the party, I looked around for adhesions in the rest of Italy. And I met Lima, who belonged to Fanfani's camp, and he said to me: 'If I switch over to Andreotti, I'm not going to come alone, but with my lieutenants, colonels, infantry, fanfares and flags.' We talked for three days non-stop, and when the day arrived for the meeting in Andreotti's office in Montecitorio, Lima really did come as the head of an army.[106]

Lima was rewarded for his transfer with the post of under-secretary at the Ministry of Finance in Andreotti's second government (July 1972–July 1973), and further posts as under-secretary there and in the ministry for the Budget. These key positions in economic ministries made him a powerful national figure in his own right, and his influence in Sicily increased correspondingly.

The silver-haired and immaculately dressed Lima, nicknamed the 'viceroy of Sicily', cut a distinguished figure at Montecitorio at this time, but the deeply tainted nature of his politics did not allow him to pursue peacefully a national career. When he was appointed to the ministry for the Budget in 1974, the eminent economist Paolo Sylos Labini, who was part of the technical committee of the ministry over which Lima was to preside, resigned in protest. He had read the details of the judicial inquiries into Lima's conduct while mayor of Palermo and decided that they were 'of such consistency' as to be incompatible with a position in government.[107] In these years, characterized by a timid reawakening of judicial activity at Palermo, no less than eleven requests to incriminate Lima reached parliament. Most were refused, and others were delayed so long as to be rendered inoperative.[108] By 1979, Lima, although still immensely powerful in Sicily, had to be content with a post as a European deputy. Even then, a dossier denouncing his links with the Mafia followed in his wake to Strasbourg.[109]

It is unlikely that the full details of Lima's connection with the Mafia will ever emerge, for this was not the sort of contact of which an astute politician would like to leave hard evidence. Buscetta maintained that Lima's father had been a 'man of honour', and a large body of testimony, both of *'pentiti'* and other witnesses, now suggests that Lima was in constant contact with the Mafia.[110] So too were his friends Nino and Ignazio Salvo, who had made a fortune as tax collectors in Sicily. All over the island the *Andreottiani* came to be known for their opportunist attitudes towards those fatal linkages between clientelism, corruption and the Mafia. They were not alone, for other factions of the DC and other parties were also involved, but the *Andreottiani* had the worst reputation and the most influence. In April 1982 Carlo Alberto dalla Chiesa, the distinguished Carabiniere general, wrote to Giovanni Spadolini that Andreotti's faction at Palermo was 'the most compromised "political family" of the city'.[111]

As for Andreotti himself, he always replied evasively or dismissively about the nature of his lieutenants' activities in Sicily. He seemed disinterested in the qualities or the reputation of his men, as long as they brought in the votes and the membership cards. Nor could it have been true, as he himself claimed later, that he cared little about his own factional power within the party and did not know what was going on in Sicily.[112] On the contrary: Andreotti was renowned for his meticulous collecting of information,[113] he visited Sicily regularly for electoral campaigns, and dedicated time at Rome to Sicilian matters. When Vito Ciancimino, one of the most disreputable of Sicilian politicians, decided to make his peace with the *Andreottiani*, he was received at Palazzo Chigi on 6 November 1976 by Andreotti himself, at that time President of the Council of Ministers, in the presence of Salvo Lima and two other leading Sicilian politicians. Lima himself defined the meeting as 'aimed at establishing a general pacification at Palermo'.[114]

e. CONFRONTATION

During and after the internecine Mafia war of 1981–3, the relationship between Cosa Nostra and the state changed. Before this time it had been rare, though not unknown, for servants of the state or politicians to be targets of the Mafia. To kill them was in fact tantamount to admitting the failure of the policy of *'avvicinamento'*. However, in the climate of instability provoked by the struggle for control of Cosa Nostra, and with the triumph of its most ferocious and confrontational wing, the *Corleonesi*, something changed for good. The *mafiosi* were richer and more sure of themselves than ever before, and these material changes wrought a subtle change in the balance of power between the men of honour and the politicians. One of the defeated bosses, Gaetano Badalamenti, had once said, 'We cannot wage war on the State';[115] the new leaders, Salvatore Riina, Bernardo Provenzano, Leoluca Bagarella were not so sure.

At the same time, a growing number of public servants showed themselves unwilling to turn a blind eye to what was going on in Sicily. There are clear parallels here with what was happening in the rest of Italy in the 1980s – the growth of arrogant illegality contrasted by the fierce determination to fight back on the part of certain minorities within the state. In a Sicilian context, the clash between these two tendencies could only mean war, and a rather unequal one at that. The list of Mafia killings in these years is a long one. Among those who died were the magistrates Cesare Terranova, Gaetano Costa and Rocco Chinnici, the policemen and *carabinieri* Giuseppe Russo, Emanuele Basile and Boris Giuliano, the regional secretary of the PCI, Pio La Torre, who had been responsible for presenting to parliament the first comprehensive anti-Mafia legislation.[116]

The attitude of Andreotti and his Sicilian lieutenants to this escalation was profoundly ambiguous. On the one hand Andreotti himself, one of the most senior politicians in Italy, could hardly do otherwise than take an official anti-Mafia stance. On the other, the power base of the *Andreottiani* depended upon the continuation of a working relationship with Cosa Nostra, however 'unreasonable' it had become. It was a difficult tightrope to walk, and there were no safety-nets.

The case of Piersanti Mattarella, the Christian Democrat president of the Sicilian region, was an early warning of the difficulties that lay ahead. Mattarella was a traditional DC politician whose father had been a leading political boss on the island in the 1950s, and whose own career had benefited accordingly. However, in 1979 Mattarella decided to change tack completely and launch a moral renewal of Sicilian Christian Democracy. This extraordinary conversion soon led, hardly surprisingly, to his complete isolation. In a secret meeting with the then minister of the Interior, Virginio Rognoni, Mattarella gave vent to his anguish and preoccupation.[117]

The conversion of Mattarella presented very serious problems for the system of collusion between politicians and Mafia which had been laboriously constructed in Sicily. In particular, it threatened the bases on which Giulio Andreotti's lieutenants operated in Sicily. On 6 January 1980 Mattarella was killed by the Mafia. After the event, Franco Evangelisti, Andreotti's closest collaborator in Rome, asked Lima his opinion about what had happened: 'He replied with a single phrase: "When agreements are struck, they have to be kept." '[118]

*

Some two years later General Carlo Alberto dalla Chiesa, the Carabiniere officer who had played the leading role in the unmasking of the Italian terrorist groups, accepted the post of prefect of Palermo. Giovanni Spadolini was then President of the Council of Ministers. Dalla Chiesa had few illusions that the struggle against the Mafia was of a completely different order to that against the Red Brigades, if for no other reason than the long-established interlinking of Mafia and politics. In the same letter to Spadolini of 2 April 1982 quoted above, dalla Chiesa asked for exceptional support from the government, but in the months that he spent in Palermo he waited in vain for a clear definition of his role and powers.[119]

Dalla Chiesa left for Palermo on the day of the assassination of the Communist Pio La Torre, 30 April 1982. His time in Palermo was an unhappy one, and he came to feel increasingly isolated as the weeks passed. On 10 August, in an interview with Giorgio Bocca, he gave vent to his deepening sense of frustration:

I have clear ideas about what needs to be done, but as you'll understand I can hardly make them public. I can only tell you that I have already illustrated these ideas to the competent authorities, and indeed some time has already passed since I did so. I hope there will be some very rapid response. If not, we cannot hope for positive results . . . I believe I have understood the new rules of the game: the powerful government servant gets killed when two conditions intertwine: he has both become too dangerous and at the same time he is isolated, and therefore killable.[120]

Bocca returned to Milan, much struck by 'this singular personality, shrewd and ingenuous, a master of the Italian diplomatic arts, but with shafts of candour that are reminiscent of a figure from the Risorgimento'.[121] Little more than three weeks later, dalla Chiesa, his young wife and their bodyguard were assassinated as they drove to a dinner appointment. Rarely in the history of the Republic had national public opinion been so shocked.

It was at this point, very belatedly, that a long fight back began. Its first act was the approval, within ten days of the death of dalla Chiesa, of La Torre's bill which introduced for the first time, as Article 416 bis of the penal code, the crime of association for criminal purposes of a specifically Mafia nature.[122] Magistrates were also given the powers to overcome bank secrecy.

Before dalla Chiesa's death, only one article of La Torre's bill of 1980 had been approved by parliament. The hasty attempt at remedy in September 1982 was typical of the upper echelons of the Italian state. In their relationship to the Mafia they were capable not of action, but only of reaction in the face of enormity.

Fortunately, at a lower level, both judicial and municipal, there followed a very concerted effort to counteract the unbridled power of the new Mafia leadership. In the early 1980s two forty-year-old Sicilian prosecuting magistrates were emerging as particularly gifted and determined in the fight against the Mafia. Both Giovanni Falcone and Paolo Borsellino were from the middle classes of Palermo (Falcone's father was a chemist, Borsellino's a pharmacist), and both came from that minority of Sicilian families which had strong traditions of service to the Italian state. Maria Falcone, Giovanni's sister, told the American journalist Alexander Stille,

Our family was very religious and very attentive to the idea of civic duty. We grew up in the cult of the Fatherland. Mamma's brother died at age eighteen in the First World War, falsifying his birth certificate so he could volunteer for the army at age seventeen. My father's brother died at age twenty-four, as a career air force official. Hearing about these relatives as children developed in us, and in Giovanni, a love of country above all. 'They served the Nation!' my father would say with reverence.[123]

In his first major case, which concerned an international heroin ring organized from Palermo, Falcone introduced new scientific methods for investigating money-laundering and banking records. But to work in the Procura of Palermo at that time was to be in constant contact with death. Both Falcone's superiors and mentors, Gaetano Costa and Rocco Chinnici, were killed by the Mafia – Costa gunned down in the street in August 1980, and Chinnici blown up by a car bomb in July 1983.

After Chinnici's death, Antonino Caponnetto, a sixty-three-year-old magistrate of Sicilian origin who had spent most of his working life in Florence, volunteered to take his place. The Higher Council of the Judiciary, much to his own and many others' surprise, appointed him to the position. Caponnetto brought many attributes to his new, horrendous job: he was a fast and methodical worker, clear-headed and calm. He was also an outsider who chose to live in monastic simplicity in a police barracks close to his work, to which he was transported in a bullet-proof car. Caponnetto quickly assembled a pool of four magistrates – Falcone, Borsellino, Giuseppe De Lello and Leonardo Guarnotta – who dedicated themselves, body and soul, over the next few years to acquiring evidence against the principal Mafia bosses.[124] It is important to note that in these labours of Sisyphus they were supported by three Christian Democrat ministers in Bettino Craxi's first government: Mino Martinazzoli, the minister of Justice, and Virginio Rognoni and Oscar Luigi Scalfaro, successively ministers of the Interior.[125]

The breakthrough for the pool came with Tommaso Buscetta's decision in July 1984 to collaborate with Giovanni Falcone. Buscetta was one of the most senior surviving Mafia bosses, with extensive contacts on three continents (North and South America as well as Europe), and he had been one of the principal coordinators of the international cocaine market.[126]

Falcone explained later the significance of Buscetta's collaboration: 'Above all he gave us a global vision, ample and long range, of the phenomenon. He gave us an essential way to read the Mafia, a language and a code.'[127]

Buscetta's testimony and the skills of the anti-Mafia pool at Palermo produced a remarkable result: the famous '*maxiprocesso*' ('maxi-trial') against the Mafia, held in 1986–7 at Palermo in a special underground bunker constructed for the purpose. Four hundred and fifty-six persons were accused of various crimes, among them legendary leaders like Luciano Liggio and Michele Greco, who had been captured in 1986. At the end of the trial in December 1987 the court found 344 defendants guilty and inflicted nineteen life sentences on Mafia leaders. It was the largest single blow ever struck against the Mafia.

In these same years the control of local government at Palermo also took a dramatic change for the better. One of the few lasting effects of De Mita's attempt to renew the DC was the support he gave to a young and radical politician, Leoluca Orlando, who became mayor of Palermo in July of 1985. With the charismatic leadership of Orlando, who was under police protection twenty-four hours a day, the anti-Mafia elements in the city took new heart. University students organized protests in favour of the magistrates, the local Jesuits tried to push the Catholic hierarchy into greater activity against the Mafia, the associationism of civil society began to assume a mass character in the city for the first time. The Palermo 'spring', as it came to be called, combining as it did a massive judicial offensive against the Mafia with many local government and civil society initiatives, was one of the most unexpected and welcome aspects of Italy in the 1980s.[128]

However, without constant and unequivocal support at a national level, it was always going to be difficult to maintain the impetus for change at Palermo. In the *maxiprocesso* the crucial link between the Mafia and the highest institutions and personalities of the state had not emerged. Buscetta had things to reveal on this count, but he was not prepared to do so at that time. The pool of anti-Mafia magistrates dissolved amid a welter of polemics. Borsellino had left to go to Marsala, and barely one month after the sentence of the *maxiprocesso*, in January 1988, Antonino Meli rather than Giovanni Falcone was chosen to replace Caponnetto, who had reached retirement age. Meli's direction of the investigation office was little short of disastrous, characterized as it was by a rapid decline in anti-Mafia investigations. Falcone left Palermo to take up a senior post in the Ministry of Justice at Rome. To add insult to injury, grave doubts began to be expressed whether the higher courts would uphold the sentence of the *maxiprocesso*. By the end of the decade, therefore, the outlook for the anti-Mafia forces was uncertain indeed.

f. HIGH AND LOW POLITICS

On 23 July 1989, Giulio Andreotti once more became President of the Council of Ministers, a post he was to continue to hold, as we have seen, until the national elections of April 1992. Until October 1990 his minister of the Interior was Antonio Gava, whose links with the Neapolitan Camorra had long been suspected, but whose complicity with it was only to emerge in full in 1993.

So dubious a coupling promised little good for the fight against Italy's various Mafias. And yet, once again, the events between 1989 and 1992 belie any facile interpretation. In 1991 and 1992 important legislation was passed against organized crime: laws giving more powers to the police in cases of kidnapping, protecting '*pentiti*' in their collaboration with the forces of order, establishing a new transparency for sub-contracting, improving the coordination of the police's anti-Mafia activity.[129] In addition, Andreotti, responding to pressure from the lawyer of murdered Carabinieri, made sure that various *mafiosi* were not released from prison while awaiting the appeal of the *maxiprocesso*.[130]

It is only possible to explain seemingly so grave a contradiction – the simultaneous dependence upon, and repression of, the Mafia – by examining the different planes of political action on which Andreotti operated, which may indeed have corresponded to different parts of his complex personality. At the level of what may be called 'high' politics, a whole series of factors pushed Andreotti into an overt anti-Mafia stance. After the killing of dalla Chiesa, the maxi-trial and the Palermo 'Spring', public opinion had been alerted as never before to the anti-Mafia struggle. In this new climate, no prime minister could be seen to be lukewarm, particularly one as suspect as Andreotti. Furthermore, the Mafia killings showed no signs of stopping. In September 1990 a young and particularly courageous magistrate called Rosario Livatino, who with very little help had been trying to bring to justice some of the thirty-five different Mafia clans in the Agrigento area, was ambushed and killed as he drove to work. He had had no police protection.[131] In August 1991 Libero Grassi, a Palermo small businessman who had made public his refusal to pay protection money, and who had appeared on national television to denounce Mafia rackets, was killed outside his home. It was in the wake of his killing, which had a profound effect on public opinion, that the new police measures against the Mafia (which Falcone had done much to prepare at the Ministry of Justice) were pushed through parliament.

In the sphere of high politics Andreotti also had another, more personal motive that encouraged him to promulgate anti-Mafia legislation. In 1992 Cossiga's term as President of the Republic would come to a close, and it had long been Andreotti's unconcealed ambition to finish his distinguished political career as President of the Republic. In order to have any chance of doing so, he badly needed the support of the left, and of the PCI–PDS in particular. Any shirking on the anti-Mafia front would cost him dear.[132]

There were, thus, driving motives at one level for Andreotti to behave in a firm and determined way. But there were others, at the level of what may be termed 'low' politics, which caused him to behave in another, and it was this conflict, never resolved, which made of him a major tragic figure. For whatever reason – the need for factional strength, the fear of blackmail, a convenient turning of the blind eye, the conviction of impunity, an obstinate belief that that was the 'way politics worked' (the historian at this point can only speculate) – he never took his distance from the lower depths of Italian politics. On the contrary, he embraced them.

In June of 1991, having just visited the Middle East and sent messages to Bush and Gorbachov on his talks with Gadafy and Assad,[133] Andreotti flew to Sicily to support Lima's and his candidates in the island's regional elections.[134] He stayed two days touring Sicily, hardly the action of a politician who cared little about his own strength within the party. Moreover, these were the days after the surprise victory of Segni's referendum campaign, and of acute political crisis at Rome. At Trapani on 11 June, before an audience of some 2,500 persons assembled at the 'Palagranata', he spoke in favour of his local candidate, duly elected, Giuseppe Giammarinaro. But who was Giammarinaro? Well known in the area for having been president of the local USL, he had been a close collaborator of Nino and Ignazio Salvo, and was widely suspected of being a 'man of honour'. On 8 November 1990, the Carabinieri of Mazara del Vallo had informed the Prefect of Trapani that they were opposed to the renewal of Giammarinaro's gun licence because 'the person in question is suspected of having had, and of still having, illegal relations and not just simple contact, with persons being investigated for Mafia activity'.[135]

To try to maintain these two levels of political action – the swift response to the national request of the Carabinieri's lawyer and the ignoring (or wilful ignorance) of these same Carabinieri's warnings about his own candidate – was a very dangerous game. For many years 'high' and 'low' politics had flowed together in the history of the Republic without the one unduly disturbing the other. This was no longer the case. The decisions being taken at the first level were increasingly limiting the freedom of movement of the second. Giulio Andreotti was caught in a trap of his own making.

It was in the summer of 1991 that tension grew over the final judicial verdict regarding the convictions and life sentences which had been passed at the end of the maxi-trial in Palermo, in December 1987. At the first level of appeal, held in Palermo in 1989, the court had rejected the so-called 'Buscetta theorem' adopted by the anti-Mafia pool, by which Mafia leaders had been convicted because they formed part of the 'Cupola' of Cosa Nostra at the time of specific murders. The final appeal was due to be heard by the Corte di Cassazione in the second half of 1991.

The *mafiosi* leaders, both inside and outside prison, were convinced that their convictions would be quashed. Numerous testimonies from within the world of Cosa Nostra have revealed that the Mafia bosses were sure that their contacts in the upper echelons of the Italian state would guide their cases to a tranquil solution. They had faith in Lima and his friends in Rome; they had faith, in particular, in the president of the first section of the Corte di Cassazione, Corrado Carnevale, who had been responsible for a whole series of judgments which had allowed *mafiosi* to go free.[136] Carnevale and his fellow judge of the first section of the Cassazione, Paolino Dell'Anno, formed part of the circle of judges who rotated around Claudio Vitalone, one of Andreotti's closest collaborators.[137]

In the event the Mafia bosses were to be disappointed. In a dramatic and little-known confrontation at the apex of the Italian state, a confrontation which constituted one of those shafts of light which occasionally illuminated its actions, the fate of the greatest trial ever held against the Mafia was wrested out of Carnevale's hands. A combination of forces – the activity of Giovanni Falcone inside the Ministry of Justice, the unexpected sympathy of the Minister of Justice, Claudio Martelli, for Falcone, the protests of the Higher Court of the Judiciary and of the parliamentary anti-Mafia commission – all worked, in the summer of 1991, to ensure a fair appeal hearing. The final decision over the composition of the Court lay with the senior judge (*il primo Presidente*) of the Cassazione, Antonio Brancaccio. In the end he imposed as President of the hearing Alfonso Valente, a judge renowned for his probity and impartiality. On 31 January 1992 it was announced that the original sentences had been upheld. The chain of collusion had been broken.

The revenge of the Mafia leaders was not long in the making. Their political friends had betrayed them, or so it seemed to them. On 12 March 1992, with the national election campaign barely open, Salvo Lima, the 'viceroy of Sicily', was assassinated in Palermo. He had been busy preparing for the arrival of Giulio Andreotti, who was due in Sicily the following day to begin electioneering. Instead Andreotti flew to Lima's funeral, which he attended ashen-faced and visibly very shaken.

Chapter 7

The State Within and the State Without

THE MISDEEDS of significant sections of the Italian political class, their widespread involvement in the practices of corruption, the collusion of a minority of them with criminal organizations, would have been enough by themselves to have brought the Italian state into disrepute by the beginning of the 1990s. Yet subjective explanations, those which ascribe to specific historical actors the overall responsibility for a given course of events, are very rarely sufficient. Structure plays an equally important role; and if it is neither easy nor perhaps even desirable to separate radically the one from the other – that is, subjects from structures – it is none the less important to examine, as best one can, the interplay between the two.[1] In the Italian case it was the structures of the state, and in particular the public administration, that offered the essential underpinning to all other discourses on the weakness of Italian democracy. The first part of this chapter is therefore dedicated to an analysis of these structural defects, while the second examines the way in which they interwove with the failings of the political class so as to create a particular image of Italy in Europe and the wider world.

The development and expansion of the state in Europe over the past decades has followed a dual trajectory, both vertical and horizontal. On the vertical axis the modern state has seen its spheres of action and its institutional presence increase both *above* and *below* its traditional national frame of reference. In other words, European states have become increasingly involved in, and bound by, supra-national institutions and organizations: those of the European Union in the first place, but also many others of a transnational

213

and global nature dealing with trade, security, environment and the like. At the same time, European nation states have increasingly devolved power to a sub-national level of government, both regional and municipal. This vertical 'stretching' of the state, upwards and downwards, has been accompanied by a similar, if not identical, process on a horizontal plane (if society is taken to be the plane of the horizon). The state has intervened in ever-increasing areas of social life: at first in those traditionally connected with the establishment of the welfare state – health, social insurance, education and housing; more recently in aspects of which William Beveridge did not even dream – gender equality, mass immigration, pollution, and so on.[2]

The net result of this expansion along two different axes has been the enormous increase in that complexity of the state to which passing reference has already been made. The state has come to resemble ever less a pyramid, with a clearly descending chain of command, and much more a network, even a patchwork. Different decisions involve different levels of the vertical axis; some are taken primarily at European and regional level; others at national, continental and global level; others still, at local level only. At the same time each sectoral area of the state has its own policy communities and policy networks which extend into society, and in which private and public interests and structures intermesh.[3] In such circumstances, the need to define public interests and public ethics has increased, but so too has the difficulty of doing so.

In the 1980s the prevailing political and academic orthodoxy in western Europe and the United States was that the nation state both needed to be 'rolled back' and was effectively on the retreat. In a decade that emphasized the values of free enterprise and the deficiencies of the public sphere, there were significant attempts, none more so than in Britain, to privatize whole areas of activity that had previously been the responsibility of the state. At the same time diverse external forces, such as the dynamism of international financial markets, the power of multinational companies, the development of supra-national European institutions, threatened to undermine the authority of single European nation states.

There was no denying the real force of these trends, but by the end of the 1990s it had become clear that the nation state had been more reshaped than reduced.[4] If the state had been 'rolled back' in some countries and in some areas, it had extended its powers in others. In Britain widespread privatization under Mrs Thatcher was accompanied by coercive centralization and increased spending on the repressive apparatuses of the state. In Belgium, by contrast, there was radical decentralization but only timid privatizing raids on the public sector.[5] Overall, as Müller and Wright have written, 'the nation state has remained for most of its citizens a primary source of welfare, order, authority, legitimacy, identity and loyalty'.[6]

1. Inside the Italian State

1.1. The Case of Italian Public Administration

For an organism as complicated and diffuse as the modern democratic state it is arduous to adopt the traditional metaphor of the body politic. But if it may be accepted that somewhere in its amorphous body the modern state has a brain, which corresponds to its government, then somewhere there is also a heart, which is its public administration and which pumps life-blood into its various limbs. Public administration is critical to the establishment of consent and legitimacy, because it is through its actions that the citizen can judge, at a daily level, the efficacy of the state. It is this organ which was weakest in the Italian case, and which most commands our attention.[7]

a. THE CULTURE OF SOCIETY AND THE NORMS OF THE STATE

One of the most important moments in the formation of the modern state was the separation of its modes of functioning and rules of conduct from those of the society which it was called upon to govern. To the one side lay the practices of the *ancien régime*, the asymmetrical relations of power founded on loyalty and reverence, on protection and submission, on faith and obedience. To the other, as Max Weber wrote, stood the triumph of impersonal over personal relations, the foundation of clearly understood rules and norms for the state's actions, the growth of the 'formal rationality' of the bureaucracy. The public administration was to be guided by principles of equality of treatment and transparency of procedures; its defining characteristics were to be precision, continuity, discipline, strictness, reliability.[8]

The absence of any such clear demarcation between the traditional culture of society and the workings of the state was to be one of the principal blights upon the development of the Italian public administration. Of course, it should be said in immediate mitigation that *no* modern bureaucracy emerged in perfect conformity with Weber's ideal-type.[9] All modern administrations function not only on the basis of law and regulation, but also on personal contact and informal relations.[10] However, it is the balance between these two elements, and the general context in which they operate, that are all important. In the Italian case, and that of southern Europe in general, the personal and the particular have always outweighed and threatened to engulf the impersonal and the impartial.

Why this should have been so is a very complicated historical question that lies beyond the scope of this book. Suffice it to say here that by the time of the post-war Republic a chasm separated the formal codes of behaviour of the public administration from its actual functioning. *In formal terms*, the actions of the civil service were minutely regulated by administrative law, whose principal objective was to safeguard the citizen against the arbitrary power of the bureaucracy. This was what has been called the 'justice-oriented' culture of Italian administration.[11] *In reality*, the habitual practice of the bureaucracy depended to a notable extent upon the exercise of discretionary power on the part of the functionary. The key term 'discretion' did not in this case signify the necessary and desirable autonomy of action of the individual civil servant within a general framework of impartiality, but rather the performance of favours in response to particularistic pressure. The speed and efficiency, indeed the very realization, of a bureaucratic act became dependent upon this sort of discretionary act, and the task of the citizen (if she or he could be called such in these circumstances) was to find the right levers to trigger that action. Naturally enough, not all citizens were equal or could exert equal pressure. Inducements to action varied, from the use of friends and relatives to the pulling of rank, to outright corruption. As a result, there came into being a profoundly *deformed relationship* between citizen and state.[12]

The social history of this deformed relationship has never been written, and still less has it been the object of study of those most qualified to comment upon it, the social anthropologists.[13] A striking exception, which must serve here as a substitute for an extended analysis, is the following account of everyday bureaucratic procedure in Naples in the 1980s. It was written by the anthropologist Amalia Signorelli, who at the time was also a member of the municipal council of the city. Her experience would appear to illustrate perfectly the general *modus operandi* outlined above, and as a sequence of events is instantly recognizable by anyone who has ever lived for any length of time in Italy:

I am in the central post office in Naples; I have to pay the telephone and electricity bills which are just about to be overdue. The queue for paying these bills is a long one, while at the next window, which is for a different service, there is nobody. Two local policemen in uniform come into the post office, go to the empty window, and extract their own and highly recognizable telephone and electricity bills. In a few minutes they have both paid and are about to leave. I cannot restrain myself. I go up to them, pull out my identification as a member of the municipal council, and contest the impropriety of what they have just done. They are perplexed; even, I would say, amazed. But from behind the window comes the chirruping voice of an all-too-willing female clerk: 'But Councillor, why didn't you come and show me your identification? I would have seen you through straight away.'[14]

Such habitual modes of behaviour in the daily operations of the bureaucracy had profound consequences for the relationships between the individual, the family, society and the state. They ensured that in the vital process of *interiorization* of codes of conduct for the public sphere, individuals were presented by the state with no constant and clear alternative to the long-standing practices of clientelism. On the contrary: patron–client relations, the exchange of favours, the use of kin and friends, became an accepted way for families to negotiate and traverse the bureaucracy. The state was not seen as either impartial or benevolent, but rather as a container of resources which individuals and families, if they found the right keys, could hope to unlock. Such a system had an undeniable logic and vivacity, even considerable human warmth, but there was little room within it for the growth of citizenship.[15]

b. THE ROOTS OF INEFFICIENCY

The weakness of the Italian public administration did not just derive from its failure to make a 'Weberian leap'. It derived also from its deep-rooted inefficiency, low productivity and disorganization. Indeed, these played a major role in pushing citizens to seek individualist and clientelistic solutions to their problems. Inefficiency, particularism and bureaucratic 'discretion' thus combined to form a vicious circle of private–public relationships from which it was very difficult to escape.

There were multiple reasons for the inefficiency of the public administration. One of the most important, already mentioned, was the dominance of a legalistic culture over one oriented to offering services. Administrative law was paramount, and every activity carried out on behalf of the state had to be set within its framework. The system was intended to safeguard the citizen against the arbitrary power of the bureaucracy, but in reality led to greater complication and inertia. In 1993 the government report on the state of the public administration observed that while in France there were 7,325 laws in force, and in Germany 5,587 (excluding the legislative activity of the Länder), in Italy the number of laws and regulations having legal status was *estimated* to be around 90,000.[16] The country suffered from a bad case of normative inflation. Legalism of this sort also led to a form of hierarchy where the lower grades of civil servants were quite unwilling to take initiatives or move outside the straitjacket of the regulations. This arid terrain of laws, statutes, circulars and internal directives was not one on which a culture of service could possibly grow, because it was essentially inward- rather than outward-looking.[17]

A second multiplicator of inefficiency was an over-developed tradition of centralism. If the Italians borrowed from the Germans the concept of the *Rechtsstaat*, the state based upon the rule of law, they took from the French the concentration of power in the major ministries of the capital. Even as late as the 1980s, the degree of autonomy which certain institutions like art galleries and museums, which elsewhere in Europe managed themselves, was non-existent. An institution of world renown like the Uffizi Gallery in Florence could not even open its own bookshop or cafeteria.[18] In the same city, it took the National Library five years to obtain from the Ministero dei Beni Culturali Venetian blinds to replace the moth-eaten curtains in the reading room; after which the blinds broke within five weeks.

Centralization went hand-in-hand with distrust. From the distant origins of the unified state, when the nation builders were faced with a fragmented and centrifugal society, the state never made the transition, not even in a democratic Republic, to trusting its citizens until such point as they proved themselves untrustworthy. Signatures had to be verified by notaries, applications for jobs had to be accompanied by numerous certificates, the task of becoming an Italian citizen either by marriage or by naturalization passed through nine and sometimes ten different offices of the state and took an average of 730 days.[19] Only with great difficulty did the practice of *'autocertificazione'*, introduced by the law no. 15 of 1968, come to be accepted by the mid-1990s in many offices of the state. All this, as must be obvious, did irreparable harm to the relationship between state and individual. If the state was unprepared to trust its citizens, then how could they trust it?

The personnel of the state were not, as we have seen,[20] more numerous than in the other major European countries, but they were often poorly distributed, both geographically and between ministries. Thus in 1993 the Ministry of Agriculture, which coordinated a constantly declining sector of the national economy, still maintained a very large administrative pay-roll, while the Ministry of the Environment, with ever-increasing responsibilities, had only a tiny staff.[21] Functionaries had a proprietary attitude to their jobs, which they regarded, usually with reason, as theirs for life. Their trade unions, highly fragmented in structure, constituted for the most part a major obstacle to reform, their prevailing attitudes being narrowly corporative. No attention was paid to building a culture of service to the public.[22] In 1994 Sabino Cassese, a scholar not given to exaggeration, described with great severity the prevailing attitudes in the public administration:

The cultural model in question is one oriented to leave things as they are, to postpone change till the morrow, to wait for others to ask, to be ready to strike a bargain. It constitutes the very antithesis of a Weberian model of administration. It is a type of civil service not based on legality and rationality, but rather on contract and convention.[23]

The vital task of creating an administrative élite, capable of imparting an ethos and an *esprit de corps* to the rest of the bureaucracy, had never been undertaken with sufficient seriousness.[24] Furthermore, the process of recruitment to the civil service, in spite of any number of formal guarantees, was deeply permeated by preferential treatment. To quote Cassese again:

In the last fifteen years, in spite of the fact that the Constitution lays down that entry to the public administration is by examination, around 60 per cent of public employees have been hired by means of temporary or 'precarious' contracts, which are then followed by permanent 'titularizations'. In this way, the bureaucrats have been able to find jobs for their relatives, following a long-standing custom of privileging family interests rather than those of the State. The political parties, in their turn, have managed to place their 'clients' in the public administration, thus fortifying their own electoral base.[25]

A last, and perhaps superfluous comment in the light of the above, regards the question of controls. In a system dominated by administrative law, the final control was recourse to law. In 1991 alone there were 110,000 appeals to administrative and financial tribunals; another 800,000 were pending (a situation to which we will have to return). The obverse side of this pathological recourse to the administrative courts was the ineffectiveness of ordinary administrative controls, above all those which performed corrective or preventive functions. The public administration seemed incapable of keeping its own house in order, a structural deficiency that was to be mercilessly revealed by the 'Tangentopoli' inquests.[26]

c. SHAFTS OF LIGHT

So black a picture can hardly go unqualified. In many parts of the public administration there were exceptions to the general pattern traced above, pockets of efficiency and impartiality, or at least of one if not of the other. Such exceptions could be found both at a macro level, in certain major institutions of the state, and at a micro one, in single offices (even post offices). There were also many examples of the individual actions of conscientious minorities.

At the institutional level, no example was more significant than that of the Bank of Italy. In the immediate post-war period its Governor, Luigi Einaudi, found the Bank deeply permeated by the culture of clientelism and nepotism. On 17 February 1945 he noted in his diary that in the Bank 'there exist various clans: one Venetian (Stringher), another Neapolitan (Azzolini), a third Apulian (Introna) . . . We are in the presence of extensive kinship ties amongst the employees, with various negative consequences.'[27] Slowly, the Bank developed a different culture, as well as evolving a more dialectical relationship with the governing parties, to which it always risked being subservient. A significant turning-point was the governorship of Guido Carli, from 1963 to 1975. Carli, as we have seen, was closely linked to the Christian Democrats and was to become Andreotti's Minister for the Treasury; but he was also deeply committed to building up the prestige of the Bank of Italy.[28]

Step by step, the Bank secured greater autonomy from the Treasury, and at the same time greater freedom for the market from both. This process, pursued sometimes in the face of considerable difficulty[29] by Carli's successors, Paolo Baffi and Carlo Azeglio Ciampi, reached a first key moment in July

1981 with the so-called 'divorce' between Bank and Treasury. The Bank was no longer obliged to buy up all residual state bonds at the end of each public auction, and the Treasury had to rely on its own resources for the financing of public spending.[30] A second turning-point came ten years later, in 1991, with the decision to allow full freedom to the Bank to fix interest rates.[31]

The relative economic autonomy of the Bank was accompanied by a cultural transformation which was of equal, if not even greater, significance. Carli built up a research office which had no equivalent in the other European central banks, and from which the top management of the Bank of Italy was regularly recruited.[32] Over a thirty-year period, the Bank's culture became that of internationalism, of profound economic professionalism, of transparency, reliability and discipline.[33] In one of the most important and delicate apparatuses of the state, a model was created which was strikingly different from that of the public administration as a whole.

There remained, of course, the delicate problem of the Bank's accountability. The greater its autonomy, the less the control that could be exercised over it by the democratically elected representatives of the people. The ideal balance between autonomy and control in such cases is probably impossible to establish. Faced with such a problem, perhaps all that a *historian* can do is to be case-specific, and to look closely at the motives of those wishing to diminish the Bank's autonomy and those wishing to increase it. On this basis, and bearing in mind the overall conditions of politics and administration in the 1980s, the relative autonomy of the Bank, and the wider cultural ramifications which accompanied it, would appear to have been a vital resource to the nation.

At a more humble level it was possible to find, even in the most ramshackle of structures, minorities of civil servants who succeeded in doing their jobs in a proper fashion. The problem, though, was that they were trapped like flies in a system whose logic and workings constantly obstructed them. If the conscientious individual was isolated for too long, exhaustion or cynicism would eventually take the place of an earlier enthusiasm.

In an interesting study dating from the early 1990s and based in the city of Rome, the sociologist Tatiana Pipan examined three very different experiences of state services on offer to the inhabitants of the capital: the student office of a university faculty, the registry office of the sixth circumscription of the capital, and a specialized department in a medium-sized hospital.[34] In the first, the administrative secretary had succeeded in transforming the office and its relations with students by adopting what Pipan has called a 'bureaucratic *maternage*'.[35] In the second, thanks to a strong group spirit, the registry worked efficiently. It managed, for example, to issue certificates within three days of request, compared to an average forty days in the other circumscriptions.[36] In the third, the dynamic and charismatic leadership of one of the consultants had led both to a high level of satisfaction on the part of the patients, and to a significant research profile, maintained by grants from the private sector.[37]

However, in all three cases there were serious drawbacks relating to the wider context in which the public employees worked. Sometimes the problems were very old, and sometimes very new. The building which housed the registry was described as 'disintegrating' and without a waiting-room for the public, which was constrained to queue outside for considerable periods of time and in all weathers. Opening hours to the public were from 8.30 a.m. to 11.30 a.m. only. The mornings were portrayed by the interviewees as 'hours of combat', between an exasperated public and be-leaguered clerks.[38]

Dysfunctions and frustrations, though, could also be directly related to innovation, in this case to the way in which information technology was being used. In both the university and the registry, computerization had led to a diminution, not an increase, of the individual functionary's autonomy and discretion, here used in the sense of being able to take decisions at a micro-level in the interests of the general public.[39] As for the hospital, only three out of the eleven departments were judged to be efficient by the direction. One of the principal problems was the need for the doctors to circumvent or ignore the complicated web of rules which rendered efficiency impossible to achieve.[40]

One of the most depressing aspects of Pipan's participant observation was the way in which these dedicated service workers viewed the functioning of public services in sections other than their own. The clerks at the registry, for instance, were convinced that the best, if not the only way for individuals or families to deal with the many disservices of the national health service (waiting lists, delays in the results of analyses, etc.) was by the mobilization of kinship networks within the USL and the hospitals. Whereas a young doctor had this to say about the general standard of public services in Italy's capital: 'It's always necessary to use networks of friendship or acquaintances. Nothing's straightforward or normal – I go there and I get served. Instead, I have to know what a certain place is like, I have to plan my approach, I have to be a whole series of things.'[41]

d. THE NEED FOR REFORM AND THE DIFFICULTY OF ACHIEVING IT

During the history of the Republic various attempts have been made to reform the public administration. However, as Giliberto Capano has shown with great clarity, the various cycles of attempted reform – that of the immediate post-war period, of the centre-left governments, of 1979–83 –

seemed ineluctably to result in adjustments to the economic and juridical status of the personnel, and little else.[42] Accurate analyses of the civil service's failings, like that of Giuseppe Medici in 1963, or major proposals for reform, like that of Massimo Saverio Giannini in 1982, were welcomed and then quietly put to one side.

In trying to explain why this was so, it is necessary to return to individual, and subjective, responsibilities. Certainly, the structures of the administration and their underlying culture were daunting in the extreme (the reformer's equivalent of the north face of the Eiger), but little help came from the political class as a whole. Administrative reform was *never*, from 1944 onwards, considered to be a priority, even when a specific ministry was created for the task. Indeed, the politicians seemed to accord the same importance to the administration as they did to Europe; and Italy's short-comings in both were, as we shall see in a moment, indelibly linked.

It was also the case that even when the will was there the way was not, or that volition and cognition rarely coincided.[43] From the Second World War onwards there circulated different versions of the myth of the 'great reform', the belief in a single grand transformative act which could resolve previous problems. Unfortunately, Italian realities proved rather recalcitrant. In an era of ever-increasing complexity of state structures, and with the culture of particularism deeply embedded both inside and outside the Italian public administration, the time for the great 'Weberian leap' had long since passed. Or, at least, the need for transparency, efficiency and equity remained, but the means of getting there could not be by a nineteenth-century model of 'rational' command.

During the period 1980–92, the two most significant pieces of legislation regarding the public administration were passed during Giulio Andreotti's last occupation of Palazzo Chigi, from 1989 to 1992: the law no. 142 of 8 June 1990 on the reorganization of local government; and the law no. 241 of 7 August of the same year, on administrative procedures and the right of access to public documents. The first introduced new areas of autonomy for local government, and defined clearly the relationships between local politicians and civil servants, granting to the first overall control and strategic planning, and to the second executive responsibilities. The second law tackled administrative procedures, and tried to lay down clear rules and limits for them. The different offices of the state were obliged to inform the public how long a procedure would take, identify a single functionary responsible for it, and grant right of access to documentation. For the first time in Italy, citizenship took on an administrative aspect.[44]

Unfortunately, both laws, and especially the second, encountered what has been called 'the obdurate and insensible resistance of the bureaucracy'.[45]

More than three years after the promulgation of the law no. 241, eighteen out of the nineteen central ministries had responded by fixing time limits for each procedure and naming the functionaries responsible for them, but only 20 per cent of local governments had done so, and only three of the twenty regional governments. Even where the letter of the law had been respected, its spirit had not. The average time which the public administration had given itself for completing procedures, many of which were disarmingly simple in content if not in form, was six months, and 8 per cent of procedures were estimated to require more than a year.[46]

In the light of these failures, it was obvious that solutions to the extremely complex problem of administrative reform were not going to be easy to come by. All over Europe in the 1980s and early 1990s different solutions were proposed for reforming state bureaucracies – reductions in size, deregulation, increased monitoring capacities from above, improved management, the dismantlement of the traditional statutory framework, and so on.[47] In Italy two themes constantly recurred, often assuming the status of magic wands. One was the introduction of information technology; the other was privatization. The first appealed to the magic of technological revolution; the second to the virtuous power of the market. The first certainly held out the hope that many frustrating and time-wasting procedures, like the paying of gas, electricity and telephone bills, could be eliminated automatically. Clerks behind windows would disappear, as would the queues and preferential treatment which the anthropologist Signorelli had observed. However, a great deal depended on *how* information technology was used, on the overall cultural and indeed political vision of those who had responsibility for its introduction. Computerization could cut both ways. If old attitudes were applied to new instruments, then the net result would be, as we have already seen, more frustration than liberation for functionaries, and a poorer quality of service.

As for privatization, it too had profoundly ambivalent qualities. The case for the privatization, in one form or another, of various parts of public services and administration formed part of a wider campaign for a major reduction of the public sector as a whole. Guido Carli, for instance, was convinced that privatizations were 'the funnel into which fifty, or perhaps sixty years of Italian history are going to flow. That was, and still is, the key to everything.'[48] The advantages were simply stated: if handled right, privatization would introduce competition, and through competition efficiency. The lackadaisical public administration of the state would be replaced by market relations, which would force up productivity, bring down inflated costs, provide incentives.[49] The selling-off of the property of the state would aid significantly the reduction of the public debt, and enlarge the profile of share-holding in the nation. Furthermore, the growth of private firms operating in what once had been the sector of public services would enrich the whole nature of Italian capitalism.

This was an attractive programme, and it will have a very familiar ring to British readers. It had significant elements of truth to it: the breaking of public monopolies in a whole series of services could indeed lead to greater efficiency and productivity. The dismantling of traditional statutory frameworks, which had been based on administrative law, could lead to greater flexibility and the end of the 'job for life' syndrome, oblivious as it was to commitment and productivity. But as the experience of more than one country in the 1980s and 1990s demonstrated, there were no guarantees of the alchemic qualities of privatization.[50] Looked at in historical terms, arguments for and against the public provision of services had a certain cyclical quality to them. In the 1940s the wave of nationalizations and the extension of state services all over western Europe had been a response, at least in part, to the inefficiency and inequity of the private sector in previous decades. Forty years later, the boot was on the other foot.

A question as complicated as this cannot be addressed adequately here. It was clear that the future lay with a greater mixture of private and public services than previously, and that it was neither possible, nor perhaps even desirable, for the state to organize directly as many services for the public as it had done in the past, especially if they were run as they were in Italy.

However, it is important to be aware of both the abdicatory and in some respects the unreal quality of many of the arguments in favour of privatization. Privatization programmes were abdicatory because they abandoned the struggle to create public ethics in favour of market mechanisms, which were not the same thing at all. They were unrealistic because they believed in a radical slimming-down of the state at a time when the state, as we have seen, was more complex and permeative than ever.[51] If the British state spent as much on the public sector at the end of Thatcherism as at the beginning, and if its civil service employed nearly as many people in 1993 as it had done in 1979, that is after fourteen years of ferociously determined majoritarian government totally committed to the private sector, then it was clear that something more than political volition was at work.[52] To put it simply, public sector services, if not industry, were here to stay. Consequently, the really crucial problem, *pace* Carli, was not to dream of abdication but of reinvention.

How this reinvention of the public sphere of service and administration was to take place gave rise to considerable discussion, and after 1992, as we shall see in the last two chapters, to the most significant attempt at reform in the whole of the twentieth century in Italy.

1.2. Family, Welfare and the State

a. WEAK CONNECTIONS

Just how necessary was the reinvention of administrative practice can be gauged by examining the relationship between Italian families and the welfare state. The 'welfare' that contemporary democratic states are prepared to offer to their populations varies widely both in content and in coverage. With regard to content, the traditional areas of intervention of modern welfare states can be simply listed: social insurance of various sorts (against unemployment, disability, sickness), pensions (principally for old age but also of other sorts), health services (both of prevention and cure), public education for children and adults, public housing, family allowances or child benefits, and finally specific assistance policies aimed at the poorest families or individuals of a national community.[53] But it is also true that the confines of public welfare services have changed constantly in the second half of the twentieth century, retracting in one area and expanding in another.

In terms of coverage, even if many welfare states are hybrids, at least three distinct models have emerged: the first is universalist, offering protection and services to the whole resident population, regardless of income, gender, occupation, etc.; the second occupational, where coverage is sectorial and dependent on employment, with contributions coming from workers, employers and the state; the third merely residual, with coverage confined to those categories of the population unable to cope or to afford private health services, insurance, etc.[54] Among the many merits of a universalist conception of public welfare is that it does not merely reflect existing socio-economic differences. Rather it responds, in positive terms, to the questions which one of the greatest scholars of the welfare state, Richard Titmuss, posed at the end of his last book: 'What effect does the system have on the social and psychological sense of community? Does it have divisive or unifying effects and in what sense and for what groups? Does it, in short, widen or diminish the concept and consciousness of "who is my neighbour"?'[55]

Within families, individual members have always had different relations, as well as needs, with respect to public welfare services. It is women who have the greatest responsibility and contact with the welfare state, accompanying young children and elderly relatives, purchasing medicines and collecting analyses, spending significant parts of their time in queues in clinics and offices. Yet very often, in historical terms, it is to male heads of families that benefits have been accorded, with women treated as their dependants.[56]

It is also true that rarely have there flourished ideas of a welfare state, even in democracies, which encourage other than a purely passive model of citizenship. Families have been treated as isolated atoms, to which protection and services are distributed from above. Forms of interaction or participation, let alone control, have been almost entirely absent, even in systems based on universal coverage. It is not only in Italy that consultant doctors sweep past on their hospital rounds, rather like medieval lords of the manor, followed by a retinue of junior doctors, while families and patients are left desperately hoping for a few words of information or of comfort. Yet it is in informal moments such as these, as much as in the formal ones of voting in local and national elections, that modern democracy is tested and often found wanting.

In the history of the Italian Republic, there had been a long tradition of only partial welfare coverage, based principally on male employment. In the field of health care and assistance, many services were offered by Catholic and private organizations rather than by the state.[57] This pattern was interrupted in a significant, even dramatic way, in the late 1960s and the 1970s. Very much in response to the social movements of that time, a culture of individual social rights came into being. The content of Italian public welfare was reinforced significantly: state maternity schools were introduced in 1968, municipal kindergartens in 1971, family advisory clinics in 1975. Above all, in 1978 the new national health service came into being. Based on universalist principles, it offered the promise of a reduction in the gross disparities of class and region, as well as an ambitious programme of preventative medicine.

During the same period the rights of individuals within families were modified profoundly by the reform of family law in 1975. Parity between the two partners in marriage was established, the head of family could be of either sex, all legal discriminations against children born out of wedlock were abolished, new guidelines were established for relations between parents and children.[58] Together with the victories in the referenda on divorce (1974) and abortion (1981), these reforms constituted a major public shift towards a more democratic definition of families, as well as a significant growth in public provision for them.

This dual impetus – towards a universalist welfare state and towards the expansion of individual rights – was not maintained, for a variety of reasons. With regard to the welfare state, the rising costs of services and insurance afflicted all the member states of the European Community in the 1970s and 1980s. The rapid growth in the number of elderly people, the cost of advanced medical technology, the increased consumption and diversity of health services, the low standards of productivity, these were all common problems with no easy solutions.

The Italian case was particular for a number of reasons.[59] Pension provision had been over-generous in certain areas, allowing for instance public service workers to 'retire' with a so-called 'baby' pension at a ridiculously early age. The national health service founded in 1978, though based on very advanced principles, could not by itself redress some of Italy's gravest and most long-standing welfare problems. It managed, for instance, to ensure that the number of hospital beds per head of population was broadly equal in the different parts of the country, but standards of health care continued to be radically different in North and South. Regions like the Veneto and Emilia-Romagna offered high standards of medicine and care, while much of the South offered the opposite.[60]

Nor was there in any way a new leap into administrative efficiency. On the contrary; the managing boards of the Unità Sanitarie Locali (local medical units) became, especially in the South, bywords for incapacity and corruption. Some 11,000 persons – presidents, vice-presidents, and board members – were appointed by the political parties at a local level. Many of them were place-men of the local spoils system, with limited technical competence or administrative skills, but considerable economic appetites.[61] Their counterparts at a national level, who were to be found in the Ministry of Health and as members of the National Commission for Medicines, organized a highly lucrative system of kickbacks involving major pharmaceutical companies. In 1994 the Court of Accounts estimated that the system of setting artificially high prices on certain medicines in return for kickbacks had alone cost the health system some 30,000 billion lire in the period 1983–93, while an estimated 15,000 billion lire had been paid in kickbacks to politicians and functionaries during the same period.[62] Thus the high noon of party government gave rise to a profound contradiction at the heart of the Italian welfare system – a universalist national health service run along clientelistic and often corrupt lines.[63]

In the 1980s and early 1990s, government welfare policy was characterized by a strategy of containment and lack of innovation. With costs rising for both legitimate and illegitimate reasons, there was no proper reformulation of welfare policy, but only piecemeal provisions: the increase in the price of prescriptions for medicines, and the introduction of charges in other areas such as tests and consultant appointments; the setting of limits to spending and the introduction of cuts in services wherever possible. Thanks to these economies, the spending on the health service as a percentage of GDP increased only modestly, from 5.6 per cent to 6.5 per cent in the period from 1980 to 1992.

The state reverted back towards *delegating* to families rather than *providing* for them.[64] One significant example of this tendency was the fate of the family advisory clinics. Set up with the intention of offering aid and advice to families as a whole, the clinics never received the priority treatment and funding which they deserved. At a time when many members of families needed expert help on a series of issues, which varied from marriage difficulties to contraception to drug abuse, from children's suffering in the event of their parents' separation to the provision of psychoanalytic care, the state offered few helping voices and fewer still welcoming institutions. By 1980 only 727 clinics had been set up, of which 72 per cent were in the Centre-North of the country. In a survey carried out in Milan in 1986, only 8 per cent of the interviewees said that they had ever used the clinics, and this in a metropolitan area where services of such a kind were most needed.[65] Many of the clinics that existed did very valuable work, but they were under-staffed and with inadequate resources.[66] A service that had been conceived as being universal in two ways – for all members of families and all classes of the population – had been transformed into little more than a residual one, directed in a very patchy way at poor mothers.

At the same time the democratic inputs from the 1970s faltered at the threshold of Italy's welfare institutions. A revealing example from a specialist sphere is that of parental involvement in the care for their premature babies in hospital. A cross-European survey of 1998 revealed that whereas 100 per cent of Swedish and British neonatal units allowed unrestricted family visiting, the corresponding number in Spain was just 11 per cent and in Italy 18 per cent. Whereas in Great Britain 89 per cent of units explicitly involved parents in ethical decisions concerning their babies, that number dropped to 19 per cent in Italy. Differences of such magnitude, occurring at a critical moment in family formation, were precious indicators of the institutional culture of a specific nation.[67]

The truth was that the ruling parties of the Republic, in spite of a great deal of rhetoric about safeguarding the family, had never evolved coherent family policies. Rather, as Chiara Saraceno has written, there developed over time 'a family politics restricted to very limited areas of intervention, circumscribed to particular social categories, often contradictory'.[68] Thus there was adequate maternity *leave*, but poor maternity *care*; infant schooling for 80 per cent of children between three and five years old, but crèches for only 5 per cent of the age group up to three years; tax deductions for a dependent spouse, but child benefits only for three or more children, and then only for dependent workers. Sometimes it was easy to discern the influence of Catholic ideology at work, as with tax rewards for married couples. At other times the state's distraction seemed to correspond to no particular choice, being rather a series of *ad hoc* and sporadic responses to pressures of different kinds.

The only clear line that emerged was that of devolving family problems to families themselves, and of tying individual members of families to each other as far as possible. This latter formed part of a long-standing tradition of Italian law relating to the family. Under the norms of the civic code, to quote Saraceno again:

Parents are economically responsible for children practically for always, if children prove incapable of providing for themselves. Brothers and sisters can be called upon to cope with each other's needs at any stage of their lives. Sons- and daughters-in-law are responsible for their parents-in-law. All this has practical consequences for social rights; it also has consequences for how individual needs and rights are viewed.[69]

Naturally, family law and family life are far from the same thing, and what may be a norm in the one sphere can be widely ignored in the other. None the less, it would be foolish to deny the reciprocal influence of the two. In Italy, the relationship between what Mary Glendon has called 'two moving systems' – the set of laws affecting families, and the patterns of behaviour that constitute the social institution of the family – tended to confirm the emphasis on the family as an institution, often at the expense of the individual within it.[70]

These attitudes and policies, or lack of them, had a number of significant consequences in the 1980s and 1990s. They meant that when average families, that is those of the urban middle classes, had need of the state, sought it out, touched it at a daily level, they were very often dissatisfied. It was true that these middle-class families used certain health services, especially preventative and specialist ones, more than poor families did.[71] Yet it would be mistaken to conclude either that they were satisfied consumers and citizens, or, more insidiously, that this imbalance would best be resolved by pushing the *ceti medi* into the use of private services, concentrating instead on residual public services for the poor. Such a solution could only destroy any sense of equity and solidarity, and of shared public provision, which the republican state had managed to impart to families in previous years.[72]

The policy of cost-containment without any overall welfare strategy, accompanied as it was in this period by widespread corruption and inefficiency, also had other consequences. It meant the limited growth of that educated and critical middle class, employed by the state and imbued with a sense of public service, which had characterized the social formation of many other modern democracies in the second half of the twentieth century.[73] Finally, if the state emitted so few convincing messages about its duties to families (while tying its members one to another), it was not easy for them in turn to develop a sense of duty towards the state. Readers who have persevered this far may perhaps recognize here one of the basic causal explanations of familism, stemming from forces *outside* the family, first advanced at the beginning of Chapter 4.[74]

b. JUSTICE AND EDUCATION

The interaction between family and state in modern Italy was subject to a great number of variables. If the general relationship broadly corresponded to that just outlined, its specific quality differed considerably according to what area of the state's activity was under examination, what broad social class the family belonged to, and what region of the country it lived in. All of these variables were significant, but none more so than the geographical one.

A particular feature of the Italian state's activity was the amount of resources that it distributed in cash payments rather than services. Cash payments, as has been seen, predominated in southern regions, as did the overall poor quality of services. In this way, the state's actual physical presence was reduced in many parts of the South, its schools and hospitals inadequate, its offices squalid and uncared for. When these conditions combined with the highest youth unemployment in Europe, then it was clear that state–family relations had all but broken down.

Whether in South or North, families encountered the state and had need of it at various stages of their life cycles. Different needs met with different responses. Here it is not possible, for reasons of space, to examine the full range of these interactions. I have chosen instead to concentrate briefly upon two of the most fundamental requests of families in modern democracies: for justice and for education.

The provision of justice is one of the most delicate of the state's functions, and the Italian Republic was woefully inadequate in this regard. Each judicial year opened with great pomp and circumstance, with the judges dressed in their ermine robes and cylindrical hats, but the solemnity of the ceremony was a poor substitute for the efficiency of the system. The actuation of both civic and penal codes was painfully slow, with cases taking an inordinate amount of time to be heard. In the history of the Republic, the length of cases showed an inexorable tendency to increase: for civil cases from an average 704 days in 1974 to 1,207 days by 1994, to which had to be added on average another 1,052 days if the case went to appeal. The official statistics for cases heard under the penal code in 1994 were measured in months: an average twenty-seven months for a first-level judgment, another forty-eight months if the case went to Appeal, and another fifty-four months if it went to the third and final level, that of the Corte di Cassazione.[75] All over Europe the due processes of justice were slowing down, but Italy was an extreme example of this tendency. As a result, an estimated two-thirds of civil law cases were abandoned before sentencing. As Jeremy Bentham once said, 'Justice delayed is justice denied.'[76]

It was also true that justice was often denied for class reasons. Italy had no system of legal aid equivalent to the British one. A new law on state funding of defence lawyers had been introduced in 1990, but its financing was derisive in comparison to the British system (even after cuts), and there was no guarantee for the poorer sections of the population of their gaining a fair hearing.[77] A newspaper article of the mid-1980s painted the following disturbing but habitual picture of chaos and distraction in the office of the Civil Tribunal in Rome:

The door of the court room is open, the judge is busy writing behind his table. A worker, victim of an industrial accident, is trying to establish his right to compensation. The lawyers present their respective cases. While this is happening, dozens of people enter and leave the court room in constant succession: lawyers asking for news of other cases, secretaries who need the judge's signature or opinion, friends of the worker, friends of friends. The plaintiff gives his version, but the verbalization of the case by the judge proceeds slowly. He is called elsewhere, then he comes back, and to make up for lost time the worker's lawyer helps him to transcribe the phrases of his client. End of the session. Case to be resumed in six months' time.[78]

The responsibility for such a state of affairs could be variously ascribed. Much of it was historic, the accumulation of decades of neglect and of the sort of administrative culture which I have described above. Much, though, can be firmly laid at the feet of the various Ministers of Justice of the 1980s and early 1990s, who were more intent, for party political reasons, on curbing the power of the prosecuting magistrates than on making the judicial system function. The jurist Sergio Chiarloni has suggested the responsibility of other actors in the legal process: the insurance companies, which often procrastinated as long as they could; the lawyers, of whom there were too many chasing too few jobs, and who thus had every interest in ensuring the duration and costs of cases;[79] the magistrates themselves, who while blessed with self-governing institutions, had done too little to put their own house in order, or reward efficiency and productivity.[80]

The net result was the creation of a highly dangerous syndrome for Italian democracy. Italians became accustomed to the fact that the redress of grievance could have as long a timespan as a whole phase in the life cycle of their families. Their resignation, though, was frequently accompanied by increased cynicism towards the state, politics, and even democracy. The state had failed in one of its most important legitimating duties, the provision of justice, and in so doing had increased perforce the desire for summary justice, exercised, if need be, by a single strong and charismatic figure.[81]

The situation with regard to schooling was rather more complex. The spread of secondary education, as has been seen in the first half of this book, was one of the most significant forces for change in Italian society. Between 1981 and 1991 the percentage of the population (of more than six years old) which had completed lower secondary schooling increased from 23.8 per cent to 30.7 per cent, and that completing upper secondary schooling from 11.5 per cent to 18.6 per cent. The percentage of graduates had crept up much more slowly (from 2.8 per cent to 3.8 per cent), but in the academic year 1991–2 a historic *sorpasso* (overtaking) had taken place: the number of women enrolled in Italian universities exceeded for the first time the number of men.[82] The slow but steady growth of educational qualifications, and especially the increase of women's education, made their influence felt in every Italian family.

Yet there was still a very long way to go, for Italy lagged far behind other nations of similar standing. In 1986 the number of her seventeen-year-olds still in education was just 46.3 per cent, compared to 49.4 per cent in Great Britain, 53.1 per cent in Spain, 79.7 per cent in France and 100.0 per cent in Germany.[83] If the disparities of gender in her educational statistics had diminished, those of geography and above all of class had not. In the 1980s in Italy 55.6 per cent of children from families of professionals, managers and entrepreneurs gained an upper secondary school diploma (the equivalent of A levels), and 24.2 per cent of them graduated. The corresponding figures for the children of workers in industry and services were only 20.8 per cent and 2.1 per cent. The family of origin was still by far the largest single determinant of educational opportunity.[84]

The quality of Italian education varied very much. Italian elementary schools were often of excellent standards, with a long tradition of dedicated female teachers.[85] Secondary education was much more patchy; the reform of lower secondary schooling, one of the achievements of the centre-left governments in the 1960s, had proved a great disappointment. Upper secondary schooling could boast some excellent *licei* and technical institutes in the major cities, but overall was disappointingly archaic, with scarce attention paid to languages and the sciences. Secondary schooling was largely populated by a demoralized staff lacking incentives. Italy had one of the lowest staff–student ratios in secondary schooling in Europe, but also the worst-paid schoolteachers of any of the economically advanced nations.[86] In the classroom, teachers showed little inventiveness, an over-dependence on costly and boring manuals, and no great desire to introduce project work into the curriculum.[87] Exams were mainly oral.

For most of the period under consideration, secondary schools had limited powers of decision-making, with a top-heavy and intrusive centralized administration holding the whip hand. Fifty-seven per cent of decisions regarding lower secondary schools were taken at national level in Italy, compared to 42 per cent in France, 5 per cent in Sweden and 2 per cent in Spain.[88]

Local-level impotence also made itself felt in the limited degree of participation of families in school life. A system of participation had been laboriously worked out in the 1970s, but it proved a substantial failure. Percentage turnout of parents for the election of their representatives was very low, and reflected the fact that a majority of parents did not identify with their children's schools, or feel that their presence in school administration could really change anything.[89]

Finally, the university system was one of Italy's weaker points, with no time limits set upon the completion of courses, the highest drop-out rate in Europe, and students graduating with painful slowness, usually in their mid to late twenties. The reforms of the early 1990s, which created a greater degree of autonomy for universities from central government, had been a step forward in theory but not in practice. Starved of adequate central government funding (in 1991 Spain spent twice as much as Italy on the university sector, and Holland three times),[90] the new autonomy seemed mainly synonymous with cuts. One of the gravest consequences of this short-sighted containment of spending was the exclusion of a whole generation of young and brilliant students from the prospect of continuing their studies beyond doctoral level. It was possible to find centres of excellence in Italian universities, as elsewhere in the Italian education system, but they were often deprived of the possibility of developing lasting traditions of research and scholarship. There were almost no funded jobs for the new generations, not even on limited-term contracts. This forced exclusion of youth from the teaching corps of the universities, presumably one of the key groups in the formation of national culture, was pregnant with consequences for the country's future.

The questions of both education and justice raise wider problems of the costs of services in modern democracies. One of the most common rebuttals against attempts to preserve and enrich the public sphere is that of the impossibility of providing adequate services without over-burdensome taxation. Another is that of the inevitable inefficiency of public services in any case. The state, in other words, cannot afford public services, except residual ones for the deprived sectors of the population, nor can it run them properly.

These points, which at the present time constitute orthodox thinking in both Italy and Britain, are not as convincing as they may seem at first sight. A society as opulent as contemporary Italy could certainly afford a rich panoply of public services, and probably would be more than happy to do so, *if* it could be convinced that such services would be run efficiently. But efficiency, as I have tried to show, has many roots, and one of the most important is that of motivation. Italy, in fact, already spent a great deal on public services, but she spent it badly, without guaranteeing some of the most elementary of needs, like that for justice, without managing to motivate her vast army of teachers, without keeping up in the sciences, without caring for families in their times of need, without fighting with determination against the great historic biases of geography and class.

c. CONCLUSIONS

It is not easy, nor even desirable, as Ferdinand Mount was at pains to point out, for governments, especially democratic governments, to try to legislate into existence specific models of families. Pluralism and diversity are the guidelines of modern democracies, not rigid conformism to pre-established models. In any case, families have the habit of going their own way, of refusing to follow, or circumventing if they can, the normative dictates of over-strong and over-imposing political authority.[91]

None the less it must be the case that democratic governments have an obligation to think about ways to further the creation of a democratic culture within families. If they succeed, then the state can become, to return to the title of this chapter, truly 'a state within'; that is, within the daily discourse of families, rather than 'a state without', exterior to families and without their active consent.

In this process, the links that are established not just between the state and families, but between the state and civil society, are of critical importance. If the state fosters rather than obstructs the growth of civil society, then it helps also to draw individual members of families into a public sphere of responsibility and solidarity. In civil society, for all its uneven texture, it is possible to develop cultures of needs and rights that are, as Laura Balbo has written, 'diffused cultures, elaborated from below, vital and innovative'.[92]

In the case of Italian democracy, the relationship between families and the state has taken two predominant forms. One was that outlined in the section on public administration: that of seeking accommodations with inefficient state mechanisms by means of personal contacts. The other was that mentioned in the chapter on civil society: the organization of spontaneous groups to fight against the state's inadequacies, often on single issues. Paradoxically, the laziness of the Italian state encouraged the activism of its civil society. But the relationship between the state, its citizens and their families, could not forever be either one long fight, or else one long underhand compromise, accompanied in both cases by expression of extreme cynicism. There had to be better ways of theorizing these relationships and of putting them into practice.

2. The Italian State and the Outside World

2.1. Italy's Foreign Policy

As with every country, Italy's relationship with the outside world was formed by a complicated mixture of her history and geography. It would probably be fair to say that the early history of the post-war period was absolutely determinant. From 1943 to 1957 crucial decisions were taken, both outside Italy and within it, which fixed the parameters of Italy's foreign policy for the next forty years. The Allied invasion of Italy in 1943, Churchill's meeting with Stalin at the Kremlin in October 1944, the beginning of the Cold War, the victory of the Christian Democrats in the national elections of April 1948, the entry of Italy into NATO in 1949, the founding of the European Economic Community in 1957 with Italy as one of its three principal members, these were the principal historical events which decided the profile of the Italian state with reference to the outside world.

Dominant were Italy's Atlantic and European choices. The nature of Italy's relationship to Europe, which was gradually to assume supreme importance, will be discussed at length in the last section of this chapter. As for its membership of the western military alliance and its links with the United States of America, Italy proved to be an extremely faithful and obedient ally. So much so, in fact, as to make her foreign policy, at least in the first three decades of the Republic, one of the least interesting and most immobile aspects of her history in the second half of the twentieth century. Hers was that 'natural laziness' which, as Carlo M. Santoro has noted, 'often accompanies the role of minor partners freed from responsibility in an asymmetrical alliance'.[93]

Yet this was far from the whole story. Italy was also a major country at the centre of the Mediterranean, the populated and opulent peninsula which divided its two basins. Its people had always looked not only to the north, to France, Switzerland, Austria and Germany, or west to the Iberian peninsula, but also east to the Balkans and the Middle East, and south to Africa.[94] Italy was, by its very geographical location, in close proximity to countries of different and contrasting cultures, of very different economic standards from its own, at this time in great demographic expansion and political turmoil. The *'mediterraneità'* of Italy was to become ever more important in the last decades of the twentieth century. Geography, in other words, had begun to reassert itself, to take its revenge upon the determining force of immediate post-war history, upon Italy's destiny as a bit player in the great ideological divide between East and West.

These shifting prospects emerged slowly during the course of the 1980s. They coincided with the ambitions and attitudes of the two men who did most to shape Italy's foreign policy in that decade, Bettino Craxi and Giulio Andreotti. Both continued, the one often in rivalry with the other, to cultivate as close a relationship as possible with the United States. Craxi was particularly anxious to reassure the Americans that the advent of the first Socialist President of the Council of Ministers in the history of the Republic would not mean any change in Italy's behaviour, and took pains to build a friendship with the American President of that time, Ronald Reagan. In 1984, in the face of considerable protests and the opposition of the Communist party, cruise missiles were installed at Comiso in Sicily.[95]

However, at the same time a new activism and autonomy began to characterize Italy's actions in the Mediterranean. In part this derived from Craxi's natural self-assertiveness and desire to make Italy count for more on an international plane, in part from Andreotti's long-standing interest in, and cultivation of, the Arab world. But above all it reflected the need to react to the explosive mixture of elements which were coming to dominate the Mediterranean. The high level of tension in the Middle East, the outrages of Palestinian terrorism, the aggressive attitudes of the Libyan dictator Colonel Gadafy, and last but not least the degree of dependence of Italy upon Arab oil, all demanded an active and autonomous response. Between 1983 and 1985 Italy took its distance from Israel, sought to work with the moderate Arab countries (Egypt, Jordan and Tunisia), and tried to build bridges with Yassar Arafat's PLO.[96]

This strategy of negotiation and appeasement contained a number of risks, not the least of which was conflict with the United States. The Americans had a very different opinion of the PLO at this time, as they did of Colonel Gadafy, and it was this divergence of views which forms the background and goes far to explain the Sigonella incident of 1985.[97] However it may be judged, the confrontation between American marines and Italian soldiers on the landing strip of the Sicilian base represented the first awakening of an independent Italian foreign policy in the Mediterranean. So, too, did the refusal in 1986 to let the USA use Italian NATO bases during the bombing of Tripoli.

The degree of change involved in these events should not be exaggerated. There was no fundamental rethink of Italy's role and responsibilities as the major democratic force in the Mediterranean, nor a desire to take any real distance from the United States. From the immediate aftermath of the Sigonella affair, with its exchange of letters beginning 'Dear Bettino' and 'Dear Ron', it was obvious that both countries were anxious to resume their relationship on the same bases as previously. Yet conditions in the Mediterranean, with its long-standing areas of tension and its new emergencies, made it impossible for Italy to fall back completely into its old absentee role. The collapse of Communism was of enormous importance for the Italian state, not only in terms of its internal politics and the fate of its Communist party, but also for its implications for the relationship between Italy and the Balkans. The arrival *en masse* of Albanian immigrants in August 1991[98] was only the first signal of how far Italy was going to be involved, whether she liked it or not, in the fate of the ex-Communist nations of the eastern Mediterranean. The disintegration of Yugoslavia and the terrible ensuing wars was to be another. Hard choices and new responsibilities awaited Italy. It was far from clear that she was prepared for either.

The last significant episode of Italian foreign policy before the major crisis of the Republic in 1992–3 was the involvement of Italian aircraft and ships in the war in the Persian Gulf. To tell the truth, the question of Italy's participation was more of internal than external significance, for the forces in Italy hostile to the war of 1991 were much broader than those which had campaigned against the installation of cruise missiles in 1984. In particular, the fervent opposition of Pope John Paul II, from his New Year message of 1991 through to his pronouncements in the middle of February (after which he much modified his tone), served to mobilize hundreds of thousands of Italian Catholics.[99] They found many points of contact with militants of the left, where pacifism had become the dominant creed in the 1980s. The debate in parliament on the war was followed with great interest, and Giulio Andreotti had to use all his skill to keep the ranks of the Christian Democrats' compact behind his motion supporting United Nations intervention.[100] As a result, a very divided nation played a very limited diplomatic and military role.

A final word must be dedicated, before passing to the relationship between Italy and Europe, to the sad history of Italy's programme of aid to developing countries (*'Cooperazione allo sviluppo'*). Even though the full details of this history have not emerged, and perhaps never will, two reasons make it important to attempt a brief reconstruction. The first is the amount of human and financial resources dedicated to the aid programme, which rendered it, as Pierangelo Isernia has written, 'perhaps the principal novelty of Italian foreign policy in the 1980s'.[101] Italy moved from spending 0.15 per cent of her GDP on aid in 1981 to 0.42 per cent in 1989. Whereas at the beginning of the decade she had been contributing 2 per cent of world aid, in 1989 that figure had risen to 6.2 per cent.[102] At a time when many other countries were cutting back their aid programmes, Italy was expanding hers.

The second reason for examining Italy's performance is that in this area Italy's foreign policy most closely resembled her domestic practice, that the 'state within' set the pattern for the 'state without', with disastrous consequences.

In 1979, in reaction to pressure from various Catholic and left-wing pressure groups, and in particular in response to Marco Pannella's and the Radical party's campaign against famine in the world, a new '*Dipartimento per la cooperazione allo sviluppo*' was set up in the Foreign Ministry. From these humanitarian beginnings, the aid programme was rapidly taken over by the ruling political parties. The PSI was particularly active in this field. In 1985, during Craxi's tenure at Palazzo Chigi, the FAI (Italian Fund for Aid) was set up. During its two years of activity, under the direction of Francesco Forte, it became a sort of Socialist monopoly.[103]

The flow of Italian funds was particularly directed towards sub-Saharan Africa, especially Somalia and Ethiopia. The choice of countries clearly followed a post-imperial pattern, but there was also much dispersion of funds in small quantities to a large number of countries.[104] In the case of Somalia, but presumably not only there, an unhealthy alliance was forged between Italian 'business politicians', Italian entrepreneurs who worked with them, and the local ruling African family, that of the dictator Siad Barre. This sort of personal networking between 'democratic' European politicians and African rulers of dubious repute had been practised for some considerable time by the French élites, and the Italians now seemed to have learned the lesson.[105]

In the case of Somalia, Paolo Pillittieri, Craxi's brother-in-law, published an interview with Siad Barre in January 1981, with a glowing preface by Craxi himself.[106] As the funds began to flow into Somalia, the country's Ministry for Cooperation passed under the direct control of Giama Barre, the brother of the dictator. In September 1985 Craxi paid a triumphal visit to Mogadishu, bringing in his wake 400 billion lire from the Italian Fund for Aid. One of the Somali opposition leaders said afterwards:

You could at least do three things: demand respect for civil rights, starting with the liberation of thousands of political prisoners; exercise a rigorous control on the way in which your aid funds are used, so that they meet the needs of the poor instead of fattening up the 'royal family'; exercise an even more rigorous control on the deployment of your military aid.[107]

Instead, from 1988 onwards, the first scandals about Italian aid began to break, first with a fertilizer factory which had cost 100 billion lire to build but never began production, and then with the construction of 3,000 useless silos in fibreglass throughout the villages of Somalia.

The picture painted for Somalia, Barre and the Socialists was not the only one in the dispiriting story of Italian aid. When an independent monitoring of 121 aid projects took place in 1993, 40 per cent of them were found to have failed completely, and of the remaining 60 per cent half functioned poorly. Only 13 per cent could be judged as satisfactory.[108]

2.2. Italy and Europe

At the end of the twentieth century Italy's image as a nation-state was ever more defined by its relation to Europe. It has long been the argument of the most distinguished historian of the European Community, Alan Milward, that the European nations who signed the Treaty of Rome in 1957 were moved to action predominantly by self-interest, by the need to 'rescue' the nation-state rather than to undermine it. Each nation agreed to surrender a limited amount of sovereignty in order to strengthen the material bases from which it derived its power and consent. Any history of the post-war European nation-state, warns Milward, 'should not start from the widespread theoretical assumption of an antithesis between nation and Community, for were it to do so it would be myth'.[109]

If these were the predominant, but by no means exclusive, motives that drove forward the process of European integration,[110] it is vital to recognize that they took different forms, and were pursued with different degrees of success in the various nation-states of the European Community. The history of the latter is made up not just of similar national self-interests combining to produce slow but steady European convergence, but also of significant and even sometimes dramatic differences in national cultures and performances.[111] And if the Franco-German axis was the iron rod that underpinned the whole structure, there was no easy coincidence, as Perry Anderson has shown, between the two countries in terms of overall aims and national publics.[112]

a. BACKGROUND

The Italian performance, it has to be said immediately, was a most erratic one. There were two basic causes for this, both of which have been encountered more than once in the course of this book. One was the quality of the Italian ruling political élite, which, with a few notable exceptions, was intensely inward-looking in character and formed for the most part of localistic and clientelistic power seekers. The other was the nature and failings of Italian public administration, which have been, at least in part, analysed above. The two were obviously interrelated and together combined to produce a very particular Italian identity in Europe.

In the complex hierarchy of priorities and actors which lies behind the setting of a national agenda, Europe was nearly always demoted by the Italian political class to a secondary place. Emblematic of this attitude was the fate of Italy's only President of the Commission before Romano Prodi, the Christian Democrat Franco Maria Malfatti. Having reluctantly accepted this key European post in 1970, Malfatti remained in Brussels the minimum necessary and resigned in March 1972 in order to concentrate, not altogether successfully, upon his political career at Rome. Nor was Italy able to present a worthy candidate to succeed him. As the *Corriere della Sera* commented at the time:

Because of the scarce enthusiasm aroused in the other European countries by the candidacy of Scarazia Mugnozza, our government will not insist that the Presidency remains an Italian prerogative. It will, therefore, not oppose the nomination of a high-ranking figure from another country for the remainder of Malfatti's mandate. According to authoritative observers, this occurrence will certainly not contribute to increasing the prestige and political weight of Italy within the institutions of the Community.[113]

Over the years, Italy's representatives in Europe were rarely at the level of importance and ability which was required, for Brussels was considered a sort of exile from the delicious intrigues and power-brokering of Montecitorio. When the major Italian politicians did arrive for the Council or other inter-governmental meetings, they were often poorly briefed and distracted. Italy was also under-represented at the highest levels of the European bureaucracy.[114]

All this meant that in the *ascending* phase of European politics, that in which national policy was formulated and then debated upon, Italy was often her own worst enemy. Maurizio Ferrera has explained this point clearly:

In order to maximize the benefits and minimize the costs of being part of the Community, it is necessary to negotiate shrewdly during the various phases that precede the taking of a decision at a European level, and to participate actively in the various committees and work groups that prepare the relevant dossiers. The success of each country in this regard depends essentially upon two conditions: the availability of well-informed and assiduous negotiators; and the ability to prepare *ex ante* (that is, before the beginning of negotiations) a sort of country-specific agenda, which establishes an order of priority for the various objectives (often in contrast with each other) of a country's internal actors (both institutional and not). These two conditions have rarely been satisfied by Italy.[115]

The result was that Italian policy came to be primarily *reactive* to the strategies of France and Germany rather than *propositive* with regard to its own national interest.[116]

As for the *descending* phase, when Italy had to implement the norms and directives of the Community, it was here that the vices of Italy's public administration which so hampered her domestically came fully into play, choking her at an international level as well. From the 1960s onwards, Italy slowly but surely acquired a reputation as the country which had most problems spending the funds ascribed to it, the weakest controls at a local level to prevent the defrauding of the Community, the most infringements and greatest delays in putting European decisions into practice.[117]

The paradoxical case of Italy's failure to spend Community funds is especially illuminating. In 1978 it was reported that Italy had been able to claim only 30 million ecus from the European Social Fund although entitled to 209 million; 79 million ecus from the Regional Fund although entitled to 158 million; and 48 million from the Farm Guidance Fund although entitled to 242 million.[118] Ten years later Italy was consistently doing worse in this respect than any of her southern European neighbours in the Community. In the years 1989—91 percentage spending of funds allotted from the Regional Fund revealed the following merit order: Spain 76 per cent, Portugal 73 per cent, Greece 71 per cent, Italy 51 per cent. An even poorer Italian performance was revealed with regard to the PIM, the long-term funding programmes for Greece and for some regions of France and Italy, offered as a compensation mechanism after Spanish and Portuguese entry into the Community. In 1987—9 the respective level of spending was the following: Greece 82 per cent, France 73 per cent, Italy 40 per cent.[119]

Administrative inadequacy clearly played a role in this lackadaisical performance. The complicated filter of Italian administrative law acted as a strong deterrent, and in the 1980s and 1990s the chaos and lack of preparation of much of southern Italian regional government proved the burial ground of many a project. Antonio Giolitti, who was Commissioner at Brussels from 1977 to 1985, and who was one of Italy's very rare representatives of real distinction at a European level, was explicit with regard to the public administration's failings in the face of the European challenge:

Belonging to the Community provided a strong stimulus to modernize and render more efficient our productive and administrative structures . . . The first responded overall in a positive fashion . . . The same could not be said for the administrative apparatus. It remained absolutely insensitive and impermeable to change, with unpropitious consequences for our efficiency, our economy, and the level and quality of our participation in European policies. In particular, I have in mind the agrarian, regional and Mediterranean policies of the Community.[120]

Yet there were strong political motives at work as well. In an interesting analysis Marco Giuliani has suggested that Europe was often viewed as a disturbance factor by Italian politicians, introducing as it did norms, directions and requirements which threatened to upset time-honoured patterns of resource distribution. The regional and PIM funds referred to above are a case in point, for Brussels required that an equal amount of funding be provided in each case by the nation-state itself. Often in Italy such an allocation of resources was inconvenient or in conflict with narrower patterns of local patronage, as were the controls that the Community wished to enforce on the spending of its funds.[121] It was better not to have the funds than to unleash external interference, better to stay out of the European mainstream than upset carefully constructed centre-periphery clienteles. Here was a case where the vertical 'stretching' of the state to a supra-national level, referred to at the beginning of this chapter, was not at all welcome.

The combination of administrative failings and political short-sightedness, of impreparation in the ascending phase and absenteeism in the descending one, meant that Italy's history in the Community was one of *relative failure*: relative that is to the performance of other countries, and relative to what she could have gained, and contributed, as one of the three major founder members. Italy's performance was not all negative. She performed a valuable role as a mediator on more than one occasion in the early history of the Community. She had a public opinion which was second to none in its enthusiasm for the European project. She had in Altiero Spinelli one of the strongest voices in favour of Europe conceived as a true federation of nations.

However, each of these points was outweighed by others which counted for more in real terms. Italy, for instance, had been unable to defend her long-term national interests in the area which had consistently consumed between two-thirds and three-quarters of the Community's budget – that of the Common Agriculture Policy (CAP). In the early decades of the Community, her 'Mediterranean' products – fruit, vegetables and oil – were consistently under-subsidized when compared to cereal production and dairy farming.[122]

Nor had Italy established the right sort of reputation in those European circles of decision-making which were to count ever more as the century drew to a close. Italy was 'unreliable'; she wanted to have a seat at every decision-making table, but once she obtained it, there was often no one to sit on it. She was very 'European' in words, but not in deeds. She wanted to press on to 'Union', but at the same time she blithely ignored the norms, directives and controls which did not suit her. If the magic hyphen that divides the word nation-state is removed, it can be seen that on an international plane Italy had difficulty in prospering as a nation because her state was in disorder. As a result, negative opinions and impressions of her gradually hardened into stereotypes as the years passed, so that her failings, even if they were occasional, came to be considered 'typical'. Such slippage was to cost her very dear.

b. FIGHTING BACK

Although a proper periodization of the history of Italy in Europe from 1957 to the present time has yet to be delineated, it is almost certainly true that the worst moment of this uneasy relationship came in the first half of the 1970s.[123] The acute social and economic crisis in the Europe of those years, which took a particularly intense form in Italy, made hers a precarious place in a stalled Community. In February 1973, Italy left the European monetary 'snake'; by 1975 she was on the outer edge of Europe, afflicted by rampant inflation and major debts with the IMF and West Germany. At the end of the decade, one informed commentator noted that Italy's inability to keep pace with the integration process had resulted in her 'being regarded as an obvious candidate for "second-tier" status in the EC'.[124]

Instead, the 1980s witnessed a determined effort to keep Italy centre-stage in Europe. Behind this fight back lay the conviction that only by being in Europe could Italy hope to solve, or at least confront, her many internal problems. The virtues of the 'external constraint' were extolled with increasing vigour, especially by those groups of economic and financial experts whose origins were often the Bank of Italy, and whose own institutional position and influence were being strengthened by the requirements of the European integration process.[125] A subtle shift was taking place in the balance of power between the leading actors of the Italian state, a shift we have already encountered when dealing with Guido Carli's role in the Andreotti governments of 1989–92. The politicians needed the experts, often in key positions of power, and the experts had their own European agenda. As Carli wrote, with disarming directness: 'the European Union represented an alternative path for the solution of problems which we were not managing to handle through the normal channels of government and parliament.'[126] Italy was to be constrained by Europe to put her house in order.

There can be little doubting the wisdom and far-sightedness of this strategy. The further the process of economic integration went, the more Italy was forced to liberalize the flows of capital, to modernize her banking system, to end over-generous subsidies to public and private firms, above all to bring her public finances into order. The effects of external constraint also went beyond mere economic advantage.[127] As European legislation developed and was enforced (by no means easily in Italy's case), it enriched Italian democracy in many ways – in the area of equal opportunities, with regard to the environment, on the issues of justice and human rights. These were often grey zones in Italy, where the internal drive to action was slow and faltering.

It was also true that many of these issues, both economic and not, were assuming global connotations and demanding global answers. Only by maintaining a constant and active presence in the Community could Italy be sure that she would have a voice in major international decision-making processes.

The case for not drifting away from Europe, as Greece was to do, was therefore of overwhelming force. However, the idea of appealing to external authority for the resolution of internal inadequacy also had its obvious weaknesses, which must be rendered explicit. If Italy was primarily in the Community not to change it, but to be changed by it, then her contribution to it as a nation always risked being a diminished and subordinate one. Furthermore, looking to Europe in this way, longing for its unqualified embrace, led to the danger of idealizing it. Such a tendency had a long history among progressive liberal intellectuals in Italy, who ran the risk, in their profound dissatisfaction with the democracy of their own country, of inventing a mythical model of it elsewhere, located rather uncertainly somewhere in north-western Europe. It was rare indeed in Italy to hear serious discussion about the possible bureaucratic tyrannies of the European Commission, of its sometimes absurd and damaging insistence on standardization, of the very serious democratic deficit that existed in the structures of the Community, of the great uncertainties regarding its future.[128]

The first step back towards Europe came in 1979, with the entry of Italy into the European Monetary System. Giulio Andreotti was Prime Minister at the time. The Bank of Italy played a leading role in the negotiations, which ended with Italy's partners agreeing to establish a two-band system, the first of which permitted currencies limited fluctuation, while the second, into which the lira was inserted, was allowed more leeway.[129]

A second, key moment came with Italy's presidency of the Community during the first six months of 1985 (the presidency rotates between members on a half-yearly basis). At the end of June 1985, a reunion of the Council of Europe, consisting of heads of governments, was held at Milan. The meeting constituted an important step towards further convergence, as well as the first of two occasions in which the British Prime Minister, Margaret Thatcher, clashed violently with her Italian counterpart.

In the wake of Jacques Delors's insistence on the need to complete the Single Market, and the Dooge committee's report on the Community's institutions, there was considerable pressure on the heads of government gathered at Milan to make some progress. However, the British delegation, under the robust leadership of the Prime Minister, was vehemently opposed to taking any steps towards further unity. There seemed little hope of headway, but on the last morning of the Council, Chancellor Kohl of Germany presented a document which requested explicitly the calling of an inter-governmental conference to revise the founding treaty of the Community.

He was immediately backed by President Mitterrand. Bettino Craxi, at the time President of the Council of Ministers, and as such President of the meeting, then took the very unusual, and for Mrs Thatcher unexpected, step of calling for a majority vote on Kohl's proposal, which passed with three votes against, those of Britain, Denmark and Greece. Mrs Thatcher commented later in her memoirs: 'To my astonishment and anger, Signor Craxi suddenly called a vote and by a majority the council resolved to establish an IGC [inter-governmental conference].'[130] The ensuing conference laid the bases for the Single Act, which became operative on 1 July 1987. It was the single most important reform of the Community since the signing of the Treaty of Rome thirty years earlier.

The outcome of the Milan Council was hailed by the Italian press as a great Italian triumph. This was rather an exaggeration, but there could be no doubt as to the increasing commitment of Italy to European questions. In November 1985, the Foreign Affairs Commission of the Chamber of Deputies voted unanimously to support Giulio Andreotti's line that Italy would only sign the new Single Act if greater powers were granted to the European parliament.[131] In the event, Italy was not able to muster sufficient support from her partners on the issue, and signed the Single Act in any case. None the less, the attention to the problem of democracy within the Community signalled a welcome, if late, recognition of an issue upon which Spinelli had insisted for many years.[132]

These were also the years in which Italy tried to render more efficient her domestic handling of European affairs. The law no. 183 of 1987 (the so-called Fabbri law) reorganized the mechanisms by which decisions were taken with regard to Europe, setting up a special Department for the coordination of Community policies as part of the prime minister's office. The new Department had responsibilities both for the 'ascending' and 'descending' phases of European policy.

A successive law (no. 86 of 1989, the so-called La Pergola law) concentrated further on the implementation process. In order to remedy Italy's woeful record in this respect, each year a special Community law (*'legge comunitaria'*), listing all the Community directives to be translated into Italian law, would be presented to parliament by the Department for the coordination of Community policies. Parliament would then undertake to approve the Community law by the end of the year. In this way, so it was hoped, Italy would soon recoup her backlog and emerge not only as an enthusiastic European nation, but also as a virtuous one.[133]

Old habits, however, die hard. The first Community law was regularly presented to parliament in March 1990, but approved only *in extremis* at the end of December. The second, that of 1991, was approved at the end of January 1992. That of 1992 was never approved at all, but was replaced by a *'mini-comunitaria'*, which was exactly what its name implied.[134] The number of infringement proceedings begun by Brussels against Italy, either for non-implementation or for incorrect application of European legislation, showed no signs of diminishing.[135] Meanwhile, Italy's rate of spending of special Community funds, thanks principally to the failings of certain southern regional governments, remained as dismal as ever.[136]

c. MRS THATCHER AND SIGNOR ANDREOTTI

Giulio Andreotti, as has already been seen, was firmly pro-European, and no part of his activity in the realm of 'high' politics was to bring him more credit.[137] During his sixth government, Italy's turn to assume the Presidency of the Community came round again, this time from July to December 1990. In the months before, important decisions had been taken which further tied Italy's fate to Europe. In January 1990 Andreotti decided to move the lira into the narrow band of currencies in the European Monetary System. Such a move was a major gamble, based on the flourishing state of the Italian economy, but also on the hope that the markets would not penalize Italy for the continuing parlous state of her public finances, and that Italian exporters would not run out of steam because of a less favourable rate of exchange. In May of the same year, free short-term movement of capital was introduced, in line with the agreement on the completion of the Single Market.[138]

Once again, the Italian Presidency of the Community in 1990 coincided with a critical phase in the history of European integration, and once again its most strenuous opponent was the British Prime Minister. Mrs Thatcher had met Giulio Andreotti at her first G7 summit meeting, and did not like him or what he stood for. In a memorable pen portrait she wrote:

Prime Minister Andreotti was no more on my wavelength than the French President. Even more than the latter, this apparently indispensable participant in Italian governments represented an approach to politics which I could not share. He seemed to have a positive aversion to principle, even a conviction that a man of principle was doomed to be a figure of fun. He saw politics as an eighteenth-century general saw war: a vast and elaborate set of parade ground manoeuvres by armies that would never actually engage in conflict but instead declare victory, surrender or compromise as their apparent strength dictated in order to collaborate on the real business of sharing the spoils. A talent for striking political deals rather than a conviction of political truths might be required by Italy's political system and it was certainly regarded as *de rigueur* in the Community, but I could not help but find something distasteful about those who practised it.[139]

Anxious to see their presidency give a tangible contribution to the integration process, the Italians called a European Council at Rome for the end of October 1990. In the preparations for the Council, Andreotti was flanked by the intelligent, hyper-active, flamboyant and unscrupulous Socialist

Minister for Foreign Affairs, Gianni De Michelis, and a large number of rather more sober economic and financial experts. Mrs Thatcher was against the Council, arguing that the leaders of the Community could not even agree on agricultural prices, let alone European integration. Not for the first time, she seriously under-estimated the forces at work on the Continent, as well as the Italian capacity to interpret them: 'As always with the Italians,' she wrote disparagingly, 'it was difficult to distinguish confusion from guile . . . but even I was unprepared for the way things went.'[140] This was a surprising admission, for things went in exactly the same way in Rome in 1990 as they had gone in Milan five years earlier; only that this time the British found themselves entirely alone.

Andreotti, having obtained the indispensable support of Helmut Kohl, persuaded the Council that Stage Two of economic and monetary union could start in January 1994.[141] He also sprang a last-minute vote for an inter-governmental conference to discuss 'political union', which in real terms meant institutional reform of the Community. Only Mrs Thatcher voted against, and returned fulminating to the Commons, where she announced in Churchillian tones that 'in my view we have surrendered enough'. *The Economist*, however, congratulated Signor Andreotti: 'He seized the chance to push for what may prove to be a historic decision. Winning agreement on EMU among eleven countries is a remarkable achievement. Only six weeks earlier a meeting of finance ministers in Rome had revealed huge differences over EMU's second stage.'[142]

The clash in Rome was to be of considerable significance in the domestic history of both Italy and Britain, and for both its protagonists. Mrs Thatcher's performance was her undoing. On 1 November 1990 Sir Geoffrey Howe, her Deputy Prime Minister and loyal servant for many years, resigned over her line on Europe. Then, on 13 November, he delivered a resignation speech, placid in tone but poisonous in content, which was to become famous in the annals of the British Parliament. He described Mrs Thatcher as

a prime minister, who seems sometimes to look upon a Continent that is positively teeming with ill-intentioned people scheming, in her words, 'to extinguish democracy', 'to dissolve our national identities', to lead us 'through the back door into a federal Europe' . . . The tragedy is – and it is for me personally, for my party, and for our whole people and for the prime minister herself, a very real tragedy – that the prime minister's perceived attitude towards Europe is running increasingly serious risks for the future of our nation . . . The time has come for others to consider their own response to the tragic conflict of loyalty with which I have myself wrestled for perhaps too long.[143]

Mrs Thatcher was already in distinct difficulty because of unpopular taxation policy and falling ratings in the opinion polls.[144] The Rome Council and Howe's memorable speech gave her opponents within her own party exactly the cue for which they had been waiting. At the leadership election held among Tory MPs on 20 November, Mrs Thatcher failed to win a convincing majority. Two days later she resigned. By the time a second European Council was held in Rome in December, John Major was the British Prime Minister.

As for Giulio Andreotti, he was able to build upon the prestige gained in Rome and went on to play a significant role in the process that led first to the agreement at Maastricht on 9–10 December 1991, and then on 7 February 1992 to the fateful signing of the Treaty bearing that same Dutch city's name.

However, if the British had stupidly isolated themselves, the Italians risked being constrained beyond their own capacities. At Maastricht all the difficulties of the strategy of the 'external constraint' were to come to the fore. The parameters for entry into the single currency were to be drawn with great rigidity. The Italians were caught in a cleft stick. On the one hand, they had to support strict criteria, for if they did not they would neither appear seriously intentioned, nor would the 'external constraint' have any real bite back at home. On the other hand, if the requirements of Maastricht were too severe, there would be no way that Italy could meet them. She would then end up isolated herself, though in a different, and more humiliating way than the British.

In the final wording of the criteria for convergence, a little leeway was introduced: an annual public deficit of more than 3 per cent of GDP and a debt-to-GDP ratio of more than 60 per cent might not be judged 'excessive' if they were seen to be declining sufficiently fast towards the required level.[145] It was something, but not very much, and the path towards meeting these criteria was going to be, as we shall see in the last two chapters of this book, a long and eventful one.

Chapter 8

Dénouement, 1992–4

O N 17 NOVEMBER 1991, the newspaper *la Repubblica* reported that Christian Democrats and Socialists were comfortably engaged in setting the pattern of politics for the new decade. They had reached agreement to govern together for the next five years, if possible with lower levels of tension than had previously been the case. 'In the next legislature the present majority can continue as before,' specified Giulio Andreotti, 'but it must do so on the basis of clear agreements, without afterthoughts.' And Antonio Gava proclaimed, rather unwisely in the event, that 'from now on we will get votes for who we are, and not simply for our anti-communism'.[1]

Instead, from the time of the national elections of April 1992 onwards, Italy witnessed a profound and dramatic crisis, which not only liquidated the old political élites and parties, but brought them into ignominious disrepute. The crisis was complex and often contradictory in nature. It was not, as 1968 had been, a unifying revolt from below, a contesting of the power and politics of one generation by another. Nor did it have at its heart a single class, or party, or social force which caused it, drove it forward and reaped its benefits. It was not confined to one sphere or sector of Italian life, nor to a merely national theatre. Indeed, viewed from differing vantage points, it presented quite diverse profiles. From the Palace of Justice of Milan it was a battle against corruption and for the restoration of the rule of law. From the Bank of Italy it was a crisis of debt, and of the lack of international confidence in the Italian economy. From Lombardy and the Veneto it was a revolt against Rome in the name of neo-localism and small-scale entrepreneurship. At Montecitorio its focus was on the demise of the old élites, and the impelling need to create new rules and modes of operation for the political system. In the fragile civil society of Palermo it was a desperate fight against Mafia power.

The many faces of the crisis rendered it almost impenetrable to contemporaries, and to none more so than its political victims. Given its complication, both the course and the outcome of the crisis were very difficult to predict, with much of the history of the years after 1992 swinging first one way and then another, and with many fateful decisions balanced on a knife edge.

For the historian, the startling events of 1992–4 present intricate problems of causation and of connection between different planes. In seeking to explain the crisis, it is as well to bear in mind a number of caveats. The first is that it is not very helpful to adopt what may be called a Cassandrian view of recent Italian history, according to which the Italian Republic has been in permanent crisis since its inception, and, riven by its many contradictions, its demise was inevitable and merely a matter of time. While only the most fervent of apologists for the Christian Democrats would attempt to deny the many and deep fault lines of the Republic, to concentrate exclusively on them impedes us from explaining both the timing of the crisis and its specific shape. Rather, as the ensuing account suggests, the crisis owed much to the virtues of Italian democracy as well as to its vices, and is indeed incomprehensible without considering both.

It is also the case that comparisons with the coterminous events in eastern Europe, comparisons which were very frequent among commentators at the time, are rather wide of the mark. If there was a 'regime' in Italy, it was not of the eastern European variety. Italy's crisis was one *within* democracy, in a country which for nearly fifty years had enjoyed free elections and universal suffrage. Civil society certainly had to struggle to affirm itself, in Italy as in Poland, but the parameters of that battle were very different in the two countries.

Lastly, it is probably a mistake to see a single key to the crisis.[2] A. J. P. Taylor enjoyed himself suggesting small, technical causes for very large events. Thus the European revolutions of 1848 were caused by the recent invention of the telegraph, and the First World War by the rigidity of the railway timetables of the era. Perhaps the Italian crisis, a much lesser event but still a very complicated one, could never have happened without the magistrate Antonio Di Pietro's computers. However, minimalism of this sort does not take us very far, and a proper explanation would have to try to follow at least three different methodological paths. The first is that of combining different levels of analysis; that is, to examine not just the political sphere but its interaction with other planes of causation – economic, social and cultural. The second is to look at the interdependence of structure and agency, without over-estimating either the role of conscious choice and action in the making of history, or the determining weight of impersonal factors; the last to strike a balance between the significance of long-term causation and that of the immediate flow of events.

In a way, much of the content of the previous chapters of this book is itself an explanation for the dramatic events of the early 1990s. However, to state this is all too easy a way out. Instead, it may be helpful to the reader if I attempt at this point to reorder and present in schematic form the central causal elements which have emerged from the previous pages. Hopefully, the relationship between the various elements of my explanation and its ordering of priorities will then become clear as this chapter unfolds.

On an international plane, it is possible to discern two causal factors of great importance, the one very specific, the other rather vague. Italy's commitment to Europe had been reinforced, as we have seen, by a whole series of choices made in the 1980s and early 1990s, and by the development of the European Community itself towards greater union. These trends acted as an increasingly formidable external constraint upon the nation's behaviour, and especially upon its political economy, an ever heavier judgement on its recent past and requirement for its future behaviour. If ever there was a necessary cause, this was it.

A second international element, of less ponderable weight, was the collapse of Communism. The failure of Gorbachov's reform projects and the dramatic events of 1989–90 had clearly devastating effects upon the Italian Communists, but also significant consequences for anti-Communists as well. Voters who had traditionally backed the governing parties, especially the Christian Democrats, as the best bulwark against the Communists felt free to experiment for the first time. But how far they would have 'floated' in any case, that is with or without the fall of the Berlin Wall, must remain an open question.[3]

In the realm of national politics and institutions, the degradation of party government in the 1980s, its widespread practice of corruption, its incapacity to carry through effective medium-range measures, its overriding smugness and arrogance, were of critical negative importance. When combined with the long-term structural failings of Italy's public administration, they produced an acute version of what had more than once been present in the history of the Italian state – the rejection of 'Rome'.[4]

However, the failings of party government and public administration were only part of the institutional story. In every part of the state, and in none more so than the judiciary, there had developed what can perhaps best be called 'virtuous minorities', recalcitrant elements who had an obstinate idea that the official morality of the Republic, its laws and Constitution should not serve merely as a figleaf to cover less codified practices. Their actions were to be an explosive element in the crisis. To their endeavours must be added, paradoxically, those of some of their opponents. The more acute members of the political élite themselves saw the case for reform, especially economic reform and that regarding Italy's performance in Europe, as well as the need to enlist the aid of 'technicians' to achieve it. Much of the history of Giulio Andreotti's last two governments was an essay in politics of this sort; not crowned by and large with success, but by a further tightening of the noose around the parties' collective necks; not reforms that served to keep the storm on the distant horizon, but rather brought it nearer.

In societal terms, disgust for the way in which party politicians ruled the country was widespread, but the two critical segments of the modern urban middle classes, which had become the majority of the country's population, found different ways of expressing their dissatisfaction. The one, entrepreneurial and localistic, with family and work often overlaying each other, had gone along with the old political parties for many years. Indeed their interests had often coincided: a blind eye turned by the state towards tax evasion, high interest rates on government bonds as a way of financing the public debt, the contribution of small industry to the commercial balance of the country – these were only some of the elements of a basic alliance between 'private dynamism and public disorder'.[5] As Carlo Trigilia has suggested, such an alliance, or perhaps better tacit understanding, served to mask and delay the crisis for some years. But once the European screws began to be turned towards cutting the annual deficit, reducing the debt and increasing income from taxation, these sections of the middle classes felt increasingly betrayed and exasperated. The state worked no better than before, it provided neither sufficient investment in infrastructures, such as new roads in the Veneto, nor efficient public administration, but it was demanding more from the productive middle classes than in the past. They reacted, especially in the North-East of the country, by seeking new political outlets as well as radical and sometimes xenophobic solutions.

The other key sector of the urban middle classes had its base in the 'caring' professions and in many sectors of public employment. They had developed, along with their counterparts in the rest of Europe, 'reflexive' and critical attitudes towards many aspects of Italy's helter-skelter modernization. Environmental pollution, the choking of city centres with private transport, indiscriminate private consumption accompanied by much public squalor – these were all elements which fuelled their critique of the politicians' failure to *govern*. Individuals and families belonging to this section of society were often left-wing or else Catholic participants in civil society. They believed, more strongly than their entrepreneurial brothers or sisters, in the affirmation of public ethics, and in national rather than local solutions. They identified strongly with the 'virtuous' elements in the Republic's history and with the minority of dissenting and reforming personnel within its institutions. The

1980s, for them, had been a decade of suffering in the face of Socialist arrogance, but they had not given up the ghost, and the crisis of 1992 came as an unexpected liberation from a pattern of political behaviour which had seemed timeless and untouchable.

The divisions just outlined are little more than broad markers, for family formation and individual beliefs do not, of course, fit so neatly into sociological pigeonholes. Uniting the majority of Italian families, though, both those of dependent workers and of the self-employed, was steadily widening educational experience. This took the form *not* of equal educational opportunity, nor even of satisfactory educational standards, but rather an increased stress on the importance of education in a world increasingly dominated by intellectual capital. The education process led to a greater awareness of what things *ought* to be like, even if they were not. The slow but steady rise in the graphs of the educated, especially among women, was one of the most significant bases for the 'moral question', which was to assume such prominence in the crisis of the early 1990s.

The last element of causation was the most violent and intractable. The growing power of organized crime, and in particular the confrontational strategy of the new leadership of the Sicilian Mafia, was a deeply destabilizing influence, particularly as part of the political class of the Republic was in covert but constant contact with it. But here, too, the causal elements were not only negative but positive in character, distinguished as they had been by Caponnetto's Palermo pool of magistrates and the new spirits of an anti-Mafia civil society which were tentatively appearing in the Palermo of the 1980s.

So much for explanation couched in the form of a list; useful but static. Of equal importance is the way these different aspects *interacted*, and how this interaction developed diachronically. The old political regime could well have survived being bombarded from one direction (it had had enough practice at it). But instead it came under attack simultaneously from many different quarters, and the often fortuitous intermingling of these different planes within a limited arc of time weakened fatally the old ruling groups. Sequentiality, then, what Oakeshott called the recounting of a 'set of happenings',[6] is also a critical part of explanation, and it is to a series of sequences that this chapter is principally dedicated. What follows is something less than history, for the events recounted are too recent and the sources too few. Hopefully, though, it is something more than a chronicle.

1. The April Elections of 1992

In the months preceding the general elections of 5–6 April 1992 there had been significant warnings for the Italian politicians, but they were not recognized as such at the time. Segni's referendum, the tightening economic climate of 1991–2, the sharp rise in votes for the Northern League at local elections, the assassination of Salvo Lima, all these in their different ways had acted as strong elements of disturbance. To them must be added the arrest in Milan on 17 February 1992 of the Socialist politician Mario Chiesa. We have already encountered Chiesa, and his confessions, in the section of this book dedicated to political corruption.[7] He was one of those politicians on-the-make who had prospered with the boom of the 1980s and the system of kickbacks which Bettino Craxi had rendered habitual in his home city of Milan. The circumstances surrounding Chiesa's arrest were interesting, both in symbolic and other terms. The Milanese magistrates had been alerted to his activities by Luca Magni, the owner of the small firm which did the contract cleaning at the Pio Albergo Trivulzio, the old people's home of which Chiesa was President. Magni, and other businessmen like him, had become accustomed to paying kickbacks directly in cash at Chiesa's office at the old people's home. There Chiesa would draw down the blind of his office window, as if in tacit recognition of the covert and illegal nature of the exchange, however much it had become standard practice. The 10 per cent he demanded and his insulting and bullying ways had become intolerable to Magni and others. The magistrate Antonio Di Pietro was informed, Magni went to pay his next *tangente* with a microphone hidden on his person and the Carabinieri close behind him, and Mario Chiesa was caught *in flagrante*, trying desperately to flush down the lavatory some 30 million lire. Rarely had one of Craxi's Socialists shown so much haste in attempting to get rid of money rather than to acquire it.[8]

The reaction of Bettino Craxi to this sequence of events was exemplary. Interviewed on 3 March 1992, he explained wearily: 'I devote myself to trying to create the conditions for the country to acquire a government which will face the difficult years we have ahead of us, [and] I find myself in front of a rogue who casts a shadow on the whole image of party which in Milan, in fifty years of activity, has never had an administrator condemned for serious crimes concerning the public administration.'[9] The 'rogue' Chiesa was taken off to the San Vittore prison, while his leader dedicated himself to the forthcoming national elections. There can be little doubt that Craxi's contemptuous dismissal of his erstwhile lieutenant was a crucial factor in provoking Chiesa to recount to the inquiring magistrates the full details of the system of *tangenti* at Milan.

The elections of April 1992 should have served to confirm the validity of the 'CAF', the political alliance between Craxi, Andreotti and Forlani. They did the opposite. The Christian Democrat share of the vote fell to its lowest ever, from 34.3 per cent to 29.7 per cent. The party had held steady in the South, but in some parts of the North, especially in the former 'white' areas, its decline was cataclysmic: it lost 18 per cent in the province of Vicenza, 12 per cent in those of Verona and Padova, 13 per cent in that of Belluno.[10] The Socialists, far from enjoying the 'long electoral wave' about which they had talked so often and for which they had waited more than a decade, lost votes, falling from 14.3 per cent to 13.6 per cent. They too performed poorly in the North and better in the South. The new PDS achieved a very modest 16.6 per cent and Rifondazione Comunista, the split-off from the rump of the party, 5.6 per cent. Taken together, their vote was lower than that achieved by the PCI at any time since the 1940s, but it was still better than many on the left had feared. By and large, their traditional heartlands in the centre of the country stayed faithful to them.

The undoubted winners of the 1992 elections were the Northern League, which increased its share of the votes from 0.5 per cent to 8.7 per cent. This was, obviously, an overwhelmingly northern vote, and it was one that repaid handsomely Bossi's strategy of trying to break out of his Lombard strongholds. The League gained a startling 25.1 per cent of the vote in Lombardy, but also 19.4 per cent in Piedmont, 18.9 per cent in the Veneto, 15.5 per cent in Liguria, and even 10.6 per cent in the traditionally left-wing Emilia-Romagna. The League's electors were a very composite group, mainly ex-DC voters, though not much interested in politics, younger than average, often self-employed, of low to average education, exasperated by the behaviour of the national parties and desirous of strong devolution if not outright autonomy for an ill-defined northern Italy.[11]

A much smaller, but still socially significant victor was a new political grouping called 'La Rete' (the Network), led by the former mayor of Palermo, Leoluca Orlando, which gained 1.9 per cent of the votes and twelve deputies. La Rete was especially strong among highly educated youth, often of Catholic background, who were heavily involved in civil society.[12] As for the extreme right, the neo-Fascists of the MSI had for the moment been unable to capitalize on the DC's discomfiture, gaining only 5.4 per cent of the vote compared to 5.9 per cent in 1987.[13]

The percentage shifts in the 1992 elections may seem relatively small to non-Italian eyes, but there can be little doubt that these were the most significant elections in Italy since 1948. The *Corriere della Sera*, immediately after the event, called them 'Earthquake elections', as did *La Stampa*. Electoral instability was higher than at any time since 1953, with nearly a third of the voters declaring after the poll that they had changed their minds with respect to previous elections.[14] The number of non-voters had increased to 17.4 per cent, a new record for Italy.[15] All in all, the 1992 result contained all the elements of a historic protest vote, not yet for anything or anybody very specific, but quite clearly against the old ruling parties and their leaders.

2. Politics and the Law

In the aftermath of the vote, the politicians met to consider their next moves. The four parties which had formed the basis of Giulio Andreotti's last government (DC, PSI, PSDI, PL) still had a technical majority of sixteen seats in the lower house, but of only one in the upper. Apart from finding a majority in parliament, they had two other difficult, but not insoluble problems. Who was to be the next President of the Council of Ministers and who the next President of the Republic? Francesco Cossiga had resigned on 25 April 1992, just one month before the end of his turbulent mandate. Giulio Andreotti or Arnaldo Forlani were the most likely candidates to succeed him, but Bettino Craxi had not exactly hidden his ambitions to become the next resident at the Quirinale – it was, after all, the Socialists' turn. Failing that, he would return to Palazzo Chigi. Craxi, Andreotti, Forlani; these were once again the familiar names in the political ring in the spring of 1992, and it seemed as if the vote of 5 April might perhaps be digested painlessly after all.

However, Rome could no longer reckon without Milan, nor the politicians without the magistrates.

The arrest of Mario Chiesa turned out not to be an isolated act, but the opening of a great campaign for legality in public life, directed and coordinated with extraordinary ability and tenacity by the chief prosecutor of Milan, Francesco Saverio Borrelli. A shy and reserved figure, but of steely determination, very much a Milanese bourgeois, enamoured of classical music and of horse-riding, Borrelli was sixty-two years old in 1992, and had become chief prosecutor in Milan four years earlier. He came from a family of magistrates, and like Giovanni Falcone had been deeply steeped in a culture of service to the state.[16] In 1993 Borrelli explained to the journalist Maria Antonietta Calabrò that those who enforced the law could not delude themselves that they were either above politics or free from them. Instead, they had to fight a dual battle: against their own prejudices, and against mere subservience to the politicians: 'It is important to be aware that a neutral interpretation of the law, a mechanical one, cannot exist. Such an awareness serves to guard oneself against the danger of being the unconscious instrument of prejudices and preconceptions . . . It's quite a subtle game, of trying to get the right dialectical equilibrium.'[17] The question of equilibrium was indeed a delicate one, and more than once, embroiled in the gargantuan and unequal battle to clean up Italian public life, it proved impossible for Borrelli and his associates to maintain the correct balance.

As the scandal of 'Tangentopoli' developed, Borrelli formed a pool of magistrates, or '*Dipartimento*' as it was officially called, dedicated entirely to exploring the innumerable highways and byways of corruption in public life in Milan. The principal members of this pool, which was destined to become even more famous than that which had operated in Palermo in the 1980s, were the assistant chief prosecutor Gerardo D'Ambrosio, and the junior prosecutors Gherardo Colombo, Piercamillo Davigo and Antonio Di Pietro. The pool was a heterogeneous group, both in social origin and in political belief. Colombo, whom we have already encountered as an undaunted and upright magistrate during the inquiries into the history of the Masonic lodge P2,[18] was an urban intellectual, very much part of that critical middle class to which I have made constant reference. Di Pietro, on the other hand, was of peasant stock from the region of Molise, an ex-policeman who had studied at night to become a magistrate. D'Ambrosio and Colombo were left-wingers, Davigo and Di Pietro on the right.[19] Borrelli forged them into a formidable team, and took pleasure in using equine imagery to describe the way he kept them under control: 'Sometimes I have left the reins quite loose on the necks of the most vivacious of my horses . . . I gave Di Pietro his head, and he did not let me down.'[20]

Both Borrelli and Colombo did not hesitate to pay tributes at an early stage to the outstanding qualities of Antonio Di Pietro as a magistrate. Not only was his mastery of information technology absolutely essential to an inquiry of this sort (into corruption in public life), but he demonstrated a great sense of pragmatism and considerable interrogatory skills. Colombo wrote: 'I believe that Di Pietro's greatest ability is his way of interrogating people. It consists not just in knowing which questions to ask, and of establishing a logical sequence which "forces" the person being interrogated to give honest answers, but also in his intuitive capacity, his way of foreseeing the answers, his theatrical touches which cannot help but involve one.'[21] And Borrelli spoke of his 'overwhelming humanity, that way of involving all those who come into contact with him, of convincing them to unburden themselves, to collaborate'.[22]

The Milan pool soon found themselves faced with an almost uncontrollable amount of information. Not only did Mario Chiesa start to collaborate from his cell at the San Vittore prison, but many figures from the world of Milanese business and the professions began to recount the details of the kickback system. The magistrates' information on the circles of corruption grew ever more detailed, involving increasingly important names in the political hierarchy of the city and the country. Borrelli did not hesitate to place them under investigation. If ever there was a moment to expose the corruption of the political system, this was it. The victory of the Northern League had greatly weakened the ruling parties in Milan and Lombardy, and it granted the magistrates the political room for manoeuvre that they desperately needed. From now on, they could no longer be muzzled, as had happened in the 1980s.

Under the stipulation of the new Code for Penal Procedure, which had been introduced in October 1989, as soon as the activities of a person came formally under investigation he or she had to be informed of the fact by the magistrates.[23] The 'Notice of Guarantee', as it came to be called, was intended to safeguard the rights of the citizen, but in the heated atmosphere of the 'Tangentopoli' inquiry it became an act of accusation in its own right. On 1 May 1992, twenty-five days after the general elections, two such Notices of Guarantee were delivered to Paolo Pillitteri, Craxi's brother-in-law and the mayor of Milan from 1986 until January 1992, and Carlo Tognoli, another former Socialist mayor of the city and minister during the last Andreotti government. Pillitteri was being investigated for receiving and corruption to the tune of nearly one billion lire, Tognoli of the receiving of some 500 million lire in the period 1984–5.[24] Then on 12 May, just twenty-four hours before the beginning of balloting by the members of parliament for the new President of the Republic, the national administrative secretary of the DC, Severino Citaristi, received the first of his many Notices, informing him that he was under investigation for illegal financing of his party.[25]

In the electric atmosphere created by this news, the members of parliament gathered at Montecitorio. The journalists Bellu and Bonsanti have described the scene: 'Today, Wednesday 13 May [1992], with the two houses of parliament sitting in solemn session, the twin tracks of Tangentopoli and of the election of the new President of the Republic are truly running very close to each other. So close, in fact, as to elide and intertwine, creating such a clash that the Speaker has difficulty in maintaining a semblance of order. The cry of "thieves, thieves" rises from the benches of the MSI, is taken up by the League, and thanks to the proceedings being televised live, finishes in the homes of every Italian family.'[26]

The following days were to be crucial for the destiny of the Italian crisis. The Old Guard knew that if they kept their nerve they could still elect one of their number as President of the Republic, and that the Quirinale was a key position from which to manage the crisis and reassert control over the magistrates. The Christian Democrats chose Forlani as their front runner. Craxi reluctantly agreed, and announced before the vote that there was a 90 per cent chance that the secretary of the DC would gain the necessary backing. On 16 May there were two secret ballots, with the quorum for election being 508 votes. On the first ballot Forlani gained only 469 votes, on the second 479. The day after, a Sunday, he withdrew his candidacy: there had been too many desertions, either from the ranks of his own party or those of its supposed allies.[27]

It was now the Socialists' turn. Craxi himself was ruled out – the developments in Milan had already begun to cast their long shadow over him, and he knew that he would never reach the necessary quorum. He put forward instead Giuliano Vassalli, former Socialist minister of Justice, no friend of the independent-minded magistrates of Milan. He came much less close than Forlani, gaining just 351 votes on 22 May 1992.

The war of attrition seemed destined to go on for some time. There was a long tradition in Italian politics of repeated balloting in the election of the President of the Republic, and sooner or later it seemed likely that the 'CAF' would persuade parliament, more from exhaustion than conviction, to elect a candidate of their choice. Giulio Andreotti, in any case, was quietly waiting his turn in the wings. However, at this point the play of contingency reached its highest level of intensity. The focus of attention once again suddenly shifted city and subject, and the multi-faceted and complex nature of the Italian crisis revealed its most terrible side.

3. Palermo

On 19 May Giovanni Falcone, who was still working at the Ministry of Justice,[28] gave an interview to the newspaper *la Repubblica*. He told the journalist Giovanni Marino: 'The enemy is always there, ready to strike. But we are not even able to agree on the election of the President of the Republic . . . Cosa Nostra commits crimes uninterruptedly, while we continue to quarrel without interruption.'[29]

Four days later, on Saturday, 23 May 1992, he flew to Palermo for the weekend, accompanied by his wife, Francesca Morvillo, who was also a magistrate. At the airport he was met by a bodyguard of seven men and three police cars. One car went ahead. Falcone himself, against the rules, took the wheel of the second, with his wife beside him, and the third car followed behind. The motorcade turned on to the *autostrada* heading for Palermo. The Mafia was waiting for them. At Capaci, just a few kilometres from the airport, Totò Riina's men, led by Giovanni Brusca, had placed more than 300 kilos of explosives in a large metal drainpipe that passed underneath the *autostrada*. As the motorcade drove past, they detonated the explosive. The three *carabinieri* in the lead car, Antonio Montinaro, Rocco Di Cillo and Vito Schifani, were killed instantly. Falcone and his wife died in hospital shortly afterwards. The official driver of the second car, who had been in the back seat, was badly injured but survived. The three bodyguards in the last car escaped with minor injuries.[30]

The 'massacre at Capaci', an event which for a moment focused the attention of the whole world upon the Italian crisis, was part of that general strategy of revenge killings by the Mafia for the '*maxiprocesso*' of Palermo, for the life sentences to which the Mafia bosses had been sentenced at its conclusion, and for the confirmation of those sentences pronounced by the Corte di Cassazione on 31 January 1992.[31] It was not a declaration of war, for that had already been declared many years previously, but a spectacular demonstration of the surveillance skills and firepower of the Mafia in that war. The Mafia leaders had carefully tracked one of the most carefully guarded men in Italy, the very symbol of the anti-Mafia struggle, caught him in a relatively unguarded moment and blown him up. In so doing, they hoped to have demonstrated both their own invincibility and the ineluctable fate that awaited all those servants of the state who stood in their way.

The reactions of the highest echelons of the state were once again, as after the killing of General Carlo Alberto dalla Chiesa in August 1982, of the knee-jerk variety. Having quarrelled and voted for days on end over who was to be the next President of the Republic, the shock wave of Falcone's death forced the joint session of the houses of parliament into precipitate action. If two weeks earlier it had been the Milanese aspect of the crisis that had rudely disturbed the rituals of Roman politics, now it was the tragedy outside Palermo that dictated the course of the crisis. On 25 May 1992 Christian Democrats, Socialists, Liberals, Social Democrats, the PDS, the Verdi, the Rete and the Radicals reached agreement on the name of Oscar Luigi Scalfaro (at that time the newly elected President of the Chamber of Deputies) for President of the Republic. It was an agreement that would have been utterly inconceivable just two days earlier.

The choice of Scalfaro was to be of profound significance for Italian politics in the 1990s. Scalfaro both was and was not a member of the Old Guard. He certainly had all the characteristics of a traditional Christian Democrat politician, and had been Minister of the Interior during both the Craxi governments. On the other hand, he was culturally very far from those 'business politicians' who had so marked the 1980s, and he was respectful of the autonomy of the magistracy. In his speech to the Chamber of Deputies of 28 May 1992, he had made his position clear on a number of issues, among which was 'Tangentopoli': 'The misuse of public money is a very serious misdemeanour; it robs and defrauds the honest citizen who pays his taxes, and undermines severely the faith of citizens in the state: there is no greater evil, no greater danger for democracy than the torbid interlacing of business and politics.'[32] The 'CAF' had not exactly got the man they wanted.

The election of the President of the Republic had been one immediate result of the killing of Falcone, his wife and his bodyguards. Another, of equal if not greater significance, was the reaction of some sections of the population of Palermo. Some 40,000 people attended the funeral in the cathedral of Palermo of the victims of the massacre at Capaci, whereas less than a year earlier, in August 1991, the family of Libero Grassi, the businessman who had dared to stand up to the Mafia, had been left almost alone to mourn him.[33] But it was not numbers that mattered so much as attitudes. The very cruelty and desperation of the conflict in Sicily seemed to provoke a reaction in which there was a noble attempt to connect family attitudes, civil society and the responsibilities of the state. In other words the linkages between these three spheres, which in much of the rest of the peninsula were to remain all too weak and undefined throughout the crisis, here emerged in an intense and admirable, albeit fleeting, form. Perhaps no document illustrates this better than the section 'The pledge', pronounced on 13 June 1992 during the prayer vigil in the packed Palermitan church of S. Giuseppe ai Teatini:

We pledge to educate our children to respect others, to have a sense of duty and a sense of justice.

We pledge not to turn a blind eye to current malpractices, lending them tacit consent simply because *'così fan tutti'*.

We pledge to renounce any privileges which could derive from contacts and help of a clientelistic or *'mafioso'* type.

We pledge to recognize justice for all as being a value superior to our own particular interest.

We pledge to not ask as a favour that which is due to us as a right . . .

We pledge not to forget Giovanni Falcone and all those who have died in the fight against the Mafia, and to remember them as if they were members of our own families who had died for us.[34]

Here, expressed in an extremely simple and direct fashion, was a code of conduct that addressed not only the problem of the individual and the Mafia, but also indicated the *via maestra* by which the family could become that 'real school of the virtues of freedom' to which John Stuart Mill had referred.[35] Here, too, was a completely different reading from the habitual one of the relationship between the citizen and the public administration.

The civil society that grew in Palermo and other parts of Sicily in these weeks, and which was unique in the history of the island, was one that had its roots in the 'Palermo Spring' of 1985–6. It was primarily middle-class,[36] a complex mixture of grass-roots Catholic activism, of ex-militants of the PCI and of the revolutionary groups of the 1970s, of feminists, of university and school students, of trade-unionists. It had all the virtues and the defects of a 'rainbow alliance' (the expression is Jessie Jackson's), all the vigour and passion and pluralism of a movement born from below, all the difficulties in making such a movement cohere and endure.

One of its most original and visually dramatic expressions was the draping, out of windows and over balconies, of old sheets on which had been sprayed a variety of slogans: 'Palermo has understood, but has the state?' 'I know, but I don't have the proof,' 'Falcone, you continue to live in our hearts,' 'Palermo wants to live.'[37] The idea had first come to a kinship group of three sisters and their daughters the night after the assassination of Falcone. A 'Sheets' committee' was formed,[38] and rapidly more and more slogans appeared, in schools as well as homes, in the historic city centre and in some of the suburbs.

The symbolic action of these months took many forms. The historian Giovanna Fiume has described just two of them. The first reinvented and modified an old trade-union tradition, the 'strike-in-reverse':

A group of citizens decide to reopen roadworks on the ring road of Palermo, incomplete after twenty years of work. They put up a sign which reads: 'Civil society assessorate: cost of the work, 000,000,000 billion lire.' A large group of volunteers sets to work weeding, moving stones, preparing verges and banks. They manage to recoup a stretch of the *autostrada*, and in so doing get rid of one of the bottlenecks which had meant long daily queues for motorists. Then they hand over the works to the Prefect of the city, as if to say, 'It's your turn now.'

The second had echoes of 1968: 'Hundreds of students from Agrigento fill the local train which is going to Racalmuto where the Mafia wars have recently been responsible for killing innocent bystanders. For an evening they take over the territory of the Mafia, with the simplicity that belongs to youth.'[39]

Obviously, the intensity of emotion and action of this time could not be sustained for long.[40] The movement, being mainly middle-class, had barely touched the popular quarters of the city where Mafia traditions were most deeply inculcated. Class and culture divided the city, and how far civil society in Palermo could put down firm roots depended to a very great extent upon the way in which the crisis developed or died at a national level.

In Sicily, though, the Mafia had not finished its work. On 19 July, a Sunday, the magistrate Paolo Borsellino went in the late afternoon to visit his mother in Palermo, in her flat in Via D'Amelio. He was accompanied to the gate of the block of flats in which she lived by five highly armed guards, one of whom was a woman, Emanuela Loi.[41] Suddenly, there was a tremendous explosion which killed all six of them instantaneously and dismembered their bodies.[42]

With the killings in Via D'Amelio, the Republican state reached the lowest point in its long and ambiguous relationship with the Mafia. If, after the massacre at Capaci, the reaction had been one of anger, now it was one of despair. In Palermo one testimony wrote of 'an infinite sadness, crowded together as we were on the steps of the Palace of Justice, the flowers we held in our hands wilting in the tremendous heat, the slogan on our tee-shirts, "enough is enough", seeming to us now like a silly piece of bravado, because we were dwarfs faced by a giant who had just demonstrated that he could do anything he wanted to'.[43]

The widow of Borsellino refused a state funeral for her husband and the police threatened not to act in the future as bodyguards for anti-Mafia magistrates. When, on 21 July 1992, the highest political authorities of the state as well as the chief of police, Vincenzo Parisi, attended the state funeral in Palermo cathedral of the four policemen and the one policewoman killed in Via D'Amelio, they were protected with great difficulty from the anger of the crowd and from many of the police themselves.[44]

The state trembled, and to all Europe it seemed as if Italy was slipping rapidly out of control. The *Observer* wrote on 26 July 1992: 'The country is in a state of chaos, a state of war. It is fast becoming the banana republic of Europe. It has the highest murder rate in the European Community, the most rampant and blatant corruption, an ailing economy, a floundering government, and an anguished and embarrassed population.'[45]

Yet Italy, including Sicily, had many hidden resources. On 23 July in Palermo 'there were ten thousand people in the streets to demonstrate their loyalty to this State, however inept and half-dismantled that it is'.[46] In Catania the young volunteers of 'Gapa', an anti-Mafia group typical of the new southern associationism, spent the entire summer working with the children of the popular quarter of San Cristoforo, where the Santapaola Mafia 'Family' ruled supreme.[47] These were minority initiatives, but highly significant none the less.

4. The Government of Giuliano Amato

Back in Rome, to continue this tale of the three cities – Milan, Rome and Palermo – in whose palaces and streets the dramatic events of 1992 were played out, the political class also demonstrated quite unexpected resources. If the problem of the Presidency of the Republic had been solved, that of the Presidency of the Council of Ministers had not. In June 1992, Bettino Craxi still hoped that his old friendship with Scalfaro and his own unceasing insistence would be rewarded with another tenure at Palazzo Chigi. Scalfaro, though, was not so sure. Too many of Craxi's closest associates were being drawn into the Milanese magistrates' net, too much evidence was accumulating which pointed directly to the Socialist leader's offices in Piazza Duomo. Scalfaro, in the first of a number of highly skilful uses of his powers as President, asked Craxi to propose another Socialist to preside over an interim government, until such time as Craxi's name would be cleared, as it surely would be. If not, he hinted, there would be no choice but to ask a

Christian Democrat like Mino Martinazzoli to take over the reins of government. Neither Arnaldo Forlani nor Giuliano Vassalli, had they been elected President of the Republic, would have dreamed of insisting on such a solution. Craxi had little option but to acquiesce, and the Old Guard had lost its last possible base for a counter-attack.

On withdrawing his own candidacy, Craxi proposed the names of three leading members of his party – Giuliano Amato, who had been Treasury Minister in the late 80s, Gianni De Michelis, the Foreign Minister until April 1992, and Claudio Martelli, Vice-President of the Council of Ministers under Andreotti. Scalfaro chose Amato, which was just as well, because both De Michelis and Martelli were shortly to be the subject of more than one judicial inquiry.

Giuliano Amato was both one of the most brilliant and most enigmatic figures in Italian politics. A distinguished professor of constitutional law, he had chosen to make a political career by serving Bettino Craxi as his Under-Secretary at the Presidency of the Council of Ministers during the years 1983–7. From this vantage point at the very centre of Craxi's web of power, Amato must have witnessed the corrosive spread of Socialist malpractice and corruption. He never denounced it, though there is no evidence that he formed part of it. Quite why he chose a figure like Craxi for his political patron and master remains a mystery, one of those conundrums wherein psychology and politics intertwine.

However, once given his own command and freed, though never completely, from Craxi's shadow, Amato displayed considerable qualities of leadership and initiative. Sworn in on 28 June 1992, his was a fragile interim government, but one presided over with quiet determination.[48]

As well as the terrible situation in Sicily, and the unwelcome activity of the Milanese magistrates, Amato was faced immediately with an economic conjuncture which combined several different elements into a single, dangerous whole. The first warning signal concerned the budget deficit. In 1991, as we have seen, the primary deficit (net of interest rates) had returned to the black, but the budget for 1992 was widely judged to be insufficient, and the long political void between the elections at the beginning of April and Amato's appointment at the end of June had allowed Italy's chronic public accounts to slip further into debt. The predicted deficit on the current account was more than 40,000 billion lire over target. Piero Barucci, Amato's Treasury Minister and one of six 'technical' members of his government, described the bleak prospect that faced the new team: 'We had to go to the G7 summit at Munich, with a completely new government . . . and explain why the figures for our public accounts bore so little resemblance to those which were in the most recent documents, and which could still be found on desks in Brussels and Washington.'[49]

One of the reasons for the Italians' discomfiture lay precisely in

Germany. Faced with a weak dollar and the risk of inflation after reunification, the Germans were absolutely determined to keep interest rates high. Italy was forced to follow suit, and this meant that interest payments on her public debt were growing at great speed.[50]

However, the most insidious element of the economic situation was what can perhaps be best described as the great post-Maastricht depression. This had both a European as well as an Italian aspect. On 2 June 1992 a referendum in Denmark had voted against the ratification of the Maastricht Treaty, and there were many signs that the French would follow suit. The euphoria that had surrounded the signing of the Treaty evaporated rapidly, and monetary union began to seem a very long way away. In the Italian case, the problems did not concern ratification,[51] but implementation. The hard truth of the 'external constraint' began to sink in. At the time of the Maastricht agreement, Italy's inflation rate was 6.9 per cent; her budget deficit 9.9 per cent of GDP, against a requirement of 3 per cent; her public debt 103 per cent of GDP, instead of 60 per cent or less; her long-term interest rate 11.9 per cent.[52] But even before the signing of the Treaty the *Financial Times* had published an editorial with the ominous title 'Italy heading for relegation'.[53] This footballing metaphor became a constant in the Italian press, both during 1992 and afterwards, and obviously touched a highly sensitive spot in the nation's history.

Other eyes, too, were watching the development of the Italian situation. Italy was in the narrow band of the EMS currencies, along with Britain, but in the jittery post-Maastricht climate there were increasing doubts as to whether either of their economic performances justified the rates of exchange of their currencies. The lira was losing ground against the mark, and the Bank of Italy was having to intervene constantly to support it. As Piero Barucci, himself a banker, wrote: 'For the financial operators . . . the exchange rate of the lira could become a market which offered unexpected profits. The Italian currency was to be studied for its weaknesses and possible developments. Henceforward, it was destined to become a prey.'[54]

Amato did what he could to buy time. One week after taking office, he summoned a Council of Ministers on a Sunday morning, 5 July 1992, and announced a drastic 'corrective measure' to the tune of some 30,000 billion lire, to be garnered both from spending cuts and further taxation.[55] He then flew off directly to Munich for the G7 meeting, where he and the other Italian representatives, even if they were not omitted from the official photograph, felt rather as if they had been. The pressure on the lira eased, but not for long.

The first weeks of Giuliano Amato's government were marked by two other events of considerable significance. The first of these was the signing on 31

July 1992 of a tripartite pact between government, employers and trade unions. As we have seen above,[56] in the 1980s the trade unions had lost their way as a major social and political protagonist. They had also quarrelled bitterly over Craxi's decision in 1984 to reduce the weight of the wage index mechanism, the so-called *'scala mobile'*. Eight years later, they had refound some sort of unity of action, and much of the merit for this belonged to the veteran leader of the CGIL, Bruno Trentin, who had convinced his union of the need to work closely with the CISL and UIL, and to establish a higher national political profile.[57]

As for the Confindustria, it too had made progress. For the first time in more than twenty years, as Liborio Mattina has shown, it had formulated a clear political strategy, in which it called for a radical overhaul of the public administration and of the relationship between the citizen and public services, immediate privatizations, reduction of the public debt, and institutional and fiscal reform.[58] Under the able leadership of a young Roman businessman, Luigi Abete, Confindustria seemed much more oriented to being a political actor than a mere lobby. It also, rather late in the day, established a code of practice, to which its members were asked to adhere.[59]

The preconditions for an agreement were thus established, and in the electric atmosphere of July 1992, Amato coaxed the two sides together and pleaded with them to move swiftly. In particular he asked Bruno Trentin to make considerable sacrifices, to abandon the *'scala mobile'* and reach a general agreement with the employers over labour costs. Only in this way, argued both Amato and Carlo Azeglio Ciampi, the Governor of the Bank of Italy, could the inflationary spiral of wages and prices be broken, and the interests of the nation be preserved.

This was not the first time in the history of the Republic that Italy's largest and most left-wing trade union had been asked to sacrifice class interests for national ones, nor the first time that it had responded positively.[60] Trentin hesitated at length before signing, because he knew how unpopular the abandonment of the *'scala mobile'*, the cherished safeguard of the real value of workers' wages, would be at the grass-roots. He also felt, justly, that Amato was not a real arbiter, but was much closer to the positions of the Confindustria than to those of the majority of the CGIL.[61]

The agreement of 31 July 1992, which led to great conflict in the CGIL, and which was widely interpreted by its base as a major defeat, came to be recognized, with the passage of time, as of historic importance. Not only was it an important international signal at a moment of considerable national crisis; it was also the start of a new political role for the unions themselves, in which consensual compromise between government, employers and trade unions became the very basis of governance.[62]

The other crucial decision of these weeks, very different in kind, was to send some 7,000 troops to Sicily in the wake of the killing of Paolo Borsellino and his bodyguard. The problem of the Mafia was not going to be solved by the army, but its presence in Palermo was of crucial psychological importance, and was recognized as such by those who were in the front line of the fight against the Mafia.[63] On 6 September Giuseppe Madonia, a leading member of the Mafia, was arrested. Five days later it was the turn of Carmine Alfieri, considered to be the head of the Neapolitan Camorra. At long last, it looked as if the state meant business, and not Mafia business.

5. 'Tangentopoli', Justice and Public Opinion

While the government tried to come to terms with the grave problems of the economy and the Mafia, that other multiplicator of crisis, judicial activity in Milan, continued its work inexorably, attracting as it did so increasing international interest.[64] On 16 July Salvatore Ligresti, the leading building constructor of the city, was arrested. As Bellu and Bonsanti wrote, 'It's an epoch-making occurrence for Milan, a sort of taking of the Bastille. Ligresti is the backroom partner of all the principal economic dynasties of the Nation.'[65] His arrest also signalled the magistrates' conviction that corruption did not flow in one direction only, from the politicians to the world of business, but also vice versa.[66]

However, very quickly the word 'Tangentopoli' became dissociated from its territorial definition of the city of Milan, and assumed a vaguer, more displaced connotation.[67] Taking courage from their Milanese colleagues' example, magistrates all over the country began to investigate those accusations of corruption in public life which they had previously ignored quietly. One of the most startling early cases concerned a PSDI *assessore* of the Comune of Rome, Lamberto Mancini, who was arrested on 10 June while receiving a kickback of 28 million lire. In itself the event was hardly by this time very noteworthy. That same morning, though, Mancini had laid a wreath on the monument to Giacomo Matteotti, whose assassination at the hands of a Fascist squad had taken place exactly seventy years earlier. Mancini had then issued a press statement specifying that his was 'a non-ritualistic homage, but one of deep respect for a man who had fought to the death against that culture of illegality which is so present even in our time'.[68]

From Reggio Calabria, where the revelations of the ex-mayor Agatino Licandro[69] led to the arrest of the leading private building constructor, Vincenzo Lodigiani, to Verona, where the Christian Democrat leadership was to be decapitated,[70] a wave of judicial activity swept through the peninsula during the following months. On 14 July 1992, Gianni De Michelis, the former Socialist Minister for Foreign Affairs and one of the Italian signatories of the Maastricht Treaty, was placed under investigation by the Venetian magistrates.[71]

For Bettino Craxi the situation was becoming quite intolerable. In a speech of 3 July to the House of Deputies he abandoned his earlier, moralizing stance, and claimed that the illegal financing of the parties was well known to be part of the Italian political system, and should be accepted as such. When this line failed to convince, he tried in August to organize a personal counter-attack against the most renowned of the Milanese prosecuting magistrates, Antonio Di Pietro. After a meeting of the Socialist leadership of 26 August, Rino Formica, the former Socialist Minister of Finances, announced, in one of the historic phrases of this period, that 'Bettino has three aces up his sleeve' which would discredit totally Di Pietro.[72] Nothing, at least for the moment, came of this menace, and the magistrates' investigations went on.

One of the principal reasons why they did so lay with the enthusiastic support that public opinion accorded them. Slogans like 'Thank you Di Pietro,' 'All power to Colombo,' 'Di Pietro, you're better than Pelé,' appeared on the walls and monuments of Milan.[73] There was widespread excitement at the prospect of some of the most arrogant figures in Italy, who had long regarded themselves as untouchable, at last being called upon to respond for their actions. A festive air pervaded many parts of Italy, as always happens when the habitual ordering of a society is suddenly brought into question.

It is possible to suggest that behind this seeming unanimity of public opinion there lay many and divergent motivations, which in turn reflected differences of class and of culture. Dependent workers of left-wing traditions rejoiced in the discomfiture of their historic opponents. The self-employed and small entrepreneurs gave vent to their pent-up fury with a political class which was taxing them increasingly at a time of recession, but which offered in return a deeply inefficient public administration. All those who had voted for the Northern League added what was for them a self-evident geographical interpretation: these were the thieves of Rome and their emissaries who were being accused and arrested. Finally, some of the educated middle classes, those who were most active in civil society, rejoiced in the forcible reaffirmation of legality and of public ethics. The convergence of interests and passions was thus a strong one, but unlikely to last.

With so many voices raised in unison, dangers of summary justice and of the infringement of civil liberties hung heavy in the air. The new Code of Penal Procedure had aimed at increasing the rights of defendants, and at destroying the old 'inquisitory' character of the Public Prosecutor. It certainly did not function in that way in the heated atmosphere of 1992–3. The *'informazione di garanzia'*, the Notice which informed a person that he or she was under investigation, functioned, as has been seen, as a sort of pre-emptive sentence. Defendants felt strongly that they had insufficient possibilities to exercise their rights of defence. The judges who had to decide on the preliminary validity of the Public Prosecutor's case were often insufficiently independent from the Prosecutor's office. Preventive imprisonment, or the threat of it, was widely used as an instrument of pressure in order to extract confession.[74] Extracts from interrogations had an uncanny habit of being reprinted in newspapers and weeklies. Some magistrates, in their eagerness to take action, made unpardonable errors.[75]

Once again, as with the question of the probity of the evidence of '*pentiti*', so with 'Tangentopoli', the debate centred around means and ends in the legal system. In 1992–3 a minority of Italian magistrates, led by those in Milan, tried to break the vicious circle of corruption in public life. Sometimes they used methods that were questionable. Sometimes they made mistakes. Nearly always their actions led to personal tragedy of a greater or lesser kind.[76] None the less, it is difficult to conclude, in overall terms, that they acted in bad faith, or to deny the impelling and important contribution they made to Italian democracy.

6. Europe and Disaster

In the autumn of 1992, the three great cities of the Italian crisis, Milan, Rome and Palermo, were joined by two others which were 'virtual', but not for this reason any less real. One, as we have just seen, was a by now omni-present 'Tangentopoli'. The other was the 'City', not in the narrow territorial sense of the one square mile in the heart of London, but a place of frenzy and of information technology inhabited by financial operators on a global scale. In the 1980s, this last city had grown correspondingly with the great transformations of the global money markets.[77] In 1992 its interest in Europe was twofold: the liberalization of flows of capital in the context of the European Single Market had improved the conditions as well as the volume of trade; and the post-Maastricht uncertainties had rendered exchange rates volatile, with the corresponding possibility of realizing significant profits. The power of this City, the way it combined iron market logic and manifest unpredictability, rendered it an awesome force. Rarely, as in the sequence of events that follows, is it so easy to discern the predominance of economic structures, and the flailing attempts of single human agents, however powerful, to combat them.

The lira, as we have just seen, had become a particular object of attention for the financial operators in the early summer of 1992. It was certainly not the only currency to attract such scrutiny, for both the French franc and sterling were under pressure, though for different reasons (if such they can be called).[78] The very stability of the European Monetary System, which had not been substantially modified in nearly six years, was being called into question. The time had come for a rapid realignment of the national currencies, before the situation got out of control.

At a secret meeting held in the Ministry of Finances in Paris on 26 August 1992, between the four European powers which were members of the G7, and at the subsequent wider reunion of EC finance ministers and Governors of national banks at Bath on 4–5 September, no agreement was reached on what should be done. Both occasions were an object lesson in the primacy of national self-interest at a time of European crisis.[79] The Germans refused to budge an inch on interest rates, given their fear of inflation. The French would not contemplate a realignment because of the negative consequences it could have on their delicately balanced referendum on the Maastricht Treaty, due on 20 September. The Italians knew that they could not avoid devaluation, but hoped that they would not be left by themselves. The British, the most obvious candidates to join them, would not even begin to contemplate such a move. Instead at Bath the blustering Norman Lamont, the Tory Chancellor of the Exchequer, repeatedly and ineffectually tried to berate Helmut Schlesinger, President of the Bundesbank, into reducing his country's interest rates.[80]

The economic representatives of the most powerful European nations therefore offered rather less than a coherent or united reaction, but in any case it must remain doubtful whether they could have saved the EMS from the menace incumbent upon it. In the week beginning Monday, 7 September 1992, there was an extraordinary speculative run against the lira. The Bundesbank, following the rules that had been agreed by the EC for such emergencies, intervened massively in support of the Italian currency. By Friday 11 September it had had enough. It had bought up some 24 billion Deutschmarks' worth of lira, and feared that these obligatory purchases would swamp its capacity to control Germany's fast-expanding money supply. Theo Waigel, the long-serving German Finance Minister, phoned Piero Barucci and said that the Bundesbank would not continue. The lira would have to devalue, hopefully not by itself.[81]

The Germans and Italians agreed therefore that the lira would devalue by 7 per cent, with the Germans reducing their interest rates very slightly. On 11 September, Giuliano Amato phoned John Major, the British Prime Minister, who was staying with the Queen at Balmoral, and asked him if Britain would consider a joint, damage-limiting initiative. The answer was a firm 'no'. The British government was content to leave Italy to go it alone.

Three days later, though, it was sterling's turn. As the *Financial Times* explained laconically: 'There was enough dissonance among policy makers to encourage fund managers and corporate treasurers to take a further shot at the ERM.'[82] On 16 September 1992, Black Wednesday, the rate of exchange of both the sterling and the lira plummeted dramatically, and both were forced not just to devalue, but to exit from the European monetary system.

The devaluation of a national currency is nearly always considered a national humiliation, and Black Wednesday was no exception, either for Italy or for Britain. In both countries the situation was made worse by the way it was handled. Amato had gone on television to present the deal with the Germans in reassuring and rational tones, almost as a triumph of Italian diplomacy, but he was immediately belied by events as the lira plummeted further downwards.[83] The British leaders, though, had been far more irresponsible, for they had behaved with considerable arrogance, convinced that there was no need for a European response, and that sterling could look after itself.[84]

Apart from wounded national pride, the greatest casualty was the spirit of Maastricht. On 20 September the French approved the Treaty by a very narrow margin, but the plans for economic and monetary union by the end of the decade had received a very severe blow. Not only was the EMS in tatters (the Spanish peseta and the Portuguese escudo were also to devalue in November), but the Germans had learned some very specific Darwinian lessons. From this time onwards they theorized a two-tier Europe; only the economically reliable nations would be allowed to join them, at least in the first instance, on the path to monetary union. And Italy? One senior European monetary official commented some months after the September débâcle: 'If you looked at all the indicators, there was one group of countries (the original members minus Italy) which stayed close to each other and another group (the newcomers with Italy) that was diverging significantly in a lasting way.'[85] The writing was on the wall, and the grand Italian strategy of the '*vincolo esterno*' lay in ruins.

7. At the Heart of the Crisis, 1992–3

a. A WINTER OF DISCONTENT
In the aftermath of the September débâcle in Europe, the Italian state once again, as in the previous July, had to endure moments of panic and discomfort. The monthly auction of state bonds (BOT) in late September had a low take-up, and the Bank of Italy had to buy heavily in order to sustain public confidence. Many people began to withdraw money from their bank accounts, and this practice extended, as the Treasury Minister noted with horror, even to the bank inside the Senate, where one afternoon he came across a queue of people waiting to withdraw their deposits.[86]

In spite of calls on Amato to resign, his government lasted another six months, and in that time it passed many useful measures, as well as many controversial ones. Immediately after what had become a free-floating devaluation, which settled the lira at around 15 per cent less than its previous value, Amato pushed very hard for budgetary reform. In the annual budget for 1993 he and Barucci proposed spending cuts and tax increases which amounted to more than 93,000 billion lire, the largest single financial intervention in the whole period under consideration. The budget, together with other measures passed by decree laws, slashed state spending in health, social insurance and other areas. As for income, new taxes were introduced on house ownership and a special 'minimum tax' for the self-employed.

After what had happened in September, there can be no doubt at all that radical steps were needed to bring the budget deficit, and if possible the public debt, under control. Amato, therefore, responded to a state of necessity. As he commented bitterly to Ciampi on 16 September 1992: 'As you can see, my dear Governor, in Italy it is only possible to take remedial measures once the roof over our heads has already fallen in.'[87]

However, his actions were highly problematic, for two principal orders of reasoning. The first was a European one. Italy was not alone, after the shocks of September, in applying a drastic programme of budget squeezing. To varying degrees, nearly all her neighbours were engaged in the same sort of operation. Such widespread action could lead only in one direction: recession. In fact, 1993 was to be a dismal year, and in Italy consumption *fell* for the first time in the whole of the post-war period, by 2.5 per cent. GDP, too, declined, by 1.2 per cent, which did nothing to help the public debt.[88]

The second reason was a domestic one. In a time of national crisis of this sort, Giuliano Amato, for all his determination and intelligence, was not the right person to be the President of the Council of Ministers. In the past he had been too close to Craxi, and in the present he was seen by left-wing forces in the trade unions and in society as being too biased towards the employers. As long as Amato was at the helm, they were unlikely to agree to economic sacrifice.

The autumn of 1992, therefore, saw a significant resurgence of a very strong tradition in Italian public culture, that of working-class protest. In spite of all the structural changes in the world of work during the 1980s, which I have attempted to analyse in Chapters 1 and 2 of this volume, the capacity for mobilization and its habitual forms had not disappeared. In September 1992 the *piazze* were full of dependent workers of one sort or another, protesting against the cuts, against the government and against their own trade-union leaders, who had signed the pact on labour costs. On 29 October, a strike called not by the trade-union leadership but by 100 factory councils brought 50,000 workers on to the streets of Milan.[89] By February 1993,

Bruno Trentin, the leader of the CGIL, was denouncing the social policies of Amato's government as 'tragic' and its plans to boost employment as 'a disgrace'.[90]

None the less, Amato battled on, and was able to chalk up a number of important initiatives in the crucial area of the reform of the state. Nearly all of these measures corresponded to that entrepreneurial approach which has been outlined above, and which sought to introduce into the public administration the productivity, efficiency and culture of the private firm.[91] Thus the first steps were taken towards privatizing the public sector giants IRI, ENI, INA and ENEL by transforming them into shareholding companies, and attempts were made to improve the health service by rationalizing the number of USLs (Local Health Authorities) and raising their productivity.

However, probably the most important of Amato's initiatives was the decree law on the reform of the public administration, announced on 22 January 1993. The contracts of all public employees were henceforth to be based on private administrative law. They were to be treated as private employees, without special job security, and were to be rewarded for productivity, rendered flexible, and sacked if necessary. Hours of opening to the public were to be extended to the afternoons. Public sector managers were to be given wider responsibilities and constant targets. The effective power of veto of the trade unions was to be drastically reduced. New Public Management had arrived in Italy. The editorial of the business newspaper *Il Sole — 24 Ore* of 23 January celebrated the changes with a familiar metaphor: 'In the great family of the public administration, home to all manner of irresponsibility, the concept of the co-relation between work and performance has been introduced for the first time. Something which was perfectly obvious to those accustomed to work in the private sphere.'[92]

As for institutional reform, very much less progress was made. Another bicameral commission, similar to that presided over by Aldo Bozzi in 1983—5, met and deliberated for a number of months under the presidency first of Ciriaco De Mita and then of Nilde Jotti. It did not manage to agree on very much. In this field Italy suffered from the conundrum ably identified by Gustavo Zagrebelsky: a constitutional reform is necessary when a political system works badly, but when a political system works badly, it will not be able to produce a reform.[93] Italy's political class also suffered from what appeared, at least from the outside, to be an obsessive concentration upon the possible merits and niceties of different electoral systems. The amount of energy and time dedicated to this argument was, obviously, at the expense of others, of equal or possibly greater importance.

However, one highly significant change did emerge from parliament just before the end of the Amato government: the new law on the election of city mayors, agreed on 25 March 1992. Passed in order to avoid a referendum on the issue, the law gave voters the right to elect their mayor directly. This provision was to have a significant effect, for the better, on the relationship between voting and political responsibility at a local level.

Finally, mention must be made of continuing developments at Palermo, developments which were not directly the responsibility of the government, but which occurred within its period of office. On 15 January 1993 a special unit of the Carabinieri, coordinated by the magistrate Ilda Boccassini, succeeded where all others had failed: it arrested the leader of the Sicilian Mafia, Totò Riina. The Carabinieri had been tipped off by Baldassare Di Maggio, a Mafia *'pentito'* whose life had been threatened by Riina and Giovanni Brusca.[94]

In this same period a new Chief Prosecutor, Gian Carlo Caselli, arrived to replace Pietro Giammanco, who had stepped down after Borsellino's killing. Like Caponnetto before him, Caselli had volunteered for the job. Piedmontese, left-wing, of working-class background, and devoutly Catholic, Caselli told the journalist Maria Antonietta Calabrò of the way in which he viewed his appointment:

In my interview of November 1992 with the Higher Council of the Judiciary, I had made it clear that if I was to go to Palermo I would do so, subjectively, in a spirit of deep humility, aware of how much I would have to learn . . . I also added a remark which might appear presumptuous, but which the Council appreciated: I said that to be an external observer of a situation like that of Palermo perhaps offered certain advantages, because in Palermo there are many 'internal' constraints, often unconscious ones . . . which are the result of practices and mechanisms which overlap with each other and have rigidified over time. It is for this reason that I was chosen for the job in Sicily.[95]

He was to prove a remarkable Chief Prosecutor, quite the most courageous and dedicated public servant in the Europe of his time.

Giuliano Amato had served his country well as Prime Minister, but it was the problem of justice, that torment of the whole political class, old and new, for all of the 1990s, that was to be his undoing. His government was already a frail one in political terms, but its composition was undermined continuously by the activities of magistrates in various parts of the country. Seven of his ministers were forced to resign during the few, but crucial, months that he held power. On 15 December 1992 his former mentor, Bettino Craxi, received the first of a series of Notices of Guarantee from the Procura di Milano, informing him that he was under investigation for corruption, receiving, and violation of the law on the public financing of political parties. Craxi defended himself by claiming that the accusations against him were all part of a political plot, a claim that was to be a constant among those accused. However, the charges against him grew ever more substantial, and in May 1994 he decided to flee the country for his villa at Hammamet in Tunisia. His most likely successor as leader of the Socialists, Claudio Martelli, who had already begun to contest Craxi's leadership, had to resign as minister of Justice when fresh revelations linked his name to an old story – that of the P2 and of the 7 million dollars which the banker Roberto Calvi had deposited in a Lugano bank account in the name of 'the Honourable Claudio Martelli on behalf of the Honourable Bettino Craxi'.[96] There seemed no end to what would be discovered or to the assault of the magistrates on the old political order. Indeed, it made a certain impression upon British readers at this time to see on the front page of the weekend supplement of the *Financial Times* a huge drawing of the Tower of Pisa depicted as a can of worms, with an accompanying article by Robert Graham entitled 'When honesty means sharing your bribes'.[97]

An end, though, was attempted. After a marathon meeting of the Council of Ministers on 5 April 1993, Giuliano Amato and Giovanni Conso, his new minister of Justice, announced the passing of four decree laws and the proposing of three bills for what was to be termed a 'political solution' to the crisis.[98] The most politically significant of these measures was immediate depenalization for the illicit financing of political parties, which was the most common and least serious of the crimes of 'Tangentopoli'.[99]

However, Amato and Conso had badly misjudged the situation. Public opinion was outraged at the prospect of what came to be called 'throwing in the sponge', and at the idea that the political class would proceed to acquit itself. That weekend, especially on Sunday, 7 March 1993, the newspapers were inundated with faxed messages of protest, the telephone exchange at the Quirinale was blocked by incoming calls, there were spontaneous meetings and assemblies in many cities. The voice of a certain civil society was making itself heard.[100]

On the same Sunday morning Eugenio Scalfari published a dramatic editorial in *la Repubblica*, accusing Amato and Conso of lying to the public.[101] In historical terms, his editorial constituted probably the single most important piece published by the newspaper during its long, constant and influential campaign in support of the magistrates of 'Tangentopoli'. Later on the same day the President of the Republic let it be known that, on exclusively constitutional grounds, he was not prepared to sign the decree law which removed the penalties for the illegal financing of the parties. Scalfaro called his a constitutional decision, but it was in reality a key political move.

Amato's government never recovered from this defeat. The magistrates took new heart and made further, clamorous decisions. On 28 March 1993 Giulio Andreotti received a Notice of Guarantee from the Chief Prosecutor of Palermo notifying him that he was under investigation for the crime of association with the Mafia.[102] The day after, the Neapolitan magistrates informed Antonio Gava, the former minister of the Interior, that he too was under investigation, for his links with the Camorra. In these weeks, as the jurist Guido Neppi Modona wrote: 'The incisiveness of the magistrates' judicial inquiries into the corrupt links between business and politics, and into the collusion between Mafia and politicians, gave the sensation that a thorough-going revolution was taking place, conducted by means of the legal instruments of the penal process.'[103]

On 18–19 April 1993 a series of referenda, which had again been promoted principally by Mario Segni, was passed with overwhelming support.[104] Seventy-five per cent of the electorate voted, and of these 82.7 per cent cast their ballots for change. The most significant referendum was that abrogating the electoral system in the Senate, a decision which obliged parliament to confront rather than to avoid the question of overall electoral reform. It was time for Amato to go. He had always opposed the path of constitutional reform by referendum, but in any case the country by this time needed a more clearly impartial President of the Council of Ministers.

b. THE CIAMPI GOVERNMENT

With the party system in absolute disarray, the road was open for Oscar Luigi Scalfaro to form a 'President's government'.[105] He chose as its head Carlo Azeglio Ciampi, the Governor of the Bank of Italy since 1979. Ciampi was born in 1920 at Leghorn; he had been a youthful partisan in the ranks of the Action Party, and was a widely respected figure, both in Italy and in Europe. At the time of the devaluation of the lira, he had wanted to resign, but had been persuaded to remain at his post;[106] just a few months later, at the age of seventy-three, he found himself as President of the Council of Ministers. With his arrival at Palazzo Chigi the tendency for the Italian 'core executive' to be dominated by non-political experts, a process already under way in the last Andreotti governments and in that of Amato, reached its apogee. Ciampi represented the very best of that particular culture enshrined in the Bank of Italy.[107] His economic expertise was invaluable at this time, but so too was his sense of social justice.

Both Scalfaro and Ciampi had wanted to include representatives of the opposition in this transitional government, and indeed in its original composition three technical experts from the PDS became ministers;[108] in addition, the Green Francesco Rutelli took over responsibility for the Environment. However, on 29 April 1993, the day after Ciampi had presented his list of ministers, the House of Deputies voted against all four requests by the Procura of Milan to proceed against Bettino Craxi (the House would have had to lift his parliamentary immunity). Only the two requests by the Procura of Rome were approved. Once again, as on 6 March, there was intense public indignation against the politicians' attempts to obstruct the magistrates' work. The PDS and the Greens immediately called upon their four ministers to resign, which they did. It was not a wise decision, for the responsibility for what had happened lay with parliament not government, and by retiring from the latter the opposition deprived itself of an important role at a crucial moment.[109]

In spite of this squally start, the Ciampi government, which was to remain in power until new national elections in March 1994, exercised a considerable calming influence on the crisis. The frenzied series of *journées* in miniature which had characterized the preceding months – 16 September 1992 ('Black Wednesday' for the lira), 15 December (Notice of Guarantee for Craxi), 15 January 1993 (arrest of Totò Riina), 5–6 March (the attempted muzzling of the magistrates by the Amato government), 28–9 March (Notices of Guarantee for Andreotti and Gava) – quietened its pace. In spite of its transitional nature and the little time available to it, or perhaps because of them both, the Ciampi government worked very well. It was relatively free from the interminable intra-party feuds of the past, and of the so-called 'party delegations' which had ensconced themselves so improperly in the Council of Ministers of previous governments. Ciampi managed to forge his ministers into a team, probably not as harmonious as he later claimed,[110] but none the less something quite new for Italian politics.

When asked in 1994 what he considered to have been the single most significant achievement of his government, Ciampi replied 'the agreement on labour costs',[111] and it is difficult to disagree with him. His equidistance from employers and employed was recognized by both, and resulted in the signing of the protocol of 3 July 1993, an ambitious and successful attempt to redefine Italian industrial relations. The protocol introduced a new incomes policy, and drew both trade unions and Confindustria into regular tripartite discussions with the government. The social peace which resulted from this far-sighted reform was to be of fundamental importance for Italy's economic recovery. However, it is worth pointing out the paradox of an unreformed trade-union movement being integrated into government at precisely the time when the political parties, under furious attack, were being ejected from it.[112]

The agreement on labour costs formed one pillar of Ciampi's economic policy. Another, in which his own reputation in Europe played an important role, consisted in the forceful reaffirmation of the strategy of the 'external constraint'. At a time when Italy seemed very far from Europe, Ciampi continued to stress unequivocally the need to work towards respecting the parameters of the Maastricht Treaty and towards eventual monetary union. The budget law for 1994 was not a harsh one, at least by Amato's standards, amounting to some 38,000 billion lire.[113] Furthermore, devaluation was not turning out to be the disaster that many had feared. As Italian goods and services cost much less on international markets (the value of the lira had continued to slip downwards until it settled at around 25 per cent less of its pre-September 1992 value), industry enjoyed an exceptional export boom and income from tourism increased. At the same time, thanks principally to the pegging of wages and salaries, in both the private and public sectors, inflation decreased significantly.[114]

A second, highly significant area of action was that concerning the public administration. In Ciampi's plans an unusual priority had been accorded to administrative reform, and in his government an unusual minister was called upon to realize it. Sabino Cassese had spent a lifetime studying the considerable problems of the Italian bureaucracy. Once in power, he belied the stereotype of the university professor and moved with the speed and energy of a whirlwind. His reforms followed a number of different paths. The first aimed to render the bureaucracy more reliable and comprehensible to its users. A 'Charter of public services' tried to make citizens aware of their rights, and established qualitative and quantitative standards of administrative behaviour. The law no. 241 of August, 1990,[115] on the transparency of administrative procedures, was re-launched with great force. So too was *autocertificazione*', the right of citizens to declare their own civil status in a number of areas, without being obliged to seek certificates to that effect from the public administration. In addition, over 100 administrative procedures were radically simplified.

Cassese's reform also tried to render administrative structures less confused and oppressive. One ministry (that of the Merchant Marine), thirteen inter-ministerial committees, and more than seventy other collegial organs were suppressed. Savings of an estimated 2,600 billion lire were achieved in less than a year. Administrative action was rendered more neutral and transparent by revolutionizing the system of internal controls, modifying the tasks of the Corte dei Conti and issuing a 'Code of behaviour for civil servants'. Finally, every effort was made to adapt the norms of the Italian bureaucracy to those of its European counterparts.[116]

Coming hard on the heels of Amato's decree law, and going considerably beyond it, Cassese's action represented the most concrete, ambitious and democratic attempt to realize bureaucratic reform in the history of the Republic. Not surprisingly, it encountered every manner of opposition – from the trade unions in defence of their corporative interests, from parts of the press, even from colleagues within the government.[117] The lack of time available, when combined with Cassese's own indomitable personality, rendered progress difficult. The reforming minister had need of ten years, not less than one, to realize his grand scheme. He received considerable support from Ciampi, but unfortunately most of the public remained unaware of, and uninvolved in, the great struggle that was taking place.[118]

The last major reform of the Ciampi government was that of the electoral system. In its making and content the law of 4 August 1993 was the very opposite of the action taken with regard to the public administration, being a rather unsatisfactory compromise between a large number of actors in parliament and government.[119] None the less, it represented a distinct move towards a majoritarian and bipolar system. Seventy-five per cent of the Senate and of the House of Deputies were to be elected on a simple majority basis and 707 single-member colleges were created for that purpose. The remaining 25 per cent of the members of parliament were to be elected by the previous method of proportional representation. An electoral system on the French model, with two turns, which would certainly have accentuated bipolarization, was discarded, as was the prospect of establishing, as in Germany, a bar of 5 per cent of the national vote for the smaller parties wishing to enter parliament.[120]

However, the gravest defect of all in the new law was its gender blindness. At this key moment in Italian politics, the transformations in women's education, their changing place in the family and their presence in the labour force, found little or no reflection in the country's institutions. On the contrary. Women candidates were to be penalized under the new system, because the parties tended to choose well-known, male candidates for single-member constituencies. Women were only 12.8 per cent of those elected in 1994, and only 9.3 per cent in 1996.[121]

While the Ciampi government moved on its reformist path, the inquiries of 'Tangentopoli' rolled relentlessly onwards. Twenty months after the arrest of Mario Chiesa, over 1,000 persons were under investigation, orders for preventive detention had been issued for more than 500 suspects, and there were more than 200 committals to trial. The investigations had touched every part of Italy's political, administrative, professional, and economic élites. Nearly 200 members of parliament were involved, many members of central and local administration, and many managers and businessmen in large and small companies.[122] One of the most startling cases concerned Duilio Poggiolini, director from 1973 onwards of the pharmaceutical Department of the Ministry of Health. The inquiring magistrates uncovered an extensive network of corruption organized from within the Ministry. Poggiolini and his wife had accumulated a fortune of many billion lire, part of which was hidden in their flat in Rome inside a lilac-coloured footstool.[123]

Senior management from FIAT was under investigation, as was Carlo De Benedetti, managing director of Olivetti. However, the greatest scandal of the summer of 1993 was that concerning the Ferruzzi group and its former managing director Raul Gardini. The Enimont affair, the fusion between Ferruzzi's Montedison and the state-owned ENI in order to form a single giant petrochemical firm, was the single largest case of corporate corruption unearthed by the pool of Milan. It led in July 1993 to the suicides of both Raul Gardini at his home and of Gabriele Cagliari, former president of ENI, in the prison of San Vittore in Milan. It also led to the spectacular televised trial of Sergio Cusani, in which leading politicians were cross-examined by Antonio Di Pietro concerning their role in the affair.[124]

Both magistrates and politicians, as well as much of public opinion, called for a solution to 'Tangentopoli', but there was no agreement over its possible content. The magistrates demanded that trials be held swiftly and clear laws be introduced to prevent future corruption. The politicians, naturally enough, were more concerned with clemency. The Ciampi government was not able to resolve this rebus, and the question of justice remained a very strong element of tension in Italian politics. The balance of powers between legislature, executive and judiciary had been severely disturbed, and no one seemed capable of creating a new equilibrium.

To complete the picture of high uncertainty and tension, mention must be made of the Mafia bombs which exploded in the summer of 1993 in some of Italy's major cities, as attempted reprisals for the state's new-found activism. On 14 May the television journalist Maurizio Costanzo, who had given ample coverage to anti-Mafia initiatives, narrowly escaped being blown up. Twelve days later a bomb exploded at night close to the Uffizi Gallery in Florence, causing five deaths and some fifty people injured. Two months later, during the night of 27–8 July, it was the turn of Milan and Rome. In the first five people were killed, and in the second the church of San Giovanni in Laterano was damaged. The Mafia was trying to send a clear message to the political authorities: if the latter did not change track, not only persons but also some of Italy's most famous monuments would be at risk.

The period of the Ciampi government also witnessed the disappearance of the two principal parties of government, the Christian Democrats and the Socialists, as well as their minor allies the Liberals, Social Democrats and Republicans. The DC had tried desperately to survive in the glacial atmosphere of 1992–3. Arnaldo Forlani had handed over the post of secretary to Mino Martinazzoli, hoping that the latter's integrity would come to the rescue of the party as Zaccagnini's had done in the 1970s. It was too late. After a few months Martinazzoli announced that the DC would abandon its name, as the PCI had done before it, and would revert to that of the first Italian mass Catholic party, Don Sturzo's Popolari.

The DC had been the principal party of Italian democracy, and it is as well to remember that fact at a time when its reputation has reached such a low ebb. The party's fidelity to representative democracy guaranteed free elections and a plural society for Italy in the post-war years. For all their integralism, the leaders of the DC in the 1940s and early 1950s did not repress the principal opposition, that of the Communists, even if pliant magistrates, adopting Fascist laws, harassed it quite severely. Sometimes the Christian Democrats were ahead of the Pope of the time in their thinking on the connection between Catholicism and democracy; sometimes they were behind him. Never, though, did they waver in their formal commitment to democracy. Not by chance did they put the word *Libertas* at the centre of their political vocabulary and on the crusaders' shield which was the electoral symbol of their party.

It was also the case that certain of their initial choices, especially that of making Italy a founder member of the European Community, were in the long term of inestimable benefit to their country. Within their own ranks, they neither believed in, nor would tolerate, the sort of personal tyranny or over-lordship which were to characterize the political forces which took their place. For all the Byzantine workings of Christian Democrat factionalism, its net result was to prevent the supremacy of a single individual, as both Amintore Fanfani and Ciriaco De Mita discovered to their cost.

However, there was a dark side to the DC which should on no account be underestimated. It consisted basically in a clientelistic mediation of the affairs of the state, a *modus operandi* which recognized no clear laws or limits, no boundaries to possible alliances forged in the name of power, money or votes, and which gradually undermined the real content of the party's commitment to democracy. Obviously, different factions and personalities, as we have seen, interpreted this *modus operandi* in different ways, and chose to draw lines of limitation in different places. Some, though, drew no lines at all, and ended deep within the secret history of the Republic.

In historical terms, the origins of these tendencies go back a long way, and should not be facilely ascribed exclusively to the 1980s. Perhaps the key moment came early on, at the end of the 1940s, with the dispersion of Dossetti's group and the distortion of its heritage. Certainly, from that time onwards there was no major organized group which proposed a clear alternative to what became standard practice within the Christian democrat state system, at both national and local level. There existed, therefore, a fundamental though often hidden contradiction in the party's praxis, between its commitment to democracy in a European context, which led in one direction, and its habitual practice, which led in another. In the very particular circumstances of 1992–3, that contradiction exploded.[125]

As for the Socialists, they did not change their name, but simply disintegrated, itself an indication of how much they had come to rely on Craxi, and into what waters he had led them. The history of the Socialist party was a much longer one than that of the DC, and the nature and aspirations of the party had changed much more dramatically over time. Its first embodiment in the history of the Republic had been as a Marxist party locked into an iron alliance with the Communists. The era of the centre-left had changed that image rapidly, as well as sowing the seeds of later degeneration. Yet the leadership of Bettino Craxi, initially welcomed by many for its vigour, youth and modernism, transformed the party beyond recognition, sucking nearly all and sundry into a vortex of corrupt and authoritarian relations. It was to be a tragedy for Italian democracy that the final expression of its ancient and glorious Socialist party should take the form and content that it did, and that so many intelligent and highly educated people within that party accepted and even welcomed this state of affairs.

c. THE LEFT FALTERS

With the demise of the principal governing parties of the Republic, and the widespread movement of public opinion which had gathered behind the magistrates, it would have been reasonable to expect the major party of opposition, the PDS, to have become the principal beneficiary of the crisis. Yet this was not to be the case.

After a very problematic start,[126] Achille Occhetto had done well to hold together the rump of the old PCI in the period 1991–3. The left-wing strongholds in the central regions of the country, which had contributed the great majority of the old Communist vote, by and large remained faithful to the new party in the 1990s.[127] However, his party never managed to expand uniformly in the rest of the country, above all in the North, and thus stake a claim to a leadership position during the crisis. The reasons for this failure are many, but it is perhaps worth isolating three in particular.

The first was that the PDS itself felt menaced by the judicial offensive. From the first weeks of 'Tangentopoli', it became clear that elements of the party had in the past been involved in the malpractices of the system. Occhetto went back to the Bolognina section of the party[128] to make a speech asking the pardon of the nation for the shortcomings of his former party. However, his gesture was not accompanied by any clear indications that the PDS really intended to come clean, or that it was prepared to reveal the skeletons in the Communist cupboard. The party seemed rather to have chosen a defensive strategy – waiting for the magistrates to find out what they could, and hoping that this did not amount to much.[129] Such a strategy may have had short-term advantages, but it failed to establish the real differences between the PDS and its opponents, and the fundamental honesty of the vast majority of its militants. At the crucial moment of the national elections of March 1994, the PDS appeared as a result to be a more compromised element of the old system than it actually was.

Second, the PDS failed almost completely to launch initiatives that would have taken the crisis away from the courts and the television screens and into everyday life. In this respect, there re-emerged an old failing of the PCI: a certain immobility and lack of imagination with respect to modern social movements and civil society. To have challenged the many closed and often corrupt corporations of society, a revolt, pacific but determined, was necessary. Strangely enough, such revolt was alien to the political culture of the PCI/PDS. Instead, after decades of entrenched opposition, caution and mediation were their hallmarks. Faced with the choice between Gramsci's political categories of the war of position and the war of manoeuvre (metaphors culled from the type of warfare waged on the western and eastern fronts during the period 1914–18),[130] there was no doubt that his heirs preferred the first. Indeed, they were culturally and temperamentally quite unprepared for the second. Yet this was probably exactly what was needed in a situation as fluid as that of 1992–3.

Finally, the left as a whole was unable to read correctly the trajectory of the crisis. This was a task of extraordinary difficulty, requiring a special political talent. With the advantage of hindsight, it is possible to suggest that the moment of maximum disorientation of the old political forces was in the spring of 1993, and that that was the time to press for a greater leadership role. Instead, as we have just seen, the PDS no sooner entered government than it exited from it. There could have been no clearer sign of its political uncertainty.

The shortcomings of the left lead naturally into what must be considered one of the central questions in the analysis of these years: why was it that the crisis, having reached a high level of intensity and of rejection of the political culture of the past, slackened, and then took a turn in a quite different direction?

Some commentators, in the light of later delusions, have chosen to answer such a question by diminishing the overall importance of the events after 1992. Marco Revelli, for instance, with his habitual incisiveness and radicalism, has written of 'the "mediocre" historical character of the crisis, perfectly in synchrony with the mediocrity of the political class that was shipwrecked by it, and with that which tried to take its place'.[131] Yet such an interpretation risks doing little justice to the first year of the crisis, deeply disturbing as it was to so many levels of Italian public life.

The reasons why the crisis did not deepen or lead to greater cultural and political transformation are, like those concerning the failure of the left, many and complex. Indeed, the two are intimately interconnected. Here I would like to offer a few preliminary suggestions by way of a conclusion to this chapter.

Unlike in 1968–9, events in Italy in 1992–3 formed no part of a wider international or European movement. Their principal protagonists were investigating magistrates, who by the very nature of their profession were punitive, but not propositive. Within their ranks they could make alliances;

both Borrelli in Milan and Caselli in Palermo continually emphasized how intimate was the link between the struggle against the Mafia and that against corruption in public life. However, even within the narrow ranks of the magistracy those involved in the investigations of 'Tangentopoli' were in a minority. There were many others who were hostile, suspicious, or with guilty consciences. Much of the history from 1994 onwards consisted of an unedifying and often incomprehensible battle between different parts of the judiciary or even single magistrates.

In order for the battle in Milan, as well as that in Palermo, to reach a successful conclusion, the reforming magistrates had to find other allies, both within the state and outside of it. They enjoyed the constant support in this period of the President of the Republic, but too many of the other institutions and personnel of the Italian state felt threatened rather than liberated by their actions. In any case, a minority of magistrates could not act as a surrogate for political leadership. That, as we have seen, was largely lacking. The PDS supported the legal offensive more than any other party did, but at the same time it was afraid of it. Furthermore, the party leadership lacked the capacity to connect the different spheres of the crisis. Cassese's attempted reform, for instance, of great historical significance for an economy dominated by services, and for the relationship between citizen and state, badly needed political support, much publicity and the mobilization of consumers. None of these was forthcoming.

However, it is always too easy to blame political leaderships, to let explanatory weight fall casually upon the shoulders of single political actors. There were deeper structural problems at work, which concerned the nature of Italian public opinion, and the limited extent of civil society. The magistrates of Milan requested a general return to legality, but this was no mean demand in the Italy of the 1990s. Interpreted literally, it would have meant many ordinary Italian families having to ask uncomfortable questions about their own behaviour, about how the dominant political culture of clientelism, nepotism, tax evasion, and so on, was *their own*. It was one thing to sit round the television and rejoice in the humiliation of Arnaldo Forlani at the hands of Antonio Di Pietro during the Cusani trial.[132] It was quite another to apply the same standards of judgement to the microprocesses which connected families to society and the state. In this respect Revelli was right when he wrote of the 'mixture of exasperation and passivity' which characterized the crisis.[133]

Chapter 9

From Berlusconi to Berlusconi, 1994–2001

_H_OWEVER UNCERTAIN the course of the crisis that had opened in 1992, there could be little doubt about its potential significance in the history of the Italian Republic. At almost every level of Italy's institutions, policy-making and political culture, questions had been asked which, if answered in a determined fashion, promised to alter significantly the nature of Italian public life. The agenda opened in 1992 was a long one: among the many items listed on it were Italy's future relationship to Europe, its party political structure, the role of the judiciary, the fight against corruption, the relationship between politicians and criminal organizations, the reform of the public administration; last but not least the balance of power between central, regional and local government. If convincing answers could be found to these problems, a new era in Italian democracy would open up. If not, there was a real risk of involution and reaction. Carlo Cattaneo, the great nineteenth-century scholar, political analyst and, briefly, revolutionary, had once written that the history of Italy was characterized by short revolutions followed by long periods of reaction. Was the period between 1994 and the new millennium going to break this mould, or confirm a long-standing tradition of brief, intense periods of aspiration and hope, followed by accommodation, and eventually by delusion?

1. Political Newcomers

The shortcomings of the left, in many ways the natural leaders, if not the initiators, of the political process that had begun in 1992, have been analysed in the previous chapter. However, they were far from the only political actors who were coming to the forefront by the middle of the decade. The old ruling parties had disappeared, and the fight was now on to take their place. It was of particular significance that Catholics, for the first time since the war, no longer felt obliged to vote for a single party. The fall of Communism had removed the necessity of sheltering behind the shield of the DC, and then the crisis of 1992–3 had removed the shield itself.[1]

Of the principal contestants for political power in these months there were three who clearly identified themselves with the Catholic tradition: the new/old Popolari, or 'People's party'; Mario Segni, who had led the referendum campaigns and abandoned the DC at the end of March 1993; and La Rete ('The Network') of Leoluca Orlando, the reforming DC mayor of Palermo. All three proved incapable of filling the great gap presented by the demise of the DC.

The Popolari were too much of the same old thing, and quarrelled incessantly among themselves, eventually fracturing into various groups, and even for a time dividing the historic site of Christian Democrat power, their palace in Piazza di Gesù, into different floors for different factions.[2] Mario Segni, without any doubt, was the most obvious candidate for success, for he had built himself an enviable reputation as an honest politician who had dared to take on the old parties. Segni, however, revealed far less political skill than anyone had imagined. He was basically a moderate, but one who seemed unable to build alliances either to his left or to his right. While he dithered, others, as we shall see, moved. Finally there was La Rete, which without doubt had the most uphill task because unlike the other two it was a radical force, with an uncompromising moral position. Yet subjective errors, especially of the charismatic but primadonna-ish Orlando, never permitted the movement really to break out of its Sicilian strongholds.[3] Even there La Rete lacked a strong material element in its programme to complement the ethical one, and reach out to a wider popular base.

Apart from the Catholics, there were other parties or groups ready to vie for the vast mass of moderate and ex-DC votes. In the summer and autumn of 1993 it appeared that the most likely candidate, apart from Mario Segni, to fill the void left by the governing parties was the Northern League. At least in the North of the country, the League appeared unstoppable at that time, with opinion polls according it around 30 per cent of the vote in all the North's major cities. In June, in the local elections for Milan, held for the first time under the new system, the League's candidate Mario Formentini was able to defeat with ease a vast and variegated front consisting of parts of the educated middle classes, Catholic volunteers, and traditional left-wing forces which had gathered around Nando dalla Chiesa, the local leader of La Rete.[4]

The fact that one of the three great capitals of the crisis was now governed by a mayor from the League was of considerable symbolic significance.

During the first year of the crisis the Northern League had behaved as a clearly subversive and secessionist force. In the aftermath of the lira crisis, a very delicate moment as we have seen, Umberto Bossi had openly invited the public not to buy state bonds, but rather to invest their money abroad. Many intellectuals began to ask themselves whether Italian national identity was strong enough to resist the centrifugal forces that the League had unleashed.[5]

When the prime minister, Giuliano Amato, imposed his new taxation on house ownership, Bossi responded by calling for a mass tax strike. However, his voters refused to follow him. Gian Franco Miglio, the League's leading intellectual at this time, has described vividly their reaction: 'We suffered a complete defeat: only an irrelevant minority followed our line . . . They told us instead, in pure Milanese dialect: "If I don't pay the tax, they'll take my house away." I can still see the long lines of Lombard taxpayers, queuing patiently under the sun in order to get the certificates with which they could go and pay the new tax. A deep-rooted fear of the vigilant taxman prevailed over any pride in civic liberty.'[6] The fears for Italy's unity thus proved devoid of substance, both in 1992 and later in the decade. In spite of all of Bossi's rhetoric, the great majority of the League's supporters were always to be reluctant to follow their leadership into illegality.

In 1993 Bossi changed tack, as he was to do frequently in these years. He presented his movement no longer as secessionist, but as a potentially national force, which would revive Italian democracy by guiding Italy out of the crisis, away from Roman government and towards a new federalist future. On this last point, regional autonomy and centre-periphery relations, the contribution of the League to opening a new discussion in the 1990s was certainly a considerable one.

In other areas, though, it was arduous indeed to present the League as a force for the renewal of Italian democracy. Bossi's own dictatorship of his party was rather similar to that of Bettino Craxi in the PSI.[7] There were also few signs that the League ever had any intention of breaking with the clientelist, nepotist and party-dominated ethos of the old regime. Quite the opposite seems to be true. Here one example will have to suffice. On 23 April 1994, *Corriere della Sera* reported that Marco Vitale, one of the leading non-League members of Formentini's local government team in Milan, in charge of the public domain, had written to his colleagues in the following terms: 'I beg each and everyone of you, whatever post you hold in the municipal government, to cease to put pressure on my department to have access to offices, private dwellings, garages, etc., for your own use or that of your relatives, in-laws, babysitters, friends or other organizations or persons to whom you are attached by ties of affection.'[8]

Quite apart from its overt racism, which was not exactly an encouraging credential for democracy, the League's own financial honesty was to be called severely into doubt. In January 1993 the party's Treasurer, Alessandro Patelli, was arrested for having accepted 200 million lire in circumstances linked to the Enimont scandal, and in October 1995 both he and Umberto Bossi were condemned by a Milanese court for the illegal financing of their party. Bossi said that to be found guilty by a court of the Italian republic was to be considered an honour, and the League's early enthusiasm for the activities of the Milanese magistrates cooled considerably.

A much more unlikely candidate for political power also made startling progress in these months. The MSI (Movimento Sociale Italiano), with its explicit nostalgia for Fascism, had always been on the margins of the Republic, almost a 'community of destiny', a party with traditional roots in both Rome and Naples, which competed in democratic elections but which *de facto* was considered outside the 'constitutional arc'.[9] In the turbulent post-'68 atmosphere of the 1972 elections it had gained 8.7 per cent of the vote, its high point in the post-war period, but had usually hovered around 6 per cent. Under the guidance of its historic leader, Giorgio Almirante, the MSI had tried, without great success, to integrate itself into the Italian political system, to build wider alliances without reneging on its Fascist past, which it acknowledged quite openly in its leaders' speeches and in the way in which its party sections were decorated.[10] As late as 17 October 1992 the party celebrated the seventieth anniversary of the March on Rome with a well-attended demonstration in Piazza Venezia in Rome, complete with Fascist hymns and Roman salutes.[11]

In the early 1990s the party was riven by internecine strife, in a re-elaboration of what had been a constant element of tension in its history. On the one side was its radical wing, led by Pino Rauti, who stressed the 'revolutionary' role of the party, its anti-Americanism and anti-capitalism, as well as the need to appeal to ex-Communist voters; on the other the young Gianfranco Fini, Almirante's protégé, who, while far from critical of the Fascist past, fully espoused the more moderate line which stressed the need to work within the democratic system. First Fini had been secretary, then Rauti, then Fini again. It was with some relief that the party's leaders greeted the results of the 1992 national elections, which showed that they had polled 5.4 per cent, losing only 0.5 per cent compared to 1987.

From this rather dismal recent history, nothing indicated that the party was destined to play a crucial role in the politics of the 1990s. On the contrary; the electoral changes, pointing as they did away from proportional representation, seemed a fatal menace to small parties like the MSI. And yet so great was the void opened up by the events of 1992–3, so anxious were ex-DC voters (but not only they) to find new political interlocutors, that the MSI not only survived but prospered. The really significant breakthrough came with the municipal elections in Rome in the autumn of 1993. Fini decided to stake his reputation by standing as mayor, and did extraordinarily well. He did not win, as Formentini had done in Milan some months earlier, but at the second ballot he gained 46.9 per cent of the vote, against the 53.1 per cent of the left's candidate, Francesco Rutelli. An excellent off-the-cuff speaker, Fini made the most of his television appearances, where he came across as intelligent, suave and reassuring. He was much aided by what seemed at the time to be a surprising endorsement from Silvio Berlusconi. As the *Financial Times* journalist Christian Tyler commented pithily, some time later: 'Fini sounds good. He looks good. Is he too good to be true?'[12] A great many Romans obviously thought not. The MSI became the largest single party in Italy's capital, and Fini tightened what was to become an iron grip upon his own party. In January 1994 he hastily held another party conference, at which he announced the formation (as Almirante had done often in the past, though without success) of an umbrella group of the right, Alleanza Nazionale (the National Alliance), under whose auspices the MSI would fight the next elections. The party's militants were not yet ready to abandon the old name, but Fini pushed hard to present himself and his organization as a new mass, right-wing democratic force in Italian politics.

2. 1994: The Year of Silvio Berlusconi

a. 'I'LL BE ON THE PITCH'

The last, and eventually largest, force to fill the void left by the old ruling parties did not even exist as a political party at the end of 1993. Silvio Berlusconi had watched the unfolding of the crisis with growing alarm. His political patron and close friend, Bettino Craxi, had been disgraced by the turn of events, and much of the Milanese business world which he knew well was being prosecuted in the trials of 'Tangentopoli'. His own business had only been marginally involved in the investigations, but it was not in the best of economic health. Fininvest's debts had grown dramatically, and in the autumn of 1993, under pressure from the banks which were the firm's principal creditors, Berlusconi appointed a new managing director, Franco Tatò.[13] The political situation grew worse by the day. The Ciampi government was actively considering a revision of the Mammì law in order to curb Berlusconi's near-monopoly of commercial television. At the beginning of December 1993, the left alliance of *'progressisti'* ('progressives') had emerged victorious in some of Italy's major cities. The new mayor of Rome, as we have seen, was Francesco Rutelli; that of Venice Massimo Cacciari; that of Naples the PDS leader Antonio Bassolino, who had defeated the MSI's candidate, Alessandra Mussolini, granddaughter of the Duce; and most remarkable of all, that of Palermo was Leoluca Orlando, who won by a landslide. Never had the left, for all its hesitations, seemed so close to power.

Silvio Berlusconi responded to this situation with the most extraordinary political 'war of movement' in the history of the Republic. For some time he had been thinking of founding a political force of his own. On 10 July 1993 there had been a secret meeting of his closest advisers at his villa at Arcore to discuss the issue; two of them Gianni Letta and Fedele Confalonieri, were against any political adventures; Marcello Dell'Utri, the managing director of Publitalia, was in favour.[14] Berlusconi, with characteristic *élan*, chose to go ahead. In order to choose the name and the image of the new organization he employed all the considerable marketing, advertising and polling techniques of Fininvest. Never in Italy had the creation of a political force been studied so minutely and scientifically, and never before had it assumed the form of a party so closely linked to a single business enterprise.[15] On 5 November the National Association of 'Forza Italia' came into being, and supporter clubs began to spring up throughout the country. However, it was only after 15 January 1994, when the President of the Republic announced new national elections for the end of March, that Berlusconi took the final plunge. On 26 January, with a gesture of considerable symbolic importance, he sent a videocassette of nine minutes and twenty-four seconds, recorded at his villa at Arcore, to Reuters, RAI and his own television channels. In it he announced:

Italy is the country I love. Here I have my roots, my hopes, my horizons. Here I have learned, from my father and from life, how to be an entrepreneur. Here I have acquired my passion for liberty . . . Never as in this moment does Italy . . . need people of a certain experience, with their heads firmly on their shoulders, able to give the country a helping hand and to make the state function . . . If the political system is to work, it is essential that there emerges a 'pole of liberty' in opposition to the left-wing cartel, a pole which is capable of attracting to it the best of an Italy which is honest, reasonable, modern. Around this pole there must gather all those forces which make reference to the fundamental principles of western democracies; in the first place the Catholic world which has contributed generously to the last fifty years of our history as a united nation . . . I tell you that we can, I tell you that we must, create for ourselves and for our children a new Italian miracle.[16]

In the critical days after 26 January 1994 Berlusconi succeeded in putting together a coalition impossible to imagine without his initiative and driving force. In the North he created 'Il Polo della libertà' ('The Pole of Liberty') in alliance with the Northern League. In the Centre and the South, where the League was not standing, he founded 'Il Polo del buon governo'

('The Pole of Good Government') together with Gianfranco Fini's National Alliance. Fini and Bossi detested each other and their parties diverged radically: the one was nationalist, with a Fascist past, convinced of the need for a strong centralized and interventionist state, with its support deriving mainly from Rome and the South; the other neolocalist and separatist, racist but not Fascist, anxious for the industrious North to be left in peace by Rome, wedded to the free market but not to the state. Such an alliance did not augur well for the future, but it served its temporary purpose magnificently. Berlusconi had understood perfectly the impelling necessities of the historical moment (and of the new electoral system), and had responded accordingly. Rarely had individual agency played so major a role in determining the course of the crisis.

Berlusconi led his own organization, Forza Italia, with a media man's eye for what was attractive, necessary and acceptable. The name itself, which was the traditional chant of the national football team's supporters, was knowingly chosen and ruthlessly exploited. The 'deep play',[17] with all its excitement, ambivalence, and commercial exploitation, had found its perfect political interpreter, an entrepreneur who also happened to be the owner of Italy's most successful team, AC Milan. Football metaphors abounded in Berlusconi's speeches, as he tried to represent politics in terms of a football match, naturally with his side winning: 'I heard that the game was getting dangerous, and that it was all being played in the two penalty areas, with the midfield being left desolately empty . . . And so we decided that we had to fill that immense space.'[18] All his language was simple and direct, the opposite of the complicated Roman political rhetoric. He had learned a lot from Umberto Bossi, but avoided the latter's vulgarity. 'Moderation' and 'balance', as Patrick McCarthy has noted, were terms that occurred again and again in these weeks.[19]

In terms of content rather than form, though the two were inextricably mixed in his case, Berlusconi advocated a basically neo-liberal economic programme, with strong Thatcherist overtones: fewer taxes, greater choices for citizens, competition and efficiency in public life, a residual welfare state.[20] The primacy of the family as *the* centre of solidarity and entrepreneurship in Italian life was strongly reasserted by Forza Italia: 'It is within families that the greatest expressions of solidarity are to be found, both quantitatively and above all qualitatively. This role of the family constitutes a precious capital with which Italy is endowed, much more so than in most other countries. We need at all costs to prevent this "natural society" being weakened drastically by assistance policies.'[21]

A particular object of attack were the magistrates in the forefront of the 'Tangentopoli' inquiry. For Berlusconi, they were 'red-robed' inquisitors: apart from their obvious political motivation (they had investigated only the right, not the left), and disrespect for citizens' rights (they had imprisoned people unwarrantedly and driven them to suicide), magistrates like Borrelli had other responsibilities, which were to weigh heavily in electoral terms: they had blocked public works' contracts at a time of recession, and their investigations had badly damaged many businesses. It was time to bring them firmly back under control.[22]

b. THE NATIONAL ELECTIONS OF MARCH 1994

The election campaign that was fought between January and March of 1994 was rather a one-sided affair. It certainly did not look that way at the time. At the beginning of the campaign the left was confident of victory, and had not yet realized that the right-wing coalition which Berlusconi had invented from out of thin air was potentially much stronger than its own. The Popolari of Martinazzoli and Mario Segni's own 'Patto per Segni' ('A Pact for Segni'), which together constituted the rump of the Catholic vote, refused to enter the 'progressive' coalition, and fought the elections by themselves. This was a fatal decision when, for the first time, 75 per cent of the seats in the Chamber of Deputies were to be determined by the first-past-the-post system. Furthermore, the natural head of the 'progressive' coalition, Carlo Azeglio Ciampi, had declined the role. The leader of the PDS, Achille Occhetto, assumed it instead, and incautiously presented the progressive leadership (eight middle-aged men, with a fair sprinkling of recycled Socialists) as 'a joyous war machine'. In reality, the coalition was too narrowly based to win what had become a substantially bi-polar electoral competition.

The real joy was on the other side. Berlusconi, as Adrian Lyttelton has written, 'ran an American-style campaign without any of the American checks and balances'.[23] The media and the other resources available to him made for a very imbalanced competition. In vain the progressives pointed to Berlusconi's past career in the shadow of Craxi, or his present failure to separate clearly business and political interests. Berlusconi replied with the promise to create 1 million new jobs. He advocated liberty *from* the state, *from* the Communists (real and imaginary), *from* excessive taxation. When in the previous November the French semiologist and marketing expert Jean-Marie Floch had been consulted by Angelo Codignoni of Fininvest on the necessary slogans for a centre-right victory, he had suggested 'sense of duty' ('We must drink the bitter chalice') and 'know-how' ('I have the necessary competence').[24] Berlusconi chose to concentrate on the second, to great effect. His appeal to many Italians lay in the fact that he was an immensely successful businessman, the incarnation of many of the individual and family dreams that had their origins in the economic 'miracle', the antithesis of the career politician who was his opponent.

When the election results were made known on the evening of 29

March 1994, the extent of Berlusconi's remarkable victory became apparent. His twin poles (of 'Liberty' and 'Good Government'), combining as they did Forza Italia, Lega Nord and Alleanza Nazionale) had between them gained 42.9 per cent of the vote for the Chamber of Deputies, which translated into 58.1 per cent of the seats. The 'progressives' (PDS, Rifondazione Comunista, La Rete, the Greens, and other smaller groupings) had gained 34.4 per cent of the vote and 33.8 per cent of the seats; the Catholic centre (Popolari and Patto Segni) 15.7 per cent of the vote, but only 7.3 per cent of the seats. Their failure to ally with either one or the other major blocs had cost them dear. In the Senate the results had gone less well for the centre-right coalition. Under Italian electoral law only those over the age of twenty-five can vote for the Senate, with the result that the strong youth vote for Berlusconi's coalition counted for less in the Senate than in the Chamber of Deputies. In the upper house the centre-right coalition had fallen just short of an overall majority (49.2 per cent of the seats).

In terms of the percentage vote for individual parties in the Chamber of Deputies, there had been an even greater fragmentation than in previous elections, confirming the limited capacity of the electoral reform to transform the multi-party political culture of the country. No party polled over 25 per cent of the votes. Forza Italia had emerged as the largest single party with 21 per cent of the vote, much less than Berlusconi's own opinion polls had predicted. Close on its heels was the PDS, with 20.4 per cent, an improvement of more than 4 per cent over its result in 1992. Fini's Alleanza Nazionale did very well indeed, becoming Italy's third largest party, with 13.5 per cent of the vote (compared with the 5.4 per cent of the MSI in 1992). The Popolari had polled 11.1 per cent, which with Segni's 4.7 per cent, was all that was left of the Christian Democrat legacy. The Northern League had taken 8.4 per cent of the vote, slightly less than in 1992, but thanks to Bossi's hard bargaining over candidates, his organization emerged as the largest in the Chamber of Deputies, with 118 seats. Rifondazione Comunista had improved its vote slightly, from 5.6 per cent to 6.1 per cent, confirming the impression that it was not a splinter group destined to extinction, but had a small but distinct following in the country. The other 'progressive' groups had performed very disappointingly, with the Greens demonstrating yet again their incapacity to become a significant force in Italian politics.

In terms of electoral geography, the result was an extraordinary one. Forza Italia and the Northern League had between them swept the North of the country. Liguria was the only region in which they had not obtained an absolute majority of the votes, and almost no deputies of the centre-left were returned to parliament from constituencies north of the Po. By contrast, the left had not only held firm in the centre of the country, but had actually increased its votes there in comparison with 1992. In the South and the islands the picture was more mixed. Some southern regions, like Basilicata, had voted strongly for the 'progressives', perhaps identifying in them a greater potential for state aid and protection than was liable to come from the 'neo-liberals' of the North. Others, like Sicily, had voted heavily for the centre-right. Coming immediately after Orlando's victory in Palermo, this was the least explicable and most disquieting of the regional results. Some analysts suggested that the Mafia vote had abstained in the Palermo municipal elections for lack of any clear political point of reference. Forza Italia's incessant attacks upon the reforming magistrates (including those of Palermo) had given them new hope. It was not that Berlusconi had chosen the Mafia, but that it had chosen him.[25]

In terms of social and gender composition, the analysis of the vote was also extremely revealing. Berlusconi had appealed principally to house-wives, to youth, to the self-employed, whether small entrepreneurs, shop-keepers or artisans. He had hoped to appeal to the educated middle class as well, because he saw himself as the natural leader of the country's modern, service-oriented élite, but the critical and 'reflexive' middle classes had voted *en masse* for the 'progressives'.[26] The structural division between the two sections of Italy's urban middle classes, as well as that between the self-employed on the one hand, and dependent workers on the other, had found a very distinct, and potentially dangerous political polarization. Even if none of the parties was dependent upon a single social class or segment of the electorate, Italy after 1994 gave the strong impression of being divided into two distinct camps, which never managed to meet, or discuss, or find points of contact.

The new parliament was, in terms of its personnel, revolutionized with respect to its predecessor; some 69 per cent of the deputies and 60 per cent of the Senators were newcomers. The number of party functionaries present in parliament declined from 26 per cent to 4.6 per cent. The full-time employment of the candidates from the various parties showed marked differences: 31.7 per cent of the PDS's candidates were school and university teachers, and another 29.3 per cent were professional politicians. Forza Italia's candidates, on the other hand, were 27.3 per cent entrepreneurs and businessmen, and 28.2 per cent lawyers and doctors. Publitalia, Berlusconi's publicity agency, alone provided some fifty members of parliament.[27]

c. BERLUSCONI IN POWER

With Silvio Berlusconi's victory in the March 1994 elections, international attention once again centred upon the Italian crisis, as it had done in 1992, at the beginning of the 'Mani Pulite' inquiries. On both occasions it had been Milan, the northern capital of the crisis, that had given birth to the new. However, the reforming magistrates and the leader of Forza Italia had nothing in common, except perhaps their love of that city. Indeed, it could be suggested that they represented two diametrically opposite images of Milan: the one as the 'moral capital' of Italy, the other as the centre of a dynamic, modern, but not necessarily very scrupulous capitalism. The two were thus inherently counterposed, and indeed were to be locked in mortal combat for the next four years.

Interest in Italy was so intense because Berlusconi's whirlwind victory seemed to suggest a new model for the gaining and exercise of power in western democracies. Many commentators talked of a new age of videocracy; others of the way in which Berlusconi had set the political example on a global scale for other media barons, the most powerful and influential figures to have emerged from the modern service sector of the economy. Democratic politics, according to this point of view, was henceforth to be a televised show, carefully orchestrated from above, and conducted as one part of an overall global profit-making business.[28]

Such views, and fears, were undoubtedly exaggerated for they over-estimated the capacity for control in plural societies whose politics are regulated by free elections. None the less they contained a kernel of truth. Viewed in the context of Italian political culture, Berlusconi represented both the very old and the very new. The old could be seen in the patron–client relations that he established with all around him, in his generous bestowal of gifts, in his formidable loyalties to family and to clan. His stubborn refusal to separate effectively his private interests from his new public duties was not only self-interest, but also a genuine incapacity to distinguish clearly between the two spheres. The Milanese magistrates' rigid and severe idea of a public sphere where there were clear and codified rules, no grey areas and no personal favours, was an anathema to him. Berlusconi had risen to great wealth and power in the 1980s through his own formidable talents as an entrepreneur, but also by his being an integral and convinced part of a modern business and political network whose values were those of an old clientelistic culture.

However, the charismatic leader of Forza Italia was not just old wine remarketed in a sleek new bottle. His close collaborator, Fedele Confalonieri, who seemed to make a habit of being rather frank about his oldest friend, had said in January 1994: 'The truth is that Berlusconi is not a political animal. He's a utopian. In another time and place he could have been an enlightened monarch. But as a democratic politician, he's decidedly anomalous.'[29]

Berlusconi's behaviour as an enlightened monarch (if that is the right expression) did not just extend to his own political organization, which lacked any form of internal democracy, and whose internal dynamics depended upon unquestioning reverence for its leader. That in itself was nothing new in Italian politics; on the contrary, it seemed to be the norm for centre-right political parties in the 1990s.[30] Rather, his originality lay with a wider project, which had no intention of abolishing democracy, but certainly wanted to change its contents and balances. Berlusconi nurtured aspirations to becoming a strong and benevolent presidential figure in a reformed Italian political system. In order to achieve that end, he had to convey clear and constant messages through all the communication networks of modern Italian society, both those in and outside of his control; not just the mass media, though these were crucial, but in all areas of consumption and leisure – in the supermarkets, in the football stadiums, in culture and in fashion. This was a formidable project for hegemony.

Formal citizenship (at least civil and political, if not social) was to remain the same, but an insinuating battle, employing the most sophisticated of marketing methods, was to be waged to establish consent and conformity at its heart. The basic lines of such a battle corresponded very well to the dominant, if not to the only, trends in European society in the 1990s: neo-liberalism as its ideological warhorse, the freedom of the individual as the basic tenet for society, ever-increasing and publicity-driven family consumption as the crucial economic motor.

In the first months after his electoral victory, Berlusconi seemed to be taking rapid steps towards achieving his objectives. In the European elections held on 12 June 1994, Forza Italia gained 30.6 per cent of the vote. Together with his two allies, Alleanza Nazionale and the Northern League, Berlusconi had just under 50 per cent of the vote. In these same weeks a wide-ranging survey, principally dedicated to religious attitudes and values, also asked if 'Italy today needs a strong man': 73.5 per cent of the survey declared that they were 'quite in agreement' or 'very much in agreement'. Such an opinion was fairly evenly spread across different ages, but in terms of geographical area, the South and the islands were most in favour (mainland South, 78.5 per cent, Sicily and Sardinia, 81.8 per cent).[31]

After this exhilarating start (AC Milan also won the European Cup that year), the experience of government turned out, against all expectations, to be sour and short-lived. Since there is little scientific literature available, and the period is so recent, it is difficult to gain a perspective on Berlusconi's period of power. However, certain lines of interpretation can perhaps be briefly suggested, within the general context of the interpretation of the crisis which has been outlined above.

The first, and most obvious, is that the actions of the government were not characterized by that competence and dynamism which Berlusconi had isolated as the core of his appeal to the electors, but rather by considerable uncertainty. Later on, Berlusconi was to coin the slogan 'They didn't let us get on with the job', but in reality he was prisoner to that same coalition he had so brilliantly created a few months previously. Umberto Bossi, in particular, proved a difficult partner. Fini and Berlusconi got on well together, for the former was profoundly grateful to the latter for having espoused his cause at an early stage, and for having brought his party in from the cold. Bossi, though, owed nothing to anyone, a situation which a master of patronage like Berlusconi found difficult to handle. Furthermore, in the European elections of June the League's share of the vote had shrunk further, to 6.6 per cent. It looked as if Forza Italia would slowly eat up the League's electorate, because on the ground rather than at Montecitorio the two parties were not allies but rivals. In the first months of the government, little priority was given to the federalism which was so close to the League's heart.

Of equal, if not greater importance, was the government's uncertainty with regard to that element which must be considered the *contrôleur* of the country's history in the 1990s: the future of Italy in Europe. It has to be said straight away that this uncertainty was mutual, because there was widespread unease in European circles, above all concerning the presence of the MSI in the government. This unease was considerably increased when, in the immediate aftermath of the elections, Gianfranco Fini defined Mussolini as 'the greatest statesman of the century'.[32] His remark was reported world-wide, and did much to harm the nascent government. Under the influence of National Alliance, the government also opened a dispute with Slovenia and Croatia regarding borders and war reparations, which did much to irritate some other EU countries, especially Germany.

With regard to Europe, hard choices of political economy faced the new executive. Was it going to abide by the 'external constraint' and continue Ciampi's strategy of trying to move Italy slowly but surely towards meeting the criteria of the Treaty of Maastricht? And if it did, how could it simultaneously hope to create a million new jobs? The Berlusconi government was very divided on this key issue. Lamberto Dini, the minister of the Treasury, and one of the few technocrats in the government, was a convinced European. He, like Ciampi, was from the Bank of Italy, though the two men were more rivals than friends. On the other hand the Foreign Minister, Antonio Martino, Forza Italia's principal economist, was like Mrs Thatcher a member of the Bruges group, and as such entirely hostile to the idea of, let alone the timetable for, monetary union. Fini, too, was rather sceptical. The most that can be said about the government's forward march towards Europe was that it was rather faltering.[33]

Equally important for the government's political economy was the fate of the tripartite pact between unions, employers and government, which had first been introduced by Amato and then developed by Ciampi. Here the Berlusconi government was at its weakest. The trade unions immediately, and not without cause, identified the new Prime Minister as a potential adversary, and their suspicions were confirmed when Berlusconi announced a reduction of dependent workers' pensions at the same time as he made tax concessions to the self-employed. His budget, which raised some 50,000 billion lire from spending cuts and taxation, appeared to ask for disproportionate sacrifices from the different social parts of the country. The government's actions gave rise to a massive mobilization in defence of workers' rights, culminating on 12 November 1994 with the largest trade union demonstration in the history of the Republic, with more than a million people filling three separate piazzas in the heart of Rome. On 1 December 1994, with the lira falling heavily against the mark, Berlusconi backtracked on pension reform, signing an agreement with the trade unions which testified to the latter's victory.[34]

The same sort of initial self-confidence and aggression, followed by retreat, characterized the government's actions with regard to the balance of power between the major institutions of the state. The new ruling parties immediately inserted their placemen and women in the key positions of the RAI, the state broadcasting company. There was nothing very new about this, however dispiriting it proved.[35] More significantly, the government also launched an attack upon the autonomy of the Bank of Italy which, as we have seen, had been one of the most delicate and important checks upon arbitrary executive action. The attack did not initially succeed, but the Bank's future was distinctly uncertain by the time the government fell.[36]

It was in his relations with the judiciary, as was to be expected, that Berlusconi entered into the deepest water. On 13 July 1994 the Council of Ministers approved a decree law, which basically put an end to the 'Tangentopoli' investigations. The outcry, in spite of the fact that the decree had been issued at the height of the summer, when most people were on holiday, was again immense. The Milanese magistrates, led by Antonio Di Pietro, appeared on television to explain their total opposition to the new attempt to snuff out their inquiries. Berlusconi's allies hesitated in the face of popular protest, and dissent from within their own ranks as well; Roberto Maroni, the League's Minister of the Interior, let it be known that he would resign if the decree went through. Umberto Bossi, eager to recoup votes in the North which had been lost to Forza Italia, supported him. Fini carefully took his distance. On 19 July the government climbed down.

Behind these various débâcles, which demonstrated clearly the strength of opposition to Berlusconi's political project, there lay a rather greyer reality. Much of Berlusconi's practice of government seemed to express an accommodation, reluctant or not, to deeply sedimented structures both within the state and outside it. He had promised a swift programme of privatization, and the free play of wider market forces, but once in power he seemed content to mark time (the MSI's statalism played a part here), and to allow the great oligarchies of the North, centred around Mediobanca, to dominate and control what privatization there was.[37] And within the state his ministers discovered that the bureaucracy had its own slow and self-protective agenda. Pino Tatarella, the MSI vice-president of the Council of Ministers and minister of Post and Telecommunications, himself very much a traditional figure plucked from the serried ranks of southern clientelism, told the journalists Di Michele and Galiani: 'The real battle is with the bureaucracy. The number one enemy of Italian politics are the high-ranking bureaucrats, who have their own network of solidarity linking the various ministries, and who can pull the rug out from beneath any government.'[38] The complexities of state formation and the weight of history did not easily coincide with simplistic ideas of marching in to run the state as a business.

The end came suddenly. On 22 November 1994, while Berlusconi was presiding over a meeting of the G7 at Naples, he was handed a Notice of Guarantee, informing him that he was under investigation by Milanese magistrates concerning possible charges of corruption. The accusations formed part of a wider inquest into the systematic bribing of the Finance police in return for them turning a blind eye to false tax returns.[39] In the following months, other grave charges were to be levied against Berlusconi himself and members of his closest entourage, especially Marcello Dell'Utri, the head of Publitalia, and Cesare Previti, Berlusconi's principal legal adviser and minister of Defence in the Berlusconi government.

The prime minister rejected every charge, and accused the Milanese magistrates of political conspiracy against him. He declared that he would continue in office. Umberto Bossi, though, had had enough. Helped on his way by Massimo D'Alema, who had replaced Achille Occhetto as secretary of the PDS, and Rocco Buttiglione of the Popolari (who was later to repent of his actions and join the Berlusconi camp), Bossi withdrew the support of the League from the government. Deprived of a majority in either house of parliament, on 22 December 1994 Berlusconi handed in his resignation to the President of the Republic, Oscar Luigi Scalfaro.

3. Intermezzo

After the sudden and ignominious collapse of the Berlusconi government, there followed a year of intense uncertainty. The President of the Republic, instead of immediately calling fresh elections, as Berlusconi and Fini insisted he should do, decided in favour of another 'Presidential government'. It was certainly within his prerogative to so decide, but the centre-right accused him of political bias, of playing for time when the opinion polls appeared favourable to Berlusconi.[40] Scalfaro remained imperturbable, and chose Berlusconi's own former minister of the Treasury, Lamberto Dini, as President of the Council of Ministers. In parliament Dini's government received the support of the former opposition, as well as the Northern League. This was a very strange state of affairs and not one that could last. Dini governed well for a year, during which time he succeeded in passing, with the support of the trade unions, the pension reform that had stymied Berlusconi.

The breathing-space of the Dini government, another of those executives dominated by technical experts, gave both right and left the chance to gather and regroup their forces. By and large, this was an opportunity which the left took much better than did the right. The new secretary of the PDS, Massimo D'Alema, realized the imperative necessity under the new electoral system of including within the left-wing coalition at least part of the Catholic forces which had fought the 1994 elections as a separate bloc, and of designating as candidate for the premiership a leader from outside the ranks of the left itself. When the Catholic economist and former president of IRI, Romano Prodi, announced his intention of standing against Berlusconi, D'Alema immediately supported him, and the 'Olive Tree' ('L'Ulivo') coalition of centre-left forces came into being.[41]

On the other hand, the centre-right of Berlusconi and Fini did not manage to operate with any great efficacy as a pole of attraction. The CCD and CDU, both of which had split away from the Popolari, joined the centre-right coalition, and Fini took another move to break with his Fascist past at his party's congress of January 1995 by dissolving the MSI and assuming formally the name of Alleanza Nazionale.[42] A small, dissenting group under the former MSI secretary, Pino Rauti, did not adhere to the new party. However, the crucial groups and names on the right escaped Berlusconi's net. He had lost Bossi and the Northern League, he had lost probably the most able minister in his government, Lamberto Dini; above all, he lost the biggest name of all, Antonio Di Pietro. The hero of 'Tangentopoli' had resigned from the magistracy in unexplained circumstances, but clearly with a political career in mind. He was the most popular man in Italy at this time, and definitely not of the left. He was not an obvious candidate to join Berlusconi's coalition, because he had been one of the magistrates who had signed the famous Notice of Guarantee to him, and he was a firm believer that the trials of 'Tangentopoli' should be brought to a proper conclusion. However, a centre-right coalition needed him if it no longer enjoyed the support of the League, and if it hoped to repeat the success of 1994. Instead Di Pietro himself was brought under investigation by the Procura di Brescia in an obscure inquiry, which revealed some not altogether transparent transactions between Di Pietro and his friends, but no penal responsibility.[43] As a result, he took no part in the coming elections, but was later to join the 'Olive Tree' coalition.

The Brescian inquiry was only the first of a number in the period

1995–6 which signalled one of the most depressing developments in the Italian crisis – conflicts between different parts of the judiciary, often for reasons which were unclear and which as a result remained incomprehensible to the general public. A sinister atmosphere was created, where no public figure seemed to be what he said he was, and where the magistracy as a whole appeared as a fractious and politically divided element within the Republic. It was difficult to distinguish whether this was a spontaneous process or a carefully organized attempt to muddy the waters.

At the end of this unedifying 'intermezzo', national elections were called once again, for 21 April 1996. Their result bore testimony to that equilibrium of different forces, both social and political, which was one of the most salient characteristics of Italy in the 1990s. The 'Olive Tree' coalition won a narrow victory. It actually polled less votes than did the centre-right, but because of the electoral system emerged as the overall winner. Its majority in the Senate was a substantial one, whereas in the Chamber of Deputies it was dependent upon the unpredictable support of Rifondazione Comunista. Such a situation was the exact opposite to that which had prevailed for the Berlusconi government in 1994, and it reflected the fact that a majority of Italian youth continued to vote for the centre-right.

Probably the crucial element in the centre-left's victory lay outside of its own ranks. The Northern League not only fought the elections alone, this time on a secessionist platform, but did better than any commentator anticipated, gaining 10.1 per cent of the votes.[44] The strength of their support in certain provinces of Lombardy and Venetia was confirmed, and all over the North their candidates for the uninominal seats drained votes away from the centre-right, with the result that the 'Olive Tree' coalition won many of the seats that the progressives had lost in 1994.

As for the individual parties, the PDS emerged narrowly as the largest force, with 21.1 per cent of the vote, closely followed by Forza Italia with 20.6 per cent. Fini's Alleanza Nazionale, with 15.7 per cent, improved on 1994 and confirmed its position as the third force in Italian politics. Rifondazione Comunista had also done well, with 8.6 per cent of the vote. Both the modest vote for the Popolari (6.8 per cent) and that for the CCD–CDU (5.8 per cent) provided further evidence that the majority of Catholic voters no longer felt obliged to vote for a political party whose primary definition was in terms of religion. The list of the outgoing prime minister, Lamberto Dini, secured an important 4.3 per cent of the vote for the centre-left.

The overall victors were undoubtedly Romano Prodi, at the head of the 'Olive Tree' coalition, and Massimo D'Alema, its principal architect. To them now belonged the task of replying to the questions which had been so dramatically posed in 1992–3.

4. The Centre-Left Governments, 1996–2001

The coalition which came to power in the spring of 1996 was rather different from the traditional centre-left governments which had dominated politics during the thirty-year period from 1962 to 1992. Gone was the hegemonic Catholic party; gone too were its Socialist allies, who had once talked the noble language of structural reform, but who had been destroyed by their acquiescence to Bettino Craxi's unsavoury vision of modern politics. In their place came the rump of the former Communist party, which now celebrated a return to government, though with a different name and in very different circumstances, for the first time since Togliatti had served in the anti-Fascist coalitions of 1944–7. Alongside the ex-Communists, though in constant competition with them, stood a whole constellation of minor parties: the Catholics of the Popolari (themselves the rump of a former great party), the Greens, the supporters of Lamberto Dini, a residual band of Socialists, and so on. The 'Olive Tree' coalition was thus highly fragmented and heterogeneous, and these characteristics were to weigh heavily upon its capacity to govern.

The Italian centre-left came to power at a time when the pendulum of politics in the major democracies of the western world had finally swung away from Republican and Conservative neo-liberalism. The victories of Clinton in the United States, Blair in Britain, Jospin in France, and finally Schroeder in Germany meant that the new Italian government found a congenial and sympathetic international environment in which to work. It has to be said, though, that the recipes for government of the 'progressives' on an international level were heavily influenced by those of their predecessors. Reagan and Thatcher had long since gone, but the force of the neo-liberal paradigm lived on in the minds and programmes of their opponents. The values of the market and of the individual continued to reign supreme: deregulation and privatization, not only of industries and banks, but also of social services, went on apace, often well beyond the limits of previous conservative regimes. The public sphere became increasingly visual and increasingly passive, dominated by commercial television, to which public broadcasting was ever more subordinate. So great was the force of this model, and so widespread the fear of losing the middle ground of the electorate, that little progress was made in the elaboration of convincing alternatives.[45]

Each of the major democracies evolved its own version of 'progressive' politics, dependent upon the traditions and political culture of the country in question.[46] The Italian case, which I examine in detail in the pages below, was a somewhat hesitant and unsatisfactory version, not lacking in individual initiatives for reform, but short of an overall vision. As Giuliano Amato, who was to be the last of the three prime ministers of this period, commented in March 2001: 'If we've suffered from a defect in these years, it has been our inability to link satisfactorily the single chapters of our reform programme to a general design, capable of involving the public, and of giving the perception of leading the country towards a better society of the future.'[47] The old Italian Communist and Socialist idea of structural reform, the laying down of stepping-stones to a socialist society, had long since been abandoned, but nothing very distinctive had taken its place.

Why was this? The fragmentation of the Italian coalition, Amato's own explanation for relative failure, certainly played a strong role. So too did the weakness of the centre-left in parliament. Unlike the Blair government in Britain, based on a single party and blessed with an overwhelming majority in the House of Commons, the 'Olive Tree' coalition had no clear majority in the House of Deputies and was dependent upon the changeable humours of Rifondazione Comunista.

These were severe limitations, but they were exacerbated by the uncertainties and theoretical weakness of the major party of the left, the PDS. As ex-Communists, the PDS leaders had serious problems both of legitimation and identity. They were anxious to show that they were responsible and moderate in government, and this made them more cautious than their French or British socialist counterparts. They were also keen to demonstrate, especially in the face of Berlusconi's constant anti-Communist tirades, that they had turned their backs decisively on the past. As a result, they abandoned the theoretical elaborations of the old PCI (the Gramscian legacy, for instance, was quietly set aside), but remained lackadaisical and vague about what to put in their place. D'Alema wrote of the need for 'a liberal revolution' and of making Italy a 'normal' country, but these were hardly the slogans necessary to give coherence and character to the centre-left's reformist programme.[48] The hegemonic ideas belonged very firmly to that group of 'technicians' and intellectuals, often originating from the Bank of Italy, who had fought to keep Italy attached to Europe. Theirs was a benign and necessary influence, but their intellectual weight was never complemented and contrasted by a similar corpus of left-wing thought. *Rinascita*, the organ of debate in the old PCI, ceased publication, as did the daily *l'Unità* for a time. Conferences substituted for hard debate. No think tank emerged on the left to undertake research and argue for reform as part of a larger strategy.[49]

Centre-left reform thus emerged as a rather *ad hoc* affair, often the result of the initiative of individual ministers, who then had to mediate and compromise constantly with other elements inside the government and the coalition. The net result was a hotchpotch. Considerable progress was made in some fields, and in some localities, but the centre-left never managed to convince the country that it knew where it wanted to go, nor to arouse enthusiasm for its policies.

a. EUROPE (AND PADANIA)

There was one major exception to what has just been said above. In the first two years of the legislature, with Romano Prodi at the head of the government, Italy staged a very determined fight to respect the economic parameters established by the Maastricht Treaty, and thus to qualify as one of the countries that would participate in the launching of European monetary union on 1 January 1999.

When Prodi took over as premier in 1996, Italy was still far from meeting the Maastricht criteria: the deficit/GDP ratio that year stood at 6.7 per cent, compared to an EMU requirement of not more than 3 per cent per annum; the level of the public debt/GDP ratio at 123.8 per cent, compared to the 60 per cent required; the level of inflation at 3.9 per cent, when it should have been no more than 1.5 per cent above the average level of the three EU countries boasting the lowest inflation rate (in 1996 an average of 2.6 per cent).[50] In spite of the good efforts of Ciampi and Dini, there was thus a very long way to go, and Italy had not even come back into the European Monetary System after the débâcle of September 1992. Her best hope was afforded by the limited flexibility introduced into Article 104c (2) of the Treaty by her own negotiators, together with their French counterparts:[51] a deficit and a public debt which were superior to the Maastricht parameters might not be judged 'excessive' if they were declining substantially and continuously towards the agreed levels.

However, there were many in Europe, with the Germans and Dutch in the front line, who were extremely sceptical about allowing Italy any leeway. The Italian public debt was too large, the lira too weak, the reordering of welfare services and pensions too half-hearted. After September 1992, there emerged a clear German preference for a two-tier Europe. A first hard core of nations could launch the Euro in 1999; the solidity of their economies would serve to protect the new currency in its early years and ensure that the disappearance of the deutschmark would not prove too traumatic. Then a second group of nations (more or less clearly indicated as southern European) could join too, after they had given ample proof of their economic stability. Hans Tietmeyer, the powerful head of the Bundesbank, warned in October 1996 that adherence to the Maastricht parameters could not be the result of 'a frenzied short-term effort, with transient results hastily patched together'.[52] Helmut Kohl was more open-minded. He had, of course, a broader vision of European unity and immense authority by this time, but even he had to ensure that he could take German public opinion with him. His Finance Minister, Theo Waigel, insisted frequently that the criteria for entry into the EMU would be interpreted strictly, and not flexibly as the Italians hoped. One EU monetary official told the *Financial Times* in

January, 1996: 'A flexible reading would mean Mr Waigel would have to eat his hat.'[53]

The road for Italy was, therefore, an uphill one. In July 1996 Prodi announced a structural fiscal adjustment of more than 32,000 billion lire, but the real showdown came in the early autumn of the same year. In mid-September the Italian prime minister visited his Spanish counterpart José María Aznar at Valencia. Although the particulars of the meeting are contested, it seems likely that Prodi proposed some sort of southern European alliance, which would press for a flexible interpretation of the Maastricht criteria, and for elongating the timetable of monetary union. Aznar, however, felt no need for Mediterranean solidarity. 'He [Prodi] wanted Spain and Italy to walk together holding hands towards Maastricht,' Aznar told the *Financial Times* in an explosive interview of 30 September, '[but] I'm not interested in holding hands. I told him we'd be there, right at the start.'[54]

To make matters worse, the *Financial Times* accompanied Aznar's interview with a first leader which cast severe doubt on Italy's capacity to meet the deadlines; her public debt was too great, and her 'history of fiscal profligacy and currency instability' rendered her unreliable. The French might be allowed a recourse to 'creative financing' to bring their national economic statistics into the requisite order, but no such opportunity should be allowed to the Italians.[55] The following day President Chirac rubbed salt into an already open wound by expressing doubts about Italy being in the first group of countries to introduce the Euro. Later in the same day he backtracked, but the damage was done.[56]

The sequence of events in the early autumn of 1996 thus had all the makings of a major crisis of European confidence in Italy. To external scepticism must be added an internal threat. The Northern League had interpreted its fine showing at the April elections as confirmation of Bossi's new line, the return to radical secessionist propaganda. Padania, whose exact dimensions were uncertain, was to seek its independence as soon as possible. The League established a shadow parliament at Mantua and a Padanian Liberation Committee, in saucy imitation of the Resistance Committee for the Liberation of Upper Italy, of 1943–5. Bossi declared that 'the North has only one problem: the South'.[57] On 15 September 1996, after a whole series of 'happenings' along the length of the river Po, supposedly the southern boundary of the new state, Bossi arrived in Venice to declare the formal independence of Padania. The event attracted widespread coverage in Europe's mass media. Martin Jacques, for instance, commented in a full-page article in the *Observer*: 'Europe's largest secessionist movement is likely to dominate Italian politics for many years.'[58]

Prodi reacted vigorously to these concurrent attacks: 'Italy's problem is a lack of unity, but at least from an economic point of view, it is without doubt a country of extraordinary capacity; . . . when it finds itself on the ropes, it always discovers the way back to revival.'[59] If this was not an iron law of Italian history, it was certainly true that Italy's peculiar brand of patriotism and capacity for action often emerged at moments of acute national crisis; even, and perhaps above all, when the latter was self-inflicted. Such had been the case in September 1992, and so it was again in September–October 1996. A significant shift of Italian policy and attitudes took place from this time onwards.

The first task was to point Italy ever more determinedly towards Europe. Not only was this essential in its own right, but it was also the best way of pulling the rug from under the League's feet. The presence of a united Italy in a single monetary union would leave little room for secessionist dreams. On his return from Valencia, Prodi had already announced the imposition of a 'tax for Europe', destined to raise another 13,000 billion lire. The government realized that there was no scope nor allies (except possibly for Greece, which counted for too little) for a possible renegotiation of Maastricht.[60] If Italy wanted to be in at the start, then it had no option but to take drastic economic measures.[61] In all, around 70,000 billion lire were garnered-in that year from spending cuts and increased taxation, the largest budget savings since Amato's emergency measures in the autumn of 1992.

Italy's national economic statistics rapidly took a turn for the better, with Carlo Azeglio Ciampi giving invaluable help to Prodi in the key role as minister of the Treasury. The former Governor of the Bank of Italy and Prime minister was very widely respected in Europe, and his sober and highly competent advocacy of Italy's case was extremely effective. Under his careful handling, on 25 November 1996 Italy re-entered the European Monetary System.

Ciampi's was not the only help that Prodi received at this critical time. The PDS leaders, Massimo D'Alema and Walter Veltroni (Vice-President of the Council of Ministers), gave him their full support. The trade union leaders, Sergio Cofferati of the CGIL, Sergio D'Antoni of the CISL, Pietro Larizza of the UIL, played an invaluable role in persuading their members to accept the austerity measures. Even Fausto Bertinotti, the leader of Rifondazione Comunista, and no friend of the 'Europe of the bankers', did little to rock the boat. The fact that the 'tax on Europe' was strongly progressive, hitting wealthier families much more than poorer ones, was interpreted as a point in Prodi's favour. So, too, was the fact that the Prime Minister refused to launch the full-scale attack on pensions and social services which many critics, both national and international, constantly invoked.[62]

On the other hand, Prodi's government had to cope with more than one section of Italian opinion hostile to the European project, in whole or in part. The greatest apparent threat was, naturally enough, from the Northern League and its closest ally, the Lega Veneta. They hoped that Europe would firmly reject the Italian candidacy. The way might then be open to split the

country, and eventually to negotiate a separate entry of the opulent and productive 'Padania' into the European Union. But were the Leagues' supporters,
in contrast to their behaviour of 1992–3, now prepared to follow Bossi down
the path of illegality? And was Bossi himself, after so much brinkmanship,
prepared actually to go over the brink? Much hung on the answer to these
questions. In May 1997, eight armed supporters of the idea of an independent
Venetia hijacked a ferry in Venice and drove their home-made armoured car
into the Piazza San Marco. They then staged an overnight occupation of the
campanile, the great belltower in the Piazza. The demonstrators were duly
arrested by units of the Italian army, and in July of the same year received
exemplary prison sentences of between four and six years.

The occupation of the *campanile* had been a spectacular publicity stunt,
and for many months its perpetrators were the heroes of the adolescents of
the schools and workshops of the Veneto.[63] However, once again the supporters of the secessionist programme shied away *en masse* from any illegal
action which would put at risk their homes and their livelihoods. The League
had adopted as its anthem Verdi's great chorus, 'Va pensiero', from the opera
Nabucco; but their own people did not suffer in the same way as the Israelites
in captivity, nor even as their own ancestors had done under the Austrians
in 1847–8. They had too much to lose, and their protest was diluted by the
many currents of modern consumption. Bossi, too, seemed content to remain
on his preferred terrain of verbal histrionics. It was indeed difficult to imagine
him taking to the northern hills armed with a Kalashnikov.

There were other oppositions to Prodi's overall project. On 24 November
1996, Berlusconi staged a major rally in Rome against the government's
economic plans. Among the highest echelons of the Italian business community there remained widespread scepticism about the impelling need to
meet the Maastricht requirements, at least in time for the first round, a
scepticism which found its focus in the influential figure of Cesare Romiti,
president of FIAT. The new Governor of the Bank of Italy, Antonio Fazio,
was also less than enthusiastic. He moved slowly and cautiously in reducing
interest rates, incurring the wrath of more than one member of the government. Prodi recalled later: 'Objectively speaking, the repeated declarations of
the Governor, though always highly competent in technical terms, seemed
to the rest of Europe like a declaration of opposition to our entry into the
single currency. I had often to deny that this was so to my European
colleagues, but it wasn't easy to reply to their objection: "If the Governor of
your own national bank doesn't believe in your entry into the Euro, how do
you expect us to believe in it?" '[64]

None the less, the government kept its nerve. Another very testing
moment came in April 1997, when the European Commission drew up its

interim report on the progress each country was making towards meeting what was increasingly considered to be the key parameter of the Maastricht Treaty, a public deficit not superior to 3 per cent of GDP. At first the Commission divided the fifteen EU countries into three groups: a leading one of five countries (Denmark, Ireland, Luxembourg, Holland and Finland), which had already reached the 3 per cent objective in 1996; a second group of eight (Belgium, Germany, Spain, France, Austria, Portugal, Sweden and Great Britain), which were well on the way to doing so; and a last group of just two, Greece and Italy, which were judged to be further behind. The writing was on the wall. After furious lobbying from the Italian government and the intervention of Italy's two excellent members of the Commission, Mario Monti and Emma Bonnino, the document was reformulated: the second group now contained all ten countries, listed in alphabetical order.[65] In the same month, as he admitted later, Prodi feared very much a new, speculative run on the lira, which would have damaged Italy's chances irretrievably.[66] But the attack did not materialize, and Italy's recouping of lost ground went on apace.

Her cause received a considerable boost with the election in May 1997 of Lionel Jospin as the new French premier. Jospin was clearly in favour of Italy's inclusion, and from this time onwards, to use Prodi's words again, France became Italy's 'convinced sponsor'.[67] The tide was turning against the Bundesbank line. Many of the countries which had been considered non-starters only a short time previously – Portugal, Spain, Italy itself – had made remarkable progress in reducing their annual deficits. Only Greece lagged further behind. There remained, though, the (for Italy) embarrassing question of public debt. In March 1998, only a few months before the final decision was to be taken, the Bundesbank published a damning report in which it judged 'insufficient' the Italian and Belgian attempts to cut their 'extremely high' levels of public debt. Belgium's debt was, in percentage terms of GDP, superior to that of Italy, but the volume of Italian debt was the greatest in the Union. Both debts showed signs of diminishing, but very slowly. If the Maastricht criteria were to be interpreted in anything but the most flexible way, Italy and Belgium could not qualify.

However, at the end of the day, as Dyson and Featherstone have written, 'compromise came on the basis of political interests overriding economic judgements'.[68] In May 1998 the EU governments decided that they had to avoid damaging splits, and that inclusion rather than exclusion should be their governing principle at such a delicate moment. Only Greece was excluded, because she had manifestly not met the key annual deficit criteria. Great Britain, Denmark and Sweden decided that they would not adhere to monetary union in the first instance, but Portugal, Spain and Italy were in. There was great rejoicing in all three countries.

*

Romano Prodi and Carlo Azeglio Ciampi, the architects of Italy's successful campaign for entry, had every reason to consider theirs a historic victory. Barely six years earlier, no one would have bet a penny or a lira on Italy sharing the same currency as France and Germany from the beginning of 2002 onwards. Italy had come a long way indeed from the depths of 1972, when she had been unable even to find a decent candidate to head the Commission. Her entry into the European monetary union was, as we have seen, far from a foregone conclusion, and the role of individual agency (and not only that of the principal *animateurs*, Prodi and Ciampi) had been particularly significant in the Italian case. A clear choice had been made, from September 1996, against all hesitation or delay; the 'Olive Tree' coalition had held firm, and public opinion had given it its support.

On the other hand, it is important not to exaggerate the size of the Italian achievement, as some of the protagonists have quite naturally tended to. Spain and Portugal had done the same, and even Greece, which seemed at one point in danger of being left permanently behind, recouped sufficiently rapidly to enter the monetary union in January 2001. All this suggests an over-determination in the historical process described above. In other words, so great were the incentives for some of the EU countries, especially the southern European ones, to put their houses in order, and so high were the possible political costs for other EU countries, especially France and Germany, of forcibly excluding them, that at the end of the day a highly flexible reading of the Maastricht criteria became almost inevitable. By May 1998, Theo Waigel had little option but to eat his hat.

Many criticisms have justly been levelled at the purely regulatory aspects of Maastricht, at its insistence on efficiency, not equity, at the absence of a parallel political process which could have given the Europeans a constitution and the foundations of a transnational democratic polity. Diplomacy more than democracy continued to be at the heart of the everyday running of the Union. Looked at from Italy's standpoint, though, the overridingly benign quality of what had taken place can hardly be over-stressed. As Mario Monti, Italy's long-serving member of the European Commission, noted in May 1998, monetary union had given Italy 'a *corpus* of rules which, if we look beyond their financial form, have a civil substance'.[69]

Finally, in March 1999, as if to crown the process of the Italian renaissance in Europe, Romano Prodi became the head of the European Commission. He did so in circumstances not of his own making, as we shall see in a moment. Furthermore, his first year in Brussels was an extremely difficult one. But Italy's presence at the heart of the Union was now a formidable one, because Mario Monti, too, stayed on in an influential position in the Commission. At last Italy was in Europe in a serious way.

b. THE PATCHWORK OF REFORMS

Only a few months after successfully taking Italy into the EMU, the Prodi government was unexpectedly brought down. Indeed, the two events were intimately linked, because once the discipline and unity necessary for the European venture had served their purpose, party politics came back with a vengeance. In October 1998, Rifondazione Comunista refused to vote Prodi's latest packet of economic measures. In the House of Deputies a motion of confidence in the government was lost, by a single vote. Massimo D'Alema, the leader of the PDS which had in the meanwhile slightly changed its name, to DS (Democratici di Sinistra), took advantage of Prodi's discomfort to take over the reins of government. He tempted into the new coalition a splinter group led by none other than Francesco Cossiga, the former President of the Republic, whom the PDS had threatened to impeach some eight years earlier. It was an unholy alliance, and not a good base on which to launch a programme of reforms. Prodi went, rather unwillingly and bitterly, to head the European Commission, and D'Alema remained premier for less than two years, until he too resigned in the wake of the unfavourable regional election results of April 2000. Giuliano Amato then became prime minister until the end of the XIIIth legislature of the Italian Republic, in March 2001.

Three premiers in just five years were obviously too many. Although nothing forbade a change of leadership, the impression given was that of a perpetuation of the old style of Italian politics, not of a new start. Constant change at the top was symptomatic of the fragility of the coalition, as well as being unconducive to what the centre-left needed most – a clear line of march.

None the less, the reformist record of these years is a significant and widespread one, though less successful than its protagonists – individual ministers of considerable political, if not governmental, experience – might have hoped. It is worth analysing briefly. The essential starting-point is the apparatuses of the state, because (as I have argued above in Chapter 6), without the radical reform of their structures, practices and culture, it was difficult to make progress in other fields. In the Ciampi government of 1993–4, Sabino Cassese had given a great initial impetus to reform of the public administration. Could that impetus now be sustained?

Responsibility for this delicate and very difficult task was entrusted primarily to Franco Bassanini, a highly technically competent politician of the DS, and one of the few who had earlier abandoned the Socialist party in protest against Bettino Craxi's methods and priorities. His efforts were concentrated mainly in three areas: the de-centralization of the public administration, with the transference of functions from the central apparatuses to regional and local government; the re-organization of the central apparatuses that remained; the simplifying of procedures, which would render less onerous citizens' and enterprises' contact with the bureaucracy. The first of these processes was launched with great vigour by the law no. 59 of 1997, to which must be added two other laws (nos. 94 and 127) of the same year, as well as a significant number of legislative decrees and norms governing the new legislation's implementation. The law no. 59 reversed the previous situation regarding areas of administrative competence by attributing to local and regional government all functions except those reserved explicitly to the state (foreign affairs, monetary policy, relations with the European Union, cultural policy, scientific research, etc.). On paper at least this was, as Brunetta Baldi has written, 'the greatest decentralization ever experimented in the history of the Italian state'.[70]

The second area of administrative reform, that of the central apparatuses, was marked by the reform of budget procedures, by the reduction of central ministries from eighteen to twelve, and by the highly successful overhauling of the personnel and activity of the key Finance ministry (primarily concerned with taxation), carried out by its Minister, Vincenzo Visco of the DS. Senior bureaucrats were also made subject to review, and could be shifted from posts that had seemed to be theirs for life.

The third major area of reform, simplification and acceleration, was marked by action on 180 procedures, and the opening of '*sportelli unici*' (literally 'single counters') in 35 per cent of Italy's communes, covering 69 per cent of its population. These '*sportelli*' made provision for a single procedure for the start-up of an economic enterprise, compared to the forty-three that had previously existed. Under the new system permission usually arrived within three months, an enormous saving of time compared to previously. In addition, the number of certificates, authorizations, etc. which each citizen had previously been required to produce was halved between 1996 and 1999.[71]

This considerable programme of reform was vitiated by a number of key weaknesses. There was never, on the part of any of the three governments of the centre-left, a clear recognition of the *priority* and *centrality* of these processes in an overall programme of reform.[72] The proposals themselves were marked by an overriding legalism, with insufficient attention being paid to the problem of changing the culture of Italian administrative practice.[73] The result was a plethora of decrees, norms, etc.; a positive 'obsession with text', as Yves Mény has called it,[74] and a lesser ability to see how things were working on the ground. The narrow, corporatist interests of the trade unions in the public sector were not curbed. Simplification had touched 180 procedures, but in central government alone nearly 5,000 others were left unreformed, and often behind a simplification lurked a new complication.[75] In order to appoint an associate professor at an Italian university in 1999, to take just one example based on personal experience, it was still necessary for the five members of the appointments committee to produce over 100 pages of minutes, and these were not considered valid unless each member of the committee signed each of the pages.

Last, but not least, administrative de-centralization was not accompanied by a corresponding move towards political federalism. It was only in the last days of the legislature, in March 2001, that parliament passed a new law decentralizing political power, and even then rights to raise taxation on a regional or local level remained limited.[76]

If we pass from the *apparatuses* of the state to the *services* it offers, it is possible to discern a pattern of considerable reforming zeal which did not, though, translate into measures which succeeded in inspiring enthusiasm or gaining widespread approval and consent. Luigi Berlinguer of the DS launched an ambitious programme of school and university reform: schools were to be freed from the oppressive control of centralized administration; the school-leaving age was to be raised, curricula to be revised and lower secondary schools, the weakest link in the Italian educational system, abolished. Twentieth-century history was to be studied systematically for the first time at a school level.

Universities, too, were granted increased autonomy. Students were no longer to amble their way through university, taking an exam or two when they felt like it, or else dropping out, but were to be constrained to graduate within three years. The Italian university was to take on a European dimension: first-degree courses, of lower standards than previously, were aimed to rectify Italy's chronic lack of graduates.

These were laudable aims, but their execution left a great deal to be desired. The reform programme had to be negotiated with, and modified by, the governing coalition. At the ministry, the bureaucracy proceeded all too slowly and inefficiently; reforms emerged in bits and pieces, with frequent changes of direction and content. By the time the legislature came to an end, five years after the educational reforms had first been announced, their realization was far from complete. Those on the ground, teachers, administrators and university professors, who tried to implement the ministerial directives, were often left disoriented and disillusioned, when not outrightly hostile.[77]

Welfare services were less touched by the reform process. In one way this was a good thing, because all over Europe 'rationalization' of the welfare state had become synonymous with its reduction. The minister for Health in the Prodi and Amato governments, Rosy Bindi, of the Catholic Popolari party, proved a combative defender of the national health service. In the face of considerable opposition, she forced hospital consultants to choose between public and private structures.[78] If they chose the first, they could still maintain private practices within the framework of the public hospitals. If they chose the second, then their activity was limited, once and for all, to private clinics.

In this way the minister intended to curb the malpractices of one of Italy's richest and least responsible corporations, accustomed for the most part to treating the public system as a secondary and subordinate activity to their private practice, while continuing to draw large salaries from the state.

In another way, though, the absence of structured reform in the Italian welfare state left a large number of important questions unanswered. In February 1996 Romano Prodi had set up a Commission, headed by Paolo Onofri, to make recommendations in this field. The Commission emphasized the perils of overspending on pensions for those on average incomes, and underspending on the most vulnerable sections of the community and those most at risk. There was also a heavy disequilibrium in Italian welfare provisions between the younger and older generations. In the summer of 1996 a lively debate took place on the Onofri proposals, but little came of them, thanks principally to the opposition of Rifondazione Comunista. In spite of strenuous attempts to improve productivity, the health system continued to be wasteful in many areas; regional governments ran up large annual deficits in their health budgets.

At the same time, it was clear that the state continued to spend *too little* on policies directed specifically at families. The very low level of fertility rates among the Italian population (discussed above in Chapter 3) never found an adequate response from the centre-left governments. Some measures were passed to help poor families with numerous offspring, but incentives to encourage and aid child-rearing remained weak. In 1996 old age pensions accounted for 52.2 per cent of total welfare spending, while spending on families was a derisory 3.6 per cent.[79]

For all their many faults, by the year 2001 Italian public educational and welfare services were far from an overall disgrace by European standards. The same could not be said of the legal system (see above, Chapter 7, pp. 230–31). One of the gravest inadequacies of the centre-left was its failure to invest sufficiently in a drastic overhaul of the administration of justice. This was a daunting task, and successive ministers of Justice were defeated by it. By the end of the legislature there was a slight improvement in the speed and efficiency with which cases were being heard, but the overall impression remained a dismal one. What reforms did take place were mainly confined to providing further guarantees for the accused, and to rendering the task of prosecuting magistrates more difficult.

Behind these tendencies lurked questions that were quintessentially political. The centre-left had to make up its mind from the very beginning whether or not it was going to give its whole-hearted support to the process of cleaning up Italian public life which had begun with the Milanese magistrates' actions of 1992. By and large, it decided against, and was quite content to allow 'Tangentopoli' to fizzle out. By April 1998, six years after the beginning of the great scandal, of the 2,970 cases connected with it, sentence had been passed in just 566, and then only at the first level of Italian justice. There had been 460 verdicts of guilty and 106 of not guilty. Of these last, however, sixty-one were caused by the statute of limitations, the expiry of the time limits set by Italian law for the hearing of cases.[80] This last tendency naturally assumed ever-greater proportions as time passed.

Most of the politicians of the centre-left, especially those belonging to the Popolari and the Greens, felt that enough was enough. There were a number of reasons for this. One was a deep-lying tendency in Italian political culture, clearly of Catholic origin, towards pardoning and forgetting. This was a tendency that had been present after 1945 when the vexed question of '*epurazione*', the punishment of ex-Fascists, had been on the agenda. It appeared again in the late 1990s, with uncanny similarity, with the argument running roughly as follows: we were all part of the system, especially the illegal financing of parties, in one way or another, the magistrates have exaggerated and have been wrong on more than one occasion, the system cannot be reformed through the law courts. It was ironic indeed that just as these views were triumphing in the Italian centre-left (they had long been dominant in the centre-right), parallel scandals in Germany and France revealed how much political corruption was a structural part of modern European democracy, and not one that could easily be swept under the carpet.[81]

Another reason for these attitudes allows us to examine a third area of possible reform in the public sphere (the first two being the state's administrative apparatuses and the services it offered). *Institutional* reform – of the form of the state, of parliament, of the balance of powers – was the issue that most exercised the Italian political class, the one to which they dedicated most energy, often at the expense of other equally important reforms. The centre-left of 1996–2001 was no exception in this respect. In January 1997, under the presidency of Massimo D'Alema, a new bicameral commission on institutional reform came into being. This was the third such commission in less than twenty years, the previous two being those of 1983–5 and 1993. Both these previous experiences had proved resounding failures.[82]

D'Alema, a politician very much in the mould of Palmiro Togliatti, shrewd and enamoured of *realpolitik*, put great store on being a constitutional reformer,[83] but knew that his commission would meet the same fate as its predecessors unless he was able to reach agreement with the opposition, and in particular with its leader, Silvio Berlusconi. It was here that the question of 'Tangentopoli' came into play. Berlusconi was primarily interested, as Gianfranco Pasquino has written, in 'a constitutional reform that scaled down the power of the magistrates both in concrete and symbolic terms'.[84] The leader of the opposition was by this time under accusation on a number of counts, and had already been convicted in the first degree for corrupting the

Financial Police and for the falsification of company accounts. Far from resigning, he continued vehemently to denounce the political plot which the magistrates had hatched against him. For Berlusconi, the fate of the bicameral commission was indissolubly linked with his own judicial position. He was open to discussing all manner of constitutional variations – semi-presidentialism, a German-style chancellorship, etc. – but the bottom line was very clear: there could be no deal without some form of guarantee for his legal future.

On this key issue, the centre-left hesitated, and its hesitation was to cost it dear. Far from taking a strong line upon the need for justice to be seen to be done and far from calling for Berlusconi's resignation, D'Alema sought to placate him as far as he could. Part of his calculation may have been that Berlusconi in 1997 seemed a weak and ineffectual leader, much preferable to the capable and popular Gianfranco Fini. D'Alema made it clear that he thought 'Tangentopoli' had gone too far. At the same time, the government moved all too slowly in introducing a law on the conflict of interests, which should have resolved the unique and embarrassing situation in which the leader of the opposition was also the owner of most of the nation's commercial television. By the end of the legislature, no such law had been passed, a damning indictment of the reforming capacity of the centre-left. As for the legal situation, in the last analysis the courts alone had the power to decide Berlusconi's fate, but the centre-left politicians could create a climate of opinion which favoured indulgence and procrastination. This they did, with disastrous results.

The bi-cameral commission met thirty-six times in plenary session, and many more at committee level. It appears that thirty-eight drafts were produced on the form of the state, nine on the form of government, twenty-seven on parliament, and just two on the judicial system. The commission inched towards agreement on a so-called 'moderated' semi-presidential system, and a new balance of powers which would rein in the powers of prosecuting magistrates. It was not enough. On 2 June 1998 Berlusconi unexpectedly declared his definite opposition to the packet of reform, and with his refusal D'Alema's elaborate constitutional card-house collapsed on the commission's table.

In fairness, not all institutional reform was concentrated in the hands of the bi-cameral commission. The local government law establishing the direct election of mayors dated back to March 1993, but its full effects were to be felt only in the following years. At one level the law did little for local democracy, because it reduced the powers of the municipal council to the advantage of the mayor. On another, identification of local government with a single, strong figure, democratically elected, increased interest and participation in politics at a local level.

Nobody made better use of these opportunities than the left-wing mayor of Naples, Antonio Bassolino, from late 1993 onwards. In what seemed a nearly impossible task – that of governing one of the most chaotic and corrupt cities of Europe – Bassolino succeeded in making his own name the symbol of the city's resurrection. The historic centre was brought back to life, Piazza del Plebiscito became its showpiece, and the former industrial area at Bagnoli, which had housed the giant steelworks of Italsider, was slowly converted into a park and riviera which was to exploit to the full its incomparable seaside position. Bassolino declared that to establish legality in the city was in itself a revolutionary act. Local government was made more transparent, and the administrative personnel, amid many difficulties, rendered more productive and responsible for its actions. Naturally, the city could not be reformed *in toto* in the course of a few years. The Camorra continued its reign in many of the historic quarters, and violent crime was almost as virulent a presence as ever. But Bassolino had given an example at local level of that clear-sighted, determined and dynamic action which was so lacking at the centre.[85]

In April 2000 the system of direct election was extended to the regions as well, with the presidents of regional councils exercising the powers of 'governors'. These were new figures in the Italian political firmament, managing huge budgets and an increasing number of functions. It remained to be seen whether they could establish as direct a link with citizens as many city mayors had done, and above all what would be the relationship between different visions of a federalist Italy – one based on its very rich urban tradition, the other on regional identification. The two were not necessarily compatible.

The centre-left, then, had attempted reform in many fields but the overall results were unconvincing. The culture of their reformism, with few exceptions, was a liberal, productivist, and rationalizing one. These were important virtues in an Italian public sphere not noted for such qualities. But they were not enough. The centre-left governed from above, with reforms or bits of reforms, norms and regulations, cascading downwards towards an essentially passive citizenship. Such a view of politics reflected the pessimism of Massimo D'Alema, profoundly convinced of the natural irresponsibility of Italian society. There was no attempt to build support and involvement from below, to create a climate of enthusiasm and involvement which could have sustained some of the more worthy initiatives of the government. In more than one sphere, as with the teachers, exactly the opposite happened. By 2001 the centre-left said that it had governed well, and in some areas it had, but in the country there was little enthusiasm for, or even knowledge of, what it had done. The long-standing tradition which identified left-wing politics with the politics of participation and grass-roots democracy, of learning citizenship through practice, had been left woefully in abeyance.

5. Postscript

On 13 May 2001, national elections took place. The centre-right, under the leadership of Silvio Berlusconi, won a famous victory. In the House of Deputies, the centre-right coalition of the 'Casa delle libertà' (literally the 'House of Liberties') gained 367 seats against the 'Olive Tree's' 248. In the upper House the victory was less marked (as in 1994), but this time the centre-right coalition had a comfortable majority, with 177 seats out of a total of 324. Berlusconi's Forza Italia returned to being the largest single party in the country, with 29.4 per cent of the proportional vote in the House of Deputies, compared to 20.6 per cent in 1996. By contrast, the left-democrats of Massimo D'Alema and Walter Veltroni slumped from their 21.2 per cent share of the vote in 1996 to just 16.6 per cent in 2001.

At the heart of the centre-right's victory was its capacity to unite its forces, whereas the centre-left entered the fray much more divided than in the previous election. Berlusconi's lieutenants patiently re-established links with Umberto Bossi's Northern League. Such an alliance had seemed totally unlikely after Bossi's desertion of Berlusconi at the end of 1994, and the subsequent animosity between the two leaders. It was Bossi, after all, who had been responsible for some of the most studied invective against Berlusconi, as well as the coining of a number of memorable nicknames such as 'BerlusKaiser'. But both parties needed the alliance to secure victory in the North, and the League had more or less come to a political dead-end after the failure of its secessionist campaign of 1996–7. Gianfranco Fini of the right-wing National Alliance, no friend of Bossi or of his ideas, acquiesced to Berlusconi's choice, as he was to do throughout this period.

The centre-left, on the other hand, suffered from two damaging divisions. Unlike in 1996, it proved impossible to reach agreement with Rifondazione Comunista on joint candidates for the House of Deputies. Relations had become very soured during the years of centre-left government. Fausto Bertinotti, the leader of Rifondazione Comunista, had been responsible for bringing down the Prodi government, thus creating the conditions of political instability which were to characterize the rest of the legislature. He and his colleagues had always reproached the centre-left for the flabbiness of their reformism. At the same time Antonio Di Pietro, the ex-magistrate and popular hero of the 'Tangentopoli' campaign, decided to fight a lonely electoral campaign, in favour of legality, against Berlusconi, and for an 'Italy of sound values'. Rifondazione gained 5 per cent of the vote, Di Pietro 3.9 per cent. These were votes which cost the centre-left dear. Many uninominal seats which would have been won if the centre-left had stayed united were lost by small percentages. And Di Pietro just failed to reach the 4 per cent quorum which would have allotted him seats under the system of proportional representation (25 per cent of the seats in the House of Deputies were still allocated in this fashion).

The election campaign, almost inevitably, concentrated on the figure of Berlusconi. This was very much what the centre-right leader himself wanted. His face was everywhere – on huge roadside posters, in the atriums of railway stations, on election bunting running down whole streets, as in the popular quarters of Naples. Forza Italia candidates were instructed not to put their own faces on posters, but always that of their leader. The centre-left tried to counter with much of the same. The handsome face of Francesco Rutelli, the former mayor of Rome, whom the centre-left had wisely chosen as the leader of their coalition, tried to stare back at Berlusconi wherever possible. But the electoral resources of the two coalitions were quite unequal. There were supposed to be rigorous rules governing election spending, but they were clearly circumvented or ignored. Berlusconi had the resources of a media empire at his disposal and acted accordingly: 18 million copies of an illustrated, 127-page booklet on his life, *Una storia italiana*, were sent to Italian families. Coverage on Berlusconi's three television channels was obviously massively in favour of the centre-right. The news coverage of the RAI was more balanced, but in other public television programmes, dedicated to commentary and satire, the control of the centre-left made itself felt. On the eve of the elections, at peak viewing time on RAI Uno, Roberto Benigni made an impassioned, very funny but quite illicit appeal to the electors to vote for the centre-left.

The most significant event in the campaign, and certainly the one which aroused most discussion at an international level, was the intervention of *The Economist*. Its issue of 28 April 2001 bore a front cover with the headline, 'Why Silvio Berlusconi is unfit to lead Italy'. There were two principal reasons, the first being his very controversial legal record. *The Economist* made a list of ten trials in which Berlusconi was under accusation, which varied from bribing financial police to the illegal financing of a political party, from the attempted corruption of magistrates to tax fraud and the breach of anti-trust laws in Spain (in connection with the television channel Telecinco). Some of these trials were still going on. In others, Berlusconi had been found guilty, but the statute of limitations (the expiry of the time allowed for the case to be heard at all three levels of Italian justice) had led to the extinguishing of the crime. In others still, he had been acquitted. For the British weekly, 'it would be unthinkable in any self-respecting democracy' that a man with such a legal record, and with judicial procedures in his regard still in full flow, could become prime minister. Furthermore, and this was the second reason, Berlusconi had never resolved his conflict of interests. His business empire, worth perhaps $14 billion, was not only in commercial television, but had ramifications in 'almost every aspect of business and public life': banking, insurance, property, publishing, advertising and football. If he won the elections, he would control 90 per cent of all television, public and commercial. Private and national interests would be inextricably intertwined and confused.

The Economist's article finished on a sombre note: 'Despite his claims that he is the shining archetype of a self-made man, Mr Berlusconi has needed a lot of help from insalubrious quarters. Though he says he wants to replace the old corrupt system, his own business empire is largely a product of it. His election as prime minister would similarly perpetuate, not change, Italy's bad old ways.'

The Economist's example was swiftly followed by major European newspapers, such as *Le Monde* and, more surprisingly, the conservative Spanish *El Mundo*. In addition to the points made by the British weekly, the European press concentrated on the disturbing prospect of having the racist Northern League in the government (which they saw as a possible repeat of the presence of Haider's Freedom Party in the Austrian government), and, to a lesser extent, on the Fascist past of the National Alliance. For the first time, an Italian election had become the object of heated discussion at the level of a newly-formed European public opinion; and one part of it clearly felt deeply alarmed that a fresh Italian anomaly was being created, which could serve as a model for the rest of Europe.

The interventions of the foreign press, overwhelmingly negative, damaged Berlusconi, but they did not stop him winning. His own party, as we have seen, scored a notable triumph, but his allies were crushed by his omni-presence. National Alliance dropped from 15.7 per cent to 12 per cent. The Northern League fell even more, from 10.1 per cent to 4 per cent. Forza Italia had eaten up much of the League's support in the North, especially the Veneto, though the League continued to be well represented in parliament thanks to the pre-electoral pact with Berlusconi. In terms of electoral geography, the centre-right regained its control over great part of the North, with the exception of Trentino-Alto Adige, some parts of Liguria and Piedmont, and pockets of centre-left resistance in Belluno, Venice and Trieste. In Puglia and Lazio the centre-right did very well, but its most spectacular coup was in Sicily, where it took every single seat for the House of Deputies.

As for the centre-left, its leader Francesco Rutelli fought a sober and honest campaign against the odds, and was rewarded with a high turn-out for his own electoral grouping, the 'Margherita' ('Daisy' or 'Marguerite', which in Italian does not sound quite as daft a name for a political party as it does in English). The 'Margherita', which included the Popular Party and others (but not the Greens who again fared disastrously) gained 14.5 per cent of the vote, which drew them much closer to the strength of the left-democrats than anyone could have anticipated. In geographical terms, the centre-left maintained its traditional strongholds in central Italy, but with reduced margins. It also did well in Basilicata and in some parts of Campania, where the influence of Antonio Bassolino, who had become President of the Region, made itself felt. In local elections, which were held in some major cities at the same time as the national ones, it narrowly held on to Rome, where Walter Veltroni became mayor, and Naples, which elected a woman mayor for the first time ever, Rosa Russo Jervolino.

Overall, it would be fair to say that the left lost the elections through their divisions, their lack of a clear line of march, their unnecessary indulgence towards Berlusconi, and their incapacity to communicate a sense of urgency and innovation. But it is also true that Berlusconi won the elections in his own right, and it is worth examining briefly why this was so. Certainly, a key factor was the quantity and quality of the resources at his disposal. His business interests, which in 1994 had shown clear signs of crisis, had been put on a far firmer footing seven years later. The ensuing cascade of funds flowed into every part of his political activity, from the rallies of Forza Italia to the sustenance of his allies. Generosity in return for loyalty and subordination was a hallmark of his actions.

Yet the reasons for his victory go deeper than cash flows, or even media control. After his bitter ejection from government in December 1994, Berlusconi had had seven years in opposition, a long time in which to learn about politics. He had surrounded himself with shrewd advisers, like Giulio Tremonti and Marcello Pera, and together they had decided on a number of long-term political initiatives, of which the reinvention of the alliance with the Northern League was the most obvious. Another was the patient work behind the scenes which led, in December 1999, to Forza Italia becoming part of the Christian Democrat group (the European People's Party) in the European parliament. Berlusconi found willing sponsors in Helmut Kohl and Aznar, both anxious to increase the numbers in their group. Not only did this give Forza Italia a Christian veneer which was a valuable asset in domestic politics; it also granted the party the European legitimation which it had previously lacked. *The Economist* might well declare Berlusconi 'unfit to govern', but a year and a half earlier senior Christian Democrat politicians in Europe had decided otherwise.

Another long-term process under way in the years of opposition was the strengthening of Forza Italia as a political party. From its origins as a shadowy grouping based on a media empire, Forza Italia was nurtured into a mass-based organization, with a significant presence in Italian society. Berlusconi's party was not a place for political discussion, nor of democracy, but it was a well-oiled machine for rallies, for the dissemination of propaganda, and for many other types of political intervention in all parts of the national territory. By May 2001 the organization was more than able to hold its own with the ailing and ageing left-democrats, whose presence in some parts of the peninsula, like Lombardy and Sicily, had become very flimsy.

To these long-term undertakings must be added the efficacy of Silvio Berlusconi's electoral campaign. Once again, as in 1994, he was extremely attuned, through the use of focus groups and other opinion-testing techniques, to the humours and desires of the electorate. His major campaigning points, which took the form of a solemn promise to the Italians, signed on television, were repeated incessantly in simple language. To British ears there was more than a little of Mrs Thatcher in all this. At the top of his list came administrative reform, the fight to put the bureaucracy at the service of Italian citizens. There followed the promise to undertake major public works, such as the bridge across the Straits of Messina, connecting Sicily to the mainland. France had built uninterruptedly in the last twenty years, Germany was refurbishing its capital at an astonishing rate; why was it that only Italy was incapable of initiatives of this sort? The answer lay in the lack of *liberty*, the key word in Berlusconi's whole campaign, the impediments created by the bureaucracy and the law, the controlling statalism of the left. The promise of major public works for the South appealed enormously in regions where the level of youth unemployment was high, and Berlusconi successfully portrayed himself as the experienced entrepreneur who could kick-start the economy of the South into action.

Other parts of his programme were also deeply appealing. Apart from the promise to lower taxes and give more choice with regard to schooling and health care, classics of the neo-liberal right, Berlusconi also declared that he would reform the justice system, which would become simpler and more efficient. The powers of investigating magistrates, who had interfered too much in the liberty of citizens, would be curbed. The leader of the centre-right ably presented himself, his friends, and other members of Forza Italia who were under investigation, as the victims of a politicized judicial system which interfered with ordinary citizens who wanted to go about their own business in peace. Finally, Italian cities were to be made safer. Illegal immigration, with its high co-relation to violent crime and prostitution, was to be eliminated.

Such a programme, with its strong accents on individual liberty and choice, on the limitation of the powers of an oppressive and inefficient state, on personal initiative in the context of public security, struck deep chords in Italian society. All that part of Italy which was instinctively entrepreneurial and individualistic, modern but vaguely Catholic, which had struggled in the course of half a century to found the material well-being of families upon hard work, self-sacrifice, and a cock-a-snook attitude towards the state, recognized itself in the smiling face of the tireless little Milanese businessman. So too did much of that poor, southern Italy which was prepared to believe his promises of putting an end to their relative deprivation. On the other hand, that Italy which believed in the growth of a civil society, in the need to curb the vertical hierarchies of patron–client relations, in the rule of law and the fight against the Mafia, in the defence of state schooling and health care, was appalled by Silvio Berlusconi's victory.

This book has been an extended argument about democracy in one great European nation, the history of what that democracy was, and the suggestion of what it could have been. I have tried to treat this fascinating theme not just in a narrowly political way, but with recourse to a wider concept of democracy, one which informs and illuminates the practices of every day life, which links society and institutions, which examines, to use an old and honourable distinction in European historiography, the connections, or lack of them, between *pays réal* and *pays légal*. However, I have also attempted to introduce a new element, and possibly a new methodology, by focusing systematically upon families as well as society and institutions, and by arguing that it is in the complex linkages or fractures between individuals, families, society and the state that modern democracy is forged or demeaned.

There is much in modern Italian society which favours the growth of a democratic culture within its families – the material wealth of a majority of the population, the striking change in the condition of many Italian women in the last three decades, spreading educational opportunity, increased access to information of every kind, the introduction of the theme of democratic participation in the recent teachings of the Catholic Church; last, but far from least, the growth of a plural and critical civil society, both in the South as well as the North of the country.

However, there is also much that threatens it – the extraordinary power and cultural penetration of the mass media, of which a very significant part belongs, in the Italian case, to a single family, that of Silvio Berlusconi; the lasting structures of closed professional corporations; the vertical ordering of relationships through clienteles, dominated nearly always by ageing male figures; the temptation to follow, in times of political uncertainty, a single charismatic leader; lastly, the lack of profitable and satisfying employment, or even employment *tout court*, for so much of Italian youth, especially that of the South.

In the 1980s the performance of the political and administrative class did little to enrich Italy's democratic culture, to encourage its civil society, to change the widespread attitudes of distrust and cynicism towards the state which permeated so many Italian families. On the contrary. So great were its misdeeds that many elements of it were swept away by that extraordinary series of events which formed the crisis of 1992–3.

From that critical season, it seemed as if a new Italy could emerge; an

Italy not radically transformed, but at least with different priorities and with a different line of march. The crisis offered the possibility of creating a public sphere in which Italian citizens could more easily espy some of democracy's virtues and not just its vices, and with which they could perhaps come to identify.

It is only just to ask, writing these last lines in the spring of 2001, what progress, if any, has been made in this direction. My answer can only be a provisional one, for any real historical judgement on the Italy of the 1990s will come much later. However, even without indulging in unnecessary pessimism, it is difficult to avoid the conclusion that many of the questions asked about Italian democracy in 1992–3 have been answered only partially, if at all. There is one clear and significant victory, which has already earned the government of the 'Olive Tree' coalition a place in Italian history – the successful fight to honour the 'external constraint', and enter into the Europe of monetary union.

It is also the case that Italy, much more than previously, has begun to take a responsible role in foreign affairs. D'Alema's handling of the Kosovo crisis, which saw a high level of Italian participation and involvement, especially in aid and peace-keeping terms, was an exemplary example. At last the very modest and frequently lampooned Italian armed services had something decent to do, and by and large did it well.[86]

The 1990s have witnessed a constant, and in one moment (1993–4) an intense, attempt to transform the greatest weakness of Italy's public sphere, that of its bureaucratic culture and practice. There can be fewer more important tests of a modern state's democratic capacity to create consent than the degree to which it succeeds in alleviating the weight of bureaucracy upon individuals and families. By the year 2001, to take up for the last time that comparison between Great Britain and Italy which I have tried to make a constant of this volume, there is every reason to suppose that while in this sphere the former has regressed, the latter has progressed. Italy has tried to climb out of the administrative pit to which its history has condemned it; in Britain, by contrast, many parts of the state's practice have sunk into that same pit, seemingly with scarce awareness of the dangers that lie therein. Italy has not yet completely turned its face on the past. So ingrained is the negative culture of its bureaucracy, and so great the resistances to change, that the whole question needs a prioritizing which it has not yet been accorded. Silvio Berlusconi, as we have seen, put administrative reform at the top of his list of election promises. Whether his government will realize that promise, or slip back into the sort of administrative culture that characterized the Christian Democrats and Socialists, will be one of its most effective tests.

The outcomes in nearly all the other areas touched centrally by the crisis of 1992–3 are either deeply uncertain, or clearly negative. The failure of the anti-corruption inquests and the isolation of the minority of reforming magistrates has already been commented upon. In another key area, the struggle against the Mafia, the result is less clear cut, either one way or the other. Since 1992, the Mafia has been dealt a series of very heavy body blows: the arrests of Totò Riina and of Giovanni Brusca; the collaboration of very many '*pentiti*', which has led to the magistrates building up an unparalleled picture of the structure and functioning of the organization; the great amount of property confiscated from Mafia bosses. However, the Mafia is more invisible than defeated. The anti-Mafia struggle has taken great strides, paying in the process a terrible cost, but even now, as the concept and practice of Mafia extends ever more beyond its original significance and geographical extension, those who are in the front line of that fight *never* receive that constant support and protection from the state which they so clearly merit and need. Nor yet has enough been done, or so it seems from the outside, to create around them that civil education and civil society which is their best protection.[87]

Furthermore, the anti-Mafia magistrates have failed to demonstrate unequivocally the links between Mafia and high-ranking politicians upon which so much of the organization's fortunes have been based. The case against Giulio Andreotti for association with the Mafia was dismissed in October, 1999.[88] His acquittal dented the prestige of the Palermo Procura, and made it much more difficult for political links to be investigated adequately. The centre-right politicians, especially those of Forza Italia, never ceased to attack the anti-Mafia magistrates, for reasons of their own.

The list of hoped-for changes only partially realized, or not realized at all, could continue for some time: the failure to legislate to ensure a much greater presence of women in Italy's institutions, which remain a firm enclave of male supremacy; the weak and ineffective measures to protect the environment; the haltering progress of educational reform (one of the great promises of the Prodi government). As for the themes that have been constantly present in this volume, the sensibility of government to civil society, the need to take seriously the relationship between families and the state, the abandonment of clientelistic and familist cultures, the bridging of the gap between formal democratic culture and everyday life, these seem all to be far down the agenda of government, if indeed they are present at all.

However, it is all too easy to attribute to the political class, both of left and of right, the sole responsibility for the failures of a state or a society. In the last analysis, the strength of a democracy in a single country does not depend only upon the capability or the integrity of its ruling élite, but also upon the culture of its families and the energy of its citizens.

Statistical Appendix

Giulio Ghellini, Paul Ginsborg and Laura Neri

The statistical appendix that we present here differs slightly from that prepared for *A History of Contemporary Italy*, for two sets of reasons. The first is that the shorter time-span analysed in this volume has allowed us to enrich the quality of the information contained in the graphs and tables. A greater and more varied quantity of statistical information is available for the last twenty years and this means that fewer problems have arisen regarding comparison over time. We have defined four thematic areas – Families, Society, Economy and State. Within each of them, the reader can find both updates of material presented in the previous volume and new information on areas not previously covered, such as the spatial proximity of Italian families (no. 8), the weight of retailing in the service sector (no. 30), the growth in advertising on television (nos. 31 and 32), etc.

In the second place, Italy's continuing integration into Europe has stimulated us to provide a greater wealth of European statistics than previously, so that Italy can be compared at the very least with the other principal EU countries (Germany, France and Great Britain). In this way the reader can find comparative statistical information on a number of the major themes analysed in this volume, such as total fertility rates (nos. 3 and 4), consumption habits (nos. 16 and 17), immigration (no. 19), etc.

As in *A History of Contemporary Italy*, we have decided for numerous tables to adopt a division of the data into four geographical areas: the North-west, the North-east and Centre, Lazio, the South and islands.* This territorial subdivision represents a variation on the famous scheme of the 'Three Italies', first proposed in 1977 by Arnaldo Bagnasco in his book of the same name. Lazio has been treated as a case apart because of the predominance of Rome in that region, with its consequent distorting effect upon regional statistics. It thus

---

* The regions contained in the three agglomerated geographical areas are the following: for the North-west, the regions of the Val d'Aosta, Piedmont, Lombardy and Liguria; the North-east and Centre comprises Trentino-Alto Adige, Veneto, Friuli-Venezia Giulia, Emilia-Romagna, Marches, Tuscany, Umbria, the Abruzzi; and the South and islands contains Molise, Puglia, Basilicata, Calabria, Sicily and Sardinia.

seemed sensible not to combine the data from other central or southern regions.

The map below this introduction shows the territorial divisions chosen, and provides the shading key used to distinguish the four regions in the subsequent graphs. We have listed the sources for the tables and explanations of them, where appropriate, in the notes to the appendix on p. 353.

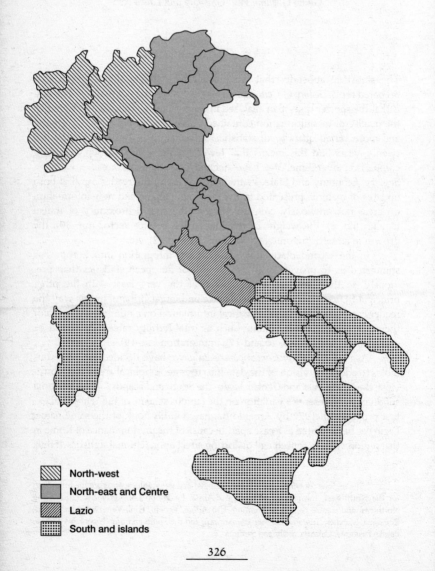

North-west

North-east and Centre

Lazio

South and islands

1 Average number of family members in Italy 1936–91

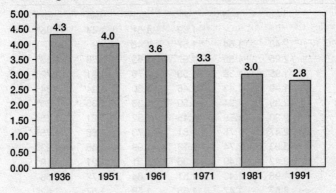

2 Family size by geographical area, 1951–91 (percentages)

	1951	1961	1971	1981	1991
Italy					
1 member	9.5	10.6	12.9	17.8	20.6
2–3 members	38.1	42.0	44.4	45.7	46.9
4 members	19.0	20.4	21.2	21.5	21.2
5 or more members	33.3	27.0	21.5	14.9	11.3
North-west					
1 member	12.5	13.7	16.1	21.3	24.3
2–3 members	45.9	49.7	49.9	49.6	50.8
4 members	19.2	19.4	20.1	19.9	18.6
5 or more members	22.4	17.2	13.9	9.2	6.2
North-east and Centre					
1 member	8.0	9.4	11.8	17.2	20.2
2–3 members	35.7	41.0	45.3	48.6	50.0
4 members	19.8	21.5	21.8	21.0	20.1
5 or more members	36.5	28.1	21.0	13.2	9.7
Lazio					
1 member	8.8	8.3	10.7	16.0	21.7
2–3 members	36.4	40.6	43.3	44.9	45.7
4 members	20.7	24.0	25.3	25.3	23.1
5 or more members	34.0	27.1	20.7	13.8	9.6
South and islands					
1 member	8.5	9.6	11.4	15.6	17.2
2–3 members	34.0	36.3	37.9	39.2	40.3
4 members	17.7	19.2	20.6	22.5	24.3
5 or more members	39.8	34.9	30.1	22.7	18.2

3   Total fertility rates in EU countries, 1970—98

	1970	1983	1988	1992	1994	1998
EUR(15)			1.59	1.51	1.44	1.45[b]
EUR(12)	2.40	1.64	1.57	1.48		
B	2.25	1.56	1.57	1.65	1.56	1.53[b]
DK	1.95	1.38	1.56	1.76	1.81	1.72[b]
D	1.99	1.43	1.46	1.30	1.24	1.34[b]
EL	2.39	1.94	1.50	1.38	1.35	1.30[b]
E	2.90	1.79	1.45	1.32	1.21	1.15[b]
F	2.47	1.78	1.81	1.73	1.66	1.75[b]
IRL	3.93	2.74	2.18	1.99	1.85	1.93[b]
I	2.42	1.49	1.36	1.31	1.21	1.19[b]
L	1.98	1.43	1.51	1.64	1.72	1.68
NL	2.57	1.47	1.55	1.59	1.57	1.62[b]
P	2.83	1.94	1.62	1.54	1.44	1.46
UK	2.43	1.77	1.82	1.79	1.74	1.72[b]
A[a]		1.54	1.44	1.49	1.44	1.34[b]
FIN[a]		1.74	1.69	1.85	1.85	1.70
S[a]		1.61	1.96	2.09	1.88	1.51

[a]Not part of the EC in 1970
[b]Provisional figures

4   Total fertility rates in EU countries (12), 1970—92

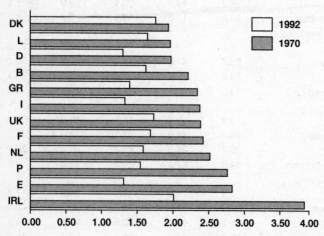

5 Separations and divorces per 1,000 marriages in Italy, by geographical area, 1981–94

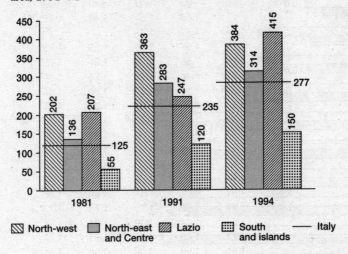

North-west North-east and Centre Lazio South and islands ——— Italy

6   Divorces per 1,000 inhabitants in EU countries (14), 1983–97

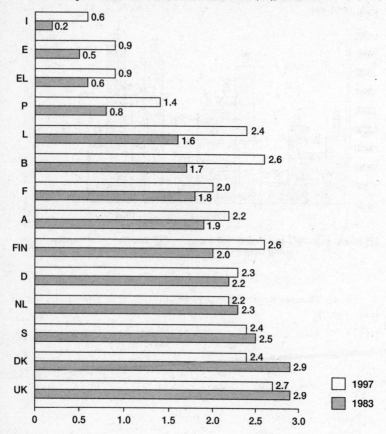

7 Live births outside marriage in EU countries (15) as percentage of all live births

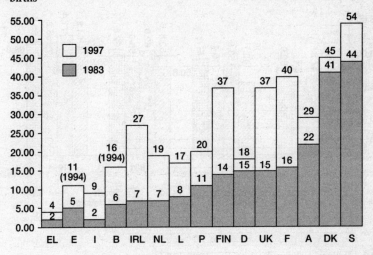

8 Average distance from mother to place of residence of married children in Italy, 1989

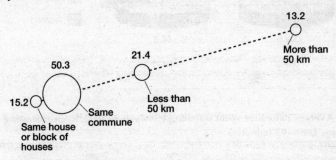

9   Home ownership in Italy, as a percentage of total households, by geographical area, 1961–91

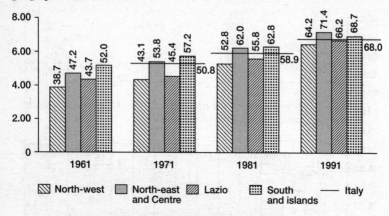

| | North-west | North-east and Centre | Lazio | South and islands | — Italy |

10   Italians' holiday destinations, 1982–98 (percentages)

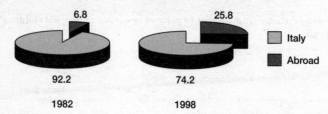

Italy
Abroad

1982 · 6.8 · 92.2
1998 · 25.8 · 74.2

11   Average daily time spent watching television in Italy, by broadcasting groups, 1988–95 (minutes)

	RAI	Fininvest	Others	Total
1988	82	65	26	173
1989	83	68	27	178
1990	95	68	26	189
1991	95	72	24	191
1992	93	87	22	202
1993	94	93	21	208
1994	99	93	21	213
1995	103	92	20	215

12   Average number of viewers at peak time (8.30–11.00 p.m.) in Italy, by broadcasting groups, 1988–99 (thousands)

	1988	1994	1999
RAI	9,868	11,859	12,133
Fininvest	4,564	10,672	10,197
Others	1,423	2,014	2,194
Total	15,855	24,545	24,524

13   Average number of viewers at peak time (8.30–11.00 p.m.) in Italy, by broadcasting groups, 1988–99 (thousands)

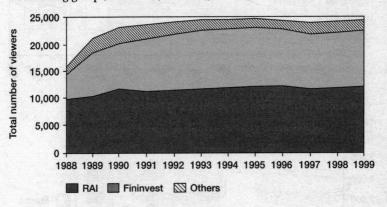

14   Cars in Italy per 1,000 inhabitants, 1951–97

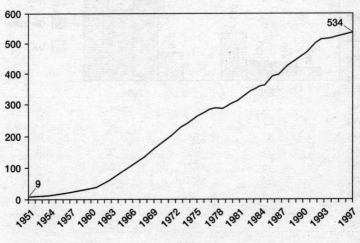

15 Passenger arrivals in Italian airports, 1967–96

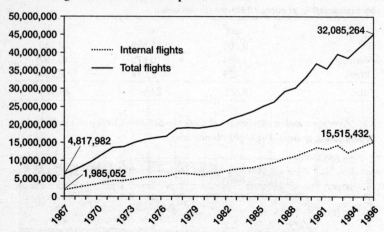

16 Number of mobile phones in 4 EU countries, 1990–94 (thousands)

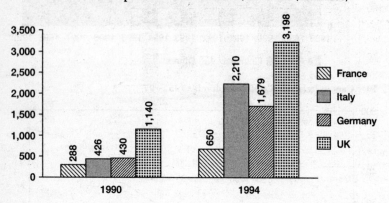

17 Expenditure on clothing and footwear in EU countries (12), 1992 (percentage of total consumption)

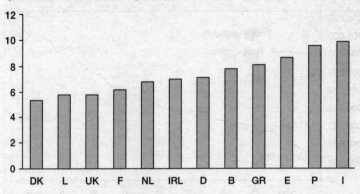

18 Percentage of the population (18–74) attending Mass or other equivalent religious service in Italy, by gender and age group, 1994

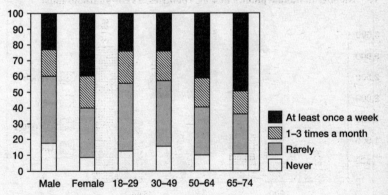

19 Non-EEA citizens living in EEA regions, as percentage of total population, 1996

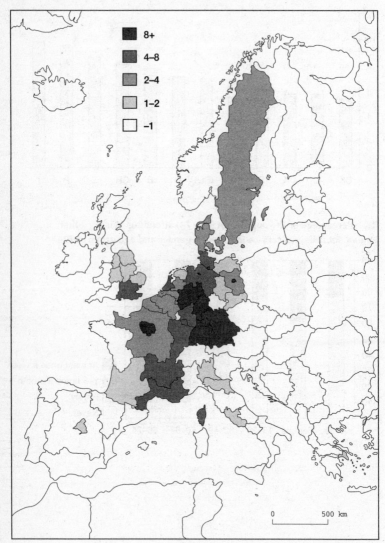

20 **Percentage of persons expressing post-materialist values in EU countries (11), 1986–7 (average figures)**

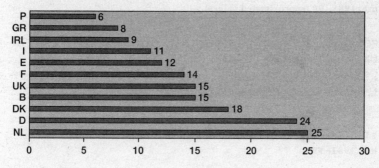

21 **Percentage of persons expressing materialist and post-materialist values in 4 EU countries, 1986–7, by age cohort (average figures)**

| | Germany | | United Kingdom | | France | | Italy | |
	mat.	post-mat.	mat.	post-mat.	mat.	post-mat.	mat.	post-mat.
15–24	9	35	13	20	26	16	25	17
25–34	14	30	22	15	32	16	25	14
35–44	20	26	20	17	32	20	32	12
45–54	18	21	19	14	40	7	42	7
55–64	20	16	26	10	37	10	44	7
65–74	28	13	30	13	48	5	48	3

22 **Composition of the working population by social class in Italy, 1951–93 (percentages)**

	1951	1971	1983	1993
Entrepreneurs, managers and professionals	2	3	3	3
Urban middle class comprising:	26	38	46	52
private sector employees	5	9	10	11
public employees	8	11	16	18
artisans	5	5	6	6
shopkeepers and traders	6	8	9	11
Peasant proprietors	31	12	8	6
Working class comprising:	41	47	43	39
agricultural workers	12	6	4	3
industrial workers	23	31	28	25
shop, transport, service-sector workers	6	10	11	11

23 Average exchange rates in Italy for some foreign currencies, in Italian lire, 1981–99 (approximated values)

	1981	1986	1991	1996	1998	1999
ECU/Euro	1,264	1,462	1,534	1,933	1,926	1,927
UK	2,284	2,187	2,187	2,409	2,877	2,940
Germany	503	687	748	1,026	987	990
France	209	215	220	302	294	295

24 Average exchange rates in Italy for some foreign currencies, in Italian lire, 1981–99

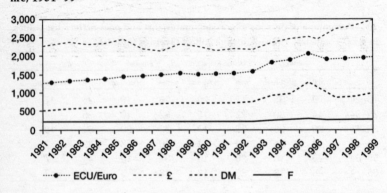

25 Consumer price trends in 4 EU countries, 1980–95

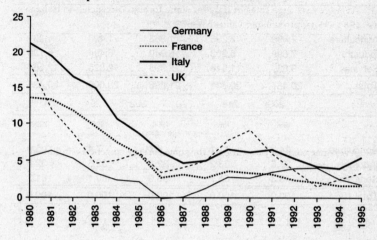

26 Number of employed per sector of the economy in Italy, 1980–98

	1980	1985	1990 (absolute values)	1995	1998
Agriculture	2,899	2,296	1,863	1,490	1,201
Industry	7,699	6,892	6,940	6,494	6,730
Services	9,889	11,548	12,593	12,025	12,504
Total	20,487	20,736	21,396	20,009	20,435

	1980	1985	1990 (percentage values)	1995	1998
Agriculture	14.1	11.1	8.7	7.4	5.9
Industry	37.6	33.2	32.4	32.5	32.9
Services	48.3	55.7	58.9	60.1	61.2
Total	100.0	100.0	100.0	100.0	100.0

27 Composition of added value by sector in Italy, 1980–98

	1980	1985	1990 (absolute values)	1995	1998
Agriculture	21,595	34,243	41,131	50,895	52,323
Industry	144,836	266,585	431,357	575,167	633,386
Services	176,794	395,118	818,291	1,133,459	1,321,648
Total	343,225	695,946	1,290,779	1,759,521	2,007,357

	1980	1985	1990 (percentage values)	1995	1998
Agriculture	6.3	4.9	3.2	2.9	2.6
Industry	42.1	38.3	33.4	32.1	31.5
Services	51.6	56.8	63.4	65.0	65.9
Total	100.0	100.0	100.0	100.0	100.0

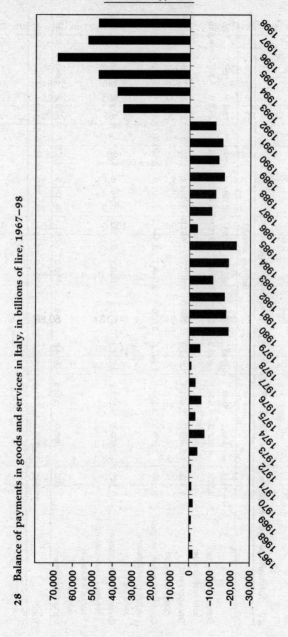

28 Balance of payments in goods and services in Italy, in billions of lire, 1967–98

29 Job units in the Italian service sector, 1987–98 (by type of activity) (thousands)

(absolute values)

	1987	1988	1989	1990	1991	1992	1993	1994	1995	1996	1997	1998
Shops, hotels, bars and restaurants	4,924.7	4,962.3	4,944.1	4,995.3	5,040.3	5,029.8	4,916.9	4,599.4	4,580.3	4,578.8	4,527.5	4,556.9
Transport and communication	1,439.3	1,465.2	1,491.4	1,513.9	1,492.0	1,480.7	1,467.0	1,384.4	1,332.5	1,365.8	1,338.4	1,366.4
Credit, insurance, estate agents, professional services	3,068.3	3,205.0	3,323.4	3,447.8	3,530.4	3,536.1	3,444.3	2,321.6	2,400.0	2,510.1	2,606.1	2,692.9
General administrative services, defence, state social insurance services	3,543.7	3,602.5	3,623.2	3,624.1	3,642.7	3,658.5	3,638.6	1,443.6	1,427.1	1,412.2	1,394.9	1,377.5
Various services	585.7	595.0	599.8	614.8	656.0	689.5	691.1	4,371.5	4,422.7	4,473.2	4,491.6	4,535.2
Total	13,561.7	13,830.0	13,981.9	14,195.9	14,361.4	14,394.6	14,157.9	14,120.5	14,162.6	14,340.1	14,358.5	14,528.9

30 Job units in the Italian service sector: the proportional share of commerce, 1998 (percentage)

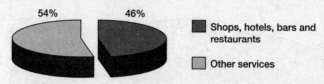

54%   46%

■ Shops, hotels, bars and restaurants

▨ Other services

31 Net advertising investments in selected mass media, Italy, 1980–99 (millions of lire)

	1980	1985	1990	1995	1999
Press	710,712	1,454,086	2,955,557	3,287,914	4,819,652
TV RAI	171,444	631,633	1,151,289	1,645,956	2,403,111
TV comm.	86,644	1,241,294	2,331,536	3,191,106	4,565,245

32 Number of advertisements on Italian television, 1982–99

	1982	1985	1990	1995	1997	1999
RAI	37,433	69,261	86,286	171,283	167,471	174,263
TV comm.	113,914	382,246	734,747	743,718	765,076	773,610

33 Persons seeking employment in Italy, by gender, 1981–98 (thousands)

	Women	Men		Women	Men
1981	1,096	799	1990	1,574	1,177
1982	1,143	909	1991	1,511	1,142
1983	1,272	992	1992	1,573	1,226
1984	1,377	1,013	1993	1,236	1,098
1985	1,358	1,023	1994	1,310	1,250
1986	1,496	1,115	1995	1,414	1,311
1987	1,604	1,228	1996	1,428	1,335
1988	1,645	1,240	1997	1,456	1,348
1989	1,646	1,220	1998	1,431	1,313

Statistical Appendix

34 Persons seeking employment in Italy, by gender, 1981–98 (thousands)

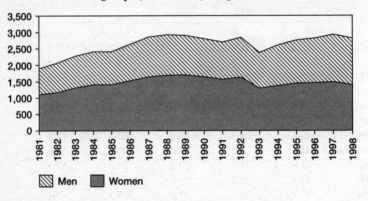

35 Rates of youth unemployment in Italy, by gender and age group, 1984–99

	15–19	20–24	25–29	Total 15–29	Total over 15
			Men		
1984	35.9	22.9	8.9	19.6	6.8
1985	37.7	24.3	9.2	20.4	7.0
1986	37.1	24.5	10.3	20.6	7.4
1987	38.2	25.9	11.9	22.1	8.1
1988	35.2	25.7	12.5	21.6	8.1
1989	34.0	25.1	12.8	21.0	8.1
1990	32.4	23.1	11.9	19.4	7.3
1991	32.2	24.4	11.5	19.4	7.5
1992	35.3	25.6	12.7	20.6	8.1
1993	30.9	25.1	12.3	19.4	7.8
1994	33.3	27.8	13.7	21.2	8.7
1995	32.7	28.8	14.7	21.9	9.2
1996	30.4	29.1	15.4	22.0	9.4
1997	30.9	28.3	16.2	22.2	9.5
1998	36.4	27.8	15.7	22.2	9.1
1999	36.1	27.4	15.2	21.5	8.8

35 Rates of youth unemployment *(contd.)* –

	15–19	20–24	25–29	Total 15–29	Total over 15
			Women		
1984	52.7	34.4	18.8	32.9	17.1
1985	53.5	35.6	19.5	33.4	17.3
1986	50.8	37.0	21.3	33.8	17.8
1987	51.4	38.1	23.6	35.0	18.7
1988	49.9	37.5	24.4	34.5	18.8
1989	48.9	36.9	24.5	33.9	18.7
1990	46.6	34.3	23.3	31.5	17.1
1991	44.7	33.0	22.9	30.2	16.8
1992	47.8	34.7	23.2	31.3	17.3
1993	43.1	32.9	19.5	27.9	14.8
1994	42.4	34.7	21.5	29.1	15.7
1995	44.2	37.4	22.9	30.9	16.6
1996	43.6	37.9	22.3	30.7	16.5
1997	43.1	38.1	23.6	31.3	16.7
1998	49.4	36.4	23.4	30.8	16.3
1999	47.6	34.9	22.6	29.5	15.7

36 GDP pro capita at market prices for 4 EU countries, 1982–94 (1985 = 100)

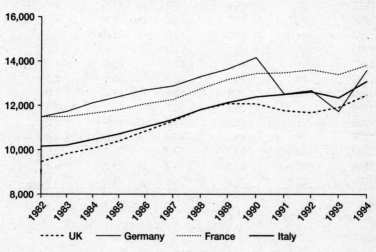

37 Overall spending on scientific research, 1981–93 (percentages of GDP)

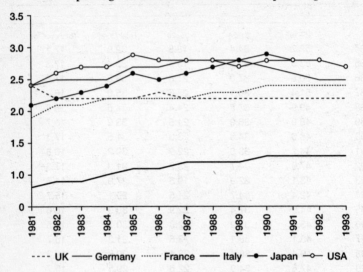

38 Elections to the Chamber of Deputies in Italy, valid votes per party, 1983–2001 (percentages)

	1983	1987	1992	1994[a]	1996[a]	2001[a]
DP	1.5	1.7				
PRC			5.6	6.1	8.6	5.0
PCI	29.9	26.6				
Comunisti Italiani						1.7
PDS/DS			16.1	20.4	21.1	16.6
La Rete			1.9	1.9		
Fed. Verdi[b]		2.5	2.8	2.7	2.5	2.2
La Margherita[c]						14.5
Radicali/Lista Pannella[d]	2.2	2.6	1.2	3.5	1.9	2.2
PSI	11.4	14.3	13.6	2.2		
PSDI	4.1	3.0	2.7			
PRI	5.1	3.7	4.4			
Lista Di Pietro						3.9
Lista Dini					4.3	
DC	32.9	34.3	29.7			
PPI[e]				11.1	6.8	
Patto Segni				4.7		
Democrazia Europea						2.4
CCD-CDU					5.8	3.2
Forza Italia				21.0	20.6	29.5
PLI	2.9	2.1	2.9			
MSI DN	6.8	5.9	5.4			
AN				13.5	15.7	12.0
Lega Nord[f]		0.5	8.7	8.4	10.1	3.9
Others with seats	1.2	1.5	1.4	1.7	0.9	
Others without seats	2.1	1.8	3.6	2.9	1.7	2.9
	100.0	100.0	100.0	100.0	100.0	100.0

[a] The statistics for 1994, 1996 and 2001 refer only to the proportional vote
[b] In 2001, allied with socialists
[c] In 2001, coalition of PPI, Democratici, Lista Dini (Rinnovamento Italiano)
[d] In 1996, Lista Pannella/Sgarbi; in 2001, Lista Pannella/Bonino
[e] In 1994, the PPI also included the CCD/CDU.
[f] In 1987, Lega Lombarda

39   Elections to the Chamber of Deputies in Italy, percentage of non-voters, 1948–2001

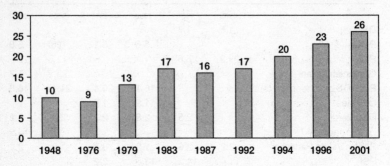

40   Level of satisfaction with the way democracy is working (percentage of those not satisfied, or not at all satisfied), certain EU countries, 1985–94

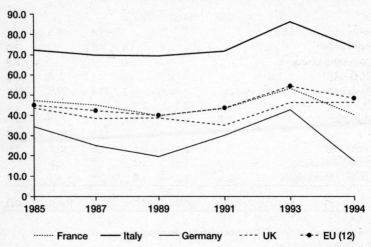

41 Educational qualifications of Italians over 6 years of age, by geographical area, 1951–91 (percentages)

	1951	1961	1971	1981	1991
Italy					
Degree	1.0	1.3	1.8	2.8	3.8
Secondary school	3.3	4.3	6.9	11.5	18.6
Middle school	5.9	9.6	14.7	23.8	30.7
Elementary school, or literate but without qualifications	76.9	76.5	71.4	58.8	44.8
Illiterate	12.9	8.3	5.2	3.1	2.1
North-west					
Degree	1.1	1.4	1.8	2.7	3.9
Secondary school	3.9	4.8	7.0	12.1	19.8
Middle school	8.6	12.7	17.4	26.6	32.8
Elementary school, or literate but without qualifications	83.6	79.3	72.5	57.8	42.8
Illiterate	2.8	1.8	1.3	0.8	0.7
North-east and Centre					
Degree	0.8	1.1	1.6	2.6	3.8
Secondary school	3.0	3.9	6.4	11.3	19.0
Middle school	5.3	8.8	14.5	23.8	30.0
Elementary school, or literate but without qualifications	81.6	80.3	74.1	60.4	46.0
Illiterate	9.3	5.9	3.4	1.9	1.2
Lazio					
Degree	2.2	2.6	3.4	4.5	5.8
Secondary school	5.4	7.0	10.2	15.6	23.8
Middle school	9.0	13.7	18.2	25.9	30.7
Elementary school, or literate but without qualifications	73.2	70.2	64.4	51.9	38.3
Illiterate	10.2	6.5	3.8	2.1	1.4
South and islands					
Degree	0.9	1.2	1.7	2.6	3.3
Secondary school	2.6	3.5	6.4	10.0	15.8
Middle school	4.0	6.9	11.5	20.9	29.7
Elementary school, or literate but without qualifications	67.7	72.1	69.6	60.1	46.9
Illiterate	24.8	16.3	10.8	6.4	4.3

42 Percentage of those in Italy with degrees or secondary-school diplomas, by geographical area, 1951–91

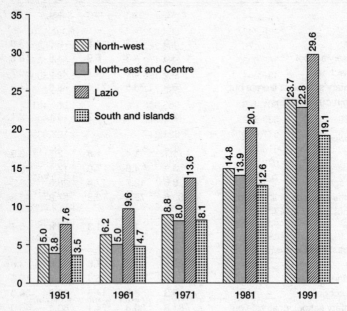

43 Number of university students in Italy, by gender, 1981/2−1996/7 (thousands)

	Women	Men	Total
1981/82	436,748	564,822	1,001,570
1982/83	444,176	556,347	1,000,523
1983/84	465,008	569,179	1,034,187
1984/85	495,344	588,156	1,083,500
1985/86	507,038	582,757	1,089,795
1986/87	501,475	563,006	1,064,481
1987/88	539,882	591,717	1,131,599
1988/89	577,618	621,217	1,198,835
1989/90	616,587	651,788	1,268,375
1990/91	672,276	686,675	1,358,951
1991/92	722,561	730,108	1,452,669
1992/93	755,631	770,987	1,526,618
1993/94	800,151	771,855	1,572,006
1994/95	836,746	766,216	1,602,962
1995/96	852,485	765,135	1,617,620
1996/97	850,477	745,165	1,595,642

44 Number of university students in Italy, by gender (women overtaking men), 1981/2−1993/4

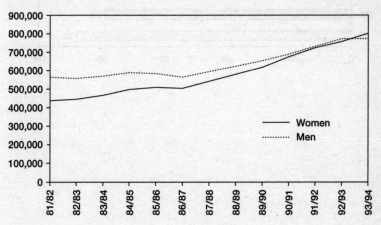

45 Population aged 25–64 by educational qualification, 4 EU countries, 1991 (percentages)

	Middle school diploma	Secondary school diploma	Degree and similar
UK	35	49	16
D	18	60	22
I	72	22	6
F	50	35	15

46 Population aged 25–34 with at least a secondary-school diploma, EU countries (10), 1991 (percentages)

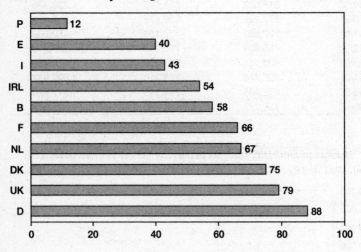

Notes to Statistical Appendix

Families

1 Average number of family members in Italy 1936–91.
Source: our elaboration of data from ISTAT.

2 Family size by geographical area, 1951–91 (percentages).
Source: our elaboration of data from ISTAT.

3 Total fertility rates in EU countries, 1970–98.
This indicator measures on average how many children a woman has from the beginning to the end of her fertility cycle (15–49 years old); data relating to Germany (D) is comprehensive also of the ex Federal Republic of Germany. This is also valid for table 6.
Source: our elaboration of data from Eurostat.

4 Total fertility rates in EU countries (12), 1970–92.
Source: our elaboration of data from table 3.

5 Separations and divorces per 1,000 marriages in Italy, by geographical area, 1981–94.
Source: our elaboration of data from ISTAT.

6 Divorces per 1,000 inhabitants in EU countries (14), 1983–97.
In this table, differently from the previous one, only divorces are taken into consideration. For Italy a clear distinction has to be made between separations and divorces. Not only do they entail two separate legal procedures, but also more than 40 per cent of separations are not converted into divorces. Data relating to Ireland (IRL) is not available, since divorce was illegal in that country for the period under consideration.
Source: our elaboration of data from Eurostat.

7 Live births outside marriage in EU countries (15), as percentage of all live births. Children born outside marriage are understood to be those born out of non-legally recognized unions.
Source: our elaboration of data from Eurostat.

8 Average distance from mother to place of residence of married children in Italy, 1989.
This table is a representation in graphic and statistical terms of a key indicator

of Italian families' 'spatial and emotional proximity', to which reference has been made in Chapter 3, pp. 74–6.
Source: our elaboration of data from ISTAT.

9 Home ownership in Italy, as a percentage of total households, by geographical area, 1961–91.
Source: our elaboration of data from ISTAT.

Society

10 Italians' holiday destinations, 1982–98 (percentages).
'Abroad' includes all those who spent holiday time solely or partially outside the national borders.
Source: our elaboration of data from ISTAT.

11 Average daily time spent watching television in Italy, by broadcasting groups, 1988–95 (minutes).
For the purposes of this table and the two following ones, the Italian population is taken to consist of individuals of more than four years old. The Auditel system surveys the presence in front of the television set of a wide sample of families (about 5,000). Each is equipped with an instrument which detects automatically the channel to which the family is tuned. However, the system requires that the number and type of viewers at any given time is indicated by a member of the family.
Source: our elaboration of data from Auditel.

12 Average number of viewers at peak time (8.30–11.00 p.m.) in Italy, by broadcasting groups, 1988–99 (thousands).
Source: our elaboration of data from Auditel.

13 Average number of viewers at peak time (8.30–11.00 p.m.) in Italy, by broadcasting groups, 1988–99 (thousands).
Source: our elaboration of data from table 12.

14 Cars in Italy per 1,000 inhabitants, 1951–97.
Data are relative to cars for which road tax has been paid in the various years under consideration.
Source: our elaboration of data from ISTAT.

15 Passenger arrivals in Italian airports, 1967–96.
These figures do not count transfers.
Source: our elaboration of data from ISTAT.

16 Number of mobile phones in 4 EU countries, 1990–94 (thousands).
Source: OECD for countries other than Italy and Telecom Italia for Italy.

17 Expenditure on clothing and footwear in EU countries (12), 1992 (percentage of total consumption).
Source: our elaboration of data from Eurostat.

18 Percentage of the population (18–74) attending Mass or other equivalent religious service in Italy, by gender and age groups, 1994.
Equivalent religious services to the Mass are considered for non-Catholics;

attendance at Mass due to funerals, weddings, etc. are not included.
Source: our elaboration of data from V. Cesareo *et al.*, *La religiosità in Italia*, Milano, 1995, pp. 340–41.

19 Non-EEA citizens living in EEA regions, as percentage of the total population, 1996. EEU = EU + EFTA (European Free Trade Association countries without Switzerland).
Statistics on foreign residents are assembled by Eurostat in cooperation with the national statistical bureaux, whose methods of data collection are not uniform. These statistics have, therefore, to be read with a certain amount of caution. It should be noted that the data does not include unregistered immigrants.
Source: Eurostat.

20 Percentage of persons expressing post-materialist values in EU countries (11), 1986–7 (average figures).
For the distinction between materialist and post-materialist values, deriving from the surveys and analyses conducted by Ronald Inglehart, see above, Chapter 4, pp. 128–9.
Data relating to Luxembourg are not available.
Source: Eurobarometer.

21 Percentage of persons expressing materialist and post-materialist values in 4 EU countries, 1986–7, by age cohort (average figures).
Source: Eurobarometer.

22 Composition of the working population by social class in Italy, 1951–93 (percentages).
The working population is defined as that group which is in work or which is actively looking for a job. There are obviously enormous obstacles to achieving a homogeneous classification of the working population by social class. This table summarizes the results of the research of Paolo Sylos Labini over the span of two decades. See his works: *Saggio sulle classi sociali*, Bari, 1974, and *Le classi sociali negli anni '80*, Bari, 1986, as well as Ginsborg, *A History*, graph 11, p. 433.
Source: P. Sylos Labini, *La crisi italiana*, Bari, 1995, p. 23.

Economy

23 Average exchange rates in Italy for some foreign currencies, in Italian lire, 1981–99.
Source: Banca d'Italia.

24 Average exchange rates in Italy for some foreign currencies, in Italian lire, 1981–99.
Source: Our elaboration of data from table 23.

25 Consumer price trends in 4 EU countries, 1980–95.
Source: OECD.

26 Number of employed per sector of the economy in Italy, 1980–98.
Source: ISTAT.

27 Composition of added value by sector in Italy, 1980–98.
Source: ISTAT.

28 Balance of payments in goods and services, Italy, in billions of lire, 1967–98.
Source: ISTAT.

29 Job units in the Italian service sector, 1987–98 (by type of activity) (thousands).
The measurement of job units is obtained by transforming the total sum of work
experience – corresponding to all persons with a job – into homogeneous units
in respect to the quantity of work undertaken. This quantity is measured by the
number of working hours effectively undertaken.
Source: ISTAT.

30 Job units in the Italian service sector: the proportional share of commerce, 1998
(percentage).
Source: our elaboration of data from ISTAT.

31 Net advertising investments in selected mass media, Italy, 1980–99 (millions of
lire).
The data presented in this table represents an estimate, undertaken by Nielsen,
of the growth of investments in advertisement, net of the discounts usually
granted on official tariffs. Nielsen is a multinational company specializing in
market research, especially in the fields of advertising and consumer behaviour.
Source: Our elaboration of data Nielsen Nasa/IBI.

32 Number of advertisements on Italian television, 1982–99.
Source: Our elaboration of data Nielsen Nasa/IBI.

33 Persons seeking employment in Italy, by gender, 1981–98 (thousands).
Source: ISTAT.

34 Persons seeking employment in Italy, by gender, 1981–98 (thousands).
Source: Our elaboration of data from table 33.

35 Rates of youth unemployment in Italy, by gender and age group, 1984–99.
The unemployment rate is a typical indicator used in the analysis of the labour
market and represents the number of persons actively seeking a job, calculated
as a percentage of the total labour force.
Source: our elaboration of data from ISTAT.

36 GDP pro capita at market prices for 4 EU countries, 1982–94 (1985 = 100).
The GDP values are expressed with reference to PPP (purchasing power
parities), calculated by the OECD to compare different countries.
Source: OECD.

37 Overall spending on scientific research, 1981–93 (percentages of GDP).
Source: *Lettere d'affari*, Centro Statistica Aziendale, no. 589.

State

38 Elections to the Chamber of Deputies in Italy, valid votes per party, 1983–2001
(percentages).
Source: Our elaboration of data from ISTAT and Ministero dell' Interno.

39 Elections to the Chamber of Deputies in Italy, percentage of non-voters, 1983–
2001.
Source: Our elaboration of data from ISTAT and Ministero dell' Interno.

40 Level of satisfaction with the way democracy is working (percentage of those not satisfied, or not at all satisfied), certain EU countries, 1985–94.

The data is taken from a questionnaire which has formed part of a survey conducted by various European research institutions from 1970 onwards. The interviewees number approximately 1,000 per country, and are asked to express their opinion about the functioning of democracy in their own country. Four typologies of answers are considered: very satisfied, satisfied, not satisfied, not at all satisfied.

Source: Eurobarometer.

41 Educational qualifications of Italians over 6 years of age, by geographical area, 1951–91 (percentages).

Source: Our elaboration of data from ISTAT.

42 Percentage of those in Italy with degrees or secondary-school diplomas, by geographical area, 1951–91.

Source: Our elaboration of data from table 41.

43 Number of university students in Italy, by gender, 1981/2–1996/7 (thousands).

Source: Our elaboration of data from ISTAT.

44 Number of university students in Italy, by gender (women overtaking men), 1981/2–1993/4.

Source: our elaboration of data from table 43.

45 Population aged 25–64 by educational qualification, 4 EU countries, 1991 (percentages).

Notwithstanding the difficulties and approximations resulting from a comparison between different educational systems, it seemed worthwhile ending with two comparative tables. The backwardness of Italy in comparison with the other major European countries emerges clearly.

Source: OCSE.

46 Population aged 25–34 with at least a secondary-school diploma, EU countries (10), 1991 (percentages).

Data for Greece and Luxembourg is not available.

Source: OCSE.

Notes

Preface

1 P. Volponi, *Memoriale*, Torino, 1991 [1st edn, 1962], pp. 33 and 41.

2 E. Berlinguer, *Austerità, occasione per trasformare l'Italia*, Roma, 1977, pp. 11–12.

3 See the oft-quoted passage where Tancredi explains to the Prince: 'If we want things to stay as they are, things will have to change'; G. di Lampedusa, *The Leopard*, London, 1963 [1st Italian edn, 1958], p. 23.

4 P. Ginsborg, *A History of Contemporary Italy*, London, 1990, pp. 401–5.

5 For an exemplary analysis, M. Revelli, 'Economia e modello sociale nel passaggio tra fordismo e toyotismo', in P. Ingrao and R. Rossanda (eds.), *Appuntamenti di fine secolo*, Roma, 1995, pp. 161–224.

6 See below, Chapter 1, pp. 7–13.

7 L. Gallino, 'Tecnologia/occupazione: la rottura del circolo virtuoso', *Quaderni di Sociologia*, vol. XXXVIII–XXXIX (1994–5), no. 7, p. 5.

8 Eurostat, *Statistiche generali dell'Unione Europea*, Luxembourg, 1996, p. 164, table 3.28.

9 For an extended discussion of this approach, see P. Ginsborg, 'Family, civil society and the state in contemporary European history: some methodological considerations', *Contemporary European History*, vol. IV (1995), no. 3, pp. 249–73.

10 S. Moller Okin, *Justice, Gender and the Family*, New York, 1989, p. 9.

11 For an original, if often superficial attempt to examine the relationships between family and economy on a global scale, see F. Fukuyama, *Trust*, New York, 1995.

12 For the relationship between emitting and receiving zones in the use of family metaphors, see F. Rigotti, *Il potere e le sue metafore*, Milano, 1992, p. 81.

13 'In these times, we often return to the expression "domestic church", which the Vatican Council made its own, and whose content we wish to ensure remains always alive and actual'; John Paul II, *Lettera alle famiglie*, Milano, 1994, p. 5, §3.

14 See below, Chapter 5, p. 148.

15 H. Seton-Watson, *The Russian Empire, 1801–1917*, Oxford, 1967, p. vi.

Notes to pages 1–3

Chapter 1: *The Italian Economy: Constraints and Achievements*

1   For the early history of the G7, see R. D. Putnam and N. Payne, *Hanging Together. The Seven-Power Summits*, London, 1984, pp. 16ff.

2   See, for instance, the emblematic title of a recent collection of essays on this subject: M. Baldassari (ed.), *The Italian Economy: Heaven or Hell?*, London, 1994. For a similar view from Paris, J. Menet-Genty, 'Forces et faiblesses de l'Italie à l'échéance de 1993', in J. Menet-Genty (ed.), *L'Economie italienne*, Paris, 1992, pp. 261–8. For the concept of the semi-periphery applied to southern Europe, G. Arrighi (ed.), *Semiperipheral Development*, London, 1985.

3   V. Zamagni, *The Economic History of Italy, 1860–1990*, Oxford, 1993, p. 365, table 12.4. For 1994, see *World Trade Organisation. Focus*, no. 2 (1995), p. 8, table 5.

4   World Trade Organisation, *Annual Report 1998*, Geneva, 1998, vol. II, p. 92, table IV.30.

5   P. Guerrieri and C. Milana, *L'Italia e il commercio mondiale*, Bologna, 1990, pp. 241ff. The Middle East accounted for 5.1 per cent of Italian trade and North Africa 7 per cent. For the change of direction in Italy's trade in the post-war period, away from southern and eastern Europe towards the Common Market and the USA, see M. De Cecco and G. G. Migone, 'La collocazione internazionale dell'economia italiana', in R. J. B. Bosworth and S. Romano (eds.), *La politica estera italiana, 1860–1985*, Bologna, 1991, pp. 184–5.

6   Guerrieri and Milana, *L'Italia e il commercio mondiale*, pp. 258–9.

7   M. Porter, *The Competitive Advantage of Nations*, London, 1990, p. 691. The countries considered by Porter were Denmark, Germany, Italy, Japan, Korea, Singapore, Sweden, Switzerland, the United Kingdom and the United States.

8   Guerrieri and Milana, *L'Italia e il commercio mondiale*, pp. 34ff. This taxonomy is based on that proposed by K. Pavitt, 'Sectoral patterns of technical change: towards a taxonomy and a theory', *Research Policy*, vol. XII (1984), no. 6, and is used in preference to a more traditional but simplistic division into high, medium and low technology sectors. Pavitt's categories have in turn been criticized for their enduring hierarchical quality and technological determinism, and their implication that 'traditional' industries are in some way residual rather than themselves being capable of technological renewal and dynamism. For a critique along these lines, see A. Ginzburg and A. Simonazzi, 'Patterns of production and distribution in Europe: the case of the textile and clothing sector', in R. Schiattarella (ed.), *New Challenges for European and International Business*, Roma, 1995, p. 272.

9   Guerrieri and Milana, *L'Italia e il commercio mondiale*, pp. 342–3. For the position up until the second quarter of 1993, see P. Guerrieri, 'La collocazione internazionale dell'economia italiana', in P. Ginsborg (ed.), *Stato dell'Italia*, Milano, 1994, p. 394.

10   World Trade Organisation, *Annual Report 1998*, vol. I, p. 124, table IV.72. Italy's

imports in textiles in the period 1980–97 diminished from 4.7 per cent to 4.1 per cent. The pre-eminent position of Hong Kong is almost entirely due to her re-exports. Much the same story can be told for clothing markets, with Italy maintaining her third place in world exports (8.4 per cent) in this sector in 1997; ibid., p. 131, table IV.80.

11 ibid., p. 101, table IV.43. Italian imports of chemical products constituted 5.6 per cent of the world total in 1980, 6.6 per cent in 1990, and 5.3 per cent in 1997.

12 The changing picture in each of the four compartments and the evolution of Italy's international specialization from 1970 to 1993 are analysed in Guerrieri, 'La collocazione internazionale', pp. 383ff.

13 C. Secchi, 'Introduzione', in C. Secchi (ed.), *L'internazionalizzazione dei servizi e l'economia italiana*, Milano, 1990, p. 11, n. 1. Not all the experts in the field are in agreement in including factor incomes in a general definition of international commerce in services. If they are excluded, the volume of world trade in services would drop from 28.5 per cent to 18.6 per cent (1986 figures). M. Kidron and R. Segal, *The State of the World Atlas*, London, 1995, p. 147, note that the value of world trade in services had doubled between 1982 and 1992, but also that many international financial transactions, transmitted electronically, often go unrecorded, especially when they are transactions between parent companies and their foreign affiliates.

14 World Trade Organisation, *Annual Report 1996*, Geneva, 1996, vol. II, pp. 164–5, which follows the guidelines laid down by the 5th edition (1993) of the *IMF Balance of Payments Manual*.

15 For overall statistics of Italy's world trade in services, see *World Trade Organisation. Focus*, no. 18 (1997), p. 9, table 6. For details of her position in the three categories of world trade in services, see World Trade Organisation, *Annual Report 1996*, vol. II, pp. 114–16, tables IV.61–3.

16 P. Genco and F. Maraschini, 'La collocazione internazionale delle società di ingegneria italiane', in F. Onida (ed.), *Il commercio internazionale dei servizi e la posizione dell'Italia*, Roma, 1989, pp. 267ff.

17 'Invisibles' include, alongside the three types of services listed above (transport, travel, and other commercial services), compensation of employees and investment income, and unilateral transfers, both public and private (such as transfers from non-resident workers).

18 This hierarchy of explanatory factors in the 'invisibles' sector follows that of R. S. Masera and S. Rossi, *La bilancia dei pagamenti*, Padova, 1993, pp. 291ff. For the growth in foreign debt see also A. Graziani, 'L'economia italiana e il suo inserimento internazionale', in *Storia dell'Italia repubblicana*, vol. III, pt 1, Torino, 1996, p. 375. For details of the deficit in energy, raw materials and agricultural products, see Masera and Rossi, *La bilancia*, p. 308, table 11.1. For a graph of Italy's balance-of-payments performance in this period, see Statistical Appendix, no. 28.

19 F. Padoa-Schioppa Kostoris, *Italy the Sheltered Economy*, Oxford, 1993, p. 225, n. 1.

20 Some British commentators claimed that the revision upwards in 1986 of Italian economic statistics, to take account of the hidden economy, was a typically Italian trick employed to allow talk of the *'sorpasso'*. However, as C. Tyler pointed out in the *Financial Times* at the time ('The statisticians remain coy', *Financial Times*, 'Survey on the Italian economy', 17 November 1987), the revision was based on the recommendations of a committee headed by Sir Claus Moser, former head of the UK's own Central Statistical Office. See also D. Verdura-Rechenmann, 'Le nouveau capitalisme: la fin des idées reçues', in Menet-Genty, *L'Economie italienne*, p. 220, who points out that the hidden economy accounted for only 4.6 per cent in a general revision upwards of 17.6 per cent in 1986. For the relative performance of Britain, Italy, Germany and France in terms of pro-capita income from 1982 to 1994, see Statistical Appendix, no. 36.

21 For EuroDisney, see 'I giostrai italiani conquistano Parigi', *Il Sole — 24 Ore*, 18 April 1992. The firm in question was that of Antonio Zamperla, which had also just won big commissions in Singapore and Hong Kong. For the story of De Benedetti and the SGB, G. Turani, *L'Ingegnere*, Milano, 1988, pp. 276—301.

22 Statistical Appendix, nos. 26 and 27.

23 Cf. W. Ochel and M. Wegner, *Service Economies in Europe*, London, 1987, p. 5.

24 T. P. Hill, 'On goods and services', *The Review of Income and Wealth*, vol. XXIII (1977), no. 3, pp. 315—38.

25 ibid., p, 317.

26 For typologies of this sort, and further discussion, Ochel and Wenger, *Service Economies in Europe*, p. 19, table 2.3; P. W. Daniels, *Service Industries in the World Economy*, Oxford, 1993, pp. 3ff.; J. N. Marshall, *Services and Uneven Development*, Oxford, 1988, pp. 12—19; C. Kassab, *Income and Equality*, New York, 1992, p. 5. In the national accounts a broad distinction is made between services destined for sale, and those that are not; see, for example, the ISTAT statistics reproduced in the Statistical Appendix, no. 29.

27 D. Siniscalco, *Beyond Manufacturing*, Torino, 1988, pp. 27—8.

28 There are, naturally, many other distinctions that can be added to the basic framework presented above. Hill, for instance, distinguishes between permanent and temporary services, between those that are reversible and irreversible, between physical and mental changes.

29 M. T. Daly, 'Transitional economic bases: from the mass production society to the world of finance', in P. W. Daniels, *Services and Metropolitan Development*, London, 1991, pp. 26 and 40; Daniels, *Service Industries in the World Economy*, pp. 14—15. See also S. Strange, *Casino Capitalism*, Oxford, 1986, and S. Strange, *Mad Money*, Manchester, 1998.

30 R. Mansell, *The New Telecommunications*, London, 1993; N. Abercrombie, *Television and Society*, London, 1996, pp. 74—104.

31 G. Esping-Andersen, 'Strutture di classe post-industriali: un confronto tra Germania, Svezia e Stati Uniti', in *Stato e Mercato*, no. 32 (1991), pp. 226–7 and 232–3.

32 Siniscalco, *Beyond Manufacturing*, argues that it is producer services that have grown most rapidly in Italy. His figures (table 2, p. 28) show producer service employment increasing from 28.8 to 41.4 per cent of all service employment between 1959 and 1982, while final trade declined slightly from 30.6 to 29.0 per cent and services for final demand dropped radically from 40.6 to 29.5 per cent. Furthermore he is convinced (p. 35) that the 'goods producing subsystems' (agricultural and energy products, manufacturing, building and construction *together* with final trade employment) still accounted for more than 65 per cent of total employment in 1982. G. Rey also emphasizes the striking increase in producer services in the 1980s; see his 'I mutamenti della struttura economica: fattori produttivi, distribuzione del reddito, domanda', in Confindustria Centri Studi, *L'Italia verso il 2000*, Roma, 1992, vol. 2, pp. 40–43. G. Sapelli, *L'Italia inafferabile*, Venezia, 1989, pp. 76–8, follows Siniscalco's lead. On the other hand, M. Paci repeatedly emphasizes the weakness of producer service employment in relation to that of other European countries, and as a percentage of total employment in the service sector in Italy; see M. Paci, 'Innovazione tecnologica, occupazione e politica sociale', in A. Ruberti (ed.), *Europa a confronto*, Bari, 1990, table 6, p. 314, which contains comparative data for the period 1978–87; M. Paci, *Il mutamento della struttura sociale in Italia*, Bologna, 1992, pp. 278–9. V. Castronovo, *Storia economica d'Italia*, Torino, 1995, p. 517, agrees with him.

33 See his interview with A. Recanatesi of February 1988, published in G. Amato, *Due anni al tesoro*, Bologna, 1990, p. 94.

34 P. L. Cotta, 'Le tecnologie e le banche', unpublished paper presented to the Convenzione Interbancaria per i problemi dell'automazione (CIPA), Roma, 29 April 1997, p. 6. Documenti CNEL, *Il terziario italiano nella competizione europea*, Roma, 1992, pp. 49ff. and 107–39. In 1989 the number of credit institutions of significant proportions was over 400, and their level of capitalization was no more than adequate; at the same date, bank employees numbered 318,000 and labour costs as a percentage of total operating costs were ten points higher in Italian banks than in those of France and Germany. For a good analysis of the structure and hierarchy of Italy's major banks in the 1990s see G. Bruno and L. Segreto, 'Finanza e industria in Italia (1963–1995)', in *Storia dell'Italia repubblicana*, vol. III, pt 1, pp. 648–56.

35 For insurance, Documenti CNEL, *Il terziario italiano*, pp. 62–3 and 77–86. For an entertaining account of the Milan stock exchange in its heady years, A. Friedman, *Ce la farà il capitalismo italiano?*, Milano, 1989, pp. 149–72.

36 See Statistical Appendix, nos. 11 and 12.

37 For details of the creation of Berlusconi's empire, see 'Dieci anni di televisione sotto il segno di Berlusconi', *Problemi dell'informazione*, vol. XV (1990), no. 4, pp. 487–622. For comparative figures on European publicity markets, W. Veltroni, *Io, Berlusconi e la RAI*, Roma, 1990, p. 121.

38 Presidenza del Consiglio dei Ministri, Dipartimento per la Funzione pubblica, *Rapporto suelle condizioni delle pubbliche amministrazioni*, Roma, 1993, p. 13.

39 Masera and Rossi, *La bilancia dei pagamenti*, p. 332, table 12.1. Taking 1970 as the base line of 100, industrial productivity in 1988 was 206.05, that of the public administration 100.91 (figure for 1987). Nominal wages had risen by 1988 to 1,459.7, compared to 1,358.6 in the public administration.

40 In September 1996 the management of the state railways was rocked by a major financial scandal with the arrest of Lorenzo Necci, the managing director. For a useful summary, see S. Carli, 'Fs, il "Progetto" finito negli scambi', *la Repubblica*, Affari e Finanza, 23 September 1996.

41 Cf. *Cultura del testo*, vol. II (1996), no. 6, which contains part of the proceedings of the Conference of January 1996 dedicated to the National Library in Florence. The Florentine library, for all its faults, was considerably more user-friendly than its Roman counterpart. For an effective critique, T. Gregory, 'Le biblioteche alla deriva', *Il Sole – 24 Ore*, 28 September 1997.

42 *Ministero per i Beni culturali e ambientali. Notiziario*, nos. 51–2 (1996), p. 19; R. De Gennaro, 'Imprenditori adottate Pompeii', *la Repubblica*, 21 September 1997. For a useful introduction, R. King, 'Italy: multi-faceted tourism', in A. M. Williams and G. Shaw (eds.), *Tourism and Economic Development*, London, 1991 [1st edn 1989], pp. 61–85.

43 For some indications on high-performing producer services in the 1980s, see G. Pellegrini, 'Integrazione e crescita dei servizi negli anni '80: l'altra faccia della ristrutturazione', *Rivista di Politica Economica*, vol. LXXI (1991), no. 4, pp. 3–21. For performance in the 1990s, World Trade Organisation, *Annual Report 1998*, vol. II, p. 139, table IV.91, and p. 47, table III.41.

44 OECD, *Economic Surveys: Italy, 1990–91*, Paris, 1991, diagram 19, 'Relative price levels in 1985 between Italy and the EC average'. Public services were by and large significantly cheaper than the EC average, though notoriously less efficient.

45 C. Secchi, 'Il turismo in Italia', in C. Secchi (ed.), *L'internazionalizzazione dei servizi*, p. 68.

46 F. Barca and I. Visco, 'L'economia italiana nella prospettiva europea: terziario protettivo e dinamica dei redditi nominali', in S. Miscossi and I. Visco (eds.), *Inflazione, concorrenza e sviluppo*, Bologna, 1993, pp. 78–9.

47 ISTAT, *Statistiche del commercio interno*, Roma, 1997, p. 13, table 1.2, and p. 14, table 1.5. The four categories of retailers were foodshops; clothing and fabrics; furniture, interior design and domestic appliances; other products and articles. Only this last category was in expansion in the period 1980–95.

48 For P. Sylos Labini's calculations, see his three books: *Saggio sulle classi sociali*, Bari, 1974, Appendix, table 2.2; *Le classi sociali negli anni '80*, Bari, 1986, Appendix, table 1.1; and *La crisi italiana*, Bari, 1995, p. 23, table 2. See also Statistical Appendix, nos. 22 and 30. For further discussion of shopkeepers, see below, Chapter 2, pp. 49ff.

49 Ginsborg, *A History*, p. 183.

50 ISTAT, *Statistiche del commercio interno*, p. 13, table 1.4; M. D'Antonio, 'Competition, development, inflation: the case of services', *Review of Economic Conditions in Italy*, no. 3 (1992), p. 334.

51 Ginzburg and Simonazzi, 'Patterns of production', pp. 262–8.

52 See below, p. 377, note 82.

53 R. E. Rowthorn and J. R. Wells, *Deindustrialisation and Foreign Trade*, Cambridge, 1987, pp. 5–6.

54 F. Barca, *Imprese in cerca di padrone*, Roma, 1994, pp. 171–2. For a good overview in English, see F. Amatori, 'Italy: the tormented rise of organizational capabilities between government and families', in A. D. Chandler, F. Amatori and J. Hikino, *Big Business and the Wealth of Nations*, Cambridge, 1997, pp. 246–76.

55 Revelli, 'Economia e modello sociale', pp. 178ff.; C. Romiti, *Questi anni alla FIAT* (ed. G. Pansa), Milano, 1988, p. 230.

56 For the events of the autumn of 1980, see Ginsborg, *A History*, pp. 403–5.

57 For some details of the firm's global activities up until 1994, see FIAT Archivio storico, *FIAT: le fasi della crescita*, Torino, 1996. For the company's relative standing in the European markets, A. Silbertson and C. P. Raymond, *The Changing Map of Industrial Europe*, London, 1996, p. 70, table 4.4. See also the important studies published to mark FIAT's centenary: C. Annibaldi and G. Berta (eds.), *Grande impresa e sviluppo italiano. Studi per i cento anni della FIAT*, 2 vols., Bologna, 1999; V. Castronovo, *FIAT. Storia di un' impresa, 1899–1999*, Milano, 1999.

58 For details of passenger transport in private cars, see Legambiente, *Ambiente Italia '93* (ed. G. Conte and G. Melandri), Roma, 1993, p. 155, table 1. See also Statistical Appendix, no. 14.

59 B. Anastasia, 'Il gruppo Zanussi: quadro storico e situazione attuale', in A. Dina (ed.), *Elettrodomestici flessibili*, Torino, 1990, pp. 34–7.

60 Bruno and Segreto, *Finanza e industria*, pp. 622–3 and 636–8.

61 Turani, *L'Ingegnere, passim*.

62 F. Barca *et al.*, *Assetti proprietari e mercato delle imprese*, Bologna, 1994, vol. I, p. 86, table 3.8.; ibid., vol. II, pp. 94–101. The large sample of mainly private companies with over fifty employees revealed the existence of four principal types of control: 'absolute', accounting for 13.8 per cent of firms; 'familial' (the components of a single family), 32.1 per cent; 'coalitional' (of non-kin partners, or of two or more closely connected families), 11.6 per cent; 'group' (a pyramid structure formed of more than one firm), 11.6 per cent. However, this last form was often little more than an *escamotage* for control concentrated in a single family firm at the top of the pyramid.

63 ibid., vol. I, pp. 205ff. See also the biting comments of M. De Cecco, 'Italia, "potenza" a gestione familiare', *la Repubblica*, Affari e Finanza, 27 February 1995.

64 OECD, *Economic Surveys, 1992–93. Italy*, Paris, 1993, p. 119, graph A1; Revelli, 'Economia e modello sociale', pp. 205–6.

65 Ginsborg, *A History*, pp. 283–5.

66 Friedman, *Ce la farà*, pp. 87—8, interview of 7 July 1989.

67 For the controversial history of this sale, A. Santagostino, *Fiat e Alfa Romeo: una privatizzazione riuscita?*, Milano, 1993. See also R. Bianchi, 'The privatisation of industry: the case of Alfa Romeo', in P. G. Corbetta, R. Leonardi and R. Y. Nanetti (eds.), *Italian Politics: a Review*, vol. I, London, 1988, pp. 109—25. For a journalistic account, very much from Prodi's point of view, R. F. Levi, *Il Professore*, Milano, 1996, pp. 94—114.

68 Some of the remaining problems emerged very clearly in the interesting testimony of G. Gallo, who was vice-president of the group from April 1991 to August 1992; see his *IRI Spa*, Milano, 1992, pp. 20ff.

69 R. Sitari, *L'Eni e le sfide del presente*, in F. Venanzi and M. Faggiari (eds.), *ENI, un'autobiografia*, Milano, 1994, pp. 302—3.

70 G. Roverato, *Nuovo Pignone. Le sfide della maturità*, Bologna, 1991.

71 OECD, *Economic Surveys, 1992—1993. Italy*, p. 119, graph A1. For Genoa, L. Caselli and A. Gozzi, 'Un'economia in declino', in A. Gibelli and P. Rugafiori (eds.), *Storia d'Italia. Le regioni. La Liguria*, Torino, 1994, pp. 901—5.

72 A. Bonomi, *Il capitalismo molecolare*, Torino, 1997, p. 61.

73 Among the principal works: M. J. Piore and C. F. Sabel, *The Second Industrial Divide*, New York, 1984; M. H. Best, *The New Competition*, Cambridge, 1990; A. Bagnasco and C. F. Sabel (eds.), *Small and Medium-Size Enterprises*, London, 1995.

74 S. Brusco and S. Paba, 'Per una storia dei distretti industriali italiani dal secondo dopoguerra agli anni novanta', in F. Barca (ed.), *Storia del capitalismo italiano*, Roma, 1997, pp. 277—8. A pioneering article was that by G. Becattini, 'Dal "settore" industriale al "distretto" industriale. Alcune considerazioni sull'unità di indagine dell'economia industriale', *Rivista di Economia e Politica Industriale*, vol. V (1979), no. 1, pp. 7—21.

75 Porter, *The Competitive Advantage*, pp. 210—25.

76 Brusco and Paba, 'Per una storia', p. 280.

77 E. and S. Bugatti, 'L'area sistema di Lumezzane', in F. Onida, G. F. Viesti and A. M. Falzoni (eds.), *I distretti industriali: crisi o evoluzione?*, Milano, 1992, pp. 345—54. Cf. M. Bongiovanni, 'Tra pentole e rubinetti l'autarchica Lumezzane', *Il Sole – 24 Ore*, 10 August 1991.

78 These are constant themes in the work of S. Brusco; see, for example, his *Piccole imprese e distretti industriali*, Torino, 1989.

79 Bongiovanni, 'Tra pentole e rubinetti'; Bonomi, *Il capitalismo molecolare*, p. 79.

80 Brusco e Paba, *Per una storia*, pp. 304—5; G. Becattini, *Distretti industriali e 'made in Italy'*, Torino, 1998, p. 138.

81 For the background to recent Italian design supremacy, see P. Sparke, *Italian Design. 1870 to the Present*, London, 1988; G. Albera and N. Monti, *Italian Modern. A Design Heritage*, New York, 1989.

82 A useful introduction is V. Balloni, 'L'industria della moda' in Ginsborg (ed.),

Stato dell'Italia, pp. 398–9. The evolution of the textile and clothing industry at an international level is traced in Ginzburg and Simonazzi, 'Patterns of production', *passim*. For an instructive comparison between small businesses in France, Britain and Italy, concentrating on textile firms in Lyons, Leicester and Como, see A. Bull, M. Pitt and J. Szarka, *Entrepreneurial Textile Communities*, London, 1993. The Como firm emerged as the most successful, with Leicester a poor third. The advantages accruing to British small business by Thatcherite attempts to revive it in the 1980s were largely wiped out by the severe economic recession from 1989 onwards.

83 Brusco and Paba, *Per una storia*, p. 286.

84 A. Pescarolo, 'Famiglia e impresa. Problemi di ricerca all'incrocio fra discipline', *Passato e Presente*, vol. XII (1994), no. 31, pp. 136–8. The author also notes a slight tendency towards 'de-familization', with the number of non-family firms exceeding for the first time those formed by horizontal kinship networks.

85 Bonomi, *Il capitalismo molecolare*, p. 37. For a welcome antidote to idealization, see F. Murray, 'Flexible specialisation in the "Third Italy"', *Capital and Class*, no. 33 (1987), pp. 84–95.

86 F. Farinelli, 'Lo spazio rurale nell'Italia di oggi', in P. Bevilacqua (ed.), *Storia dell'agricoltura italiana in età contemporanea*, vol. I, *Spazi e paesaggi*, Venezia, 1989, p. 231.

87 Istituto G. Tagliacarne, *Divari territoriali dello sviluppo agricolo nel decennio 1980–1990*, Milano, 1994, p. 18.

88 Farinelli, 'Lo spazio rurale', p. 233. For the massive use in the Po valley of pesticides and fertilizers, which had 'overturned the delicate environmental equilibrium of the most fertile land in our country', see C. Donnhauser, 'Agricoltura', in Lega per l'Ambiente, *Ambiente Italia. Rapporto 1989* (ed. G. Melandri), Torino, 1989, pp. 170–80. The provinces of Novara, Vercelli and Pavia were known as a sort of ecological Bermuda Triangle, with the largest consumption of weedkillers in Italy.

89 P. De Castro and R. Deserti, 'Imprese multinazionali, strategie di mercato e nuovi scenari del sistema agro-alimentare italiano', *Rivista di Politica Agraria*, vol. XIII (1995), no. 3, pp. 4–8, and especially tables 1, p. 4, and 3, p. 7. Certain markets in dynamic expansion such as sugar, biscuits, pasta, beer, coffee, frozen foods and prepared sauces had assumed 'a decidedly oligopolistic character'.

90 G. Giacomini and P. Bertolini, 'Vecchi e nuovi problemi dell'agricoltura italiana', *Rivista di Politica Agraria*, vol. XII (1994), no. 6, p. 9, table 6.

91 R. Fanfani, 'Il rapporto agricoltura-industria tra passato e presente', in P. P. D'Attorre and V. Zamagni (eds.), *Distretti, imprese, classe operaia*, Milano, 1992, p. 71.

92 World Trade Organisation, *Annual Report 1996*, vol. II, p. 73, table IV.2. Cf. R. Fanfani, 'Agricoltura italiana e CEE', in Ginsborg (ed.), *Stato dell'Italia*, p. 651.

93 A recent and interesting analysis of the question is that of G. Di Sandro, 'Quante sono le aziende agrarie: tre milioni o tre-quattrocentomila?', *Rivista di Politica*

Agraria, vol. XII (1994), no. 6, pp. 29–36. For a rather different view, in which restricted size is seen as the crippling problem of Italian agriculture, G. Colombo and E. Bassanelli, *Quale futuro per l'agricoltura italiana?*, Bologna, 1995.

94 For the ten-year-long Italian failure to respect the milk quotas established by the EEC, the frauds involved and the subsequent scandal, see the reconstruction in ibid., pp. 28–53.

95 NOMISMA, *Rapporto 1993 sull'agricoltura italiana*, Bologna, 1993, p. 298.

96 CENSIS, 'L'imprenditore agricolo nella trasformazione dell'agricoltura', in *Rapporto sulle prospettive economiche del settore agro-alimentare nel 1993*, Roma, 1993.

97 Colombo and Bassanelli, *Quale futuro*, pp. 169 and 192–4. For the earlier history of the Federconsorzi, see Ginsborg, *A History*, pp. 171–2, and above all M. Rossi-Doria, *Rapporto sulla Federconsorzi*, Bari, 1961.

98 The new Ministry was named that of Agricultural and Food Resources, but then changed again in 1997 to that of Agricultural Policies.

99 NOMISMA, *Rapporto 1993*, pp. 410ff.; G. Colombo, 'Quale politica per lo spazio rurale?', *Rivista di Politica Agraria*, vol. XII (1994), no. 2, pp. 3–12. See also the observations of P. Bevilacqua concerning the rich potential for biological agriculture in many parts of the south, as well as the possibility of the revival and marketing of certain traditional products; P. Bevilacqua, 'Riformare il Sud', *Meridiana*, no. 31 (1998), pp. 42–3.

100 SVIMEZ, *Rapporto 1991 sull'economia del Mezzogiorno*, Bologna, 1991, table 6, p. 33. These official figures must be handled with care, because they cannot take into account the considerable amount of 'black' and casual work undertaken by southern youth. None the less, the gravity of youth unemployment in the South is not in question.

101 N. Boccella, 'Mezzogiorno più lontano dal Nord', in Ginsborg (ed.), *Stato dell'Italia*, p. 430.

102 C. Trigilia, *Sviluppo senza autonomia*, Bologna 1994 [1st edn 1992], p. 61. At the end of the 1980s state spending in the South was 34.7 per cent of the national total, slightly less than the South's percentage of total population.

103 ibid., pp. 62–3.

104 The history of the 'southern question', as has been asserted recently, is a history of aggregations and distinctions, not of homologies. See the interesting collection of essays edited by R. Lumley and J. Morris, *The New History of the Italian South*, Exeter, 1997.

105 G. F. Viesti, 'Che succede nell'economia del Mezzogiorno? Le trasformazioni 1990–1995', *Meridiana*, nos. 26–7 (1996), pp. 123–6; Trigilia, *Sviluppo senza autonomia*, pp. 47–54 and 99–114. Trigilia distinguishes between provinces of rapid industrial growth (L'Aquila, Campobasso, Chieti, Teramo, Isernia, Bari, Lecce and in part Avellino and Pescara), and those largely dependent on the building trade for their economic progress (Catania, Ragusa, Sassari and in part Avellino and Bari).

106 Viesti, 'Che succede', pp. 115–16.

107 This is not to say that *all* of the state's 'extraordinary intervention' in the South in previous decades was an unqualified failure. For a recent and detailed collection of essays which breaks much new ground, see L. D'Antone (ed.), *Radici storiche ed esperienza dell'intervento straordianrio nel Mezzogiorno*, Roma, 1996.

108 N. Ajello, 'Mezzogiorno di fuoco', *L'Espresso*, vol. XXX (1984), no. 45, 11 November. By 1995 certain regions of the Italian South – Campania, Basilicata and Calabria – had reached levels of unemployment which were inferior in the European Union only to certain peripheral regions in Spain. At the same time levels of GDP per capita in these same Italian regions were superior to those in many parts of Spain, Portugal, Greece and Ireland; Eurostat, *Statistiche generali*, 1996, pp. 67–77 and 157–67 (the statistics for GDP per capita are for 1993).

109 Boccella, 'Mezzogiorno più lontano dal Nord', p. 430.

110 A. Graziani, 'Mezzogiorno oggi', *Meridiana*, no. 1 (1987), p. 214. For a detailed picture of southern state subsidies at the beginning of the 1980s, N. Boccella, *Il Mezzogiorno sussidiato*, Milano, 1982.

111 Trigilia, *Sviluppo senza autonomia*, pp. 90–91.

112 The areas of the South most infested by criminal organizations were also those with high levels of unemployment and sparse economic development. It was difficult, though, as A. Becchi has remarked, to decide which was the cause of the other; A. Becchi, 'Le politiche per il Mezzogiorno', *Meridiana*, no. 31 (1998), p. 56.

113 Trigilia, *Sviluppo senza autonomia*, pp. viiiff. and 75ff.

114 Viesti, 'Che succede', p. 127. For developments in the 1980s, see S. Cafiero, 'Dopo la "Cassa" ', in S. Cafiero, *Transizione e attualità del meridionalismo*, Bologna, 1989, pp. 159–64.

115 SVIMEZ, *L'industrializzazione del Mezzogiorno: la FIAT a Melfi*, Bologna, 1993, pp. 16ff. for the 'programmatic contract' between FIAT and the Ministry, 18 April 1991. With such high levels of subsidies, it was feared that the EEC would intervene to block the agreement, and Sir Leon Brittan, the commissioner then responsible for this sector, did open a case against FIAT in October 1991; by November 1992, however, the Commission had given its approval. With the opening of the Melfi factory, and continued production at Pomigliano d'Arco, more FIAT cars were being produced in the South than in the North.

116 ibid., pp. 42–3.

117 E. Barone and R. S. Masera, 'Index-linked bonds from an academic, market and policy-making standpoint', in M. De Cecco, L. Pecchi and G. Piga (eds.), *Managing Public Debt*, Cheltenham, 1997, pp. 122–3, table 6.1: 'Italy's public accounts: the question of their sustainability'.

118 L. Spaventa, 'Introduction', in F. Giavazzi and L. Spaventa, *High Public Debt: the Italian Experience*, Cambridge, 1988, pp. 4–5.

119 See below, Chapter 2, pp. 50–51.

120 L. Pennacchi (ed.), *Le ragioni dell'equità*, Bari, 1994, p. 14. For a historical overview, M. G. Rossi, 'Il problema storico della riforma fiscale in Italia', *Italia Contemporanea*, no. 170 (1988), pp. 5–19.

121 See below, Chapter 7, pp. 227ff.

122 Amato, *Due anni al Tesoro*, p. 15.

123 Graziani, 'L'economia italiana e il suo inserimento internazionale', p. 374, and 'Introduzione', in A. Graziani (ed.), *La spirale del debito pubblico*, Bologna, 1988, pp. 9–10.

124 E. Scalfari, 'Lo stato fallisce, i partiti ingrassano', *la Repubblica*, 17 September 1991.

125 For a detailed analysis of these decisions, see below, Chapter 7, pp. 244ff.

126 Sir W. Temple, *Observations upon the United Provinces of the Netherlands*, Oxford, 1972 [1673], p. 123, quoted by I. Hont, 'Free trade and the economic limits to national politics: neo-Machiavellian political economy reconsidered', in J. Dunn (ed.), *The Economic Limits to Modern Politics*, Cambridge, 1990, p. 55.

127 Barca and Visco, 'L'economia italiana nella prospettiva europea', p. 25.

128 Cf. UNDP (United Nations Development Programme), *Human Development Report 1991*, Oxford, 1991. The UNDP attempted to define human development not only in terms of income but also in relation to other criteria such as health, education, degree of liberty and the quality of the physical environment.

129 Quoted in L. R. Brown and H. Kane, *Full House. Reassessing the Earth's Population Carrying Capacity*, London, 1995, p. 30. For the accumulated environmental tensions deriving from population explosion and over-consumption, see A. Rahman, N. Robins and A. Roncerel (eds.), *Exploding the Population Myth: Consumption versus Population*, Bruxelles, 1993.

130 Italy may have occupied fifth or sixth place in the world's economic rankings, but in the Human Development Index drawn up by UNDP, based on four principal criteria – life expectancy, adult literacy, average number of years at school and income per capita – Italy slipped down into twenty-second place; UNDP, *Human Development Report 1994*, Oxford, 1994, p. 129, table 1.

131 UNDP, *Human Development Report 1991*, p. 22.

132 For a sensitive discussion of these issues, A. Schmidt, 'The new world order, incorporated: the rise of business and the decline of the nation-state', *Daedalus*, Spring 1995, pp. 75–106.

133 For a discussion of the Italian role in international cooperation for development, see below, Chapter 7, pp. 237ff.

Chapter 2: *The Social Hierarchies of a Prosperous Nation*

1 H. Mendras, *La Seconde révolution française (1965–1984)*, Paris, 1988, p. 44.

2 G. Sapelli, *L'Italia inafferabile*, Venezia, 1989, p. 118.

3 P. Marcenaro and V. Foa, *Riprendere tempo*, Torino, 1982, pp. 33–4 and 73.

4 The most forceful treatment of this theme is that of U. Beck, *Risk Society*, London, 1992 [original edn *Risikogesellschaft*, Frankfurt am Main, 1986]. For further discussion of the themes raised by Beck's work, see U. Beck, A. Giddens and S. Lash, *Reflexive Modernisation*, Cambridge, 1994.

5 W. Scobie, 'La dolce Italia', *Observer*, 15 November 1987.

6 A. Cobalti and W. Schizzerotto, *La mobilità sociale in Italia*, Bologna, 1994, p. 77, table 3.3. Other studies on social mobility in Italy include A. Barbagli, V. Capecchi and A. Cobalti, *La mobilità sociale in Emilia-Romagna*, Bologna, 1988; H. M. A. Schadee and A. Schizzerotto, *Social Mobility of Men and Women in Contemporary Italy*, Trento, 1990; A. De Lillo, 'La mobilità sociale assoluta', *Polis*, vol. III (1988), no. 1, pp. 19–51.

7 T. W. Smith, 'Inequality and welfare', in R. Jowell *et al.*, *British Social Attitudes. Special International Report*, London, 1989, p. 67. Other European countries included in this comparison were West Germany, Britain, Hungary and the Netherlands. Italy's actual, as opposed to perceived, social mobility, appeared in this survey as much more limited.

8 A. Cobalti, 'La mobilità sociale in Italia e negli altri paesi europei', in M. Paci (ed.), *Le dimensioni della disuguaglianza*, Bologna, 1993, pp. 63–8.

9 ibid., p. 66.

10 J. Rifkin, *The End of Work*, New York, 1995. For a less extreme view, though hardly a less pessimistic one, see L. Gallino, *Se tre milioni vi sembran pochi*, Torino, 1998; in particular his reasoned scepticism with regard to any easy application of recent American employment patterns to the European case.

11 M. Mafai, 'Ora la paura della povertà contagia i "colletti bianchi"', *la Repubblica*, 1 April 1996.

12 S. Scamuzzi, 'La percezione della disuguaglianza sociale', in Paci (ed.), *Le dimensioni*, pp. 68ff., with reference to Eurisko surveys of 1987 and 1992.

13 S. J. Rose, *Social Stratification in the United States*, New York, 1992. The data was derived from the March 1990 annual Bureau of the Census Current Population Survey of 60,000 households.

14 As Peter Donaldson has commented: 'Extreme disparities in income are dwarfed by those in the ownership of personal wealth . . . however great the differential between the average worker and the average managing director, it is nothing compared with the income gap between "earned" and "unearned" income resulting from ownership of wealth'; P. Donaldson, *The Economics of the Real World*, London, 1984 (3rd edn), pp. 185 and 188.

15 'To achieve that we call in Procrustes, a cruel host whose custom it was to adapt the height of his guests to the size of the bed in the guest room'; J. Pen, *Income Distribution*, London, 1971, p. 48.

16 The emphasis is Pen's; ibid., p. 51.

17 ibid., p. 52: 'The rear of the parade is brought up by a few participants who are

Notes to pages 34–6

measured in miles. Indeed, they are figures whose height we cannot even estimate: their heads disappear into the clouds and probably they themselves do not even know how tall they are' (p. 53).

18 M. Geri and L. Pennacchi, 'La distribuzione del reddito', in Paci (ed.), *Le dimensioni*, pp. 169–96, especially table 4.1, p. 176. Their methodology derives from that suggested by D. R. Cameron, 'Politics, public policy and distributional inequality: a comparative analysis', in I. Shapiro and G. Reeher (eds.), *Power, Inequality and Democratic Politics*, Boulder, Colorado, 1988. For another recent and detailed analysis, which comes to similar conclusions, A. B. Atkinson, L. Rainwater and T. Smeeding, *Income Distribution in European Countries*, Working Paper no. 9535, University of Cambridge, Department of Applied Economics, 1995.

19 Geri and Pennacchi, 'La distribuzione', pp. 190–91. As in other western countries, the Italian disequalities of *wealth* were even greater than those of *income*. Bank of Italy figures for 1987 show that the top 10 per cent of Italian families, which held 26.4 per cent of overall individual income, had 35 per cent of overall financial wealth (ibid., p. 189).

20 J. Scott, *Gender and the Politics of History*, New York, 1988, p. 42.

21 Sylvia Walby, in her *Theorizing Patriarchy*, London, 1995 [1st edn 1990], p. 20, has suggested that the analysis of patriarchy must address the following broad range of structures: waged work, housework, sexuality, culture, violence and the state. She also argues for a distinct shift in patriarchal oppression of women from the private to the public sphere in the course of the twentieth century (ibid., pp. 173–201).

22 For the debate on Italy's radical decline in reproduction, see below, Chapter 3, pp. 69–73. In the cohort of students born between 1952 and 1967, for the first time the number of graduate women exceeded that of men (5.4 per cent against 5.2 per cent), as did the number of girls with upper secondary school diplomas (34.3 per cent against 30.2 per cent); A. Schizzerotto, 'La scuola è uguale per tutti', in Ginsborg (ed.), *Stato dell'Italia*, p. 560. For the importance of the 1991 equal opportunities legislation, C. Valentini, *Le donne fanno paura*, Milano, 1997, p. 111.

23 A. Perulli, 'Com'è cambiata l'occupazione', in Ginsborg (ed.), *Stato dell' Italia*, p. 443.

24 Presidenza del Consiglio dei Ministri, Dipartimento per la Funzione pubblica, *Rapporto sulle condizioni delle pubbliche amministrazioni*, Roma, 1993, p. 235, table 3.4.1.

25 M. Piazza, 'Il rischio di una nuova marginalità', in Ginsborg (ed.), *Stato dell'Italia*, p. 271.

26 *Eurostat Yearbook '95*, Bruxelles–Luxembourg, 1995, p. 105.

27 G. Malerba, 'La donna nella famiglia e nel lavoro: i risultati di una analisi cross-country', in G. Rossi and G. Malerba (eds.), *La donna nella famiglia e nel lavoro*, Milano, 1993, pp. 57–8. For recent comparative studies, see also M. D. Garcia-Ramon and J. Monk (eds.), *Women of the European Union*, London/New York, 1996.

28 See P. David and G. Vicarelli (eds.), *Donne nelle professioni degli uomini*, Milano, 1993.

29 I. Bertaux Wiame, C. Borderias and A. Pesce, 'La forza dell'ambiguità, traiettorie sociali di donne in Italia, Francia e Spagna', *Inchiesta*, vol. XVIII (1988), no. 82, p. 21; and above all L. Balbo, 'La doppia presenza', *Inchiesta*, vol. VIII (1978), no. 32, pp. 3–6.

30 R. Crompton, 'Women's employment and the "middle class"', in T. Butler and M. Savage (eds.), *Social Change and the Middle Classes*, London, 1995, p. 67.

31 G. Contini, 'Gestirsi il proprio tempo', in Ginsborg (ed.), *Stato dell'Italia*, pp. 249–53.

32 For an analysis of this gendered occupational segregation for the city of Bologna, based on the national census of 1991, see M. Barbagli and M. Pisati, *Rapporto sulla situazione sociale a Bologna*, Bologna, 1995, pp. 65–72. One survey of 1993 from the Milanese hinterland, covering women between the ages of twenty and fifty-five who lived alone, found over 50 per cent of them were middle-ranking white-collar workers. Out of a sample of 104 women, only one was a manager and two were professionals. Most were very critical of their work conditions and career prospects; see B. Beccalli, 'Introduzione', in G. Achilli *et al.*, *Vivere sole*, Milano, 1994, pp. 13–22, as well as M. Cacioppo *et al.*, *La donna sola: aspetti e scelte di vita*, Milano, 1994.

33 A. M. Chiesi, 'Disuguaglianze sociali nell'uso del tempo', in Paci (ed.), *Le dimensioni*, p. 220.

34 For the Swedish model, see below, Chapter 3, p. 73.

35 P. Feltrin and S. La Mendola, 'I lavori manuali non operai: il caso delle donne delle pulizie', *Prospettiva sindacale*, vol. XIX (1988), no. 69, pp. 63–102.

36 L. Balbo, 'Crazy quilts', in G. Statera (ed.), *Consenso e conflitto nella società contemporanea*, Milano, 1982, p. 231.

37 For an analysis of these tendencies, Valentini, *Le donne*, pp. 129–51.

38 See, among others, M. Molyneux, 'Beyond the domestic labour debate', *New Left Review*, no. 116 (1979), pp. 3–27; H. I. Hartmann, 'The unhappy marriage of Marxism and Feminism: towards a more progressive union', in L. Sargent (ed.), *Women and Revolution*, Boston, 1981, pp. 1–42. For a good summary of 'dual-systems theory', the attempted synthesis of Marxist and radical feminist theory, see Walby, *Theorizing Patriarchy*, pp. 5–7.

39 One of the most innovative attempts to redraw the lines dividing society (in this case French society), principally on the basis not just of economic divisions but also of cultural capital and consumption patterns, is to be found in P. Bourdieu, *Distinction*, London, 1994 [original edn, *La Distinction, critique sociale du jugement*, Paris, 1979]. See also his 'What makes a social class? On the theoretical and practical existence of groups', *Berkeley Journal of Sociology*, vol. XXXII (1987), pp. 1–17.

40 See M. Paci, 'I mutamenti della stratificazione sociale', in *Storia dell'Italia repubblicana*, vol. III, pt 1, Torino, 1996, pp. 707–8.

41 K. Marx, *Misère de la philosophie*, Paris, 1847.

42 Cf. A. O. Hirschman, *Exit, Voice, and Loyalty*, Cambridge, Mass., 1970.

43 F. Tamburini, *Misteri d'Italia*, Milano, 1996, p. 183. Aldo Ravelli (1911—95) had survived the concentration camp of Mauthausen (ibid., pp. 51ff.), and many other vicissitudes. His extended conversation with Tamburini, which he allowed to be published only after his death, constitutes a rare glimpse of the attitudes and actions of at least one part of the *grande borghesia*.

44 S. Cingolani, *Le grandi famiglie del capitalismo italiano*, Bari, 1990, pp. 6ff., 22ff., and 69—70. In this period also, nearly all the Italian pharmaceutical industry was taken over by foreign multinationals.

45 This widely accepted thesis has recently been presented in attractive form by A. Friedman; see both his *Angelli and the Network of Italian Power*, London, 1988, and his *Ce la farà il capitalismo italiano?*, Milano, 1989.

46 Cingolani, *Le grandi famiglie*, p. 90.

47 F. Tamburini, *Un siciliano a Milano*, Milano, 1992, p. 73. Cuccia died on 23 June 2000, aged ninety-two.

48 Ginsborg, *A History*, pp. 145—67.

49 G. Andreotti, *A ogni morte di Papa*, Milano, 1980.

50 This aphorism first appeared in Andreotti's journal *Concretezza*, vol. V (1959), no. 12, 16 June, p. 4.

51 Quoted, without a specific reference, in M. Franco, *Andreotti visto da vicino*, Milano, 1993 [1st edn 1989], p. 46.

52 Even Berlusconi, who was certainly not considered part of the '*buon salotto*', did not hesitate to pay tribute to the man he considered its prince. In August 1989 Berlusconi's closest friend and adviser, Fedele Confalonieri, used an appropriately feudal imagery to describe the relationship between the two men: 'The emperor calls, the duke responds, and takes with him the list of lands that he has conquered, as well as a hunting trophy or two. And from the heights of his throne the emperor smiles and is amused at so unpredictable and intelligent a knight.' S. Pende, 'L'amico Fedele', in *L'Europeo*, vol. XLV (1989), nos. 33—4, 25 August, p. 48.

53 C. Thomas, 'Family and kinship in Eaton Square', in F. Field (ed.), *The Wealth Report*, London, 1979, pp. 129—59.

54 A precious documentation of these habits has come into the public domain through the revelations and holiday photographs of Stefania Ariosto, the sometime fiancée of Vittorio Dotti, a lawyer who was one of Berlusconi's closest advisers. For a more analytical approach, see A. Corso, 'Quelli della vela', *la Repubblica*, Affari e Finanza, 8 May 1992, who divides the Italian owners of large sailing yachts into three groups: those interested in regattas, those in cruises, and those in antique ships.

55 A. Chiesi, 'Il sistema delle associazioni industriali e la specificità del caso italiano', in A. Martinelli (ed.), *L'azione collettiva degli imprenditori italiani*, Milano, 1994, pp. 199—201, 208 and 374, n. 5.

56 A. Martinelli and L. Lanzalaco, 'L'organizzazione degli interessi imprenditoriali e il sistema politico. La logica dell'influenza', in ibid., p. 343.

57 C. Donolo, 'L'erosione delle basi morali nella società italiana', *Quaderni di Sociologia*, vol. XXXVIII–XXXIX (1994–5), no. 8, p. 61.

58 See, for instance, the stimulating chapter entitled 'Reflexive subjects' in S. Lash and J. Urry, *Economies of Signs and Space*, London, 1994, pp. 31–59.

59 Mendras, *La Seconde révolution*, p. 55.

60 For crucial elements in the formation of this tradition, see J. Harris, *Private Lives, Public Spirit*, Oxford, 1993. For the formation of 'expressive professionals', B. Martin, *A Sociology of Contemporary Cultural Change*, Oxford, 1981, pp. 185–233. Growth and change in public sector employment is analysed in R. Parry, 'Britain: stable aggregates, changing composition', in R. Rose (ed.), *Public Employment in Western Nations*, Cambridge, 1985, pp. 195–233.

61 Rose (ed.), *Public Employment*, pp. 63, 105, 134, 172. In the Italian case, if private health personnel are added, the 1961 total is 276,000.

62 For a further discussion of these themes, see below, Chapter 7.

63 See the articles published in *Polis*, vol. VII (1993), no. 1: A. Schizzerotto, 'Le classi superiori in Italia: politici, imprenditori, liberi professionisti e dirigenti', pp. 5–13; A. Schizzerotto, 'La porta stretta: classi superiori e processi di mobilità', pp. 15–43; H. M. A. Schadee and L. Saviori, 'Il matrimonio e le frequentazioni sociali delle classi superiori', pp. 45–68; G. C. Rovati, 'Imprenditori e dirigenti tra cultura d'impresa e cultura politico-sociale', pp. 69–91.

64 In particular, the existence of the 'service class' is hotly debated, and the very term is likely to lead to confusion between, on the one hand, all those who work in services and on the other the much narrower category, which Schizzerotto has in mind, of upper and middle management. It is worth noting also that both Karl Renner, who coined the term, and John Goldthorpe, who is its most renowned advocate, used it to include both professionals and managers. For a discussion of these issues of labelling, see T. Butler, 'The debate over the middle classes', in Butler and Savage (eds.), *Social Change*, pp. 27ff.

65 Schizzerotto, 'Le classi superiori in Italia', p. 8.

66 A. Bernacchi, M. Mascini and M. Moussanet, *Crisi? No grazie*, Milano, 1994, p. 148.

67 There was distinct evidence of a distancing of small entrepreneurs from the shopfloor of their factories in the 1990s, for a whole series of reasons connected with growth and the need for greater efficiency; see M. Franchi, V. Rieser, 'Le categorie sociologiche nell'analisi del distretto industriale: tra comunità e razionalizzazione', *Stato e Mercato*, no. 33 (1991), pp. 451–76.

68 L. Tulli, 'Ingrandire la stalla, allargare il magazzino', *Altrochemestre*, no. 1 (1994), pp. 8–9. Silvana's daughter Ester commented in the course of the interview: 'My mother is a slave to work, for her nothing else exists, it's absurd, this can't be what life is about. I want to work as a secretary with fixed office hours.'

69 P. P. Poggi, 'La Lega secondo natura', *Iter*, vol. II (1992), nos. 5–6, p. 152.

70 For a further discussion of these processes, see Chapter 4, p. 107 and Chapter 5, pp. 174–8.

71 G. Brosio, *The Regulation of Professions in Italy*, Roma, 1997 (Fondazione Eni Enrico Mattei, Nota di Lavoro 36.97), p. 9, table 1; L. Speranza and W. Tousijn, 'Le libere professioni' in Paci (ed.), *Le dimensioni*, p. 82. However, 197,600 of these were nurses. The groupings whose members for the most part clearly belonged to the upper middle classes were as follows: doctors and dentists, 346,013; engineers, 121,625; architects, 70,763; lawyers, 70,413; journalists, 72,214; accountants, 46,000. To this list must be added university professors, who are not, however, a recognized profession in Italy, but rather public employees.

72 W. Tousijn, 'Tra stato e mercato: le libere professioni in una prospettiva storico-evolutiva', in W. Tousijn (ed.), *Le libere professioni in Italia*, Bologna, 1987, pp. 38–9.

73 E. Durkheim, *Lezioni di sociologia. Fisica dei costumi e dei diritti*, Milano, 1973, p. 33 [original edn *Leçons de sociologie*, Paris, 1950].

74 A common distinction between entrepreneurs and managers is that the first group displays a talent for innovation, while the second has a talent for organization. But Giancarlo Rovati has warned against any over-simplification, stressing instead the heterogeneity of the world of both managers and entrepreneurs, and the importance of generational differences; 'Imprenditori e dirigenti', p. 70.

75 P. Gagliardi and B. A. Turner, 'Aspects of Italian management', in D. J. Hickson (ed.), *Management in Western Europe*, Berlin and New York, 1993, p. 151. See also G. Sapelli, 'The Italian crises and capitalism', *Modern Italy*, vol. I (1995), no. 1, pp. 86–7, where he makes a fundamental distinction between the management culture of northern Europe, based on universalist values, a low level of class segregation and a respect for the impersonality of the market and state, and that of southern Europe, where clientelism, familism and traditional non-meritocratic deference dominate.

76 M. Deaglio, *La nuova borghesia e la sfida del capitalismo*, Bari, 1991, especially pp. 41–64.

77 For some similar, though not identical, ideas on the new élite of symbolic analysts in the United States, see R. Reich, *The Work of Nations*, New York, 1991, pp. 169–240; and, on a global level, under the general umbrella of 'professional society', H. Perkin, *The Third Revolution*, London, 1996.

78 P. Perulli, *Atlante metropolitano*, Bologna, 1991, pp. 143ff.

79 A mine of information is to be found in G. P. Prandstaller (ed.), *Le nuove professioni del terziario*, Milano, 1994 (4th enlarged edn).

80 Paci, *Il mutamento*, p. 285, table 18. Cobalti and Schizzerotto give a similar figure, 22.4 per cent, for the traditional 'urban petite bourgeoisie', and a very detailed breakdown of the categories that constitute it (principally artisans with 0–14 dependants, as well as 'self-employed in the commercial and services' sectors);

La mobilità sociale, pp. 216–17 and Appendix 1, pp. 251–2. According to the statistics of Sylos Labini (see Statistical Appendix, no. 22), only 29 per cent of the workforce in 1993 were white-collar workers in the public and private sectors. Overall, though, his 'urban middle classes' account for 52 per cent of the working population.

81 See in particular the work of G. Esping-Andersen: 'Strutture di classe post-industriali', pp. 219–47, and 'Occupazioni o classi sociali: esiste un proletariato postindustriale?', *Polis*, vol. VII (1993), pp. 453–75.

82 Cobalti and Schizzerotto, *La mobilità sociale*, p. 216, give some indication of this when they note that their category of 'urban petite bourgeoisie' was in Italy more than twice the size of that of any other country in their comparative survey (the other countries being Hungary, Sweden, France, Great Britain (without Wales), Ireland, Poland, W. Germany). See also Statistical Appendix, nos. 29 and 30.

83 See, for example, J. Morris, *The Political Economy of Shopkeeping in Milan, 1886–1922*, Cambridge, 1993. A good introduction to the commercial sector in Italy is to be found in C. Barberis, *La società italiana*, Milano, 1995 (2nd revised edn), pp. 350–73.

84 The survey was reported in F. Recanatesi, 'Compro, vendo, evado', *la Repubblica*, 17 January 1984. For some European comparisons, see Barberis, *La società*, p. 362, table 3. In 1991 there existed in Italy 171 shops for every 10,000 inhabitants (one for every 59 inhabitants), in Spain 134, in France 97, in Germany 85, in Great Britain 81.

85 For meat consumption, see *Eurostat Yearbook '95*, p. 136; for pharmaceuticals, CENSIS, *Consumi e spesa farmaceutica*, Milano, 1997, p. 47, figure 3 and pp. 61ff. for some international comparisons.

86 See, for example, 'Il fisco vola alto sopra i 40 milioni', *Il Sole – 24 Ore*, 19 October 1996. For an even worse situation a decade earlier, see T. Oldani, 'I miserabili', *Panorama*, vol. XXVI (1988), no. 1173, pp. 68–77 (for 1984–5); A. Forbice and G. C. Fornari, *I bugiardi del fisco*, Roma, 1985, and A. Tagliacozzo, *Per una sociologia dell'evasione fiscale*, Roma, 1984.

87 Some indications on the diffusion of state bonds for the years 1992–3 are to be found in L. Cannari and G. D'Alesio, 'Composizione e distribuzione della ricchezza delle famiglie', in N. Rossi (ed.), *La transizione equa*, Bologna, 1994, pp. 267–8, tables 4–9, and pp. 276–7.

88 For a balanced view of the relative advantages of small shops and supermarkets, see G. Pini, 'Grande distribuzione, modelli di consumo e costi sociali', *Commercio*, vol. XVI (1994), no. 52, pp. 87–110.

89 A. Perulli, 'Com'è cambiata l'occupazione', p. 446.

90 M. Mafai, 'Ora la paura della povertà contagia i "colletti bianchi"', *la Repubblica*, 1 April 1996.

91 ibid. For a sociological profile of bank clerks, see E. Campelli and E. Testi, *I bancari*, Roma, 1988.

92 Presidenza del Consiglio dei Ministri, Dipartimento per la Funzione pubblica, *Rapporto sulle condizioni*, p. 41.

93 Between 1973 and 1989 women increased their presence in the schools from 83 per cent to 90 per cent of elementary teachers, 63 per cent to 70 per cent in lower secondary schools, and 48 per cent to 52 per cent in the upper secondary schools; see M. Dei, 'Insegnanti, parola d'ordine: insoddisfazione', in Ginsborg (ed.), *Stato dell'Italia*, p. 574. For the percentage breakdown of national public sector employment in 1992, see F. P. Cerase, *I dipendenti pubblici*, Bologna, 1994, p. 26, table 2.1.

94 ibid., pp. 107–62.

95 This was my very strong impression after taking part in four large further-training courses in the period 1994–7.

96 A. Cavalli, 'Valori, orientamenti politici e opinioni nella politica scolastica', in A. Cavalli (ed.), *Insegnare oggi*, Bologna, 1992, p. 220.

97 G. Gervasio Carbonaro and G. Paoletti Sbordoni, *La qualità possibile. Educazione, cultura, servizi sociali nel territorio*, Firenze, 1995, p. 14.

98 See Statistical Appendix, no. 22.

99 Bagnasco, *L'Italia*, p. 27.

100 Revelli, 'Economia e modello sociale', pp. 185ff.

101 G. Bonazzi, *Il tubo di cristallo*, Bologna, 1993, pp. 185–6.

102 M. Revelli, *Lavorare in FIAT*, Milano, 1989, pp. 125ff.

103 On the delicate balance between autonomy (of the worker) and control (by the firm), see G. C. Cerruti and V. Rieser, *Fiat: qualità totale e fabbrica integrata*, Roma, 1991, pp. 52–5.

104 B. Trentin, *Il coraggio dell'utopia*, Milano, 1994, pp. 16–18 and 36–7.

105 Revelli, 'Economia e modello sociale', *passim*.

106 M. L. Blim, *Made in Italy*, New York, 1990, p. 194. His research was carried out in 'San Lorenzo Marche', 'one of a half-dozen key shoe production towns in the Marche', with a population of 7,000.

107 See above, p. 19.

108 Ginsborg, *A History*, p. 322.

109 P. Giovannini, 'Trasformazioni sociali e crisi di rappresentanza', in P. Giovannini (ed.), *I rumori della crisi*, Milano, 1993, pp. 238–9.

110 R. Edwards, P. Garonna and E. Pisani (eds.), *Il sindacato oltre la crisi*, Milano, 1988. In this period an Italian trade-union delegation on a visit to Britain was received briefly by Mrs Thatcher at 10 Downing Street. A leading British trade-unionist who accompanied the delegation confided afterwards to his Italian counterpart that only the protocol of the Italian visit had constrained the Prime Minister to allow a British trade-unionist to cross the threshold of her official residence. I owe this anecdote to Vittorio Foa.

111 A. Accornero, *La parabola del sindacato*, Bologna, 1992, p. 251. For a critique of trade-union organization, ibid., pp. 213ff.

112 ibid., pp. 259ff.

113 G. Ricordy, *Senzadiritti*, Milano, 1990, pp. 9–10.

114 ibid., pp. 13–28.

115 P. Perulli (ed.), *Piccole imprese metropolitane*, Milano, 1990, pp. 42–3. See also the article in the same volume by E. Baptiste and A. Michelsons, 'Artigianato e piccole imprese nell'area ovest di Torino', especially p. 122.

116 Letter from F. Capalbo to U. Galimberti, in *la Repubblica delle donne*, 8 April 1997.

117 N. Negri and C. Saraceno, *Politiche contro la povertà in Italia*, Bologna, 1996, p. 12.

118 G. B. Sgritta and G. Innocenzi, 'La povertà', in Paci (ed.), *Le dimensioni*, pp. 261–70, offer an exceptionally clear account of the different methodologies and results.

119 Commissione d'indagine sulla povertà e l'emarginazione, *Secondo rapporto sulla povertà in Italia* (ed. G. Sarpellon), Milano, 1992, pp. 30ff.; and Negri and Saraceno, *Politiche contro*, pp. 121–2, table 3.1, for the figures for 1994.

120 Commissione d'indagine, *Secondo rapporto*, p. 35.

121 ibid., p. 37, table 8. Among the elderly population, it was women living alone who were most vulnerable. One's previous working life, and the pension deriving from it, were decisive for the quality of life when over sixty-five. Most old women in the Italy of the 1990s had very discontinuous employment patterns or had worked only in the home.

122 E. Pugliese, *Sociologia della disoccupazione*, Bologna, 1993, pp. 147–90.

123 Eurostat, *Statistiche generali dell'Unione Europea (1997)*, Luxembourg, 1997, pp. 154–5.

124 E. Mingione, 'La disoccupazione giovanile', in Paci (ed.), *Le dimensioni*, pp. 251ff.

125 Pugliese, *Sociologia della disoccupazione*, p. 152.

126 P. Romito, 'La depressione delle donne, ovvero la radicalizzazzione dell'oppressione quotidiana', *Inchiesta*, vol. XVIII (1988), no. 81, pp. 48–53.

127 See A. Becchi, 'Città e forme di emarginazione', in *Storia dell'Italia repubblicana*, vol. III, pt 1, pp. 837–929, and especially the comparison between Turin and Naples, p. 907.

128 Ginsborg, *A History*, pp. 438–9, for the case of Quarto Oggiaro in Milan.

129 For documentation on Le Piagge, see the excellent local journal *L'Altracittà*.

130 Ministry of Interior figures for 1990 estimated at around 300,000 the number of Italian drug addicts, mainly male and mainly in the great cities and the North of the country; N. Negri, 'L'esclusione sociale', in Paci (ed.), *Le dimensioni*, pp. 294ff. Obviously, not all addicts came from the urban peripheries. For Naples, see below, Chapter 5, pp. 122–3.

131 Ruffolo, *Lo sviluppo dei limiti*, p. 57. Nor did they fit Ruffolo's own description of them as 'disorganized and turbulent, of the late Roman Empire'.

132 For a reflection on the synonyms and metaphors used in connection with immigration to Italy, see J. ter Wal, 'Il linguaggio del pregiudizio etnico', *Politica ed Economia*, vol. XXII (1991), no. 4, pp. 33–48.

133 L. Mauri and G. A. Micheli, 'Flussi immigratori in Italia: una scheda documentaria', in L. Mauri and G. A. Micheli (eds.), *Le regole del gioco*, Milano, 1992, pp. 213ff. Another measurement of the same year was provided by the national census; see ISTAT, *La presenza straniera in Italia*, Roma, 1993, pp. 33ff., which gave a total number of 519,613 resident and non-resident foreign citizens (this figure excluded those staying in hotels, etc. for less than a month). Of these 99,166 were from the European Community (see also table 2.3, p. 40).

134 Official Eurostat figures (which obviously could not take into account illegal and non-registered immigrants) offered the following picture for non-EEA (European Economic Area) citizens present in the major western European countries in 1992 (EEA = EU + EFTA countries, but not Switzerland): Germany, 4,176,000; France, 2,273,000 (1990 figures); UK, 1,200,000; Netherlands, 549,000; Italy, 418,000; *Eurostat Yearbook '95*, p. 68. See also Statistical Appendix, no. 19.

135 For the different strands of immigration to Milan, see G. Barile *et al.*, *Tra due rive*, Milano 1994, and especially the excellent article of A. Marchetti, 'La nuova immigrazione a Milano. Il caso senegalese', ibid., pp. 241–366. Four regions – Lazio, Lombardy, Tuscany and Venetia – absorbed 52.3 per cent of immigration in 1991 (ISTAT, *La presenza straniera*, p. 34). Major cities tended to have a mix of ethnic groups, but smaller ones sometimes found themselves with an intense immigration from one country alone. Thus 71 per cent of the immigrants to Rieti by 1992 were from Morocco, 85 per cent to Trapani were Tunisians, 50 per cent to Ravenna were Senegalese (Mauri and Micheli, 'Flussi immigratori', p. 218).

136 E. Biagi, 'Niente spaghetti', *Corriere della Sera*, 12 August 1991.

137 On 12 August 1991, those still in the stadium at Bari were offered a pair of jeans, a T-shirt, MS cigarettes and 50,000 lire if they would go peacefully. Most did, but the 1,000 who resisted to the last were eventually allowed to stay 'temporarily'. It thus appeared that the most violent of the immigrants had been the most leniently treated by the Italian authorities.

138 Often these women took the place of Italian family members, while their own families paid a heavy price. For an interesting analysis see J. Andall, 'Catholic and state construction of domestic workers: the case of Cape Verdean women in Rome in the 1970s', in H. Koser and H. Lutz (eds.), *The New Migration in Europe: Social Constructions and Social Realities*, London, 1997, pp. 124–42.

139 Pugliese, *Sociologia della disoccupazione*, p. 176.

140 Ginsborg, *A History*, p. 222.

141 F. Gatti, 'Centrale, guerra dei binari', *Corriere della Sera* (Cronaca di Milano), 16 March 1993. At the Stazione Termini in Rome, violence was also the norm, but the most remarked-upon phenomenon was the great gathering in the early evening of Sunday of the Somali community, in front of the station. As the anthropologist Pietro Clemente has commented, 'As evening falls, Stazione Termini is not a place that is frightening, as some believe. On the contrary, it is reassuring, because it becomes a Somali village, it has the serenity of

a village. It is when the immigrants go away that it is time to be afraid';
P. Clemente, 'Immigrati: incroci di sguardi', in Ginsborg (ed.), *Stato dell'Italia*,
p. 244. See also M. Cuffaro, 'Roma dopo mezzanotte', *il manifesto*, 2 September
1990.

142 For the treatment of these themes with respect to the southern and eastern
shores of the Mediterranean, see above all M. Livi Bacci, 'Introduzione', in
M. Livi Bacci and F. Martuzzi Veronesi (eds.), *Le risorse umane del Mediterraneo*,
Bologna, 1990, pp. 11–40.

143 See the discussion between M. Livi Bacci, A. Lonni and E. Pugliese, 'Immigrazione
e razzismo nel Mediterraneo', *Passato e Presente*, vol. XVI (1998), no. 43,
pp. 15–34.

144 P. Tabet, *La pelle giusta*, Torino, 1997, p. 24.

145 L. Balbo and L. Manconi, *I razzismi reali*, Milano, 1992, pp. 30–40.

146 'Immigrati in Italia, un'aggressione al giorno', *la Repubblica*, 12 June 1997.

147 F. Mazzonis, 'Un problema capitale', in Ginsborg (ed.), *Stato dell'Italia*, p. 108.

148 See, for example, V. De Lucia, *Se questa è una città*, Roma, 1992, and M. Pazienti,
Roma e la sua regione urbana, Milano, 1995.

Chapter 3: *Families and Consumption*

1 P. Nichols, *Italia, Italia*, London, 1973, p. 227.

2 *The Economist*, vol. CCCXV (1990), no. 7656, 'Survey of Italy', p. 14.

3 J. Finch, 'Kinship and friendship', in Jowell *et al. British Social Attitudes. Special
International Report*, p. 101.

4 Pietro Clemente kindly told me of these attitudes, which he encountered while
conducting anthropological research on immigrants to Rome from the Maghreb.
If family relations in the Maghreb are now going through a period of rapid
transformation, the force and pervasiveness of the traditional endogamic family,
based on preferential marriages between parallel cousins on the male side, remain
one of the fundamental long-term characteristics of the region. See C. Lacoste-
Dujardin, 'La famiglia', in G. Calchi Novati (ed.), *Maghreb*, Milan, 1991,
pp. 188–200.

5 A. Cherlin and F. F. Furstenberg Jr, 'The changing European family', *Journal of
Family Studies*, vol. IX (1988), no. 3, pp. 291–2.

6 See Statistical Appendix, nos. 3 and 4; A. Santini, 'La fecondità', in Barbagli and
Saraceno (eds.), *Lo stato delle famiglie*, pp. 113–21; A. Golini, 'Le tendenze
demografiche dell'Italia in un quadro europeo', in A. Golini (ed.), *Tendenze
demografiche e politiche per la popolazione*, Bologna, 1994, pp. 17–18, especially
p. 29, table 2; and A. Golini and A. Silvestrini, 'Cambiamenti familiari e relazioni
generazionali: una lettura demografica', in P. P. Donati (ed.), *Quarto rapporto
CISF sulla famiglia in Italia*, Milano, 1995, p. 92 and p. 417, table 5b.

7 M. Livi Bacci, 'Introduzione', in Livi Bacci and Martuzzi Veronesi (eds.), *Le
risorse umane del Mediterraneo*, pp. 11–40. In 1993 Greece had a total

fertility rate of 1.38, Portugal 1.53 and Spain 1.24; see *Eurostat Yearbook '95*, p. 50.

8 G. C. Blangiardo, 'Il problema della dentalità in Italia: intensità, conseguenze, proposte di intervento', in P. P. Donati (ed.), *Secondo rapporto sulla famiglia in Italia*, Milano, 1991, p. 157. This is not to say that a modest reversal of trends is impossible; for the Swedish case, see below, p. 73.

9 ibid., p. 170.

10 See Statistical Appendix, no. 1.

11 For a useful discussion of old age and dependency ratios in Italy, see Fondazione Giovanni Agnelli, *Italy Toward 2001*, Torino, 1990, pp. 19–20 and 154–9. At a wider European level, Tony Judt has commented: 'Once the baby boomers begin to retire (around A D 2010), the presence of a huge, frustrated, bored, unproductive and ultimately unhealthy population of old people could become a major social crisis. It should already be a matter of some concern that the far-right populist parties of Jörg Haider in Austria and Jean-Marie Le Pen in France do notably better among unemployed youth and the insecure aged than among employed persons in the prime of life'; T. Judt, *A Grand Illusion?*, New York, 1996, p. 101.

12 G. Guazzini, 'Dimensione ideale della famiglia e calendario ideale delle nascite', in R. Palomba (ed.), *Vita di coppia e figli*, Firenze, 1987, p. 51.

13 M. Livi Bacci, 'Esiste davvero una seconda transizione demografica?', in G. A. Micheli (ed.), *La società del figlio assente*, Milano, 1995, p. 96, makes the important qualifying point that Italy's contraception revolution was only a partial one, at least as far as the adoption of the contraceptive pill was concerned. By 1987 still only 7 per cent of Italian women of reproduction age were using it, as opposed to 10 per cent in Spain and 30 per cent in France. See also L. Roussel, 'La famille en Europe occidentale: divergences et convergences', *Population*, vol. XLVII (1992), no. 1, table 8, p. 145.

14 See below, pp. 79–80. For changes in Great Britain, suggesting a slow change in male attitudes across time and generation, J. Gershuny, M. Goodwin and S. Jones, 'The domestic labour revolution: a process of lagged adaptation', in M. Anderson, F. Bechhofer and J. Gershuny (eds.), *The Social and Political Economy of the Household*, Oxford, 1994, pp. 151–97.

15 See, above all, L. Balbo, 'La doppia presenza', *Inchiesta*, vol. VIII (1978), no. 32, pp. 3–6, and M. Bianchi, 'Oltre il "doppio lavoro" ', ibid., pp. 7–11. For a discussion of the three cohorts of Italian women who since 1965 have reduced significantly their childbearing, and the differences between them, see C. Saraceno, 'Fecondità, famiglia e lavoro', in Micheli (ed.), *La società*, pp. 187–201.

16 Golini and Silvestrini, 'Cambiamenti familiari', p. 91, table 2.1. The percentage of those married among young women aged twenty-two had been 41.8 per cent in 1981; it had dropped to just 21.2 per cent by 1991.

17 ibid., p. 104, n. 12.

18 G. Pietropolli Charmet, *Un nuovo padre*, Milano, 1995, pp. 146–7.

19 G. Dalla Zuanna, 'Meglio soli. Famiglia e natalià in Italia', *Il Mulino*, vol. XLIV (1995), no. 357, p. 115. As for old people, statistics for the city of Bologna show a very limited increase for those in old people's homes in the period 1981–91. In 1991 only 0.7 per cent of men and 1.8 per cent of women over the age of sixty were in institutions. Even for those over the age of eighty-five the respective percentages were still only 4.4 per cent of men and 10 per cent of women; M. Barbagli and M. Pisati, *Rapporto sulla situazione sociale a Bologna*, Bologna, 1995, pp. 203ff.

20 For Neapolitan families, see V. Capecchi and E. Pugliese, 'Due città a confronto: Bologna e Napoli', *Inchiesta*, vol. VIII (1978), nos. 35–6, pp. 21ff.

21 P. Filippucci, *Presenting the Past in Bassano*, unpublished PhD Dissertation, University of Cambridge, 1992, p. 153.

22 However, in the South there was a more marked tendency for young men, once they had found work, to leave the family home; and also for young women, whether employed or not, to get married at an earlier age than in the Centre-North of the country; S. Piccone Stella, 'I giovani in famiglia', in Barbagli and Saraceno (eds.), *Lo stato delle famiglie*, pp. 154–8.

23 Eugenia Scabini makes the important point that research in various countries shows that the choice not to have children is rarely a choice as such, but rather a putting-off of the decision until it is too late – certainly for two children, and often for one; E. Scabini, 'Aspettative di un figlio e catene generazionali', in Micheli (ed.), *La società*, p. 205.

24 For the low level of family allowances and their constant variations over the decades, see Golini, 'Le tendenze demografiche dell'Italia in un quadro europeo', pp. 39–40.

25 Here, too, we can trace a direct legacy of Catholic social teaching, to the effect that small children were best at home with their mothers, or, failing that, at school in the care of the nuns. Attitudes to, and care of, childbirth still left a great deal to be desired. The anthropologist Victoria Goddard noted for Naples in the late 70s: 'In a maternity clinic serving a working-class population, women at different stages of labour were packed into a small ward . . . No pain relief was offered and no physical contact or movement was encouraged. The midwife made regular visits to the ward, admonishing women for complaining and pointing out that pain was what motherhood was about'; V. Goddard, *Gender, Work and Family in Naples*, Oxford/Washington DC, 1996, pp. 188–9. For a further discussion of state–family relations, see below, Chapter 7.

26 For Italy under Fascism, see V. De Grazia, *How Fascism Ruled Women*, Berkeley, 1992, especially Ch. 3, 'Motherhood', and C. Saraceno, 'Redefining maternity and paternity: gender, pronatalism and social policies in Fascist Italy', in G. Bock and P. Thane (eds.), *Maternity and Gender Policies*, London, 1991, pp. 196–212. For Germany under Nazism, C. Koonz, *Mothers in the Fatherland*, New York, 1986; G. Bock, 'Antinatalism, maternity and paternity in National Socialist racism', in Bock and Thane (eds.), *Maternity*, pp. 233–55; and the eye-witness account of C. Kirkpatrick, *Nazi Germany: its Women and Family Life*, Indianapolis,

1938. For the contrasting experiences of France and Britain in the inter-war years. S. Pedersen, *Family, Dependence and the Origins of the Welfare State*, Cambridge, 1993. For Franco's Spain, M. Nash, 'Pronatalism and motherhood in Franco's Spain', in Bock and Thane (eds.), *Maternity*, pp. 160—77.

27 *Eurostat Yearbook '95*, p. 50. For a reflection on the Swedish and Italian cases, A. Pinnelli, 'Modernizzazione socio-economica, condizione femminile e nuovi comportamenti familiari e procreativi', *Stato e Mercato*, no. 36 (1992), pp. 401—28. In 1989, for example, the Swedish government offered putative working mothers the possibility of having one long unbroken spell of maternity leave if they had a second child within thirty months of the birth of the preceding one.

28 Louis Roussel veers dangerously close to this position when he argues in favour of a general demographic convergence of European countries, with Sweden always leading the way, and the South of the continent always catching up the North; Roussel, 'La famille en Europe occidentale', pp. 145—50. For a less idealized vision of Swedish family life, and some sharp distinctions between Denmark, Norway and Sweden, see A. Leira, *Welfare States and Working Mothers*, Cambridge, 1992.

29 In Bologna in the 1990s the total fertility rate hovered around the 0.80 children per woman mark; Barbagli and Pisati, *Rapporto*, p. 198.

30 In Italy, unlike in the majority of other European countries, it is necessary for a divorcing couple to have recourse to two separate judicial acts — separation and then divorce — with an obligatory three years between them; more than 40 per cent of separations are never transformed into divorces. See G. Maggioni, 'Le separazioni e i divorzi', in Barbagli and Saraceno (eds.), *Lo stato delle famiglie*, pp. 233—5. See also Statistical Appendix, nos. 5 and 6. The recent Eurobarometer survey, *Europeans and the Family*, Bruxelles, 1994, p. 71, table 3.14, revealed that Italians, along with the Greeks and Portuguese, felt most negatively about the consequences for children of the divorce of parents who did not get on together any more. The Spaniards, on the other hand, as in many other parts of this opinion poll, were much nearer the EU average. This apparently more rapid evolution of Spanish public opinion serves to warn against any over-homogeneous southern European model.

31 A. L. Zanatta, 'Le famiglie con un solo genitore', in Barbagli and Saraceno (eds.), *Lo stato delle famiglie*, pp. 249—50. See also OECD, *Lone Parent Families*, Paris, 1990, especially p. 29, table 2.1, on the incidence of lone-parent families in Europe.

32 *Eurostat. Statistics in Focus. Population and Social Conditions*, 1995, no. 8, p. 4, table 2.1, on the incidence of lone-parent families in Europe.

33 J. Finch, 'Kinship and friendship', pp. 91—2.

34 L. Diena, *Gli uomini e le masse*, Torino, 1960, p. 73.

35 It was E. Littwack who first coined this expression; see his two articles 'Occupational mobility and extended family cohesion' and 'Geographic mobility and extended family cohesion', both in *American Sociological Review*, vol. XV (1960), nos. 1 and 3, pp. 9—21 and 385—94. M. Paci had already suggested the ubiquity

of this form in urban Italy in his *La struttura sociale italiana*, Bologna, 1982, pp. 69–79, and in particular p. 76, table 5. See also F. Bugarini and G. Vicarelli, 'Interazione e sostegno parentale in ambiente urbano', *Rassegna Italiana di Sociologia*, vol. XX (1979), no. 1, pp. 464–93. For evidence on the role of grandparents in a more traditional Calabrian setting (Zaccanopoli, province of Catanzaro) in the 1980s, see M. Minicuci, *Qui e altrove*, Milano, 1989, p. 294.

36 L. Balbo, M. P. May and G. A. Micheli, *Vincoli e strategie nella vita quotidiana*, Milano, 1990, p. 25 and p. 33, table 1.8. The survey did not stipulate exactly who were considered 'closest relatives'. Interesting regional differences have emerged over which set of grandparents (or parents, in the absence of a third generation) received more attention – those of the woman or those of the man. For a detailed treatment of this problem see M. Barbagli, 'Linee di parentela', *Polis*, vol. V (1991), no. 1, pp. 5–19; M. Barbagli, 'I genitori di lei e quelli di lui. Una ricerca sui rapporti di parentela in Emilia-Romagna', ibid., pp. 71–83; A. Oppo, 'Madri, figlie e sorelle: solidarietà parentali in Sardegna', ibid., pp. 21–48; S. La Mendola, 'I rapporti di parentela in Veneto', ibid., pp. 49–70.

37 P. De Sandre, 'Quando i giovani lasciano la famiglia', *Studi Interdisciplinari sulla Famiglia*, no. 7 (1986), p. 74, table 4. The statistics for Italy are for 1983 and for the other countries for 1982.

38 Cavalli and De Lillo, *Giovanni anni '90*, pp. 211–13.

39 Pinnelli, 'Modernizzazione socio-economica', p. 417, has a useful discussion of housing markets in different European countries. In Sweden and Denmark nearly half of all accommodation was available for rent.

40 See A. Cavalli and O. Galland (eds.), *Youth in Europe*, London, 1995, and Piccone Stella, 'I giovani in famiglia', pp. 151–3.

41 The Eurisko survey of 1986 revealed that 97.7 per cent of Italians described their families as 'very' or 'quite' united (72.3 per cent opted for the first and 27.4 per cent for the second); A. Calvi (ed.), *Indagine sociale italiana. Rapporto 1986*, Milano, 1986, p. 159, table 5.3.

42 G. De Rita, 'L'impresa famiglia', in P. Melograni and L. Scaraffia (eds.), *La famiglia italiana dall'Ottocento ad oggi*, Bari, 1988, pp. 383–416.

43 De Rita concentrated his attention on the process of enrichment of Italian families, a process which he extended rather arbitrarily to all sections of the population in these years.

44 ibid., p. 416.

45 D. Tettamanzi, 'Famiglia chiesa domestica', in A. Alessandri *et al.*, *La 'Familiaris Consortio'*, Città del Vaticano, 1982, pp. 222–34.

46 For transitions in patriarchy, see F. Bimbi, 'Il patriarcato: un privilegio senza legittimazione?', in F. Bimbi and G. Castellano (eds.), *Madri e padri*, Milano, 1992, pp. 191–200.

47 P. Nava, 'Emilia-Romagna: a una svolta la cultura dei servizi', in Ginsborg (ed.), *Stato dell'Italia*, p. 159.

48 For a British discussion of this point, with reference to middle-class couples, see the article by K. Backett, 'The negotiation of fatherhood', in C. Lewis and M. O'Brien (eds.), *Reassessing Fatherhood*, London, 1987, pp. 74—90.

49 C. Bertolo, 'Modelli culturali e pratiche sociali tra passato e presente', in Bimbi and Castellano (eds.), *Madri e padri*, pp. 55—9, on reactions to paternity among young fathers in Emilia-Romagna.

50 Pietropolli Charmet, *Un nuovo padre*, p. 76. For Zaccanopoli, in the province of Catanzaro, Minicuci, *Qui e altrove*, p. 290.

51 E. Rosci, 'Le lunghe adolescenze dell'Italia d'oggi', in Ginsborg (ed.), *Stato dell'Italia*, p. 302.

52 H. Pitkin, *The House That Giacomo Built*, Cambridge, 1985, p. 213.

53 Goddard, *Gender*, p. 188.

54 For a stimulating recent discussion of the role of the Virgin Mary, see L. Accati, 'Il marito della santa. Ruolo paterno, ruolo materno e politica italiana', *Meridiana*, no. 13 (1992), pp. 79—105. An excellent general introduction is M. Warner, *Alone of All Her Sex*, London, 1976 (new edn with 'Afterthoughts', 1990). See also Goddard, *Gender*, pp. 191ff. For an interesting collection of essays, mainly located in earlier centuries, see G. Fiume (ed.), *Madri*, Venezia, 1995.

55 E. Bernhard, 'Il complesso della Grande Madre' [1960], in E. Bernhard, *Mitobiografia*, Milano, 1969, p. 171. For a very informative discussion of the significance of the massive statues of mothers, *matres matutae*, to be found in the Museum of Capua in Campania, see S. Vegetti Finzi, 'Il mito delle origini', in S. Lagorio, S. Vegetti Finzi and L. Ravasi, *Se noi siamo la terra*, Milano, 1996, pp. 54—60.

56 A. Parsons, 'Is the Oedipus complex universal?', in A. Parsons, *Belief, Magic and Anomie*, New York, 1969, pp. 3—66.

57 ibid., pp. 46—7.

58 ibid., pp. 44 and 52.

59 ibid., p. 51.

60 ISTAT, *Indagini multiscopo sulle famiglie, anni 1993—94. Aspetti della vita quotidiana*, vol. II, Roma, 1996, pp. 52ff.

61 L. Laurenzi, 'Appesi alle gonne della mamma', *la Repubblica*, 18 February 1997. See also A. Gumbel, 'Italian men cling to mamma', *Speak Up*, vol. 13 (1997), no. 3, pp. 30—32.

62 More recently there have been some variations on this theme, as with a 'Zigulì' advertisement of 1995, delightfully described by Oreste Del Buono ('Mamma sciattona con pallina di frutta', *L'Espresso*, vol. XLI (1995), no. 6, p. 173): 'We see a mother who moves from one room to another and only stops in front of the oven, which seems, hardly reassuringly, to be about to go up in flames. Her knees give way and she slips towards the floor. There she would remain, overwhelmed by the demands of home and office, did not her son intervene affectionately to break her fall. As she falls, he offers her a Zigulì, the famous fruit pastille. Anxiety, tiredness, sweat, feelings and resentments, all disappear

in a hug between the two. With a laugh that conveys abandonment and liberation, the mother becomes the same age as her son.'

63 See the comments of the Catholic theologian E. Ruffini, 'La teologia di fronte alle problematiche della famiglia nella tensione tra "pubblico" e "privato"', in Università Cattolica del Sacro Cuore, *La coscienza contemporanea tra "pubblico" e "privato"*, Milano, 1979, p. 158.

64 R. Palomba and L. L. Sabbadini, 'Differenze di genere e uso del tempo nella vita quotidiana', in Paci (ed.), *Le dimensioni*, pp. 223 and 226, tables 6.6 and 6.7.

65 ibid., p. 224.

66 It would be more than possible to suggest that Italian mothers shared these characteristics with those in other major southern European and Christian countries, both orthodox and Catholic. Interesting elements of comparison between Spanish and Italian families are suggested in T. Jurado Guerrero and M. Naldini, 'Is the South so different? Italian and Spanish families in comparative perspective', in M. Rhodes (ed.), *Southern European Welfare States*, London, 1997, pp. 42–66. See also D. S. Reher, *Perspectives on the Family in Spain, Past and Present*, Oxford, 1997, and I. Alberdi (ed.), *Informe sobre la situación de la familia en España*, Madrid, 1995. For illuminating similarities and contrasts with Islamic motherhood in the Mediterranean, with special reference to Algeria, see A. Bouhdiba, *Sexuality in Islam*, London, 1985, Ch. 13, 'In the kingdom of the mother', pp. 212–30.

67 The negative and positive roles of Italian grandparents have been sensitively analysed by S. Vegetti Finzi, *Il romanzo della famiglia*, Milano, 1992, pp. 303ff. See also the interesting article based on recent research in Tuscany: F. Budini Gattai and T. Musatti, 'Grandmothers' involvement in grandchildren's care: attitudes, feelings and emotions', *Family Relations*, vol. XLVIII (1999), no. 1, pp. 35–42.

68 Scabini, 'Aspettative di un figlio', p. 204.

69 V. Padiglione and C. Pontalti, 'Fra le generazioni modelli di connessione simbolica', in Donati (ed.), *Quarto rapporto*, p. 199.

70 *Europeans and the Family*, p. 85, table 4.6. The British place in this list may be somewhat of a surprise, both to Italian and to British readers.

71 The most forceful statement of the dangers inherent in a family turned inward upon itself comes from C. C. Harris, 'The changing relation between family and societal form in western society' (1977), in M. Anderson (ed.), *Sociology of the Family*, Harmondsworth, 1980 (2nd edn), p. 399: 'the resultant concentration of creative and emotional energies within this small compass constitutes what I shall term the family's *implosion* or "the bursting inward of a vessel by external pressure".'

72 S. Nirenstein, 'Muro in famiglia', *la Repubblica*, 30 January 1995. The survey was conducted in Rome, Naples and Milan with a sample of 887 young women and men. For feelings among youth of isolation and solitude that penetrated the family itself, see P. Di Nicola and M. De Bernart, 'Generazioni di genitori e

generazioni di figli; mondi incomunicabili?', in Donati (ed.), *Quarto rapporto*, p. 281.

73 L. Balbo, 'Un caso di capitalismo assistenziale: la società italiana', *Inchiesta*, vol. VII (1977), no. 28, p. 13.

74 S. De Matteis, 'Storie di famiglia. Appunti e ipotesi antroplogiche sulla famiglia a Napoli', *Meridiana*, no. 17 (1993), pp. 137–8. Our knowledge of contemporary Neapolitan families is unusually rich thanks to the articles collected and introduced by Gabriella Gribaudi in this same number of *Meridiana*. See her 'Familismo e famiglia a Napoli e nel Mezzogiorno', ibid., pp. 13–42; S. Alvino, 'Nel cuore di Montecalvario: "un vicinato di parenti" ', pp. 113–36; and also L. Grilli, 'Nei vicoli di Napoli. Reti sociali e percorsi individuali', *Meridiana*, no. 15 (1992), pp. 223–47. For the self-sacrificing life of a middle-class housewife in the same city, see 'Comunque mi sono annullata (l'esperienza di una casalinga napoletana raccolta da G. Contini)', in Ginsborg (ed.), *Stato dell'Italia*, pp. 303–5.

75 G. Ingrassia, *Indagine campionaria sui principali aspetti socio-economici della città di Palermo con particolare riferimento alla povertà economica*, Trapani, 1988, pp. 62–4.

76 E. Mingione, 'Economia informale, strategie formali e Mezzogiorno', *Inchiesta*, vol. XVI (1986), no. 74, p. 1.

77 M. Mafai, 'Napoli a gonfie Vele', *la Repubblica*, 17 September 1995.

78 G. De Luca, 'Noi abbattiamo le Vele', *la Repubblica* (Neapolitan edition), 20 March 1991, for the report of a group of health workers to the USL 41; see also O. Lucarelli, 'Finalmente le finestre per uscire dal ghetto', *la Repubblica* (Neapolitan edition), 19 March 1991.

79 An interesting discussion of these changes, as they were reflected in the advertising of the time, is to be found in L. Minestroni, *Casa dolce casa*, Milano, 1996, pp. 36ff.

80 See the fine description in S. Lanaro, *Storia dell'Italia repubblicana*, Venezia, 1992, pp. 253–4.

81 Such a distinction is difficult to draw, not only because the luxuries of yesterday rapidly become the necessities of today, but also because needs are perforce socially determined. Colin Campbell, in his outstanding book *The Romantic Ethic and the Spirit of Modern Consumerism*, Oxford, 1987, makes a number of attempts to distinguish between the two (see, for example, pp. 37ff. and pp. 59–60). He stresses, for example, the way in which 'the original contrast between need and want can be related to the difference between activities which aim to relieve discomfort and those which yield pleasure' (p. 59); and again (p. 60) 'pleasure and utility are very different concepts, relating to contrasting aspects of human conduct'. However, such stark distinctions seem unsustainable when related to the consumption of everyday life. An air-conditioning machine, for instance, is both utilitarian and pleasurable.

82 See, for example, U. La Malfa, 'Problemi e prospettive dello sviluppo economico italiano. Nota aggiuntiva, presentata al Parlamento dal Ministro del Bilancio il 22 maggio 1962', in U. La Malfa, *Discorsi parlamentari*, Roma, 1963, p. 783.

83 A. K. Sen, 'Why does poverty persist in rich countries?', in P. Giudicini and G. Pieretti (eds.), *Urban Poverty and Human Dignity*, Milano, 1994, pp. 98–9.

84 The analogy is Sen's.

85 See C. D'Apice, *L'arcipelago dei consumi*, Bari, 1981, pp. 65ff. None the less, taking the decade as a whole (see pp. 86–7, table 7), Italian private consumption increased by an average 3 per cent, while that in the UK did so only by 2.1 per cent.

86 Campbell, *The Romantic Ethic*, p. 89, and more in general pp. 77–95.

87 ibid., p. 76.

88 For the statistic for 1996, see CENSIS, *Rapporto sulla situazione sociale del Paese. 1996*, Milano, 1996, p. 546, table 3. The information on the 1980s is to be found in R. Biorcio and M. Maneri, 'Consumi e società: dagli anni Ottanta agli anni Novanta', in M. Livolsi (ed.), *L'Italia che cambia*, Firenze, 1993, p. 188, table 2. Stereo hi-fis spread more slowly but steadily: from 34.0 per cent of families in 1986 to 47.6 per cent in 1992.

89 See Statistical Appendix, no. 15.

90 CENSIS, *Rapporto 1996*, p. 546, table 3.

91 Biorcio and Maneri, 'Consumi e società', p. 201, table 7. For the percentage of family income reserved for clothing and footware in the various countries of the European Union, see Statistical Appendix, no. 17.

92 Biorcio and Maneri, 'Consumi e società', p. 201, table 7.

93 A. Silberston and C. P. Raymond, *The Changing Map of Industrial Europe*, London, 1996, p. 46 and table 3.2, for world pharmacy drug sales in January–September 1993. Italy was in third place after Germany and France, a long way ahead of Britain. Lower prices in southern Europe were part, but not all of the explanation of this pattern. For an authoritative and alarming account of the misuse and inutility of many pharmaceutical drugs in contemporary Italy, see G. Traversa, 'Cittadini sottoposti a rischi inutili', in Ginsborg (ed.), *Stato dell'Italia*, pp. 310–13.

94 An invaluable guide to the state of health of the Italian nation is to be found in the annual reports edited by M. Geddes, *La salute degli italiani*, Roma, 1990, onwards.

95 See Statistical Appendix, no. 9.

96 Filippucci, *Presenting the Past*, p. 142.

97 N. Riza, 'Il palinsesto come fattore di produzione. Evoluzione delle logiche di programmazione nell'emittenza commerciale', *Problemi dell'Informazione*, vol. XV (1990), no. 4, p. 530.

98 D. Forgacs, *Italian Culture in the Industrial Era, 1880–1980*, Manchester, 1990, pp. 184–5.

99 V. Packard, *Hidden Persuaders*, New York, 1957.

100 For an interesting analysis, R. Grandi, *Come parla la pubblicità*, Milano, 1987, especially p. 14.

101 Calvi (ed.), *Indagine sociale*, p. 172 and table 5.14, p. 173.

102 On consumption as emulation, see T. Veblen, *The Theory of the Leisure Class*, London, 1899.

103 Biorci and Maneri, 'Consumi e società', pp. 191–9. Their typology is based on data from the Eursiko 'Sinottica' surveys of 1986 and 1990, and derives from responses to a large number of questions concerning consumer habits; see the methodological note, pp. 205–7. For some comparisons, CENSIS, *Consumi '87*, Milano, 1987; CENSIS, *Consumi '90*, Milano, 1990; G. P. Fabris and V. Mortara, *Le otto Italie*, Milano, 1986.

104 J. C. Agnew has identified two principal strands in the critique of consumerism: the first, English, 'extends from Thomas Carlyle's caustic denunciations of advertising puffery through George Orwell's even grimmer ruminations a century later', the second, Continental, moves from Marx's discussion of commodity fetishism to the work of Lukacs, Walter Benjamin and the Frankfurt school. 'These two traditions of criticism differ in important respects, but they both picture western history and culture – time and space – as invaded and colonized by commodities and commodity-relations': J. C. Agnew, 'Coming up for air: consumer culture in historical perspective', in J. Brewer and R. Porter (eds.), *Consumption and the World of Goods*, London, 1993, p. 20. There is, of course, a third important strand, the Catholic one.

105 See, for instance, his comments on the fate of the Portuguese revolution of the 1970s: 'The Portuguese people has celebrated the 1st May . . . with a freedom, an enthusiasm and a sincerity as if the last time had been only yesterday. But it is to be expected that five years of "consumerist fascism" will radically change things': P. P. Pasolini, *Scritti corsari*, Milano, 1981 [1st edn 1977], 11 July 1974, p. 76.

106 Agnew, 'Coming up for air', p. 34.

107 D. Miller, *Material Culture and Mass Consumption*, Oxford, 1987, p. 77. For Miller's use of 'sublation', derived from Hegel's *Phenomenology of the Spirit*, see pp. 19–33.

108 E. Berlinguer, *Austerità, occasione per trasformare l'Italia*, Roma, 1977, p. 18.

109 E. Berlinguer, *Economia, stato, pace: l'iniziativa e le proposte del PCI* (Rapporto, conclusioni e documento politico del XVI congresso), Roma, 1983, p. 23. For a further discussion of Berlinguer's treatment of these themes, see M. D'Alema and P. Ginsborg, *Dialogo su Berlinguer* (ed. M. Battini), Firenze, 1994, pp. 71ff.

110 On the question of refuse and its disposal, see above all G. Viale, *Un mondo usa e getta*, Milano, 1994.

111 Conversation with the author; Firenze, September 1985.

112 F. Piselli, *Parentela ed emigrazione*, Torino, 1981, p. 159.

113 A. Hirschman, *Shifting Involvements*, Princeton, 1978, p. 46.

114 Campbell, *The Romantic Ethic*, p. 216: 'As there is no good [historical reason] for assuming that a one-way trend governs such changes, it would seem reasonable to postulate a *recurso* pattern of generation – degeneration – regeneration to have typified the last two hundred years. Thus, if Romanticism did originally

make hedonism possible, then the spirit of hedonism has subsequently also functioned to give rise to further outbursts of romantic fervour.'

115 ibid.

116 For a further discussion of television, see below, Chapter 5, pp. 108—12.

117 M. P. Comand and M. Santucci, 'Il consumo addomesticato', in F. Casetti (ed.), *L'ospite fisso*, Milano, 1995, pp. 179—81.

118 Cf. the comments and illustrations in Minestroni, *Casa dolce casa*, pp. 97—101, where she talks of the bathroom's conversion from a 'place of physical needs' to a 'site for body care' (p. 97).

119 See also the comments of Francesco Casetti, 'Quasi di casa. Mass media, televisione e famiglia', in F. Casetti (ed.), *L'ospite fisso*, p. 16: 'Sometimes it is the content of the programme which makes the audience react, but at others it is purely marginal aspects, such as the tone of voice of the presenter, the clothes of a guest, or the furnishings in the house of the hero of the telefilm.'

120 C. Lasch, *Haven in a Heartless World*, New York, 1977, p. xxiii.

121 For a discussion of the 'general potential' of goods, see Miller, *Material Culture*, p. 109.

122 An expansion that incidentally led to the presence of a significant number of English language teachers in Italy, many of whom settled permanently in the country. The influx, in its social origins, wealth, and ideology, was in stark contrast to traditional British residents in Italian cities, and brought a welcome breath of fresh air.

123 This was clearly an element of progress, even if there were heavy costs attached. Women, much more than men, risked a rapid deterioration in their living standards. In addition the freedom of adults often meant the suffering of children. For a passionate and convincing treatment of the need to defend vulnerable children as the basis of constructing citizenship, see P. Hewitt, 'Re-inventing citizenship: the role of family policy', in C. Crouch and D. Marquand (eds.), *Reinventing Collective Action*, Oxford, 1995, pp. 103—11.

124 See, for example, G. Dall'Orto, *Manuale per coppie diverse*, Roma, 1994.

125 Cf. Cavalli and De Lillo, *Giovani anni Novanta*, pp. 213—14.

126 For a detailed discussion of these issues, with reference to the Valdelsa in Tuscany, see P. Ginsborg, 'I cambiamenti della famiglia in un distretto industriale italiano, 1965—1997', in P. Ginsborg and F. Ramella (eds.), *Un'Italia minore*, Firenze, 1999, pp. 109—54.

127 Cf. C. Sieder and M. Mitterauer, 'The reconstruction of the family life course', in R. Wall *et al.*, *Family Forms in Historic Europe*, Cambridge, 1983, p. 310.

128 A. Bagnasco, *L'Italia in tempo di cambiamento politico*, Bologna, 1996, p. 56. He continues (p. 59): 'Certain types of family, including the "contractual" one, favour the growth of a free associationism, for they create the cultural bases for it.'

Chapter 4: *Civil Society and Mass Culture*

1 For two important introductions to the history of the term 'civil society', see M. Riedel, 'Der Begriff der "Bürgerlichen Gesellschaft" und des Problem seines geschichtlichen Ursprungs', in M. Riedel, *Studien zu Hegels Rechtsphilosophie*, Frankfurt am Main, 1969, pp. 135–66; and N. Bobbio, 'Società civile', in N. Bobbio, N. Matteucci and G. F. Pasquino (eds.), *Dizionario politico*, Torino, 1983, pp. 1084–90.

2 'Civil society affords a spectacle of extravagance and misery as well as the physical and ethical corruption common to both'; G. W. F. Hegel, *Elements of the Philosophy of Right* (ed. A. W. Wood), Cambridge, 1991, p. 222, §185. For an excellent recent Italian commentary, see C. Mancina, *Differenze nell'eticità*, Napoli, 1991, pp. 161–211.

3 'If you assume given stages of development in production, commerce or consumption, you will have a corresponding form of social constitution, a corresponding organization, whether of the family, of the estates or of the classes – in a word, a corresponding civil society'; letter to P. V. Anenkov, 28 December 1846, in K. Marx and F. Engels, *Collected Works*, vol. XXXVIII, London, 1982, p. 96.

4 For a good summary, see J. L. Cohen and A. Arato, *Civil Society and Political Theory*, Cambridge, Mass., 1992, Ch. 1. See also Z. A. Pelczynski, 'Solidarity and "the rebirth of civil society" in Poland, 1976–81', in J. Keane (ed.), *Civil Society and the State*, London, 1988, pp. 361–80.

5 M. Walzer, 'Introduction', in M. Walzer (ed.), *Towards a Global Civil Society*, Providence/Oxford, 1995, p. 1. Other recent treatments of the term include V. Pérez-Díaz, *The Return of Civil Society*, Cambridge, Mass., 1993; E. Gellner, *Conditions of Liberty*, London, 1994; J. A. Hall (ed.), *Civil Society*, Oxford, 1995; J. Keane, *Civil Society. Old Images, New Visions*, London, 1998.

6 G. Calvi, 'Presentazione del Rapporto 1986', in G. Calvi (ed.), *Indagine sociale italiana. Rapporto 1986*, Milano, 1987, p. 11. A Eurobarometer survey of the same year revealed that while only 10 per cent of Germans considered their co-nationals not very trustworthy or not at all trustworthy, the corresponding figure for Spaniards was 16 per cent, for Greeks 25 per cent, and for Italians a startling 35 per cent, which increased to 45 per cent in the South and islands; *Eurobarometer*, no. 25, June 1986, pp. 26–33. For 'furbizia', see the convincing definition of John Davis in his anthropological study of one village in the Basilicata in 1973: 'The quality *furbo* – foreseeing all the possibilities, having the strength of purpose to ignore the moral and affective claims of a partner and to take advantage of his gullible, or trusting, or slow-witted nature – is much admired in Pisticci and is inculcated at an early age'; J. Davis, *Land and Family in Pisticci*, London, 1973, p. 23.

7 M. Revelli, *Le due destre*, Torino, 1996, p. 17.

8 R. Inglehart, *The Silent Revolution*, Princeton, 1977.

9 Loredana Sciolla offers a useful definition in her 'Identità e mutamento culturale

nell'Italia di oggi', in V. Cesareo (ed.), *La cultura dell'Italia contemporanea*, Torino, 1990, p. 38.

10 For societies and states of this sort, see above all N. Mouzelis, *Politics in the Semi-Periphery*, London, 1986, which deals with the Balkans, Greece and Latin America; see also his 'Modernity, late development and civil society', in Hall (ed.), *Civil Society*, pp. 224–49.

11 See in particular G. Gribaudi, 'Il paradigma del "familismo amorale" ', in P. Macry and A. Massafra (eds.), *Fra storia e storiografia*, Bologna, 1994, pp. 337–54; G. Gribaudi, 'Familismo e famiglia a Napoli', ibid., pp. 13–42.

12 P. Ginsborg, 'Familismo', in Ginsborg (ed.), *Stato dell'Italia*, pp. 78–82; Bagnasco, *L'Italia in tempi di cambiamento politico*, pp. 55–60; C. Trigilia, 'Conclusioni: associazionismo e nuovo Mezzogiorno', in C. Trigilia (ed.), *Cultura e sviluppo*, Roma, 1995, pp. 223–5.

13 E. Banfield, *The Moral Basis of a Backward Society*, Glencoe, Ill., 1958, p. 10. Banfield's 'predictive hypothesis' was that the villagers 'acted as if they were following this rule: "Maximize the material, short-run advantage of the nuclear family; assume that all others will do likewise" ' (ibid., p. 83).

14 See the excellent collection of articles in the Appendix to D. De Masi's Italian edition of Banfield, *Le basi morali di una società arretrata*, Bologna, 1976, and in particular A. Pizzorno, 'Familismo amorale e marginalità storica, ovvero perché non c'è niente da fare a Montegrano', ibid., pp. 237–53.

15 For Milanese working-class families in the early 70s, see L. Balbo, *Stato di famiglia*, Milano, 1976, pp. 132–3. In Britain the concept of 'privatism' is that most akin to 'familism'. For its use, see the famous study of Luton workers by J. Goldthorpe *et al.*, *The Affluent Worker*, 3 vols., London, 1968–9. A revisitation of Luton and a contesting of the privatism thesis is to be found in F. Devine, *Affluent Workers Revisited*, Edinburgh, 1992.

16 Ginsborg, 'Familismo', p. 79.

17 N. Bobbio, 'La fine della prima Repubblica' (interview with S. Vertone), *Europeo*, yr XLVI (1990), no. 52, 28 December, p. 107.

18 Banfield, *Le basi morali*, p. 10.

19 Rosci, 'Le lunghe adolescenze', p. 302.

20 The structure of Gabriella Gribaudi's explanation, for instance, belongs very much to this external form of causality; see 'Il paradigma', p. 352.

21 B. Croce, *Teoria e storia della storiografia*, Bari, 1973 [1st edn Napoli, 1917], p. 325.

22 For a sophisticated treatment of the new estates at Milan in this period and the problem of familism, see J. Foot, 'The family and the "Economic Miracle": social transformation, work, leisure and development at Bovisa and Comasina (Milan), 1950–1970', *Contemporary European History*, vol. IV (1995), no. 3, pp. 315–38.

23 J. S. Mill, 'The subjection of women', in J. S. Mill, *On Liberty and Other Essays*, Oxford, 1991 [1st edn 1869], p. 510.

24 S. De Matteis, 'Storie di famiglia. Appunti e ipotesi antropologiche sulla famiglia a Napoli', *Meridiana*, no. 17 (1993), p. 142.

25 See, for example, E. Deniaux, *Clientèles et pouvoir à l'époque de Cicéron*, Rome, 1993. For an interesting comparison between modern clientelism and that of Ancient Rome, see L. Roniger, 'Modern patron–client relations and historical clientelism. Some clues from Ancient Republican Rome', *Archives Européennes de Sociologie*, vol. XXIV (1983), no. 1, pp. 63–95.

26 D. Mack Smith, 'The Latifundia in modern Sicilian history', *Proceedings of the British Academy*, vol. LI (1965), pp. 85–124. For a recent detailed treatment of the Barracco *latifondo* in Calabria, see M. Petrusewicz, *Latifondo*, Padova, 1989.

27 'Patronage may not always and necessarily be illegal or corrupt, and it does have its own pride and morality; but though it may despise the official morality as hypocritical, fraudulent or effeminate, it nevertheless knows that it is not itself *the* official morality'; E. Gellner, 'Patrons and clients', in E. Gellner and J. Waterbury (eds.), *Patrons and Clients in Mediterranean Societies*, London 1977, p. 3. For a strong emphasis on this point in an Italian context, see J. Walston, *The Mafia and Clientelism*, London, 1988. A recent and acute study of patronage is to be found in D. Moss, 'Patronage revisited: the dynamics of information and reputation', *Journal of Modern Italian Studies*, vol. 1 (1995), no. 1, pp. 58–93.

28 A. Signorelli, 'L'incertezza del diritto. Clientelismo politico e innovazione nel Mezogiorno degli anni '80', *Problemi del Socialismo*, 1988, nos. 2–3, p. 258.

29 A. Signorelli, 'Patroni e clienti', in C. Pasquinelli (ed.), *Potere senza stato*, Roma, 1986, pp. 156–7. Obviously, the simple vertical diadic relationship between patron and client expands in any complex society into a diffuse system involving alternative clientelistic networks, with large numbers of clients and competing patrons. Major studies of the southern Italian clientelist use of state resources include P. Allum, *Politics and Society in Post-war Naples*, Cambridge, 1973; M. Caciagli *et al.*, *Democrazia cristiana e potere nel Mezzogiorno*, Firenze, 1977; J. Chubb, *Patronage, Power and Poverty in Southern Italy*, Cambridge, 1982.

30 I completely agree with Amalia Signorelli that much of the general literature on clientelism, especially anthropological and sociological, has presented in a profoundly ambiguous way the relative advantages of the system to patron and to client, and has systematically under-presented the gulf that separates them in terms of power and economic resources; see A. Signorelli, *Chi può e chi aspetta*, Napoli, 1983, pp. 27ff.

31 See Gellner and Waterbury (eds.), *Patrons and Clients, passim*; the remarks by G. Sapelli on what he calls 'Neo-caciquism', in G. Sapelli, *Southern Europe since 1945*, London, 1995, pp. 111–22; N. Mouzelis, 'Class and clientelistic politics: the case of Greece', *Sociological Review*, vol. XXVI (1978), pp. 471–97.

32 Signorelli, 'L'incertezza del diritto', p. 267.

33 See the necessarily cautionary remarks on this point made by P. Bevilacqua in 'La mafia e la Spagna', *Meridiana*, no. 13 (1992), p. 116.

34 L. Franchetti, *Condizioni politiche e amministrative della Sicilia*, Roma, 1993 [1st edn 1877], pp. 39—41.

35 Andreotti's specific objection on this occasion was to the speech of Cesare Merzagora, the then President of the Senate, in which he praised Enrico De Nicola for having written only one letter of recommendation in his whole life; see Andreotti's column 'Zanzariera' in *Concretezza*, vol. III (1957), no. 22, p. 6.

36 T. W. Smith, commenting on a seven-country survey of 1987, wrote: 'Italy differs in giving more weight to connections – "knowing the right people" (ranked second) and "political connections" (ranked fifth) – than does any of the other nations'; T. W. Smith, 'Inequality and welfare', in Jowell *et al.*, *British Social Attitudes*, p. 68 and table 4.2, pp. 80—81. See also S. Scamuzzi, 'La percezione della disuguaglianza sociale', in Paci (ed.), *Le dimensioni*, p. 73, table 1.6.

37 The institutions of *comparaggio* or *comparatico*, which first flourished in the whole of Europe between the third and the ninth century A D, were still of considerable significance in rural Italy in the second half of the twentieth. Spiritual kinship has both a vertical and horizontal element: the relationship of *comparaggio* between the godparent and the child (vertical) and that of *compadrinaggio* between the child's real parents and his spiritual ones (horizontal). Often, though, vertical relationships dominated both, as local notables were chosen as godparents in order to insert the child into a solid structure of patron–client relations. In her study of three communities in Calabria during the 1980s, Fortunata Piselli shows how political figures, especially the mayor, 'go hunting for godchildren'; F. Piselli, 'Il comparatico politico', *L'Uomo*, vol. XI (1987), no. 1, pp. 137—59. On the other hand, in another Calabrian village, Zaccanopoli, Minicuci found in the same period the strong survival of horizontal and more egalitarian relations among parents and godparents; Minicuci, *Qui e altrove*, p. 303. More generally, see J. H. Lynch, *Godparents and Kinship in Early Medieval Europe*, Princeton, 1986; I. Signorini, *Padrini e compari*, Torino, 1981; and the excellent case study by R. A. Miller and M. G. Miller, 'The golden chain. A study of the structure, function and patterning of *comparatico* in a south Italian village'; *American Ethnologist*, vol. V (1978), no. 1, pp. 116—36.

38 G. Greco, 'Potere e parentela nella Sicilia nuova', *Quaderni di Sociologia*, vol. XIX (1970), no. 1, pp. 3—41.

39 For the well-known formulation of the idea of Italian subcultures, see G. Galli *et al.*, *Il comportamento elettorale in Italia*, Bologna, 1968, p. 320.

40 'Allocuzione di S.S. Pio XII alla gioventù maschile di A.C.I. sulle gravi necessità dell'ora presente', *La Civiltà Cattolica*, vol. XCVII (1946), 4 May, p. 170.

41 G. Galli, 'Il PCI, la DC, e la cultura istituzionalizzata in Italia', in A. Manoukian (ed.), *La presenza sociale del PCI e della DC*, Bologna, 1968, p. 648.

42 P. Scoppola, *La "nuova cristianità" perduta*, Roma, 1985, pp. 31—4. The phrase 'eschatological reserve' is that of E. Passerin D'Entrèves, in 'Recenti studi sull'Azione Cattolica in Italia fra Ottocento e Novecento', *Studium*, vol. L (1954), no. 4, p. 231, quoted in Scoppola, *La 'nuova cristianità'*, p. 34.

43 Signorelli, 'Patroni e clienti', p. 155; Accati, 'Il marito della santa', *passim*; see also the remarks of Giovanna Tatò in V. Foa *et al.*, *Le virtù della Repubblica*, Milano, 1994, pp. 74–5: 'Catholic culture is, *par excellence*, the culture of mediation . . . in Italy there exist hundreds of saints, many of them offering "specialized" services. They are the link between the devoted or the desperate individual and the absolute and distant power of God. Similarly, in the public administration and in politics you can find the patron who serves as mediator between the client and the potentate.'

44 See M. Caciagli, 'Quante Italie? Persistenze e trasformazioni delle culture politiche subnazionali', *Polis*, vol. II (1988), no. 3, pp. 429–57.

45 The outstanding account of this decline and absorption, with regard to Communist culture, is S. Gundle, *Between Hollywood and Moscow*, Durham/London, 2000.

46 For a detailed questionnaire in Milan in the mid-1970s, see B. Barbero Avanzini and C. Lanzetti, *Problemi e modelli di vita familiare*, Milano, 1980, especially pp. 194–223 and 244–5.

47 See the vivid description in G. Galli, *Il bipartitismo imperfetto*, Bologna, 1966, pp. 272–3.

48 P. Allum and I. Diamanti, *'50/'80, vent'anni*, Roma, 1986, pp. 37–8 and 103ff. The questionnaire was of 1954.

49 Filippucci, *Presenting the Past*, p. 184.

50 R. Siebert, *E' femmina, però è bella*, Torino, 1991, pp. 344–5.

51 M. Minicuci, 'La casa natale, la casa sognata: Zaccanopoli', in F. Faeta (ed.), *L'architettura in Italia. Calabria*, Bari, 1984, p. 157; Siebert, *E' femmina*, p. 345. For neighbours' relations in Milan, see the interesting study by A. Mutti, *Il buon vicino*, Bologna, 1992.

52 S. Duncan, 'The diverse worlds of European patriarchy', in M. D. García Ramon and J. Monk (eds.), *Women of the European Union*, London/New York, 1996, pp. 74–110.

53 Calvi (ed.), *Indagine sociale italiana*, pp. 160ff.

54 ibid., p. 172. See also table 5.8, p. 165.

55 R. D. Putnam (with R. Leonardi and R. Y. Nanetti), *Making Democracy Work*, Princeton, 1993.

56 ibid., p. 5.

57 ibid., pp. 5–6.

58 ibid., p. 83.

59 ibid., Ch. 4, 'Tracing the roots of the civic community', pp. 121–62.

60 See Ginsborg, *A History*, pp. 233–5. The classic text is A. Bagnasco, *Tre Italie. La problematica territoriale dello sviluppo italiano*, Bologna, 1977.

61 G. Becattini and G. Bianchi, 'Sulla multiregionalità dello sviluppo economico italiano', *Note Economiche*, nos. 5–6 (1992), pp. 22 and 37. For Lombardy, see P. Natale, 'Lega Lombarda e insediamento territoriale: un'analisi ecologica', in

R. Mannheimer (ed.), *La Lega Lombarda*, Milano, 1991, pp. 83–121. For an acute analysis covering the whole of the North, I. Diamanti, *La Lega*, Roma, 1993, pp. 41ff.

62 See, for instance, the reflections of Padre Alessandro Zanotelli and Monsignor Giovanni Nervo, reported in Stella, *Schei*, p. 194.

63 Statistical Appendix, no. 11.

64 Calvi (ed.), *Indagine sociale italiana*, p. 173.

65 K. R. Popper and J. Condry, *Cattiva maestra televisione*, Roma, 1996 [1st edn 1994]; N. Bobbio, G. Bosetti and G. Vattimo, *La sinistra nell'era del karaoke*, Roma, 1994, especially pp. 36–42.

66 Popper and Condry, *Cattiva maestra*, p. 44.

67 T. De Mauro, 'La cultura', in A. Gambino *et al.*, *Dal '68 a oggi*, Bari, 1979, p. 196.

68 J. Meyrowitz, *No Sense of Place*, Oxford, 1985, p. 90.

69 See for example p. 66: 'Hierarchies will be undermined by new media that expose what were once the private spheres of authorities'; or again, p. 64: 'the more a medium of communication tends to merge informational worlds, the more the medium will encourage egalitarian forms of interaction'. The attempt to connect, in rather mechanical fashion, changes in the form of media and wider social transformation begs rather too many questions.

70 For a sensitive discussion of this point in an Italian context, see P. Ortoleva, *Un ventennio a colori*, Firenze, 1995.

71 P. Laslett, 'Elusive intimacy', *Times Literary Supplement*, no. 4639, 28 February 1992, p. 15.

72 B. Gunther and M. Svennevig, *Behind and in Front of the Screen*, London, 1987, p. 75.

73 The structure of television ownership, at least in a British context, is well explained in R. Abercrombie, *Television and Society*, London, 1996, pp. 74–108.

74 Calvi (ed.), *Indagine sociale italiana*, p. 172.

75 S. Lash and J. Urry, *Economies of Signs and Space*, London, 1994, p. 16: 'post-modernist time is based on a sort of video paradigm, where attention spans are short, and events jumbled out of narrative order via re-wind, fast forward and channel hopping.'

76 R. Giudicci, *Periferie: le voci dei cittadini*, Milano, 1993, p. 149.

77 M. Augé, *Non-lieux*, Paris, 1992.

78 Robert Putnam has recently produced disturbing evidence from the United States to support this view. Television watching and 'civic disengagement' were intimately linked. 'Viewers,' concluded Putnam, 'are homebodies'; R. D. Putnam, 'Bowling alone: America's declining social capital', *Journal of Democracy*, vol. VI (1995), no. 1, pp. 64–78.

79 C. Gallucci, 'Sola contro un dannato Biscione', *L'Espresso*, vol. XLI (1995), no. 11, 17 March, pp. 47–50.

80 For an interesting reflection on contemporary Italian journalism, see R. Lumley,

'Peculiarities of the Italian newspaper', in D. Forgacs and R. Lumley (eds.), *Italian Cultural Studies*, Oxford, 1996, pp. 199–215, as well as R. Lumley, *Italian Journalism*, Manchester, 1996.

81 M. Wolf, 'Mass media', in Ginsborg (ed.), *Stato dell'Italia*, p. 587.

82 S. Gundle, 'Television in Italy', in J. Coleman and B. Rollett (eds.), *Television in Europe*, Exeter, 1997, p. 72. Gundle's view of the overall performance of RAI 3 in these years is rather more positive than mine.

83 U. Eco, 'A guide to the neo-television of the 1980s', in Z. G. Baranski and R. Lumley (eds.), *Culture and Conflict in Postwar Italy*, London, 1990, pp. 245–55.

84 For Bernabei's excellent memoirs, see E. Bernabei (with G. Dell'Arti), *L'uomo di fiducia*, Milano, 1999, especially pt 2, 'Alla Rai (1961–74)', pp. 75–211.

85 M. Serra, 'Pomeriggio tivù', *L'Unità*, 14 January 1996.

86 C. Geertz, *The Interpretation of Cultures*, New York, 1973, pp. 448–51. Cockfighting in Bali, the object of his study, is 'set aside from [everyday] life as "only a game" and reconnected to it as "more than a game"' (ibid., p. 450). Geertz uses the expression 'deep play' in its Benthamite sense, that is play in which the stakes are so high that it is, from a utilitarian standpoint, irrational for men to engage in it at all (ibid., p. 432). It would be forcing a point to use this definition for Italian football, even though there are some aspects of it which would comfort such an interpretation. Instead, I use it in the looser sense, also adopted by Geertz, as being revelatory of elements of a deeper culture.

87 A. Signorelli, 'Il tifo e la città virtuale', in A. Signorelli, *Antropologia urbana*, Milano, 1996, p. 194.

88 A. Dal Lago and R. Moscati, *Regalateci un sogno*, Milano, 1992, p. 21.

89 G. P. T. Finn, 'Football violence: a societal psychological perspective', in R. Giulianotti, N. Bonney and M. Hepworth (eds.), *Football, Violence and Social Identity*, London/New York, 1994, p. 93. He adds: 'Both players and supporters are socialized into a culture of quasi-violence: a culture that accepts aggression and violence as central to the game but accompanies this acceptance with all manner of inconsistencies, uncertainties, qualifications and disagreements. For this reason it is more accurately described as a culture of quasi-violence than as a culture of violence' (p. 103).

90 Signorelli adds: 'The *machismo* of the ultras is not only physical courage, strength, aggressivity; it is also the capacity for self-control and the ability to demonstrate predatory skills with regard to the women present'; 'Il *tifo* e la città virtuale', p. 191.

91 Comand and Santucci, 'Il consumo addomesticato', p. 175.

92 For one example among many, see the amusing article by G. Mura, 'Arbitri, ribellatevi', *la Repubblica*, 10 February 1998: 'Thanks to them, to these sewer rats, *sentina omnium malorum*, we all feel much better.'

93 Geertz, *The Interpretation of Cultures*, pp. 423–4.

94 Quoted in N. Porro, *Identità, nazione, cittadinanza*, Roma, 1995, p. 118.

95 ibid., p. 109.

96 ibid., table 4, p. 117. For the contrast with France, whose international results were much more modest in this period, but whose population was much more active in sporting terms, see J. Defrance and C. Pociello, 'Structure and evolution in the field of sports in France', *International Review for the Sociology of Sport*, vol. XXVIII (1993), no. 1, pp. 1–21.

97 Porro, *Identità*, pp. 124–5. In the same period the number of gyms increased from 7,340 to 19,674, and the number of covered tennis-courts and swimming-pools from 719 to 3,830.

98 For this boom and diversification, see S. Pivato, 'Sport: verso nuove forme di consumo', in Ginsborg (ed.), *Stato dell'Italia*, pp. 629–31.

99 C. Lasch, *The Culture of Narcissism*, New York, 1980.

100 Porro, *Identità*, p. 185, table 12. See also, for a longer time sweep, P. Quirino, 'I consumi in Italia dall'Unità ad oggi', in *Storia dell'economia italiana* (ed. R. Romano), vol. III, Torino, 1991, p. 234, table 20, 'Spesa del pubblico per le manifestazioni sportive, 1951–85'.

101 Maria Grazia, 'Interclub', in Dal Lago and Moscati, *Regalateci un sogno*, p. 74.

102 Quoted by Signorelli, 'Il *tifo* e la città virtuale', p. 189.

103 N. Ferlat, *L'ultima curva*, Torino, 1985, *passim*.

104 Dal Lago and Moscati, *Regalateci un sogno*, p. 65. In order to transport 26,000 fans for the final of the Champions' League in Barcelona in 1989, the club chartered a ship, twenty-five aeroplanes and 450 buses.

105 ibid., pp. 44–5.

106 E. Gamba, 'Se lascia la Spagna pronto il Parma', *la Repubblica*, 12 March 1997. In the end, as is well known, Ronaldo went to Inter.

107 G. Simonelli and A. Ferrarotti, *I media nel pallone*, Milano, 1995, p. 116.

108 E. Audisio, 'Un borghese felice di giocare', *Il Venerdì di Repubblica*, 11 June 1993. See also the revealing interview with Baggio's mother, M. Auriti, 'Il mio bimbo d'oro ha un solo difetto: è buddista', *Oggi*, vol. L (1994), no. 3, 24 January.

109 As must be obvious to my readers, this paragraph is based on the personal experience of following my eldest son's team on its peregrinations through Tuscany in the regional and provincial championships of his age group.

110 Wolf, 'Mass media', p. 590.

111 D. Forgacs, 'Cultural consumption, 1940s to 1990s', in Forgacs and Lumley (eds.), *Italian Cultural Studies*, p. 285.

112 P. P. Pasolini, *Lettere luterane*, Torino, 1976, p. 92, and also pp. 53–4, 80–83, 85–91.

113 De Mauro, 'La cultura', p. 171.

114 For an in-depth analysis of these themes, F. Ramella, 'Istruzione, generazioni e cambiamento sociale', in P. Ginsborg and F. Ramella (eds.), *Un'Italia minore*, Firenze, 1999, pp. 185–244.

115 G. Turnaturi, *Associati per amore*, Milano, 1991, p. 90.

116 D. Della Porta, *Movimenti collettivi e sistema politico in Italia*, Bari, 1996, p. 9.

117 I. Colozzi, 'Società civile e terzo settore', in P. P. Donati (ed.), *La società civile in Italia*, Milano, 1997, pp. 123–58; and S. Zamagni, 'Economia civile come forza di civilizzazione per la società italiana', ibid., pp. 159–92. Cf. Revelli, *Le due destre*, pp. 211–27.

118 L. Passerini, 'Gender relations', in Forgacs and Lumley (eds.), *Italian Cultural Studies*, p. 152.

119 For the account of one woman's search, which at the same time was historical research, in these years, see the work of the Catanese historian E. Baeri, *I lumi e il cerchio*, Roma, 1992.

120 A. Rossi-Doria, 'Introduzione' to M. C. Marcuzzo and A. Rossi-Doria (eds.), *La ricerca delle donne*, Torino, 1987, p. 36.

121 A. Rossi-Doria, 'Una rivoluzione non ancora compiuta', in Ginsborg (ed.), *Stato dell'Italia*, p. 263.

122 A. Rossi-Doria, 'Introduzione', p. 37.

123 Turnaturi, *Associati per amore*, p. 38.

124 P. Balistreri, 'La società mafiosa', *MicroMega*, 1990, no. 5, p. 170. The neglect of public spaces was well described by the German journalist Valeska von Roques when she made a pilgrimage to Palma di Montechiaro (province of Agrigento), once the summer residence of Giuseppe Tomasi di Lampedusa, and the small town to which he had given the name 'Donnafugata' in *The Leopard*; V. von Roques, *L'ora dei gattopardi*, Milano, 1996 [original edn *Die Stunde der Leoparden*, München, 1994].

125 Signorelli, *Chi può e chi aspetta*.

126 ibid., p. 82.

127 ibid., p. 141: '40 young people had ceased their education at the lower secondary school or earlier; 114 had completed all or part of their upper secondary school education; and as many as 148 were enrolled at the university.'

128 Signorelli, 'L'incertezza del diritto', p. 265.

129 Signorelli, *Chi può e chi aspetta*, p. 178. They were often in bitter conflict with their parents, whom they found apathetic, gossipy, stuck in their ways.

130 The information for this paragraph is taken from Trigilia (ed.), *Cultura e sviluppo*, which is dedicated entirely to charting the phenomenon of associationism in the South, and which contains articles by I. Diamanti, F. Ramella and Trigilia himself.

131 See J. and P. Schneider, 'Dalle guerre contadine alle guerre urbane: il movimento antimafia a Palermo', *Meridiana*, no. 25 (1996), pp. 50–76; A. Blando, 'Percorsi dell'antimafia', ibid., pp. 77–92; and F. Ramella, C. Trigilia, 'Associazionismo e mobilitazione contro la criminalità organizzata nel Mezzogiorno', in L. Violante (ed.), *Mafia e società italiana. Rapporto '97*, Bari, 1997, pp. 24–46.

132 Trigilia, 'Conclusioni: associazionismo e nuovo Mezzogiorno', in Trigilia (ed.), *Cultura e sviluppo*, pp. 193 and 225–7.

133 R. King and J. Killingbeck, 'Agriculture and land use in central Basilicata', *Land Use Policy*, 1990, no. 1, p. 20; and R. King and J. Killingbeck, 'Carlo Levi, the Mezzogiorno and emigration: fifty years of demographic change at Aliano', in *Geography*, vol. LXXIV (1989), no. 2, pp. 128–43.

134 Filippucci, *Presenting the Past*, p. 193.

135 ibid., p. 195.

136 ibid., p. 196.

137 ibid., p. 197.

138 ibid., p. 166.

139 For some illuminating observations on this theme, G. Simmel, *Conflict and the Web of Group Affiliations*, New York, 1955, pp. 125–94.

140 See, for example, L. Ricolfi, S. Scamuzzi and L. Sciolla, *Essere giovani a Torino*, Torino, 1988, pp. 41–2.

141 Padre Alessandro Zanotelli, interviewed by Stella in *Schei*, p. 197.

142 The best diachronic analysis of these different waves of commitment in the 1980s and early 1990s is to be found in Della Porta, *Movimenti collettivi*, Chs. 4 and 5, pp. 91–166.

143 ARCI, *Come Dove Quando*, Milano, 1996, p. 152. None the less more than half the membership was still concentrated in two regions, Emilia-Romagna and Tuscany.

144 M. Diani, 'Dalla ritualità delle subculture alla libertà dei reticoli sociali', *Democrazia e Diritto*, vol. XXXII (1992), pp. 206–7 and p. 213.

145 T. Parks, *Italian Neighbours*, London, 1994 [1st edn 1992], p. 246.

146 Istituto di Ricerche Educative e Formative (IREF), *Rapporto sull'associazionismo sociale 1995* (ed. A. Valentini), Roma, 1995, p. 47. IREF had also published a similar report for the years 1983, 1985, 1989 and 1991.

147 R. Inglehart, *Cultural Shift in Advanced Industrial Society*, Princeton, 1990.

148 For the original development of these value indicators, see Inglehart, *The Silent Revolution*, pp. 39–43.

149 Inglehart, *Valori e cultura politica*, pp. 88ff., especially figure 2.5, p. 88.

150 ibid., pp. 90–91, and in particular table 2:2, whose content is reproduced in the Statistical Appendix, nos. 20 and 21.

151 For the data on 1994, R. Inglehart, *Modernisation and Postmodernisation*, Princeton, 1997, p. 140, graph 5.4, and also p. 157, table 5.2, which shows Italy's rapid shift in the period 1981–90.

152 The most important parts of the document are published in D. Tettamanzi and D. Del Rio, *Una fatica da cristiani*, Casale Monferrato, 1993, pp. 162–75. For a discussion of the genesis and reception of the document, ibid., pp. 75–9.

153 ibid., p. 175.

154 Pius XII, 'Allocuzione ai padri di famiglia (18 Sett. 1951)', in *Insegnamenti pontifici*, vol. 1, *Il matrimonio*, Roma, 1957, p. 371.

155 For a discussion of this contribution, see Ginsborg, *A History*, pp. 173–5.

156 John Paul II, *Familiaris consortio*, Bologna, 1994 [1st edn 1981], p. 45 (para. 42). There is a specific section in the work (paras. 42–8, pp. 45–50) entitled 'Participation in the development of civil society'. However, it must be noted that John Paul II's later *Lettera alle famiglie*, Roma, 1994, hardly mentions the duties of Catholic families to a wider society. For a Catholic discussion and commentaries upon *Familiaris Consortio*, see A. Alessandri *et al.*, *La 'Familiaris Consortio'*, Città del Vaticano, 1982. A useful introduction is M. Toso, *Famiglia, lavoro e società nell'insegnamento sociale della Chiesa*, Roma, 1994.

157 G. Savagnone, *La Chiesa di fronte alla mafia*, Milano, 1995, p. 112.

158 John Paul II, at the end of the Holy Mass at Agrigento, 9 May 1993, *L'Osservatore Romano*, 10–11 May 1993.

159 A. Riccardi, *Intransigenza e modernità*, Bari, 1996, pp. 103–4.

160 A. Bazzari, 'Servizi sperimentali della Caritas ambrosiana: segni di evangelizzazione', in A. Bausola *et al.*, *Cultura e fede nell'Italia del Nord*, Milano, 1992, p. 199.

161 F. Garelli, 'Religione e modernità: il caso italiano', in Fondazione Agnelli, *La religione degli europei*, Torino, 1992, p. 77.

162 C. M. Martini, *Farsi prossimo*, Milano, 1985, pp. 85–6.

163 Bazzari, 'Servizi sperimentali della Caritas', pp. 203ff.

164 It is interesting to note that a recent survey showed that Italians valued the Church more for its social and educational activities than for its religious ones; see F. Garelli, 'Gli italiani e la Chiesa', in V. Cesareo *et al.*, *La religiosità in Italia*, Milano, 1995, pp. 247–50.

165 John Paul II, *Alle donne*, Milano, 1995, p. 6.

166 John Paul II, *Familiaris Consortio*, paras. 5 and 17, pp. 9–10 and 25–6.

167 For these arduous analogies between the Christian family and the Christian Church, see the very interesting reflections contained in a group of essays dedicated to the family theology of Antonio Rosmini: C. Riva *et al.*, *La società domestica*, Roma, 1982.

168 Riccardi, *Intrasigenza e modernità*, pp. 100–101.

169 See, for instance, the beginning of the autobiography of its charismatic leader: R. Formigoni, *Io e un milione di amici*, Milano, 1988, pp. 9–21. See also M. Vitali and A. Pisoni, *Comunione e liberazione*, Milano, 1988.

170 K. Steigleder and M. Di Giacomo, *L'Opus Dei vista dall'interno*, Torino, 1986; and the entry 'Opus Dei', in C. Andres and G. Deuzler, *Dizionario storico del Cristianesimo*, Milano, 1992, pp. 474–5.

171 See A. Riccardi, 'Cattolicesimo', in Ginsborg (ed.), *Stato dell'Italia*, pp. 67–71.

172 M. Politi, 'La Chiesa in allarme: "Roma città pagana" ', *la Repubblica*, 2 October 1996.

173 For an introduction in English to the cult of Padre Pio, J. Gallagher, *Padre Pio. The Pierced Priest*, London, 1995.

174 L. Dani, *Domanda e offerta religiosa*, Padova, 1986.

175 ibid., p. 101.

176 ibid., p. 41.

177 ibid., pp. 83ff.

178 P. Nicotri, *Tangenti in confessionale*, Venezia, 1993.

179 ibid., p. 97.

180 ibid., p. 63.

181 ibid., p. 55.

182 ibid., p. 69.

183 Salvador Giner makes this fundamental point in his article, 'Civil society and its future', in Hall (ed.), *Civil Society*, pp. 301–25.

184 N. Bobbio, 'Sulla nozione di società civile', in *De Homine*, no. 24 (1968), pp. 34ff.

185 ibid., p. 35.

186 For further details, see below, Chapter 7, pp. 231–3.

187 This is a point well made by Loredana Sciolla, 'Identità e mutamento culturale', p. 60.

188 G. A. Almond and S. Verba, *The Civic Culture*, Princeton, 1963.

Chapter 5: *A Blocked Political System, 1980–92*

1 For a discussion of this theme, R. S. Flickinger and D. T. Studlar, 'The disappearing voters? Exploring declining turn-out in western European elections', in *Western European Politics*, vol. XV (1992), no. 2, pp. 1–16.

2 J. Dunn, 'Conclusion', in J. Dunn (ed.), *Democracy: the Unfinished Journey*, Oxford, 1992, pp. 264–5.

3 For the introduction of regional government, see Ginsborg, *A History*, p. 327 and P. Allum, *Italy: Republic without Government?*, London, 1973, pp. 225–38. Putnam, *Making Democracy Work, passim*, is certainly the best and most detailed comparison of the performance of Italy's various regional governments (with the exception of those enjoying a special Statute – Sicily, Sardinia, Val D'Aosta, Trentino-Alto Adige and Friuli Venezia-Giulia).

4 D. Hine, *Governing Italy*, Oxford, 1993, p. 2.

5 G. Amato, 'Conto poco e lo so, vi racconto perché', *la Repubblica*, 23 July 1988.

6 The Catholic scholar, R. Orfei, in his *L'occupazione del potere*, Milano, 1976, was the first to use this image systematically.

7 For a good introduction, see G. Pasquino, 'La partitocrazia', in G. Pasquino (ed.), *La politica italiana. Dizionario critico, 1945–1995*, Bari, 1995, pp. 341–54.

8 In the academic world the most fervent supporter of this thesis has been the sociologist Alessandro Pizzorno. See his 'Le difficoltà del consociativismo', in Alessandro Pizzorno, *Le radici della politica assoluta*, Milano, 1993, pp. 285–313, and 'Dopo il consociativismo', in *MicroMega*, 1995, no. 2, pp. 236–60. The term 'consociationalism' was first termed by Arend Lijphart in his *Democracy in Plural Society*, New Haven, 1977, but he abandoned the term in his later work, *Democracies*, New Haven, 1984, in favour of 'consensual government', which he counterposed to 'majoritarian government'.

9 Ginsborg, *A History*, p. 388, for more details.

10 ibid., p. 155. For a balanced account of this process, see Hine, *Governing Italy*, pp. 174ff., but also M. Giuliani, 'Meaures of consensual law-making: the Italian "Consociativismo"', *Poleis. Quaderno di Ricerca*, no. 12, 1996.

11 Hine, *Governing Italy*, pp. 174–5.

12 See C. Laubier (ed.), *The Condition of Women in France: 1945 to the Present*, London, 1990, p. 117. The best analysis of the granting of votes to women in Italy in 1946 is A. Rossi-Doria, *Diventare cittadine*, Firenze, 1996.

13 ibid., pp. 103–4.

14 For an introduction to patriarchy in the modern democratic state, see Walby, *Theorising Patriarchy*, pp. 150–72.

15 A. Buttafuoco, 'Cittadine italiane al voto', *Passato e Presente*, vol. XV (1997), no. 40, p. 7. For the distant origins of this exclusion, sited in the political thought of the seventeenth-century English revolution, see C. Pateman, 'The fraternal social contract', in Keane (ed.), *Civil Society and the State*, pp. 101–27, and C. Pateman, *The Sexual Contract*, Cambridge, 1988.

16 G. Pasquino, 'Il pentapartito', in Pasquino (ed.), *Politica italiana*, p. 349.

17 The President of the Republic is elected by a college consisting of the members of the two houses of parliament and three representatives from each region, with the exception of Val d'Aosta, which has just one. For the in-fighting connected with Pertini's election, see A. Baldassare and C. Mezzanotte, *Gli uomini del Quirinale*, Bari, 1985, pp. 220–27.

18 P. Barile, 'Presidente della Repubblica: la prassi di Pertini', *Quaderni Costituzionali*, vol. I (1981), no. 2, pp. 365–75.

19 For the figure of Sindona, see above all C. Stajano, *Un eroe borghese*, Torino, 1991, pp. 44–92.

20 For the structure of the Masons in Italy in the 1970s, and references to P2 before its discovery, see S. Flamigni, *Trame atlantiche*, Milano, 1996, and A. Cecchi, *Storia della P2*, Roma, 1985.

21 *Commissione parlamentare d'inchiesta sulla Loggia massonica P2*, vol. I, pt 4, p. 1118, testimony of Col. V. Bianchi.

22 Flamigni, *Trame atlantiche*, Appendix, for the complete list of names found; and Flamigni, 'La loggia P2', in *Storia d'Italia. Annali 12. La criminalità* (ed. L. Violante), Torino, 1997, p. 425.

23 *Commissione parlamentare d'inchiesta sulla Loggia massonica P2*, quater I/I, vol. I, pt 1, p. 358.

24 For the very chequered career of Roberto Calvi and his close contacts with both the Vatican and the Socialists, see the detailed reconstruction by R. Cornwell, *God's Banker*, London, 1983.

25 G. Colombo, *Il vizio della memoria*, Milano, 1996, pp. 57—9. Colombo's testimony, which is not limited just to this episode, is invaluable in the reconstruction of the history of the P2, but it must be remembered that his book was written some fifteen years after the event.

26 M. Costanzo, 'Parla, per la prima volta, il "signor P2"', *Corriere della Sera*, 5 October 1980.

27 *Commissione parlamentare d'inchiesta sulla Loggia massonica P2*, vol. VII, pt 1, p. 196. The two documents have been published in Cecchi, *Storia della P2*, pp. 241—70.

28 See the careful construction of the facts in A. Silj, *Il malpaese*, Roma, 1994, pp. 245—50.

29 ibid., pp. 331—56.

30 For the probable lack of contact between the P2 and the CIA, and the disinterest of the latter, see the convincing evidence reproduced from the archives of the CIA in C. Gatti, *Rimanga tra noi*, Milano, 1991, pp. 200 and 224ff. Francesco Cossiga, later to be President of the Republic, gave a very American-oriented interpretation of the P2 in an interview of some years later: 'The P2 was an American import. There is no doubt that Gelli was not the real head of the Lodge . . . The head was a person who was a reference-point for the Americans and who managed to put pro-American generals into key positions'; G. Riva, 'Cossiga: la P2 viene dagli USA e Gelli non era il capo', in *Il Giorno*, 24 August 1993. Whether this is true or not, it is worth pointing out that the secret service chiefs of the time, all of whom were in the P2, had been appointed in a supposedly 'democratic' shake-up of the services in 1977, when Giulio Andreotti was President of the Council of Ministers, and Francesco Cossiga Minister of the Interior.

31 *Commissione parlamentare d'inchiesta sulla Loggia massonica P2*, Sigla no. 2, *Relazione conclusiva di maggioranza dell'on.* Tina Anselmi, p. 164.

32 See the minority report written by Massimo Teodori; ibid., no. 2, bis/1.

33 Flamigni, 'La loggia P2', pp. 453—5.

34 M. Caciagli, 'Il resistibile declino della Democrazia cristiana', in G. F. Pasquino (ed.), *Il sistema politico italiano*, Bari, 1985, p. 121. In the elections of 1983, only 37.4 per cent of Christian Democrat votes came from the South.

35 F. Anderlini, 'La Dc: iscritti e modello di partito', in *Polis*, vol. III (1989), no. 2, p. 295, table 5, and p. 296.

36 'Intervento al XV Congresso nazionale della DC, Roma, 5 Maggio 1982, nella sintesi presentata da "Il Popolo"', published in C. De Mita, *Ragionando di politica*, Milano, 1984, p. 19.

37 See, for example, his 'Relazione al Consiglio nazionale della DC, Roma 15 Ottobre 1982', ibid., especially pp. 66–71.

38 See A. Becchi, 'The difficult reconstruction in Irpinia', in S. Hellman and G. F. Pasquino (eds.), *Italian Politics: A Review*, vol. VII, London, 1992, pp. 110–28. See also the interesting study by S. Pappalardo, *Un terremoto per amico*, Milano, 1994, pp. 348–443.

39 C. De Mita, *Intervista sulla Dc* (ed. A. Levi), Bari, 1986, p. 147. For an acute analysis of the motives for the defeat of De Mita, see J. Chubb, 'The Christian Democratic Party: reviving or surviving?', in R. Leonardi and R. Y. Nanetti (eds.), *Italian Politics: A Review*, vol. I, London, 1986, pp. 69–86.

40 Diamanti and Riccaboni, *La parabola del voto bianco*, pp. 41 and 64, table 3.17.

41 N. Machiavelli, *Il Principe*, Torino, 1977, ch. XV, p. 75. It is interesting in this context to note Craxi's own preface to *The Prince*, of September 1988, in B. Craxi, *Un'onda lunga* (ed. U. Intini), Imola, 1988. At a certain point (p. 243) he deprecated 'that all-too-convenient Machiavellianism which has aspired to construct a personal and private set of laws for the powerful, and another for ordinary people, one for who governs, and another for who is governed'.

42 For an introduction to Machiavellianism in the context of contemporary Italian politics, see G. F. Pasquino, 'Machiavellismo', in Ginsborg (ed.), *Stato dell'Italia*, pp. 92–4.

43 B. Craxi, 'Guardando al passato "Tiremm Innanz" (discorso per il 140esimo anniversario delle Cinque Giornate)', in B. Craxi, *Un'onda lunga*, p. 70.

44 A. Padellaro and G. Tamburrano, *Processo a Craxi*, Milano, 1993, p. 35. For a convincing portrait of the 'yuppie' and Socialist Milan of these years, see M. Andreoli, *Andavamo in Piazza Duomo*, Milano, 1993.

45 Cf. B. Craxi, 'Leninismo e socialismo', in *I nodi della sinistra* (ed. D. Argeri), Roma, 1980, pp. 22–32. This article first appeared in *L'Espresso*, vol. XXIV (1978), no. 34.

46 B. Visentini, 'Craxi, perché ti leghi alla DC', *la Repubblica*, 4 January 1992.

47 L. Cafagna, *Una strana disfatta*, Venezia, 1996, p. 132. See also A. Lepre, *Storia della prima repubblica*, Bologna, 1993, pp. 297ff.

48 Barone and Masera, 'Index-linked bonds', p. 123, table 6.1. For inflation, C. Nardi Spiller, *La dinamica inflattiva nell'economia italiana*, Padova, 1994, pp. 83–91 and 139, table 26.

49 Barone and Masera, 'Index-linked bonds', p. 123, table 6.1.

50 'Craxi: ecco il mio governo'; electoral forum with B. Craxi published in *la Repubblica*, 1 April 1992.

51 For a precise documenting of the various phases of the new agreement, see Presidenza del Consiglio dei Ministri, *Rapporti nuovi*, Roma, 1984.

52 Cf. F. J. Piason, 'Italian foreign policy: the *Achille Lauro* affair', in Leonardi and Nanetti (eds.), *Italian Politics*, vol. I, pp. 146–63; and above all A. Cassese, *Il caso 'Achille Lauro'*, Roma, 1987.

53 For the reformism of the 1970s, see Ginsborg, *A History*, pp. 326–31 and

387–95. The historian Giovanni Sabbatucci has argued that any Socialist projects for reform were seriously weakened by the fact that many of the most serious Socialist intellectuals had taken their distance from Craxi by the middle of the 1980s; G. Sabbatucci, *Il riformismo impossibile*, Bari, 1991, p. 119.

54 For the work of the commission, see in particular P. Scoppola, *La repubblica dei partiti*, Bologna, 1997 [1st edn 1991], pp. 439–49. For the public administration, G. Morcaldo, *La finanza pubblica in Italia*, Bologna, 1993, p. 94, n. 12.

55 See the interview with G. P. Pansa, *la Repubblica*, 18 October 1984.

56 C. D'Orta, 'Ambiente e danno ambientale: dalla giurisprudenza della Corte dei Conti alla legge sul Ministero dell'Ambiente', in *Rivista Trimestrale di Diritto Pubblico*, vol. XXXVII (1987), no. 1, pp. 60–112; and F. Miracco, 'In morte della legge Galasso', *il manifesto*, 15 January 1989.

57 A. Pace, 'La radiotelevisone in Italia con particolare riguardo alla emittenza privata', *Rivista Trimestrale di Diritto Pubblico*, vol. XXXVII (1987), no. 3, p: 623.

58 In the absence of any legislation, it is possible to discern different strategies and attitudes on the part of the three major private television entrepreneurs of the time. Edilio Rusconi (Rete 4) and Mario Formenton of the Mondadori group (Italia 1) were convinced that anti-trust legislation was on its way, and that they could not stray too far from local transmission. Rusconi told a Senate committee in 1988 that he had thought it best to follow the provisions of American law, because they seemed the most logical! These allowed for the ownership of not more than five UHF and two VHF stations. Formenton chose a syndication strategy, with a federation of a number of autonomous local stations. Only Berlusconi risked total illegality, buying up local stations in the whole of the peninsula, ensuring clear reception, and explicitly establishing a national network; see G. Fiori, *Il venditore*, Milano, 1995, pp. 94–104.

59 A. Statera, 'Silvio Berlusconi', in N. Ajello *et al.*, *Perché loro*, Bari, 1984, p. 217.

60 G. Ruggeri and M. Guarino, *Berlusconi*, Milano, 1994, p. 31, and G. Lazzarini, 'Una favola italiana', in *Tv Sorrisi e Canzoni*, vol. XXXIX (1990), no. 52, 30 December, pp. 46–53.

61 The best reconstruction of this extraordinary event and its aftermath is to be found in Fiori, *Il venditore*, pp. 105–20, upon which my own account is heavily dependent.

62 ibid., p. 109.

63 P. Martini, 'Molti affari, molta politica', in *Problemi dell'Informazione*, vol. XV (1990), no. 4, pp. 518–20.

64 See, for instance, B. Craxi, 'Madrid, Lisbona, Parigi. E noi?' [1977], in B. Craxi, *Il rinnovamento socialista*, Venezia, 1991, pp. 165–9.

65 Transcription from the soundtrack of the RAI 1 programme, *Tribuna politica*, 15 December 1981. Reprinted in A. Tatò (ed.), *Conversazioni con Berlinguer*, Roma, 1984, p. 271.

66 For the overwhelming conviction among militants of the PCI that socialism existed in the USSR, see M. Barbagli and P. G. Corbetta, 'Una tattica e due

strategie. Inchiesta sulla base del PCI', *Il Mulino*, vol. XXVII (1978), no. 260, pp. 922–67. Their data is of 1977–8. For reactions of the base of the party to Berlinguer's break with Moscow, see G. P. Pansa, *Ottobre, addio*, Milano, 1982.

67 Cf. G. Fiori, *Vita di Enrico Berlinguer*, Roma, 1992 [1st edn Bari, 1989], p. 468.

68 E. Berlinguer, 'Relazione al XIV congresso', in *XIV congresso del Partito comunista italiano: Atti e risoluzioni*, Roma, 1975, p. 19.

69 D'Alema and Ginsborg, *Dialogo su Berlinguer*, p. 39.

70 The last possible, but still unlikely, moment for such unity was in the early 70s, when Francesco De Martino, the then leader of the PSI, proposed a united party, though obviously not under the Communist banner. See A. Occhetto, *Il sentimento e la ragione*, Milano, 1994, pp. 81–2, and also G. Vacca, *Vent'anni dopo*, Torino, 1997, p. 181.

71 For a useful selection of Berlinguer's writings on this theme, see W. Veltroni, *La sfida interrotta*, Milano, 1994, pp. 77–90.

72 See P. Ginsborg, 'Le riforme di struttura nel dibattito degli anni Cinquanta e Sessanta', *Studi Storici*, vol. XXXIII (1992), nos. 2–3, pp. 653–68.

73 An interesting critique of the party on some of these themes is L. Balbo, 'Falsa demitizzazione: il PCI e la vita quotidiana', in L. Balbo *et al.*, *Lettere da vicino*, Torino, 1986, pp. 3–14.

74 J. Wyles, 'Fleshing out a new identity', *Financial Times*, 31 July 1989.

75 For these innovations in Communist culture, see U. Curi, *Lo scudo di Achille*, Milano, 1989, pp. 49–64. For the relationship between feminism and the PCI, see L. Turco, 'Differenza sessuale e liberazione umana', *Critica Marxista*, vol. XXVII (1989), nos. 1–2, pp. 97–126, and G. Buffo, 'Le donne comuniste tra emancipazione e differenza', ibid., pp. 167–76.

76 At the XVIIIth Congress of March 1989 a long message from Gorbachov was screened to the delegates, and received a standing ovation.

77 Occhetto, *Il sentimento e la ragione*, p. 63. See also the precious testimony of A. Asor Rosa, *La sinistra alla prova*, Torino, 1996, pp. 111–43.

78 ibid., p. 126. See also G. Chiaromonte, *Col senno di poi*, Roma, 1990, p. 217. For the view from outside, M. J. Bull, 'The unremarkable death of the Italian Communist party', in R. Catanzaro and F. Sabetti (eds.), *Italian Politics: A Review*, vol. V, London, 1991, pp. 23–39.

79 The early months of the party are well analysed by Stephen Hellman, 'The difficult birth of the Democratic Party of the Left', in Hellman and Pasquino (eds.), *Italian Politics*, vol. VII, pp. 68–86. See also the interesting analysis by D. I. Kertzer, *Politics and Symbols. The Italian Communist Party and the Fall of Communism*, New Haven/London, 1996; and P. Ignazi, *Dal PCI al PDS*, Bologna, 1992.

80 The early career of the Gavas, father and son, was carefully dissected by Percy Allum in *Politics and Society, passim*. See also M. Caprara, *I Gava*, Milano, 1975. For the 1980s, P. and F. Allum, 'The resistible rise of the new Neapolitan

Camorra', in S. Gundle and S. Parker (eds.), *The New Italian Republic*, London and New York, 1996, pp. 234–46; and F. Barbagallo, *Napoli fine Novecento*, Torino, 1997.

81 Giulio Andreotti, whose faction had grown steadily in strength, as it expanded from Lazio into Campania and above all Sicily, had originally supported De Mita for secretary. The two men, though, were increasingly at loggerheads through the 1980s, as they clashed over the need to reform the party in Sicily and over Andreotti's ambitions to become President of the Republic. As for Bettino Craxi, he had never hidden his hostility to De Mita, nor his ambition to emarginate the 'left' of the DC, nor his desire to find more congenial interlocutors within that party.

82 The best account is M. Caciagli, 'The 18th DC Congress: from De Mita to Forlani and the victory of "neodoroteism"', in Catanzaro and Sabetti (eds.), *Italian Politics*, vol. V, pp. 8–22.

83 'La dichiarazione d'intenti di Arnaldo Forlani al XVIII congresso nazionale della DC', in F. Malgeri (ed.), *Storia della Democrazia Cristiana*, vol. V, Roma, 1989, pp. 105–6.

84 A. Carini and A. Calabrò, 'Giulio e la sua guardia di Palazzo', *la Repubblica, Affari e Finanza*, 31 January 1992. The article also contains an accurate map of Andreotti's place-men in the public sector at that time.

85 M. Mafai, 'Andreotti fra croce e palazzo', *MicroMega*, 1990, no. 2, pp. 56–64.

86 E. Scalfari, 'Il Signore delle mosche vi ha preso l'anima', *la Repubblica*, 4 April 1993.

87 Mafai, 'Andreotti', p. 63.

88 See, for instance, P. Craveri, *La Repubblica dal 1958 al 1992*, Torino, 1995, p. 960.

89 This is the thesis which is strongly argued in one of the best analyses of the Italian crisis, M. Cotta and P. Isernia (eds.), *Il gigante dai piedi di argilla*, Bologna, 1996. In their 'Premessa' (p. 9), they write: 'The overall picture is that of a decreasing capacity of the parties to guide Italian politics in changed circumstances and in the face of new problems.' See also M. Cotta, 'La crisi del governo di partito all'italiana', ibid., pp. 11–52, where the failure of Italian party government to address middle-range issues of reform (neither the micropolitics of patronage nor the macropolitics of ideological debate) is discussed in detail.

90 Without the Republican party.

91 Many laws in Italy bear the names, at least in informal terms, of their principal promoters.

92 In contrast to most Italian politicians and public figures, both Amato and Carli have written informative memoirs of this period: G. Amato, *Due anni al Tesoro*, Bologna, 1990; and G. Carli, *Cinquant'anni di vita italiana*, Bari, 1993, especially pp. 385ff. Carli's work, given its long time-span and the frankness of its views, is particularly valuable for historians; see the comments of D. Preti, 'Gli ammonimenti di un governatore di "classe". L'Italia repubblicana nella testimonianza di Guido Carli', *Italia Contemporanea*, no. 199 (1995), pp. 297–326.

93 Carli, *Cinquant'anni*, p. 398. And elsewhere: 'Old friends, like Bruno Visentini, but not only he, pointed an accusing finger at me immediately: "You, with your prestige, are giving cover to a government which is the expression of the political will not to change." These were criticisms which I can now recognize, calmly, to have contained a part of the truth'; ibid., p. 386.

94 Ginsborg, *A History*, pp. 265–7.

95 R. Lombardi, 'Una nuova frontiera per la sinistra', in V. Parlato (ed.), *Spazio e ruolo del riformismo*, Bologna, 1974, p. 66.

96 Fiori, *Il venditore*, pp. 174ff., again supplies a splendid account, this time as a participant observer, since he was a Senator for the Sinistra Independente.

97 Apart from the support of the Socialists, Berlusconi could count on the loyalty of the MSI. Throughout the 1980s the neo-Fascists had helped to keep as low as possible the level of advertising on the three public channels of the RAI, so that the Fininvest channels could profit accordingly. Certain MSI deputies, like Franco Servello, were rewarded for their labours with considerable amounts of television time at the time of the 1987 elections; Fiori, *Il venditore*, pp. 122–3.

98 The journalist Giampaolo Pansa found a white-faced Gianni Letta, one of Berlusconi's closest collaborators, in the Senate's Press gallery, doing his sums: ' "For us, the cost of the amendment won't be less than 400 billion lire . . . This is the end of commercial television" '; G. P. Pansa, *L'intrigo*, Milano, 1990, p. 250. For the campaign against the interruption of films for commercial breaks, see Veltroni, *Io e Berlusconi, passim*.

99 For an earlier discussion of this syndrome, see Ginsborg, *A History*, pp. 330 and 391.

100 J. Foot, 'The logic of contradiction: migration control in Italy and France, 1980–93', in R. Miles and D. Thranhardt (eds.), *Migration and European Integration*, London, 1995, pp. 142–3. By the cut-off date of May 1990, 220,240 previously illegal immigrants had regularized their position. Most came from the North and the Centre of the country, while in the South the connection between organized crime and illegal labour deterred many immigrants from coming forward.

101 Cf. U. Leone, 'Le politiche dell'ambiente', in V. Di Donna and A. Vallario (eds.), *L'ambiente. Risorse e rischi*, Napoli, 1994, pp. 267–8. For Ruffolo's own views, see his *La qualità sociale*, Bari, 1985, especially pp. 155–6.

102 OECD, *Economic Surveys: Italy (1991)*, p. 92; F. Cavazzuti, 'Privatisation: false starts and frustrated takeoffs', in Hellman and Pasquino (eds.), *Italian Politics*, vol. VII, p. 148.

103 For Carli's hesitations, see M. Monti, 'Guido Carli, l'Europa, la memoria', in *Scritti in onore di Guido Carli*, Milano, 1995, p. 329.

104 Barone and Masera, 'Index-linked bonds', p. 123, table 6.1; L. Verzichelli, 'Le politiche di bilancio: il debito pubblico da risorsa a vincolo', in Cotta and Isernia (eds.), *Il gigante*, p. 215, fig. 5.6.

105 Carli, *Cinquant'anni*, pp. 389 and 393.

106 For a collection of Cossiga's *bons mots* of this time, see G. Turani (ed.), *Anche i presidenti si incazzano*, Milano, 1991.

107 A. Mitchison, 'Method or madness?', *The Independent Magazine*, 29 February 1992. She added: 'he can come across as an agreeable old buffer: full of old-fashioned affability, ponderous anecdotes and the slow speech of powerful men who brook no interruption.'

108 From the interview on RAI 3 with the journalist Giancarlo Santalmassi, 21 March 1991; quoted in both G. M. Bellu and S. Bonsanti, *Il crollo*, Bari, 1993, p. 78, and G. P. Pansa, *Il regime*, Milano, 1991, p. 168.

109 For the events of 1964 see Ginsborg, *A History*, pp. 276–8. For Cossiga's own self-defence, F. Cossiga, *Il torto e il diritto* (ed. P. Chessa), Milano, 1993.

110 A detailed and accurate reconstruction of these events is F. Ferraresi, 'A secret structure codenamed Gladio', in Hellman and Pasquino (eds.), *Italian Politics*, vol. VII, pp. 29–48. F. Casson, *Lo stato violato*, Venezia, 1994, publishes in appendix (pp. 175–98) his valuable 'Sentenza conclusiva dell'istruttoria sull'organizzazione Gladio, 10 Ott. 1991'. See also G. M. Bellu and G. D'Avanzo, *I giorni di Gladio*, Milano, 1991.

111 For a passionate denouncement of the British 'secret state', see E. P. Thompson, *Writing by Candlelight*, London, 1980, pp. 149–80, and especially pp. 151–2. The 1976 United States Senate report on the CIA, drawn up by Frank Church, revealed the existence of the Office of Policy Coordination, set up in 1948, which was funded and staffed by the CIA, and which had responsibility, among other things, for setting up 'stay behind' networks. For the spreading of the Gladio scandal to other European countries see, for example, R. Norton-Taylor, 'The Gladio file: did fear of communism throw West into the arms of terrorists?', *Guardian*, 5 December 1990.

112 S. Bonsanti, 'Andreotti ha fretta. "E' ora di chiudere il caso Gladio"', *la Repubblica*, 9 January 1991.

113 Cossiga surmised, and he was not along in doing so, that the Machiavellian Andreotti had allowed the Gladio story to emerge so that he could discredit Cossiga, perhaps force him to resign ahead of time, and then with the support of the Communists himself become President of the Republic. The complicated relationship between the two men was given another twist when Cossiga made Andreotti a life Senator, a gesture which was also variously interpreted. One of the most delicate questions regarding Gladio was its connection with General De Lorenzo's 'counter-insurgent' Piano Solo of 1964. It was known that De Lorenzo's plan envisaged the arrest of trade-union and left-wing leaders and their deportation to the same Sardinian military base at Capo Marragiu which served as the training ground for Gladio.

114 The magistrate Casson, in his Sentence of October 1991, had accused of political conspiracy and of the constitution of illegal armed groups the former chief of the SISMI (the name given to one branch of the Italian secret services after the reform of 1977), Admiral Fulvio Martini, and the last head of Gladio, General Paolo Inzerilli. The papers then passed to Rome, where the chief Procurator,

Ugo Giudiceandrea, judged the accusations to be unfounded and asked for the case to be dropped (F. Scottoni, ' "Gladio, nessuna cospirazione" ', *la Repubblica*, 1 February 1992).

115 This point is strongly argued by Casson in his 'Sentenza' (*Lo stato violato*, pp. 177ff.), as well as by the Republican Libero Gualtieri, the President of the parliamentary commission of inquiry on bomb outrages, in his report on Gladio published in *l'Unità*, 29 January 1992.

116 Casson, 'Sentenza', in *Lo stato violato*, p. 188. For some elements in the career of Stone, who seemed a moderate in comparison to Graham Martin, Nixon's ambassador in Italy from 1969 to 1973, see Gatti, *Rimanga tra noi*, pp. 113—18. Casson also produced strong circumstantial evidence to suggest that at least one of the arms deposits of Gladio (no. 203 at Aurisina) had been systematically used to supply extreme right-wing terrorists during the period of the strategy of tension (ibid., p. 194).

117 For full details of these initiatives, see G. F. Pasquino, 'The electoral reform referendums', in F. Anderlini and R. Leonardi (eds.), *Italian Politics: A Review*, vol. VI, London, 1992, pp. 9—24.

118 For an excellent basic outline of this and other aspects of the electoral system, see D. Wertman, 'The Italian electoral process: the elections of June 1976', in H. R. Penniman (ed.), *Italy at the Polls*, Washington DC, 1977, pp. 41—79 and especially pp. 48 and 74—7; an outstanding local research (on Naples) is the chapter 'Patronage and the preference vote', in Allum, *Politics and Society*, pp. 153—91; and an interesting broader view is S. H. Barnes and G. Sani, 'Mediterranean political culture and Italian politics: an interpretation', *British Journal of Political Science*, vol. IV (1974), no. 3, pp. 289—303.

119 For his account of the campaign, M. Segni, *La rivoluzione interrotta*, Milano, 1994.

120 None the less, as Pasquino has pointed out, without the mass strength of the PCI/PDS and the organizational know-how of the Radicals, who were old hands at referenda, the quorum of signatures would not have been reached; Pasquino, 'La promozione dei referendum', p. 53.

121 ibid., p. 52.

122 P. McCarthy, 'The referendum of 9 June', in Pasquino and Hellman (eds.), *Italian Politics*, vol. VII, p. 21.

123 B. Palombelli, 'Io ci spero, ma è l'ultima volta' (interview with A. Occhetto), *la Repubblica*, 25 June 1991.

124 In fact, as Ilvio Diamanti has been at pains to chart, it was the Liga Veneta, not Bossi's organization, which first made a national breakthrough in 1983. For a scrupulous reconstruction of the electoral and geographical fortunes of the various Leagues in their early years, see Diamanti, *La Lega*, pp. 19—54.

125 No less an authority than Gianfranco Miglio, the most important Lombard intellectual to back the League, was absolutely explicit on this point; G. F. Miglio, 'Vocazione e destini dei lombardi', in G. F. Miglio, *Io, Bossi e la Lega*, Milano, 1994, pp. 73 and 89.

126 See, for example, the remarks of Umberto Bossi in a forum organized by *la Repubblica* with the leaders of the League, published in the newspaper on 19 May 1990.

127 This condemnation of the Risorgimento did not stop the League appropriating some of its history. The revolt of the inhabitants of the Lombardo-Venetian kingdom against Austrian rule in March 1848 was compared to the League's incipient revolt against Rome, and the decision of many Milanese in early 1848 to refrain from smoking in order not to pay the Austrian tax on tobacco was cited favourably as the precursor of the League's own advocacy of tax evasion.

128 See G. De Luna, 'Dalla spontaneità all'organizzazione: la resistibile ascesa della Lega di Bossi', in G. De Luna (ed.), *Figli di un benessere minore*, Firenze, 1994, p. 50.

129 In a research conducted by the Istituto Poster in 1992–3, quoted in Diamanti, *La Lega*, pp. 105–7, 'intolerance towards southerners' emerged as by far the largest single factor contributing to sympathy for the League. For a further discussion of this theme, R. Biorcio, *La Padania promessa*, Milano, 1997, pp. 133–44.

130 U. Bossi, 'Intervento al primo congresso nazionale della Lega Lombarda, Segrate, 8–9 dicembre 1989'; quoted in Balbo and Manconi, *I razzismi reali*, p. 84. His attitude to homosexuals was also revelatory (ibid., p. 85): 'I have expelled at most six people from the party. Among them was a lad who was trustworthy and with the right values, but he was homosexual. How many of the major parties have self-declared homosexuals, i.e. effeminate weaklings, in key posts?'; from an interview with S. Pende, 'Fratelli d'Italia, diventiamo cugini', in *L'Europeo*, vol. XLVI (1990), no. 37, 14 September 1990. See also the revealing section in Biorcio, *La Padania*, pp. 145–65.

131 Lumezzane was atypical in its allegiance to the Christian Democrats, a loyalty that can at least in part be explained by the fact that the parish priest was the brother of Giovanni Prandini, a powerful figure in the national party, who was to become Minister of Public Works.

132 Diamanti, *La Lega*, p. 31, table 1, and pp. 38–40.

133 Among the few authors who attempt to deal with this theme, see R. Cartocci, *Fra Lega e Chiesa*, Bologna, 1994, and the journalist G. Pajetta, *Il grande camaleonte*, Milano, 1994, pp. 13–37.

134 F. Bozzini, *Destini incrociati*, Roma, 1997, p. 271.

135 De Luna, 'Dalla spontaneità', pp. 48–9.

136 G. Pajetta, 'Consiglieri in Carroccio', *il manifesto*, 2 September 1990.

Chapter 6: *Corruption and the Mafia*

1 The Teardo case is analysed in detail by D. della Porta in her *Lo scambio occulto*, Bologna, 1992. For Turin, see L. Marini, 'La corruzione politica', in *Storia d'Italia. Annali 12. La criminalità* (ed. L. Violante), Torino, 1997, pp. 355–6, as well as

the account of one of the principal figures involved, A. Zampini, *Io corruttore*, Napoli, 1993.

2 G. Migliorino, 'Speculazioni edilizie e tangenti tra le accuse agli esponenti socialisti arrestati a Savona', in *Corriere della Sera*, 16 June 1983.

3 D. della Porta and Y. Mény, 'Democrazia e corruzione' in D. della Porta and Y. Mény (eds.), *Corruzione e democrazia. Sette paesi a confronto*, Napoli, 1995, p. 6.

4 The best discussion of 'moral costs' is that of A. Pizzorno, 'Introduzione', in della Porta, *Lo scambio occulto*, pp. 14–16. See also S. Rose Ackerman, *Corruption*, New York, 1978.

5 Pizzorno, 'Introduzione', pp. 24ff., who emphasizes that such politicians frequently had limited initial capital, whether this was measured in monetary or social or technico-scientific terms.

6 Cf. CENSIS, *Rapporto sulla situazione sociale del paese. 1996*, Milano, 1996, p. 497, table 1, where the number of employees in local government is given as 685,500 persons.

7 Bozzini, *Destini incrociati*, p. 263.

8 These were only some of the mechanisms at work; for an exhaustive and revealing analysis, D. della Porta and A. Vannucci, *Corruzione politica e amministrazione pubblica*, Bologna, 1994, pp. 83–172.

9 For Savona, Marini, 'La corruzione politica', p. 357; for Rome, P. Boccacci, 'Ecco l'assessore dieci per cento', *la Repubblica*, 15 November 1991; for Milan, D. della Porta, 'Milan: immoral capital', in S. Hellman and G. F. Pasquino (eds.), *Italian Politics: A Review*, vol. VIII, London, 1993, pp. 98–115.

10 Corte dei Conti, *Relazioni al Parlamento relative agli anni 1987–1992*, Roma, 1992, vol. II, 1989, p. 407; quoted in della Porta and Vannucci, *Corruzione politica*, p. 107.

11 As Alberto Asor Rosa has commented: 'at a certain point it becomes difficult to distinguish if a person is stealing for the cause or for himself (most frequently he steals for himself and for the cause; for himself because in any case that serves the cause; for the cause because through it he serves himself)'; *La sinistra*, p. 146.

12 The minutes of the interrogations of Mario Chiesa of 23, 27 and 30 March 1992 were published, in nearly complete form, under the title 'Confessioni che cambiano la storia', in *L'Espresso*, vol. XXXVIII (1992), no. 26, 28 June, pp. 12ff. For further details of Chiesa's career and the ambience in which he moved, see the long and fascinating interview he gave to the journalist Marcella Andreoli; Andreoli, *Andavamo in Piazza Duomo, passim*.

13 See della Porta, 'Milan', pp. 111ff.; for Colombo, G. Bevilacqua, 'Colombo: sì al condono', *La Stampa*, 26 August 1993; for Chiesa, 'Confessioni', p. 18.

14 Carli, *Cinquant'anni*, pp. 366–74.

15 A recent and valuable account of these connections is to be found in Barbagallo, *Napoli fine Novecento*.

16 For a memorable portrait of one such carrier of bags, see Daniele Lucchetti's film of 1990, *Il Portaborse*.

17 Patrick McCarthy, in his acute and accessible *The Crisis of the Italian State*, London, 1997 [1st edn 1995], insists, I think mistakenly, on collating the two, making clientelism a subspecies of corruption. See, for instance, p. 61: 'Beginning in 1992 clientelism, the special kind of corruption that lay at the heart of the postwar regime, was exposed daily . . .'

18 Mény and della Porta, in their treatment of this issue, tend to go too far in the opposite direction to that of McCarthy, and to delineate separations that are too rigid ('Democrazia e corruzione: verso un'analisi comparata', in *Corruzione e democrazia*, pp. 234–5). For instance, their suggestion that political corruption involves 'an exchange between public decision-making and the payment of money' while clientelism is the exchange of 'protection for consent' is altogether too limited a description of the latter. It is enough to take the example of the widespread distribution of state invalidity pensions through clientelistic networks to realize that the lines of demarcation are by no means so clear. Similarly, when they maintain that 'only in the case of clientelism is it possible to perceive a vertical distinction, with the subordination of a clientes [*sic*] to a patron', they seem to ignore much of their own evidence of the rigidly vertical structuring of many of the networks of political corruption.

19 In this context it is as well to recall the comments of Ernest Gellner, already cited in Chapter 4, n. 27 with regard to patronage in the Mediterranean. See also the furher discussion of these issues in Moss, 'Patronage revisited', pp. 59–61.

20 See Caciagli (ed.), *Democrazia Cristiana e potere nel Mezzogiorno*, p. 273; I have already quoted this example in my *A History*, p. 179. For evidence of kickbacks and other forms of corruption being discovered at the same hospital in 1987, see della Porta, *Lo scambio occulto*, pp. 118–21. The two incidents, separated by twenty-four years, provide a clear indication of the environmental continuities linking clientelism and corruption.

21 Chiesa, 'Confessioni', p. 21.

22 Della Porta, *Lo scambio occulto*, p. 52, quoting the description of the Teardo clan offered by the prosecutors of the Tribunal of Savona in their 'Sentenza-ordinanza di rinvio a giudizio', of 1984.

23 N. Andriolo, 'Vuoi essere assunto alle Poste? Se sei amico del sottosegretario DC', *l'Unità*, 12 June 1992. The local PDS senator who denounced this state of affairs was Lorenzo Gianotti.

24 Della Porta, 'Milan', p. 103.

25 G. Locatelli and D. Martini, *Mi manda papà*, Milano, 1991, pp. 189–91. See also C. Valentini, 'Quei due si parlano in cinese?', in *Panorama*, vol. XXIV (1986), no. 1074, 16 November, pp. 50–52.

26 The headquarters of the PSI in Milano was at via Bagutta 12, and this was also the address of two charitable foundations presided over by Anna Craxi, the wife

of Bettino, who temporarily befriended Mario Chiesa before his fall from grace; Andreoli, *Andavamo in Piazza Duomo*, pp. 159ff. Chiesa recalled: 'One would have to have been stupid not to understand the influence that the circle of women around Anna had upon Bettino, who was very much their friend' (ibid., p. 162).

27 Locatelli and Marini, *Mi manda papà*, p. 165.

28 Della Porta and Mény, 'Democrazia e corruzione', pp. 4—5.

29 Cafagna, *Una strana disfatta*, pp. 138—9.

30 Andreoli, *Andavamo in Piazza Duomo*, p. 166.

31 ibid., p. 164.

32 Cafagna, *Una strana disfatta*, p. 143.

33 See A. Giovagnoli, *Il partito italiano. La Democrazia Cristiana dal 1942 al 1994*, Bari, 1996, p. 264.

34 Della Porta, 'Milan', p. 103.

35 A. Licandro and A. Varano, *La città dolente*, Torino, 1993. Italstat, with a turnover of over 5,000 billion lire in the year 1990, was by far the largest company, public or private, in the building industry; see P. Della Seta and E. Salzano, *L'Italia a sacco*, Roma, 1993, p. 33.

36 Licandro and Varano, *La città*, p. 20.

37 ibid.

38 ibid., pp. 23—31, for Licandro's extended account of this meeting.

39 ibid., p. 31.

40 ibid., pp. 31—3.

41 Della Seta and Sacco, *L'Italia a sacco*, pp. 27—8.

42 According to research carried out by the Ministero del Bilancio in 1991, only 58 per cent of state museums were effectively open to the public. Throughout the 1980s the number of paying visitors to state museums remained stationary. Italy spent more on '*beni culturali*' than did the other major European countries, but even so this amounted in 1987 to a paltry 0.33 per cent of GDP. See L. Bobbio, 'Le politiche dei beni culturali in Europa: una comparazione', in L. Bobbio (ed.), *Le politiche dei beni culturali in Europa*, Bologna, 1992, p. 12; see also p. 36, table 2, and L. Bobbio, 'La politica dei beni culturali in Italia', ibid., p. 208.

43 A. Becchi, 'Opere pubbliche', *Meridiana*, no. 9 (1990), p. 232.

44 See *Stato della Costituzione* (ed. G. Neppi Modona), Milano, 1995, pp. 344—64. For a more critical view of these developments, C. Guarnieri, *Magistratura e politica in Italia*, Bologna, 1993, pp. 93—147.

45 Foa *et al.*, *Le virtù della Repubblica*, *passim*. The best outline of the continuities between Fascism and the Republic is C. Pavone, 'La continuità dello Stato. Istituzioni e uomini' [1974], now reprinted with other essays in C. Pavone, *Alle origini della Repubblica*, Torino, 1995.

46 A. Pizzorusso, *L'organizzazione della giustizia in Italia*, Torino, 1990, pp. 167–8.

47 T. Jean-Pierre, 'Come si manipolano i giudici in Francia', *MicroMega*, 1993, no. 5, pp. 69–72, as well as his interview in the *Observer*, 17 July 1994. Also, more generally, the invaluable work of Y. Mény, *La corruption de la République*, Paris, 1992.

48 D. Nelken, 'A legal revolution? The judges and *Tangentopoli*', in Gundle and Parker (eds.), *The New Italian Republic*, p. 194.

49 P. Borgna and M. Cassano, *Il giudice e il principe*, Roma, 1997, pp. 125–46 and 188.

50 For the very changed climate of those years, see M. Ramat (ed.), *Storia di un magistrato*, Roma, 1986; Casson, *Lo stato violato*, p. 9.

51 For differing views, A. Pizzorusso, 'Correnti della magistratura e politicizzazione', *Quaderni della Giustizia*, vol. VI (1986), no. 62, pp. 4–9; and Guarnieri, *Magistratura e politica in Italia*, pp. 97ff. On Magistratura Democratica, S. Pappalardo, *Gli iconoclasti*, Milano, 1987.

52 See the valuable diary of these events by Baffi himself, published after his death by Massimo Riva; P. Baffi, 'Cronaca di un'infamia, *Panorama*, vol. XXVIII (1990), no. 1242–3, 11 February, pp. 121–47.

53 ibid., entries for 23 March and 11 April 1979.

54 ibid., p. 120, letter to Massimo Riva.

55 See the excellent article by the jurist Tullio Padovani, 'La soave inquisizione. Osservazioni e rilievi a proposito delle nuove ipotesi di "ravvedimento"', *Rivista Italiana di Diritto e Procedura Penale*, vol. XXIV (1981), no. 2, pp. 529–45.

56 See the accurate reconstruction by M. V. Foschini and S. Montone, 'Il processo Tortora', in *Storia d'Italia. Annali 12*, pp. 685–713.

57 Tortora's reflections during the last period of his life can be found in S. De Gregorio, *Tortora, morire d'ingiustizia*, Napoli, 1988, especially pp. 183–8.

58 Cf. L. Ferrajoli, 'La prova diabolica', in *Politica ed Economia*, vol. XXI (1990), nos. 7–8, pp. 9–11; C. Ginzburg, *Il giudice e lo storico*, Torino, 1991.

59 M. Del Gaudio, *La toga strappata*, Napoli, 1992, p. 17, letter of 15 March 1981.

60 ibid., p. 30, letter of 14 June 1983.

61 The offensive dates from the very beginning of the decade; see V. Zagrebelsky, 'La polemica sul Pubblico Ministero e il nuovo Consiglio Superiore della Magistratura', *Quaderni Costituzionali*, vol. I (1981), no. 2, pp. 391–9.

62 G. Di Federico, 'The crisis of the justice system and the referendum on the judiciary', in R. Leonardi and P. G. Corbetta (eds.), *Italian Politics: A Review*, vol. III, London, 1989, pp. 25–49. For the Socialists, see also C. Guarnieri, 'The judiciary in the Italian political crisis', in M. Bull and M. Rhodes (eds.), *Crisis and Transition in Italian Politics*, London, 1997, pp. 164–5.

63 G. C. Caselli, 'La cultura della giurisdizione', *MicroMega*, 1993, no. 5, pp. 15–16.

64 Franchetti, *Condizioni politiche*, pp. 14ff.

65 G. Falcone, *Cose di Cosa Nostra*, Milano 1993 [1st edn 1991], p. 9.

66 ibid., p. 37.

67 D. Gambetta, *The Sicilian Mafia*, Cambridge, Mass., 1993, p. 7.

68 P. Bevilacqua, 'La Mafia e la Spagna', *Meridiana*, no. 13 (1992), pp. 118—19.

69 Falcone, *Cose di Cosa Nostra*, p. 49.

70 'Testimonianza di Tommaso Buscetta resa al giudice istruttore di Palermo Giovanni Falcone *et alii*, July—Aug. 1984', vol. I, pp. 115—17, quoted in Gambetta, *The Sicilian Mafia*, p. 121.

71 Gambetta insists on calling the Mafia an 'industry', and protection a 'commodity' (ibid., p. 53), but I think this is confusing. Protection is basically a service not a good, and the Mafia, *if* it can be compared with any tranquillity to legal economic structures, can certainly be called an 'enterprise' but with difficulty an 'industry'. It is true that Franchetti called it an 'industry of violence', but his was a late-nineteenth-century use of the term, embracing indiscriminately all economic activities, or even activity in general.

72 Hill, 'Goods and services', p. 318. The element of non-consensual activity is that which perhaps most distinguishes Mafia economic activity from that of a nominally legal service enterprise.

73 J. and P. Schneider, 'Mafia, antimafia and the question of Sicilian culture', *Politics and Society*, vol. XXII (1994), no. 2, p. 245. For a compelling account of the way a Mafia protection racket operates, F. Abate, *Capo d'Orlando. Un sogno fatto in Sicilia*, Roma, 1993, especially pp. 15—22.

74 P. Bevilacqua, 'Mafia spa e DC', *L'Unità*, 17 May 1993.

75 Gambetta, *The Sicilian Mafia*, pp. 57—8.

76 Tribunale di Palermo, *Sentenza istruttoria contro Spatola + 119* (Giudice Istruttore G. Falcone), quoted in S. Lupo, *Storia della mafia*, Roma, 1993, p. 212.

77 'Testimonianza resa alla Commissione parlamentare antimafia, XI° legislatura', 4 December 1992, p. 513; quoted in Lupo, *Storia della mafia*, p. 212.

78 P. Arlacchi, *Gli uomini del disonore*, Milano, 1992, p. 126. Calderone told his brother Antonino: '"Wasn't I right to not want too many brothers, too many cousins and close kin in the Family? They always end up trying to gain command. Blood will out, and comes before every other loyalty. And you can't reason with it, it destroys everything it finds in its way"' (ibid., p. 126).

79 Falcone, *Cose di Cosa Nostra*, p. 60.

80 See, for instance, a peasant's testimony to Danilo Dolci: 'They are all honey and bees these *mafiosi*, smiling and affable to talk to, as if they were teachers in the same school. But all the time they're watching their own backs'; D. Dolci, *Spreco*, Torino, 1960, p. 133. See also, for the Calabrian context, Piselli, 'Il comparato politico', p. 143.

81 U. Santino, 'L'omicidio mafioso', in G. Chinnici and U. Santino, *La violenza programmata*, Milano, 1989, p. 291.

82 The *mafioso* Salvatore Contorno told Falcone: 'Only I can spill my own blood,' and Falcone commented: 'It is indeed a strange concept of honour that which

insists in delegating to no other the task of killing one's own kin'; Falcone, *Cose di Cosa Nostra*, p. 31.

83 ibid., p. 61. The tragic relations between a father who was a 'man of honour' and a son who was committed to the anti-Mafia struggle are recounted in F. Bortolotta Impastato, *La mafia in casa mia* (eds. A. Puglisi and U. Santino), Palermo, 1987. See also S. Vitale, *Nel cuore dei coralli. Peppino Impastato, una vita contro la mafia*, Soveria Mannelli, 1995.

84 R. Siebert, *Le donne, la mafia*, Milano, 1994, pp. 228–41. See also her chapter on the family (pp. 47–78), where she insists quite rightly on certain fundamental differences between Mafia Families and real ones and comments (p. 57), 'the *mafiosi* themselves are the first to exploit ably the apparent identicalness of that which is not identical at all'.

85 Arlacchi, *Gli uomini del disonore*, p. 165. See also C. Longrigg, *Mafia Women*, London, 1997.

86 Valeria Pizzini-Gambetta suggests that Mafia gender norms 'regulate behaviour in three domains: safety and secrecy; testing Mafia members' qualities as protectors; and enhancing their reputation'; V. Pizzini-Gambetta, 'Gender norms in the Sicilian Mafia', in M. L. Arnot and C. Usborne, *Gender and Crime in Modern Europe*, London, 1999, p. 264 and Appendix B, p. 271.

87 Siebert, *Le donne, la mafia*, pp. 62–3.

88 Arlacchi, *Gli uomini del disonore*, p. 116.

89 U. Santino, 'Economia della droga. Traffico di stupefacenti, mafia e organised crime', *Segno*, nos. 31–2 (1982), pp. 25–49; Lupo, *Storia della Mafia*, p. 211, according to whom heroin coming from Sicily covered 80 per cent of the East Coast market of the United States by 1982.

90 Santino, 'L'omicidio mafioso', pp. 290ff. The war began on 23 April 1981 with the killing of Stefano Bontate.

91 N. dalla Chiesa, *Delitto imperfetto*, Milano, 1984, p. 225.

92 I. Sales, *La camorra, le cammore*, Roma, 1992, and F. Barbagallo, *Il potere della camorra (1973–1998)*, Torino, 1999. For the kinship structure of one Camorra band in the *quartieri spagnoli* of Naples, see Gribaudi, 'Familismo e famiglia', pp. 33–9.

93 Commissione Parlamentare Antimafia, XI Legislatura, *Rapporto sulla Camorra (21 Dicembre 1993)*, Roma, 1994, pp. 46–7. No sooner had the clans composing the Nuova Famiglia won the war against Cutolo than they began an internecine struggle of their own.

94 L. Violante, *Non è la piovra*, Torino, 1994, p. 90.

95 The most detailed treatment is to be found in M. Massari, *La Sacra Corona Unita*, Bari, 1998.

96 Commissione Parlamentare Antimafia, XI Legislatura, 'Relazione sui rapporti tra mafia e politica (6 Aprile 1993)', p. 60; now published, with a preface by N. Tranfaglia, as Commissione Parlamentare Antimafia, *Mafia e politica*, Bari,

1993, p. 107 (the quotation was especially in relation to the lodges of Piazza del Gesù).

97 Violante, *Non è la piovra*, pp. 260–61. For the 1986 figures, CENSIS, *A metà decennio. Riflessione e dati sull'Italia dall'80 all'85*, pp. 87–8. See also, CENSIS and CDS, *Contro e dentro*, Milano, 1992, and G. M. Rey, 'Analisi economica ed evidenza empirica dell'attività illegale in Italia', in S. Zamagni (ed.), *Mercati illegali e mafie*, Bologna, 1993, pp. 15–55.

98 See above, Chapter 2, pp. 39–40 and n. 43.

99 Commissione Parlamentare d'Inchiesta sul Fenomeno della Mafia in Sicilia, VI Legislatura, *Relazione conclusiva, 4 Feb. 1976*, Roma, 1976, p. 270, letter of 13 April 1951.

100 P. Pezzino, 'Intervento', in D. Gambetta, S. Lupo, P. Pezzino and N. Tranfaglia, 'La mafia e la sua storia. Radici locali e dimensione internazionale', *Passato e Presente*, vol. XII (1994), no. 31, p. 38.

101 Chubb, *Patronage, Power*, pp. 67–8 and 128–58 for an unrivalled picture of these years.

102 Violante, *Non è la piovra*, p. 155.

103 'Commissione Parlamentare Antimafia, XI Legislatura, seduta 13 luglio 1993, resoconto stenografico dell'audizione del collaboratore della giustizia Pasquale Galasso, p. 2229'; quoted in Violante, *Non è la piovra*, p. 258.

104 The term 'ecomafia' was first coined by the Legambiente in 1994. See also A. Cianciullo and E. Fontana, *Ecomafia*, Roma, 1995, and E. Fontana, 'Le ecomafie', in L. Violante (ed.), *Mafie e antimafie. Rapporto '96*, Bari, 1996, pp.197–205.

105 The best reconstruction of the history of the parliamentary anti-Mafia commissions is N. Tranfaglia, 'Introduzione', in Tranfaglia, *Mafia, politica e affari*, pp. ix–xxxii.

106 S. Bonsanti, 'Giulio e Salvo, "nozze d'Argento" ', *la Repubblica*, 23 October 1992.

107 'Procura di Palermo, memoria depositata dal pubblico ministero nel procedimento penale n. 3538/94 N.R., instaurato nei confronti di Andreotti Giulio', now published as *La vera storia d'Italia*, Napoli, 1995, p. 147. The text of Sylos Labini's letter was published in *Corriere della Sera*, 21 December 1974.

108 For further details, see V. Vasile, 'Salvo Lima', in E. Ciconte, I. Sales and V. Vasile, *Cirillo, Ligato e Lima* (ed. N. Tranfaglia), Bari, 1994, p. 237 and n. 43. The early accusations which had so alarmed Sylos Labini referred principally to the period 1960–62, when Lima was mayor of Palermo. One of them concerned the granting of jobs in the Municipality, without an open and fair competition, to the sons and daughters of members of the 'Provincial Control Commission', the same administrative organ which had the responsibility of supervising the activities of the Municipality. The prefect Bevivino, called upon in November 1963 to inquire into the building boom at Palermo, 'documented the construction of an extraordinary castle of falsifications, which culminated in the concession of 2,500 construction permits out of a total of 4,000 to three old age pensioners, who were mere front men for members of Cosa Nostra or entrepreneurs strongly

suspected of having Mafia sympathies'; Commissione Parlamentare Antimafia, *Mafia e politica*, p. 104.

109 The dossier was the work of the tireless Centro Siciliano di Documentazione 'Giuseppe Impastato', headed by Umberto Santino, and was based in particular on the documentation and judgements of the minority report of 1976, signed among others by Cesare Terranova and Pio La Torre, to the parliamentary inquiry on the Mafia in Sicily; see U. Santino (ed.), *Un amico a Strasburgo*, Palermo, 1984, as well as the same author's comments in U. Santino, *La mafia interpretata*, Sovorio Mannelli, 1995, p. 137 and n. 8, p. 159. Giulio Andreotti, in his *Cosa loro*, Milano, 1995, p. 61, defends Lima's actions to the hilt.

110 See the details contained in 'La richiesta degli ordini di custodia cautelare nei confronti dei presunti mandanti dell'omicidio Lima, firmata dai magistrati della Procura Distrettuale Antimafia di Palermo, 11 Oct. 1992', now published as *Delitto Lima. L'atto di accusa dei giudici di Palermo*, Agrigento, n.d.

111 Letter of 2 April 1982, now published in full in N. dalla Chiesa, *Delitto imperfetto*, Milano, 1984, pp. 32—3. Later evidence on this 'family', collected by the magistrates of Palermo, makes for disconcerting reading. See *La vera storia d'Italia*, p. 887, as well as the very detailed confession of a doctor from Palermo, Gioacchino Pennino, who was also a prominent local politician (ibid., pp. 791—870).

112 He wrote in 1995: 'I have always maintained that the polemics relative to Lima had their principal origin in the special situation of Palermo, a city in whose politics, it must be added, I have never dabbled that much' (Andreotti, *Cosa loro*, p. 30). As for the importance of Sicily to his faction, Andreotti wrote: 'to argue that the factional support I received from Sicily in some way freed me from a "ghetto" in Lazio is simply ridiculous' (ibid., p. 64). However, if the political gains to be had from enlarging his faction to Sicily were really so limited, it may reasonably be asked why he welcomed so controversial a crew aboard his ship. Nor was this a passing acquaintance, for it lasted twenty-four years and was not then interrupted by Andreotti's choice.

113 As he wrote himself: 'I am a rather orderly sort of person and I keep note in my personal archives even of the Christmas greetings that I send and receive'; *Cosa loro*, p. 93.

114 Commissione Parlamentare Antimafia, *Mafia e politica*, p. 118 and n. 75.

115 *La vera storia d'Italia*, p. 10.

116 Lupo, *Storia della mafia*, pp. 216—17.

117 Testimony of Virginio Rognoni, 11 June 1981, now published in part in *La vera storia d'Italia*, p. 735.

118 Testimony of Franco Evangelisti, 1 July 1993, now published in part in ibid., p. 149.

119 Dalla Chiesa, *Delitto imperfetto*, pp. 32—3.

120 The interview is republished in full in ibid., pp. 225—30.

121 ibid., p. 226, and Bocca's testimony to the judge Giovanni Falcone, now published in *Mafia. L'atto d'accusa dei giudici di Palermo* (ed. C. Stajano), Roma, 1986, p. 235.

122 The article of the penal code reads: 'The association is of a specifically mafia nature when those who form part of it make use in the associational tie of intimidatory force, and of the methods of subjugation and conspiracy of silence that derive therefrom, in order to gain, either directly or indirectly, the management or in whatever manner the control, of economic activities, concessions, authorizations, sub-contracts and public services, so as to realize, for themselves or for others, illicit profits or advantages.'

123 A. Stille, *Excellent Cadavers*, London, 1995, pp. 23–4. Stille's book, which deals principally with the lives of Falcone and Borsellino, is enriched by a large number of interviews with the protagonists, both minor and major, of his story.

124 A. Caponnetto, *I miei giorni a Palermo*, Milano, 1992, *passim*, and p. 37 in particular for his valuable pen portraits of Borsellino and Falcone.

125 ibid., p. 46.

126 For a pen portrait of Buscetta, C. Sterling, *The Mafia*, London, 1990, pp. 67–76. In October 1983, when Buscetta was arrested in Rio de Janeiro, the head of the Brazilian anti-drug squad announced that he was the principal coordinator of the cocaine traffic between Brazil, Bolivia, Peru, Colombia, Europe and the United States.

127 Falcone, *Cose di Cosa Nostra*, p. 41.

128 L. Orlando, *Palermo* (ed. C. Fotia and A. Roccuzzo), Milano, 1990, pp. 64–6. See also Greco, *Studenti a Palermo*, pp. 83–4 and Appendix II, pp. 129–36, for student attitudes to the Mafia. For the Jesuits, E. Pintacuda, *Palermo palcoscenico d'Italia*, Palermo, 1986, *passim*, and p. 56 for his description of the new associationism in the city in 1984–5.

129 Violante, *Non è la piovra*, p. 210.

130 Andreotti, *Cosa loro*, pp. 16–17 and 29.

131 His story is told in detail by N. dalla Chiesa, *Il giudice ragazzino*, Torino, 1992.

132 Bonsanti, 'Giulio e Salvo'. For the relationships between Andreotti and the Mafia, see also S. Lupo, *Andreotti, la mafia, la storia d'Italia*, Roma, 1996; P. Allum, 'Statesman or godfather? The Andreotti trials', in R. D'Alimonte and D. Nelken (eds.), *Italian Politics. A Review*, vol. 12, Boulder, Colorado, 1997, pp. 219–32.

133 A. Flores D'Arcais, ' "Shamir non insulti l'Onu" ', *la Repubblica*, 6 June 1991.

134 In between he had found time to visit Frosinone, one of his great factional strongholds in the Lazio region: 'The President is a bit tired; for more than sixty times, with mechanical courtesy, he has just presented the "Conca d'Oro" prize to the same number of distinguished inhabitants of Frosinone'; M. Ricci, ' "Sì, andrò a votare" ', *la Repubblica*, 9–10 June 1991.

135 The Carabinieri's letter is part of a detailed report prepared by the prosecuting magistrates of Palermo, published in *La vera storia d'Italia*, pp. 891–6.

136 One of the most controversial of these was the annulling of the sentences passed on those accused of the killing in May 1980 at Monreale, near Palermo, of

Emanuele Basile, a young captain in the Carabinieri. Basile had been killed by the Mafia while walking home from a party, with his four-year-old daughter in his arms. The reason given for the annulling of the sentence was the irregular way in which the date for the extraction of the names of the jury had been communicated to one of the defence lawyers. Even one of Carnevale's closest collaborators over many years in the first section of the Corte di Cassazione, Dr Pasquale Molinari, admitted that such an irregularity had never previously been considered of sufficient gravity to annul a whole trial; deposition of Dr Molinari of 31 March 1994, published in *La vera storia d'Italia*, p. 273.

137 From 1986 onwards both Andreotti and Carnevale formed part of the General Council of the Fiuggi Cultural Foundation, Andreotti being its President. As late as 14 May 1994 Carnevale, in a taped telephone conversation, was recorded as telling a friend that Vitalone had assured him of the firm support of Andreotti for Carnevale's application to become President of the Roman Court of Appeal. In a deposition of 16 September 1993 Vittorio Sbardella, Andreotti's one-time lieutenant in Roman politics, told the Palermo magistrates: 'the real lynch-pin for his [Andreotti's] relations with the Salvo cousins on the one hand, and the Corte di Cassazione on the other, was indeed Claudio Vitalone'; *La vera storia d'Italia*, pp. 277 and 773–5.

Chapter 7: *The State Within and the State Without*

1 For an illuminating guide to this difficult enterprise see P. Anderson, 'Agency', in P. Anderson, *Arguments within English Marxism*, London, 1980, pp. 16–58, and his 'Structure and subject', in P. Anderson, *In the Tracks of Historical Materialism*, London, 1983, pp. 32–55.

2 See the very useful analysis of L. Bobbio, *La democrazia non abita a Gordio*, Milano, 1996, pp. 49–55, especially fig. 1, p. 50, and fig. 2, p. 54.

3 ibid., pp. 55ff.

4 See W. C. Müller and V. Wright, 'Reshaping the state in western Europe: the limits to retreat', in W. C. Müller and V. Wright, *The State in Western Europe. Retreat or Redefinition?*, London, 1994, pp. 1–11.

5 For a series of articles comparing the Belgium and the Italian political situations, see the special number of *Res Publica* (Belgian Journal of Political Science), vol. XXXVIII (1996), no. 2, and especially L. De Winter, D. della Porta, and K. Deschouwer, 'Comparing similar countries: Italy and Belgium', pp. 215–35.

6 Müller and Wright, 'Reshaping the state', p. 10. Their conclusions regarding the fundamental stability of the nation-states of western Europe echo the opinions expressed by Stanley Hoffman more than a decade earlier in his 'Reflections on the nation-state in western Europe today', in *Journal of Common Market Studies*, vol. XXI (1982), nos. 1–2, pp. 21–37.

7 For medicine and the body politic, some passing reflections in Rigotti, *Il potere e le sue metafore*, pp. 54–5, and F. Rigotti, *Metafore della politica*, Bologna, 1989, pp. 61ff.

8 M. Weber, *Politik als Beruf, Wissenschaft als Beruf*, Berlin, 1919; M. Weber, 'Bureaucracy', ch. 8, in H. H. Gerth and C. Wright Mills, *From Max Weber: Essays in Sociology*, London, 1967, pp. 196–244.

9 Cf. F. Braudel, *Civiltà materiale, economia e capitalismo*, vol. II, *I giochi dello scambio*, Torino, 1981, p. 555 [orig. edn *Civilisation matérielle et capitalisme, XVe–XVIIIe siècle. Les jeux de l'échange*, Paris, 1979], where reference is made to 'the incomplete State which makes itself complete as best it can, unable by itself to exercise all its rights, to fulfil all its functions'.

10 For the constant process of 'negotiated compromise' in the contemporary French bureaucracy, see F. Depuy and J. C. Thoenig, *Sociologia dell'azione burocratica*, Bologna, 1986 [orig. edn *Sociologie de l'administration française*, Paris, 1983], especially pp. 83–5.

11 B. Dente, 'La cultura amministrativa italiana negli ultimi 40 anni', in B. Dente, *Politiche pubbliche e pubblica amministrazione*, Rimini, 1989, pp. 147ff.

12 For an earlier formulation of this relationship, see Ginsborg, *A History*, p. 149.

13 An interesting analysis of 'micro-corruption', based on a survey of newspaper articles in *La Stampa* and *la Repubblica* for the period 1976–91, is to be found in F. Cazzola, *L'Italia del pizzo*, Torino, 1992.

14 Signorelli, 'L'incertezza del diritto', pp. 261–2.

15 In a provocative article, G. F. Miglio returns to the Weberian distinctions of North and South, Protestant and Catholic, in order to suggest that the attempt to impose 'rational' bureaucracies upon the Mediterranean countries was a profound mistake; 'Una Repubblica "mediterranea"?' [1987], in G. F. Miglio, *Le regolarità della politica*, Milano, 1988, vol. II, pp. 1095–1104.

16 Presidenza del Consiglio dei Ministri, Dipartimento della Funzione pubblica, *Rapporto sulle condizioni*, p. 23. Other estimates, such as that of the Servizio Studi of the Chamber of Deputies, updated to 17 October 2000, puts the number much lower, at 13,000 laws and 27,000 regulations having legal status. Even so, the normative inflation afflicting the Italian state is hardly in question. See S. Cassese, 'Le leggi sono troppe, ma la Camera non lo sa', *Il Sole – 24 ore*, 19 March 2001; and Cassesse, 'Un centro-sinistra senza più senso critico', ibid., 24 March 2001.

17 Cf. Presidenza del Consiglio dei Ministri, Dipartimento della Funzione Pubblica, *L'organizzazione dei ministeri*, Roma, 1994, p. 7: 'The functions of the state are regulated and distributed among its organs by a highly disparate collection of acts, laws, regulations, circulars, directives, deliberations of interministerial committees, functional orders, etc. Some of these acts are not even published.'

18 The reasons for such a state of affairs are analysed in L. Bobbio, 'La peculiarità dell' ordinamento museale italiano nel contesto europeo e il dibattito sulla sua riforma', in P. A. Valentino (ed.), *L'immagine e la memoria*, Roma, 1992, pp. 41–63.

19 Presidenza del Consiglio dei Ministri, Dipartimento della Funzione Pubblica, *Rapporto sulle condizioni*, pp. 441–5. The ten sections were: Comune, Prefettura, Questura or Comando Carabinieri, Divisione Cittadinanza Ministero dell'Interno, Casellario Giudiziale, Dipartimento PS, Ministero Affari Esteri,

Consiglio di Stato (occasionally), Ufficio Legislativo Ministero dell'Interno, Gabinetto Ministro dell'Interno.

20 See above, Chapter 2, p. 52.

21 The details of their respective lists of personnel make for instructive reading; see Presidenza del Consiglio dei Ministri, Dipartimento della Funzione Pubblica, *L'organizzazione dei ministeri*, pp. 641–60 and 1071–81. The first (Agriculture) had 199 directors, the second thirty-seven; the first 200 'employees for waiting-room duties and auxiliary services', the second twenty-eight.

22 F. P. Cerase, *Un'amministrazione bloccata*, Milano, 1990, pp. 26ff., who notes that even with regard to the principal national unions a profound gap existed between official statements of principle and actual practice within the public administration. For an interesting case study, by no means unsympathetic to the trade unions, of the macroscopic penalties paid by the public as a result of a strike in 1984 of twenty-one clerks at the Ministry of the Treasury's '*Centro meccanografico*' at Latina, see T. Pipan, *Lo sciopero contro l'utente*, Torino, 1988.

23 S. Cassese, 'Il sistema amministrativo italiano, ovvero l'arte di arrangiarsi', in S. Cassese and C. Franchini (eds.), *L'amministrazione pubblica italiana*, Bologna, 1994, pp. 18–19.

24 In 1972 the category of '*Dirigenza*' had been instituted, with its own 'statute' and higher salaries. But it was judged by Cassese to have been a failure, being both too numerous and lacking in a real capacity to lead the rest of the administration; ibid., pp. 14–15. See also B. Dente, 'Introduzione', in B. Dente (ed.), *Le politiche pubbliche in Italia*, Bologna, 1990, p. 22. For a Franco-Italian comparison in a key moment for possible administrative reform, see P. Ginsborg, 'Resistenza e riforma in Italia e Francia, 1943–48', *Ventesimo Secolo*, vol. II (1992), nos. 5–6, pp. 311–12.

25 Cassese, 'Il sistema amministrativo italiano', p. 17. Naturally, the patient and difficult work of tracing these kinship and clientele links has not been, and perhaps never will be, undertaken systematically. For some indications in the case of regional government in Basilicata in the 1980s, see Cerase, *L'amministrazione*, pp. 211–12. See also Presidenza del Consiglio, Dipartimento per la Funzione Pubblica, *Rapporto sulle condizioni*, p. 45. For the 'social-therapeutic' role of the Italian public administration, see the important recent work of G. Melis, *Storia dell'amministrazione italiana, 1861–1993*, Bologna, 1996.

26 S. Cassese, 'Le disfunzioni dei controllori amministrativi', in S. Cassese (ed.), *I controlli nella Pubblica Amministrazione*, Bologna, 1993, p. 21. See also G. D'Auria, 'I controlli', in Cassese and Franchini (eds.), *L'amministrazione*, pp. 79–96.

27 L. Einaudi, *Diario 1945–1947*, Bari, 1993, p. 142. See also ibid., p. 201, for his description of a similar situation in the Banco di Napoli.

28 For his role as 'councillor to the Prince', see E. Addis, 'Banca d'Italia e politica monetaria: la riallocazione del potere fra stato, mercato e Banca Centrale', *Stato e Mercato*, n. 19 (1987), p. 83.

29 See above, Chapter 6, p. 192.

30 Addis, 'Banca d'Italia', p. 87. The other principal steps in the 1970s were the

introduction of a free auction for the sale of government bonds, the equalization of reserve requirements across credit institutions, the issuing of new bonds over a range of rates and terms to maturity. See also P. Formica, *L'autonomia della Banca centrale nel corso degli anni settanta e ottanta*, Messina, 1993.

31 See above, Chapter 5, p. 165.

32 Addis, 'Banca d'Italia', p. 89. A period of study abroad was considered essential for the young managers of the Bank. Indeed, for many years the Bank recruited to its ranks by advertising a number of scholarships for study in foreign institutions, and then offered the successful candidates jobs on their return.

33 See the tribute to Carli by Gordon Richardson, the former Governor of the Bank of England: 'by common consent he led the transformation of the Banca d'Italia into a modern central bank which is everywhere recognized as a pillar of stability and integrity and is admired among its peers for its intellectual distinction'; Richardson's speech is published without title in G. Agnelli *et al.*, *In ricordo di Guido Carli (Atti del convegno BNL-ABI)*, Roma, 1994, pp. 77–86 (the quotation is from p. 86).

34 T. Pipan, *Il labirinto dei servizi*, Milano, 1996.

35 ibid., pp. 49–66. 'bureaucratic *maternage*' was here conceived as the actions of the female secretaries in looking after the students, taking care of them, sometimes inviting them into the 'back office' so as to have more time to deal with their needs and queries.

36 ibid., p. 68.

37 The unit in question was a gastro-enterological one, and its research was funded mainly by pharmaceutical companies. The management of the hospital described the unit as being run with 'Swedish' efficiency (ibid., p. 87).

38 ibid., pp. 72ff. 'It's like being in the trenches, with the assault coming in the morning.' The aptness of this First World War imagery was confirmed by the fact that here too the war was on two fronts. The distracted and distant generals were represented by the administration, who sometimes left yet more norms and circulars on the clerks' desks, with no instructions as to what they meant or how to implement them.

39 ibid., pp. 64 and 125.

40 ibid., p. 100.

41 ibid., pp. 103 and 119.

42 G. Capano, *L'improbabile riforma*, Bologna, 1992.

43 It may be suggested that reform in this field, as in others, rotated around the relationship between three verbs: '*sapere*' (the knowing awareness of what needed to be done); '*volere*' (the willingness to act upon such awareness); '*potere*' (the effective possibilities for the realization of a reform programme).

44 G. della Cananea, 'Il cittadino e la pubblica amministrazione', in Cassese and Franchini (eds.), *L'amministrazione*, p. 190.

45 Melis, *Storia*, p. 529.

46 For a detailed and illuminating analysis of the administration's response to this key law, Presidenza del Consiglio dei Ministri, Dipartimento per la Funzione Pubblica, *L'attuazione della legge 7 agosto 1990, n. 241, e la semplificazione dei procedimenti amministrativi*, Roma, 1994.

47 V. Wright, 'Reshaping the state: the implications for public administration', in Müller and Wright (eds.), *The State in Western Europe*, pp. 110–17.

48 Carli, *Cinquant'anni*, p. 396. For another eloquent advocacy of the advantages of privatization, seen though from the left, Cavazzuti, 'Privatisation', pp. 145–58.

49 Not by chance, some of the most vociferous opponents of this step were those politicians and trade unionists most interested in preserving parts of the public administration as their own private fiefdoms.

50 See the incisive pages in Hutton, *The State We're In*, pp. 217ff. For an international analysis, D. Siniscalco *et al.*, *Privatizzazioni difficili*, Bologna, 1999.

51 Vincent Wright, one of the foremost experts of European public administration, came to the following conclusions on these points: 'Too much current radical reform of the public sector is obsessed with efficiency, narrowly defined, and is based on a simplistic view of bureaucracy, a naïve view of the market, an idealized view of the private sector, an insensitivity to the hidden costs of reform, an over-optimism about outcomes, and, perhaps more fundamentally, a misleading view of the state'; Wright, 'Reshaping the state', pp. 128–9. He also points out the dangers of the demoralization of civil servants and the sapping of the public sector ethos, rooted in profoundly internalized 'standards of public conduct' – a point made by the House of Commons Public Accounts Committee in 1993 (ibid., p. 127).

52 ibid., pp. 110 and 130, n. 21.

53 See P. Johnson, 'The welfare state', in R. Floud and D. McCloskey (eds.), *The Economic History of Britain since 1700*, vol. III, Cambridge, 1994, p. 288, fig. 10.1.

54 I have followed here the distinctions outlined with exemplary clarity by Maurizio Ferrera (*Modelli di solidarietà*, Bologna, 1993, pp. 76–102), but have added a 'residual' category which is based, as Richard Titmuss suggested, 'on the premise that there are two "natural" (or socially given) channels through which an individual's needs are properly met; the private market and the family. Only when these break down should social welfare institutions come into play and then only temporarily' (*Social Policy*, London, 1974, pp. 30–31). Ferrera prefers to treat very limited welfare states, like that of the United States, as 'underdeveloped' and 'exceptional'. See also another renowned tripartite typology: G. Esping-Andersen, *The Three Worlds of Welfare Capitalism*, New York, 1990.

55 Titmuss, *Social Policy*, pp. 140–41. Suffering from terminal cancer, Titmuss was treated in 1972–3 at Westminster Hospital, London. The 'Postscript' to *Social Policy* describes that National Health treatment and ends with the following words, which encapsulate perfectly the values of equity and solidarity which were at the heart of his conception of a 'welfare state': 'Amongst all the other experiences I had, another which stands out is that of a young West Indian from

Trinidad, aged 25, with cancer of the rectum. His appointment was the same as mine for radium treatment – 10 o'clock every day. Sometimes he went into the Theratron Room first; sometimes I did. What determined waiting was quite simply the vagaries of London traffic – not race, religion, colour or class' (pp. 150–51).

56 Pedersen, *Family, Dependence*, pp. 338–41.

57 See Ginsborg, *A History*, pp. 151–2 and 226–7. For the projects and hopes of those years, G. Berlinguer, *Una riforma per la salute*, Bari, 1979. See also U. Ascoli (ed.), *Welfare state all'italiana*, Bari, 1984, pp. 5–52 and A. Piperno, 'La politica sanitaria', ibid., pp. 153–80; at a comparative level, M. Paci, *Pubblico e privato nei moderni sistemi di Welfare*, Napoli, 1989.

58 For a detailed discussion, both of the strongly innovative areas of the new law, and also of its continuing deficiencies with regard to gender equality, D. Vincenzi Amato, 'Il diritto della famiglia', in Barbagli and Saraceno (eds.), *Lo stato delle famiglie*, pp. 37–52.

59 For the history of the Italian welfare state, see above all Ferrera, *Modelli di solidarietà*, pp. 201–72.

60 See, for instance, L. Greco *et al.*, 'Indagine sulla migrazione Sud-Nord del bambino ammalato', *Rivista Italiana di Pediatria*, vol. XI (1985), no. 3, pp. 287–95. Official statistics suggested that at least 25,000 sick children from the South were admitted every year to pediatric wards in the Centre-North. For hospital beds per head of population, Berlinguer, *Storia e politica*, p. 213. The same levelling process was true for spending per capita, which in 1984–85 amounted to 692,828 lire in the South, 805,568 in the Centre, and 721,022 in the North (ibid.).

61 M. Ferrera, 'La composizione partitica e socioprofessionale dei comitati di gestione della legislatura 1980–1985', in M. Ferrera and G. Zincone (eds.), *La salute che noi pensiamo*, Bologna, 1986, pp. 227–40. For a detailed analysis of corrupt practices in the USL no. 35 of Catania, della Porta, *Lo scambio occulto*, pp. 106–11 and 118–21.

62 Ferrera, 'La partitocrazia della salute', in Cotta and Isernia (eds.), *Il gigante*, p. 67.

63 That this mix was not particular only to Italy is a thesis sustained with conviction by Maurizio Ferrera in his suggestive article, 'The "southern model" of welfare in social Europe', *Journal of European Social Policy*, vol. VI (1996), no. 1, pp. 25ff. The other main traits that he identifies in a southern European model are a highly fragmented and 'corporatist' income maintenance system, as well as a marked collusion between public and private services, often to the great advantage of the latter.

64 G. Esping-Andersen, *Social Foundations of Postindustrial Economies*, Oxford, 1999, examines the way in which welfare regimes allocate welfare obligations to families, or by contrast attempt to alleviate individuals' reliance on family resources. He suggests a bi-modal model, with the Nordic welfare states far ahead of their European counterparts, whether British, continental or southern

European. For spending on health services in Italy in the 1980s see Ferrera, 'La partitocrazia della salute', pp. 60–64. For comparative statistics, OECD, *New Orientations in Social Policy*, Paris, 1994.

65 Martinotti *et al.*, *Milano ore sette*, p. 10. For the situation in 1980, see C. Cardia, 'Relazione', in G. Leonardi and L. Violante (eds.), *Quale famiglia?*, Roma, 1980, p. 13. For the daunting problems of a popular quarter of Benevento in the early 1980s, see A. Calzone, A. M. Pozzutto and R. Sorice, *Indagine territoriale nel bacino di utenza di un consultorio familiare*, Benevento, n.d. [1983?]. Of the women interviewed, only 17 per cent used the *consultorio*, mainly for paediatric, gynaecological and contraceptive advice.

66 See, for example, the work and publications of the UCIPEM (Unione Consultori Prematrimoniali e Matrimoniali).

67 M. Cuttini *et al.*, 'Parental visiting, communication, and participation in ethical decisions: a comparison of neonatal unit policies in Europe', *Archives of Disease in Childhood, Fetal and Neonatal Edition*, vol. LXXXI (1999), no. 2, pp. 84–9.

68 C. Saraceno, 'Le politiche per la famiglia', in Barbagli and Saraceno (eds.), *Lo stato delle famiglie*, p. 301. See also the article by the same author, 'The ambivalent familism of the Italian welfare state', *Social Politics*, vol. I (1994), no. 1, pp. 60–82.

69 Saraceno, 'Le politiche per la famiglia', p. 309. The reference here is to the system of alimony and maintenance payments, the Italian regulation of which is more extensive than in other European countries. See in particular the articles 433–48 of the civil code, as well as the commentary of A. Della Valle, *Delle persone e della famiglia. Artt. 231–455. Commentario*, Milano, 1989, pp. 401–26.

70 M. Glendon, *The Transformation of Family Law*, Chicago, 1989, p. 5. For a historical introduction, P. Ungari, *Storia del diritto di famiglia in Italia (1796–1942)*, Bologna, 1974.

71 C. Ranci and P. Ielasi, 'L'uso dei servizi sociali e sanitari', in Paci (ed.), *Le dimensioni*, pp. 416–20 and 422–3.

72 See the highly relevant analyses and considerations of P. Belli, 'Effetti redistributivi del Servizio sanitario nazionale', in Paci (ed.), *Le dimensioni*, pp. 436–7. Cf. O. De Leonardis, 'I welfare mix. Privatismo e sfera pubblica', *Stato e mercato*, no. 46 (1996), pp. 51–75.

73 See above, Chapter 2, pp. 44.

74 See above, Chapter 4, p. 98.

75 ISTAT, *Statistiche giudiziarie civili, anno 1994*, Roma, 1996, pp. 49–50, table 3.5, and ISTAT, *Statistiche giudiziarie penali 1994*, annuario no. 3, Roma, 1995, pp. 214–16, table 4.5.

76 For the number of abandoned civil cases, see the splendid article by S. Chiarloni, 'La giustizia civile e i suoi paradossi', *Storia d'Italia. Annali no. 14, Legge, Diritto, Giustizia*, Torino, 1998, pp. 401–83.

77 ibid., p. 405.

78 S. Mazzocchi, 'Giustizia, viaggio nella preistoria', *la Repubblica*, 28 January 1986.

See also the two successive articles of 30 January and 1 February. That little had changed more than ten years later can be seen from another newspaper cutting, chosen at random, from another Tribunal in another city, this time Florence: 'In the great chaos of the Tribunal the witnesses begin to rebel . . . and have signed the following declaration: "The undersigned, part of the 86 witnesses summoned for the audience scheduled for 9 a.m., draw the attention of the authorities once again to the preoccupying misfunctioning of the judicial machinery, of which, unfortunately, they are testimonies. At one o'clock, after more than four hours of waiting, still nothing was known about whether the hearing was to take place or not. Above all, this trial has been going on since 1993 and has not even reached a first level of judgment'; F. Selvati, 'Tribunale, la rivolta dei testimoni', *la Repubblica* (cronaca di Firenze), 5 February 1998.

79 Chiarloni, 'La giustizia civile', pp. 440–46.

80 ibid., p. 464. See also pp. 446–9. The just increase in the autonomy of junior magistrates, suggests Chiarloni, had left senior magistrates with insufficient powers to increase productivity in their offices.

81 See below, Chapter 9, p. 296. Even without considering this extreme solution, clauses had been introduced in many commercial transactions which envisaged forms of rapid protection and tutelage. However, as Chiarloni notes, such provisions invariably favoured the more powerful and privileged social groups ('La giustizia sociale', pp. 421–2 and 428–30).

82 See Statistical Appendix, tables 41–4.

83 OECD figures quoted in M. Dei, 'Cambiamento senza riforma: la scuola secondaria superiore negli ultimi trent'anni', in S. Soldani and G. Turi (eds.), *Fare gli italiani*, Bologna, 1993, vol. 2, p. 92. A decade later, the gap will have doubtless narrowed, but much more slowly than was needed. See also Statistical Appendix, tables 45–6.

84 See the important article by A. Schizzerotto, 'La scuola è uguale per tutti?', in Ginsborg (ed.), *Stato dell'Italia*, pp. 558–61. His figures are of 1985. In the early 1990s 56.6 per cent of Italian families declared that they had fewer than twenty-five books in their homes, and 23 per cent none at all; T. De Mauro, *Idee per il governo. La scuola*, Bari, 1995, p. 9.

85 They also compared favourably, in terms of the amount taught, on an international level; see G. C. Gasperoni, 'Quanto si impara a scuola?', in Ginsborg (ed.), *Stato dell'Italia*, p. 564.

86 De Mauro, *Idee per il governo*, pp. 46–7, tables 11–12, where teachers' income is compared in dollar terms. The absence of significant monetary increments during a teaching career was another striking feature of the Italian system. For staff–student ratios, F. Fabbroni *et al.*, *Scuola '93*, Bari, 1994, p. 64.

87 For reflections on many of these aspects, see the acts of the National Commission for secondary school reform, set up in 1997: 'Le conoscenze fondamentali per l'apprendimento dei giovani nella scuola italiana nei prossimi decenni', *Studi e Documenti degli Annali della Pubblica Istruzione*, no. 78 (1997), and in particular

the intervention of C. Pontecorvo, pp. 384–96. For some remarks on the teaching of history, see my intervention in the same commission (ibid., pp. 417–24).

88 OECD, *Education at a Glance*, Paris, 1992, quoted in M. Barbagli, 'Nella scuola secondaria le radici delle disfunzioni dell'università', in Ginsborg (ed.), *Stato dell'Italia*, p. 566. See also P. Trivellato, 'La scuola "reale": questioni critiche e condizioni per cambiare', *Quaderni di Sociologia*, vol. XXXVII (1993), no. 6, p. 17.

89 See A. Cicocca, 'Le famiglie: quadro sintetico della ricerca', in C. Cedrone (ed.), *Centralità e qualità dell'istruzione*, Firenze, 1990, p. 133.

90 De Mauro, *Idee per il governo*, p. 43, table 7.

91 F. Mount, *The Subversive Family*, London, 1982. For an interesting comparison of family policies in twenty-two countries, A. H. Gauthier, *The State and the Family*, Oxford, 1996.

92 L. Balbo, 'Una cultura dei diritti quotidiani', in L. Balbo (ed.), *Time to Care*, Milano, 1987, p. 131.

93 C. M. Santoro, 'La politica estera del Partito Socialista', in C. M. Santoro, *L'Italia e il Mediterraneo*, Milano, 1988, p. 127.

94 C. M. Santoro, *La politica estera di una media potenza*, Bologna, 1991, p. 38.

95 P. Isernia, 'Bandiera e risorse: la politica estera negli anni Ottanta', in Cotta and Isernia (eds.), *Il gigante*, pp. 160–65. Cf. C. Seton-Watson, 'La politica estera della Repubblica italiana', in R. J. B. Bosworth and S. Romano (eds.), *La politica estera italiana (1860–1985)*, Bologna, 1991, p. 352. The decision to install the missiles had already been taken by the House of Deputies in October 1981, but with a slim majority of 244 votes against 225.

96 For further details see G. P. Calchi Novati, 'Mediterraneo e questione araba nella politica estera italiana', *Storia dell'Italia repubblicana*, vol. II, pt 1, Torino, 1995, pp. 235–7.

97 For the details of the incident, see above, Chapter 5, p. 153.

98 See above, Chapter 2, p. 63.

99 For John Paul II's message of 1 January 1991, which had been declared a day of global peace, see *La Traccia*, vol. XII (1991), no. 1, pp. 8–13. For his speech during his visit to the parish of S. Dorotea, Roma, 17 February 1991, in which he stated categorically, 'We are not pacifists, we do not want peace at any cost', ibid., no. 2, p. 176. Cf. M. Donovan, 'Catholic "pacifism" and the Gulf War; pluralism, cohesion and politics', in Hellman and Pasquino (eds.), *Italian Politics*, vol. VII, pp. 159–72. By mid-February it was clear that the radicalism of the Pope had been reined in by the alarmed reaction of the Catholic hierarchy.

100 The debates of 16 January and 21 February 1991 were the most intense moments of parliamentary discussion; see Camera dei Deputati, *La guerra del Golfo Persico*, Roma, 1991, vol. II, pp. 661ff. and 1032ff.

101 P. Isernia, *La cooperazione allo sviluppo*, Bologna, 1995, p. 18.

102 ibid.

103 A. Del Boca, *Una sconfitta dell'intelligenza*, Bari, 1993, p. 31.

104 Isernia, *La cooperazione*, p. 248 and table 5.9, pp. 250 and 287.

105 See the interesting article by J. F. Médard, 'Francia-Africa: affari di famiglia', in della Porta and Mény, *Corruzione e democrazia*, pp. 29–48.

106 P. Pillitteri, *Somalia '81*, Milano, 1981. It must be noted that the PCI also initially backed the regime of Siad Barre; Del Boca, *Una sconfitta*, pp. 15–17.

107 Del Boca, *Una sconfitta*, p. 40.

108 Isernia, *La cooperazione*, pp. 338–9, table 6.9. Cf. M. Aden Sheikh and P. Petrucci, *Arrivederci a Mogadiscio*, Roma, 1994 [1st edn 1991], pp. 214–15, for the fertilizer factory of Tecnipetrol, and M. Yusuf Hasan, *Somalia* (ed. R. Balducci), Roma, 1993, pp. 172–3, for the silos and other scandals. For the very critical report of August 1993, drawn up by the then Foreign Minister, Nino Andreatta, see G. Schettino, 'Tutte le vergogne della cooperazoine', *la Repubblica*, 6 August 1993.

109 A. S. Milward *et al.*, *The European Rescue of the Nation-State*, London, 1992, p. 5. European integration, suggests Milward, was 'a new form of agreed international framework created by the nation-states to advance particular sets of national domestic policies which could not be pursued, or not be pursued so successfully, through the already existing international framework of cooperation between interdependent states, nor by renouncing international interdependence' (ibid., p. 182).

110 For some very significant caveats see P. Anderson, 'Under the sign of the interim', *London Review of Books*, vol. XVIII (1996), no. 1, pp. 13–17, now republished in P. Gowan and P. Anderson (eds.), *The Question of Europe*, London/New York, 1997, pp. 51–71.

111 For a lively debate upon the correct weighting of similitude and diversity, and the overall Italian performance, see F. Romero, 'L'Europa come strumento di *nation-building*: storia e storici dell'Italia repubblicana', *Passato e Presente*, vol. XIV (1996), no. 36, pp. 19–32; and P. Ginsborg, 'L'Italia e l'Unione europea', ibid., no. 37, pp. 85–92. For a strong Spanish espousal of the theme of general convergence, at both a socio-economic and political level, see S. Giner, 'The rise of a European society', *Revue Européenne des Sciences Sociales*, vol. XXXI (1993), no. 95, p. 161. But Giner also reminds us that north-west Europe has followed one set of related roots to convergence, none of them identical, southern Europe another, and the East another still.

112 Anderson, 'Under the sign', pp. 58ff.

113 G. F. Ballardin, 'Crea problemi al M.E.C. la successione di Malfatti', *Corriere della Sera*, 20 March 1972.

114 G. Pridham, 'Italy', in C. and K. J. Twitchett (eds.), *Building Europe: Britain's Partners in the EEC*, London, 1981, pp. 96–7.

115 M. Ferrera, 'Italia: aspirazioni e vincoli del "quarto grande" ', in M. Ferrera (ed.), *Le dodici Europe*, Bologna, 1991, p. 87.

116 A point forcefully made by R. Galli and S. Torcasio, *La partecipazione italiana alla politica agraria comunitaria*, Bologna, 1976, pp. 245–6.

117 D. J. Hine, 'Italy and Europe: the Italian presidency and the domestic management of European Community affairs', in Anderlini and Leonardi (eds.), *Italian Politics*, vol. VI, pp. 50–68. For a succinct and convincing analysis of the relationship between Italian public administration and the CEE, see C. Franchini, 'La fatica di stare in Europa', in Ginsborg (ed.), *Stato dell'Italia*, pp. 503–6.

118 'Look at it our way', *The Economist*, vol. CCLXXIV (1980), no. 7120, 16 February, p. 57.

119 M. Giuliani, 'Il processo decisionale italiano e le politiche comunitarie', *Polis*, vol. VI (1992), no. 2, p. 315, table 5.

120 A. Giolitti, *Lettere a Marta*, Bologna, 1992, p. 211.

121 Giuliani, 'Il processo decisionale', pp. 331–8. There remains the problem of why Greece, with a very similar political culture of centre-periphery clienteles, has been so much more efficient in spending Community funds; for some indications, see T. Galeros, 'Politique structurelle communautaire: l'expérience de la Grèce', in A. Predieri (ed.), *Fondi strutturali e coesione economica e sociale nell'Unione europea*, Milano, 1996, pp. 225–38.

122 Statistics charting the levels of guarantee spending by the EEC between 1962 and 1967 reveal that whereas 53.64 million units of spending on agriculture (the measure adopted by the PAC) were dedicated to cereals (including rice), and 30.85 million on dairy products, only 9.28 million were given over to 'fats and oils' and a derisory 0.19 million to fruit and vegetables; J. S. Marsh and P. J. Swanney, *Agriculture and the European Community*, London, 1980, p. 86, table 8(b). For the period up to 1962, see G. Laschi, *L'agricoltura italiana e l'integrazione europea*, Berne, 1999; for the more recent period, Fanfani, *L'agricoltura*, ch. 3.

123 See M. Telò, 'L'Italia nel processo di costruzione europea', *Storia dell'Italia repubblicana*, vol. III, pt 1, p. 213.

124 Pridham, 'Italy', p. 81. See also De Cecco and Migone, 'La collocazione internazionale', p. 188.

125 See the important article by K. Dyson and K. Featherstone, 'Italy and EMU as a "*vincolo esterno*": empowering the technocrats, transforming the state', *South European Society and Politics*, vol. I (1996), no. 2, pp. 272–99.

126 Carli, *Cinquant'anni*, p. 435.

127 M. Dassù and A. Missiroli, 'L'Italia nell'Unione europea: un bilancio e qualche prospettiva', *Europa Europe*, vol. V (1996), no. 1, pp. 16–17.

128 These problems are confronted with great intellectual force by Perry Anderson in his 'The Europe to come', first published in *London Review of Books*, vol. XVIII (1996), no. 2, pp. 3–8, now in Gowan and Anderson (eds.), *The Question of*

Europe, pp. 126–45. For the democratic deficit, see in particular W. Godley, 'The hole in the treaty', ibid., pp. 173–7.

129 M. V. Agostini, 'Italy and its Community policy', in *International Spectator*, vol. XXV (1990), no. 4, p. 348. The opposition to the move was considerable, ranging from the PCI to the Confindustria; even the Bank of Italy was more cautious than the Foreign Ministry.

130 M. Thatcher, *The Downing Street Years*, London, 1993, pp. 549–51. I am grateful to Perry Anderson for having drawn my attention to this source; see his 'The Europe to come', pp. 128–9.

131 Agostini, 'Italy and its Community policy', p. 351.

132 See for instance his speech of 9 July 1985, in the presence of Bettino Craxi; A. Spinelli, *Discorsi al parlamento europeo, 1976–86* (ed. P. Virgilio Dastoli), Bologna, 1987, p. 359. In the formulation of the Single Act, Jacques Delors and the majority of the heads of government preferred to put the accent on more efficient decision-making in the Community, rather than on an extension of democracy and an increased role for the European Parliament.

133 For the law of 1987, Agostini, 'Italy and its Community policy', p. 353. For that of 1989, Ferrera, 'Italia', pp. 85ff.

134 For details of the fate of the annual Community laws, see M. Giuliani, 'Italy', in D. Rometsch and W. Wessels (eds.), *The European Union and Member States*, Manchester, 1996, p. 123, table 5.3. One hundred and thirty-four directives were included in the law of 1990, ninety-five in that of 1991, and only thirty-three in that of 1992. Nor were the great majority transposed directly, but rather legislative power was delegated by parliament to the government. See the letter of alarm written by Jacques Delors to Giulio Andreotti on 28 January 1992, 'Caro Giulio, così non va', *la Repubblica*, 7 February 1992, and Andreotti's reply 'Eccellenza, non siamo gli ultimi', *Il Sole – 24 Ore*, 17 February 1992.

135 Giuliani, 'Italy', p. 126, fig. 5.5, for the years 1987–92.

136 Cf. F. Papitto, 'La Cee boccia le nostre regioni', *la Repubblica*, 1 August 1991, in which the regional governments of Lazio, Liguria, Calabria, Campania, Puglia and Sicily were identified as the principal culprits; F. Papitto, 'Così l'Italia perde i miliardi della Cee', *la Repubblica*, 12 March 1992; G. Pelosi, 'Emergenza fondi strutturali in Italia', *Il Sole – 24 Ore*, 17 February 1992.

137 The testimonies to this effect come from impeccable sources. Guido Carli in his memoirs pays tribute to Andreotti's role (*Cinquant'anni*, pp. 362 and 404). So too does Tommaso Padoa-Schioppa, who as a high-ranking official of the Bank of Italy was to have a key role in drawing up the Maastricht Treaty; M. Pirani, ' "Nei prossimi quattro mesi l'Italia si gioca tutto" ' (Intervista a Tommaso Padoa-Schioppa), *la Repubblica*, 18 April 1997. For the group of Italian *tecnici* at work in 1990–91, see the analysis of Dyson and Featherstone, 'Italy and EMU', *passim*.

138 Agostini, 'Italy and its Community policy', p. 349.

139 Thatcher, *The Downing Street Years*, p. 70.

140 ibid., pp. 765–76.

141 To this effect Andreotti based his actions upon a report prepared for the Council by Guido Carli, now published in R. A. Cangelosi and V. Grassi, *Dalle Comunità all'Unione*, Milano, 1996, pp. 108–12. See also the eye-witness account of the Council by Carli himself (*Cinquant'anni*, p. 404).

142 'Rows at the Rome summit', *The Economist*, vol. CCCXVII (1990), no. 7679, 3 November, p. 23. The positive contribution of the Italian presidency was further underlined by a second meeting of the European Council in Rome on 14–15 December 1990. However, exaggerated claims for Italy's role should be treated with some care. The Italians could move as far or as little as the Franco-German alliance allowed them, a point revealed very clearly by the tone and content of a joint letter from Kohl and Mitterrand to Andreotti of 6 December 1990 on the question of political unity. The text is published in Cangelosi and Grassi, *Dalle Comunità all'Unione*, pp. 113–15.

143 'The savaging', *The Economist*, vol. CCCXVII (1990), no. 7681, 17 November, p. 40.

144 On 16 November 1990 an opinion poll published in *The Times* was the first of several to suggest that the Conservatives would overtake Labour if Michael Heseltine, Mrs Thatcher's principal opponent, were to replace her as Prime Minister.

145 Dyson and Featherstone, 'Italy and EMU', p. 288. For the interventions of Tommaso Padoa-Schioppa in this crucial period, see his *L'Europa verso l'unione monetaria*, Torino, 1992.

Chapter 8: *Dénouement, 1992–4*

1 G. L. Luzi, 'La DC ringrazia Craxi ma avverte "Se fai un patto devi mantenerlo" ', *la Repubblica*, 17 November 1991.

2 This is very much the tendency of some distinguished Italian scholars who have addressed the problem of the causation of the crisis. For the sociologist Pizzorno, consociationalism is the lonely explanatory giant (see his *Le difficoltà del consociativismo, passim*); for the historian Massimo L. Salvadori the lack of political alternation since Unification led perforce to a series of regime crises, of which 1992 was only the latest (*Storia d'Italia e crisi di regime*, Bologna, 1994). For the political scientists Cotta and Isernia it is 'party government' (*'il governo dei partiti'*) which was the principal stone thrown into the pond of the Republic (the metaphor is theirs). The latter authors do, however, allow for the possibility of different ripples being caused by other stones (*Il gigante*, pp. 419–20). The historian Pietro Scoppola, in his *La repubblica dei partiti*, Bologna, 1991, also concentrates his attention on the political sphere. Aurelio Lepre delineates briefly but interestingly two crises, one economic and the other political, which fortunately for Italy did not coincide (*Storia della prima repubblica*, pp. 339–41). The most convincing attempt to explain the crisis at more than one level of analysis remains, in my opinion, that of Luciano Cafagna, *La grande slavina*, Venezia, 1993.

3 As far as I am aware there is no opinion poll which specifically asked electors at

the time of the 1992 elections how great an influence the collapse of Communism had had upon their way of voting. I must thank Anna Bosco and Paolo Segatti for help in trying to track down such a poll.

4 Leonardo Morlino and Marco Tarchi have pointed rightly to a 'chronic, widespread dissatisfaction that had existed since the end of the 1940s in various different formats but which was only able to manifest itself fully in the early 1990s'; see their article 'The dissatisfied society: the roots of political change in Italy', in *European Journal of Political Research*, vol. XXX (1996), no. 1, p. 43. See also Statistical Appendix, no. 40, for details of the Eurobarometer surveys on the 'Level of satisfaction with the functioning of democracy' for the period 1985–93, which show Italian dissatisfaction at over 70 per cent throughout the period, more than twenty percentage points higher than the average in the European Union.

5 C. Trigilia, 'Dinamismo privato e disordine pubblico. Politica, economia e società locali', in *Storia dell'Italia repubblicana*, vol. II, pt 1, Torino, 1995, especially pp. 770–77.

6 M. Oakeshott, *Rationalism in Politics*, London, 1962, p. 157.

7 See above, Chapter 6, p. 182.

8 For these details, see the depositions of various businessmen to the Milanese Procura, reproduced in A. Carlucci, *Tangentomani*, Milano, 1992, pp. 30ff. For Chiesa's arrest, E. Nascimbeni and A. Pamponara, *Le mani pulite*, Milano, 1992, pp. 13–14.

9 Quoted in Bellu and Bonsanti, *Il crollo*, p. 122.

10 G. Sani, '1992: la destrutturazione del mercato elettorale', in *Rivista Italiana di Scienza Politica*, vol. XXII (1992), no. 3, pp. 554–5. For the detailed analysis of the 'white' areas, Diamanti and Riccaboni, *La parabola del voto bianco*, pp. 167–87, especially p. 177, table 7. The vote for the Lega was significantly higher in the smaller centres than in the provincial capitals.

11 The above description is based on the analysis made by R. Mannheimer, 'L'elettorato della Lega Nord', *Polis*, vol. VII (1993), no. 2, pp. 253–76. See also P. G. Corbetta, 'La Lega e lo sfaldamento del sistema', ibid., pp. 229–52.

12 A survey on La Rete published in *Iter*, no. 4 (1992), pp. 7–98, revealed that of the 487 members of the movement in its sample, 30.4 per cent had degrees and 52.8 per cent upper secondary school diplomas. Their previous experience of civic organization came from cultural associations, parish circles, pacifist groups, etc. White-collar workers, students, professionals and teachers accounted for 71 per cent of membership; 55.5 per cent were below thirty-five years old, and another 24.4 per cent between thirty-five and forty-five (ibid., pp. 27–8).

13 The votes for the Greens, the Liberals and the Republicans all increased a little, while that for the Social Democrats declined. For the full results, see Statistical Appendix, no. 38.

14 Corbetta, 'La Lega e lo sfaldamento del sistema', pp. 231–3.

15 See Statistical Appendix, no. 39, for the percentage of non-voters from 1983–96.

16 See his long interview with the journalist M. A. Calabrò, *In prima linea*, Milano 1993, pp. 1–35. Educated in Florence, he admired Milan for its 'European vocation, and its rather Protestant tendency to consider riches and success as a proof of divine grace' (p. 6).

17 ibid., pp. 29–30. See also M. Andreoli, *Borrelli direttore d'orchestra*, Milano, 1998.

18 See above, Chapter 5, p. 144.

19 For Piercamillo Davigo, see his *La giubba del re. Intervista sulla corruzione* (ed. D. Pinardi), Bari, 1998.

20 Calabrò, *In prima linea*, p. 21.

21 Colombo, *Il vizio della memoria*, p. 133.

22 Calabrò, *In prima linea*, p. 18.

23 For the new Code, see L. Ferrajoli, 'Anatomie di una riforma', in *MicroMega*, 1989, no. 4, pp. 23–34; G. Colombo, 'The new code of criminal procedure', in Catanzaro and Sabetti (eds.), *Italian Politics*, vol. V, pp. 55–68.

24 M. Brambilla and G. Buccini, 'Chiesa inguaia i due ex sindaci Psi', *Corriere della Sera*, 3 May 1992. On 30 April Epifanio Li Calzi, previously a Communist *assessore* in the Milanese local government, and Sergio Soave, former President of the Lombard League of Cooperatives, were both arrested; 'Milano, tangenti, arrestati due del Pds', ibid., 1 May 1992.

25 'Tangenti: tocca al tesoriere DC', ibid., 13 May 1992. He was accused of having illegally received for party funds some 700 million lire.

26 Bellu and Bonsanti, *Il crollo*, pp. 152–3.

27 There were, of course, at this stage a lot of old scores to settle. In particular, the 'left' of the DC had not forgotten their humiliations under the rule of the 'CAF'. See the series of articles with eloquent titles in *Corriere della Sera*, 17 May 1992: G. Credazzi, 'Doppia imboscata e mistero finale'; F. Proietti, 'DC alla ricerca di voti perduti'; F. Merlo, 'Lasciamo fare allo Spirito Santo'; S. Vertone, 'Giochi di un Palazzo sordo al Paese'.

28 See above, Chapter 6, p. 209. The work of Falcone in the Ministry, as we have already seen, was of great value in orienting the apparatuses of the state towards a more constant and efficient intervention against the Mafia. However, it seems to me that there are clear traces in Falcone's statements at that time of the influence that Roman politics was exercising upon him, just as he exercised influence upon them. In other words, just as it has often been said that Falcone 'converted' Claudio Martelli to the anti-Mafia struggle, so Martelli seems to have accentuated that part of Falcone most attracted by *realpolitik*. See for instance his long interview in *Il Sole – 24 Ore*, 7 April 1991, where he presents a quite reductionist view of the relationships between political parties and Mafia backing.

29 'Cosa Nostra è pronta a colpire', *la Repubblica*, 24 May 1992 (interview originally of 19 May for the Neapolitan edition of the newspaper).

30 For a scrupulous reconstruction, based on the documentation of the prosecuting magistrates of Caltanisetta, who were responsible for handling the case, see Stille, *Excellent Cadavers*, pp. 353–4. For the testimony of Giovanni Brusca, see S. Lodato, *'Ho ucciso Giovanni Falcone'*, Milano, 1999, especially pp. 86–107.

31 See above, Chapter 6, pp. 212.

32 Discourse of O. L. Scalfaro at Montecitorio, published in *Corriere della Sera*, 29 May 1992.

33 For much of the account that follows, see the fine book of R. Alajmo, *Un lenzuolo contro la mafia*, Palermo, 1993.

34 'Falcone . . . oltre la morte. La Parola di Dio ci interpella', Veglia di preghiera, S. Giuseppe a Teatini, 13 June 1992. And from another part of the same document: 'God created man and woman, and with them the family. And He desired the family to be the cradle of love and of Communion. In our island today the name of the family has been offended! It indicates a group of persons intent on realizing crimes, oppression, illicit gain, death. But what we want is that from the family, the real family, there will emerge the victorious reply.' I must thank Nicoletta Silvestri for bringing me a copy of this document from Palermo.

35 See above, Chapter 4, p. 99.

36 See the analysis of the American anthropologists Jane and Peter Schneider, themselves participants and observers of these events; Schneider and Schneider, 'Dalle guerre contadine', p. 59.

37 The use of a white sheet conjured up many images. For Giovanna Fiume, 'The sheet that the newspaper photographs show, bloodstained and covering lifeless bodies, a veil for the discomposure of a violent death, that sheet we have washed and bleached and draped over the balconies of our houses' ('Introduzione' to Alajmo, *Un lenzuolo*, p. 5). For the Schneiders, the sheets were the opposite 'of the embroidered linen of the trousseau of a respectable bride, which symbolizes not only status but also sexual purity' ('Dalle guerre contadine', p. 58). While in moments of despair it seemed to the journalist Roberto Alajmo as if the sheets were hung out 'as if they were the white flags of surrender' (Alajmo, *Un lenzuolo*, p. 27).

38 ibid., p. 28: '4 June [1992]: at the first reunion there are fourteen people. An analysis of those present makes it difficult to present a standard portrait of the "sheeter": tendentially middle-class, tendentially left-wing, tendentially convinced that to be on the left does not mean much, any more.'

39 Fiume, 'Introduzione', p. 7.

40 None the less, civil society in Palermo made considerable progress. In July 1993, the journalist Enrico Deaglio registered the fact that as many as 120 different groups had adhered to the demonstration of 23 May 1993, the first anniversary of the death of Falcone; E. Deaglio, *Raccolto rosso*, Milano, 1993, p. 195.

41 The other four were Agostino Catalano, Walter Cusina, Vincenzo Li Muli and Claudio Traina; Stille, *Excellent Cadavers*, p. 372. Emanuela Loi, twenty-five years old, was from Sestu near Cagliari: ' "She was brave, but she hadn't made the police force her choice for life. And every time she came home on leave, she repeated: 'I don't want to stay in Palermo, it's too dangerous. I hope they'll soon let me return to Sardinia.' " Virgilio Loi, a retired railway worker, remembers his daughter in this way. First a training as an elementary teacher, with many sacrifices made in order to gain the diploma; then no work to be found in the schools, and enrolment in the police as a second-best. And her younger sister, Claudia, who has the same diploma, is now a hairdresser, and is waiting for her application to enter the police force to be accepted'; A. Pinna, 'Emanuela, maestrina in divisa', *Corriere della Sera*, 21 July 1992.

42 'Several days earlier, his security detail had asked that a "no parking" zone be created in the area to protect against the possibility of car bombs, but the request had not been examined by the committee in charge of government security in Palermo'; Stille, *Excellent Cadavers*, p. 372.

43 Testimonianza di 'Gabbi, artigiana', in Alajmo, *Un lenzuolo*, p. 71.

44 M. Breda, 'Benedetti morti, esplode l'ira', *Corriere della Sera*, 22 July 1992. Cf. P. Guzzanti, 'A Palermo la Norimberga dello Stato', *La Stampa*, 22 July 1992.

45 P. Hillmore, 'Land of illustrious corpses', *Observer*, 26 July 1992.

46 Alajmo, *Un lenzuolo*, p. 78.

47 F. Erbani, 'Sud, miracolo di Natale', *la Repubblica*, 20 December 1995. Draped from the balconies of the school which served as their headquarters was a sheet bearing the words: 'Every murder murders the future of our children.'

48 See R. Graham, 'Subtle Doctor moves into Italy's political front line', and 'Doctor Subtle's twin pillars', *Financial Times*, 22 June and 16 July 1992: 'With his glasses perched precariously on the end of his nose and his aloof air, the 54-year-old constitutional law expert has always looked more at home delivering academic lectures than giving speeches at Socialist party meetings. He talks quietly and listens silently.' The number of ministers in Amato's government was twenty-four, compared to the previous thirty-one, and thirty-five under-secretaries compared to the previous sixty-nine.

49 P. Barucci, *L'isola italiana del tesoro*, Milano, 1995, p. 29. See also his account of the meeting the day after the government was sworn in, at which Carlo Azeglio Ciampi, the then Governor of the Bank of Italy, warned of the gravity of Italy's economic situation (ibid., p. 327). Barucci's memoirs continue the tradition of those of Amato and Carli, although I find it difficult to understand why only *Treasury* Ministers seem able to write informative insider accounts of Italian politics.

50 Barone and Masera, 'Index linked bonds', p. 123, table 6.1, for the marked increase of the weight of interest repayments in 1991–2.

51 M. Balducci, 'Italy and the ratification of the Maastricht Treaty', in F. Laursen

and S. Van Hoonacker (eds.), *The Ratification of the Maastricht Treaty*, Dordrecht, 1994, pp. 195–202.

52 Menet-Genty, 'Forces et faiblesses', p. 226.

53 14 January 1992. Andreotti's budget for 1992 came in for harsh criticism: 'It anticipates GDP growth of 2.3 per cent in 1992, for example, higher than the OECD's optimistic forecast of 2 per cent; it does not incorporate the higher cost of debt service imposed by the recent rise in interest rates, from 11.5 to 12 per cent; and it relies on further revenue from privatization, if the politicians can agree on what to privatize.'

54 Barucci, *L'isola italiana*, p. 23.

55 ibid., pp. 29 and 327–34. Barucci offers many interesting background details to this emergency budget, as well as to Amato's intense way of working.

56 Chapter 2, pp. 57–8.

57 These themes were particularly evident at the 12th Congress of the CGIL in 1991, where Trentin stressed the importance of 'co-determination', of the trade unions having a role in the formation of Italy's political economy, both at a national and international level. See C. A. Mershon, 'The crisis of the CGIL: open division in the 12th National Congress', in Hellman and Pasquino (eds.), *Italian Politics*, vol. VII, pp. 87–109.

58 L. Mattina, 'Abete's Confindustria: from alliance with the DC to multiparty appeal', in Hellman and Pasquino (eds.), *Italian Politics*, vol. VIII, pp. 151–64. Abete had been elected on 27 May 1992, after Cesare Romiti, the favoured candidate of the industrialists, had made it clear that he intended to stay at FIAT.

59 See the discussion in *Quale impresa*, May and September 1992.

60 For the precedents of Giuseppe Di Vittorio in 1945–6, and of Luciano Lama in 1978, see Ginsborg, *A History*, pp. 95–6 and 389.

61 Trentin, *Il coraggio dell'utopia*, pp. 165–81. His account of the dramatic negotiations of these days is full of indignation against those who had forced him into what he considered to have been an impossible position. In the end he signed, as he explained on 1 August, for three basic reasons: to avoid a new government crisis 'at such a dramatic moment for the country', to prevent a division between the CGIL and the other two major unions, to keep Socialists and ex-Communists united within the CGIL; 'Ho fatto di tutto. Ho perso. Non posso fingere', *Corriere della Sera*, 2 August 1992. See also R. M. Locke, '*Eppure si tocca*: the abolition of the scala mobile', in Mershon and Pasquino (eds.), *Italian Politics*, vol. IX, pp. 185–96.

62 For an interesting comparative study, E. Gualmini, 'L'evoluzione degli assetti concertativi in Italia e in Germania', *Rivista Italiana di Scienza Politica*, vol. XXVII (1997), no. 1, pp. 101–50.

63 See the testimony of the journalist Giuliana Saladini in Alajmo, *Un lenzuolo*, pp. 88–9.

64 See for instance the long article by Pia Hinckle, 'The bribery mess in Milan', *Newsweek*, 1 June 1992.

65 Bellu and Bonsanti, *Il crollo*, p. 190. Ligresti was on the board of Enrico Cuccia's Mediobanca, the Ferruzzis' Ferfin and Carlo De Benedetti's Cofide.

66 More than a month earlier Antonio Di Pietro had made this point very plain to a shocked annual assembly of the Confindustria: 'Choose which camp you're in, isolate and denounce the cases of misconduct, this is what "positive" responsibility is about'; R. Armeni, B. Ugolini, ' "Voi non siete vittime" ', *l'Unità*, 6 June 1992. For an analysis of the flows of corruption, see above, Chapter 6.

67 For this change of meaning, J. Foot, 'From Boomtown to Bribesville. The images of the city, Milan, 1980–1997', shortly to be published in J. Foot, *Milan and the Miracle*, Oxford, 2001, pp. 157–80.

68 G. Gentili, ' "Evviva gli onesti" e poi incassa la mazzetta', *Corriere della Sera*, 11 June 1992.

69 See above, Chapter 6, pp. 188–9, for a detailed account of the Licandro case.

70 The full force of the Veronese inquiries was only to emerge in the spring of 1993. The Chief Prosecutor in Verona, Papalia, commented at that time: 'Corruption had got to such a point that it was bound to explode by itself'; quoted in Bozzini, *Destini incrociati*, p. 273.

71 For the judicial and other adventures of De Michelis and another Venetian potentate, Carlo Bernini, some useful indications in the journalistic account by R. Canteri and F. Peruffo, *Il Doge e il Sultano*, Trento, 1993.

72 S. Folli, 'Craxi: non sono impaziente ma . . .', *Corriere della Sera*, 27 August 1992.

73 In turn, this popular support greatly aided the progress of the investigations. As three of the Milanese magistrates wrote in 1993: 'Before this sea-change in mentality, the inquiring magistrate . . . found it impossible to connect the evidence he had accumulated, and thus expand the inquiry. In the present conditions all this has been greatly facilitated'; G. Colombo, P. C. Davigo and A. Di Pietro, 'Noi obbediamo alla legge, non alla piazza', *MicroMega*, 1993, no. 5, p. 10.

74 For an exchange of opinions on these and other points between Giovanni Maria Flick, who was later to become minister of Justice, and Francesco Saverio Borrelli, see G. M. Flick, *Lettera a un procuratore della Repubblica*, Milano, 1993, pp. 3–13. The judge of 'the preliminary inquiries' had the responsibility of controlling the actions of the Public Prosecutor and of deciding upon requests for imprisonment, the confiscation of goods, etc.; that of 'the preliminary hearing' of deciding upon the initial validity of the case in question.

75 Certain of these cases, seen from the point of view of the defendants, are described in C. Giovanardi, *Storie di straordinaria ingiustizia*, Roma, 1997.

76 In a country where concepts of honour and of *'figura'* were very deep-rooted, the ignominy of public exposure could be particularly hard to bear. As in all modern democracies, the liberties accorded to the mass media led to great abuses. The situation in Italy was exacerbated at this time by the absence of any

law safeguarding privacy. On 2 September 1992 a socialist deputy from Brescia, Sergio Moroni, committed suicide. He left a letter in which he explained his decision: 'I hope above all that [my gesture] can ensure that others, in the same conditions, will be able to avoid the moral anguish that I have suffered in these weeks, and the summary justice (by television or in the piazzas of this country), which transforms a Notice of Guarantee into a pre-emptive sentence of guilt'; quoted in Bellu and Bonsanti, *Il crollo*, pp. 203–4.

77 See above, Chapter 1, p. 8.

78 The franc was in difficulty because of the uncertainty of the outcome of the referendum on Maastricht, due on 20 September; sterling because of the depth of Britain's long-lasting economic recession, which showed no signs of lessening. Italy's position, in turn, was further weakened on 13 August, when the American agency Moody's announced that it had downgraded by two points Italy's investment-security rating.

79 See Piero Barucci's interesting account (*L'isola italiana*, pp. 47–58 and 344–59), especially of the meeting in Paris.

80 P. Norman and L. Barber, 'The monetary tragedy of errors that led to currency chaos', *Financial Times*, 11 December 1992. 'Faced with Mr Lamont's battering ram tactics, Mr Schlesinger nearly walked out. Some days later, he complained that he had been asked four times to cut rates and had to reply "No" four times "when only once should have done".' For an entertaining and informed account of the events of September 1992, written by an insider deeply hostile to Economic and Monetary Union, see B. Connolly, *The Rotten Heart of Europe*, London, 1995, pp. 138–66.

81 Barucci, *L'isola italiana*, pp. 347–8 and P. Norman, 'The day Germany planted a currency time bomb', *Financial Times*, 12–13 December 1992. For the wider context of German actions, which points an accusing finger at the Bundesbank, C. Hefeker, 'German monetary union, the Bundesbank and the EMS collapse', in *Banca Nazionale del Lavoro. Quarterly Review*, vol. XLVII (1994), no. 191, pp. 379–98. In the same week that marked the demise of the lira, both the Finnish markka and the Swedish krona had also come under intense speculative pressure.

82 Norman and Barber, 'The monetary tragedy'. Helmut Schlesinger had taken a quiet revenge on the British by letting it be known after the lira devaluation that he felt further realignment would probably be necessary. For information on who was doing the speculating, Connolly, *The Rotten Heart*, p. 154.

83 For the feeling of national humiliation and incredulity at Amato's presentation of events, see the editorial by Eugenio Scalfari, 'Dopo la Spagna e sotto alla Grecia', *la Repubblica*, 15 September 1992.

84 On 3 September 1992 the British Treasury had made arrangements to borrow $14.5 billion, and had declared 'once again the government's clear determination and ability to maintain sterling's position in the ERM at the existing central rate regardless of the outcome of the French referendum on the Maastricht Treaty'; Connolly, *The Rotten Heart*, pp. 140–41.

85 Norman, 'The day Germany planted'. In a severe editorial of 7 October 1992, the *Financial Times* commented: 'In some quarters there has been *Schadenfreude* at the self-inflicted wounds of a country which has for years been bankrupt in all but name; in others, relief at seeing an end to the make-believe of a state with a budget deficit nearly triple the EC average aspiring to join a monetary union within seven years.'

86 Barucci, *L'isola italiana*, p. 64. For the auction of BOT, ibid., p. 63.

87 ibid., p. 358.

88 D. Marsh, 'Europe adds a fiscal choke to monetary grip', *Financial Times*, 8 October 1992; S. Trevisani, 'Per il '93 la CEE avverte: "Esplode la disoccupazione" ', *l'Unità*, 1 December 1992.

89 G. Laccabò, 'La lezione dei 50 mila di Milano', and R. Armenni, 'E un giorno, all' improvviso, sono riemersi i Consigli', *l'Unità*, 30 October 1992.

90 V. Sivo, ' "Il governo è nudo davanti alla crisi" ', *la Repubblica*, 13 February 1993. In the same weeks there were widespread protests by shopkeepers and the self-employed against the 'minimum tax'.

91 See above, Chapter 7, pp. 222–3.

92 Published with the not very encouraging title 'Per lo statale suona la campana', *Il Sole – 24 Ore*, 23 January 1993. See also A. Orioli, 'Nel pubblico impiego salta il mito del "posto sicuro" ', ibid. For a different point of view, cf. F. Bassanini, 'La riforma del pubblico impiego', *l'Unità*, 5 March 1993. The decree law introduced for the first time the right to employment in the public administration for a stipulated number of handicapped persons.

93 G. Zagrabelsky, 'Adeguamenti e cambiamenti della Costituzione', in *Scritti in onore di Vezio Crisafulli*, Padova, 1985, vol. 2, pp. 927–8. For a revealing sample of the non-official minutes of the deeply inconclusive meetings of the Commissione bicamerale, F. Geremicca, ' "Caro presidente, non siamo computer" e i sessanta rinviano', *la Repubblica*, 19 November 1992.

94 For the background to Riina's capture, see the extraordinary testimony of one of the officers of the special unit of the Carabinieri most closely involved in the operation: M. Torrealta, *Ultimo*, Milano, 1995.

95 Calabrò, *In prima linea*, p. 99.

96 See above, Chapter 5, p. 145. The text of the sentence of 29 July 1994 which condemned, at the first level of judgment, Bettino Craxi, Claudio Martelli, Licio Gelli, Leonardo Di Donna and Silvano Larini for concourse in the fraudulent bankrupting of the Banco Ambrosiano is now available in: Tribunale di Milano, IIIa sezione penale, *UBS-Lugano.633369 'Protezione'*, Milano, 1996.

97 *Financial Times*, 27–8 February 1993. As Roberto Mongini, former vice-president of the Milan Airports Authority, told Graham: 'The reception centre at San Vittore prison has become like the foyer at La Scala – where you see anyone and everyone.'

98 F. Coppola, 'Via da Tangentopoli', *la Repubblica*, 6 March 1993.

99 Among the political class, there was widespread indignation that this should be treated on a par with crimes like extortion and corruption, both because the illegal financing of parties had become commonplace, and because it did not involve personal gain. On the other hand, it was the parties themselves who had passed the 1974 law on their own financing, who had not amended it in the interim, and who had taken no steps to set ceilings on political expenses. Furthermore, the line dividing personal gain from illicit party financing was by no means as clear as the politicians tried to make out. For a detailed analysis of this terrain cf. M. Rhodes, 'Financing party politics in Italy: a case of systemic corruption', in Bull and Rhodes (eds.), *Crisis and Transition*, pp. 54–80.

100 Cf. the detailed reconstruction of M. Fuccillo, 'Suona il tam, tam, l'Italia non ci sta', *la Repubblica*, 9 March 1993: 'No trace will remain in the history books of those two elderly ladies in a cake-shop of the capital at eleven o'clock in the morning on Sunday 7 March 1993, who muttered to each other a single phrase of four words: *"Bisogna fare qualcosa"* ("We must do something . . .").'

101 E. Scalfari, 'Il governo dello scippo', *la Repubblica*, 7 March 1993.

102 For the definition of this crime, and the context in which it came into being, see above, Chapter 6, p. 207; for Andreotti and the Mafia, ibid., pp. 204–12.

103 G. Neppi Modona, 'Ruolo della giustizia e crisi del potere pubblico', *Quaderni di Sociologia*, vol. XXXVII (1993), no. 5, p. 7.

104 For the campaign, Segni, *La rivoluzione interrotta*, pp. 204ff.; G. Ambrosini, *Referendum*, Torino, 1993. For the wider problems of the political use of referenda, M. Fedele, *Democrazia referendaria*, Roma, 1994.

105 G. F. Pasquino and S. Vassallo, 'The government of Carlo Azeglio Ciampi', in Mershon and Pasquino (eds.), *Italian Politics*, vol. IX, pp. 55–74.

106 Barucci (*L'isola italiana*, pp. 382–3) publishes Ciampi's letter of resignation of 14 September 1992.

107 The formation of that culture is discussed above in Chapter 7, pp. 219–20.

108 They were Augusto Barbera as minister for Relations with Parliament, Vincenzo Visco as minister of Finance, and Luigi Berlinguer as minister for the University and for Scientific Research. Among the other 'technicians' were Piero Barucci, who continued at the Treasury, and Luigi Spaventa as minister of Finances.

109 Looking back on these events in April 1994, Ciampi went as far as to say: 'Italian history changed course on 29 April 1993; that was the great error of the PDS'; and one of his closest collaborators, Antonio Maccanico, in the same interview, traced the defeat of the left at the elections of 1994 to this cause. While not wishing to underestimate the gravity of the error, such a line of argument seems to me to risk ascribing to a single political action an excessive explanatory weight; G. Valentini, 'Ciampi, il primo giorno di "libertà"', *la Repubblica*, 18 April 1994. For these events seen from the viewpoint of the PDS, cf. Occhetto, *Il sentimento e la ragione*, pp. 116–19.

110 'The fusion between "experts" and politicians was entirely successful and the

general level of cohesion was perfect'; E. Scalfari, ' "Il nuovo eravamo noi" ' (interview with C. A. Ciampi), *la Repubblica*, 8 May 1994.

111 ibid.

112 This is a point made forcibly by Michael Braun, 'The confederated trade unions and the Dini government', in M. Caciagli and D. I. Kertzer (eds.), *Italian Politics: A Review*, vol. XI, London, 1996, p. 219. For details of the agreement of 31 July 1993, Locke, *'Eppure si tocca'*, pp. 185–96.

113 Another 9,000 billion lire needs to be added to this figure, the result of 'corrective' measures taken on 21 May 1993; cf. C. A. Ciampi, 'Dalla recessione alla ripresa: un anno di governo dell'economia', *Il Mulino*, vol. XLIV (1995), no. 357, p. 79.

114 The programme of privatizations also went ahead, though more slowly than its advocates would have liked. It is important, though, to note the plight of the South; lacking a significant number of exporting industries, it bore the burdens of recession and public service cuts without benefiting from devaluation. There was also a significant lack of government intervention in the South between the suppression of the old system of extraordinary expenditure and the new measures for depressed areas which were drawn up only in 1996; Viesti, 'Che succede nell'economia del Mezzogiorno?', pp. 103–4.

115 See above, Chapter 7, pp. 222–3.

116 The details of these reforms are taken from Cassese's own illuminating article, 'Il difficile mestiere di ministro della Funzione pubblica', in *Riformare la Pubblica Amministrazione. Italia, Gran Bretagna, Spagna, Stati Uniti*, Torino, 1995, pp. 135–6. Cf. also Melis, *Storia dell'amministrazione*, pp. 530–34. Some 500 people were involved in the preparation of the reforms, and thirty-five volumes of studies were published by the 'Dipartimento della Funzione pubblica' in 1993–4.

117 For the opposition of Nicola Mancino of the Popolari, who was afraid of the electoral costs of bureaucratic reform, see Barucci, *L'isola italiana*, p. 181. A particular cause for controversy was the fact that, for reasons of speed and efficiency, most of the measures Cassese envisaged were included in the Budget law for 1994.

118 Cassese wrote later: 'The most significant failure consisted in not having attracted the interest of the consumers. We had succeeded in getting public opinion on our side, but the voice of the consumers was not listened to by the administration and by the authorities in general. The direct action of giving a new sovereignty to citizens and of reducing the expense of the machine of state had both benefits and costs. The cost was paid and consisted in the negative reaction of the bureaucracy. But such an action, which asked the consumers of public services to control those who performed them, should have had a greater echo among the consumers themselves'; Cassese, 'Il difficile mestiere', p. 150. The question remains, though, of the degree to which the consumers were themselves aware of being called to arms, and of what instruments of effective control were made available to them.

119 Giorgio Napolitano, as president of the Chamber of Deputies, insisted with determination on a deadline of 5 August 1993 for the approval of the new electoral law; for his account of these months, G. Napolitano, *Dove va la Repubblica*, Milano, 1994.

120 For further details and comments see, among others, R. D'Alimonte and S. Bartolini, ' "Electoral transition" and party system change in Italy', in Bull and Rhodes (eds.), *Crisis and transition*, pp. 110–34; S. Parker, 'Electoral reform and political change in Italy, 1991–1994', in Gundle and Parker (eds.), *The New Italian Republic*, pp. 40–56; S. Warner and D. Gambetta, *La retorica della riforma*, Torino, 1994; R. S. Katz, 'The 1993 parliamentary electoral reform', in Mershon and Pasquino (eds.), *Italian Politics*, vol. IX, pp. 93–112.

121 Buttafuoco, 'Cittadine italiane al voto', p. 6; Valentini, *Le donne fanno paura*, pp. 173ff.

122 Neppi Modona, 'Ruolo della giustizia', p. 6. For an accurate analysis of the involvement of members of the 1992 parliament in 'Tangentopoli', see L. Ricolfi, *L'ultimo parlamento*, Roma, 1993. A complete juridico-historical account of the investigations of 'Tangentopoli', which would require an enormous work of reconstruction, has yet to be undertaken.

123 S. Montanaro and S. Ruotolo, *Mister e Lady Poggiolini*, Napoli, 1994.

124 For an interesting linguistic analysis of that trial, see P. P. Giglioli, S. Cavicchioli, and G. Fede, *Rituali di degradazione*, Bologna, 1997. A businessman and financier, Cusani had been a close collaborator of Raul Gardini, and had been arrested and imprisoned in relation to the Enimont scandal. He refused to collaborate with the magistrates, and asked for an immediate trial. The Procura of Milan separated his case from the rest of the highly complicated investigation and the trial opened on 28 October 1993. In December a number of politicians were cross-examined as testimonies or accessories to the facts; among them were Altissimo, Cirino Pomicino, Craxi, Forlani and Martelli. For the judicial sentence at first level concerning the Enimont 'maxi-bribe', see Tribunale di Milano, Quinta Sezione Penale, *La maxitangente Enimont*, Milano, 1997.

125 For an interesting obituary of the party, rather different from mine, written by a Catholic historian who was himself involved in attempts to reform the DC, see P. Scoppola, *La Repubblica dei partiti*, pp. 502ff., and also Giovagnoli, *Il partito italiano*, p. 282.

126 See above, Chapter 5, pp. 159–61.

127 Why this was so, in contrast to the abandonment of the DC by its former Venetian and Lombard strongholds, is a complicated question which merits further research. Certainly, efficient local government and deep-rooted traditions played important roles, but by themselves they are insufficient to explain the continuation of a very strong left-wing vote in Emilia-Romagna, Tuscany, Umbria and the Marches, in both the elections of 1994 and those of 1996. For the beginnings of a more complex and society-oriented explanation, see P. Ginsborg and F. Ramella (eds.), *Un'Italia minore*, Firenze, 1999.

128 See above, Chapter 5, p. 160.

129 Occhetto's own version of 1994 is rather different, and puts the accent on the PDS as the victim of unfounded and politically motivated investigations by certain magistrates; *Il sentimento e la ragione*, pp. 23–4. There can be no doubt that the PDS was at times the object of inquiries which were later revealed as unfounded or of dubious motivation, but there is equally little doubt of the involvement of parts of the party in 'Tangentopoli'. See the discussion above, Chapter 6, pp. 187–8.

130 A. Gramsci, *Selections from the Prison Notebooks* (eds. Q. Hoare and G. Nowell Smith), London, 1971, especially pp. 238–9.

131 Revelli, *Le due destre*, p. 17.

132 The transcription of parts of that cross-examination is reproduced in the Appendix of Giglioli, Cavicchioli and Fede, *Rituali di degradazione*, pp. 211–27.

133 Revelli, *Le due destre*, p. 17.

Chapter 9: *From Berlusconi to Berlusconi, 1994–2001*

1 I. Diamanti, 'Identità e comportamento di voto. L'unità e la fedeltà non sono più virtù', in P. Corbetta and A. M. L. Parisi (ed.), *A domanda risponde*, Bologna, 1997, pp. 317–60.

2 For a fascinating insider's account of this unedifying process, see the diary, written between 1990 and 1996, by the Catholic historian Gabriele De Rosa: *La transizione infinita*, Bari, 1997.

3 For Orlando, see Peter Robb's convincing pen portrait in his *Midnight in Sicily*, Potts Point, 1996, pp. 40ff.

4 A fine description of this campaign is to be found in C. Stajano, *Il disordine*, Torino, 1993, pp. 5–82. Nando dalla Chiesa was the son of the Carabiniere general who had been murdered by the Mafia in Palermo in the summer of 1982.

5 See, for example, G. E. Rusconi, *Se cessiamo di essere una nazione*, Bologna, 1993.

6 Miglio, *Io, Bossi e la Legha*, pp. 34–5.

7 Gian Franco Miglio was an eloquent, but not solitary, testimony to this fact. Cf. Biorcio, *La Padania promessa*, pp. 236–48.

8 E. Soglio, 'Assessori della Lega, basta raccomandazioni', *Corriere della Sera*, 23 April 1994.

9 M. Tarchi, *Dal MSI ad AN*, Bologna, 1997, p. 28. For a recent and detailed reconstruction of the post-war history of the MSI, see P. Ignazi, *Il polo escluso*, Bologna, 1998.

10 In May 1994, in the Nomentano party section in Rome of which Fini was a member, 'Mussolini reigns like a monarch in every room. His portrait, either in profile or full-face, with or without helmet, is to be found on every wall and behind the desks of the section's officers'; A. Longo, 'La svolta di Fini si ferma in sezione', *la Repubblica*, 8 May 1994.

11 P. Ignazi, *Postfascisti?*, Bologna, 1994, p. 93. In a survey conducted by the same author at the XVIth Congress of the MSI in 1990, concerning the beliefs of its militants, the four assertions that met with the most favour were: 'The United States is an imperialist power' (94 per cent); 'the family is the pillar of society' (90 per cent); 'the reproduction habits of immigrants threaten our national identity' (79 per cent); 'discipline is the basis of the social order' (74 per cent). Sixty-four per cent of the sample declared itself anti-Zionist, and 25 per cent antisemitic; ibid., pp. 80–89, especially p. 84, table 5.

12 C. Tyler, 'The three phases of Fini', *Financial Times*, 18 February 1995. The article was written on the occasion of Fini's first official visit to London.

13 See, for example, H. Simonian, 'Berlusconi facing pressure to trim sails', *Financial Times*, 8 June 1993.

14 Cf. the informative 'Cronologia' published in D. Mennitti (ed.), *Forza Italia. Radiografia di un evento*, Roma, 1997, p. 281.

15 G. Riotta, 'Il segreto della vittoria è "la strategia da judo" ', *Corriere della Sera*, 30 March 1994; P. McCarthy, 'Forza Italia: the new politics and old values of a changing Italy', in Gundle and Parker (eds.), *The New Italian Republic*, pp. 130–46; and the detailed reconstruction of C. Golia, *Dentro Forza Italia*, Venezia, 1997, pp. 27ff.

16 S. Berlusconi, 'Costruiamo un nuovo miracolo', *Il Giornale*, 27 January 1994. For a commentary on the speech and its staging, see M. Deni and F. Maresciani, 'Analisi del primo discorso di Berlusconi. Indagine semiotica sul funzionamento discorsivo', in M. Livolsi and U. Volli (eds.), *La comunicazione politica tra prima e seconda Repubblica*, Milano, 1995, pp. 227–41.

17 See above, Chapter 4, pp. 112–19.

18 E. Semino and M. Masci, 'Politics is football: metaphor in the discourse of Silvio Berlusconi', *Discourse and Society*, vol. VII (1996), no. 2, p. 248. His other preferred metaphors were military and biblical.

19 McCarthy, *The Crisis of the Italian State*, p. 165.

20 See, for example, his speech of 6 February 1994, at the Palafiera di Roma: 'The fundamental concept is that of leaving to the State everything that cannot be attributed to private enterprise, and to accord to the private sphere everything that, in a regime based on competition, can cost less and whose quality can be improved. The idea that inspires us is that of being able to give each citizen the liberty to choose which school to send his children to, which clinic or hospital to be cured in, which company to insure with. All this, naturally, accompanied by a constant effort to ameliorate the services offered to the weakest categories in our society'; S. Berlusconi, 'Un nuovo miracolo italiano', in Mennitti (ed.), *Forza Italia*, p. 216.

21 G. Urbani, 'Alla ricerca del buongoverno – Appello per la costruzione di un' Italia vincente' [not dated, but of the last weeks of 1993], ibid., p. 211.

22 Cf. J. Arias, 'Il fascino del nuovo', *MicroMega*, 1994, no. 2, pp. 54–5.

23 A. Lyttelton, 'Italy: the triumph of TV', *New York Review of Books*, vol. XLI (1994), no. 14, p. 28.

24 'Cronologia', in Mennitti (ed.), *Forza Italia*, p. 283.

25 The scientific literature on the 1994 elections is very considerable. See, among others, I. Diamanti and R. Mannheimer (eds.), *Milano a Roma*, Roma, 1994; *Rivista Italiana di Scienza Politica*, vol. XXIV (1994), no. 3 (special issue dedicated to the elections); S. Bartolini and R. D'Alimonte (eds.), *Maggioritario ma non troppo*, Bologna, 1995; G. Pasquino (ed.), *L'alternanza inattesa*, Catanzaro, 1995; the section 'La politica', in Ginsborg (ed.), *Stato dell'Italia*, pp. 652–88.

26 See the very useful analysis of G. Calvi and A. Vannucci, *L'elettore sconosciuto*, Bologna, 1995, based on a sample of 4,655 cases. Alleanza Nazionale, Rifondazione Comunista, and the Lega Nord were the parties which had the highest percentage of young people among their voters, while the Popolari and the Pact for Segni were those which had the oldest electorate. The electorate of the League and of Alleanza Nazionale were disproportionately male. For Berlusconi's insistence on the importance of attracting the educated élite (he himself had graduated with maximum votes), see Lyttelton, 'Italy the triumph of TV', p. 28.

27 L. Verzichelli, 'Gli eletti', in Bartolini and D'Alimonte (eds.), *Maggioritario ma non troppo*, p. 414, table 6. For the social composition of the candidates, L. Mattina, 'I candidati', in *Rivista Italiana di Scienza Politica*, vol. XXIV (1994), no. 3, p. 564, table 6. For Publitalia, L. Gray and W. Howard, 'Forza Italia. Il partito americano', in M. Fedele and R. Leonardi (eds.), *La politica senza i partiti*, Roma, 1996, p. 99.

28 For some interesting points in this context, as well as references to the German debate on Berlusconi's victory, see J. Seisselberg, 'Conditions of success and political problems of a "media-mediated personality-party": the case of Forza Italia', *West European Politics*, vol. XXIX (1996), no. 4, pp. 714–43.

29 P. Corrias, M. Gramellini and C. Maltese, *1994. Colpo grosso*, Milano, 1994, p. 94, interview with the authors, 21 January 1994.

30 An interesting and informed analysis of the functioning of Forza Italia is offered by Golia, *Dentro Forza Italia*, *passim*. For the organization's lack of internal democracy, see the 'Prefazione' to the same book by Paolo Ceri, pp. 8–14. On the wider and thorny problem of the lack of democratic controls within modern political parties, some indications in Seisselberg, 'Conditions of success', pp. 717–18, who rather overestimates though the degree of inner democracy historically present in left-wing mass membership parties.

31 Cesareo *et al.*, *La religiosità in Italia*, pp. 314–15. No breakdown of the difference between the two islands was listed here.

32 A. Statera, 'Il migliose resta Mussolini', *La Stampa*, 1 April 1994.

33 For a defence of Martino, see E. Rogati, 'Il governo Berlusconi tra nazionalismo e federalismo', *Politica Internazionale*, vol. XXIII (1995), nos. 1–2, pp. 46–53. Of a diverse opinion, F. Rampini, 'L'Italia svalutata', in *Il Mulino*, vol. XLIV (1995), no. 1, pp. 92–102.

34 Braun, 'The confederated trade unions', pp. 224–5.

35 S. Gundle, 'Rai and Fininvest in the year of Berlusconi', in R. S. Katz and P. Ignazi (eds.), *Italian Politics. A Review*, vol. X, Boulder, Colorado, 1996, pp. 195–218.

36 R. Graham, 'Test of independence for Bank of Italy', and 'Berlusconi seeks to control central bank appointments', *Financial Times*, 13 May and 4 July 1994. The government had issued a statement claiming its right to make senior appointments in the Bank, thus breaking with the latter's traditions.

37 A. Friedman, 'The economic elites and the political system', in Gundle and Parker (eds.), *The New Italian Republic*, pp. 269–70; F. Cavazzuti, 'The uncertain path of privatisation', in Katz and Ignazi (eds.), *Italian Politics*, vol. X, pp. 169–82.

38 S. Di Michele and A. Galiani, *Mal di destra*, Milano, 1995, pp. 81–2.

39 The accusations were levied against Silvio Berlusconi and his brother Paolo. According to the Procura of Milan, its investigation 'had taken as its point of departure the testimony of the Vice-Brigadier Di Giovanni, who had come to offer his evidence spontaneously to the Procura'; see the case presented by the magistrates on 14 October 1995, published in its entirety in Tribunale di Milano e Palermo, *Le mazzette della Fininvest*, Milano, 1996 (for Di Giovanni, p. 27). That kickbacks had been paid for a sum of at least 330 million lire was not in contention. Paolo Berlusconi admitted immediately that the money had been handed over, but maintained that he had been forced to pay up because the Financial Police had threatened him with 'an unjustified expansion of their enquiries to include a meticulous control of formal irregularities' (ibid., p. 96). He added that his brother had never been informed: 'The structure of the Fininvest group, leaving aside titular posts, has a precisely designated division of responsibilities; I personally manage all that concerns tactics and strategy, while Silvio Berlusconi has responsibility for the overall global strategy of the group' (ibid., p. 104).

40 For the dynamics of the support for the five principal parties from December 1994 onwards, see G. Sani and P. Segatti, 'Programmi, media e opinione pubblica', *Rivista Italiana di Scienza Politica*, vol. XXVI (1996), no. 3, pp. 460–61.

41 M. Gilbert, 'The Oak Tree and the Olive Tree', in Caciagli and Kertzer (eds.), *Italian Politics: A Review*, vol. XI, pp. 101–17.

42 See Ignazi, *Il polo escluso*, pp. 447ff., and Tarchi, *Dal MSI ad AN*, pp. 139ff. Both authors underline the total control which the new statute of the party accorded to its leader. Even the national directory of the party was 'designated by the president'.

43 In May 1998 Di Pietro was again accused by the Brescian magistrates, this time for corruption in his handling of the case against the financier Pierfrancesco Pacini Battaglia. For his successful defence, see A. Di Pietro, *Memoria*, Milano, 1999.

44 For the results of the 1996 elections, see Statistical Appendix, no. 38. For a detailed analysis of the League's performance, I. Diamanti, 'La Lega Nord, dal successo alla secessione', in I. Diamanti and M. Lazar (eds.), *Stanchi di miracoli*, Milano, 1997, pp. 221–35. For an overall view of the results, R. Mannheimer, 'Eppur si muove. Opinione pubblica e offerta politica', ibid., pp. 159–79.

45 P. Anderson, 'Renewals', *New Left Review* (New Series), no. 1 (2000), pp. 5—24; C. Leys, 'Public sphere and media', *Socialist Register*, Rendlesham, 1999, pp. 314—35. For a spirited rebuttal of accusations of insufficiency, A. Giddens, *The Third Way and Its Critics*, Oxford, 1999.

46 For a particularly successful country-specific adaptation, see A. Hemerijck and J. Visser, 'The Dutch model: an obvious candidate for the "Third way"?', *Archives Européennes de Sociologie*, vol. XL (1999), no. 1, pp. 103—21.

47 M. Giannini, 'Le Cassandre sono servite' (interview with G. Amato), *la Repubblica*, 2 March 2001.

48 See M. D'Alema (with C. Velardi and G. Cuperlo), *Un paese normale*, Milano, 1995. The old Italian Communist party, whatever its faults, had always been characterized by a high level of theoretical elaboration, and by the attempt to analyse the trends of modern capitalism.

49 D. Stone, M. Garnett and A. Denham (eds.), *Think Tanks across Nations: a Comparative Approach*, Manchester, 1998. For Italy, C. Radaelli and D. Martini, 'Think tanks, advocacy coalitions and policy change: the Italian case', ibid., pp. 59—81.

50 G. Mazzoleni, *La corsa all'Euro*, Roma, 1998, p. 124.

51 K. Dyson and K. Featherstone, *The Road to Maastricht: Negotiating Economic and Monetary Union*, Oxford, 1999, p. 528. The Italians (principally Guido Carli and Mario Draghi from the Treasury) also pushed successfully for the EU Commission to be entrusted with the task of evaluating the degree of convergence achieved by member states, in the hope that the Commission would be as inclusive as possible.

52 F. M. Signorelli, 'Tietmayer gela le speranze dell'Italia', *la Repubblica*, 17 October 1996.

53 L. Barber, 'When the countdown faltered', *Financial Times*, 27 January 1996.

54 D. White and T. Burns, 'Still everything to play for' (interview with J. M. Aznar), *Financial Times*, 30 September 1996.

55 'Italy's budget and EMU', *Financial Times*, 30 September 1996.

56 'Chirac attacca l'Italia, poi si ferma', *Corriere della Sera*, 2 October 1996. See also the interesting article of the same day by the newspaper's Paris correspondent, A. Guatelli: 'Il premier dà lezioni, ma è prigioniero della Bundesbank'.

57 R. Bianchini, 'Il Senatur: Nord e Sud due monete diverse', *la Repubblica*, 26 May 1996.

58 M. Jacques, 'Italy's showman threatens to bring the house down', *Observer*, 15 September 1996.

59 R. R., 'Prodi agli alleati: vedrete i sorci verdi', *Corriere della Sera*, 2 October 1996.

60 For the Greek case, see the perceptive article by L. Tsoukalis, 'Greece in the EU: domestic reform coalitions, external constraints and high politics', in A. Mitsos and E. Mossialos (eds.), *Contemporary Greece and Europe*, Aldershot, 2000, pp. 37—51. There is more than one similarity with Italy. Thus Tsoukalis writes (p. 42): 'many Greeks consider the EU as a protection mechanism against

their own bad, collective self and also a kind of insurance, inadequate though admittedly it may be, against external risks.'

61 Maurizio Cotta, in an interesting analysis which uses Hirschman's well-known categories of 'exit', 'voice' and 'loyalty', dates from this period Italy's change of attitude from 'voice' (an attempt to influence or change the terms of entry) to 'loyalty', or even 'submission', with regard to the process of economic integration; M. Cotta, 'Le élite politiche nazionali di fronte all'integrazione', *Il Mulino*, vol. XLVII (1998), no. 377, pp. 450ff.

62 F. Bertinotti, 'Le due sinistre devono dialogare', *l'Unità*, 29 September 1996.

63 Information based on a conversation with Francesco Selmin, schoolteacher at Este.

64 M. Giannini, 'Siamo arrivati al traguardo nonostante Romiti e Fazio' (interview with R. Prodi), *La Repubblica*, 30 December 1998. The costs of Italy staying out of, or being excluded from, the EMU were carefully spelled out by G. Bonvicini *et al.*, 'Italy's difficult road into the EU hard core', *International Spectator*, vol. XXXII (1997), nos. 3–4, pp. 3–20.

65 F. Papitto, 'Bruxelles meno dura con l'Italia', *la Repubblica*, 23 April 1997.

66 R. Prodi, 'Siamo arrivati al traguardo nonostante Romiti e Fazio', *la Repubblica*, 30 December 1998.

67 ibid.

68 Dyson and Featherstone, *The Road to Maastricht*, p. 533.

69 M. Monti, editorial, *Corriere della Sera*, 3 May 1998.

70 B. Baldi, 'La politica di riforma del centro-periferia', in G. Di Palma, S. Fabbrini and G. Freddi (eds.), *Condannata al successo?*, Bologna, 2000, p. 133.

71 F. Bassanini, 'La riforma della pubblica amministrazione in Italia', paper presented at the 3rd Conference of Ambassadors, Roma, 26 July 2000, tables, pp. 6–10. I must thank the Minister for personally making available this paper to me.

72 Indeed Bassanini himself was shifted from his ministerial position in the first period of D'Alema's premiership, with a resulting stagnation in the reform process and a public row in May 1999 between Bassanini and the new Minister for Administrative Reform, Piazza; G. Capano, 'Le politiche amministrative: dall'improbabile riforma alla riforma permanente', in Di Palma *et al.* (eds.), *Condannata al successo?*, p. 168, n. 11.

73 This is a point made by both S. Cassese, 'La riforma della pubblica amministrazione italiana', *Il Lavoro nella Pubblica Amministrazione*, vol. III (2000), no. 6, pp. 12–13, and G. Capano, 'Le politiche amministrative', p. 197.

74 Y. Mény, 'Le riforme amministrative in Italia e in Europa', in SPISA, *Le riforme amministrative italiane: un confronto europeo*, Bologna, 2000, p. 18.

75 See Confindustria: Centro Studi, *L'Italia da semplificare*, 3 vols., Bologna, 1998, especially vol. 1, *Le istituzioni* (ed. S. Cassese and G. Galli).

76 A. Manzella, 'La legge sul federalismo: architrave per la Repubblica', *la Repubblica*, 1 March 2001.

77 G. Gasperoni, 'The uncertain renewal of Italian education', in L. Bardi and M. Rhodes (eds.), *Italian Politics: A Review*, vol. 13, Oxford, 1998, pp. 227–48.

78 F. Maino, *La politica sanitaria*, Bologna, 2001, pp. 250ff. Bindi lost her place in the government when Amato became prime minister, being replaced by a distinguished senior consultant, Franco Veronesi.

79 M. Ferrera and E. Gualmini, *Salvati dall'Europa?*, Bologna, 1999, p. 116. For the Onofri report, ibid., pp. 110–14.

80 'Sei anni di Mani pulite', *la Repubblica*, 7 April 1998.

81 S. J. Pharr and R. D. Putnam (eds.), *Disaffected Democracies*, Princeton, 2000; E. U. Savona and L. Mezzanotte, *La corruzione in Europa*, Roma, 1988; D. della Porta and A. Vannucci, *Un paese anormale*, Roma-Bari, 1999.

82 See above, Chapter 8, p. 273.

83 See his book on the opportunities opened up by the bicameral commission: M. D'Alema (with G. Cuperlo), *La grande occasione*, Milano, 1997.

84 G. Pasquino, 'A postmortem for the Bicamerale', in D. Hine and S. Vassallo (eds.), *Italian Politics: A Review*, vol. XIV, Oxford, 2000, p. 102.

85 A. Ghirelli, *Napoli dalla guerra a Bassolino*, Napoli, 1998, pp. 167ff.; A. Bassolino, *La repubblica delle città*, Roma, 1996.

86 T. Amendola and P. Isernia, 'Continuità e mutamento nella politica estera italiana', in Di Palma *et al.* (eds.), *Condannata al successo?*, pp. 365–400.

87 G. C. Caselli and A. Ingroia, *L'eredità scomoda*, Milano, 2001.

88 On this acquittal, see P. Ginsborg, 'Assoluzioni all'italiana', *la Repubblica*, 30 October 1999.

Bibliography

Abate, F., *Capo d'Orlando. Un sogno fatto in Sicilia*, Roma, 1993.

Abercrombie, R., *Television and Society*, London, 1996.

Accati, L., 'Il marito della santa. Ruolo paterno, ruolo materno e politica italiana', in *Meridiana*, no. 13 (1992), pp. 79–105.

Accornero, A., *La parabola del sindacato*, Bologna, 1992.

Achilli, G., *et al.*, *Vivere sole*, Milano, 1994.

Addis, E., 'Banca d'Italia e politica monetaria: la riallocazione del potere fra stato, mercato e Banca Centrale', *Stato e Mercato*, no. 19 (1987), pp. 73–95.

Aden Sheikh, M., and Petrucci, P., *Arrivederci a Mogadiscio*, Roma, 1994 [1st edn 1991].

Agnelli, G., *et al.*, *In ricordo di Guido Carli (Atti del convegno BNL–ABI)*, Roma, 1994.

Agnew, J. C., 'Coming up for air: consumer culture in historical perspective', in Brewer and Porter (eds.), *Consumption and the World of Goods*, q.v., pp. 19–39.

Agostini, M. V., 'Italy and its Community policy', in *The International Spectator*, vol. XV (1990), no. 4, pp. 347–55.

Ajello, N., 'Mezzogiorno di fuoco', *L'Espresso*, vol. XXX (1984), no. 45, 11 November.

Ajello, N., *et al.*, *Perché loro*, Bari, 1984.

Alajmo, R., *Un lenzuolo contro la mafia*, Palermo, 1993.

Albera, G., and Monti, N., *Italian Modern. A Design Heritage*, New York, 1989.

Alberdi, I. (ed.), *Informe sobre la situación de la familia en España*, Madrid, 1995.

Alessandri, A., *et al.*, *La 'Familiaris Consortio'*, Città del Vaticano, 1982.

Allum, P., *Italy: Republic without Government?*, London, 1973.

—— *Politics and Society in Post-war Naples*, Cambridge, 1973.

—— 'Statesman or Godfather? The Andreotti trials', in D'Alimonte and Nelken (eds.), *Italian Politics. A Review*, vol. XII, q.v., pp. 219–32.

Allum, P. and F., 'The resistible rise of the new Neapolitan Camorra', in Gundle and Parker (eds.), *The New Italian Republic*, q.v., pp. 234–46.

Allum, P., and Diamanti, I., '50/'80, vent'anni*, Roma, 1986.

Almond, G. A., and Verba, S., *The Civic Culture*, Princeton, 1963.

Bibliography

Alvino, S., 'Nel cuore di Montecalvario: "un vicinato di parenti"', *Meridiana*, no. 17 (1993), pp. 113–36.

Amato, G., *Due anni al tesoro*, Bologna, 1990.

Amatori, F., 'Italy: the tormented rise of organizational capabilities between government and families', in Chandler, Amatori and Hikino, *Big Business and the Wealth of Nations*, q.v., pp. 246–76.

Ambrosini, G., *Referendum*, Torino, 1993.

Amendola, T., and Isernia, P., 'Continuità e mutamento nella politica estera italiana', in Di Palma *et al.* (eds.), *Condannata al successo?*, q.v., pp. 365–400.

Anastasia, B., 'Il gruppo Zanussi: quadro storico e situazione attuale', in Dina (ed.), *Elettrodomestici flessibili*, q.v., pp. 11–89.

Andall, J., 'Catholic and state construction of domestic workers: the case of Cape Verdean women in Rome in the 1970s', in Koser and Lutz (eds.), *The New Migration in Europe: Social Constructions and Social Realities*, q.v., pp. 124–42.

Anderlini, F., 'La DC: iscritti e modello di partito', in *Polis*, vol. III (1989), no. 2, pp. 277–304.

Anderlini, F., and Leonardi, R. (eds.), *Italian Politics: A Review*, vol. VI, London, 1992.

Anderson, M. (ed.), *Sociology of the Family*, Harmondsworth, 1980 (2nd edn).

Anderson, M., Bechhofer, F., and Gershuny, J. (eds.), *The Social and Political Economy of the Household*, Oxford, 1994.

Anderson, P., 'Agency', in Anderson, *Arguments within English Marxism*, q.v., pp. 16–58.

—— *Arguments within English Marxism*, London, 1980.

—— 'The Europe to come', in Gowan and Anderson (eds.), *The Question of Europe*, q.v., pp. 126–45 [1st edn in *The London Review of Books*, vol. XVIII (1996), no. 2, pp. 3–8].

—— *In the Tracks of Historical Materialism*, London, 1983.

—— 'Renewals', *New Left Review* (New Series), no. 1 (2000), pp. 5–24.

—— 'Structure and subject', in Anderson, *In the Tracks of Historical Materialism*, q.v., pp. 32–55.

—— 'Under the sign of the interim', in Gowan and Anderson (eds.), *The Question of Europe*, q.v., pp. 51–71 [1st edn in *London Review of Books*, vol. XVIII (1996), no. 1, pp. 13–17].

Andreoli, M., *Andavamo in Piazza Duomo*, Milano, 1993.

—— *Borrelli direttore d'orchestra*, Milano, 1998.

Andreotti, G., *A non domanda rispondo*, Milano, 1999.

—— *A ogni morte di Papa*, Milano, 1980.

—— *Cosa loro*, Milano, 1995.

—— 'Una "marcia" mancata', in *Concretezza*, vol. V (1959), no. 12, p. 4.

—— 'Zanzariera', in *Concretezza*, vol. III (1957), no. 22, p. 6.

Andres, C., and Deuzler, G., *Dizionario storico del Cristianesimo*, Milano, 1992.

Annibaldi, C., and Berta, G. (eds.), *Grande impresa e sviluppo italiano. Studi per i cento anni della FIAT*, 2 vols., Bologna, 1999.

ARCI (Associazione Ricreativa Culturale Italiana), *Come Dove Quando*, Milano, 1996.

Arias, J., 'Il fascino del nuovo', *MicroMega*, 1994, no. 2, pp. 53–9.

Arlacchi, P., *Gli uomini del disonore*, Milano, 1992.

Arnot, M. L., and Usborne, C. (eds.), *Gender and Crime in Modern Europe*, London, 1999.

Arrighi, G. (ed.), *Semiperipheral Development*, London, 1985.

Ascoli, U. (ed.), *Welfare state all' italiana*, Bari, 1984.

Asor Rosa, A., *La sinistra alla prova*, Torino, 1996.

Atkinson, A. B., Rainwater, L., and Smeeding, T., *Income Distribution in European Countries*, Working Paper no. 9535, University of Cambridge, Department of Applied Economics, Cambridge, 1995.

Audisio, E., 'Un borghese felice di giocare', *Il Venerdì di Repubblica*, 11 June 1993.

Augé, M., *Non-lieux*, Paris, 1992.

Auriti, M., 'Il mio bimbo d'oro ha un solo difetto: è buddista', *Oggi*, vol. L (1994), no. 3, 24 January, pp. 86–9.

Backett, K., 'The negotiation of fatherhood', in Lewis and O'Brien (eds.), *Reassessing Fatherhood*, q.v., pp. 74–90.

Baeri, E., *I lumi e il cerchio*, Roma, 1992.

Baffi, P., 'Cronaca di un'infamia', *Panorama*, vol. XXVIII (1990), no. 1242–3, 11 February, pp. 121–47.

Bagnasco, A., *L'Italia in tempi di cambiamento politico*, Bologna, 1996.

—— *Tre Italie. La problematica territoriale dello sviluppo italiano*, Bologna, 1977.

Bagnasco, A., and Sabel, C. F. (eds.), *Small and Medium-Size Enterprises*, London, 1995.

Balbo, L., 'Un caso di capitalismo assistenziale: la società italiana', *Inchiesta*, vol. VII (1977), no. 28, pp. 3–18.

—— 'Crazy quilts', in Statera (ed.), *Consenso e conflitto nella società contemporanea*, q.v., pp. 217–42.

—— 'Una cultura dei diritti quotidiani', in Balbo (ed.), *Time to Care*, q.v., pp. 121–36.

—— 'La doppia presenza', *Inchiesta*, vol. VIII (1978), no. 32, pp. 3–6.

—— 'Falsa demitizzazione: il PCI e la vita quotidiana', in Balbo *et al.*, *Lettere da vicino*, q.v., pp. 3–14.

—— *Stato di famiglia*, Milano, 1976.

Balbo, L. (ed.), *Time to Care*, Milano, 1987.

Balbo, L., and Manconi, L., *I razzismi reali*, Milano, 1992.

Bibliography

Balbo, L., May, M. P., and Micheli, G. A., *Vincoli e strategie nella vita quotidiana*, Milano, 1990.

Balbo, L., *et al.*, *Lettere da vicino*, Torino, 1986.

Baldassare, A., and Mezzanotte, C., *Gli uomini del Quirinale*, Bari, 1985.

Baldassari, M. (ed.), *The Italian Economy: Heaven or Hell?*, London, 1994.

Baldi, B., 'La politica di riforma del centro-periferia', in Di Palma *et al.* (eds.), *Condannata al successo?*, q.v., pp. 113–52.

Balducci, M., 'Italy and the ratification of the Maastricht Treaty', in Laursen and Van Hoonacker (eds.), *The Ratification of the Maastricht Treaty*, q.v., pp. 195–202.

Balistreri, P., 'La società mafiosa', *MicroMega*, 1990, no. 5, pp. 169–83.

Balloni, V., 'L'industria della moda', in Ginsborg (ed.), *Stato dell'Italia*, q.v., pp. 398–9.

Banfield, E., *The Moral Basis of a Backward Society*, Glencoe, 1958 (Italian edn *Le basi morali di una società arretrata*, ed. D. De Masi, Bologna, 1976).

Baptiste, E., and Michelsons, A., 'Artigianato e piccole imprese nell'area ovest di Torino', in Perulli (ed.), *Piccole imprese metropolitane*, q.v., pp. 103–41.

Baranski, Z. G., and Lumley, R. (eds.), *Culture and Conflict in Postwar Italy*, London, 1990.

Barbagallo, F., *Napoli fine Novecento*, Torino, 1997.

—— *Il potere della camorra (1973–1998)*, Torino, 1999.

Barbagli, A., Capecchi, V., and Cobalti, A., *La mobilità sociale in Emilia-Romagna*, Bologna, 1988.

Barbagli, M., 'I genitori di lei e quelli di lui. Una ricerca sui rapporti di parentela in Emilia-Romagna', *Polis*, vol. V (1991), no. 1, pp. 71–83.

—— 'Linee di parentela', *Polis*, vol. V (1991), no. 1, pp. 5–19.

—— 'Nelle scuola secondaria le radici delle disfunzioni dell'università', in Ginsborg (ed.), *Stato dell'Italia*, q.v., pp. 565–8.

Barbagli, M., and Corbetta, P. G., 'Una tattica e due strategie. Inchiesta sulla base del PCI', *Il Mulino*, vol. XXVII (1978), no. 260, pp. 922–67.

Barbagli, M., and Pisati, M., *Rapporto sulla situazione sociale a Bologna*, Bologna, 1995.

Barbagli, M., and Saraceno, C. (eds.), *Lo stato delle famiglie in Italia*, Bologna, 1997.

Barberis, C., *La società italiana*, Milano, 1995 (2nd revised edn).

Barbero Avanzini B., and Lanzetti, C., *Problemi e modelli di vita familiare*, Milano, 1980.

Barca, F., *Imprese in cerca di padrone*, Roma, 1994.

Barca, F. (ed.), *Storia del capitalismo italiano*, Roma, 1997.

Barca, F., and Visco, I., 'L'economia italiana nella prospettiva europea: terziario protettivo e dinamica dei redditi nominali', in Miscossi and Visco (eds.), *Inflazione, concorrenza e sviluppo*, q.v., pp. 21–91.

Barca, F., *et al.*, *Assetti proprietari e mercato delle imprese*, 3 vols., Bologna, 1994.

Bardi, L., and Rhodes, M. (eds.), *Italian Politics. A Review*, vol. XIII, Oxford, 1998.

Bibliography

Barile, G., *et al.*, *Tra due rive*, Milano, 1994.

Barile, P., 'Presidente della Repubblica: la prassi di Pertini', *Quaderni Costituzionali*, vol. I (1981), no. 2, pp. 365–75.

Barnes, S. H., and Sani, G., 'Mediterranean political culture and Italian politics: an interpretation', *British Journal of Political Science*, vol. IV (1974), no. 3, pp. 289–303.

Barone, E., and Masera, R. S., 'Index-linked bonds from an academic, market and policy-making standpoint', in De Cecco, Pecchi and Piga (eds.), *Managing Public Debt*, q.v., pp. 117–47.

Bartolini, S., and D'Alimonte, R. (eds.), *Maggioritario ma non troppo*, Bologna, 1995.

Barucci, P., *L'isola italiana del tesoro*, Milano, 1995.

Bassolino, A., *La repubblica delle città*, Roma, 1996.

Bausola, A., *et al.*, *Cultura e fede nell'Italia del Nord*, Milano, 1992.

Bazzari, A., 'Servizi sperimentali della Caritas ambrosiana: segni di evangelizzazione', in Bausola *et al.*, *Cultura e fede nell'Italia del Nord*, q.v., pp. 199–206.

Becattini, G., 'Dal "settore" industriale al "distretto" industriale. Alcune considerazioni sull'unità di indagine dell'economia industriale', *Rivista di Economia e Politica Industriale*, vol. V (1979), no. 1, pp. 7–21.

—— *Distretti industriali e 'made in Italy'*, Torino, 1998.

Becattini, G., and Bianchi, G., 'Sulla multiregionalità dello sviluppo economico italiano', *Note Economiche*, 1992, nos. 5–6, pp. 19–39.

Beccalli, B., 'Introduzione', in Achilli, *et al.*, *Vivere sole*, q.v., pp. 13–22.

Becchi, A., 'Città e forme di emarginazione', in *Storia dell'Italia repubblicana*, vol. III, pt 1, q.v., pp. 837–929.

—— 'Opere pubbliche', *Meridiana*, no. 9 (1990), pp. 223–43.

—— 'Le politiche per il Mezzogiorno', *Meridiana*, no. 31 (1998), pp. 45–62.

—— 'The difficult reconstruction in Irpinia', in Hellman and Pasquino (eds.), *Italian Politics: A Review*, vol. VII, q.v., pp. 110–28.

Beck, U., *Risk Society*, London, 1992 [original edn *Risikogesellschaft*, Frankfurt am Main, 1986].

Beck, U., Giddens, A., and Lash, S., *Reflexive Modernisation*, Cambridge, 1994.

Belli, P., 'Effetti redistributivi del Servizio sanitario nazionale', in Paci (ed.), *Le dimensioni della disuguaglianza*, q.v., pp. 424–37.

Bellu, G. M., and Bonsanti, S., *Il crollo*, Bari, 1993.

Bellu, G. M., and D'Avanzo, G., *I giorni di Gladio*, Milano, 1991.

Berlinguer, E., *Austerità occasione per trasformare l'Italia*, Roma, 1977.

—— 'Relazione al XIV° congresso', in *XIV° congresso del Partito comunista italiano: Atti e risoluzioni*, q.v., pp. 15–76.

Berlinguer, G., *Una riforma per la salute*, Bari, 1979.

Bibliography

Berlusconi, S., *Discorsi per la democrazia*, Milano, 2000.

—— *L'Italia che ho in mente*, Milano, 2000.

—— 'Un nuovo miracolo italiano', in Mennitti (ed.), *Forza Italia. Radiografia di un evento*, q.v., pp. 212–19.

Bernabei, E., and Dell'Arti, G., *L'uomo di fiducia*, Milano, 1999.

Bernacchi, A., Mascini, M., and Moussanet, M., *Crisi? No grazie*, Milano, 1994.

Bernhard, E., 'Il complesso della Grande Madre' [1960], in Bernhard, *Mitobiografia*, q.v., pp. 168–79.

—— *Mitobiografia*, Milano, 1969.

Bertaux Wiame, I., Borderias, C., and Pesce, A., 'La forza dell'ambiguità, traiettorie sociali di donne in Italia, Francia e Spagna', *Inchiesta*, vol. XVIII (1988), no. 82, pp. 21–7.

Bertolo, C., 'Modelli culturali e pratiche sociali tra passato e presente', in Bimbi and Castellano (eds.), *Madri e padri*, q.v., pp. 47–78.

Best, M. H., *The New Competition*, Cambridge, 1990.

Bevilacqua, P., 'La mafia e la Spagna', *Meridiana*, no. 13 (1992), pp. 105–28.

—— 'Riformare il Sud', *Meridiana*, no. 31 (1998), pp. 19–44.

Bevilacqua, P. (ed.), *Storia dell'agricoltura italiana in età contemporanea*, vol. I, *Spazi e paesaggi*, Venezia, 1989.

Bianchi, M., 'Oltre il "doppio lavoro"', *Inchiesta*, vol. VIII (1978), no. 32, pp. 7–11.

Bianchi, R., 'The privatisation of industry: the case of Alfa Romeo', in Corbetta, Leonardi and Nanetti (eds.), *Italian Politics: A Review*, vol. II, q.v., pp. 109–25.

Bimbi, F., 'Conclusion', in Bimbi and Castellano (eds.), *Madri e padri*, q.v., pp. 161–200.

Bimbi, F., and Castellano, G. (eds.), *Madri e padri*, Milano, 1992.

Biorcio, R., *La Padania promessa*, Milano, 1997.

Biorcio, R., and Maneri, M., 'Consumi e società: dagli anni Ottanta agli anni Novanta', in Livolsi (ed.), *L'Italia che cambia*, q.v., pp. 185–208.

Blando, A., 'Percorsi dell'antimafia', *Meridiana*, no. 25 (1996), pp. 77–92.

Blim, M. L., *Made in Italy*, New York, 1990.

Bobbio, L., *La democrazia non abita a Gordio*, Milano, 1996.

—— 'La peculiarità dell'ordinamento museale italiano nel contesto europeo e il dibattito sulla sua riforma', in Valentino (ed.), *L'immagine e la memoria*, q.v., pp. 41–63.

—— La politica dei beni culturali in Italia', in Bobbio (ed.), *Le politiche dei beni culturali in Europa*, q.v., pp. 149–214.

—— 'Le politiche dei beni culturali in Europa: una comparazione', in Bobbio (ed.), *Le politiche dei beni culturali in Europa*, q.v., pp. 11–70.

Bobbio, L. (ed.), *Le politiche dei beni culturali in Europa*, Bologna, 1992.

Bibliography

Bobbio, N., 'La fine della prima Repubblica' (interview with S. Vertone), *Europeo*, vol. XLVI (1990), no. 52, 28 December.

—— 'Società civile', in Bobbio, Matteucci and Pasquino (eds.), *Dizionario politico*, q.v., pp. 1084–90.

—— 'Sulla nozione di società civile', *De Homine*, no. 24 (1968), pp. 19–36.

Bobbio, N., Bosetti, G., and Vattimo, G., *La sinistra nell'era del karaoke*, Roma, 1994.

Bobbio, N., Matteucci, N., and Pasquino, G. F. (eds.), *Dizionario politico*, Torino, 1983.

Boccella, N., 'Mezzogiorno più lontano dal Nord', in Ginsborg (ed.), *Stato dell'Italia*, q.v., pp. 429–31.

—— *Il Mezzogiorno sussidiato*, Milano, 1982.

Bock, G., 'Antinatalism, maternity and paternity in National Socialist racism', in Bock and Thane (eds.), *Maternity and Gender Policies*, q.v., pp. 233–55.

Bock, G., and Thane, P. (eds.), *Maternity and Gender Policies*, London, 1991.

Bonazzi, G., *Il tubo di cristallo*, Bologna, 1993.

Bonomi, A., *Il capitalismo molecolare*, Torino, 1997.

Bonvicini, G., *et al.*, 'Italy's difficult road into the EU hard core', *The International Spectator*, vol. XXXII (1997), nos. 3–4, pp. 3–20.

Borgna, P., and Cassano, M., *Il giudice e il principe*, Roma, 1997.

Bortolotta Impastato, F., *La mafia in casa mia*, eds. A. Puglisi and U. Santino, Palermo, 1987.

Bosworth, R. J. B., and Romano, S. (eds.), *La politica estera italiana, 1860–1985*, Bologna, 1991.

Bouhdiba, A., *Sexuality in Islam*, London, 1985.

Bourdieu, P., *Distinction*, London, 1994 [original edn *La Distinction, critique sociale du jugement*, Paris, 1979].

—— 'What makes a social class? On the theoretical and practical existence of groups', *Berkeley Journal of Sociology*, vol. XXXII (1987), pp. 1–17.

Bozzini, F., *Destini incrociati*, Roma, 1997.

Braudel, F., *Civiltà materiale, economia e capitalismo*, vol. II, *I giochi dello scambio*, Torino, 1981 (original edn *Civilisation matérielle et capitalisme, XVe–XVIIIe siècle. Les jeux de l'échange*, Paris, 1979).

Braun, M., *L'Italia da Andreotti a Berlusconi*, Milano, 1995.

—— 'The confederated trade unions and the Dini government', in Caciagli and Kertzer (eds.), *Italian Politics: A Review*, vol. XI, q.v., pp. 205–22.

Brewer, J., and Porter, R. (eds.), *Consumption and the World of Goods*, London, 1993.

Brosio, G., *The Regulation of Professions in Italy*, Roma, 1997.

Brown, L. R., and Kane, H., *Full House. Reassessing the Earth's Population Carrying Capacity*, London, 1995.

Bibliography

Bruno, G., and Segreto, L., 'Finanza e industria in Italia (1963–1995)', in *Storia dell'Italia repubblicana*, q.v., vol. III, pt 1, pp. 499–694.

Brusco, S., *Piccole imprese e distretti industriali*, Torino, 1989.

Brusco, S., and Paba, S., 'Per una storia dei distretti industriali italiani dal secondo dopoguerra agli anni novanta', in Barca (ed.), *Storia del capitalismo italiano*, q.v., pp. 265–334.

Budini Gattai, F., and Musatti, T., 'Grandmothers' involvement in grandchildren's care: attitudes, feelings and emotions', *Family Relations*, vol. XLVIII (1999), no. 1, pp. 35–42.

Buffo, G., 'Le donne comuniste tra emancipazione e differenza', *Critica Marxista*, vol. XXVII (1989), nos. 1–2, pp. 167–76.

Bugarini, F., and Vicarelli, G., 'Interazione e sostegno parentale in ambiente urbano', *Rassegna Italiana di Sociologia*, vol. XX (1979), no. 1, pp. 464–93.

Bugatti, E. and S., 'L'area sistema di Lumezzane', in Onida, Viesti and Falzoni (eds.), *I distretti industriali: crisi o evoluzione?*, q.v., pp. 345–54.

Bull, A., Pitt, M., and Szarka, J., *Entrepreneurial Textile Communities*, London, 1993.

Bull, M. J., 'The unremarkable death of the Italian Communist Party', in Catanzaro and Sabetti (eds.), *Italian Politics: A Review*, vol. V, q.v., pp. 23–39.

Bull, M. J., and Rhodes, M. (eds.), *Crisis and Transition in Italian Politics*, London, 1997.

Butler, T., 'The debate over the middle classes', in Butler and Savage (eds.), *Social Change*, q.v., pp. 26–40.

Butler, T., and Savage, M. (eds.), *Social Change and the Middle Classes*, London, 1995.

Buttafuoco, A., 'Cittadine italiane al voto', *Passato e Presente*, vol. XV (1997), no. 40, pp. 5–11.

Caciagli, M., 'The 18th DC Congress: from De Mita to Forlani and the victory of "neodoroteism"', in Catanzaro and Sabetti (eds.), *Italian Politics: A Review*, q.v., vol. V, pp. 8–22.

—— 'Quante Italie? Persistenze e trasformazioni delle culture politiche subnazionali', *Polis*, vol. II (1988), no. 3, pp. 429–57.

—— 'Il resistibile declino della Democrazia cristiana', in Pasquino (ed.), *Il sistema politico italiano*, q.v., pp. 101–27.

Caciagli, M., and Kertzer, D. I. (eds.), *Italian Politics: A Review*, vol. XI, London, 1996.

Caciagli, M., *et al.*, *Democrazia cristiana e potere nel Mezzogiorno*, Firenze, 1977.

Cacioppo, M., *et al.*, *La donna sola: aspetti e scelte di vita*, Milano, 1994.

Cafagna, L., *La grande slavina*, Venezia, 1993.

—— *Una strana disfatta*, Venezia, 1996.

Cafiero, S., 'Dopo la "Cassa"', in Cafiero, *Transizione e attualità del meridionalismo*, q.v., pp. 159–64.

—— *Transizione e attualità del meridionalismo*, Bologna, 1989.

Bibliography

Calabrò, M. A., *In prima linea*, Milano, 1993.

Calchi Novati, G., 'Mediterraneo e questione araba nella politica estera italiana', *Storia dell'Italia repubblicana*, vol. II, pt 1, q.v., pp. 197–263.

Calchi Novati, G. (ed.), *Maghreb*, Milano, 1991.

Callagher, J., *Padre Pio. The Pierced Priest*, London, 1995.

Calvi, A. (ed.), *Indagine sociale italiana. Rapporto 1986*, Milano, 1986.

Calvi, G., 'Presentazione del Rapporto 1986', in Calvi (ed.), *Indagine sociale italiana. Rapporto 1986*, q.v., pp. 9–14.

Calvi, G., and Vannucci, A., *L'elettore sconosciuto*, Bologna, 1995.

Calzone, A., Pozzutto, A. M., and Sorice, R., *Indagine territoriale nel bacino di utenza di un consultorio familiare*, Benevento, n.d. [1983?].

Camera dei Deputati, *La guerra del Golfo Persico*, Roma, 1991.

Cameron, D. R., 'Politics, public policy and distributional inequality: a comparative analysis', in Shapiro and Reeher (eds.), *Power, Inequality and Democratic Politics*, q.v.

Campbell, C., *The Romantic Ethic and the Spirit of Modern Consumerism*, Oxford, 1987.

Campelli, E., and Testi, E., *I bancari*, Roma, 1988.

Cangelosi, R. A., and Grassi, V., *Dalle Comunità all'Unione*, Milano, 1996.

Cannari, L., and D'Alessio, G., 'Composizione e distribuzione della ricchezza delle famiglie', in Rossi (ed.), *La transizione equa*, q.v., pp. 245–77.

Canteri, R., and Peruffo, F., *Il Doge e il Sultano*, Trento, 1993.

Capano, G., *L'improbabile riforma*, Bologna, 1992.

—— 'Le politiche amministrative: dall' improbabile riforma alla riforma permanente', in Di Palma *et al.* (eds.), *Condannata al successo?*, q.v., pp. 153–98.

Capecchi, V., and Pugliese, E., 'Due città a confronto: Bologna e Napoli', *Inchiesta*, vol. VIII (1978), nos. 35–6, pp. 3–54.

Caponnetto, A., *I miei giorni a Palermo*, Milano, 1992.

Caprara, M., *I Gava*, Milano, 1975.

Cardia, C., 'Relazione', in Leonardi and Violante (eds.), *Quale famiglia?*, q.v., pp. 11–23.

Carli, G., *Cinquant'anni di vita italiana*, Bari, 1993.

Carlucci, A., *Tangentomani*, Milano, 1992.

Cartocci, R., *Fra Lega e Chiesa*, Bologna, 1994.

Caselli, G. C., 'La cultura della giurisdizione', *MicroMega*, 1993, no. 5, pp. 15–18.

Caselli, G. C., and Ingroia, A., *L'eredità scomoda*, Milano, 2001.

Caselli, L., and Gozzi, A., 'Un'economia in declino', in Gibelli and Rugafiori (eds.), *Storia d'Italia. Le regioni. La Liguria*, q.v., pp. 885–916.

Casetti, F., 'Quasi di casa. Mass media, televisione e famiglia', in Casetti (ed.), *L'ospite fisso*, q.v., pp. 13–33.

Casetti, F. (ed.), *L'ospite fisso*, Milano, 1995.

Bibliography

Cassese, A., *Il caso 'Achille Lauro'*, Roma, 1987.

Cassese, S., 'Il difficile mestiere di ministro della Funzione pubblica', in *Riformare la Pubblica Amministrazione. Italia, Gran Bretagna, Spagna, Stati Uniti*, q.v., pp. 135–56.

—— 'Le disfunzioni dei controlli amministrativi', in Cassese (ed.), *I controlli nella Pubblica Amministrazione*, q.v., pp. 13–21.

—— 'La riforma della pubblica amministrazione italiana', in *Il Lavoro nella Pubblica Amministrazione*, vol. III (2000), no. 6.

—— 'Il sistema amministrativo italiano, ovvero l'arte di arrangiarsi', in Cassese and Franchini (eds.), *L'amministrazione pubblica italiana*, q.v., pp. 13–21.

Cassese, S. (ed.), *I controlli nella Pubblica Amministrazione*, Bologna, 1993.

Cassese, S., and Franchini, C. (eds.), *L'amministrazione pubblica italiana*, Bologna, 1994.

Casson, F., *Lo stato violato*, Venezia, 1994.

Castronovo, V., *FIAT. Storia di un'impresa, 1899–1999*, Milano, 1999.

—— *Storia economica d'Italia*, Torino, 1995.

Catanzaro, R., and Sabetti, F. (eds.), *Italian Politics: A Review*, vol. V, London, 1991.

Cavalli, A., 'Valori, orientamenti politici e opinioni sulla politica scolastica', in Cavalli (ed.), *Insegnare oggi*, q.v., pp. 207–38.

Cavalli, A. (ed.), *Insegnare oggi*, Bologna, 1992.

Cavalli, A., and De Lillo, A., *Giovani anni Novanta*, Bologna, 1993.

Cavalli, A., and Galland, O. (eds.), *Youth in Europe*, London, 1995.

Cavazzuti, F., 'The uncertain path of privatisation', in Katz and Ignazi (eds.), *Italian Politics: A Review*, vol. X, q.v., pp. 169–82.

—— 'Privatisation: false starts and frustrated takeoffs', in Hellman and Pasquino (eds.), *Italian Politics: A Review*, vol. VII, q.v., pp. 145–58.

Cazzola, F., *L'Italia del pizzo*, Torino, 1992.

Cecchi, A., *Storia della P2*, Roma, 1985.

Cedrone, C. (ed.), *Centralità e qualità dell'istruzione*, Firenze, 1990.

CENSIS (Centro Studi investimenti sociali), *A metà decennio. Riflessione e dati sull'Italia dall'80 all'85*, Milano, 1986.

—— *Consumi e spesa farmaceutica*, Milano, 1997.

—— *Consumi '90*, Milano, 1990.

—— *Consumi '87*, Milano, 1987.

—— 'L'imprenditore agricolo nella trasformazione dell'agricoltura', in *Rapporto sulle prospettive economiche del settore agro-alimentare nel 1993*, Roma, 1993.

—— *Rapporto sulla situazione sociale del paese. 1996*, Milano, 1996.

CENSIS (Centro Studi investimenti sociali) and CDS (Centro nazionale di prevenzione e difesa sociale), *Control e dentro*, Milano, 1992.

Cerase, F. P., *Un'amministrazione bloccata*, Milano, 1990.

—— *I dipendenti pubblici*, Bologna, 1994.

Bibliography

Ceri, P., 'Prefazione', in Golia, *Dentro Forza Italia*, q.v., pp. 8–14.

Cerruti, G. C., and Rieser, V., *Fiat: qualità totale e fabbrica integrata*, Roma, 1991.

Cesareo, V. (ed.), *La cultura dell'Italia contemporanea*, Torino, 1990.

Cesareo, V., *et al.*, *La religiosità in Italia*, Milano, 1995.

Chandler, A. D., Amatori, F., and Hikino, J., *Big Business and the Wealth of Nations*, Cambridge, 1997.

Cherlin, A., and Furstenberg Jr., F. F., 'The changing European family', *Journal of Family Studies*, vol. IX (1988), no. 3, pp. 291–7.

Chiarloni, S., 'La giustizia civile e i suoi paradossi', in *Storia d'Italia. Annali 14*, q.v., pp. 401–83.

Chiaromonte, G., *Col senno di poi*, Roma, 1990.

Chiesa, M., 'Confessioni che cambiano la storia', in *L'Espresso*, vol. XXXVIII (1992), no. 26, 28 June.

Chiesi, A. M., 'Disuguaglianze sociali nell'uso del tempo', in Paci (ed.), *Le dimensioni della disuguaglianza*, q.v., pp. 215–20.

—— 'Il sistema delle associazioni industriali e le specificità del caso italiano', in Martinelli (ed.), *L'azione collettiva degli imprenditori italiani*, q.v., pp. 197–230.

Chinnici, G., and Santino, U., *La violenza programmata*, Milano, 1989.

Chubb, J., 'The Christian Democratic party: reviving or surviving?', in Leonardi and Nanetti (eds.), *Italian Politics: A Review*, vol. I, q.v., pp. 69–86.

—— *Patronage, Power and Poverty in Southern Italy*, Cambridge, 1982.

Ciampi, C. A., 'Dalla recessione alla ripresa: un anno di governo dell'economia', *Il Mulino*, vol. XLIV (1995), no. 357, pp. 71–82.

Cianciullo, A., and Fontana, E., *Ecomafia*, Roma, 1995.

Ciocca, A., 'Le famiglie: quadro sintetico della ricerca', in Cedrone (ed.), *Centralità e qualità dell'istruzione*, q.v., pp. 133–6.

Ciconte, E., Sales, I., and Vasile, V., *Cirillo, Ligato e Lima*, ed. N. Tranfaglia, Bari, 1994.

Cingolani, S., *Le grandi famiglie del capitalismo italiano*, Bari, 1990.

Clemente, P., 'Immigrati: incroci di sguardi', in Ginsborg (ed.), *Stato dell'Italia*, q.v., pp. 244–5.

Cobalti, A., 'La mobilità sociale in Italia e negli altri paesi europei', in Paci (ed.), *Le dimensioni della disuguaglianza*, q.v., pp. 63–8.

Cobalti, A., and Schizzerotto, W., *La mobilità sociale in Italia*, Bologna, 1994.

Cohen, J. L., and Arato, A., *Civil Society and Political Theory*, Cambridge (Mass.), 1992.

Coleman, J., and Rollett, B. (eds.), *Television in Europe*, Exeter, 1997.

Colombo, G. (Gherardo), 'The new code of criminal procedure', in Catanzaro and Sabetti (eds.), *Italian Politics: A Review*, vol. V, q.v., pp. 55–68.

—— *Il vizio della memoria*, Milano, 1996.

Bibliography

Colombo, G. (Gherardo), Davigo, P. C., and Di Pietro, A., 'Noi obbediamo alla legge, non alla piazza', *MicroMega*, 1993, no. 5, pp. 7–14.

Colombo, G. (Giovanni), 'Quale politica per lo spazio rurale?', *Rivista di Politica Agraria*, vol. XII (1994), no. 2, pp. 3–12.

Colombo, G. (Giovanni), and Bassanelli, E., *Quale futuro per l'agricoltura italiana?*, Bologna, 1995.

Colozzi, I., 'Società civile e terzo settore', in Donati (ed.), *La società civile in Italia*, q.v., pp. 123–58.

Comand, M. P., and Santucci, M., 'Il consumo addomesticato' in Casetti (ed.), *L'ospite fisso*, q.v., pp. 155–82.

Commissione d'Indagine sulla Povertà e l'Emarginazione, *Secondo rapporto sulla povertà in Italia*, ed. G. Sarpellon, Milano, 1992.

Commissione Parlamentare Antimafia, XI Legislatura, *Rapporto sulla Camorra (21 Dicembre 1993)*, Roma, 1994.

—— 'Relazione sui rapporti tra mafia e politica (6 Aprile 1993)' (now published, with a preface by N. Tranfaglia, as Commissione Parlamentare Antimafia, XI Legislatura, *Mafia e politica*, Bari, 1993).

Commissione Parlamentare d'Inchiesta Sulla Mafia, *Camorra, politica, pentiti, atti della Commissione parlamentare d'inchiesta sulla mafia*, Soveria Mannelli, 1994.

Confindustria: Centro Studi, *L'Italia da semplificare*, 3 vols., Bologna, 1998.

Confindustria: Centri Studi, *L'Italia verso il 2000*, 2 vols., Roma, 1992.

Connolly, B., *The Rotten Heart of Europe*, London, 1995.

Contini, G., 'Comunque mi sono annullata', in Ginsborg (ed.), *Stato dell'Italia*, q.v., pp. 303–5.

—— 'Gestirsi il proprio tempo', in Ginsborg (ed.), *Stato dell'Italia*, q.v., pp. 249–53.

Corbetta, P. G., 'La Lega e lo sfaldamento del sistema', *Polis*, vol. VII (1993), no. 2, pp. 229–52.

Corbetta, P. G., and Leonardi, R. (eds.), *Italian Politics: A Review*, vol. III, London, 1989.

Corbetta, P. G., Leonardi, R., and Nanetti, R. Y. (eds.), *Italian Politics: A Review*, vol. II, London, 1988.

Corbetta, P. G., and Parisi, A. M. L. (eds.), *A domanda risponde*, Bologna, 1997.

Cornwell, R., *God's Banker*, London, 1983.

Corrias, P., Gramellini, M., and Maltese, C., *1994. Colpo grosso*, Milano, 1994.

Corte dei Conti, *Relazioni al Parlamento relative agli anni 1987–1992*, Roma, 1992.

Cossiga, F., *Il torto e il diritto*, ed. P. Chessa, Milano, 1993.

Cotta, M., 'La crisi del governo di partito all'italiana', in Cotta and Isernia (eds.), *Il gigante dai piedi di argilla*, q.v., pp. 11–52.

—— 'Le élite politiche nazionali di fronte all'integrazione', *Il Mulino*, vol. XLVII (1998), no. 377, pp. 445–56.

Bibliography

Cotta, M., and Isernia, P. (eds.), *Il gigante dai piedi di argilla*, Bologna, 1996.

Cotta, P. L., 'Le tecnologie e le banche', unpublished paper presented to the Convenzione Interbancaria per i Problemi Dell'Automazione (CIPA), Roma, 29 April 1997.

Craxi, B., 'Guardando al passato "Tiremm Innanz" (discorso per il 140esimo anniversario delle Cinque Giornate)' in Craxi, *Un'onda lunga*, q.v., pp. 69–85.

—— 'Leninismo e socialismo', in *I nodi della sinistra*, ed. D. Argeri, Roma, 1980, pp. 22–32 [1st edn in *L'Espresso*, vol. XXIV (1978), no. 34].

—— 'Madrid, Lisbona, Parigi. E noi?' (1977) in Craxi, *Il rinnovamento socialista*, q.v., pp. 165–9.

—— *Il rinnovamento socialista*, Venezia, 1991.

—— *Un'onda lunga*, ed. U. Intini, Imola, 1988.

Croce, B., *Teoria e storia della storiografia*, Bari, 1973 [1st edn Napoli, 1917].

Crompton, R., 'Women's employment and the "middle class"', in Butler and Savage (eds.), *Social Change and the Middle Classes*, q.v., pp. 58–75.

'Cronologia', in Mennitti (ed.), *Forza Italia. Radiografia di un evento*, q.v., pp. 279–302.

Crouch, C., and Marquand, D. (eds.), *Reinventing Collective Action*, Oxford, 1995.

Cultura del testo, vol. II (1996), no. 6, which contains part of the proceedings of the Conference of January 1996 dedicated to the National Library in Florence.

Curi, U., *Lo scudo di Achille*, Milano, 1989.

Cuttini, M., *et al.*, 'Parental visiting, communication, and participation in ethical decisions: a comparison of neonatal unit policies in Europe', *Archives of Disease in Childhood, Fetal and Neonatal Edition*, vol. LXXXI (1999), no. 2, pp. 84–9.

D'Alema, M., and Ginsborg, P., *Dialogo su Berlinguer*, ed. M. Battini, Firenze, 1994.

D'Alimonte, R., and Bartolini, S., '"Electoral transition" and party system change in Italy', in Bull and Rhodes (eds.), *Crisis and Transition*, q.v., pp. 110–34.

D'Alimonte, R., and Nelken, D. (eds.), *Italian Politics. A Review*, vol. XII, Boulder, Colorado, 1997.

Dalla Chiesa, N., *Delitto imperfetto*, Milano, 1984.

—— *Il giudice ragazzino*, Torino, 1992.

Dal Lago, A., and Moscati, R., *Regalateci un sogno*, Milano, 1992.

Dalla Zuanna, G., 'Meglio soli. Famiglia e natalità in Italia', *Il Mulino*, vol. XLIV (1995), no. 357, pp. 111–18.

Dall'Orto, G., *Manuale per coppie diverse*, Roma, 1994.

Daly, M. T., 'Transitional economic bases: from the mass production society to the world of finance', in Daniels, *Services and Metropolitan Development*, q.v., pp. 26–43.

Dani, L., *Domanda e offerta religiosa*, Padova, 1986.

Bibliography

Daniels, P. W., *Service Industries in the World Economy*, Oxford, 1993.

—— *Services and Metropolitan Development*, London, 1991.

D'Antone, L. (ed.), *Radici storiche ed esperienza dell'intervento straordinario nel Mezzogiorno*, Roma, 1996.

D'Antonio, M., 'Competition, development, inflation: the case of services', *Review of Economic Conditions in Italy*, 1992, no. 3, pp. 309–39.

D'Apice, C., *L'arcipelago dei consumi*, Bari, 1981.

Dassù, M., and Missiroli, A., 'L'Italia nell'Unione europea: un bilancio e qualche prospettiva', *Europa Europe*, vol. V (1996), no. 1, pp. 7–27.

D'Attorre, P. P., and Zamagni, V. (eds.), *Distretti, imprese, classe operaia*, Milano, 1992.

David, P., and Vicarelli, G. (eds.), *Donne nelle professioni degli uomini*, Milano, 1993.

Davigo, P., *La giubba del re. Intervista sulla corruzione*, ed. D. Pinardi, Bari, 1998.

Davis, J., *Land and Family in Pisticci*, London, 1973.

Deaglio, E., *Raccolto rosso*, Milano, 1993.

Deaglio, M., *La nuova borghesia e la sfida del capitalismo*, Bari, 1991.

De Castro, P., and Deserti, R., 'Imprese multinazionali, strategie di mercato e nuovi scenari del sistema agro-alimentare italiano', *Rivista di Politica Agraria*, vol. XIII (1995), no. 3, pp. 4–8.

De Cecco, M., and Migone, G. G., 'La collocazione internazionale dell'economia italiana', in Bosworth and Romano (eds.), *La politica estera italiana, 1860–1985*, q.v., pp. 147–96.

De Cecco, M., Pecchi, L., and Piga, G. (eds.), *Managing Public Debt*, Cheltenham, 1997.

Defrance, J., and Pociello, C., 'Structure and evolution in the field of sports in France', *International Review for the Sociology of Sport*, vol. XXVIII (1993), no. 1, pp. 1–21.

De Grazia, V., *How Fascism Ruled Women*, Berkeley, 1992.

De Gregorio, S., *Tortora, morire d'ingiustizia*, Napoli, 1988.

Dei, M., 'Cambiamento senza riforma: la scuola secondaria superiore negli ultimi trent'anni', in Soldani and Turi (eds.), *Fare gli italiani*, q.v., vol. II, pp. 87–128.

—— 'Insegnanti, parola d'ordine: insoddisfazione', in Ginsborg (ed.), *Stato dell'Italia*, q.v., pp. 572–5.

Del Boca, A., *Una sconfitta dell' intelligenza*, Bari, 1993.

Del Buono, O., 'Mamma sciattona con pallina di frutta', *L'Espresso*, vol. XLI (1995), no. 6.

De Leonardis, O., 'I welfare mix. Privatismo e sfera pubblica', *Stato e Mercato*, no. 46 (1996), pp. 51–75.

Del Gaudio, M., *La toga strappata*, Napoli, 1992.

De Lillo, A., 'La mobilità sociale assoluta', *Polis*, vol. III (1988), no. 1, pp. 19–51.

Della Cananea, G., 'Il cittadino e la pubblica amministrazione', in Cassese and Franchini (eds.), *L'amministrazione pubblica italiana*, q.v., pp. 185–202.

Della Porta, D., 'Milan: immoral capital', in Hellman and Pasquino (eds.), *Italian Politics. A Review*, vol. VIII, q.v., pp. 98–115.

—— *Movimenti collettivi e sistema politico in Italia*, Bari, 1996.

—— *Lo scambio occulto*, Bologna, 1992.

Della Porta, D., and Mény, Y. (eds.), *Corruzione e democrazia. Sette paesi a confronto*, Napoli, 1995.

—— 'Democrazia e corruzione', in Della Porta and Mény (eds.), *Corruzione e democrazia. Sette paesi a confronto*, q.v., pp. 1–7.

Della Porta, D., and Vannucci, A., *Corruzione politica e amministrazione pubblica*, Bologna, 1994.

—— *Un paese anormale*, Roma/Bari, 1999.

Della Seta, P., and Salzano, E., *L'Italia a sacco*, Roma, 1993.

Della Valle, A., *Delle persone e della famiglia. Artt. 231–455. Commentario*, Milano, 1989.

De Lucia, V., *Se questa è una città*, Roma, 1992.

De Luna, G., 'Dalla spontaneità all'organizzazione: la resistibile ascesa della Lega di Bossi', in De Luna (ed.), *Figli di un benessere minore*, q.v., pp. 21–80.

De Luna, G. (ed.), *Figli di un benessere minore*, Firenze, 1994.

De Matteis, S., 'Storie di famiglia. Appunti e ipotesi antropologiche sulla famiglia a Napoli', *Meridiana*, no. 17 (1993), pp. 137–62.

De Mauro, T., 'La cultura', in Gambino *et al.*, *Dal'68 a oggi*, q.v., pp. 167–218.

—— *Idee per il governo. La scuola*, Bari, 1995.

De Mita, C., *Intervista sulla DC*, ed. A. Levi, Bari, 1986.

—— *Ragionando di politica*, Milano, 1984.

Deni, M., and Maresciani, F., 'Analisi del primo discorso di Berlusconi. Indagine semiotica sul funzionamento discorsivo', in Livolsi and Volli (eds.), *La comunicazione politica tra prima e seconda Repubblica*, q.v., pp. 227–41.

Deniaux, E., *Clientèles et pouvoir à l'époque de Cicéron*, Roma, 1993.

Dente, B., 'La cultura amministrativa italiana negli ultimi 40 anni', in Dente, *Politiche pubbliche e pubblica amministrazione*, q.v., pp. 139–72.

—— 'Introduzione', in Dente (ed.), *Le politiche pubbliche in Italia*, q.v., pp. 9–50.

—— *Politiche pubbliche e pubblica amministrazione*, Rimini, 1989.

Dente, B. (ed.), *Le politiche pubbliche in Italia*, Bologna, 1990.

De Rita, G., 'L'impresa famiglia', in Melograni and Scaraffia (eds.), *La famiglia italiana dall'Ottocento ad oggi*, q.v., pp. 383–416.

De Rosa, G., *La transizione infinita*, Bari, 1997.

De Sandre, P., 'Quando i giovani lasciano la famiglia', *Studi Interdisciplinari sulla Famiglia*, no. 7 (1988), pp. 63–84.

Devine, F., *Affluent Workers Revisited*, Edinburgh, 1992.

De Winter, L., Della Porta, D., and Deschouwer, K., 'Comparing similar countries:

Italy and Belgium', *Res Publica* (Belgian Journal of Political Science), vol. XXXVIII (1996), no. 2, pp. 15–35.

Diamanti, I., 'Identità e comportamento di voto. L'unità e la fedeltà non sono più virtù', in Corbetta and Parisi (eds.), *A domanda risponde*, q.v., pp. 317–60.

—— *La Lega*, Roma, 1993.

—— 'La Lega Nord, dal successo alla secessione', in Diamanti and Lazar (eds.), *Stanchi di miracoli*, q.v., pp. 221–35.

Diamanti, I., and Lazar, M. (eds.), *Stanchi di miracoli*, Milano, 1997.

Diamanti, I., and Mannheimer, R. (eds.), *Milano a Roma*, Roma, 1994.

Diamanti, I., and Riccamboni, G., *La parabola del voto bianco*, Vicenza, 1992.

Diani, M., 'Dalla ritualità delle subculture alla libertà dei reticoli sociali', *Democrazia e Diritto*, vol. XXXII (1992), no. 2, pp. 199–221.

Di Donna, V., and Vallario, A. (eds.), *L'ambiente. Risorse e rischi*, Napoli, 1994.

'Dieci anni di televisione sotto il segno di Berlusconi', *Problemi dell'Informazione*, vol. XV (1990), no. 4, pp. 487–622.

Diena, L., *Gli uomini e le masse*, Torino, 1960.

Di Federico, G., 'The crisis of the justice system and the referendum on the judiciary', in Leonardi and Corbetta (eds.), *Italian Politics: A Review*, vol. III, q.v., pp. 25–49.

Di Lampedusa, G., *The Leopard*, London, 1963 [1st Italian edn 1958].

Di Michele, S., and Galiani, A., *Mal di destra*, Milano, 1995.

Dina, A. (ed.), *Elettrodomestici flessibili*, Torino, 1990.

Di Nicola, P., and De Bernart, M., 'Generazioni di genitori e generazioni di figli; mondi incomunicabili?', in Donati (ed.), *Quarto rapporto CISF sulla famiglia in Italia*, q.v., pp. 259–98.

Di Palma, G., Fabbrini, S., and Freddi, G. (eds.), *Condannata al successo?*, Bologna, 2000.

Di Pietro, A., *Intervista su Tangentopoli*, ed. G. Valentini, Roma/Bari, 2000.

—— *Memoria*, Milano, 1999.

Di Sandro, G., 'Quante sono le aziende agrarie: tre milioni o tre-quattrocentomila?', *Rivista di Politica Agraria*, vol. XII (1994), no. 6, pp. 29–36.

Documenti CNEL (Consiglio Nazionale dell'Economia e del Lavoro), *Il terziario italiano nella competizione europea*, Roma, 1992.

Dolci, D., *Spreco*, Torino, 1960.

Donaldson, P., *The Economics of the Real World*, London, 1984 (3rd edn).

Donati, P. P. (ed.), *Quarto rapporto CISF sulla famiglia in Italia*, Milano, 1995.

—— *Secondo rapporto sulla famiglia in Italia*, Milano, 1991.

—— *La società civile in Italia*, Milano, 1997.

Donnhauser, C., 'Agricoltura', in Lega per l'Ambiente, *Ambiente Italia. Rapporto 1989*, ed. Melandri, q.v., pp. 170–80.

Bibliography

Donolo, C., 'L'erosione delle basi morali nella società italiana', *Quaderni di Sociologia*, vol. XXXVIII–XXXIX (1994–95), no. 8, pp. 56–76.

Donovan, M., 'Catholic "pacifism" and the Gulf War: pluralism, cohesion and politics', in Hellman and Pasquino (eds.), *Italian Politics: A Review*, vol. VII, q.v., pp. 159–72.

D'Orta, C., 'Ambiente e danno ambientale: dalla giurisprudenza della Corte dei Conti alla legge sul Ministero dell'Ambiente', in *Rivista Trimestrale di Diritto Pubblico*, vol. XXXVII (1987), no. 1, pp. 60–112.

Duncan, S., 'The diverse worlds of European patriarchy', in García-Ramon and Monk (eds.), *Women of the European Union*, q.v., pp. 74–110.

Dunn, J., 'Conclusion', in Dunn (ed.), *Democracy: the Unfinished Journey*, q.v., pp. 264–5.

Dunn, J. (ed.), *Democracy: the Unfinished Journey*, Oxford, 1992.

—— *The Economic Limits to Modern Politics*, Cambridge, 1990.

Dupuy, F., and Thoenig, J. C., *Sociologia dell'azione burocratica*, Bologna, 1986 [original edn *Sociologie de l'administration française*, Paris, 1983].

Durkheim, E., *Lezioni di sociologia. Fisica dei costumi e dei diritti*, Milano, 1973 [original edn *Leçons de sociologie*, Paris, 1950].

Dyson, K., and Featherstone, K., 'Italy and EMU as a *"vincolo esterno"*: empowering the technocrats, transforming the state', *South European Society and Politics*, vol. I (1996), no. 2, pp. 272–99.

—— *The Road to Maastricht: Negotiating Economic and Monetary Union*, Oxford, 1999.

Eco, U., 'A guide to the neo-television of the 1980s', in Baranski and Lumley (eds.), *Culture and Conflict in Postwar Italy*, q.v., pp. 245–55.

Economia, stato, pace: l'iniziativa e le proposte del PCI (Rapporto, conclusioni e documento politico del XVI congresso), Roma, 1983.

Edwards, R., Garonna, P., and Pisani, E. (eds.), *Il sindacato oltre la crisi*, Milano, 1988.

Einaudi, L., *Diario 1945–1947*, Bari, 1993.

Esping-Andersen, G., 'Occupazioni o classi sociali: esiste un proletariato postindustriale?', *Polis*, vol. VII (1993), pp. 453–75.

—— *Social Foundations of Postindustrial Economies*, Oxford, 1999.

—— 'Strutture di classe post-industriale: un confronto tra Germania, Svezia e Stati Uniti', in *Stato e Mercato*, no. 32 (1991), pp. 219–48.

—— *The Three Worlds of Welfare Capitalism*, New York, 1990.

Eurobarometer survey, *Europeans and the Family*, Bruxelles, 1994.

Eurostat, *Statistiche generali dell'Unione Europea (1996)*, Luxembourg, 1996.

—— *Statistiche generali dell'Unione Europea (1997)*, Luxembourg, 1997.

Eurostat. Statistics in Focus. Population and Social Conditions, 1995, no. 8.

Eurostat Yearbook 1998–99, Bruxelles-Luxembourg, 1999.

Bibliography

Fabbroni, F., *et al.*, *Scuola '93*, Bari, 1994.

Fabris, G. P., and Mortara, V., *Le otto Italie*, Milano, 1986.

Faeta, F. (ed.), *L'architettura popolare in Italia. Calabria*, Bari, 1984.

Falcone, G., *Cose di Cosa Nostra*, Milano, 1993 [1st edn 1991].

Fanfani, R., 'Agricoltura italiana e CEE', in Ginsborg (ed.), *Stato dell'Italia*, q.v., pp. 650–51.

—— 'Il rapporto agricoltura-industria tra passato e presente', in D'Attorre and Zamagni (eds.), *Distretti, imprese, classe operaia*, q.v., pp. 33–74.

—— *L'agricoltura in Italia*, Bologna, 1998.

Farinelli, F., 'Lo spazio rurale nell'Italia di oggi', in Bevilacqua (ed.), *Storia dell'agricoltura italiana in età contemporanea*, vol. I, *Spazi e paesaggi*, q.v., pp. 229–48.

Fedele, M., *Democrazia referendaria*, Roma, 1994.

Fedele, M., and Leonardi, R. (eds.), *La politica senza i partiti*, Roma, 1996.

Feltrin, P., and La Mendola, S., 'I lavori manuali non operai: il caso delle donne delle pulizie', *Prospettiva sindacale*, vol. XIX (1988), no. 69, pp. 63–102.

Ferlat, N., *L'ultima curva*, Torino, 1985.

Ferrajoli, L., 'Anatomie di una riforma', in *MicroMega*, 1989, no. 4, pp. 23–34.

—— 'La prova diabolica', in *Politica ed Economia*, vol. XXI (1990), nos. 7–8, pp. 9–11.

Ferraresi, F., 'A secret structure codenamed Gladio', in Hellman and Pasquino (eds.), *Italian Politics: A Review*, vol. VII, q.v., pp. 29–48.

Ferrera, M., 'La composizione partitica e socioprofessionale dei comitati di gestione della legislatura 1980–1985', in Ferrera and Zincone (eds.), *La salute che noi pensiamo*, q.v., pp. 227–40.

—— 'Italia: aspirazioni e vincoli del "quarto grande"', in Ferrera (ed.), *Le dodici Europe*, q.v., pp. 73–92.

—— *Modelli di solidarietà*, Bologna, 1993.

—— 'La partitocrazia della salute', in Cotta and Isernia (eds.), *Il gigante dai piedi di argilla*, q.v., pp. 53–72.

—— 'The "southern model" of welfare in social Europe', *Journal of European Social Policy*, vol. VI (1996), no. 1, pp. 17–37.

Ferrera, M., and Gualmini, E., *Salvati dall'Europa?*, Bologna, 1999.

Ferrera, M. (ed.), *Le dodici Europe*, Bologna, 1991.

Ferrera, M., and Zincone, G. (eds.), *La salute che noi pensiamo*, Bologna, 1986.

FIAT Archivio storico, *FIAT: le fasi della crescita*, Torino, 1996.

Field, F. (ed.), *The Wealth Report*, London, 1979.

Filippucci, P., *Presenting the Past in Bassano*, unpublished Ph.D. Dissertation, University of Cambridge, 1992.

Bibliography

Finch, J., 'Kinship and friendship', in Jowell, Witherspoon and Brook (eds.), *British Social Attitudes. Special International Report*, q.v., pp. 87–104.

Finn, G. P. T., 'Football violence: a societal psychological perspective', in Giulianotti, Bonney and Hepworth (eds.), *Football, Violence and Social Identity*, q.v., pp. 90–128.

Fiori, G., *Il venditore*, Milano, 1995.

—— *Vita di Enrico Berlinguer*, Roma, 1992 [1st edn Bari, 1989].

Fiume, G., 'Introduzione' to Alajmo, *Un lenzuolo contro la mafia*, q.v., pp. 5–7.

Fiume, G. (ed.), *Madri*, Venezia, 1995.

Flamigni, S., 'La loggia P2', in *Storia d'Italia. Annali 12*, q.v., pp. 421–60.

—— *Trame atlantiche*, Milano, 1996.

Flick, G. M., *Lettera a un procuratore della Repubblica*, Milano, 1993.

Flickinger, R. S., and Studlar, D. T., 'The disappearing voters? Exploring declining turn-out in western European elections', in *Western European Politics*, vol. XV (1992), no. 2, pp. 1–16.

Floud, R., and McCloskey, D. (eds.), *The Economic History of Britain since 1700*, 3 vols., Cambridge, 1994.

Foa, V., et al., *Le virtù della Repubblica*, Milano, 1994.

Fondazione Giovanni Agnelli, *Italy Toward 2001*, Torino, 1990.

—— *La religione degli europei*, Torino, 1992.

Fontana, E., 'Le ecomafie', in Violante (ed.), *Mafie e antimafie. Rapporto '96*, q.v., pp. 197–205.

Foot, J., 'The family and the "Economic Miracle": social transformation, work, leisure and development at Bovisa and Comasina (Milan), 1950–1970', *Contemporary European History*, vol. IV (1995), no. 3, pp. 315–38.

—— 'The logic of contradiction: migration control in Italy and France, 1980–93', in Miles and Thränhardt (eds.), *Migration and European Integration*, q.v., pp. 132–58.

—— *Milan since the Miracle. City, Culture and Identity*, Oxford, 2001.

Forbice, A., and Fornari, G. C., *I bugiardi del fisco*, Roma, 1985.

Forgacs, D., 'Cultural consumption, 1940s to 1990s', in Forgacs and Lumley (eds.), *Italian Cultural Studies*, q.v., pp. 273–90.

—— *Italian Culture in the Industrial Era, 1880–1980*, Manchester, 1990.

Forgacs, D., and Lumley, R. (eds.), *Italian Cultural Studies*, Oxford, 1996.

Formica, P., *L'autonomia della Banca centrale nel corso degli anni settanta e ottanta*, Messina, 1993.

Formigoni, R., *Io e un milione di amici*, Milano, 1988.

Foschini, M. V., and Montone, S., 'Il processo Tortora', in *Storia d'Italia. Annali 12*, q.v., pp. 685–713.

Franchetti, L., *Condizioni politiche e amministrative della Sicilia*, Roma 1993 [1st edn 1877].

Franchini, C., 'La fatica di stare in Europa', in Ginsborg (ed.), *Stato dell'Italia*, q.v., pp. 503–6.

Franci, M., and Rieser, V., 'Le categorie sociologiche nell'analisi del distretto industriale: tra comunità e razionalizzazione', *Stato e Mercato*, no. 33 (1991), pp. 451–76.

Franco, M., *Andreotti visto da vicino*, Milano, 1993 [1st edn 1989].

Friedman, A., *Agnelli and the Network of Italian Power*, London, 1988.

—— *Ce la farà il capitalismo italiano?*, Milano, 1989.

—— 'The economic elites and the political system', in Gundle and Parker (eds.), *The New Italian Republic*, q.v., pp. 263–72.

Fukuyama, F., *Trust*, New York, 1995.

Gagliardi, P., and Turner, B. A., 'Aspects of Italian management', in Hickson (ed.), *Management in Western Europe*, q.v., pp. 149–65.

Galeros, T., 'Politique structurelle communautaire: l'expérience de la Grèce', in Predieri (ed.), *Fondi strutturali e coesione economica e sociale nell'Unione europea*, q.v., pp. 225–38.

Galli, G., *Il bipartitismo imperfetto*, Bologna, 1966.

—— 'Il PCI, la DC, e la cultura istituzionalizzata in Italia', in A. Manoukian (ed.), *La presenza sociale del PCI e della DC*, q.v., pp. 617–75.

Galli, G., *et al.*, *Il comportamento elettorale in Italia*, Bologna, 1968.

Galli, R., and Torcasio, S., *La partecipazione italiana alla politica agraria comunitaria*, Bologna, 1976.

Gallino, L., *Se tre milioni vi sembran pochi*, Torino, 1998.

—— 'Tecnologia/occupazione: la rottura del circolo virtuoso', *Quaderni di Sociologia*, vol. XXXVIII–XXXIX (1994–95), no. 7, pp. 5–15.

Gallo, G., *IRI Spa*, Milano, 1992.

Gallucci, C., 'Sola contro un dannato Biscione', *L'Espresso*, vol. XLI (1995), no. 11, 17 March.

Gambetta, D., *The Sicilian Mafia*, Cambridge, Mass., 1993.

Gambetta, D., Lupo, S., Pezzino, P., and Tranfaglia, N., 'La mafia e la sua storia. Radici locali e dimensione internazionale', *Passato e Presente*, vol. XII (1994), no. 31, pp. 19–40.

Gambino, A., *et al.*, *Dal'68 a oggi*, Bari, 1979.

García-Ramon, M. D., and Monk, J. (eds.), *Women of the European Union*, London/ New York, 1996.

Garelli, F., 'Gli italiani e la Chiesa', in Cesareo *et al.*, *La religiosità in Italia*, q.v., pp. 237–64.

Bibliography

—— 'Religione e modernità: il caso italiano', in Fondazione Giovanni Agnelli, *La religione degli europei*, q.v.

Gasperoni, G. C., 'Quanto si impara a scuola?', in Ginsborg (ed.), *Stato dell'Italia*, q.v., pp. 563–5.

Gatti, C., *Rimanga tra noi*, Milano, 1991.

Gauthier, A. H., *The State and the Family*, Oxford, 1996.

Geddes, M., *La salute degli italiani*, Roma, 1990.

Geertz, C., *The Interpretation of Cultures*, New York, 1973.

Gellner, E., *Conditions of Liberty*, London, 1994.

—— 'Patrons and clients', in Gellner and Waterbury (eds.), *Patrons and Clients in Mediterranean Societies*, q.v., pp. 1–6.

Gellner, E., and Waterbury, J. (eds.), *Patrons and Clients in Mediterranean Societies*, London, 1977.

Genco, P., and Maraschini, F., 'La collocazione internazionale delle società di ingegneria italiane', in Onida (ed.), *Il commercio internazionale dei servizi e la posizione dell'Italia*, q.v., pp. 265–96.

Geri, M., and Pennacchi, L., 'La distrubuzione del reddito', in Paci (ed.), *Le dimensioni della disuguaglianza*, q.v., pp. 169–96.

Gershuny, J., Goodwin, M., and Jones, S., 'The domestic labour revolution: a process of lagged adaptation', in Anderson, Bechhofer and Gershuny (eds.), *The Social and Political Economy of the Household*, q.v., pp. 151–97.

Gerth, H. H., and Wright Mills, C. (eds.), *From Max Weber: Essays in Sociology*, London, 1967.

Gervasio Carbonaro, G., and Paoletti Sbordoni, G., *La qualità possibile. Educazione, cultura, servizi sociali nel territorio*, Firenze, 1995.

Ghirelli, A., *Napoli dalla guerra a Bassolino*, Napoli, 1998.

Giacomini, G., and Bertolini, P., 'Vecchi e nuovi problemi dell'agricoltura italiana', *Rivista di Politica Agraria*, vol. XII (1994), no. 6, pp. 3–16.

Giavazzi, F., and Spaventa, L., *High Public Debt: the Italian Experience*, Cambridge, 1988.

Gibelli, A., and Rugafiori, P. (eds.), *Storia d'Italia. Le regioni. La Liguria*, Torino, 1994.

Giddens, A., *The Third Way*, Oxford, 1998.

—— *The Third Way and its Critics*, Oxford, 1999.

Giglioli, P. P., Cavicchioli, S., and Fede, G., *Rituali di degradazione*, Bologna, 1997.

Gilbert, M., 'The Bassanini laws: a half-way house in local government reform', in Hine and Vassallo (eds.), *Italian Politics: A Review*, vol. XIV, q.v., pp. 139–56.

—— 'The Oak Tree and the Olive Tree', in Caciagli and Kertzer (eds.), *Italian Politics: A Review*, vol. XI, q.v., pp. 101–17.

Giner, S., 'Civil society and its future', in Hall (ed.), *Civil Society*, q.v., pp. 301–25.

—— 'The rise of a European society', *Revue Européenne des Sciences Sociales*, vol. XXXI (1993), no. 95, pp. 151–65.

Bibliography

Ginsborg, P., 'I cambiamenti della famiglia in un distretto industriale italiano, 1965–1997', in Ginsborg and Ramella (eds.), *Un'Italia minore*, q.v., pp. 109–54.

—— 'Familismo', in Ginsborg (ed.), *Stato dell'Italia*, q.v., pp. 78–82.

—— 'Family, civil society and the state in contemporary European history: some methodological considerations', *Contemporary European History*, vol. IV (1995), no. 3, pp. 249–73.

—— *A History of Contemporary Italy*, London, 1990.

—— 'Intervento', in National Commission for secondary school reform, 'Le conoscenze fondamentali per l'apprendimento dei giovani nella scuola italiana nei prossimi decenni', q.v., pp. 417–24.

—— 'L'Italia e l'Unione europea', *Passato e Presente*, vol. XIV (1996), no. 37, pp. 85–92.

—— 'Resistenza e riforma in Italia e Francia, 1943–48', *Ventesimo Secolo*, vol. II (1992), nos. 5–6, pp. 297–319.

—— 'Le riforme di struttura nel dibattito degli anni Cinquanta e Sessanta', *Studi Storici*, vol. XXXIII (1992), nos. 2–3, pp. 653–68.

Ginsborg, P. (ed.), *Stato dell'Italia*, Milano, 1994.

Ginsborg, P., Ragazzini, D., and Tassinari, G. (eds.), *Enti locali, società civile e famiglia nell'educazione in Toscana*, Firenze, 1996.

Ginsborg, P., and Ramella, F. (eds.), *Un'Italia minore*, Firenze, 1999.

Ginzburg, A., and Simonazzi, A., 'Patterns of production and distribution in Europe: the case of the textile and clothing sector', in Schiattarella (ed.), *New Challenges for European and International Business*, q.v., pp. 261–83.

Ginzburg, C., *Il giudice e lo storico*, Torino, 1991.

Giolitti, A., *Lettere a Marta*, Bologna, 1992.

Giovagnoli, A., *Il partito italiano. La Democrazia Cristiana dal 1942 al 1994*, Bari, 1996.

Giovanardi, C., *Storie di straordinaria ingiustizia*, Roma, 1997.

Giovannini, P., 'Trasformazioni sociali e crisi di rappresentanza', in Giovannini (ed.), *I rumori della crisi*, q.v., pp. 235–66.

Giovannini, P. (ed.), *I rumori della crisi*, Milano, 1993.

Giudicci, R., *Periferie: le voci dei cittadini*, Milano, 1993.

Giudicini, P., and Pieretti, G. (eds.), *Urban Poverty and Human Dignity*, Milano, 1994.

Giuliani, M., 'Italy', in Rometsch and Wessels (eds.), *The European Union and Member States*, q.v., pp. 105–33.

—— 'Measures of consensual law-making: the Italian "Consociativismo", *Poleis. Quaderno di Ricerca*, no. 12, 1996.

—— 'Il processo decisionale italiano e le politiche comunitarie', *Polis*, vol. VI (1992), no. 2, pp. 307–42.

Giulianotti, R., Bonney, N., and Hepworth, M. (eds.), *Football, Violence and Social Identity*, London/New York, 1994.

Bibliography

Glendon, M., *The Transformation of Family Law*, Chicago, 1989.

Goddard, V., *Gender, Work and Family in Naples*, Oxford/Washington DC, 1996.

Godley, W., 'The hole in the treaty', in Gowan and Anderson (eds.), *The Question of Europe*, q.v., pp. 173–7.

Goldthorpe, J., *et al.*, *The Affluent Worker*, 3 vols., London, 1968–9.

Golia, C., *Dentro Forza Italia*, Venezia, 1997.

Golini, A., 'Le tendenze demografiche dell'Italia in un quadro europeo', in Golini (ed.), *Tendenze demografiche e politiche per la popolazione*, q.v., pp. 17–78.

Golini, A. (ed.), *Tendenze demografiche e politiche per la popolazione*, Bologna, 1994.

Golini, A., and Silvestrini, A., 'Cambiamenti familiari e relazioni generazionali: una lettura demografica', in Donati (ed.), *Quarto rapporto CISF sulla famiglia in Italia*, q.v., pp. 89–126.

Gowan, P., and Anderson, P. (eds.), *The Question of Europe*, London/New York, 1997.

Gramsci, A., *Selections from the Prison Notebooks*, eds. Q. Hoare and G. Nowell Smith, London, 1971.

Grandi, R., *Come parla la pubblicità*, Milano, 1987.

Gray, L., and Howard, W., 'Forza Italia. Il partito americano', in Fedele and Leonardi (eds.), *La politica senza i partiti*, q.v.

Graziani, A., 'L'economia italiana e il suo inserimento internazionale', in *Storia dell'Italia repubblicana*, q.v., vol. III, pt 1, pp. 349–402.

—— 'Introduzione', in Graziani (ed.), *La spirale del debito pubblico*, q.v.

—— 'Mezzogiorno oggi', *Meridiana*, no. 1 (1987), pp. 201–18.

Graziani, A. (ed.), *La spirale del debito pubblico*, Bologna, 1988.

Greco, G., 'Potere e parentela nella Sicilia nuova', *Quaderni di Sociologia*, vol. XIX (1970), no. 1, pp. 3–41.

Greco, L., *et al.*, 'Indagine sulla migrazione Sud-Nord del bambino ammalato', *Rivista Italiana di Pediatria*, vol. XI (1985), no. 3, pp. 287–95.

Gribaudi, G., 'Familismo e famiglia a Napoli e nel Mezzogiorno', in *Meridiana*, no. 17 (1993), pp. 13–42.

—— 'Il paradigma del "familismo amorale"', in Macry and Massafra (eds.), *Fra storia e storiografia*, q.v., pp. 337–54.

Grilli, L., 'Nei vicoli di Napoli. Reti sociali e percorsi individuali', *Meridiana*, no. 15 (1992), pp. 223–47.

Gualmini, E., 'L'evoluzione degli assetti concertativi in Italia e in Germania', *Rivista Italiana di Scienza Politica*, vol. XXVII (1997), no. 1, pp. 101–50.

Guarnieri, C., 'The judiciary in the Italian political crisis', in Bull and Rhodes (eds.), *Crisis and Transition in Italian Politics*, q.v., pp. 157–75.

—— *Magistratura e politica in Italia*, Bologna, 1993.

Guazzini, G., 'Dimensione ideale della famiglia e calendario ideale delle nascite', in Palomba (ed.), *Vita di coppia e figli*, q.v., pp. 39–51.

Bibliography

Guerrieri, P., 'La collocazione internazionale dell'economia italiana', in Ginsborg (ed.), *Stato dell'Italia*, q.v., pp. 379–87.

Guerrieri, P., and Milana, C., *L'Italia e il commercio mondiale*, Bologna, 1990.

Gumbel, A., 'Italian men cling to mamma', *Speak Up*, vol. XIII (1997), no. 3, pp. 30–32.

Gundle, S., *Between Hollywood and Moscow*, Durham/London, 2000.

—— 'Rai e Fininvest nell'anno di Berlusconi', in Katz and Ignazi (eds.), *Italian Politics. A Review*, vol. X, q.v., pp. 195–218.

—— 'Television in Italy', in Coleman and Rollett (eds.), *Television in Europe*, q.v.

Gundle, S., and Parker, S. (eds.), *The New Italian Republic*, London/New York, 1996.

Gunther, B., and Svennevig, M., *Behind and In Front of the Screen*, London, 1987.

Hall, J. A. (ed.), *Civil Society*, Oxford, 1995.

Harris, C. C., 'The changing relation between family and societal form in western society' (1977), in Anderson (ed.), *Sociology of the Family*, q.v., pp. 396–413.

Harris, J., *Private Lives, Public Spirit*, Oxford, 1993.

Hartmann, H. I., 'The unhappy marriage of Marxism and Feminism: towards a more progressive union', in Sargent (ed.), *Women and Revolution*, q.v., pp. 1–42.

Hefeker, C., 'German monetary union, the Bundesbank and the EMS collapse', in *Banca Nazionale del Lavoro. Quarterly Review*, vol. XLVII (1994), no. 191, pp. 379–98.

Hegel, G. W. F., *Elements of the Philosophy of Right* (ed. A. W. Wood), Cambridge, 1991.

Hellman, S., 'The difficult birth of the Democratic Party of the Left', in Hellman and Pasquino (eds.), *Italian Politics: A Review*, vol. VII, q.v., pp. 68–86.

Hellman, S., and Pasquino, G. F. (eds.), *Italian Politics: A Review*, vol. VII, London, 1992.

—— *Italian Politics: A Review*, vol. VIII, London, 1993.

Hemerijck, A., and Visser, J., 'The Dutch model: an obvious candidate for the "Third Way"?', *Archives Européennes de Sociologie*, vol. XL (1999), no. 1, pp. 103–21.

Hewitt, P., 'Re-inventing citizenship: the role of family policy', in Crouch and Marquand (eds.), *Reinventing Collective Action*, q.v., pp. 103–11.

Hickson, D. J. (ed.), *Management in Western Europe*, Berlin/New York, 1993.

Hill, T. P., 'On goods and services', *The Review of Income and Wealth*, vol. XXIII (1977), no. 3, pp. 315–38.

Hinckle, P., 'The bribery mess in Milan', *Newsweek*, 1 June 1992.

Hine, D., *Governing Italy*, Oxford, 1993.

—— 'Italy and Europe: the Italian presidency and the domestic management of European Community affairs', in Anderlini and Leonardi (eds.), *Italian Politics: A Review*, vol. VI, q.v., pp. 50–68.

Hine, D., and Vassallo, S. (eds.), *Italian Politics: A Review*, vol. XIV, Oxford, 2000.

Hirschman, A. O., *Exit, Voice, and Loyalty*, Cambridge, 1970.

—— *Shifting Involvements*, Princeton, 1978.

Hoffman, S., 'Reflections on the nation-state in western Europe today', *Journal of Common Market Studies*, vol. XXI (1982), nos. 1–2, pp. 21–37.

Hont, I., 'Free trade and the economic limits to national politics: neo-Machiavellian political economy reconsidered', in Dunn (ed.), *The Economic Limits to Modern Politics*, q.v., pp. 41–120.

Ignazi, P., *Dal PCI al PDS*, Bologna, 1992.

—— *Il polo escluso*, Bologna, 1998.

—— *Postfascisti?*, Bologna, 1994.

'Il fenomeno della Rete in Sicilia', *Iter*, no. 4 (1992), pp. 7–98.

Inglehart, R., *Cultural Shift in Advanced Industrial Society*, Princeton, 1990.

—— *Modernisation and Postmodernisation*, Princeton, 1997.

—— *The Silent Revolution*, Princeton, 1977.

Ingrao, P., and Rossanda, R. (eds.), *Appuntamenti di fine secolo*, Roma, 1995.

Ingrassia, G., *Indagine campionaria sui principali aspetti socio-economici della città di Palermo con particolare riferimento alla povertà economica*, Trapani, 1988.

Isernia, P., 'Bandiera e risorse: la politica estera negli anni Ottanta', in Cotta and Isernia (eds.), *Il gigante dai piedi di argilla*, q.v., pp. 139–88.

—— *La cooperazione allo sviluppo*, Bologna, 1995.

IREF (Istituto di Richerche Educative e Formative), *Rapporto sull'asociazionismo sociale 1995*, ed. A. Valentini, Roma, 1995.

ISTAT (Istituto Nazionale di Statistica), *Indagini multiscopo sulle famiglie, anni 1993–94. Aspetti della vita quotidiana*, vol. II, Roma, 1996.

—— *La presenza straniera in Italia*, Roma, 1993.

—— *Statistiche del commercio interno*, Roma, 1997.

—— *Statistiche giudiziarie civili, anno 1994*, Roma, 1996.

—— *Statistiche giudiziarie penali 1994*, annuario no. 3, Roma, 1995.

Istituto G. Tagliacarne, *Divari territoriali dello sviluppo agricolo nel decennio 1980–1990*, Milano, 1994.

Jean-Pierre, T., 'Come si manipolano i giudici in Francia', *MicroMega*, 1993, no. 5, pp. 69–72.

John Paul II, *Alle donne*, Milano, 1995.

—— *Familiaris consortio*, Bologna, 1994 [1st edn 1981].

—— *Lettera alle famiglie*, Roma, 1994.

—— 'Message' of 1 January 1991, in *La Traccia*, vol. XII (1991), no. 1, pp. 8–13.

—— 'Speech on the occasion of his visit to the parish of S. Dorotea, Roma, 17 February 1991', in *La Traccia*, vol. XII (1991), no. 2, p. 176.

Johnson, P., 'The welfare state', in Floud and McCloskey (eds.), *The Economic History of Britain since 1700*, vol. III, q.v., pp. 284–317.

Jowell, R., Witherspoon, S., and Brook, L., *British Social Attitudes. Special International Report*, London, 1989.

Judt, T., *A Grand Illusion?*, New York, 1996.

Jurado Guerrero, T., and Naldini, M. 'Is the South so different? Italian and Spanish families in comparative perspective', in Rhodes (ed.), *Southern European Welfare States*, q.v., pp. 42–66.

Kassab, C., *Income and Equality*, New York, 1992.

Katz, R. S., 'The 1993 parliamentary electoral reform', in Mershon and Pasquino (eds.), *Italian Politics: A Review*, vol. IX, q.v., pp. 93–112.

Katz, R. S., and Ignazi, P. (eds.), *Italian Politics: A Review*, vol. X, Boulder, Colorado, 1996.

Keane, J., *Civil Society. Old Images, New Visions*, London, 1998.

Keane, J. (ed.), *Civil Society and the State*, London, 1988.

Kertzer, D. I., *Politics and Symbols. The Italian Communist Party and the Fall of Communism*, New Haven/London, 1996.

Kidron, M., and Segal, R., *The State of the World Atlas*, London, 1995.

King, R., 'Italy: multi-faceted tourism', in Williams and Shaw (eds.), *Tourism and Economic Development*, q.v., pp. 61–85.

King, R., and Killingbeck, J., 'Agriculture and land use change in central Basilicata', *Land Use Policy*, 1990, no. 1, pp. 7–26.

—— 'Carlo Levi, the Mezzogiorno and emigration: fifty years of demographic change at Aliano', in *Geography*, vol. LXXIV (1989), no. 2, pp. 128–43.

Kirkpatrick, C., *Nazi Germany: its Women and Family Life*, Indianapolis, 1938.

Koonz, C., *Mothers in the Fatherland*, New York, 1986.

Koser, H., and Lutz, H. (eds.), *The New Migration in Europe: Social Constructions and Social Realities*, London, 1997.

Lacoste-Dujardin, C., 'La famiglia', in Calchi Novati (ed.), *Maghreb*, q.v., pp. 188–200.

Lagorio, S., Vegetti Finzi, S., and Ravasi, L., *Se noi siamo la terra*, Milano, 1996.

La Malfa, U., *Discorsi parlamentari*, Roma, 1963.

—— 'Problemi e prospettive dello sviluppo economico italiano. Nota aggiuntiva, presentata al Parlamento dal ministro del Bilancio il 22 maggio 1961', in La Malfa, *Discorsi parlamentari*, vol. II, q.v., pp. 779–97.

La Mendola, S., 'I rapporti di parentela in Veneto', *Polis*, vol. V (1991), no. 1, pp. 49–70.

Lanaro, S., *Storia dell'Italia repubblicana*, Venezia, 1992.

Bibliography

Lasch, C., *The Culture of Narcissism*, New York, 1980.

—— *Haven in a Heartless World*, New York, 1977.

Laschi, G., *L'agricoltura italiana e l'integrazione europea*, Berne, 1999.

Lash, S., and Urry, J., *Economies of Signs and Space*, London, 1994.

Laslett, P., 'Elusive intimacy', *Times Literary Supplement*, no. 4639, 28 February 1992, p. 15.

Laubier, C. (ed.), *The Condition of Women in France: 1945 to the Present*, London, 1990.

Laursen, F., and Van Hoonacker, S. (eds.), *The Ratification of the Maastricht Treaty*, Dordrecht, 1994.

Lazzarini, G., 'Una favola italiana', in *TV Sorrisi e Canzoni*, vol. XXXIX (1990), no. 52, 30 December, pp. 46–53.

Legambiente, *Ambiente Italia '93*, ed. G. Conte and G. Melandri, Roma, 1993.

Lega per l'Ambiente, *Ambiente Italia. Rapporto 1989*, ed. G. Melandri, Torino, 1989.

Leira, A., *Welfare States and Working Mothers*, Cambridge, 1992.

Leonardi, G., and Violante, L. (eds.), *Quale famiglia?*, Roma, 1980.

Leonardi, R., and Corbetta, P. G. (eds.), *Italian Politics: A Review*, vol. III, London, 1989.

Leonardi, R., and Nanetti, R. Y. (eds.), *Italian Politics: A Review*, vol. I, London, 1986.

Leone, U., 'Le politiche dell'ambiente', in Di Donna and Vallario (eds.), *L'ambiente. Risorse e rischi*, q.v., pp. 251–70.

Lepre, A., *Storia della prima repubblica*, Bologna, 1993.

Levi, R. F., *Il Professore*, Milano, 1996.

Lewis, C., and O'Brien, M. (eds.), *Reassessing Fatherhood*, London, 1987.

Leys, C., 'Public sphere and media', in *Socialist Register*, Rendlesham, 1999, pp. 314–35.

Licandro, A., and Varano, A., *La città dolente*, Torino, 1993.

Lijphart, A., *Democracies*, New Haven, 1984.

—— *Democracy in Plural Society*, New Haven, 1977.

Littwack, E., 'Geographic mobility and extended family cohesion', *American Sociological Review*, vol. XXV (1960), no. 3, pp. 385–94.

—— 'Occupational mobility and extended family cohesion', *American Sociological Review*, vol. XXV (1960), no. 1, pp. 9–21.

Livi Bacci, M., 'Esiste davvero una seconda transizione demografica?', in Micheli (ed.), *La società del figlio assente*, q.v., pp. 90–104.

—— 'Introduzione', in Livi Bacci and Martuzzi Veronesi (eds.), *Le risorse umane del Mediterraneo*, q.v., pp. 11–40.

Livi Bacci, M., Lonni, A., and Pugliese, E., 'Immigrazione e razzismo nel Mediterraneo', *Passato e Presente*, vol. XVI (1998), no. 43, pp. 15–34.

Livi Bacci, M., and Martuzzi Veronesi, F. (eds.)., *Le risorse umane del Mediterraneo*, Bologna, 1990.

Bibliography

Livolsi, M. (ed.), *L'Italia che cambia*, Firenze, 1993.

Livolsi, M., and Volli, U. (eds.), *La comunicazione politica tra prima e seconda Repubblica*, Milano, 1995.

Locatelli, G., and Martini, D., *Mi manda papà*, Milano, 1991.

Locke, R. M., '*Eppure si tocca*: the abolition of the scala mobile', in Mershon and Pasquino (eds.),*Italian Politics: A Review*, vol. IX, q.v., pp. 185–96.

Lodato, S., '*Ho ucciso Giovanni Falcone*', Milano, 1999.

Lombardi, R., 'Una nuova frontiera per la sinistra', in Parlato (ed.), *Spazio e ruolo del riformismo*, q.v., pp. 65–74.

Longrigg, C., *Mafia Women*, London, 1997.

'Look at it our way', *The Economist*, vol. CCLXXIV (1980), no. 7120, 16 February.

Lumley, R., *Italian Journalism*, Manchester, 1996.

—— 'Peculiarities of the Italian newspaper', in Forgacs and Lumley (eds.), *Italian Cultural Studies*, q.v., pp. 199–215.

Lupo, S., *Andreotti, la mafia, la storia d'Italia*, Roma, 1996.

—— *Storia della mafia*, Roma, 1993.

Lynch, J. H., *Godparents and Kinship in Early Medieval Europe*, Princeton, 1986.

Lyttelton, A., 'Italy: the triumph of TV', *New York Review of Books*, vol. XLI (1994), no. 14.

Machiavelli, N., *Il Principe*, Torino, 1977 [1532].

Mack Smith, D., 'The Latifundia in modern Sicilian history', *Proceedings of the British Academy*, vol. LI (1965), pp. 85–124.

Macry, P., and Massafra, A. (eds.), *Fra storia e storiografia*, Bologna, 1994.

Mafai, M., 'Andreotti fra croce e palazzo', *MicroMega*, 1990, no. 2, pp. 56–64.

Mafia. L'atto d'accusa dei giudici di Palermo, ed. C. Stajano, Roma, 1986.

Maggioni, G., 'Le separazioni e i divorzi', in Barbagli and Saraceno (eds.), *Lo stato delle famiglie in Italia*, q.v., pp. 233–5.

Maino, F., *La politica sanitaria*, Bologna, 2001.

Malerba, G., 'La donna nella famiglia e nel lavoro: i risultati di un' indagine cross-country', in Rossi and Malerba (eds.), *La donna nella famiglia e nel lavoro*, q.v., pp. 49–90.

Malgeri, F. (ed.), *Storia della Democrazia Cristiana*, Roma, 1989.

Mancina, C., *Differenze nell'eticità*, Napoli, 1991.

Mannheimer, R., 'L'elettorato della Lega Nord', *Polis*, vol. VII (1993), no. 2, pp. 253–76.

—— 'Eppur si muove. Opinione pubblica e offerta politica', in Diamanti and Lazar (eds.), *Stanchi di miracoli*, q.v., pp. 159–79.

—— *La Lega Lombarda*, Milano, 1991.

Manoukian, A. (ed.), *La presenza sociale del PCI e della DC*, Bologna, 1968.

Bibliography

Mansell, R., *The New Telecommunications*, London, 1993.

Marcenaro, P., and Foa, V., *Riprendere tempo*, Torino, 1982.

Marchetti, A., 'La nuova immigrazione a Milano. Il caso senegalese', in Barile, *et al.*, *Tra due rive*, q.v., pp. 241–366.

Marcuzzo, M. C., and Rossi-Doria, A. (eds.), *La ricerca delle donne*, Torino, 1987.

Marini, L., 'La corruzione politica', in *Storia d'Italia Annali 12*, q.v., pp. 323–72.

Marsh, J. S., and Swanney, P. J., *Agriculture and the European Community*, London, 1980.

Marshall, J. N., *Services and Uneven Development*, Oxford, 1988.

Martin, B., *A Sociology of Contemporary Cultural Change*, Oxford, 1981.

Martinelli, A. (ed.), *L'azione collettiva degli imprenditori italiani*, Milano, 1994.

Martinelli, A., and Lanzalaco, L., 'L'organizzazione degli interessi imprenditoriali e il sistema politico. La logica dell'influenza', in Martinelli (ed.), *L'azione collettiva degli imprenditori italiani*, q.v., pp. 317–64.

Martini, C. M., *Farsi prossimo*, Milano, 1985.

Martini, P., 'Molti affari, molta politica', in *Problemi dell'Informazione*, vol. XV (1990), no. 4, pp. 513–28.

Martinotti, G., *et al.*, *Milano ore sette: come vivono i milanesi*, Milano, 1988.

Marx, K., *Misère de la philosophie*, Paris, 1847.

Masera, R. S., and Rossi, S., *La bilancia dei pagamenti*, Padova, 1993.

Massari, M., *La Sacra Corona Unita*, Bari, 1998.

Mattina, L., 'Abete's Confindustria: from alliance with the DC to multiparty appeal', in Hellman and Pasquino (eds.), *Italian Politics: A Review*, vol. VIII, pp. 151–64.

—— 'I candidati', in *Rivista Italiana di Scienza Politica*, vol. XXIV (1994), no. 3, pp. 549–86.

Mauri, L., and Micheli, G. A., 'Flussi immigratori in Italia: una scheda documentaria', in Mauri and Micheli (eds.), *Le regole del gioco*, q.v., pp. 213–30.

Mauri, L., and Micheli, G. A. (eds.), *Le regole del gioco*, Milano, 1992.

Mazzoleni, G., *La corsa all'Euro*, Roma, 1998.

Mazzonis, F., 'Un problema capitale', in Ginsborg (ed.), *Stato dell'Italia*, q.v., pp. 108–14.

McCarthy, P., *The Crisis of the Italian State*, London, 1997 [1st edn 1995].

—— 'Forza Italia: the new politics and old values of a changing Italy', in Gundle and Parker (eds.), *The New Italian Republic*, q.v., pp. 130–46.

—— 'The referendum of 9 June', in Hellman and Pasquino (eds.), *Italian Politics*, vol. VII, pp. 11–28.

Médard, J. F., 'Francia-Africa: affari di famiglia', in della Porta and Mény (eds.), *Corruzione e democrazia*, q.v., pp. 29–48.

Melis, G., *Storia dell'amministrazione italiana, 1861–1993*, Bologna, 1996.

Melograni, P., and Scaraffia, L. (eds.), *La famiglia italiana dall'Ottocento ad oggi*, Bari, 1988.

Mendras, H., *La Seconde révolution française (1965–1984)*, Paris, 1988.

Menet-Genty, J. (ed.), *L'Economie italienne*, Paris, 1992.

—— 'Forces et faiblesses de l'Italie à l'échéance de 1993', in Menet-Genty (ed.), *L'Economie italienne*, q.v., pp. 261–68.

Mennitti, D. (ed.), *Forza Italia. Radiografia di un evento*, Roma, 1997.

Mény, Y., *'La corruption de la République'*, Paris, 1992.

—— 'Le riforme amministrative in Italia e in Europa', in SPISA, *Le riforme amministrative*, q.v.

Mershon, C. A., 'The crisis of the CGIL: open division in the 12th National Congress', in Hellman and Pasquino (eds.), *Italian Politics: A Review*, vol. VII, q.v., pp. 87–109.

Mershon, C. A., and Pasquino, G. F. (eds.), *Italian Politics: A Review*, vol. IX, Oxford, 1995.

Meyrowitz, J., *No Sense of Place*, Oxford, 1985.

Micheli, G. A. (ed.), *La società del figlio assente*, Milano, 1995.

Miglio, G. F., *Io, Bossi e la Lega*, Milano, 1994.

—— *Le regolarità della politica*, 2 vols., Milano, 1988.

—— 'Una Repubblica "mediterranea"?', in Miglio, *Le regolarità della politica*, q.v., vol. II, pp. 1095–1104.

—— 'Vocazione e destini dei lombardi', in Miglio, *Io, Bossi e la Lega*, q.v., pp. 73–96.

Miles, R., and Thränhardt, D. (eds.), *Migration and European Integration*, London, 1995.

Mill, J. S., *On Liberty and Other Essays*, Oxford, 1991 [1st edn 1869].

—— 'The subjection of women', in Mill, *On Liberty and Other Essays*, q.v., pp. 469–582.

Miller, D., *Material Culture and Mass Consumption*, Oxford, 1987.

Miller, R. A., and Miller, M. G., 'The golden chain. A study of the structure, function and patterning of *comparatico* in a south Italian village', *American Ethnologist*, vol. V (1978), no. 1, pp. 116–36.

Milward, A. S. *et al.*, *The European Rescue of the Nation-State*, London, 1992.

Minestroni, L., *Casa dolce casa*, Milano, 1996.

Mingione, E., 'La disoccupazione giovanile', in Paci (ed.), *Le dimensioni della disuguaglianza*, q.v., pp. 251–9.

—— 'Economia informale, strategie formali e Mezzogiorno', *Inchiesta*, vol. XVI (1986), no. 74, pp. 1–3.

Minicuci, M., 'La casa natale, la casa sognata: Zaccanopoli', in Faeta (ed.), *L'architettura popolare in Italia. Calabria*, q.v., pp. 143–59.

—— *Qui e altrove*, Milano, 1989.

Ministero per i Beni culturali e ambientali. Notiziario, nos. 51–2 (1996).

Miscossi, S., and Visco, I. (eds.), *Inflazione, concorrenza e sviluppo*, Bologna, 1993.

Bibliography

Mitchison, A., 'Method or madness?', *The Independent Magazine*, 29 February 1992.

Mitsos, A., and Mossialos, E. (eds.), *Contemporary Greece and Europe*, Aldershot, 2000.

Moller Okin, S., *Justice, Gender and the Family*, New York, 1989.

Molyneux, M., 'Beyond the domestic labour debate', *New Left Review*, no. 116 (1979), pp. 3–27.

Montanaro, S., and Ruotolo, S., *Mister e Lady Poggiolini*, Napoli, 1994.

Monti, M., 'Guido Carli, l'Europa, la memoria', in *Scritti in onore di Guido Carli*, q.v., pp. 327–30.

Morcaldo, G., *La finanza pubblica in Italia*, Bologna, 1993.

Morlino, L., and Tarchi, M., 'The dissatisfied society: the roots of political change in Italy', in *European Journal of Political Research*, vol. XXX (1996), no. 1, pp. 41–63.

Morris, J., *The Political Economy of Shopkeeping in Milan, 1886–1922*, Cambridge, 1993.

Moss, D., 'Patronage revisited: the dynamics of information and reputation', *Journal of Modern Italian Studies*, vol. I (1995), no. 1, pp. 58–93.

Mount, F., *The Subversive Family*, London, 1982.

Mouzelis, N., 'Class and clientelistic politics: the case of Greece', *Sociological Review*, vol. XXVI (1978), pp. 471–97.

—— 'Modernity, late development and civil society', in Hall (ed.), *Civil Society*, q.v., pp. 224–49.

—— *Politics in the Semi-Periphery*, London, 1986.

Müller, W. C., and Wright, V., 'Reshaping the state in western Europe: the limits to retreat', in Müller and Wright (eds.), *The State in Western Europe. Retreat or Redefinition?*, q.v., pp. 1–11.

Müller, W. C. and Wright, V. (eds.), *The State in Western Europe. Retreat or Redefinition?*, London, 1994.

Murray, F., 'Flexible specialisation in the "Third Italy"', *Capital and Class*, no. 33 (1987), pp. 84–95.

Mutti, A., *Il buon vicino*, Bologna, 1992.

Napolitano, G., *Dove va la Repubblica*, Milano, 1994.

Nardi Spiller, C., *La dinamica inflattiva nell'economia italiana*, Padova, 1994.

Nascimbeni, E., and Pamponara, A., *Le mani pulite*, Milano, 1992.

Nash, M., 'Pronatalism and motherhood in Franco's Spain', in Bock and Thane (eds.), *Maternity and Gender Policies*, q.v., pp. 160–77.

Natale, P., 'Lega Lombarda e insediamento territoriale: un'analisi ecologica', in Mannheimer, *La Lega Lombarda*, q.v., pp. 83–121.

National Commission for secondary school reform, 'Le conoscenze fondamentali per l'apprendimento dei giovani nella scuola italiana nei prossimi decenni', *Studi e Documenti degli Annali della Pubblica Istruzione*, no. 78 (1997).

Bibliography

Nava, P., 'Emilia-Romagna: a una svolta la cultura dei servizi', in Ginsborg (ed.), *Stato dell'Italia*, q.v., pp. 156–60.

Negri, N., 'L'esclusione sociale', in Paci (ed.), *Le dimensioni della disuguaglianza*, q.v., pp. 293–323.

Negri, N., and Saraceno, C., *Politiche contro la povertà in Italia*, Bologna, 1996.

Nelken, D., 'A legal revolution? The judges and *Tangentopoli*', in Gundle and Parker (eds.), *The New Italian Republic*, q.v., pp. 191–205.

Neppi Modona, G., 'Ruolo della giustizia e crisi del potere pubblico', *Quaderni di Sociologia*, vol. XXXVII (1993), no. 5, pp. 6–30.

Nichols, P., *Italia, Italia*, London, 1973.

Nicotri, P., *Tangenti in confessionale*, Venezia, 1993.

NOMISMA, *Rapporto 1993 sull'agricoltura italiana*, Bologna, 1993.

Oakeshott, M., *Rationalism in Politics*, London, 1962.

Occhetto, A., *Il sentimento e la ragione*, Milano, 1994.

Ochel, W., and Wegner, M., *Service Economies in Europe*, London, 1987.

OECD (Organization for Economic Cooperation and Development), *Economic Surveys: Italy, 1990–91*, Paris, 1991.

—— *Economic Surveys, 1992–93: Italy*, Paris, 1993.

—— *Education at a Glance*, Paris, 1992.

—— *Lone Parent Families*, Paris, 1990.

—— *New Orientations in Social Policy*, Paris, 1994.

Oldani, T., 'I miserabili', *Panorama*, vol. XXVI (1988), no. 1173, pp. 68–77.

Onida, F., 'Does there still exist an external constraint on Italian economic growth?', *Review of Economic Conditions in Italy*, 1993, no. 1, pp. 31–80.

Onida, F. (ed.), *Il commercio internazionale dei servizi e la posizione dell'Italia*, Roma, 1989.

Onida, F., Viesti, G. F., and Falzoni, A. M. (eds.), *I distretti industriali: crisi o evoluzione?*, Milano, 1992.

Oppo, A., 'Madri, figlie e sorelle: solidarietà parentali in Sardegna', *Polis*, vol. V (1991), no. 1, pp. 21–48.

Orfei, R., *L'occupazione del potere*, Milano, 1976.

Orlando, L., *Palermo*, ed. C. Fotia and A. Roccuzzo, Milano, 1990.

Ortoleva, P., *Un ventennio a colori*, Firenze, 1995.

Pace, A., 'La radiotelevisone in Italia con particolare riguardo alla emittenza privata', *Rivista Trimestrale di Diritto Pubblico*, vol. XXXVII (1987), no. 3, pp. 615–57.

Paci, M., 'Innovazione tecnologica, occupazione e politica sociale', in Ruberti (ed.), *Europa a confronto*, q.v., pp. 287–337.

—— 'I mutamenti della stratificazione sociale', in *Storia dell'Italia repubblicana*, vol. III, pt 1, q.v., pp. 697–776.

Bibliography

—— *Il mutamento della struttura sociale in Italia*, Bologna, 1992.

—— *Pubblico e privato nei moderni sistemi di Welfare*, Napoli, 1989.

—— *La struttura sociale italiana*, Bologna, 1982.

Paci, M. (ed.), *Le dimensioni della disuguaglianza*, Bologna, 1993.

Packard, V., *Hidden Persuaders*, New York, 1957.

Padellaro, A., and Tamburrano, G., *Processo a Craxi*, Milano, 1993.

Padiglione, V., and Pontalti, C., 'Fra le generazioni modelli di connessione simbolica', in Donati (ed.), *Quarto rapporto CISF sulla famiglia in Italia*, q.v., pp. 187–220.

Padoa-Schioppa Kostoris, F., *Italy the Sheltered Economy*, Oxford, 1993.

Padoa-Schioppa, T., *The Road To Monetary Union in Europe*, Oxford, 1994 [Italian edn *L'Europa verso l'unione monetaria*, Torino, 1992].

Padovani, T., 'La soave inquisizione. Osservazioni e rilievi a proposito delle nuove ipotesi di "ravvedimento"', *Rivista Italiana di Diritto e Procedura Penale*, vol. XXIV (1981), no. 2, pp. 529–45.

Pajetta, G., *Il grande camaleonte*, Milano, 1994.

Palomba, R. (ed.), *Vita di coppia e figli*, Firenze, 1987.

Palomba, R., and Sabbadini, L. L., 'Differenze di genere e uso del tempo nella vita quotidiana', in Paci (ed.), *Le dimensioni della disuguaglianza*, q.v., pp. 220–30.

Pansa, G. P., *L'intrigo*, Milano, 1990.

—— *Ottobre, addio*, Milano, 1982.

—— *Il regime*, Milano, 1991.

Pappalardo, S., *Gli iconoclasti*, Milano, 1987.

—— *Un terremoto per amico*, Milano, 1994.

Parker, S., 'Electoral reform and political change in Italy, 1991–1994', in Gundle and Parker (eds.), *The New Italian Republic*, q.v., pp. 40–58.

Parks, T., *Italian Neighbours*, London, 1994 [1st edn 1992].

Parlato, V. (ed.), *Spazio e ruolo del riformismo*, Bologna, 1974.

Parry, R., 'Britain: stable aggregates, changing composition', in Rose (ed.), *Public Employment in Western Nations*, q.v., pp. 185–233.

Parsons, A., *Belief, Magic and Anomie*, New York, 1969.

—— 'Is the Oedipus complex universal?', in Parsons, *Belief, Magic and Anomie*, q.v., pp. 3–66.

Pasolini, P. P., *Lettere luterane*, Torino, 1976.

—— *Scritti corsari*, Milano, 1981 [1st edn 1977].

Pasquinelli, C. (ed.), *Potere senza stato*, Roma, 1986.

Pasquino, G. F., 'The electoral reform referendums', in Anderlini and Leonardi (eds.), *Italian Politics: A Review*, vol. VI, q.v., pp. 9–24.

—— 'Machiavellismo', in Ginsborg (ed.), *Stato dell'Italia*, q.v., pp. 92–4.

—— 'La partitocrazia', in Pasquino (ed.), *La politica italiana. Dizionario critico, 1945–1995*, q.v., pp. 341–54.

—— 'Il pentapartito', in Pasquino (ed.), *La politica italiana. Dizionario critico, 1945–1995*, q.v., pp. 355–63.

—— 'A postmortem for the Bicamerale', in Hine and Vassallo (eds.), *Italian Politics: A Review*, vol. XIV, q.v., pp. 101–20.

Pasquino, G. F. (ed.), *L'alternanza inattesa*, Catanzaro, 1995.

—— *La politica italiana. Dizionario critico, 1945–1995*, Bari, 1995.

—— *Il sistema politico italiano*, Bari, 1985.

Pasquino, G. F., and Vassallo, S., 'The government of Carlo Azeglio Ciampi', in Mershon and Pasquino (eds.), *Italian Politics: A Review*, vol. IX, q.v., pp. 55–74.

Passerin D'Entrèves, E., 'Recenti studi sull'Azione Cattolica in Italia fra Ottocento e Novecento', *Studium*, vol. L (1954), no. 4, pp. 228–44.

Passerini, L., 'Gender relations', in Forgacs and Lumley (eds.), *Italian Cultural Studies*, q.v., pp. 144–59.

Pateman, C., 'The fraternal social contract', in Keane (ed.), *Civil Society and the State*, q.v., pp. 101–27.

—— *The Sexual Contract*, Cambridge, 1988.

Pavitt, K., 'Sectoral patterns of technical change: towards a taxonomy and a theory', *Research Policy*, vol. XII (1984), no. 6.

Pavone, C., *Alle origini della Repubblica*, Torino, 1995.

—— 'La continuità dello Stato. Istituzioni e uomini', in Pavone, *Alle origini della Repubblica*, q.v., pp. 70–159.

Pazienti, M., *Roma e la sua regione urbana*, Milano, 1995.

Pedersen, S., *Family, Dependence and the Origins of the Welfare State*, Cambridge, 1993.

Pelczynski, Z. A., 'Solidarity and "the rebirth of civil society" in Poland, 1976–81', in Keane (ed.), *Civil Society and the State*, q.v., pp. 361–80.

Pellegrini, G., 'Integrazione e crescita dei servizi negli anni '80: l'altra faccia della ristrutturazione', *Rivista di Politica Economica*, vol. LXXI (1991), no. 4, pp. 3–21.

Pen, J., *Income Distribution*, London, 1971.

Pende, S., 'L'amico Fedele', in *L'Europeo*, vol. XLV (1989), nos. 33–4, 25 August.

—— 'Fratelli d'Italia, diventiamo cugini', in *L'Europeo*, vol. XLVI (1990), no. 37, 14 September.

Pennacchi, L. (ed.), *Le ragioni dell'equità*, Bari, 1994.

Penniman, H. R. (ed.), *Italy at the Polls*, Washington DC, 1977.

Pérez-Díaz, V., *The Return of Civil Society*, Cambridge, Mass., 1993.

Perkin, H., *The Third Revolution*, London, 1996.

Perulli, P., *Atlante metropolitano*, Bologna, 1991.

Perulli, P. (ed.), *Piccole imprese metropolitane*, Milano, 1990.

Bibliography

Pescarolo, A., 'Famiglia e impresa. Problemi di ricerca all'incrocio fra discipline', *Passato e Presente*, vol. XII (1994), no. 31, pp. 127–42.

Petrusewicz, M., *Latifondo*, Padova, 1989.

Pezzino, P., *Mafia: industria della violenza*, Firenze, 1995.

Pharr, S. J. and Putnam, R. D. (eds.), *Disaffected Democracies*, Princeton, 2000.

Piason, F. J., 'Italian foreign policy: the *Achille Lauro* affair', in Leonardi and Nanetti (eds.), *Italian Politics: A Review*, vol. I, q.v., pp. 146–63.

Piazza, M., 'Il rischio di una nuova marginalità?', in Ginsborg (ed.), *Stato dell'Italia*, q.v., pp. 266–72.

Piccone Stella, S., 'I giovani in famiglia', in Barbagli and Saraceno (eds.), *Lo stato delle famiglie in Italia*, q.v., pp. 154–8.

Pietropolli Charmet, G., *Un nuovo padre*, Milano, 1995.

Pillitteri, P., *Somalia '81*, Milano, 1981.

Pini, G., 'Grande distribuzione, modelli di consumo e costi sociali', *Commercio*, vol. XVI (1994), no. 52, pp. 87–110.

Pinnelli, A., 'Modernizzazione socio-economica, condizione femminile e nuovi comportamenti familiari e procreativi', *Stato e Mercato*, no. 36 (1992), pp. 401–28.

Pintacuda, E., *Palermo palcoscenico d'Italia*, Palermo, 1986.

Pinto, C., *La fine di un partito. Il PSI dal 1992 al 1994*, Roma, 1999.

Pio XII, 'Allocuzione ai padri di famiglia (18 Sett. 1951)', in *Insegnamenti pontifici*, vol. I, *Il matrimonio*, Roma, 1957, p. 371.

—— 'Allocuzione di S.S. Pio XII alla gioventù maschile di A.C.I. sulle gravi necessità dell'ora presente', *La Civiltà Cattolica*, vol. XCVII (1946), vol. II, 4 May, p. 170.

Piore, M. J., and Sabel, C. F., *The Second Industrial Divide*, New York, 1984.

Pipan, T., *Il labirinto dei servizi*, Milano, 1996.

—— *Lo sciopero contro l'utente*, Torino, 1988.

Piperno, A., 'La politica sanitaria', in Ascoli (ed.), *Welfare state all'italiana*, q.v., pp. 153–80.

Piselli, F., 'Il comparatico politico', *L'Uomo*, vol. XI (1987), no. 1, pp. 137–59.

—— *Parentela ed emigrazione*, Torino, 1981.

Pitkin, H., *The House That Giacomo Built*, Cambridge, 1985.

Pivato, S., 'Sport: verso nuove forme di consumo', in Ginsborg (ed.), *Stato dell'Italia*, q.v., pp. 629–31.

Pizzini-Gambetta, V., 'Gender norms in the Sicilian Mafia', in Arnot and Usborne (eds.), *Gender and Crime in Modern Europe*, q.v., pp. 257–76.

Pizzorno, A., 'Le difficoltà del consociativismo', in Pizzorno, *Le radici della politica assoluta*, q.v., pp. 285–313.

—— 'Dopo il consociativismo', in *MicroMega*, 1995, no. 2, pp. 236–60.

—— 'Familismo amorale e marginalità storica, ovvero perché non c'è niente da fare a Montegrano', in Banfield, *Le basi morali di una società arretrata*, q.v., pp. 237–52.

—— 'Introduzione', in della Porta, *Lo scambio occulto*, q.v., pp. 14–16.

—— *Le radici della politica assoluta*, Milano, 1993.

Pizzorusso, A., 'Correnti della magistratura e politicizzazione', *Quaderni della Giustizia*, vol. VI (1986), no. 62, pp. 4–9.

—— *L'organizzazione della giustizia in Italia*, Torino, 1990.

Poggi, P. P., 'La Lega secondo natura', *Iter*, vol. II (1992), nos. 5–6, pp. 138–61.

Pontecorvo, C., 'Intervento', in National Commission for secondary school reform, 'Le conoscenze fondamentali per l'apprendimento dei giovani nella scuola italiana nei prossimi decenni', q.v., pp. 384–96.

Popper, K. R., and Condry, J., *Cattiva maestra televisione*, Roma, 1996 [1st edn 1994].

Porro, N., *Identità, nazione, cittadinanza*, Roma, 1995.

Porter, M., *The Competitive Advantage of Nations*, London, 1990.

Prandstaller, G. P. (ed.), *Le nuove professioni del terziario*, Milano, 1994 (4th enlarged edn).

Predieri, A. (ed.), *Fondi strutturali e coesione economica e sociale nell'Unione europea*, Milano, 1996.

Presidenza del Consiglio dei Ministri, *Rapporti nuovi*, Roma, 1984.

Presidenza del Consiglio dei Ministri, Dipartimento per la Funzione Pubblica, *L'attuazione della legge 7 agosto 1990, n. 241, e la semplificazione dei procedimenti amministrativi*, Roma, 1994.

—— *L'organizzazione dei ministeri*, Roma, 1994.

—— *Rapporto sulle condizioni delle pubbliche amministrazioni*, Roma, 1993.

Preti, D., 'Gli ammonimenti di un governatore di "classe". L'Italia repubblicana nella testimonianza di Guido Carli', *Italia Contemporanea*, no. 199 (1995), pp. 297–326.

Pridham, G., 'Italy', in Twitchett and Twitchett (eds.), *Building Europe: Britain's Partners in the EEC*, q.v., pp. 80–118.

'Procura di Palermo, memoria depositata dal pubblico ministero nel procedimento penale n. 3538/94 N.R., instaurato nei confronti di Andreotti Giulio' (now published as *La vera storia d'Italia*, q.v.).

Pugliese, E., *Sociologia della disoccupazione*, Bologna, 1993.

Putnam, R. D., *Bowling Alone*, New York, 2000.

Putnam, R. D., and Payne, N., *Hanging Together. The Seven-Power Summits*, London, 1984.

Putnam, R. D. (with Leonardi, R., and Nanetti, R. Y.), *Making Democracy Work*, Princeton, 1993.

XIV Congresso del Partito comunista italiano: Atti e risoluzioni, Roma, 1975.

Bibliography

Quirino, P., 'I consumi in Italia dall'Unità ad oggi', in *Storia dell'economia italiana*, ed. R. Romano, q.v., vol. III, pp. 201–78.

Radaelli, C., and Martini, D., 'Think tanks, advocacy coalitions and policy change: the Italian case', in Stone, Garnett and Denham (eds.), *Think Tanks across Nations*, q.v., pp. 59–81.

Rahman, A., Robins, N., and Roncerel, A. (eds.), *Exploding the Population Myth: Consumption versus Population*, Bruxelles, 1993.

Ramat, M. (ed.), *Storia di un magistrato*, Roma, 1986.

Ramella, F., 'Famiglia, istruzione e società civile: uno studio del caso', in Ginsborg, Ragazzini and Tassinari (eds.), *Enti locali, società civile e famiglia nell'educazione in Toscana*, q.v., pp. 87–113.

—— 'Istruzione, generazioni e cambiamento sociale', in Ginsborg and Ramella (eds.), *Un'Italia minore*, q.v., pp. 185–244.

—— 'Still a "Red subculture?" Continuity and change in central Italy', in *South European Society and Politics*, vol. V (2000), no. 1, pp. 1–24.

Ramella, F., and Trigilia, C., 'Associazionismo e mobilitazione contro la criminalità organizzata nel Mezzogiorno', in Violante (ed.), *Mafia e società italiana. Rapporto '97*, q.v., pp. 24–46.

Rampini, F., 'L'Italia svalutata', in *Il Mulino*, vol. XLIV (1995), no. 1, pp. 92–102.

Ranci, C., and Ielasi, P., 'L'uso dei servizi sociali e sanitari', in Paci (ed.), *Le dimensioni della disuguaglianza*, q.v., pp. 410–24.

Reher, D. S., *Perspectives on the Family in Spain, Past and Present*, Oxford, 1997.

Reich, R., *The Work of Nations*, New York, 1992.

Revelli, M., *Le due destre*, Torino, 1996.

—— 'Economia e modello sociale nel passaggio tra fordismo e toyotismo', in Ingrao and Rossanda (eds.), *Appuntamenti di fine secolo*, q.v., pp. 161–224.

—— *Lavorare in FIAT*, Milano, 1989.

Rey, G. M., 'Analisi economica ed evidenza empirica dell'attività illegale in Italia', in Zamagni (ed.), *Mercati illegali e mafie*, q.v., pp. 15–55.

—— 'I mutamenti della struttura economica: fattori produttivi, distribuzione del reddito, domanda', in Confindustria Centri Studi, *L'Italia verso il 2000*, q.v., vol. II, pp. 3–55.

Riccardi, A., 'Cattolicesimo', in Ginsborg (ed.), *Stato dell'Italia*, q.v., pp. 67–71.

—— *Intransigenza e modernità*, Bari, 1996.

'La richiesta degli ordini di custodia cautelare nei confronti dei presunti mandanti dell'omicidio Lima, firmata dai magistrati della Procura Distrettuale Antimafia di Palermo, 11 Oct. 1992' (now published as *Delitto Lima. L'atto di accusa dei giudici di Palermo*, Agrigento, n.d.).

Ricolfi, L., *L'ultimo parlamento*, Roma, 1993.

Ricolfi, L., Scamuzzi, S., and Sciolla, L., *Essere giovani a Torino*, Torino, 1988.

Ricordy, G., *Senzadiritti*, Milano, 1990.

Riedel, M., 'Der Begriff der "Bürgerlichen Gesellschaft" und des Problem seines geschichtlichen Ursprungs', in Riedel, *Studien zu Hegels Rechtsphilosophie*, q.v., pp. 135–66.

—— *Studien zu Hegels Rechtsphilosophie*, Frankfurt am Main, 1969.

Rifkin, J., *The End of Work*, New York, 1995.

Riformare la Pubblica Amministrazione. Italia, Gran Bretagna, Spagna, Stati Uniti, Torino, 1995.

Rigotti, F., *Metafore della politica*, Bologna, 1989.

—— *Il potere e le sue metafore*, Milano, 1991.

Riva, C., *et al.*, *La società domestica*, Roma, 1982.

Rizza, N., 'Il palinsesto come fattore di produzione. Evoluzione delle logiche di programmazione nell'emittenza commerciale', *Problemi dell'Informazione*, vol. XV (1990), no. 4, pp. 529–540.

Rhodes, M., 'Financing party politics in Italy: a case of systemic corruption', in Bull and Rhodes (eds.), *Crisis and Transition in Italian Politics*, q.v., pp. 54–80.

Rhodes, M. (ed.), *Southern European Welfare States*, London, 1997.

Robb, P., *Midnight in Sicily*, Potts Point, 1996.

Rogati, E., 'Il governo Berlusconi tra nazionalismo e federalismo', *Politica Internazionale*, vol. XXIII (1995), nos. 1–2, pp. 46–53.

Romero, F., 'L'Europa come strumento di *nation-building*: storia e storici dell'Italia repubblicana', *Passato e Presente*, vol. XIV (1996), no. 36, pp. 19–32.

Rometsch, D., and Wessels, W. (eds.), *The European Union and Member States*, Manchester, 1996.

Romiti, C., *Questi anni alla FIAT*, ed. G. P. Pansa, Milano, 1988.

Romito, P., 'La depressione delle donne, ovvero la radicalizazzione dell'oppressione quotidiana', *Inchiesta*, vol. XVIII (1988), no. 81, pp. 48–53.

Roniger, L., 'Modern patron–client relations and historical clientelism. Some clues from Ancient Republican Rome', *Archives Européennes de Sociologie*, vol. XXIV (1983), no. 1, pp. 63–95.

Rosci, E., 'Le lunghe adolescenze dell'Italia d'oggi', in Ginsborg (ed.), *Stato dell'Italia*, q.v., pp. 301–5.

Rose, R. (ed.), *Public Employment in Western Nations*, Cambridge, 1985.

Rose, S. J., *Social Stratification in the United States*, New York, 1992.

Rose-Ackerman, S., *Corruption*, New York, 1978.

Rossi, G., and Malerba, G. (eds.), *La donna nella famiglia e nel lavoro*, Milano, 1993.

Rossi, M. G., 'Il problema storico della riforma fiscale in Italia', *Italia Contemporanea*, no. 170 (1988), pp. 5–19.

Rossi, N. (ed.), *La transizione equa*, Bologna, 1994.

Rossi-Doria, A., *Diventare cittadine*, Firenze, 1996.

—— 'Introduzione', in Marcuzzo and Rossi-Doria (eds.), *La ricerca delle donne*, q.v., pp. 7–29.

—— 'Una rivoluzione non ancora compiuta', in Ginsborg (ed.), *Stato dell'Italia*, q.v., pp. 262–6.

Rossi-Doria, M., *Rapporto sulla Federconsorzi*, Bari, 1961.

Roussel, L., 'La famille en Europe occidentale: divergences et convergences', *Population*, vol. XLVII (1992), no. 1, pp. 133–52.

Rovati, G. C., 'Imprenditori e dirigenti tra cultura d'impresa e cultura politico-sociale', *Polis*, vol. VII (1993), no. 1, pp. 69–91.

Roverato, G., *Nuovo Pignone. Le sfide della maturità*, Bologna, 1991.

'Rows at the Rome summit', *The Economist*, vol. CCCXVII (1990), no. 7679, 3 November, p. 23.

Rowthorn, R. E., and Wells, J. R., *Deindustrialisation and Foreign Trade*, Cambridge, 1987.

Ruberti, A. (ed.), *Europa a confronto*, Bari, 1990.

Ruffini, E., 'La teologia di fronte alle problematiche della famiglia nella tensione tra "pubblico" e "privato"', in Università Cattolica del Sacro Cuore, *La coscienza contemporanea tra 'pubblico' e 'privato'*, q.v., pp. 141–75.

Ruffolo, G., *La qualità sociale*, Bari, 1985.

—— *Lo sviluppo dei limiti*, Bari, 1994.

Ruggeri, G., and Guarino, M., *Berlusconi*, Milano, 1994.

Rusconi, G. E., *Se cessiamo di essere una nazione*, Bologna, 1993.

Sabbatucci, G., *Il riformismo impossibile*, Bari, 1991.

Sales, I., *La camorra, le camorre*, Roma, 1992.

Salvadori, M. L., *Storia d'Italia e crisi di regime*, Bologna, 1994.

Sani, G., '1992: la destrutturazione del mercato elettorale', in *Rivista Italiana di Scienza Politica*, vol. XXII (1992), no. 3, pp. 539–66.

Sani, G., and Segatti, P., 'Programmi, media e opinione pubblica', *Rivista Italiana di Scienza Politica*, vol. XXVI (1996), no. 3, pp. 459–82.

Santagostino, A., *Fiat e Alfa Romeo: una privatizzazione riuscita?*, Milano, 1993.

Santini, A., 'La fecondità', in Barbagli and Saraceno (eds.), *Lo stato delle famiglie in Italia*, q.v., pp. 113–21.

Santino, U., 'Economia della droga. Traffico di stupefacenti, mafia e organised crime', *Segno*, nos. 31–2 (1982), pp. 25–49.

—— *La mafia interpretata*, Soverio Mannelli, 1995.

—— 'L'omicidio mafioso', in Chinnici and Santino, *La violenza programmata*, q.v., pp. 191–379.

Santino, U. (ed.), *Un amico a Strasburgo*, Palermo, 1984.

Santoro, C. M., *L'Italia e il Mediterraneo*, Milano, 1988.

—— 'La politica estera del Partito Socialista', in Santoro, *L'Italia e il Mediterraneo*, q.v., pp. 105–35.

—— *La politica estera di una media potenza*, Bologna, 1991.

Sapelli, G., *L'Italia inafferabile*, Venezia, 1989.

—— 'The Italian crises and capitalism', *Modern Italy*, vol. I (1995), no. 1, pp. 82–96.

—— *Southern Europe since 1945*, London, 1995.

Saraceno, C., 'The ambivalent familism of the Italian welfare state', *Social Politics*, vol. I (1994), no. 1, pp. 60–82.

—— 'Fecondità, famiglia e lavoro', in Micheli (ed.), *La società del figlio assente*, q.v., pp. 187–201.

—— 'Le politiche per la famiglia', in Barbagli and Saraceno (eds.), *Lo stato delle famiglie in Italia*, q.v., pp. 301–10.

—— 'Redefining maternity and paternity: gender, pronatalism and social policies in Fascist Italy', in Bock and Thane (eds.), *Maternity and Gender Policies*, q.v., pp. 196–212.

Sargent, L. (ed.), *Women and Revolution*, Boston, 1981.

'The savaging', *The Economist*, vol. CCCXVII (1990), no. 7681, 17 November, p. 40.

Savagnone, G., *La Chiesa di fronte alle mafia*, Milano, 1995.

Savona, E. U., and Mezzanotte, L., *La corruzione in Europa*, Roma, 1998.

Scabini, E., 'Aspettative di un figlio e catene generazionali', in Micheli (ed.), *La società del figlio assente*, q.v., pp. 202–8.

Scamuzzi, S., 'La percezione della disuguaglianza sociale', in Paci (ed.), *Le dimensioni della disuguaglianza*, q.v., pp. 68–75.

Schadee, H. M. A., and Saviori, L., 'Il matrimonio e le frequentazioni sociali delle classi superiori', *Polis*, vol. VII (1993), no. 1, pp. 45–68.

Schadee, H. M. A., and Schizzerotto, A., *Social Mobility of Men and Women in Contemporary Italy*, Trento, 1990.

Schiattarella, R. (ed.), *New Challenges for European and International Business*, Roma, 1995.

Schizzerotto, A., 'Le classi superiori in Italia: politici, imprenditori, liberi professionisti e dirigenti', *Polis*, vol. VII (1993), no. 1, pp. 5–13.

—— 'La porta stretta: classi superiori e processi di mobilità, *Polis*, vol. VII (1993), no. 1, pp. 15–43.

—— 'La scuola è uguale per tutti?', in Ginsborg (ed.), *Stato dell'Italia*, q.v., pp. 558–61.

Schmidt, A., 'The new world order, incorporated: the rise of business and the decline of the nation-state', *Daedalus*, Spring, 1995, pp. 75–106.

Schneider, J. and P., 'Dalle guerre contadine alle guerre urbane: il movimento antimafia a Palermo', *Meridiana*, no. 25 (1996), pp. 50–76.

—— 'Mafia, antimafia and the question of Sicilian culture', *Politics and Society*, vol. XXII (1994), no. 2, pp. 237–58.

Sciolla, L., 'Identità e mutamento culturale nell'Italia di oggi', in Cesareo (ed.), *La cultura dell'Italia contemporanea*, q.v., pp. 35–69.

Scoppola, P., *La 'nuova cristianità' perduta*, Roma, 1985.

—— *La repubblica dei partiti*, Bologna, 1997 [1st edn 1991].

Scritti in onore di Guido Carli, Milano, 1995.

Scritti in onore di Vezio Crisafulli, 2 vols., Padova, 1985.

Scott, J., *Gender and the Politics of History*, New York, 1988.

Secchi, C., *L'internazionalizazzione dei servizi e l'economia italiana*, Milano, 1990.

—— 'Introduzione', in Secchi (ed.), *L'internazionalizazzione dei servizi e l'economia italiana*, q.v., pp. 11–34.

—— 'Il turismo in Italia', in Secchi (ed.), *Turismo, società e lavoro*, q.v., pp. 48–71.

Segni, M., *La rivoluzione interrotta*, Milano, 1994.

Seisselberg, J., 'Conditions of success and political problems of a "media-mediated personality-party": the case of Forza Italia', *West European Politics*, vol. XIX (1996), no. 4, pp. 714–43.

Semino, E., and Masci, M., 'Politics is football: metaphor in the discourse of Silvio Berlusconi', *Discourse and Society*, vol. VII (1996), no. 2, pp. 243–69.

Sen, A. K., 'Why does poverty persist in rich countries?', in Giudicini and Pieretti (eds.), *Urban Poverty and Human Dignity*, q.v., pp. 97–106.

Seton-Watson, C., 'La politica estera della Repubblica italiana', in Bosworth and Romano (eds.), *La politica estera italiana (1860–1985)*, q.v., pp. 331–60.

Seton-Watson, H., *The Russian Empire, 1801–1917*, Oxford, 1967.

Sgritta, G. B., and Innocenzi, G., 'La povertà', in Paci (ed.), *Le dimensioni della disuguaglianza*, q.v., pp. 261–88.

Shapiro, I., and Reeher, G. (eds.), *Power, Inequality and Democratic Politics*, Boulder, Colorado, 1988.

Siebert, R., *Le donne, la mafia*, Milano, 1994.

—— *E' femmina, però è bella*, Torino, 1991.

Sieder, C., and Mitterauer, M., 'The reconstruction of the family life course', in Wall *et al.*, *Family Forms in Historic Europe*, q.v., pp. 309–45.

Signorelli, A., *Antropolgia urbana*, Milano, 1996.

—— *Chi può e chi aspetta*, Napoli, 1983.

—— 'L'incertezza del diritto. Clientelismo politico e innovazione nel Mezzogiorno degli anni '80', *Problemi del Socialismo*, 1988, nos. 2–3, pp. 256–72.

—— 'Patroni e clienti', in Pasquinelli (ed.), *Potere senza stato*, Roma, 1986, pp. 151–62.

—— 'Il *tifo* e la città virtuale', in Signorelli, *Antropolgia urbana*, q.v., pp. 179–94.

Bibliography

Signorini, I., *Padrini e compari*, Torino, 1981.

Silberston, A., and Raymond, C. P., *The Changing Map of Industrial Europe*, London, 1996.

Silj, A., *Il malpaese*, Roma, 1994.

Simmel, G., *Conflict and the Web of Group Affiliations*, New York, 1955.

Simonelli, G., and Ferrarotti, A., *I media nel pallone*, Milano, 1995.

Siniscalco, D., *Beyond Manufacturing*, Torino, 1988.

Siniscalco, D. *et al.*, *Privatizzazioni difficili*, Bologna, 1999.

Sitari, R., 'L'Eni e le sfide del presente', in Venanzi and Faggiari (eds.), *ENI, un'autobiografia*, q.v., pp. 300–12.

Smith, T. W., 'Inequality and welfare', in Jowell *et al.*, *British Social Attitudes. Special International Report*, q.v., pp. 59–86.

Soldani, S., and Turi, G. (eds.), *Fare gli italiani*, Bologna, 1993.

Sparke, P., *Italian Design. 1870 to the Present*, London, 1988.

Spaventa, L., 'Introduction', in Giavazzi and Spaventa, *High Public Debt: the Italian Experience*, q.v., pp. 4–5.

Spinelli, A., *Discorsi al parlamento europeo, 1976–86*, ed. P. Virgilio Dastoli, Bologna, 1987.

Stajano, C., *Il disordine*, Torino, 1993.

—— *Un eroe borghese*, Torino, 1991.

Statera, A., 'Silvio Berlusconi', in Ajello *et al.*, *Perché loro*, q.v., pp. 195–218.

Statera, G. (ed.), *Consenso e conflitto nella società contemporanea*, Milano, 1982.

Statistiche generali dell'Unione Europea, Luxembourg, 1996.

Stato della Costituzione, ed. G. Neppi Modona, Milano, 1995.

Steigleder, K., and Di Giacomo, M., *L'Opus Dei vista dall'interno*, Torino, 1986.

Stella, G. A., *Schei*, Milano, 1996.

Sterling, C., *The Mafia*, London, 1990.

Stille, A., *Excellent Cadavers*, London, 1995.

Stone, D., Garnett, M., and Denham, A. (eds.), *Think Tanks across Nations: a Comparative Approach*, Manchester, 1998.

Storia dell'economia italiana, ed. R. Romano, Torino, 1991.

Storia dell'Italia repubblicana, ed. F. Barbagallo *et al.*, 3 vols., Torino, 1994–7.

Storia d'Italia. Annali 12. La criminalità, ed. L. Violante, Torino, 1997.

Storia d'Italia. Annali 14. Legge, diritto, giustizia, Torino, 1998.

Strange, S., *Casino Capitalism*, Oxford, 1986.

—— *Mad Money*, Manchester, 1998.

'Survey of Italy', *The Economist*, vol. CCCXV (1990), no. 7656.

Bibliography

SVIMEZ (Associazione per lo sviluppo dell'industria nel Mezzogiorno), *L'industrializazzione del Mezzogiorno: la FIAT a Melfi*, Bologna, 1993.

—— *Rapporto 1991 sull'economia del Mezzogiorno*, Bologna, 1991.

Sylos Labini, P., *Le classi sociali negli anni '80*, Bari, 1986.

—— *La crisi italiana*, Bari, 1995.

—— *Saggio sulle classi sociali*, Bari, 1974.

Tabet, P., *La pelle giusta*, Torino, 1997.

Tagliacozzo, A., *Per una sociologia dell'evasione fiscale*, Roma, 1984.

Tamburini, F., *Misteri d'Italia*, Milano, 1996.

—— *Un siciliano a Milano*, Milano, 1992.

Tarchi, M., *Dal MSI ad AN*, Bologna, 1997.

Tatò, A. (ed.), *Conversazioni con Berlinguer*, Roma, 1984.

Telò, M., 'L'Italia nel processo di costruzione europea', *Storia dell'Italia repubblicana*, vol. III, pt 1, q.v., pp. 129–248.

Temple, W., *Observations upon the United Provinces of the Netherlands*, Oxford, 1972 [1673].

Tettamanzi, D., 'Famiglia chiesa domestica', in Alessandri *et al.*, *La "Familiaris Consortio"*, q.v., pp. 222–34.

Tettamanzi, D., and Del Rio, D., *Una fatica da cristiani*, Casale Monferrato, 1993.

Thatcher, M., *The Downing Street Years*, London, 1993.

Thomas, C., 'Family and kinship in Eaton Square', in Field (ed.), *The Wealth Report*, q.v., pp. 129–59.

Thompson, E. P., *Writing by Candlelight*, London, 1980.

Titmuss, R., *Social Policy*, London, 1974.

Torrealta, M., *Ultimo*, Milano, 1995.

Toso, M., *Famiglia, lavoro e società nell'insegnamento sociale della Chiesa*, Roma, 1994.

Tousijn, W., 'Tra stato e mercato: le libere professioni in una prospettiva storico-evolutiva', in Tousijn (ed.), *Le libere professioni in Italia*, q.v., pp. 13–54.

Tousijn, W. (ed.), *Le libere professioni in Italia*, Bologna, 1987.

Tranfaglia, N., 'Introduzione', in Tranfaglia, *Mafia, politica e affari*, q.v., pp. ix–xxxii.

—— *Mafia, politica e affari*, Bari, 1990.

Traversa, G., 'Cittadini sottoposti a rischi inutili', in Ginsborg (ed.), *Stato dell'Italia*, q.v., pp. 310–13.

Trentin, B., *Il coraggio dell'utopia*, Milano, 1994.

Tribunale di Milano, Quinta Sezione Penale, *La maxitangente Enimont*, Milano, 1997.

Tribunale di Milano, Terza Sezione Penale, *UBS-Lugano.633369 'Protezione'*, Milano, 1996.

Tribunali di Milano e di Palermo, *Le mazzette della Fininvest*, Milano, 1996.

Bibliography

Trigilia, C., 'Conclusioni: associazionismo e nuovo Mezzogiorno', in Trigilia (ed.), *Cultura e sviluppo*, q.v., pp. 193–227.

—— 'Dinamismo privato e disordine pubblico. Politica, economia e società locali', in *Storia dell'Italia repubblicana*, vol. II, pt 1, q.v., pp. 711–77.

—— *Sviluppo senza autonomia*, Bologna 1994 [1st edn 1992].

Trigilia, C. (ed.), *Cultura e sviluppo*, Roma, 1995.

Trivellato, P., 'La scuola "reale": questioni critiche e condizioni per cambiare', *Quaderni di Sociologia*, vol. XXXVII (1993), no. 6, pp. 5–25.

Tsoukalis, L., 'Greece in the EU: domestic reform coalitions, external constraints and high politics', in Mitsos and Mossialos (eds.), *Contemporary Greece and Europe*, q.v., pp. 37–51.

Tulli, L., 'Ingrandire la stalla, allargare il magazzino', *Altrochemestre*, no. 1 (1994), pp. 8–9.

Turani, G. (ed.), *Anche i presidenti si incazzano*, Milano, 1991.

—— *L'Ingegnere*, Milano, 1988.

Turismo, società, lavoro, Trento, 1987.

Turco, L., 'Differenza sessuale e liberazione umana', *Critica Marxista*, vol. XXVII (1989), nos. 1–2, pp. 97–126.

Turnaturi, G., *Associati per amore*, Milano, 1991.

Twitchett, C. and K. J. (eds.), *Building Europe: Britain's Partners in the EEC*, London, 1981.

UNDP (United Nations Development Programme), *Human Development Report 1991*, Oxford, 1991.

—— *Human Development Report 1994*, Oxford, 1994.

Ungari, P., *Storia del diritto di famiglia in Italia (1796–1942)*, Bologna, 1974.

Università Cattolica del Sacro Cuore, *La coscienza contemporanea tra 'pubblico' e 'privato'*, Milano, 1979.

Vacca, G., *Vent'anni dopo*, Torino, 1997.

Valentini, C., *Le donne fanno paura*, Milano, 1997.

—— 'Quei due si parlano in cinese?', in *Panorama*, vol. XXIV (1986), no. 1074, pp. 50–52.

Valentino, P. A. (ed.), *L'immagine e la memoria*, Roma, 1992.

Vasile, V., 'Salvo Lima', in Ciconte, Sales and Vasile, *Cirillo, Ligato e Lima*, q.v., pp. 187–270.

Veblen, T., *The Theory of the Leisure Class*, London, 1899.

Vegetti Finzi, S., 'Il mito delle origini', in Lagorio, Vegetti Finzi and Ravasi, *Se noi siamo la terra*, q.v., pp. 54–60.

—— *Il romanzo della famiglia*, Milano, 1992.

Veltroni, W., *Io, Berlusconi e la RAI*, Roma, 1990.

—— *La sfida interrotta*, Milano, 1994.

Venanzi, F., and Faggiari, M. (eds.), *ENI, un'autobiografia*, Milano, 1994.

La vera storia d'Italia, Napoli, 1995.

Verdura-Rechenmann, D., 'Le nouveau capitalisme: la fin des idées reçues', in Menet-Genty (ed.), *L'Economie italienne*, q.v., pp. 219–30.

Verzichelli, L., 'Gli eletti', in Bartolini and D'Alimonte (eds.), *Maggioritario ma non troppo*, q.v., pp. 401–25.

—— 'Le politiche di bilancio: il debito pubblico da risorsa a vincolo', in Cotta and Isernia (eds.), *Il gigante dai piedi di argilla*, q.v., pp. 189–240.

Viale, G., *Un mondo usa e getta*, Milano, 1994.

Viesti, G. F., 'Che succede nell'economia del Mezzogiorno? Le trasformazioni 1990–1995', *Meridiana*, nos. 26–27 (1996), pp. 91–130.

Vincenzi Amato, D., 'Il diritto della famiglia', in Barbagli and Saraceno (eds.), *Lo stato delle famiglie*, q.v., pp. 37–52.

Violante, L., *Non è la piovra*, Torino, 1994.

Violante, L. (ed.), *Mafia e società italiana. Rapporto '97*, Bari, 1997.

—— *Mafie e antimafie. Rapporto '96*, Bari, 1996.

Vitale, S., *Nel cuore dei coralli. Peppino Impastato, una vita contro la mafia*, Soveria Mannelli, 1995.

Vitali, M., and Pisoni, A., *Comunione e liberazione*, Milano, 1988.

Volponi, P., *Memoriale*, Torino, 1991 [1st edn 1962].

Von Roques, V., *L'ora dei gattopardi*, Milano, 1996 [original edn *Die Stunde der Leoparden*, Munchen, 1994].

Wal, J. ter, 'Il linguaggio del pregiudizio etnico', *Politica ed Economia*, vol. XII (1991), no. 4, pp. 33–48.

Walby, S., *Theorizing Patriarchy*, London, 1995 [1st edn 1990].

Wall, R., *et al.*, *Family Forms in Historic Europe*, Cambridge, 1983.

Walston, J., *The Mafia and Clientelism*, London, 1988.

Walzer, M., 'Introduction' in Walzer (ed.), *Towards a Global Civil Society*, q.v., 1995, pp. 1–4.

Walzer, M. (ed.), *Towards a Global Civil Society*, Providence/Oxford, 1995.

Warner, M., *Alone of All Her Sex*, London, 1976 (new edn with 'Afterthoughts', 1990).

Warner, S., and Gambetta, D., *La retorica della riforma*, Torino, 1994.

Weber, M., 'Bureaucracy', in Gerth and Wright Mills (eds.), *From Max Weber: Essays in Sociology*, q.v., pp. 196–244.

—— *Politik als Beruf, Wissenschaft als Beruf*, Berlin, 1919.

Wertman, D., 'The Italian electoral process: the elections of June 1976', in Penniman (ed.), *Italy at the Polls*, q.v., pp. 41–79.

Williams, A. M., and Shaw, G. (eds.), *Tourism and Economic Development*, London, 1991 [1st edn 1989].

Wolf, M., 'Mass media', in Ginsborg (ed.), *Stato dell'Italia*, q.v., pp. 587–92.

World Trade Organisation. Focus, no. 2 (1995).

World Trade Organisation. Focus, no. 18 (1997).

Wright, V., 'Reshaping the state: the implications for public administration', in Müller and Wright (eds.), *The State in Western Europe*, q.v., pp. 110–17.

WTO (World Trade Organisation), *Annual Report 1996*, Genève, 1996.

—— *Annual Report 1998*, Genève, 1998.

Yusuf Hasan, M., *Somalia*, ed. R. Balducci, Roma, 1993.

Zagrebelsky, G., 'Adeguamenti e cambiamenti della Costituzione', in *Scritti in onore di Vezio Crisafulli*, q.v., vol. II, pp. 915–35.

Zagrebelsky, V., 'La polemica sul Pubblico Ministero e il nuovo Consiglio Superiore della Magistratura', *Quaderni Costituzionali*, vol. I (1981), no. 2, pp. 391–9.

Zamagni, S., 'Economia civile come forza di civilizzazione per la società italiana', in Donati (ed.), *La società civile in Italia*, q.v., pp. 159–92.

Zamagni, S. (ed.), *Mercati illegali e mafie*, Bologna, 1993.

Zamagni, V., *The Economic History of Italy, 1860–1990*, Oxford, 1993.

Zampini, A., *Io corruttore*, Napoli, 1993.

Zanatta, A. L., 'Le famiglie con un solo genitore', in Barbagli and Saraceno (eds.), *Lo stato delle famiglie in Italia*, q.v., pp. 248–56.

Index

Index